A History *of the* Book *in* America

VOLUME 4

Print in Motion

The Expansion of
Publishing and Reading
in the United States,
1880–1940

A History of the Book in America
David D. Hall, General Editor

. . .

VOLUME 1
The Colonial Book in the Atlantic World
edited by Hugh Amory and David D. Hall

VOLUME 2
An Extensive Republic:
Print, Culture, and Society in the New Nation
edited by Robert A. Gross and Mary Kelley

VOLUME 3
The Industrial Book, 1840–1880
*edited by Scott E. Casper, Jeffrey D. Groves,
Stephen W. Nissenbaum, and Michael Winship*

VOLUME 4
Print in Motion:
The Expansion of Publishing and Reading
in the United States, 1880–1940
edited by Carl F. Kaestle and Janice A. Radway

VOLUME 5
The Enduring Book:
Print Culture in Postwar America
*edited by David Paul Nord, Joan Shelley Rubin,
and Michael Schudson*

. . .

EDITORIAL BOARD
*David D. Hall (chair), Hugh Amory,
Scott E. Casper, Ellen S. Dunlap, James N. Green,
Robert A. Gross, Jeffrey D. Groves, Philip F. Gura,
John B. Hench, Carl F. Kaestle, Mary Kelley,
Marcus A. McCorison, Stephen W. Nissenbaum,
David Paul Nord, Janice A. Radway, Joan Shelley Rubin,
Michael Schudson, Michael Winship*

A History of the Book in America

VOLUME 4

Print in Motion

The Expansion of Publishing and Reading in the United States, 1880–1940

EDITED BY

Carl F. Kaestle and Janice A. Radway

Published in Association with
the American Antiquarian Society
by The University of North Carolina Press
Chapel Hill

Publication of this book was assisted by a grant
from the William R. Kenan Jr. Charitable Trust.

© 2009
The University of North Carolina Press
All rights reserved
Set in Bulmer by Tseng Information Systems, Inc.
Manufactured in the United States of America

The paper in this book meets the guidelines
for permanence and durability of the Committee on
Production Guidelines for Book Longevity of the
Council on Library Resources.

The University of North Carolina Press has been a member
of the Green Press Initiative since 2003.

Library of Congress Cataloging-in-Publication Data
Print in motion : the expansion of publishing and reading in the United
States, 1880-1940 / edited by Carl F. Kaestle and Janice A. Radway.
p. cm. — (A history of the book in America ; v. 4)
Includes bibliographical references and index.
ISBN 978-0-8078-3186-1 (alk. paper)
1. Book industries and trade—United States—History—19th century. 2. Book industries
and trade—United States—History—20th century. 3. Publishers and
publishing—United States—History—19th century. 4. Publishers and
publishing—United States—History—20th century. 5. Books and reading—
United States—History—19th century. 6. Books and reading—United States—
History—20th century. I. Kaestle, Carl F. II. Radway, Janice A., 1949-
Z473.P75 2008
381'.450020973—dc22
2008027802
13 12 11 10 09   5 4 3 2 1
THIS BOOK WAS DIGITALLY PRINTED.

CONTENTS

Contributors · xiii
Editors' and Authors' Acknowledgments · xv

Prologue · 1
Carl F. Kaestle and Janice A. Radway

Section I. Print in Motion

CHAPTER 1
A Framework for the History of Publishing and
Reading in the United States, 1880–1940 · 7
Carl F. Kaestle and Janice A. Radway

CHAPTER 2
Seeing the Sites: Readers, Publishers,
and Local Print Cultures in 1880 · 22
Carl F. Kaestle

Section II. The Publishing Trades

Introduction · 49
Carl F. Kaestle and Janice A. Radway

CHAPTER 3
The Rise of a National Book Trade System
in the United States · 56
Michael Winship

CHAPTER 4
The Expansion of the National Book Trade System · 78
James L. W. West III

CHAPTER 5
Copyright in Transition · 90
Peter Jaszi and Martha Woodmansee

CHAPTER 6
Diverging Paths: Books and Magazines
in the Transition to Corporate Capitalism · 102
Richard Ohmann

CHAPTER 7
From Partisanship to Professionalism:
The Transformation of the Daily Press · 116
Richard L. Kaplan

CHAPTER 8
Persistence of Vision: Partisan Journalism
in the Mainstream Press · 140
Michael Schudson

CHAPTER 9
Unruly Servants: Machines, Modernity,
and the Printed Page · 151
Megan Benton

CHAPTER 10
Ambivalent Advertising: Books, Prestige,
and the Circulation of Publicity · 170
Ellen Gruber Garvey

Section III. The Social Uses of Print

Introduction · 193
Carl F. Kaestle and Janice A. Radway

CHAPTER 11
Learned and Literary Print Cultures in an Age
of Professionalization and Diversification · 197
Janice A. Radway

CHAPTER 12
Crafting a Communications Infrastructure: Scientific
and Technical Publishing in the United States · 234
Marcel Chotkowski LaFollette

CHAPTER 13
The Government as Publisher · 260
Charles A. Seavey with Caroline F. Sloat

CHAPTER 14
Gilded-Age Consensus, Repressive Campaigns, and Gradual Liberalization:
The Shifting Rhythms of Book Censorship · 276
Paul S. Boyer

CHAPTER 15
Distinctive Media: The European Ethnic Press in the United States · 299
Sally M. Miller

CHAPTER 16
Exiles, Immigrants, and Natives: Hispanic Print Culture
in What Became the Mainland of the United States · 312
Nicolás Kanellos

CHAPTER 17
Reading, Writing, and Resisting:
African American Print Culture · 339
James P. Danky

CHAPTER 18
An Outpouring of "Faithful" Words:
Protestant Publishing in the United States · 359
William Vance Trollinger Jr.

CHAPTER 19
Two Ambitious Goals:
American Jewish Publishing in the United States · 376
Jonathan D. Sarna

CHAPTER 20
Running the Ancient Ark by Steam:
Catholic Publishing · 392
Una M. Cadegan

Section IV. Readers and Reading

PART A. INSTITUTIONS

Introduction · 411
Carl F. Kaestle and Janice A. Radway

CHAPTER 21
From McGuffey to Dick and Jane: Reading Textbooks · 415
Richard L. Venezky with Carl F. Kaestle

CHAPTER 22
The American Public Library: Construction
of a Community Reading Institution · 431
Wayne A. Wiegand

CHAPTER 23
The Great Libraries · 452
Phyllis Dain

PART B. READING IN SITU

Introduction · 471
Carl F. Kaestle and Janice A. Radway

CHAPTER 24
Aflame with Culture: Reading and Social Mission
in the Nineteenth-Century White Women's
Literary Club Movement · 476
Elizabeth Long

CHAPTER 25
Reading and Race Pride:
The Literary Activism of Black Clubwomen · 491
Elizabeth McHenry

CHAPTER 26
Making Meaning: Analysis and Affect
in the Study and Practice of Reading · 511
Joan Shelley Rubin

Epilogue · 528
Carl F. Kaestle and Janice A. Radway

Notes · 537

Bibliographical Essay · 623

Index · 649

FIGURES & TABLES

Figures

2.1. Opening day, Philadelphia Centennial Exhibition, 1876 · 23
2.2. Trial of Johnson Whittaker, *Harper's Weekly*, 1880 · 36
3.1. Canvassing book for proposed biography of P. T. Barnum · 66
3.2. Prospectus for an edition of the collected poems of Longfellow · 68
3.3. Linotype machine · 73
3.4. Printer's account book entry with details of use of Monotype machine · 75
4.1. Advertisement for Armed Services Edition of *Boston Adventure*, 1944 · 82
4.2. Bantam paperback edition of *The Great Gatsby*, 1945 · 86
6.1. Advertisements for new books and other products, 1900 · 105
6.2. Advertisement for Kodak cameras, 1902 · 111
7.1. Newspaper press room, 1942 · 122
7.2. Newsstand with foreign-language newspapers, 1941 · 124
7.3. Bench warmers, Union Square, 1908 · 126
7.4. Composing room and Linotype machines, 1902 · 129
9.1. Linotype operators, 1909 · 153
9.2. Modernist design by Douglas C. McMurtrie · 158
9.3. Traditional and modern advertisements by Jim Clarke for Raymond & Whitcomb, 1933 · 160
9.4. Traditional design by Daniel Berkeley Updike · 163
10.1. Harper and Brothers, a list of important new books, 1896 · 174
10.2. Advertisement for *Lovers Once but Strangers Now*, 1890 · 176
10.3. Prentice-Hall advertisement for *Refugee*, 1940 · 180
10.4. Poster advertising film of *Grapes of Wrath*, 1940 · 181

10.5. Advertisement for "Dr. Eliot's Five-Foot Shelf of Books," 1910 · 183

12.1. Popular representation of science in the 1920s · 247

12.2. *Man in a Chemical World*, 1937 · 249

12.3. Representations of the scientist in *Man in a Chemical World*, 1937 · 250

12.4. *Microbe Hunters*, 1926 · 254

13.1. *Big Trees Folio, Geologic Atlas of the United States* · 267

13.2. *Excavation and Repair of Sun Temple*, 1916 · 270

13.3. "Migrant Mother and Children," by Dorothea Lange · 273

14.1. Illustrated cover, *National Police Gazette*, 1879 · 280

14.2. Tobacco advertisement, circa 1880 · 281

14.3. Comstock's commission as a special agent for the Post Office Department, 1875 · 282

14.4. Cover and table of contents, *American Mercury*, April 1926 · 290

14.5. Cover and table of contents, *The Little Review*, July–August 1920 · 292

15.1. *Allentown Friedens-Bote*, 1888 · 303

15.2. *Svoboda* (Ukrainian National Association), 1918 · 309

16.1. Ricardo Flores Magón (1874–1922) · 318

16.2. *Voz de la Mujer*, 6 September 1907 · 320

16.3. *Revista Católica*, 27 January 1884 · 332

17.1. Flora Sengstack holds a copy of *Chicago Defender*, 1921 · 352

17.2. Newsboy selling *Chicago Defender*, 1942 · 353

17.3. *Negro World*, 18 December 1926 · 355

18.1. Sister Aimée preaching, 1938 · 364

18.2. Scofield Reference Bible, 1909 · 368

18.3. Title page and frontispiece, *Ben-Hur: A Tale of the Christ*, 1899 · 373

19.1. Cover of *Thirty-five Years of Jewish Endeavor*, 1924 · 378

19.2. *Thirty-five Years of Jewish Endeavor*, colophon · 379

20.1. *Catholic Gems*, 1887 · 394

20.2. *Catholic World*, April 1900 · 396

20.3. Index of Forbidden Books notice in *The Downfall*, 1902 · 400

20.4. *The Rosary Made Easier*, 1929 · 401

21.1. *Appleton's School Readers: The Third Reader*, 1877 · 416

21.2. *Swinton's Fourth Reader*, 1883 · 422

21.3. *More Streets and Roads*, 1942 · 429

22.1. New York State Library School, 1888 class portrait · 434

22.2. Eliza Kent Branch (Toledo Public Library), floor plans, 1917 · 439

22.3. Chicago Public Library circulation desk, circa 1920 · 440

23.1. Library of Congress Building, exterior and reading room, 1897 · 460

23.2. New York Public Library, main reading room, circa 1911 · 464

23.3. Sterling Memorial Library, Yale University, 1990 · 469

25.1. YMCA reading room and office, La Boca, Florida, circa 1900 · 495

25.2. Five women around a table with books, circa 1900 · 497

25.3. Young woman reading, 1880s · 502

25.4. Seated woman reading, 1880s · 509

E.1. Cover of *Astounding Stories*, April 1935 · 531

E.2. Cover of *Lost Horizon*, 1939 · 532

E.3. Televisions at New York World's Fair, 1939 · 534

Tables

1.1. Daily papers in English, 1880–1930 · 12

2.1. Top-selling periodicals in 1880 · 38

3.1. New titles and editions, 1880–1916 · 60

6.1. Pages of book ads in publishers' monthly magazines, 1880–1890 · 104

11.1. Principal scholarly publications of research universities, 1906 · 205

19.1. Jewish publications by decade, 1850–1899 · 382

CONTRIBUTORS

MEGAN BENTON is humanities fellow at Pacific Lutheran University.
PAUL S. BOYER is Merle Curti Professor of History Emeritus at the University of Wisconsin at Madison.
UNA M. CADEGAN is associate professor of history and director of the American studies program at the University of Dayton.
PHYLLIS DAIN is professor emerita of Library Service at Columbia University.
JAMES P. DANKY retired from the State Historical Society of Wisconsin but continues to teach for the University of Wisconsin at Madison's School of Journalism and Mass Communication.
ELLEN GRUBER GARVEY is associate professor of English at New Jersey City University.
PETER JASZI is professor of law, Washington College of Law at American University.
CARL F. KAESTLE is University Professor and Professor of Education, History, and Public Policy emeritus at Brown University.
NICOLÁS KANELLOS is Brown Foundation Professor of Spanish and director of Recovering the U.S. Hispanic Literary Heritage Program at the University of Houston.
RICHARD L. KAPLAN is an editor/writer with ABC-Clio Publishing, Santa Barbara, California.
MARCEL CHOTKOWSKI LAFOLLETTE is an independent historian in Washington, D.C.
ELIZABETH LONG is professor of sociology at Rice University.
ELIZABETH MCHENRY is associate professor of English at New York University.
SALLY M. MILLER is professor emerita of history at the University of the Pacific.
RICHARD OHMANN is professor emeritus of English at Wesleyan University.
JANICE A. RADWAY is Walter Dill Scott Professor of Communication and professor of American studies and gender studies at Northwestern University.
JOAN SHELLEY RUBIN is professor of history at the University of Rochester.
JONATHAN D. SARNA is Joseph H. & Belle R. Braun Professor of American Jewish History at Brandeis University.

MICHAEL SCHUDSON is distinguished professor of communication at the University of California at San Diego and professor of communication in the Graduate School of Journalism, Columbia University.

CHARLES A. SEAVEY retired as associate professor, School of Information Science & Learning Technologies at the University of Missouri, Columbia.

WILLIAM VANCE TROLLINGER JR. is associate professor of history and director of the Core Integrated Studies Program at the University of Dayton.

RICHARD L. VENEZKY was Unidel Professor of Educational Studies at the University of Delaware at the time of his death in June 2004.

JAMES L. W. WEST III is Edwin Erle Sparks Professor of English at Pennsylvania State University.

WAYNE A. WIEGAND is F. William Summers Professor of Library and Information Studies and professor of American studies at Florida State University.

MICHAEL WINSHIP is Iris Howard Regents Professor of English at the University of Texas at Austin.

MARTHA WOODMANSEE is professor of English and law at Case Western Reserve University.

EDITORS' & AUTHORS' ACKNOWLEDGMENTS

The editors wish to thank the National Endowment for the Humanities for its support of the multivolume project, *A History of the Book in America*. Without this support, we could not have received the nurturing, evolving, expert help that the board of editors provided to each set of volume editors and from which we benefited greatly. We also wish to thank the general editor of the project, Professor David D. Hall of the Harvard Divinity School, for his leadership, guidance, and support throughout this volume's long gestation and production. Similarly, great thanks are due to the American Antiquarian Society (AAS), which housed and staffed the project. In particular we thank Ellen Dunlap, president of the society, for her active support of the project and her patience with its pace. For his countless contributions and suggestions, we also thank John B. Hench, vice president for collections and programs at AAS, now retired. Caroline Sloat, director of scholarly publications at AAS, worked tirelessly and expertly to facilitate the completion of this volume, especially in its last stages, supporting us and attending to countless editorial details. Two outside readers undertook full-scale reviews of the manuscript that proved both encouraging and very helpful. Our thanks to Alice Fahs and Ann Fabian, although the remaining shortcomings and infelicities remain ours. Also, our thanks to Katherine S. Simpson at AAS for her detailed and expert help with the illustrations.

Generous funding from the National Endowment for the Humanities made it possible for the editors and many of the contributors to meet for crucial face-to-face discussions and supported the work of the projcct's editorial board. Further financial support has been provided by The Elisabeth Woodburn Fund of the Antiquarian Booksellers' Association of America, American Booksellers' Association, the Richard A. Heald Fund, the James J. Colt Foundation, the John Ben Snow Memorial Trust, and the Center for the Book in the Library of Congress. We are most grateful for these contributions.

The coeditors thank each other for friendship, mutual support, some fun, and a great deal of learning along the way. We thank our life partners, Liz Hollander and Laurie Shannon, for their support and love and patience.

. . .

Carl Kaestle wishes to thank The Spencer Foundation for supporting his research on the history of literacy and print culture, in particular for two research grants that led to the publication of *Literacy in the United States: Readers and Reading since 1880* (New Haven: Yale University Press, 1990) and to this volume. Additional funds for research and editorial assistance for this volume were provided by grants awarded to Carl Kaestle by Kathryn Spoehr and Mary Fennell, successive deans of the faculty, Brown University, and by Warren Simmons, director of the Annenberg Institute for School Reform at Brown University. For research assistance, thanks to Helen Damon-Moore, Anne Durst, Marc Goulden, Lawrence Stedman, Dina Stephens, Katherine Tinsley, and William Vance Trollinger Jr. at the University of Wisconsin; to Joshua Rubin, Michelle Rosenthal, Sarah Hodges, and Katherine Crawford at the University of Chicago; and to Jennifer Meeropol, Karen Inouye, Tia Malkin, Lesley Caccamese, Jason Barnosky, Jesse Stout, Ani Mukherji, and Tom Jundt at Brown University. Special thanks are due to our expert editorial assistants at Brown University, Deborah Brown, Shana Newman, Angela Mazaris, and Jessica McCrory.

. . .

Janice Radway wishes to thank Carl F. Kaestle and Alice Fahs for their comments on an earlier version of chapter 11. She also wishes to thank research assistants Rod Frey and Arnal Dayaratna for their help with the research for the same chapter. Finally, she also thanks Jonathan Flatley, Jennifer Parchesky, Erin Smith, Katherine Stubbs, and Trysh Travis for conversations about middlebrow culture and the literary field during the years this book was being planned and assembled.

. . .

Individual contributors wish to add the following particular acknowledgments:

Megan Benton is indebted to Brittany Kesselman for a wealth of valuable material on the effects of mechanization within the industry in the 1880s and 1890s and to the insightful advice of media and technology historian Lisa Gitelman.

James Danky observes that his essay could not have existed without the research assistance of Story Lee Matkin-Rawn and, earlier, Michael Kwas, both of the University of Wisconsin at Madison. He expresses his gratitude also to Cheryl Knott Malone of the University of Arizona, Randall Burkett of Emory University, and Paul Hass of Madison.

Peter Jaszi would like to thank Dean Claudio Grossman of the Washington College of Law for generous research support.

Nicolás Kanellos thanks the Rockefeller Foundation for all of the support for researching the history of the Hispanic book in America.

Richard Kaplan wishes to thank Michael Schudson for continual support and inspiration.

Marcel Chotkowski LaFollette gratefully acknowledges research suggestions and comments on her draft from Lawrence Badash, Eugene Garfield, Elizabeth Knoll, Marc Rothenberg, and Jeffrey K. Stine.

Elizabeth Long would like to thank Chandler Davidson, Lynne Huffer, Bill Martin, Helena Michie, and Carol Quillen of Rice University and the editors of this volume for their conceptual and editorial help with her essay.

Elizabeth McHenry wishes to thank the National Endowment for the Humanities and the National Humanities Center for fellowship support, which allowed her to pursue this project.

Joan Shelley Rubin thanks the John Simon Guggenheim Memorial Foundation for supporting the early stages of her research.

Charles Seavey would like to thank Caroline Sloat and the editors of the volume for their assistance with the final version of this essay.

William Vance Trollinger Jr. thanks Tim Dillon of the University of Dayton for research assistance.

Richard Venezky thanks the Unidel Foundation for providing time for this work and the two editors of this volume for their thoughtful suggestions on the chapter. Carl F. Kaestle, who assumed responsibility for the revision of this essay after Richard Venezky's untimely death, wishes to thank David Pearson of the University of California at Berkeley for his assistance.

Wayne Wiegand thanks Carl Kaestle and Janice Radway for their editorial suggestions.

. . .

Portions of Richard Ohmann's essay in this volume appeared in his book, *The Commercialization of the University, the Professions, and Print Culture* (Middletown: Wesleyan University Press, 2003). The editors and Richard Ohmann wish to thank Wesleyan University Press for permission to reprint those portions here.

Portions of Jonathan Sarna's essay in this volume appeared as "Jewish Culture Comes to America," *Jewish Studies* 42 (2003–4): 45–57. The editors and Professor Sarna wish to thank the World Council for Jewish Studies for permission to reprint those portions here.

Prologue

Carl F. Kaestle and Janice A. Radway

. . .

Broad, synthetic histories are notoriously difficult to write no matter what the focus of the narrative. They are even more of a challenge, however, when they are largely unprecedented—as this one is. To our knowledge, there is only one attempt at a comprehensive history of book publishing in the United States during the pivotal period of 1880–1940, and its treatment is more descriptive than analytical.[1] Despite laudable work on different aspects of publishing history,[2] there is no consensus about how to frame a comprehensive history of the book in this period. If such a history is to be attempted, decisions that must be justified intellectually have to be made about what counts as an instance of book history. It is also crucial to offer, at the outset, certain formulations about the relationship between the history of the book and its surrounding social context because those understandings will continually affect how far afield one looks for factors that influenced, affected, or even "caused" key events in the narrative. When the narrative is to be crafted collaboratively and is only one part of a larger project, the difficulty is multiplied exponentially. *Print in Motion: The Expansion of Publishing and Reading in the United States, 1880–1940* is the result of a sustained effort to meet these many challenges. Our introduction is designed both to explain how we approached those challenges and to describe the key terms and conceptual frameworks that have guided our efforts.

It is important to note first that, although our volume appears in a series entitled *A History of the Book in America*, we have broadened our focus in order to look at the production, circulation, and use of print in a general sense, that is, to include magazines, newspapers, and other forms. While the essays in this volume do address key developments in the history of book publishing in the period 1880–1940, they also attend to the changing and complex relationships across different print forms. Additionally, some of the essays consider the relation between print and institutions like schools, government bureaucracies, and corporate businesses. Our canvas is further broadened by our interest not only in the production and distribution of print but also in its reception by readers and uses by readers. Thus, several of the essays look at the use of print forms in everyday lives. Although evidence about the history of reading is hard to come by and is often sketchy, we nonetheless examine the complex processes by which readers created meaning from texts. Finally, we investigate how social practices of reading may have changed during our period, when print was so spectacularly set in motion, circulating more quickly, more cheaply, and more widely to ever-increasing numbers of individuals and groups.

The first part of our introduction ventures some very basic generalizations about the economic, social, and cultural trends that exerted pressure on the practices of print production and use during this period. In it, we attempt to describe the social context for print: the larger environment within which publishing was organized, technologies of printing were invented, and innovative forms and institutions emerged to circulate new messages to new audiences. Our goal is to situate the development of a "culture of print" in a larger narrative about social change in the United States during this period, a period characterized at once by expanding markets, national consolidation, and social upheaval.

Necessarily, then, chapter 1 offers a highly schematic metanarrative. We consider such a narrative both an inescapable and daunting part of our charge. It is daunting in part because the expansion of print produced both consolidation *and* diversification. The explosive growth of print and print channels during this period enabled many more individuals and groups to gain access to the public sphere of print, thereby leaving us records with conflicting points of view about the period in question that complicate efforts at generalization. It is important to remember that people adapted print to their *particular* uses and employed it to make sense of their *local* experience, even as that local experience was increasingly mediated by connection to national institutions, markets, social trends, and symbolic forms.

The second part of chapter 1 defines our key terms and presents our conceptual framework for understanding how the production, circulation, and use of print changed during the period. This framework emerged from our early effort to wrestle with the complexities and contradictions evident in even the most cursory recounting of what happened to publishing and reading in this sixty-year span. In that effort we developed a general argument about a crucial tension within the larger culture of print between centripetal forces of concentration and integration on the one hand and centrifugal forces of multiplication and diversification on the other. Indeed, greatly accelerated attempts at standardization, mass marketing, and cultural consolidation developed simultaneously with widening access to print by both writers and readers. Expanded access enabled individuals and groups beyond the book-oriented, educated elites to shape print to their own social, political, and cultural interests.

During this period, more tightly integrated, nationally oriented print forms and institutions emerged that were devoted to assembling and addressing larger and larger audiences. Inextricably bound up with the creation of a consumer culture and its requisite technologies and institutions, these new forms and the establishments responsible for them—from ad agencies to book clubs to syndicated newspaper features—exploited economies of scale and speed to augment opportunities for realizing profits from the business of printing and publication. Simultaneously, however, the same technological innovations and changes in the distribution of literacy that fueled the rise of the mass press in the United States also enabled the proliferation of smaller, more narrowly focused, local print cultures that drew together publishers, writers, readers, and a range of support personnel around shared interests, investments, goals, and intentions. Some of these print cultures were professional and technical, circulating highly specialized content to a small set of trained experts. Others were oriented around emerging leisure-time pursuits and united people with specific hobbies and interests who were scattered across the country. Still others were oriented explicitly toward the practice and publication of dissent, as people challenged the status quo in the nationally oriented, mass-market press.

We tracked the results produced by the expansion of print, and we realized that they were the effects of simultaneous, contrapuntal pressures toward concentration and proliferation. This conclusion pushed us to complicate the traditional framework of book history, which tends to conceptualize book production principally as a matter of transmission and communication. As a consequence, the traditional framework—famously defined and graphically represented as a circuit by Robert Darnton—tends to concentrate agency in authors and publishers and to render readers and consumers secondary and subordinate to them.[3] The circuit metaphor, we believe, cannot capture the myriad ways in which a range of actors, not limited to writers and readers, sought to use print. As we have already indicated, they could do so precisely because the accelerated generation and circulation of printed forms in this period made print both more essential and more available as a technology of group formation and of power more generally.

Indeed, we argue—first in the introduction and later throughout the volume—that between 1880 and 1940 the production, distribution, and consumption of print was so pervasive a part of daily life in the United States that it became the habitual arena for the achievement of all sorts of purposes, from business to religion, from leisure to organizational life. Our general goal with the volume has been to trace people's efforts to enlist print in the pursuit of a range of social purposes. In a sense, then, our real subject is the social and political struggles that occurred within and over the larger culture of print that developed during the period 1880 to 1940.

The social conflicts of our period were pervasive and consequential. The struggling parties used every means at their disposal to gain advantage and to make their views heard. In some cases, these struggles were carried out *through* printed pages and books; in others, what resulted was a conflict *over* the very "order of books," a phrase coined by Roger Chartier to suggest that, while "the book always aims at installing order," it is "not all powerful, however, when it comes to annulling the reader's liberty."[4] In our period, contending parties sought to broaden and diversify literacy training and education and to exploit new mass production technologies in order to challenge the traditional connection between books and educated elites. It is no coincidence that during this period higher education for women and African Americans developed and eventually flourished, thereby encouraging the creation of literatures that illuminated the abilities of people previously excluded from the domains of legitimate book culture.

As a way of complicating the metanarrative suggested in chapter 1, chapter 2 seeks to balance our interest in grand forces of social change and in the establishment of a larger culture of print by discussing specific details of local print cultures in 1880, just as the sweeping changes we chronicle in the rest of the volume were taking off. This chapter seeks to provide a ground-level account of locally sited producers and readers of print. It employs the notion of the "site" to emphasize the intersection of particular readers; their immediate social location; the printed materials available and reading practices typical of that location; and the histories, needs, capabilities, and intentions they brought to their engagement with print. Suggestive rather than exhaustive, the sites described in chapter 2 illustrate something of the range of ways that writing, publishing, and reading functioned for the individuals drawn into the nascent culture of print in 1880.

Section I

Print in Motion

CHAPTER 1

A Framework for the History of Publishing and Reading in the United States, 1880–1940

Carl F. Kaestle and Janice A. Radway
. . .

Social Change and the Culture of Print

Stability has been elusive in all societies undergoing economic growth, technological change, immigration, political contention, and shifting international circumstances. From high offices to local neighborhoods, people have attempted to maintain order in response to multiple sources of diversity, conflict, and incoherence. Although these warring tendencies have been present in all industrial societies, the pace and consequences of change have been more dramatic in some periods than in others. Such was the case between 1880 and 1940, when the United States experienced changes so fundamental that everything was transformed, from the production and purchasing of goods to social relations, to the nature of institutions and modes of communication.

Increasing productivity and faster transportation gave rise to national-scale businesses, which in turn spawned national brand-name products, advertising, and infrastructures of distribution. Educational activity mushroomed, from new research universities that incubated new disciplines to the humble one-room schoolhouses that lifted African American literacy rates. High school attendance was unevenly distributed but increased from less than 5 percent in 1880 to more than 50 percent in 1940.[1]

Immigration brought ethnic conflict as well as economic strength. Class consciousness became more pronounced as both the working class and the emerging middle class sought to define their roles in the new economic order. Recently freed slaves and other people of color were integrated into the economy, usually in subordinate positions, a process that caused much opposition but nonetheless achieved an unjust durability across our period. Efforts to achieve order were implemented through force, the uses of capital, the legal system, organizational innovation, persuasion, politics, and legislation. Because the people who sought to manage these changes articulated ideal systems and goals, historians must beware of equating their hyperrational schemes with daily reality. It is difficult to estimate the impact of these systems and goals on the messy experience of ordinary life. Not everyone worked in a large factory, and not everyone could afford to ride on a railroad. Nonetheless, increases in the speed of production and transportation affected everyone in myriad ways.

Across the six decades of this watershed period beginning in 1880, the printed word became the sine qua non of influence and organization. In a culture of print, the printed word acted as both an instrument and an expression of change, whether directed toward more orderliness or toward new assertions. As the nation expanded geographically and consolidated economically, print became a key handmaid of nationalization and professionalization. At the same time, the printed word could drive wedges of dissent into the structures of national firms and professional organizations.

People born in 1880 faced breathtaking changes, decade after decade. Contemporaries commented upon the pace of change continually. For years, historians, too, have made the pace of change a major theme in their analysis of this period. The title of Robert Wiebe's 1967 book, *The Search for Order*, long ago became the watchword of this interpretation.[2] Alfred Chandler's equally famous title, *The Visible Hand*, was taken up for its ability to summarize changes in the organization of the manufacturing and distribution of goods.[3] Alan Trachtenberg's introduction of the term "incorporation" also proved consequential, as his book, *The Incorporation of America*, traced the cultural consequences of processes of integration.

In these decades a key shift in the legal institution of incorporation occurred. The emphasis was no longer on granting charters to organizations pursuing the public interest but rather on granting privileges to business enterprises in order to facilitate their large-scale capital transactions. Nicholas Murray Butler, president of Columbia University, hailed the limited-liability corporation as "the greatest single discovery of modern time."[4] As Trachtenberg argued, though, incorporation was also social and cultural, as the expansion of national markets across the land, accompanied by new and tighter hierarchies of control, affected people's understanding of—and in some cases resistance to—the forces of integration.

James Beniger also focused on the concept of control in his effort to make sense of this period. The increasing efficiency of production and speed of transportation, he argued, provided the potential for a national economy but created a crisis in the way constituent processes were managed."[5] By the 1890s a "control revolution" had begun, fostering new communication devices, networks, and practices, as well as supporting activities such as storage, advertising, and market research.

Continuing the story beyond World War I, Ellis Hawley argued further that problems of control and integration persisted into the 1920s and 1930s.[6] These included a legacy of ethnic tension; rising class consciousness, centered in the relations between management and labor; the dramatic collapse of the financial system in the 1930s; and the contending visions of a reordered society that came with that crisis. By the end of the period the acceptance of collective bargaining and the rudiments of a welfare state stood side by side with continued business prestige and influence.

These familiar historical interpretations have survived subsequent years of scholarship, though they have been complicated in recent years by the work of Sven Beckert, Claudia Goldin, and Michael Denning, among others.[7] Still, the concepts of control and integration remain useful in grappling with the daunting complexity of order and disorder during this period, and a brief, elementary review of key dates and developments in the history of such integration can provide a scaffolding for our discussion of the culture of print.

Until the development of steamboats and railroads, the distribution of goods had been essentially limited to the speed of draft animals. As manufacturing became more efficient, this limitation became more serious. In the decades before the Civil War, railroads crisscrossed the industrial Northeast and sent out spurs into the South and the Midwest. In the 1840s the number of miles of rail surpassed miles of canals.[8] Costs declined as speed increased. In 1870 the Bessemer process allowed the production of steel at dramatically reduced prices, from $168 per ton in 1868 to $31 per ton by 1884, enabling the great steel producers and railroad magnates to become partners in a transportation revolution.[9] In 1869 the famous golden spike joined the eastern and western pieces of the first transcontinental rail line, and by 1900 there were four competing strands from coast to coast.[10]

When the scope and speed of distribution reached these grand proportions, the stage was set for national corporations. The modern corporation expanded horizontally, buying up competitors and moving outward geographically; at the same time it expanded vertically, linking with enterprises that supplied raw materials, transportation, packaging, finishing, distribution, and other processes. This expansion was the central event in the rise of corporate capitalism, and it created two further needs: better communications and a new cadre of administrators.

Several rapidly evolving technological innovations facilitated the communications revolution. A simple list of inventions does not convey the timing of the transformation, because there were delays between the initial invention of a device, its improvement, its diffusion into general business use, and its availability for ordinary consumer use. Indeed, as one development built upon and then augmented another, the pace of change quickened. Samuel Morse patented the telegraph in 1837; by midcentury it had connected large cities, facilitating the transmission of news and business transactions.[11] Initially spurred by the Civil War, the development of Western Union accelerated telegraphy even more in the later nineteenth century. In 1870 the firm had about 4,000 offices handling 9 million messages. By 1910 there were almost 25,000 offices processing 75 million messages.[12] Building upon Marconi's introduction of long-wave telegraphy in 1895, transatlantic wireless communication began in 1901, extending the reach of the nation and its culture beyond its borders.[13]

Alexander Graham Bell patented the telephone in 1876. At first his device was limited to short distances, and Bell remained uncertain about its future communications use. Nonetheless, by 1880 the American Bell Telephone organization had installed 54,000 telephones in major cities, about one for each 1,000 people in the population. By 1910 there were 7.6 million phones, about eighty-two for every 1,000 people.[14] Edison added another device for transmitting sound with his invention of the phonograph in 1877, which was given its most popular commercial form in the 1890s with the gramophone of Emile Berliner, who advertised that even a faithful dog was fooled by the recording of "his master's voice." As the twentieth century progressed, other devices for recording and transmitting messages in fast, standardized formats were developed, including shorthand, the typewriter, and the Dictaphone.[15]

During the 1920s, commercial radio broadcasting exploded on the scene once the technology emerged from its association with ham radio enthusiasts and the military. Dominated by music programs, with a smattering of drama, comedy, and talk shows, early radio was governed tightly to avoid social and political criticism. Most stations were owned by large corporations like General Electric and Westinghouse. They were in turn dependent upon public authorities, thus guaranteeing, in the words of early radio commentator H. V. Kaltenborn, that radio's influence went "towards stabilization rather than change."[16]

These developments made it possible to hurl words across great distances. Meanwhile, changes in the world of print production dramatically changed magazines and newspapers. With the advent of national brands and national markets, innovative publishers like S. S. McClure and Edward Bok perceived that one could sell magazines at less than cost by carrying more advertising. During the "magazine revolution" of the 1890s, the cover price of popular magazines plummeted. While the old-fashioned best sellers, *Harper's* and *Scribners'*, cost fifty cents, the upstarts like *McClure's* and *Ladies' Home Journal* cost fifteen cents. As Richard Ohmann has so aptly put it, the publishers sold the magazines to the reader for a low price, but they sold the reader's attention to companies who wanted to sell goods.[17] As a result, advertising became more prominent in magazines, woven intermittently throughout the articles and features.

Change accelerated in newspapers also. Fiercely competing publishers like Joseph Pulitzer and William Randolph Hearst developed the "new journalism," which aimed at providing entertaining, low-cost daily newspapers for a mass audience. Technology did not "cause" change but enabled it, and the results were dramatic. German immigrant watchmaker and tinkerer Ottmar Mergenthaler invented a typesetting machine in 1884 and improved it sufficiently to warrant a debut at the *New York Tribune* as the "Linotype" in 1886. The machine was in widespread use by the mid-1890s.[18] Improvements in stereotype plates, which in rotary printing replaced movable type, allowed a further speedup of printing time during the 1890s, when the volume of papers produced per hour tripled.[19] At the same time, the improvements in wood-pulp paper production vastly increased the supply and lowered the price of newsprint, from $138.00 per ton in 1880 to $42.00 in 1899.[20] Editors like Hearst now knew they could succeed with a morning paper costing one penny.

The magazine revolution and the new journalism dovetailed with the development of corporate capitalism. The availability of faster, cheaper production and transportation had many of the same effects on these print forms as on the production of other goods. Magazines that embraced advertising became a key tool in the development of consumer capitalism. Newspapers—one of America's most ubiquitous and local institutions—proliferated even further in the late nineteenth century. As the twentieth century progressed, though, even as the number of readers increased, the number of papers decreased due to the decline of competing papers in smaller towns, along with the greater outreach of the big urban papers. The number of English-language daily papers shot up from 850 in 1880 to 1,967 in 1900, to a peak of 2,042 in 1910 and then declined slightly to 1,942 in 1930. While the number of papers declined from 1910 to 1930, the total daily circulation increased from 22.4 million to 39.6 million (see table 1.1). Paralleling the consolidation in the industry were several other trends that integrated newspapers and challenged their local character. Among these developments were newspaper chains, wire services, and syndicated materials, from comics to columns. People in Maine and people in California shared many more features in their newspapers by 1940 than they had in 1880, from the "Katzenjammer Kids" to Walter Lippmann's influential political columns.[21]

Book production did not undergo this transformation to the same degree or the same way. Books were not repeatable, periodical items, despite publishers' attempts to market several books by the same author as a set or to group similar pieces of fiction in a series or "library." Because books were not clearly "consumed" the way magazines and newspapers were, they did not serve as a good

TABLE 1.1. Daily papers in English, 1880–1930

	1880	1900	1910	1930
Number of English-language dailies	850	1,967	2,042	1,942
Number of cities with dailies	389	915	1,207	1,402
Percentage of cities with competing dailies	61.4	61.1	57.1	20.6
Total daily circulation (millions)	3.1	15.1	22.4	39.6

Source: Adapted from Edwin Emery, *The Press and America: An Interpretative History of the Mass Media*, 3rd ed. (Englewood Cliffs, N.J.: Prentice-Hall, 1972), 443.

vehicle for commercial advertisements. Thus, big-city firms that specialized in books continued to dominate the book trade, treating each title essentially as a new and different product. Of course, change was constant, but changes in book publishing were neither as abrupt nor as structural as those wrought upon the other print forms by the communications revolution and the development of corporate capitalism.

As the century progressed, however, an exciting intellectual development animated the book industry. A group of new publishers based in New York nurtured the rise of literary modernism. With its set of iconoclastic, aesthetic principles and its critical social stance, modernism produced much of the energy in the high-literary book business from the 1910s to the 1930s. In these same decades other publishers finally learned how to market books more like periodicals and to tie them to social goals conveyed by advertisements. The best-known pioneer was the Book-of-the-Month Club, established in 1926. In separate analyses, Janice Radway and Joan Shelley Rubin have dissected the serious, principled efforts of the club's selection committee as it tried to define a middlebrow criterion of excellence. In the marketing of monthly book choices, however, the Book-of-the-Month Club tied its enterprise to the same advertising techniques used to sell soap and automobiles. Readers were urged to keep up with the fast-paced, modern world and impress their friends by reading the books selected by the club.[22]

Coterminous with the rapid innovations in the communication of sound and the production of print was an explosion of the visual. Chromolithography made inexpensive color graphics available by the 1870s for use on sheet music covers, book jackets, and pictures for the walls of working-class homes, somewhat rattling cultural commentators, who feared that ordinary people would either become overly excited by all the swirling, colorful illustrations or falsely believe they had acquired culture through cheap reproductions.[23] Another visual breakthrough was made with the development of the Kinetograph camera and the Kinetoscope viewing machine by Edison's protégé, W. K. L. Dickson. In the 1890s and first decade of the twentieth century, brief motion pictures were shown in Kinetoscope parlors and vaudeville halls. By 1905 many companies were developing equipment and began producing longer films with actual stories, spawning the nickelodeon halls.[24] Building on the popularity of such sensationally popular films as Edwin Porter's *Great Train Robbery* of 1903, many nickelodeons discontinued vaudeville acts and devoted themselves entirely to motion pictures. By 1907 attendance at nickelodeons was estimated in the millions per day.[25] Reacting to this explosion of interest, cultural critics worried about the allegedly subversive and salacious effects of all this visual stimulation.[26]

Meanwhile, the visual revolution altered newspapers and magazines through the development of halftone reproduction of photographs, building on "the golden age of wood engraving," when the number and quality of illustrations was already increasing in the old leading magazines like *Harper's* and *Century*. The editor of the *Century Magazine*, Richard Watson Gilder, warned his publishers that *Harper's* was stealing his engravers, learning their secrets, and outspending *Century* on illustrations.[27] New and improved processes, such as zinc engravings and the halftone reproduction of lithographs and other graphics increased the speed and quality of such illustrations.[28] However, the successful application of the halftone process to photographs soon overshadowed these developments.

First developed by Frederick Ives at Cornell University in the 1870s, halftone photographic reproduction used a screen to rephotograph the original photo and reduce it to a series of patterned dots of differing sizes. Thus rendered, the images could be sent by wire; when reproduced on paper, the areas with large dots close together appeared black or dark gray, and the areas with smaller dots and more space between them appeared light gray or white, thus re-creating a version of the photograph. Perfected as a method through the 1890s, halftone was widely adopted in the production of both magazines and newspapers. Not all commentators saw this as progress. Richard Gilder, defending the old traditions, saw photographs as the centerpiece of a "recording tendency" in American life and letters, from cheap chromolithographs to realism in fiction. It was, he lamented, a "religion of the commonplace."[29]

"Commonplace," indeed. By the 1920s the new-fashioned print, sound, and motion-picture media provided many ways to reach mass audiences. The revolution in print, auditory, and visual communication allowed more frequent and faster communication and strengthened the possibilities for a national popular culture. The new media also raised questions about the nature of reality and the nature of American life. Were photographs real? Were they visual tricks? Were they art? Was the rapid pace of life throwing American values out of focus? Would the new media undermine the morals of ordinary people? Would they serve nefarious motives of elite people? The media both expressed and caused such anxieties; at the same time, they facilitated the creation of a national economy and a national consumer culture.

Managing the production, marketing, and distribution of goods in this new national arena required a new cadre of administrators and professionals. In creating and training such a cadre, corporate capitalists created a virtually new social class, one that Marx had not anticipated. They were salaried, not owners, capitalists without capital. They were factory managers, sales experts, engineers, architects, lawyers, accountants, advertising executives, and personnel managers, and they scurried to professionalize their training, their work, and their status. Such administrators and facilitators existed not only in the big manufacturing companies but in supporting firms and institutions. The implementation of new technologies, for example, was assisted crucially by organizations like the Railway Mail Service, Western Union, the Bell System, and the Associated Press.[30]

To be sure, the United States was not suddenly and entirely integrated into corporate capitalism in the last two decades of the nineteenth century. Although historian Frederick Jackson Turner famously proclaimed the "end of the frontier" in America in 1894, the western states and territories remained principally occupied with farming and mining.[31] The area included large numbers of people of color, and their relationship to expanding capitalism was mediated by negotiations over land. The new social and economic order was ushered in at the local level by white settlers and businessmen from the East, in their day-to-day encounters with the indigenous population, through land purchases, court disputes about ownership, the creation of public school systems, and the like. In the process the lives of Latino Americans in the Southwest were disastrously reordered, their culture challenged, and their property rights subverted. The lives of Native Americans were similarly reordered, after the cessation of outright warfare, through broken treaties and reforms directed against tribal culture, such as the Dawes General Allotment Act of 1887 and the establishment of boarding schools intended to "kill the Indian and save the man."[32] In the South, the end of Reconstruction ushered in a new era of resubordination for African Americans, entailing their relegation to the lowest economic levels and the withdrawal of their political rights.

Thus, even as new ideologies of American nationalism coalesced during this era, the country's actual population was becoming more diverse, augmented as it was by waves and waves of immigrants from southern and eastern Europe as well as from Asia and Latin America. At the same time, the country's African

American population migrated in large numbers from the South to the North, thereby producing increased diversity within densely concentrated urban areas. More and more women also made their way into the public worlds of work and print. The interaction between this more diversified population and the consolidating tendencies of various commercial, juridical, and bureaucratic institutions led to significant forms of social unrest. It also led to the creation of alternate, diverse, locally generated bodies of knowledge situated within evolving subcultures and countercultures that helped people to make sense of these charged interactions. In sum, processes of concentration and consolidation were always accompanied by countervailing processes of diversification and specialization and sometimes by outright contestation.

Key Terms and a Conceptual Framework

Our framework for ordering the histories of printing, publishing, and reading developed out of our earliest efforts to trace the role these activities played in a society characterized by deepening polarities. We have found the term "culture of print" a useful shorthand descriptor for this period's social formation in part because the tensions between social integration and disintegration, between order and disorder, and between incorporation and diversity were themselves played out with the indispensable assistance of proliferating print practices and reading formations. Indeed, the vertical and horizontal integration characteristic of the limited-liability corporation, as well as the nationalization of both consumption and American popular culture, could not have been managed without the extension and rapid circulation of print technologies and forms. At the same time, neither could alternative forms of identification and affiliation have multiplied so easily without the widening access to print provided by economies of scale and speed as well as by the extension of schooling to previously excluded populations, rising literacy rates, the creation of foreign-language newspapers, alternative presses, and a range of specialized print forms. As much as the period 1880 to 1940 was an age of incorporation in search of order, so, too, was it one of proliferating, ubiquitous, nearly inescapable print — print that was everywhere set in motion to suit multiple and diverse purposes.

Culture of print captures our sense that print and publication became indispensable to the business of American life during this period and, as a result, more formally integrated with other institutions, practices, and associations. Indeed, reams of published timetables, rate schedules, manuals, and regulations were essential to the expansion and maturation of the national transportation and communications networks that made the new integrated corporations possible. Trade journals played an ever-increasing role in advertising new technologies to managers. Equally essential was the development of an ad-driven, nationally oriented, mass-market press that sought to persuade Americans to consume the products churned out by diversifying industries and showed them how to use them in new formations of bourgeois life. Printed forms, reports, and legislative instruments were similarly critical to the growth of the increasingly bureaucratic administrative state. Finally, a more elaborate scholarly apparatus for circulating research results nationally and internationally emerged during this era, as did a textbook industry that supported the schools that were necessary to produce the more literate, more highly educated individuals needed for work in an increasingly specialized society.

Access to printed materials, however, did not guarantee that the user would necessarily be integrated into a more fully ordered and coordinated society. Indeed, the aforementioned economies of scale and speed enabled the production of cheaper and cheaper books, magazines, and newspapers, a development that put these forms into the hands of people who previously were denied access to both the literacy and the literary tools of the powerful. Cheaper books and more literacy presented a diverse people with opportunities for the reading of varied material. In time, these developments fueled the imaginations of women, freed slaves, and working-class individuals, all of whom sought to make sense of their relationship to the emerging forms of American life and to articulate their own interests.

As more and more Americans became habituated to the presence of printed materials in their daily lives, publishing, printing, and reading activities appeared to many a natural route to the realization of a range of interests, investments, and desires. Some expressed their views by founding magazines or journals, small presses or alternative newspapers; others decided to write for such organs or to subscribe to them as a way of pursuing their own interests and to augment their sense of themselves as distinct people. Still others saw economic opportunity in the range of supporting businesses necessary to the smooth functioning of the publishing industry. They moved into papermaking, binding, book design, bookselling, and library work in increasing numbers; some even created new businesses like book wholesaling, advertising firms, and literary agencies. As these activities multiplied exponentially in the years after 1880, what emerged in addition to the mass-market newspapers, magazines, and books—which so many scholars of print have emphasized as characteristic of this age—was a variety of *specialized* networks for printing, publishing, and circulating material that often were quite focused and had more narrow audiences.

We have decided to include these networks in our category of "local print cultures" not to identify them with particular geographic areas or to suggest that they were sequestered outside the larger culture of print, but rather to emphasize the *particularity* of certain networks that joined readers, writers, publishers, and various supporting individuals together in a set of activities that articulated certain shared interests.

"Culture" is used to refer to the *habituated* nature of the social relations, practices, traditions, assumptions, and beliefs that characterized these specialized networks. Thus, when targeted forms of print attracted both habitual readers and contributors to their pages and together they developed shared ways of reading and writing about a circumscribed set of topics, they created local print cultures that were instrumental in articulating specific forms of affiliation and could even generate new identities and new communities.

The centralizing tendencies inherent in the creation of nationally oriented news syndicates and mass-market magazines aimed at a nation of middle-class consumers were checked somewhat by the contrapuntal effects of the emergence of print forms targeting, among others, non-English speakers, African Americans, working-class readers, women, people with particular religious views and affiliations, socialists, imagists, and a range of others who had reason to question dominant cultural formations and the views and values that underwrote them. At the same time, print forms also helped to define and gather people together as physicians, plumbers, stamp collectors, engineers, farmers, clubwomen, psychologists, and others who were marked off from the mainstream less by their questioning of it than by their possession of technical knowledge and special expertise. The culture of print that emerged in the decades after 1880, like American society more generally, was pushed and pulled by contradictory pressures that, on the one hand, led to greater centralization and intensified nationalism and, on the other, produced differentiation, specialization, and alternative forms of identification.

Because some of these local print cultures tried to maintain their distance from mainstream print networks, they could be clearly defined, insular in focus, and relatively homogeneous in their orientation. Others were more fluid and more permeable. In either case, when people bought, read, or wrote print matter, they had complex reasons for doing so that were not necessarily contiguous with the intentions of those who had read or written in the same venue before them. And sometimes they used those print forms in ways wholly oblique to their producers' intentions. It is well known, for instance, that the pages of magazines like *Munsey's*, *Ainslee's*, and *Cosmopolitan* were often cut up for use in scrapbooks, as pictures for framing, as wallpaper, or as packing material.

Thus, even as we have attempted to track the regularities and trends that ordered Americans' many interactions with printed materials during this period, so too have we attempted to take note of the irregularities—that Americans also read, wrote, bought, sold, categorized, shelved, and recommended print matter to others for a host of reasons, not all of them in keeping with what might have been expected. What, we have asked ourselves, did people hope to gain from their expanded access to a range of print materials? What exactly did they *do* with the words they wrote, printed, and read? How did print culture function for them at the particular site where they engaged it? Our interest in the active and adaptive use of print led to our emphasis that not only individuals who were traditionally conceived as producers of print—that is, publishers and writers—operated as *agents* in the history of print culture. Whether as writers, editors, publishers, printers, designers, wholesalers, advertisers, literary agents, or readers, millions of Americans used print culture for their own purposes. They used print to make a living, to gather information, to indulge in pleasure, to develop a certain understanding of their identity and a capacity for voice in the public arena, and to constitute specific communities—in short, to get things done.

Our sense of this rich complexity of the culture of print between 1880 and 1940 prompted our reservations about the usefulness for this period of Robert Darnton's circuit metaphor as a device for conceptualizing the history of print culture. Despite Darnton's willingness to concede, on the one hand, that the process of book production involves many different actors and, on the other, that it should not be conceived in linear fashion as proceeding simply from author to publisher to printer to reader, we believe that the graphic representation of the process tends to reinstate this simple trajectory. It thus runs the risk of simplifying the highly complex and contentious social practices that circulated in, around, and through print culture during this period. The metaphor of the circuit implies a view from above that homes in on the object being circulated rather than the social actors involved in the process, on the social milieu within which they operated, and their complex reasons for involving themselves in the culture of print in the first place.

We think this tends to reduce print culture to a system of communication alone rather than attend to it as a complex network of socially organized practices. We worry that, by privileging the idea of communication, Darnton's circuit metaphor inadvertently tends to privilege authors and the act of writing as the real point of origin of the process rather than to recognize that the industrialized yet articulated publishing industry of the late nineteenth and early twentieth centuries drew many to it who were less interested in the meaning of any particular product turned out by the industry than in what they could accomplish economically, socially, culturally, or ideologically by inserting themselves at a particular point or site in the larger process. We think it important *not* to erase these other, complex forms of agency when seeking to understand the array of activities that both constituted print culture and contended with each other over its use and effects.

We approach the history of print culture from the point of view of the practices and intentions of multiple actors who involved themselves in the production and use of print, the sites at which they took place, and the multiple effects of these activities. We are especially interested in the production, use, control, and limitation of print. By "production," we mean all those activities involved in generating print products from writing and editing to printing and publishing. We try to avoid privileging one aspect of the larger process over another. We use the abstract term "use" to refer to the many ways people turned to print culture to accomplish particular ends. Writers and readers were both "users" of print culture in that they sought to employ magazines, books, and newspapers to accomplish particular ends — that is, to address others, to learn, to constitute a sense of the self, or to express their beliefs. Thus the notion of "use" covers everything from writing to reading, bookselling to library work, advertising to home decoration and display.

Finally, in seeking to understand how print has been controlled and limited, we have attempted to take account of the fact that print was a key technology of power during this period. Interested parties to its production and use struggled with each other over what could appear in print just as they struggled over who should be given access to particular sorts of print products. Editors rejected inappropriate submissions for their publications; librarians sought to restrict the number of novels that patrons could check out at any given time; local governments tried to censor the publication and distribution of material they deemed pornographic; settlement house workers taught English to immigrants to insure their assimilation; and some elite universities attempted to deny higher education to Jews. All of these actors sought to control how print was used and by whom.

Because we think these struggles over books and print culture are essential to any effort to understand how they functioned during our period, we believe it is essential to construe "the history of the book" in its broadest sense. Therefore, although we attend carefully to the privileged arena of trade book publishing, we also pay attention to the production of magazines, newspapers, government pamphlets and reports, and religious books and ephemera, as well as non-English print forms. If we had featured only bound books as the heart of our story, without attending to the way the bound book's cultural dominance was contested by the existence of other print forms, we would have favored the activities of social and cultural elites. The distribution of book readers, after all, is not random; book reading in the United States tends to correlate with education and wealth. In fact, there were far more readers of newspapers and magazines in the late nineteenth and early twentieth centuries than there were readers of books. Thus we have attempted to make sense here of the changing relationship between books and other forms as well as of the ways in which the disempowered and disadvantaged sought access to print culture often through the use of print forms that either were newer or possessed less social status than the trade publishing network.

In sum, we conceptualize the culture of print of the period 1880 to 1940 as a complex, highly articulated system, entered into by different actors at different points for various and multiple purposes. Because our view emphasizes multiple functions as well as the existence of loosely coupled parts and interlocking subsystems, it is not easily captured through the use of a single metaphor; nor can it be effectively diagrammed. Still, despite our emphasis on the proliferation of semiautonomous and specialized local print cultures, we continually return to the idea of print culture as something of a system to emphasize that publication and print practices became habituated, ritualized, and increasingly integrated during these years. Indeed, to gain access to the world of print, one had to possess certain knowledge, capacities, contacts, and strategies. One had to know how, when, and where to seek entry to an already functioning process governed by particular protocols and gate-keeping procedures. And one learned that information by participating in other arenas of print culture.

The consolidation of the culture of print in these years did not lead to the creation of a single, homeostatically calibrated system governing all publication. Nonetheless, as printed texts became more and more essential to diverse arenas of American life and as opportunities for generating profit from print culture increased, many agents tried to coordinate more effectively the making, distribution, and consumption of printed texts. The drive for efficiency and speed in this process led not only to the creation of new distribution agencies and outlets, such as the American News Company, drug and department store book departments, and book clubs, but also to the creation of new mediating and coordinating agents like newspaper syndicates, newspaper book review sections, and literary agents. Although no single institution or single set of intentions governed this process of innovation, the ultimate effect was that different businesses coordinated their efforts, worked more closely together, and thereby subsidized each other's efforts.

As a result, they increased the possibility that a single text would be circulated redundantly through different nodes of what looked increasingly to some like a single integrated system. A text might appear first as a magazine or newspaper short, migrate later through trade distribution outlets as a traditional hardbound book, materialize as the subject of a review in a newspaper book review section or as an object of "chat" on a radio book program, reappear later as a cheap reprint, and then emerge finally in yet another form as a Hollywood film. As this kind of coordination increased, the processes of integration became so noticeable that "massification" became a subject of significant commentary and criticism. This culminated in the "mass culture" debate and eventually in the creation of university departments of communication designed to study what Theodor Adorno and Max Horkheimer presciently named "the culture industry."

The process of integration was, however, uneven and imperfect. The increasing mobility and extension of print made possible by technological and organizational innovation had multiple and contradictory effects. The word "motion" in our title is meant to refer to the ways in which the mobility of print forms not only was intensified and sped up but also extended geographically. Railroads, syndicates, the telegraph, the telephone, better and more plentiful distribution outlets—together, these forces enabled print materials to be produced and circulated more cheaply and more quickly. At the same time, these innovations and the economies they permitted also enabled producers of print to reach out beyond the local geographic area in search of sometimes larger, sometimes more-specific audiences. Thus, even as print culture contributed to the consolidation of nationalism during this period, so, too, did it challenge the primacy of affiliation based solely on residence. Specialized, targeted print forms gathered people together from across the nation on the basis of interests not directly tied to where people resided. In this way the larger culture of print proliferated new, cross-cutting possibilities for the construction of identities and the creation of communities that were sometimes generated in response to racialized, gendered, and sexualized hierarchies of power, and sometimes through elected affinity based on shared interests. It is, finally, this tension between centralization, concentration, and standardization on the one hand, and specialization, small-scale production, and the diversification of published reading material on the other that stands at the very heart of the story we have to tell here. In the end, the culture of print that flourished between 1880 and 1940 displayed bristling diversity despite the dominance of powerful mechanisms of consolidation.

CHAPTER 2

Seeing the Sites
Readers, Publishers, and Local Print Cultures in 1880

Carl F. Kaestle

In 1876 the largest crowd in American history—186,000 people—gathered in Philadelphia to celebrate the nation's centennial[1] (figure 2.1). On opening day, all eyes were on the huge engine built by George Corliss of Rhode Island. Standing before it, the novelist William Dean Howells called it "an athlete of steel and iron, without a superfluous ounce of metal on it." When President Ulysses Grant threw the switch, the engine began churning out power for thirteen acres of assorted machines, making everything from shoes to wallpaper. Warned by their ministers to avoid the nude paintings from France and Italy, most American visitors reveled in machinery and inventions: electric lights, telephones, and typewriters.[2]

Four years later, the centennial was only a memory, but the country's prospects actually looked much better. Businesses had recovered from the depression that had begun in 1873. American commentators celebrated the spread of public libraries, the development of a respectable American literature, the proliferation of local newspapers, and the opening of the transcontinental railroad. Delivering on the dreams of the centennial exhibits, Thomas Edison displayed the first workable electric streetlight at Menlo Park in 1880. That same year, industrialist George Pullman, who had purchased the Corliss engine from the Philadelphia exposition to run the factories that would make his railroad cars, created what he believed would be an ideal company town, just south of Chicago.[3]

In 1880 as well, the Ivory Soap Company first announced that its soap was "99 and 44/100 percent pure." Ivory joined Royal Baking Powder and Lydia Pinkham's Vegetable Compound among America's original national brands, harbingers of the budding nationwide consumer market. Ayer's Advertising Company of Philadelphia performed in 1880 the nation's first market survey—for a threshing machine sales campaign in the Midwest.[4] The country was being drawn together by business, transportation, and print media.

Yet elite Anglo-Americans had not forgotten the depression of the 1870s and

FIGURE 2.1. On the opening day of the Philadelphia Centennial Exhibition, 10 May 1876, stands for speakers and a choir for the opening ceremonies were erected on the terraces of the Art Gallery and the Main Building. The crowd gathered under umbrellas to listen. Print and Picture Collection, The Free Library of Philadelphia.

labor's confrontations with industrial management. Some remarked anxiously on the new surge of immigration, which included more people from southern and eastern Europe, poorer and more culturally different from Anglo-Americans than earlier immigrants had been. Other racial and ethnic minorities were also outside the cultural and economic mainstream, and women's activities were proscribed in many respects. Members of these groups strove to assert and institutionalize their aspirations through African American colleges, Latino-American publications, Native American treaty struggles, and female assertions of authorial status. The restoration of white governments in the South represented a shaky sectional truce and boded ill for African Americans. All of these agitations bubbled beneath the not-quite-placid surface of Victorian culture in 1880. Catching their breath after a difficult decade, Victorian Americans mustered a nervous confidence.

How did these cultural, economic, technological, and political crosscurrents affect the worlds of publishing and reading? This chapter explores the production and uses of print in 1880, revealing a wide diversity of practices, customs, and conditions. Before the tour begins, two preliminaries may be helpful. First, a discussion of some key concepts will help establish an interpretive approach consistent with the framework presented in chapter 1. Then, some national-level data on education and literacy in the United States in 1880 will provide context.

Some Key Concepts

Producers and Readers

This volume focuses not only on the production of printed material but also on how readers used and interpreted print. It is an article of faith in print studies today that texts have no meaning without readers and thus that we cannot know what a reader thought about a text without direct evidence. Although this is an exciting theory, evidence on the readers' side is sparse. Readers often leave few tracks. Not only is the evidence more abundant on the producers' side, but also the scale of the enterprise is greater. Michel de Certeau underscores this point when he talks about the "strategies" of production and the "tactics" of interpretation.[5] In modern times the production of print has been aimed at large audiences, but interpretation is by definition a small-scale phenomenon. For the student of print, this raises the alarming possibility of a chaos of limitless interpretations. Fortunately, readers employ tactics to interpret text, some of which are shaped by shared histories, cultures, ideologies, and predicaments. Scholars have therefore argued that we can discern groups of people with similar backgrounds and interests who are likely to interpret a given text in similar ways.

A Culture of Print

The thesis of this volume is that American culture from 1880 to 1940 was increasingly a "culture of print," that is, a culture that was knit together and defined by the printed word. Many factors encouraged the expansion and standardization of mainstream printed materials, but it was not a simple story of growing consensus or homogenization. Dissident groups and newly active producers of print constantly added their diverse voices. Meanwhile, economic, political, and cultural life increasingly was embedded in the printed word, which circulated faster, more cheaply, and more widely than ever before. Such a culture of print not only expanded publishing and reading but also produced a lot of thinking about the nature and purposes of print, ranging from formal essays about the nation's book trades and reading publics to informal discussions carried on at sites of print production or where people talked about their reading.

What are here called "local print cultures" involved traditions, values, experiences, practices, infrastructures, and ideologies that provided common purposes and understandings within certain groups of print producers and readers. On the production side, some authors, publishers, and editors shared traditions, values, practices, and goals that drove their work. That work depended upon financial and material capital whose organization and particular application created incentives and constraints on the process. The personal and cultural experiences of the producers also conditioned their purposes and practices. Those were in turn pursued at different sites where particular modes of communication and leadership, operating procedures, and beliefs about audiences prevailed. For example, one might contrast the local print culture of a radical press putting out a weekly paper in a Chicago basement with that of the *Chicago Tribune* just up the street. They had different economics, social relations, purposes, practices, and clients.

Like producers, readers were influenced by social class, income, and education, as well as by the history and social beliefs of their communities. Depending upon their literacy level, their past experience with a range of different texts, and even their attitudes toward particular kinds of books, people varied in how and where they read as well as whether they read alone or with others. Their interpretive practices and procedures varied, too, depending on whether they were reading to learn, to revisit familiar truths and valued stories, or merely to while away a few moments in the middle-class parlor or on a streetcar bustling them toward work. Some readers wrote extensively about what their books meant to them as solitary readers, and others discussed favorite texts with friends or family, thus aligning their reading with that of their peers. In both cases, however, readers applied certain interpretive tactics and evaluative judgments reflective of their particular social location. Examples of scholarship on local cultures of reading and how they affected interpretation and use include Janice Radway's work on the readers of romance novels; Christine Pawley's book on the institutions of literacy in Osage, Iowa, in the late nineteenth and early twentieth centuries; and David Nord's research on the Protestant readers of the *Chicago Tribune* in the 1910s.[6] To be sure, there was often much overlap in the assumptions and values of producers of print and their readers, but we cannot *assume* congruence without evidence of the readers' interpretations.

Core and Periphery

Readers, obviously, are more dispersed than producers. Ultimately, scholars of print history need to find a way to move through space and time, examining the production and uses of print across the whole country and across the whole population, in order to understand patterns and trends in print production and reading practices, and the extent and nature of variations across differently situated social groups. Where to begin?

There are some existing models to consider. The traditional approach in the history of the book begins with publishing houses, discusses professional trends within the zone of production, and casts only occasional glances beyond, into the zones of consumption. The cultural view behind this model was spoofed in Saul Steinberg's famous *New Yorker* magazine cartoon depicting New Yorkers' myopic view of the United States as seen from Ninth Avenue, in which Tenth Avenue in New York looms large, with a rather barren continent beyond the Hudson, featuring Chicago and the Pacific Ocean.[7]

The academic version of this "core and periphery" model, however, has some merit. After all, by 1880 New York City *was* the center of the publishing trade and had huge influence. Still, the relationship between the core and the periphery was neither one-way nor fixed. Indigenous publications' relation to the mainstream was partly independent, partly reactive, and partly reciprocal. Much activity and meaning remained outside the hegemony of the central system of cultural production and marketing. A site that was peripheral for one person may have been the core for another. If you were the young Charles Scribner, who inherited his family's publishing firm in 1879, you might not have noticed the founding in 1882 of the new periodical called *El Tiempo* in Las Cruces, New Mexico. But if you were an intellectual living in New Mexico, like the editor Severino Trujillo, you probably focused on just such developments in publishing. The railroad had reached New Mexico in 1879, bringing with it the ominous beginnings of Anglo immigration and economic domination but simultaneously enabling the independent Spanish-language press to expand. Eighteen new Hispanic periodicals began in the 1880s.[8] From New Mexico, New York receded invisibly past the far horizon.

Sometimes influential publishers took up print materials that originated far from the mainstream, as when Alfred Knopf became a patron of the Harlem Renaissance in the 1920s, or when Longman's published Isabel de Palencia's autobiography about the Spanish Civil War in 1940.[9] Capitalism had many niches, and the commercial culture of a diverse nation assimilated a wide range of material, often changing it in the process. But it was a two-way street. Such aspirations and adaptations were complex on both sides. On the elite patron's side, there was often a desire to recognize diverse, creative voices while making them commercially attractive. For authors, there was generally a resolve to achieve recognition without capitulation. Lawrence Levine has written subtly about the effects of acculturation on black music, parsing seemingly paradoxical processes of give-and-take. For example, producers of phonograph recordings exerted pressure on African American artists to make their music more accessible to whites. At the same time, recordings brought distinctive, regional black music to more people, to new migrants in the region, and to blacks in other regions. In the end, Levine concludes, "records can be seen as bearers and preservers rather than primarily destroyers of folk traditions."[10]

Many of the same complexities and the same pathos that occurred in the case of music also occurred in the history of African American writing. Houston Baker recently revisited Alain Locke's famous anthology of 1925, *The New Negro*, and concluded that it achieved for African American culture an "irreversible shift from the medieval to the modern," a critical shift from a southern rural identity to a cosmopolitan Harlem, a fusion of "class and mass," a simultaneous maintenance and transformation of the "folk sound," through "poetic mastery." The authors in Locke's anthology, considered a manifesto of the Harlem Renaissance, were working within a "fluid field" of possibilities and were seeking new definitions of African American identity.[11] In the process, as James Danky notes in chapter 17, they distanced themselves from many ordinary black readers.

In sum, the core-periphery model risks privileging the core and missing much of the story of print culture in the periphery, but when it is seen as a subtle two-way dialogue, it can lead us to explore some important truths about economic power and the emergence of mass print culture.[12]

The Importance of the Site

It is easier to decenter New York than to find a new organizing principle for this volume. The "core" and "periphery" model is seductive, at once unavoidable and insufficient. It must be supplemented, however, by thick descriptions of diverse sites away from the core.[13] The choice of sites is governed by researchers' interests and assumptions, which should be made as explicit as possible, and by the availability of evidence. Historians are always beholden to the remnants of the past, and the remnants are more revealing at some sites than at others.

Several conclusions about what is important in the history of print culture have influenced the selection of sites in this chapter and this volume. For example, magazines and newspapers had greater readership than books. The sites highlighted in this chapter, therefore, were selected because they might provide evidence about these various print forms and their readers. In addition, hundreds of published autobiographies of people from diverse economic circumstances were consulted in an effort not only to identify those which discussed authors' reading practices but also to develop descriptions of the sites of their early reading.

Chapter 1's theoretical framework highlighted four functions involving text: producing, using, controlling, and limiting. The analysis of 1880 presented in this chapter surveys sites where one can assess those functions. When Carlo Barsotti established *Il Progresso* in New York City in 1880, for example, he began *producing* text. Indeed, *Il Progresso* eventually became the largest Italian-language daily in the United States and a substantial business. Simultaneously, of course, Barsotti was *using* print to assert his views, for example, against those of the rival paper, *L'Eco*. At the same time, through his editorial stance, he was *controlling* print. He rejected some views and promoted others. Finally, he was *limiting* his audience by publishing the paper in Italian, serving Italian speakers.[14]

In sum, this chapter emphasizes the importance of *site* in exploring print production and reading. Whether considering a modest home in small-town, upstate Michigan or the back-alley offices of the fledgling *Il Progresso* in New York City, the chapter's goal is to enter into the historical site and explore the material conditions and the local print cultures influencing that place. This overview moves from site to site quickly, but many of the examples are drawn from studies or archival sources that present rich depictions of reading and publishing in 1880.

Education, Literacy, and the Book Trade in 1880

Before we examine specific sites, some national statistics describing levels of education, literacy, and the production of print are relevant, as these form the raw materials for a national culture of print. By 1880 most white Americans attended school for at least a few years. Of the white children ages five to nineteen, about 62 percent were enrolled in 1880. For children of other races enrollment equaled 34 percent.[15] The length of the school year and the average daily attendance had both been rising steadily. While most children received at least a few years of education, the school-leaving age was strongly influenced by family characteristics, including parents' occupation, education, ethnicity, and recency of immigration.[16]

Free public schooling for whites had been available in most areas for several decades. Schooling and other forms of instruction were sufficient to produce widespread, rudimentary adult literacy in the United States by 1880. Only

9 percent of native-born whites over the age of ten reported that they could not write. The figure for foreign-born whites was 12 percent. Among the population of color, a majority of whom were former slaves, 70 percent said that they were unable to write, but that proportion declined rapidly after 1880.[17] Rudimentary education and literacy, then, were widespread, although there was a large but decreasing racial divide.

Higher education was much sparser. Secondary school enrollment was probably less than 5 percent of the population aged between fourteen and seventeen, and the reported college enrollment was about 116,000, about 2 percent of the population aged from eighteen to twenty-two. Thus, many Americans possessed basic reading ability while a more elite corps was educated to higher literacy, a two-tiered situation Lauren and Daniel Resnick have called "industrial literacy."[18]

With a population of 50 million, the United States had about 1,000 daily newspapers; aggregate daily circulation totaled 3.5 million. Among those papers, there were modest indicators of consolidation and standardization. About one-third of small-town papers purchased "readyprint" pages of national news stories from metropolitan suppliers. In addition, some city papers traveled miles into the hinterland to subscribers, relying heavily on railroads for distribution. Telegraphs carried common news stories to papers all over the country, and the Associated Press, despite some spirited competition, became the major supplier of these news items.[19] Nonetheless, newspapers were more local in content than books and more local in advertising than magazines. The Census Bureau's extensive survey of the industry in 1880 commented on the strikingly local nature of the American press, noting that newspapers were published in 2,073 of the country's 2,605 counties.[20] Indeed there were no newspaper chains and little syndicated material at this time. Local newspapers played a Janus-like role as a result, acting as arbiters between their locale and the emerging national culture.[21]

In addition to the daily newspapers, there were about 10,000 other periodicals, including magazines and weekly newspapers. Most periodicals—78 percent—were devoted to politics, news, and family reading, followed by religious publications, constituting about 5 percent. Within that category, Methodists, Roman Catholics, and Baptists were the biggest producers. The world of newspapers and magazines was largely an English-speaking world. Only 7 percent of all periodicals were in other languages, with German leading strongly.[22] The heyday of the foreign-language press was yet to come.

In the world of books, as in commerce more generally, 1880 brought modest prosperity after the damaging economic crisis of the 1870s. A Boston correspondent wrote to the trade journal *Publishers' Weekly* in January that "the outlook in the book world is quite encouraging." Taking "the pulse of the trade" the following September, the editors of *Publishers' Weekly* celebrated "the buoyancy of the entire bookselling interests."[23]

While the publishers and booksellers applauded the economic recovery and the associated boom in book sales, they fretted over the lack of a satisfactory distribution system. The book industry still depended heavily on direct subscription sales by itinerant book salesmen to individual readers, a legacy of the agrarian early republic. In the late nineteenth and twentieth centuries, retail bookstores and then book clubs that used the mails would become increasingly important. In 1880 books usually went from publishers to consumers in two stages: first, traveling booksellers and bookstore operators bought the books, usually at biannual trade sales. In September 1880, for example, the fall trade sale in New York City attracted buyers not only from San Francisco, Cleveland, Chicago, and Cincinnati but from Binghamton, New York; Nashville, Tennessee; and other smaller places. For seven days Houghton Mifflin, Appleton, Charles Scribner's Sons, and their competitors sold large lots of their books to the highest bidders.[24] In the second stage of the distribution process, the middlemen then sold books to individual consumers through local bookstores or door-to-door sales. Book publishers complained that the trade fairs disrupted the price structure for books, and those in regional centers complained that the fairs concentrated all the sales in the cities where the large publishers were located. Many industry spokespeople concluded that the fairs were an uneven, outmoded distribution mechanism. Indeed, the fairs declined in the 1880s and were gone by the turn of the century.[25]

In the area of libraries, clear-cut progress was noted. The American Library Association had been formed in 1876, and the federal government's inventory of public libraries in the same year showed that the public lending library was coming into its own. It counted about 3,000 libraries in the states and territories; while Idaho had only 1, New York had nearly 500.[26] Most library collections had fewer than 3,000 volumes, and there were sharp differences in access by race and region and on the urban-rural dimension.[27] Still, by 1880 the public library was developing an institutional presence and an architectural identity.

Simultaneously, the public high school became the dominant form of secondary education in the United States, surpassing private academies in the 1880s. Racial and class biases affected high schools as well as libraries, limiting access and opportunities, but Victorian commentators nonetheless touted high schools and public libraries as signs of progress. Gradually and unevenly, then, libraries and high schools spread education and literacy, promoting Anglo-American Protestant history, literature, and values. The values promoted by families, churches, and printed publications diverged strongly from this mainstream in some locations and were profoundly in tune with it in others. In the latter settings, print performed an accommodating and supportive role, not a jarring or transformative one. Our tour of America's literacy environments begins at just such a site.

Readers: The Tour Begins

Born in Salisbury, North Carolina, Hope Summerell was ten years old in 1880. Her father was a physician; her well-educated mother provided almost all of Hope's education at home. Hope's reading connected her to the outside world but was mediated by her parents' values, southern identity, and Anglo-American standards of literature. In her mother's library, Hope found works by Shakespeare, Scott, Thackeray, Dickens, Emerson, Tennyson, and Austen. When she was five, Hope received from an aunt her first book, *Alice in Wonderland*. In her memoir she recalls sitting on the porch with her new possession, captivated by the picture of the White Rabbit.[28] Neither bookish nor shy, Hope played with the neighborhood children, chafed at some of her assignments, and enjoyed her childhood. The influences available to Hope enculturated her into the outlook and literary repertoire of an educated southern woman. Her reading fare was focused on classics and steady sellers. Reading was a constant activity, and on occasion it could be sensual. Referring to a popular magazine for youngsters, she recalled, "*St. Elmo*, devoured of a summer's afternoon, along with many soft peaches, in a convenient crotch of a tree, was indeed a glorious feast." Hope also read dime novels, "purloined," as she said, from her brother.[29]

This was a conservative print environment, offering much "good" literature with an admixture of harmless "trash." In Hope's autobiography we see a child encountering seamlessly reinforced social messages and, as an adult, a woman who heartily approved of her cultural upbringing. Nonetheless, her willing enculturation was not preordained. If we had a hundred memoirs of young women with reading experiences similar to Hope's, there would be some central tendencies, but doubtless much interesting variation as well.

At our next site we can glimpse young women constructing a more professional, incipiently feminist interpretation of virtually the same print materials. The Hamilton sisters of Fort Wayne, Indiana, were privileged. Like Hope Summerell, they had an intense interest in reading.[30] Members of a prominent family, the sisters were educated at home by their mother through the 1870s and 1880s until they were sent off, one by one, to Miss Porter's School in Connecticut. At home, their education was virtually synonymous with their family reading activities. They read aloud, made up plays about characters in books, and used fictional characters as codes in their private family discourse.

The sisters focused on "good" literature, including works by Dickens, Eliot, Thackeray, and Scott. There were also contemporary novels, somewhat lower in the sisters' literary hierarchy but attractive nonetheless. The Hamiltons' reading provided escape, entertainment, and the acquisition of cultural capital, but the most striking purpose, according to historian Barbara Sicherman, was their use of fiction to imagine their futures as women in the Victorian world. They did not identify with conventional, subordinate female characters; they identified instead with venturesome, independent female and sometimes male characters. Their parents' approval of higher education and careers for young women reinforced such affinities. In this case, book culture supported family culture, but in a way that strained against the dominant values of the society. Edith Hamilton became a leading author of books about classical mythology; her sister Alice became a physician involved in public health and the first female professor at Harvard University. Their younger sisters—and the cousins who actively shared their family reading circle—pursued careers in teaching, art, settlement work, and architecture.[31]

Not all privileged youths, of course, followed in their parents' footsteps. M. Carey Thomas's ideas diverged radically from those of her parents, who were devout Quakers. Thomas's developing sense of art, gender, and sexuality went down another path. She decided as an adolescent in Baltimore that marriage represented the loss of both independence and meaningful work. By the time she had completed college and embarked on a trip to Europe in 1879, Thomas had concluded that a close, committed relationship with a woman could be the perfect solution to the conflict between love and career.[32] She had come to this realization through a complicated course of reading and relationships that set her at odds with the mainstream with respect to intimate relationships, art, and morals. By the time of her European sojourn, Thomas and her companion Mamie Gwinn were devotees of the English poet Algernon Swinburne and the French novelist Théophile Gautier, both of whom advocated the independence of art from moral constraints and encouraged the exploration of erotic pleasure, including passionate relationships between women.[33]

Rather than hide all of her unconventional notions from her mother, Thomas tried to present some of them in acceptable ways—for she loved her mother and wished no breach. In the summer of 1880 she let her mother know that she was attending theater—forbidden to strict Quakers—and that she was reading books considered improper by some, such as Émile Zola's *Nana*, a frank account of a courtesan that had just appeared that year. She reassured her mother that she found *Nana* and books like it "stupid," but "like the theater, so long as I had not read them . . . they possessed an attraction which has now *utterly* vanished."[34]

Carey Thomas was part of a cultural avant-garde. Her experience demonstrates the powerful role reading could have in the constitution of the self, but, as is so often the case, even this more rebellious self was constituted in a social context and in light of other readers' reactions. In negotiating delicate truces with her parents, she prepared herself for success in the academic world, first as a scholar and eventually as the president of Bryn Mawr College.

For children of immigrants and people of color, the contrast between the family culture and the choices presented outside the family could be even starker and even more consequential. In 1880 Emma Goldman was eleven years old and lived in St. Petersburg, Russia. When her very traditional father tried to marry her off at age fifteen, Emma protested, whereupon her father threw her French grammar into the fire, exclaiming, "All a Jewish daughter needs to know is how to prepare gefültefish, cut noodles fine, and give the man plenty of children." But Emma "wanted to study, to know life, to travel." In 1885, after many ferocious arguments with her father, she immigrated to Rochester, New York, to live with an aunt. By the following year, she had read accounts in socialist newspapers about the Haymarket riot in Chicago. At political meetings, Emma heard fiery speeches against the execution of the Haymarket anarchists, reinforcing the passion that emanated from her reading. From the moment her father burned her French grammar to the moment she delivered her first radical speech, one can see how people and books shaped Emma Goldman's trajectory toward radical concepts of personal freedom and social justice.[35]

The memoirs of two African American readers illustrate a different kind of conflict: how to relate to the print matter and cultural repertoire endorsed by the white world. James Corrothers grew up in South Haven, Michigan, a tiny lumber town eighty miles northeast of Chicago. His grandfather raised him, presiding over prayers, hymns, and Scripture reading morning and evening. Corrothers was the only person of color in the public schools. Looking back on it, he saw this as an advantage: "I grew up in an atmosphere of pure speech. . . . I have never talked Negro dialect, nor done plantation antics. My speech and ways were those of the white community about me." Eventually Corrothers regretted that this had isolated him from "the masses of my race," but as a young man, he evidenced more pride about his standard English than regret about his distance from ordinary black life.[36] Well into his career, working as a writer for the *Chicago Daily News* and the *Chicago Journal*, Corrothers said he "detested Negro dialect." When Corrothers encountered the writings of the black poet Paul Laurence Dunbar, however, he became a convert. Corrothers declared that "Negro dialect attained a new dignity and beauty." Here, he said, "was splendid material which I had overlooked." Corrothers attempted dialect writing himself, but, because he had made himself a virtual outsider to black dialect, he did not, he admitted, do it very well.[37]

The autobiography of Ida B. Wells, who turned eighteen in 1880, depicts the reconciliation of white Anglo-American culture and the experiences of ordinary black people in a quite different way. Born the daughter of slaves in Holly Springs, Mississippi, Wells grew up amid the turbulence of Reconstruction. She attended a school established by the Freedmen's Bureau, for which her father served as a trustee, and she became an enthusiastic reader, eventually finishing all the books in the library. Ida read Dickens, Alcott, the Brontes, and Shakespeare, but never, she said, "anything about Negroes."[38] Nonetheless, she learned early about the rights of African Americans and the dangers of asserting those rights. When her father rejected pressure from his landlord to vote for the Democratic ticket, he returned from the polls to find his workshop locked and his carpenter's tools confiscated. The family had to relocate and start over. Wells knew that the "Ku Klux Klan" meant "something fearful," and she remembered her mother fretting while her father went to political meetings.[39]

As a young woman in the 1880s Ida Wells moved to Memphis, where she began writing articles. She took over the *Evening Star* when the editor went to Washington, and she began writing a weekly column in a Baptist publication that reached people in the hinterland.[40] As an editor and a crusader against lynching, Ida Wells spent her life bridging two worlds: first, the world of ordinary people who sought help, an enterprise that taught her the virtue of direct, simple writing and speaking; and, second, the world of power—the power of journalism as a weapon against the power of unlawful violence. Her entrée to this elite realm owed much to her parents' devotion to education and social justice, the opportunity of a good school and library, and her voracious appetite for reading.

It should be clear from these examples that individual readers were shaped by the print matter presented to them, but over time they also had opportunities to revise their interpretations and change their values. In this process they were influenced not only by parents but also by friends, siblings, and members of organizations. These were interpretive groups—the Hamilton family, Emma Goldman's political mentors, and Carey Thomas's college friends—comprising people who shared similar life experiences, who talked about their reading, and who were inclined to have similar reactions. Although an individual's interpretation of a particular text is not predictable, these memoirs demonstrate the social nature of reading: the shaping influence of the circumstances the reader brought to the text, and of the conversations readers had with other readers.

Publishers: The Tour Continues

Like readers, *publishers* were not wholly independent of each other, and their practices were affected by economics, technology, and ideology. With respect to technology, for instance, the invention and spread of the Linotype in the 1880s made typesetting faster and cheaper, allowing publishers to strive for larger, more dispersed audiences. Other changes that influenced producers of print quite broadly were the passage of an international copyright law, changes in the postal service, the development of telegraph news services, and increases in literacy through public schooling. Producers of print also had local traditions and practices—local print cultures. For example, although the New York producers of cheap "story papers" were competitors, they shared many practices and beliefs regarding writing, design, content, and marketing. Similarly, men in the top publishing houses and elite review journals of New York, Boston, and Philadelphia, at once competitors and colleagues, shared many literary standards, practices, concepts, and contacts.

The chapter's tour resumes, then, with a focus on some publishers and editors. Newspapers were the most widely read and most local print form,[41] and it is important to note the existence of significant interplay between the national and the local by following a major news story through the pages of newspapers around the country. One such story in 1880 was the Whittaker scandal at West Point. Johnson Whittaker, the only black cadet at the military academy in 1880, accused three unknown attackers of assaulting him as he slept in the barracks, mutilating him around the ears, and leaving him on the floor bleeding. Initial press coverage was sympathetic to the cadet, but soon the academy's superintendent and the attending surgeon accused Whittaker of fabricating the incident to avoid an examination he feared he would fail. Whittaker denied the charges and asked for an inquiry. A review panel supported General John Schofield, the superintendent, and Whittaker was confined to his quarters. However, Schofield soon faced a storm of criticism. President Rutherford B. Hayes got involved, and, after many behind-the-scenes discussions within the cabinet, transferred Schofield to the frontier. Whittaker was then court-martialed and convicted, but upon review the army's judge advocate general overturned that decision. At this point, charges against Whittaker were dropped, but he was expelled permanently from the academy for having performed poorly on his philosophy examination (figure 2.2).[42]

Readers' capacity to learn about this episode was heavily influenced by their newspapers' editorial slant and depth of coverage. The *Atlanta Constitution*, for example, had a general position on race relations in the North: that social equality among the races was impossible and undesirable; that northerners were

FIGURE 2.2. The trial of the black West Point cadet, Johnson Whittaker, received wide coverage in the southern and northern press. *Harper's Weekly*, 1 May 1880. Courtesy of HarpWeek.

hypocrites because in fact they treated African Americans worse than southerners did; and that, therefore, northerners should stop preaching to the South.[43] The Whittaker story provided an opportunity to sound these themes. The *Atlanta Constitution* quickly picked up on the accusations that Whittaker had fabricated the incident, and its editors used sarcastic, alliterative titles for their headlines as the story unfolded, such as "The Carved Cadet," and "Whittled Whittaker."[44] They accused northern Republicans of trying to use the story to "attack the South."[45] After the inquiry found against Whittaker, the *Constitution* commented that "West Point has Whittaker by the ears."[46]

Moving to the West, we find the regional character of San Francisco's *Evening Bulletin* striking for a different reason. There was simply much less coverage of national politics and Washington events. Typical items included local weather, finance, shipping, and West Coast political news.[47] The paper often compressed its coverage of national news under the heading, "Telegraphic Sparks from Washington." On 8 April this column reported briefly on the Whittaker scandal, stating that "Cadet Whittaker is very indignant at the suspicion that he mutilated himself, and has asked for a Court of Inquiry," adding, "The affair grows more perplexing." On 22 April the paper wrote an editorial, consistent with its Republican affiliation, condemning West Point and supporting Whittaker. After that, it generally emphasized testimony about Whittaker's good character.[48]

A brief swing through rural Illinois can illustrate variety within a region. The *Ogle County Press*, published in Polo, Illinois, attempted to include all the subjects covered by big-city papers by keeping them very brief. National stories like the Whittaker scandal were covered in short paragraphs off the front page. The brevity of the news articles tended to curtail editorializing. On Whittaker, for example, the initial three-sentence article read: "during the night of the fifth a colored cadet at West Point was attacked, in the barracks, by three masked men, bound hand and foot, and mutilated about the ears. It was believed the outrage was perpetrated by classmates of the victims. The matter was being investigated."[49] This seems to place the paper on Whittaker's side, but only one further short mention of the Whittaker affair appeared. Such brief coverage left much room for puzzlement by Ogle County readers.

The *Quincy Daily Whig*, located in a larger town, contained a large volume of advertising but, like the *Ogle County Press*, attempted to cover both national and local news. It had whole sections of news about various eastern centers, often noting that the material was copied from big-city newspapers. Whittaker was covered first on 7 April, in a brief notice, calling the episode an "outrage." The next week a longer story in the *Whig* approvingly quoted a *New York Times* article. The *Times* queried "whether West Point academy is a school for the training of soldiers to whose advantages all American citizens are entitled on a footing of exact equality, or a seminary of aristocratic pretension and nursery of snobs in uniform."[50]

Whether noncommittal, like the *Ogle County Press*, or partisan, like the *Quincy Daily Whig*, these small rural papers could not afford the space to give readers the complex details involved in the Whittaker saga. The *New York Times*, in contrast, was in the thick of the action. With the space and the intention to cover news thoroughly, the editors printed thirty-nine stories on the Whittaker incident. As with the *Atlanta Constitution*, regional context affected coverage. The *Times* had run many stories on southern cruelty to black citizens, decrying white southerners for lynching, economic oppression, and obstructing blacks' right to vote.[51] The first Whittaker story, on 7 April, entitled "Villainy at West Point," quotes Whittaker's statement about the attack in great detail, including his attackers' alleged remark that they wanted to "mark" him like farmers mark hogs in the South. In April and May the *Times* covered details of the investigation and printed several stories on Whittaker's good character and academic abilities.[52] When the Court of Inquiry in late May decided against Whittaker, however, the disappointed *Times* editors simply quoted their findings.[53]

TABLE 2.1. Top-selling periodicals in 1880

Rank	Title	Type	Circulation (est.)
1	*New York Weekly*	Literary	200,000
2	*Youth's Companion*	Youth	150,000
3	*Saturday Night*	Literary	150,000
4	*Harper's Weekly*	Literary	120,000
5	*Scribner's Monthly*	Literary	117,000
6	*Farm and Fireside*	Agricultural	103,000
7	*Home and Farm*	Agricultural	100,000
8	*Fireside Companion*	Literary	92,000
9	*Delineator*	Fashion	85,000
10	*American Agriculturist*	Agricultural	75,000

Source: Tabulated from N. W. Ayer and Son, *American Newspaper Annual* (Philadelphia, Pa.: N. W. Ayer and Son, 1880). Ayer's circulation estimates were largely unverified in the early years of that advertisers' guide to publications, including the 1880s and 1890s. Because they were largely supplied by the editors of the periodicals, they should be treated with some skepticism.

With a national election heating up, the Whittaker story faded. Whittaker returned to the South, where he was a teacher and principal in various black academies during the rest of his career. The coverage of this case in local newspapers provides a clear-cut example of how texts can constrain readers' interpretations. Local print cultures, with varying resources and ideological orientations, produced texts that provided readers with very different materials for understanding the scandal.

Magazines also helped people interpret events occurring beyond their communities. In 1880 there were about 3,000 periodicals in the United States.[54] They came into people's homes through the mail system, mostly by railroad. Less local than newspapers, magazines tended to rely on special identities — like occupations or religious beliefs — to unite readers across space. Three of the ten top-circulation magazines in 1880, for example, were agricultural magazines (see table 2.1).

Their pages exude a strong sense of community promoted by the editors. The May 1880 edition of the *American Agriculturalist* featured an article on the importance of rest and "intelligent recreation" at noontime, accompanied by an elaborate illustration evoking healthy activities for noon hour on a farm, including, of course, reading. The *American Agriculturalist*'s letters section carried an extensive discussion of barbed wire, newly introduced in the late 1870s. Mr. R. Noyes, of Coles County, Illinois, reported that all the railroads were using barbed wire to protect their tracks from wandering livestock. "As to its being 'barbarous,' I have never known an animal really hurt with it." Disagreeing, L. B. Goodwin, of Rock Island County, Illinois, said that his neighbor's valuable mare got frightened and ran against the barbs, suffering "cuts reaching the bone." Louis Vorus of Coffey County, Kansas, thought he knew the solution. He recommended sharp, straight barbs "but not long enough to penetrate the vital part of any living thing."[55]

Religious periodicals had different but interesting ways to reach their audiences. Some of these—like Sunday School magazines and daily devotional aids—penetrated local communities because they were useful in actual religious practices. There were also religious newspapers representing denominational viewpoints, children's periodicals, and religiously oriented family magazines. The number of subscribers to the larger religious periodicals in 1800 totaled about 73,000 for the *Sunday School Journal* (Methodist), about 64,000 for the *Christian Advocate* (Methodist), and about 60,000 for the *Pilot* (Catholic).[56]

There were also hundreds of smaller, specialized religious journals, each claiming 1,000 to 10,000 subscribers, such as *Southern Churchman* (Richmond, Virginia; Episcopal), *Africo-American Presbyterian* (Wilmington, North Carolina; Presbyterian), *Lutherische Herold* (New York City; Lutheran), and *Hebrew Observer* (San Francisco; Jewish).

Noting the increasing popularity of weekly story papers, some Catholic editors in New York inaugurated in 1880 a weekly, the *Illustrated Catholic American*, as "a guide and teacher, quite as much as a delight and recreation." It opened its series on "eminent Catholic Americans" with an article about Cardinal McCloskey of New York. That issue also featured the first installment of a serialized novel, *Victor's Crucifix*, which would, the editors predicted, produce "tears of pity and admiration," and, "in very big type, for little people just beginning to read, the astonishing adventure of Toto in Angel Land."[57] The editors wanted a pious magazine but also a magazine that would connect with their readers' ethnic and historical identities. Their magazine included conventional story paper fare, including serialized fiction, advertisements, and travel items, but piety was the central feature of the print culture that drove their enterprise.[58]

Most story papers went for excitement, not piety. Serialized novels were their main content, and they were hugely popular. Street and Smith's *New York Weekly* had the highest circulation of any periodical in the country in 1880. The front page of the 23 February 1880 issue began "Irene's Vow," by Bertha Clay, and "The Death-Trail," a Buffalo Bill story. On the back pages there were ongoing installments of four other serials.[59] The editors saw their readers as enthusiasts of lively fiction who wanted a lot of adventure, romance, and travel in their stories. Many story paper serials became dime novels shortly after the serial versions ended. Edward Judson, writing under the pseudonym of Ned Buntline, wrote hundreds of "Buffalo Bill" installments, most of which became dimes, and some of which were translated into various immigrant languages, such as French and Polish.[60] Like the English readers of Dickens's serial fiction, hundreds of Buffalo Bill enthusiasts would line up at the offices of *New York Weekly* on Rose Street, waiting to find out how the swashbuckling hero got out of the predicament in which Buntline had left him the previous week.[61]

Another popular story paper writer was Horatio Alger, known by 1880 as the author of *Ragged Dick* and *Luck and Pluck*. Alger wrote similar rags-to-riches stories over and over again, including sixteen serialized novels in the *New York Weekly* between 1872 and 1889.[62] His 1880 contribution to dime literature was *The Young Explorer*, in which the hero, young Ben Stanton, is orphaned without much of an inheritance and decides to go West to the Sierra Nevada, where he has adventures, makes friends, and finds gold. In the preface, Alger encourages young readers to emulate Ben's "manliness and fidelity to duty."[63]

Amid all these white male virtues in dime novels, negative stereotypes of others were common. Buffalo Bill killed "savages" every time he turned around. In Alger's *Young Explorer*, the hero comes across a "Chinee" in the gold fields, and asks him where he sleeps at night. "Me sleep on glound," replies the man. Other dime novels referred to Mexican Americans as "greasers."[64] These stereotypes suggest that the intended audience was white. But what else can we say about the audience for the story papers and dime novels?

Francis Smith, the editor of *New York Weekly*, aimed at both a female and a male audience, by placing romances and detective mysteries in almost every issue.[65] In contrast, W. H. Bishop, writing a snobby article in the *Atlantic Monthly*, claimed that the audience for story papers was mainly "boys," but he went on to say that while standing outside a shop specializing in story papers he had observed "a middle aged woman," "a shop-girl on her way home" and a female servant "from one of the good houses on the side streets" entering the shop. Furthermore, he admitted, some story papers included serialized fiction from such respectable popular novelists as Mrs. Southworth and wound up "on the table of so many boudoirs, far indeed removed from the lower classes."[66] Recent scholar Nan Enstad found pervasive references to dime novel reading among women factory workers from the 1880s through the early twentieth century.[67]

There is, then, much anecdotal evidence of both male and female readership. On the issue of social class, some writers claim that the audience for dimes was largely middle class, others that it was mainly working class. It seems that the audience was both. According to Bishop, the stationers' shops that sold dimes could be found not only in "the more prosperous" neighborhoods uptown, but in the German immigrant neighborhoods and in the Five Points slum. Also, there were frequent reports in the press of rough young boys who read story papers or dime novels and were inspired to commit crimes.⁶⁸ Bishop thought that such alarms about dimes were exaggerated. Nonetheless, he identified the main audience as "working class" and expressed his contempt for their mental ability. They were "not reflective." Their "lack of culture is a continuous childhood."⁶⁹ Although Michael Denning agrees that the audience was working class, he does not share Bishop's view of the readers as simpleminded. Rather, he argues, many dime novels were intermittently subversive, providing opportunity for workers to reflect upon their grinding experiences with capitalism.⁷⁰

The evidence suggests that cheap serial fiction appealed to a variety of readers, often for quite different reasons—escape, reflection, romantic diversion, violence, and suspense. No scholar will win the argument about the "real" readers or the "real" functions of inexpensive fiction. Despite their reputation for superficiality and stereotyping, dimes and story papers were diverse, and a single text could serve different purposes for different readers.

In high-literary circles there was a similar relationship between serialized fiction and full-length novels. Published by major book publishers, magazines like *Harper's*, *Scribner's*, and the *Atlantic* advertised, reviewed, and serialized books, including those published by their own parent companies. Prominent literary figures of the day—Henry James, William Dean Howells, Harriet Beecher Stowe, Helen Hunt Jackson, and others—all serialized their tales. Looking in detail at a single year, 1880, reveals some of the mundane activities of these famous authors in their pursuit of income from writing. James and Howells, dubbed the "new School," were busy articulating and advancing ideas about realism.⁷¹ On the cutting edge of American highbrow fiction, James took time out from writing *Portrait of a Lady* to publish a short, mediocre novel entitled *Confidence* in February 1880.⁷² Howells, in contrast, published his *Undiscovered Country* in 1880, a major work that the *New York Post* described as having a "power which belongs to very few novels of our time."⁷³ Both of these novels were serialized prior to their publication as books, *Confidence* in *Scribner's Monthly*, and *Undiscovered Country* in the *Atlantic Monthly*. Mark Twain was suffering in 1880 from a writer's block over *Huckleberry Finn*, so, like James, he published a little-remembered trifle, called *A Tramp Abroad*.⁷⁴

One of the most influential and controversial authors in America was the Frenchman, Émile Zola. In 1880 Zola produced not only a theoretical treatise called *The Experimental Novel* but also a hugely popular and controversial novel called *Nana*. Early in the novel it is clear that Nana sleeps with her rich male friends for material gain. In late Victorian America, gaining the opprobrium of book reviewers did not require an author to describe sexual activity but only to describe promiscuous people without condemning them. The *Atlantic* called *Nana* "shameless" and "disgusting," while the reviewer in the *American Book-*

seller called it "unpleasant," "nauseating," and "sensational."[75] It sold like hotcakes.

Meanwhile, at the Century Association in New York, artists and their patrons discussed the future of poetry and the pros and cons of the new naturalism in novels. There was no cause to worry about propriety here. Samuel Clemens called the Century the "most unspeakably respectable Club in the United States." On a visit there he said he had "averaged the heads, and they were three sizes larger than the style of heads I have been accustomed to."[76] All of the 500 members were men, most of them old New Yorkers of Protestant lineage, including patrons of the arts, patrician publishers, and the artists themselves, including in 1880 Frederick Law Olmstead, Albert Bierstadt, and Winslow Homer. One member recalled the handsome poet Edmund Stedman, darting from one "coterie" to another, shaping the print culture of elite New York City.[77]

Women authors were precluded from membership in the Century Association, but they made abundant contributions to the book scene in 1880 — from the steady-selling classics of Harriet Beecher Stowe and Louisa May Alcott, to the highly regarded work of Helen Hunt Jackson, Sarah Orne Jewett, and Constance Woolson, to the popular fiction of Mrs. Southworth, and the racy novels of "Ouida," the pen-name of Louise de la Ramée. When Henry Houghton held a dinner in 1877 for the leading authors appearing in the *Atlantic* and had not invited even the most prestigious women who wrote for that periodical, like Harriet Beecher Stowe, there was some public protest. Houghton made a lame excuse — "We were afraid to ask, for fear we should be refused" — but in 1880 he relented and invited Stowe, Jackson, and others to a celebratory breakfast.[78]

Between this world of highbrow novels and that of story papers and dimes lay a great body of popular novels. When star authors published new books, publishers tried to capitalize on their celebrity by reissuing their previous works, often in new, cheaper editions. The initial publicity for Anna Katharine Green's second mystery novel, *Strange Disappearance*, published in 1880, built upon the fabulous success of her first book, *The Leavenworth Case*, which had appeared in 1878, the work of a young unknown. Putnam had taken a chance and published it. It proved a smash, hailed as the first great American mystery novel.[79] The plot of *The Leavenworth Case* raced forward from the first page, with a wily police detective, fainting witnesses, and a succession of suspects. While its tone owed much to romance novels, Green's emphasis on sleuthing, physical evidence, and deduction took its cue from French and English mystery writers.

Good mysteries found niches at different brow levels. The tales of the leading French mystery writer, Émile Gaboriau, were often serialized and then put into cheap paper editions. His *Monsieur LeCoq*, published in the United States in

1880, was, according to his American publisher, "for sale at all bookstores, news stands and on all the railroads."[80] Yet these mysteries were reviewed in highbrow literary journals, sometimes with begrudging praise. The *Nation*, for example, called *Monsieur LeCoq* "the most labyrinthine of detective stories" and promised that "no one who likes these will begin it and leave it unfinished."[81]

Other genres and topics also tapped large audiences. The end of southern Reconstruction in 1876 spawned romanticized accounts of the reconciliation of North and South, as well as some works that criticized the South. In January 1880 *Publishers' Weekly* reported that Albion Tourgée's controversial novel about the evils of the Ku Klux Klan, *A Fool's Errand* (1879), was the talk of Washington, "a second *Uncle Tom's Cabin*." "President Hayes has bought ten copies of it, and every member of the cabinet had something to say about it." By August 1880 the trade journals reported that more than 100,000 copies had been sold, and that Tourgée was working on a second book about the South.[82] *Bricks without Straw* appeared in September 1880, with an initial printing of 25,000 and sales soon reaching 50,000. It provided novelistic background for the massive exodus of black migrants northward, a hot topic of conversation in the wake of 1880 Senate hearings by the alarmist Senator Daniel Voorhees of Indiana.[83]

Both steady sellers and new titles about the life of Christ were prominent in 1880. The most successful of these was *The Life of Christ*, by the English clergyman F. W. Farrar.[84] Its appeal came from Farrar's union of the separate stories of the Gospels into a single narrative, augmented by materials from his extensive research and travels to the Holy Land.[85] At least four other lives of Christ were advertised in 1880, some claiming big sales.[86] However, the blockbuster in this mode was Lew Wallace's potboiler *Ben Hur*, about a life nearby that of Christ, also published in 1880.

In a completely secular and spicier vein, Louise de la Ramée, as "Ouida," wrote one novel after another, depicting the degenerate lives of thinly disguised celebrities. The trade press's reports of the author's movements in Europe as she gathered information for new titles created a buzz in 1880 over the anticipated arrival of *The Moths*.[87] Her books sold well, though patrician library censors and highbrow reviewers routinely deplored them. "Odorous," said the *Nation*.[88] Yet they were mentioned favorably as enjoyable "trash" in middle-class memoirs and were in demand at public libraries. With readers inclined variously toward piety, romance, action, or reflection, the market for middlebrow books was diverse.

Although the history of publishing often focuses on new titles, much actual reading centered on old books. The Bible was the most popular book of all, and copies of the Bible remained in families for generations. Even new Bibles presented text that remained stable over centuries. Then there were the classics, from Milton to Dickens, so prevalent in the memoirs of those raised to appreciate the Anglo-American canon. In August 1880, for example, Lovell offered, at $1.00 each, *Robinson Crusoe, Don Quixote, Pilgrim's Progress, Ivanhoe,* and *Gulliver's Travels,* as well as the poets Shakespeare, Milton, Byron, Scott, Tennyson, Pope, Dante, Homer, and others.[89] "Steady sellers" remained in print for decades after their first publication. In 1880 these included the fiction of Mrs. Southworth, Henry Ward Beecher, and Elizabeth Phelps Ward. Publishers regularly reissued and advertised classics and steady sellers, but readers could also get them from friends and family.

Moreover, by 1880 public lending libraries were commonplace. Like home libraries, however, public libraries did not contain a random sampling of books. Their collection policies were the result of an arbitration between the producers and the readers of books, creating hierarchies of value and principles of inclusion and exclusion. Because the public library was a rather new institution in 1880, this was highly contested terrain. The overwhelming demand, everyone agreed, was for fiction, especially popular fiction, which some deemed too salacious or violent or otherwise morally suspect. In the fledgling *Library Journal* in 1879, Samuel Green argued for the outright exclusion of all dime novels as well as the novels of Ouida, which "leave a taint on a pure mind." He considered borderline the popular books of "Oliver Optic" (William Adams), as well as novels by Gautier, Horatio Alger, and Mrs. Southworth.[90] Many libraries reported that they did indeed censor these and other books.[91] But more latitudinarian voices weighed in. William Poole, director of the Chicago Public Library, argued that questionable fare would lead readers to better and more challenging reading. Many library leaders agreed.[92]

As new institutions in 1880, public libraries prompted both publicity and debate. In the coming decades they expanded, unevenly but impressively, and the debates about which books should be on their shelves and in their patrons' hands moderated but did not disappear. The public library became an important instrument in the accelerating circulation of books, and library collections represented an evolving compromise between the "good" literature recommended by America's guardians of virtue and the diverse fiction that most library users wanted to read.

Conclusion

The cardinal principle of the new history of print culture is that readers and producers of print meet in the text. This tour of publishing and reading sites in 1880 suggests that the production of a text and each encounter between a reader and that text are complex events. Both the text and the reader come to that intersection carrying various values, histories, ideological assumptions, and goals—some of them overlapping, some divergent. The producers' agendas may differ from or compete with those of readers. The author, the publisher, the editor, the illustrator, the printer, the advertiser, and the bookseller try to capture the reader's attention. Many mediators attempt to influence the reader as well: parents, teachers, librarians, booksellers, and peers. In the 1880s, as in all periods, an unpredictable mix of agency and constraint guided the readers' selection, understanding, and appropriation of meaning.

Section II

The Publishing Trades

Introduction

Carl F. Kaestle and Janice A. Radway
. . .

The publishing trades were profoundly affected by the economic, social, and cultural forces that transformed every aspect of American life between 1880 and 1940, thus creating a "culture of print." Technological changes in transportation and communication, economic integration, professionalization, and bureaucratization all helped to change the country's trade in words. Although these forces affected each aspect of print differently, the trade itself was transformed from a collection of independent, interacting businesses into a system of loosely integrated parts.

As the population exploded and dispersed geographically across the continent, many in the trade sought to profit from newfound access to readers and the opportunities it presented. These increasingly coordinated efforts both intentionally and inadvertently intensified the commercial orientation of American publishing. Throughout the period examined here, publishers also thoroughly transformed and multiplied the commodities they offered. This section aims to trace schematically the histories of the main publishing trades and to track the business of integration within the trades themselves, among them, and in their relation to the developing consumer economy. It also tracks the transformation of publishing from a trade, principally, in words, text, and printed books, to a trade in subsidiary rights and fungible "content," diversifying print forms, audience attention, images, and social, cultural, and political prestige.

This is not to suggest, of course, that prior to 1880 American publishing was not commercially oriented. Notwithstanding the traditional trade's famously clubby tone, its reputation as a gentlemanly pastime, or its literary orientation and investment in the public interest, publishers still sought to regularize and systematize their relationships with writers while maximizing sales through predictable relationships with readers. Both Richard Ohmann and Ellen Garvey reveal in chapters 6 and 10, in fact, that in the years before 1880 some of the most prestigious literary houses had created periodicals that acted both as "vestibules to the house" and as elaborate advertising vehicles for their lists of titles. This commercial synergy was augmented in the years after 1880 by increasingly integrated relationships between branches of the publishing trade and by the appearance of wholesalers, traveling book salesmen, literary agents, and book club promoters who fostered the meshing of gears in an ever more complex, industrialized, and bureaucratized system of publishing.

Michael Winship argues in chapter 3 that, between 1880 and 1940, a highly articulated national book trade system was established in the United States. Characterized by the exploitation of technological changes in printing and paper manufacture, that business was always challenged more by the problem of distribution than by the problem of production. This tendency was exacerbated by the explosion and extension of the population after 1880 and accordingly, Winship suggests, the history of publishing is "largely the history of how the book trade addressed the problem of distribution and . . . costs, prices, and discounts."

Winship's chapter tracks the transformation of family-owned publishing "houses" into modern business corporations characterized by internal differentiation, bureaucracy, and financial reorganization. These corporations, he finds, professionalized and sought to regularize their operations, thereby increasing the predictability of their profits. The growing importance of *Publishers' Weekly* demonstrates the increasingly professional and integrated character of the trade. Winship similarly traces the transformation of the distribution infrastructure as the search for audiences and profit intensified. Publishers relied increasingly on wholesalers and jobbers, commercial travelers, and modernized bookstores that helped readers to choose books by organizing their wares according to topic rather than publisher.

In 1913 the trade was finally recognized as "big business," he suggests, when the U.S. Supreme Court ruled that the publishers' net-pricing system violated the Sherman Antitrust Act against monopoly and restraint of trade. Despite the setback, however, American publishers continued to increase title production and sought to place the trade on sound economic footing by working out an international copyright agreement and by finding ways to utilize various media in multiple venues for advertising and marketing. What this produced, Winship suggests (and as Martha Woodmansee and Peter Jaszi detail further in chapter 5), was a growing sense that the right to publish a work was not "integral and whole." Copyright, rather, was "differentiated and several" and consisted of subsidiary rights to newspaper and magazine publication as well as to translation, movie adaptation, book club publication, and paperback reissue. Literary agencies developed accordingly as a way to manage literary property that was abstract and fungible, able to migrate from form to form and medium to medium.

Examining the subsequent development of the traditional book trade, James L. W. West III documents in chapter 4 how literary agents and other mediators expanded the potential of literary property. He traces the growing emphasis on the commodity status of text, underscoring the pressures levied on writers and publishers by commercial forces and opportunities. Although the emergence of a range of new-style publishers in the twenties and the thirties countered this trend, changes in copyright law and in other branches of the publishing business strengthened the commercial orientation of the trade and slowly began to erode the power of individual authors to control their work.

In chapter 5 Woodmansee and Jaszi argue that the rhetoric of Romantic authorship was used by the courts persistently in copyright cases. Ironically, it was not to strengthen the hand of individual authors but rather to shore up the commercial claims of the corporations that published them. This trend was presaged by the emergence of the "work for hire" doctrine, which assigned "effective cause" to corporations whose salaried writers wrote catalogs and manuals and fleshed out dime novel plots. Woodmansee and Jaszi see this early development as consistent with the later articulation of the 1891 International Copyright Law, which "operated to consolidate the elite publisher's and printers' authority over the production and circulation of printed texts." Copying restrictions and the doctrine of "substantial similarity" claimed to protect authors' rights but actually "safeguarded existing commercial interests and provided legal security for new developments in information commerce."

The term "information commerce" effectively captures the changes then taking place even more intensively in other branches of the publishing trades. Magazines reorganized their financial support in the 1890s, shifting their emphasis from the production of the physical object itself to the sale of their readers' attention, sold en bloc to manufacturers who advertised in their pages. In doing so, Richard Ohmann suggests in chapter 6, they drastically altered their product. They evolved from being literary institutions closely related to book publishers to being midwives for an emerging consumer capitalism. Ad-driven magazines linked readers and manufacturers, publicized new commodities, and instructed their readers in using these products as part of a more modern life. Thus, they subordinated the textual material they published to their function as critical intermediaries between production and consumption.

Ohmann argues that book publishers began to adopt some of the same practices as their magazine and newspaper competitors. They, too, focused on finding writers to implement their ideas, commodifying talent by circulating authors' writing among a range of media and product categories. Although eventually willing to work with literary agencies, publishers only reluctantly capitulated to the book clubs, which they saw initially as competitors.

Ohmann concludes, however, somewhat differently from Winship, that despite such developments book publishing remained distinct from other branches of the trade. Books, he suggests, continued "to arrive on the market as thousands of discrete commodities each year that readers would buy or not, with little carry-over from previous purchases." Because the distinctiveness of each title made advertising difficult, houses could not develop reader loyalty to the house as a brand and thus had little to offer to advertisers. Heavily invested in the literary aspects of the trade, some book publishers thus resisted the new corporate and marketing environments.

Ohmann's essay emphasizes principally the last two decades of the nineteenth century, whereas Winship traces changes through the first two decades of the twentieth century, when book publishers made some commercial innovations. Still, many resisted what Ohmann calls "the commodification of text and talent," opening the marketplace to struggles over all aspects of book publication, from the design of the object to methods of audience access.

Before examining those struggles, however, this section of the volume considers another of the publishing trades ascendant in the last decades of the nineteenth century—the newspaper industry. Richard Kaplan and Michael Schudson trace the growing commercialism of the daily press, its intensifying connection to the evolving consumer economy, its increasingly significant role in information commerce, and the changing ways journalists adapted their business to the economic, social, and cultural situation. They demonstrate that newspapers, too, helped to incorporate America and to integrate the printing and publishing trades. This is especially significant because far more Americans read newspapers than books in the years after the turn of the century.

In chapter 7 Kaplan documents the expansion of the press as it evolved from serving only elite interests and readers to addressing a broader, national, more diverse audience. Driven by the pursuit of profits and advertising, by 1910, newspapers were "full-scale incorporated companies, paying dividends to stockholders, and embarking on consolidation into extended media chains." Although each paper initially aligned with a particular political party, newspapers gradually abjured their earlier partisanship so as not to alienate potential readers and key advertisers, adopting instead what Kaplan calls "an impersonal, unified authoritative discourse." This "objective" discourse facilitated the decline of political party power and helped to shift social authority to the administrative bureaucracies of corporations and the national state. Papers suppressed overtly politicized discourse (or relegated it to the editorial page or columns of personal opinion), replacing it with the expert pronouncements of a range of professional and technical elites. By the 1920s newspapers were perhaps the most widely read print form in America. They had become, Kaplan suggests, vehicles for the organization and administration of consumer markets and unofficial though highly efficient partisans of the national state.

Schudson makes this argument explicitly in chapter 8, tracing the varied ways in which the commercially oriented press maintained its political role and authority despite mediating key debates between manufacturers, advertisers, and consumers. Newspapers did this by modernizing their operations and by diversifying their pages to resemble the new department stores captivating middle-class America. Like Kaplan, Schudson notes that as the newspapers increased their commercial orientation and mass audience, they argued against overt political advocacy. As Schudson shows, however, despite the increasing invocation of this ideology, profit-oriented newspapers tried to serve diverse readers' interests by becoming "conversational parlors, with multiple voices and multiple conversations conducted simultaneously." This created the appearance of diversity and enabled publishers, editors, reporters, and columnists to express political views. At the same time, Schudson suggests, because a paper's political coverage depended heavily on access to government authorities, journalists often befriended men in power. Columnists, in particular, depended on "their central location in a network of Washington insiders." And, as Schudson shows so effectively, columnists like Walter Lippmann regularly used their insider status "to advance the candidacy, career, or policies of favored politicians without public declaration." In effect, then, the newspapers in this period consolidated and maintained their political and cultural authority by taking on an essential role in the new consumer society and by touting "objectivity" while often promoting the political agendas of elites in power.

Despite the integration of America's culture of print as an essential component in the new consumer economy, resistance continued to percolate in some branches of the trade. This was especially true within book publishing circles, where some resisted commercial pressures, insisting that the book was not a commodity. Megan Benton examines these struggles in chapter 9, analyzing technological developments in printing and changes in typeface design. Ellen Garvey follows in chapter 10 with an account of book publishers' ambivalence about the usefulness of advertising and publicity in selling books. In both cases, the debate centered on the effects of technological innovation and increased commercialism on the cultural status of the written word, on the printed book itself, and on the fate of the literary.

Tracing the contradictory effects of increased mechanization on the production of print, Benton notes that widespread adoption of mechanized typesetting and halftone engraving augmented the speed and lowered the price of book production. At the same time, it also led to the creation of objects that, to many observers, seemed lacking in aesthetic quality. This led to a vociferous debate between two different groups of designers about the role technology should play in print production.

On one side, modernist celebrants of "machine civilization" elaborated an ideology of typographic modernism that recommended "streamlined speed, simplicity, standardization, precision, [and] economy." It was mostly the new magazines that adopted the latest machine technologies, proudly sporting coated papers, Linotype composition, and halftone images. Their typefaces had a no-nonsense functionality, enabling quick perusal of the page. Later, advocates of a "new typography" made these typefaces more sophisticated, seeking "innovative departures from convention . . . designed to enhance legibility in short, streamlined bursts." In the American context, typographic modernism was largely associated with entrepreneurial and industrial enterprise.

On the other side of this debate, traditionalists advocated a return to typefaces that evoked the values of the turn-of-the-century Arts and Crafts movement. Opposed to the utilitarianism associated with mechanization, they sought "to restore the timelessly calming qualities of reasoned order, beauty, and peace to the printed page." They launched a renaissance in type design, adapting traditional typefaces to the demands of the modern era, siding with those in the book trade rather than with magazinists, and frequently collaborating with the producers of fine books. Traditionalist typographers defined the book in explicit opposition to the magazine and to the tastes of a mass audience that seemed to prefer titillation and information over aesthetic contemplation.

In chapter 10, Ellen Garvey makes a parallel argument. Although the book industry was eventually affected by corporate methods and styles, there remained considerable ideological investment in the singular character of books, in what Janice Radway has elsewhere called their "auratic" quality."[1] Indeed many booksellers continued to insist that each published title was "the unique utterance of an autonomous individual who had composed from within, who expressed highly personal aims, and who therefore created a book chiefly valuable for its original content and idiosyncratic style."[2] Given this investment, Garvey suggests, it is not surprising that conventional wisdom in the book trade dictated that books could not be advertised like soap, toothpaste, or automobiles, even while some mass-market publishers were experimenting with the new advertising and publicity methods.

Struggles within the trade to define the book and its proper audience continued between 1880 and 1940. Traditionalists argued that each book should find its own, unique audience via word of mouth. They believed that readers bought books not only for the uniqueness of the text itself but also for the quality of the corresponding material object, its paper, typeface design, and the nature of its binding. When publishers like these eventually used advertising, they often touted the author's prominence or expertise and the cultural prestige attached to books more generally.

More modern advertising practices were generally employed in the book trade by the more commercially oriented publishers that targeted the mass audience. In addition to the contents of the books, they marketed what those books could do for and to their readers. In effect, book advertising began to shift attention away from the book and its author, focusing instead on the reader and the reading experience. Increasingly, book publishers traded in what communication theorists have called "uses and gratifications," that is, they marketed emotion and experience rather than the object that produced it. In effect, by adopting modern advertising methods, book publishers altered the nature of the commodity they were selling.

Indeed, Garvey goes on to show that the book trade slowly reoriented itself around readers and profit maximization, while making increasing use of advertising techniques and modern publicity methods. As a result, additional synergies developed between the trade and other media forms. Garvey shows that by the end of the period under investigation here, most trade publishers had adopted modern public relations techniques and deliberately sought to produce best sellers. They also created a bandwagon effect by repackaging the "content" of their books in newspaper, magazine, and radio format. In effect, as Garvey writes, "they shaped books' subject matter as a transferable commodity."

By the end of our period, then, copyright law, the advent of modern ad-driven magazines and newspapers, and the widespread adoption of advertising and public relations techniques had together produced a transformation in literary property and in the nature of the commodities marketed by the publishing trades. Increasingly, those trades operated together, exchanging highly fungible literary "content" among them, thereby contributing to what Richard Ohmann has characterized as "the unity of the cultural field." We shall see in the next section, however, that despite the loose integration of the publishing trade during this period and the redundant circulation of material among them, diversity persisted in the culture of print. That diversity arose from the use of the publishing trade for other than commercial motives. It was also a function of the fact that those who actually read and used printed materials often did so for unpredictable and surprising reasons. Before we assess the impact of these contrary forces, however, we turn to the halting but inexorable integration of the publishing trades and American culture more generally.

CHAPTER 3

The Rise of a National Book Trade System in the United States

Michael Winship

. . .

An editorial in the 6 January 1900 issue of *Publishers' Weekly* reflected on the state of publishing in the United States, noting "the wonderful development through utilization of natural forces, [such] as steam and electricity" and "the corresponding development in education" that had resulted in books having been "printed in such enormous quantities for the widest popular sale." It further noted, "the contrast between that first general catalogue issued in 1804 and the portly Publishers' Trade List Annual of to-day is sufficient evidence of this extraordinary development in our own country." But according to the editors, progress had not been even and all was not well:

> It is to be regretted that, particularly in the last quarter of a century, the methods of the book trade in America, in England, and elsewhere have not only failed to keep pace with book production, but have actually shown retrogression. The fact that the public library has grown to be a great and almost universal institution, within that period, does not account for the diminution of books stores [*sic*] and book distributing facilities in most of the smaller places ... libraries have probably not decreased, and have perhaps increased, the actual sale of books. The facility given by the mails for the distribution of books has partly accounted for the lack of growth, if not the diminution, of local book stores, so that in many places the "old bookseller" is no more.[1]

This complaint, which sounds eerily familiar even today, demonstrates that book distribution has often posed a more difficult problem for publishers than book production. This was especially true in a country like the United States, in which production facilities, largely concentrated in eastern urban publishing centers, had to reach a diverse population spread over an extensive area. The history of American publishing has revolved around efforts to solve the problem of distribution. Costs, prices, and discounts were major concerns.

In an 1880 editorial, for example, the editors at *Publishers' Weekly* advised:

It seems to us that this is the opportunity the trade has long been waiting for—an opportunity which suggests a means of returning to better business methods. The natural tendency would be of course to put up retail prices, or at least to make higher retail prices on new books as they are published. The high discounts would still offer the old temptations to undersellers. We would suggest that the wiser plan would be to hold to the present prices, stiffen them up, and make discounts closer. It will not then be possible for undersellers to make the marked reduction they now offer from advertised prices, and the "usual discounts" can with abundant reason be at least checked.[2]

Despite these problems of pricing, the editors were hopeful for the future. Business was booming, both within the book trade and more generally. After the recessions of the 1870s, reform and prosperity finally seemed possible.

Growth in Trade Publishing

Between 1880 and 1916, the year before the country became involved in World War I, a distinctive national book trade system emerged. This was a period of rapid growth in the United States, both generally and for the publishing industry. The population more than doubled, exceeding 100 million by 1916. The annual number of new titles and new editions grew sixfold, from 2,076 in 1880 to 13,470 in 1910, but falling to 10,445 by 1916. More generally, the total output value of "magazines, newspapers, misc. paper supplies, etc." increased at a similar rate, growing from $61.5 million in 1879 to $352.2 million in 1916.[3]

With the nation expanding both demographically and geographically during these years, the challenge of reaching an extensive national market forced the book trade to adopt modern business models of organization. Many of the major American trade publishers had been founded before the Civil War as family enterprises or limited partnerships and were run on an ad hoc basis. As the second—and, in a few cases, the third—generation of proprietors took charge of these firms, most were expanded and structured more rationally. Growth brought a need for increased capital to what had traditionally been an undercapitalized business, causing many firms to reorganize as private corporations: Lippincott in 1885, Harper in 1896 and again in 1900, Appleton in 1900, Scribner in 1904, and Houghton Mifflin in 1908. Growth brought increased internal organization, with separate departments overseeing such functions as editing, production, distribution, advertising, and publication of school books. A new class of professional managers supervised these departments and their specialized staffs.[4]

Emblematic of this evolution, though hardly typical, was the fate of the Harper firm. Founded in 1817, it remained a family concern until 1890 when Fletcher Harper Jr. died, leaving no son or third-generation heir to take over his role or stake in the firm. That same year his cousin, Joseph W. Harper, announced that he would retire in 1894 and would use only half of his total equity of $296,000 to cover his son's partnership in the firm, receiving the other half himself in four annual payments. To remedy the problem, the firm reluctantly agreed to sell off its primary and secondary school texts for more than half a million dollars to the American Book Company, a textbook trust formed by several leading education publishers. Nevertheless, with the contraction of the money supply and the depression that followed the Panic of 1893, as well as declining profits from its magazines and loss of income from textbook sales, the firm found itself increasingly in financial straits.

In 1896 the Harper firm turned to J. P. Morgan & Co., one of the world's leading financial bankers, for new capital. Morgan insisted that the firm reorganize and incorporate; he would hold most of the stock in the new corporation as collateral for loans. When the Harpers were unable to meet their interest payments in 1899, Morgan brought in an outsider to manage the firm. The S. S. McClure Company had run a successful international publishing syndicate since 1884, had published a popular mass-market magazine since 1893, and had joined with Frank N. Doubleday in 1897 to found the book publishing firm of Doubleday & McClure Company. Morgan and McClure agreed to install McClure's longtime associate John S. Phillips as manager of the Harper firm. Returning in October from a summer in Europe, however, McClure found that the Harper debt was in danger of swallowing up his total profits for the year. Undeterred, McClure proposed to merge S. S. McClure Company and Doubleday & McClure Company into a single corporation capitalized at an additional half million dollars. Frank Doubleday rejected the plan, however, forcing McClure to cancel his agreement with Morgan to purchase the Harper firm.

The Harpers next turned to Colonel George Harvey. After serving as the managing editor at the *New York World*, Harvey had turned to financing and directing electric streetcar companies and, in 1899, had purchased the venerable *North American Review*. With Morgan's approval, Harvey was brought in as president and managing director. Once he took the firm through receivership, he recapitalized and reorganized it according to modern business standards: Harvey hired his former colleague from the *New York World* as general manager and secretary of the board of directors and appointed professionals to such key positions as treasurer, head of accounting, and manager of periodical circulation. He sold off the college textbooks and scholarly reference works divisions to the American Book Company, and in the book manufacturing plant he replaced most of the hand compositors with Linotype machines. The Harper heirs were, for the most part, relieved of their duties, and their desks moved upstairs to the old composing room — many subsequently resigned. A framed photograph of J. Pierpont Morgan hung prominently in Harvey's office.[5]

If such events indicated that publishing was becoming big business, other developments also reflected the growth and increased complexity of the book trade. One was increased trade consolidation in a few East Coast cities — predominantly in New York, emerging as the nation's financial capital, but also in Boston and Philadelphia. In the Midwest, Chicago became an important wholesale center, reflecting its position as a node in the growing rail network. Numerous East Coast firms established branch offices in Chicago and also located regular agents or branches in other cities across the nation. Furthermore, specialized wholesale jobbing firms, such as the American News Company and Baker & Taylor of New York and A. C. McClurg of Chicago, grew in importance during these years, systematizing the process of book distribution.

Another significant development was the emergence of R. R. Bowker Company as the semiofficial publisher of the book trade. Bowker's *Publishers' Weekly* was first issued in 1873 and quickly evolved to become the chief American book trade periodical, providing a systematic record of new publications and a forum for exchange of information and opinion. Additionally, Bowker provided a whole range of supplemental publications: the *Annual American Catalogue* cumulated and indexed the listings in *Publishers' Weekly* by year, which was then further cumulated from time to time. The *Publishers' Trade List Annual* provided additional access to books through a single yearly volume containing each individual publisher's current trade catalog. The annual *American Educational Catalogue* was a separate publication of the list from the August education issue of *Publishers' Weekly*. Bowker also published the *Library Journal*, the "Official Organ of the American Library Association," and *Literary News*, an "Eclectic Review of Current Literature." The firm served as agent for numerous other bibliographical publications, including the annual *English Catalogue* published in London by Sampson Low, Marston & Co.[6] The range of Bowker's publications indicates not just the growing complexity of the book trade but also its increased self-consciousness and professionalism.

These developments did not, however, change the fundamental fact that large trade houses remained general publishers, maintaining varied lists of publications covering a broad range of subjects and genres. A classified list of the publications of Houghton Mifflin from 1905 to 1906, for example, divides the firm's output into 21 categories, from "archaeology" to "household books" to "travel and description," many of which were further divided into numerous subsections. An earlier catalog from Harper includes more than 100 subject or

TABLE 3.1. New titles and editions, 1880–1916

	1880		1890	
Philosophy	22	1.1%	11	0.2%
Religion	239	11.5%	467	10.2%
Sociology, Economics	99	4.8%	183	4.0%
Law	62	3.0%	458	10.0%
Education, Philology	131	6.3%	399	8.8%
Science	56	2.7%	93	2.0%
Technical Books (Useful Arts)	63	3.0%	133	2.9%
Medicine, Hygiene	114	5.5%	117	2.6%
Agriculture, Gardening, Domestic Economy	43	2.1%	29	0.6%
Business	—	0.0%	—	0.0%
Fine Arts	44	2.1%	135	3.0%
Music	24	1.2%	—	0.0%
Games, Sport	32	1.5%	82	1.8%
General Literature, Essays	106	5.1%	183	4.0%
Poetry, Drama	111	5.3%	168	3.7%
Fiction	292	14.1%	1,118	24.5%
Juvenile	270	13.0%	408	8.9%
History	72	3.5%	153	3.4%
Geography, Travel	115	5.5%	162	3.6%
Biography	151	7.3%	218	4.8%
Humor and Satire	30	1.4%	42	0.9%
Miscellaneous	—	0.0%	—	0.0%
Total	2,076		4,559	

Source: This table is based primarily on that printed in Hellmut Lehmann-Haupt, Lawrence C. Wroth, and Rollo G. Silver, *The Book in America: A History of the Making and Selling of Books in the United States*, 2nd ed. (New York: R. R. Bowker, 1951), 321, but discrepancies in the figures for 1910 and 1916 have been corrected by reference to the original data presented in *Publishers' Weekly* 79 (28 January 1911): 211–12, and *Publishers' Weekly* 91 (27 January 1917): 257.

genre headings in its index.[7] Although a number of firms did limit their lists—concentrating on such special fields as medicine and science (Lea & Febiger), agriculture (Orange, Judd), or drama (Samuel French)—these specialized firms never gained the importance or prominence of the large general trade houses. Although various trade houses had recognized specialties—novels, especially by British authors (Harper), handbooks and travel literature (Appleton), or New England authors and outdoor or nature writing (Houghton Mifflin)—none restricted themselves to limited categories or had exclusive control over any of them. Instead, these firms issued works of all subjects and genres, competing with each other in what often proved to be an oversupplied market.

	1900		1910		1914		1916	
	101	1.6%	265	2.0%	408	3.4%	322	3.1%
	448	7.0%	943	7.0%	1,032	8.6%	755	7.2%
	269	4.2%	784	5.8%	1,038	8.6%	767	7.3%
	543	8.5%	678	5.0%	507	4.2%	274	2.6%
	641	10.1%	623	4.6%	598	5.0%	583	5.6%
	184	2.9%	711	5.3%	677	5.6%	639	6.1%
	153	2.4%	707	5.2%	669	5.6%	689	6.6%
	218	3.4%	544	4.0%	542	4.5%	516	4.9%
	76	1.2%	332	2.5%	506	4.2%	540	5.2%
	—	0.0%	150	1.1%	229	1.9%	272	2.6%
	167	2.6%	245	1.8%	310	2.6%	238	2.3%
	—	0.0%	100	0.7%	112	0.9%	113	1.1%
	51	0.8%	145	1.1%	194	1.6%	127	1.2%
	543	8.5%	2,042	15.2%	732	6.1%	461	4.4%
	400	6.3%	752	5.6%	902	7.5%	860	8.2%
	1,278	20.1%	1,539	11.4%	1,053	8.8%	932	8.9%
	527	8.3%	1,010	7.5%	633	5.3%	670	6.4%
	257	4.0%	565	4.2%	581	4.8%	754	7.2%
	192	3.0%	599	4.4%	542	4.5%	354	3.4%
	274	4.3%	645	4.8%	604	5.0%	469	4.5%
	34	0.5%	49	0.4%	—	0.0%	—	0.0%
	—	0.0%	42	0.3%	141	1.2%	110	1.1%
	6,356		13,470		12,010		10,445	

General trade houses were the major advertisers in *Publishers' Weekly*. Their business affairs provided the bulk of its news, and their new publications and editions were regularly noted, listed, and reviewed. Their output as a whole is represented by table 3.1. These figures again demonstrate the persistence of a wide-ranging output of trade publications over this period. Certain trends seem logical—the growth in importance of technical books and books in the new social sciences and the relative parallel decline of religious books, for instance. Others are more surprising—the decline in the importance of "juvenile" books and especially of "fiction" after the latter's domination of the trade's output at century's end. Some of these anomalies undoubtedly reflect the nature of the data that were reported and the sample presented here, failing to account for the size of print runs, which presumably varied from genre to genre. Furthermore, many specialized or minor firms opted not to inform *Publishers' Weekly* of their new publications or were irregular in doing so.

Many trade houses also continued to supplement their book lists with general interest periodicals, usually monthly literary magazines that allowed publishers to communicate with readers directly. As Richard Ohmann shows in chapter 6, the names of many of these magazines—*Appleton's Journal, Harper's Monthly, Lippincott's Magazine, Putnam's Monthly, Scribner's Magazine*—emphasized their close ties with parent firms, serving not only to showcase a publisher's writers but also, by means of serials, excerpts, reviews, notices, and advertisements, to encourage reader awareness of a firm's publications. At century's end, with the emergence of mass magazines that increasingly drew support from general advertising rather than subscriptions, these literary periodicals lost circulation but not cultural prestige. Those that survived eventually became independent of their parent firms.[8]

Trade Publishing and Distribution through Retail Bookstores

Throughout the period, distribution and pricing remained central concerns of the book trade. The problem of getting books out to a dispersed and diverse population was exacerbated by both national growth and book trade consolidation. First and foremost, trade publishers addressed this problem with a wholesale trade system. New publications and those from the backlists were sold at a discount—typically 40 percent—to a network of specialized retail bookstores in cities and towns across the nation. These retailers had the right of return for credit should any book remain unsold after an established period of time. Both the rate of discount and the terms for return were negotiable, and discounts particularly became a contentious issue within the book trade.

As the nineteenth century progressed, the book trade, like other American businesses, modified the management of its wholesale trade. Prior to the Civil War, regular semiannual or annual "trade sales" were held in the major publishing centers of New York, Philadelphia, Boston, and Cincinnati. These auction sales were strictly limited to members of the trade, attracting buyers and retailers from around the country to a central location and serving not only as an important means of book distribution but also as a place where credit could be regulated and information exchanged.[9] Although the trade-sale system persisted to the very end of the century, publishers also increasingly relied on commercial travelers (salesmen) to visit individual retail bookstores across the country and take orders to be supplied by a firm's branch offices and warehouse depots. Travelers provided publishers a direct link to retailers and also gathered information on the state of the trade and the taste of book purchasers outside the major publishing centers. Nevertheless, their importance is difficult to assess, as in 1914 even the largest publishing firms employed only four travelers, each covering extensive territories. Specialized wholesaling firms, or jobbers, were also important agents of distribution, relying on traveling salesmen, and eventually branch offices and warehouse depots, to link numerous publishers and retailers.[10]

During this period, retail bookshops were strikingly different from their modern form; as with traditional department stores, customers relied less on their own browsing than on the service and knowledge of salespeople to choose their books.[11] While new arrivals were displayed on tables easily accessible to customers, the majority of stock was stored in shelves and cupboards with drawers placed around the walls, often separated from the main floor by sales counters. Many stores also arranged stock not by subject or genre but by publisher or supplier, giving the store's staff greater control over the inventory. In addition to books, many stores also sold a range of periodicals, as well as an assortment of stationery, games, and fancy goods. Some also increased business by means of a circulating library. Bookshops also were encouraged to manage their own publicity in the effort to attract customers, by means not just of window displays, posters, and bulletin boards but also through advertisements in local newspapers.

Publishers often jeopardized the discounting system required to support this sales infrastructure by selling their books at a small discount directly to individual customers by mail or subscription, thereby competing directly with the jobbers and retail bookshops that underpinned the distribution system. In turn, bookshops frequently offered customers small discounts off the nominal retail price of books in their stock. Furthermore, department stores and other large retailers also increasingly began offering cut-rate prices on remainders and books bought at trade sales in large quantities and at deep discounts.

The American Publishers' Association and the American Booksellers' Association, formed in 1900 and 1901 respectively, prompted major trade publishers and retailers to develop a net-pricing system. Thus, certain books were to be designated as "net" books and would be made available only at nationally uniform retail prices. Publishers were prohibited from distributing to retail outlets that charged a different price. Although novels were initially exempt from the net system, after 1909 they too were published increasingly as net books. The resulting regularity and stability in prices benefited the book trade but only at a higher cost to the consumer.

Department stores with large book selections, particularly R. H. Macy, quickly challenged these attempts at price maintenance. In 1901 Macy, which refused to abide by the net-pricing system, found that the publishers were attempting to cut off the store's supply. In retaliation, Macy sought out jobbers and other suppliers willing to provide it with book stock through roundabout means. In turn, the publishers sought to secure the net-pricing system by cutting off these firms, but the system ultimately depended upon voluntary cooperation and was legally unenforceable. Realizing this, in 1902 Macy turned to the courts for relief, and after a series of decisions and further appeals in both state and federal jurisdictions, the Supreme Court declared in a unanimous decision on 1 December 1913 that the net-pricing system violated the Sherman Antitrust Act's provisions against monopoly and restraint of trade. Subsequently Macy was awarded $140,000 in damages, and in 1914 the American Publishers' Association folded.[12]

The failure of the net-pricing system ensured that an open market with a large circulation of inexpensive books was characteristic of the American book trade. Such a model was preferable to a system that offered high-priced books in a highly regulated market with restricted but predictable sales — a system typified in Great Britain. The Supreme Court ruling also suggests that trade publishing was seen as a part of big business in the United States and shared in the trends toward corporate consolidation and market regulation.

Alternative Means of Distribution

Although trade books were sold through retail bookshops, other outlets were needed to reach a growing and widely dispersed population. Indeed, although the number of bookstores recorded in lists prepared for the trade in 1859 and in 1914 grew in absolute terms from 1,090 to 3,501, the growth in population meant that the number of people served on average by each had risen from around 15,000 to 28,000.[13] In many places, especially those too small to support a specialized bookstore, books must have been available for sale only as a small part of the stock in a general or department store, or at a newsagent, making jobbers crucial suppliers to such nonspecialist merchants. Public libraries also became significant during this period, a development signaled by the professionalization of librarianship, the formation of the American Library Association in 1876, and the Carnegie Corporation's financial support of new free libraries.[14]

In addition to the wholesale system of distribution through retail bookshops, several other methods were developed for reaching the book-buying public. While the general trade houses often utilized these alternative means of distribution, they also left room for other publishing firms that specialized in them and thereby challenged and complemented the trade publishing system.

One method of distribution that flourished during these years, although rooted in the earliest years of American publishing, was the use of subscription sales by agents who canvassed door-to-door, collecting orders for books. Books intended for subscription sale were not generally available for purchase in retail bookshops and were therefore outside the trade publishing system. In many cases books were not manufactured or bound until after orders had been received. A number of specialized subscription publishers sprang up—Hartford in particular became a center for subscription publishing. Together the publishers formed an alternative distribution network across the nation. It did not share the trade publishers' East Coast concentration; its dispersed nature is reflected in surviving copies of books sold by subscription, among which the same work will often have been issued with as many as a dozen different title-page imprints, each representing a different subscription firm and place of publication.[15]

Most subscription books were large and heavy, with a characteristic look; they were illustrated and usually packaged in an ornate binding. Indeed, the customer usually had the choice of a range of bindings at different costs (figure 3.1). Subscription books also tended to specialize in certain subject matters: typical genres were household manuals, encyclopedia, and handbooks, collections of biographical sketches, Civil War memoirs, and accounts of natural disasters. The subscription trade involved many firms each publishing a limited number of titles. Sales figures for a particular title could be very high indeed. *The Personal Memoirs of General U. S. Grant*, a two-volume work published in 1885 by a Hartford firm in which Mark Twain was a partner, is a prime example. Orders for 300,000 sets had been collected as early as four months before the manufacturers delivered the first volume, and by early 1866 sales had reached 325,000. It went on to become a spectacular best seller.[16] Most subscription works were less exceptional, but many had sales in the tens of thousands.

Subscription agents, who often pursued their work in a temporary or casual way, were usually provided with a prospectus or sample book to use as a prop in their sales pitch. Orders were passed on to the publisher, which supplied copies to the agent, who in turn delivered them to customers and collected payments, receiving a commission—or extra copies of the work to sell—in remuneration. The advantage of subscription selling was that it allowed publishers to reach out directly to the large group of customers, both rural and urban, who could not or did not frequent bookshops. This feature attracted Mark Twain, who, unlike other major literary figures of the period, often preferred this means of distribution. Its success depended, however, on the skill of the subscription agent, who proved difficult to supervise and control: if many were effective and dedicated salesmen, others no doubt brought halfhearted energy or limited honesty to their work. Commonly, subscription publishers attempted to manage their agents by providing instructional pamphlets or even by inserting colored slips in the prospectus with a printed sales pitch that could be memorized by the agent.[17]

THE UNIQUE STORY OF A MARVELLOUS LIFE!!!

THE ONLY NEW, RELIABLE AND DULY AUTHORIZED LIFE OF

P. T. BARNUM

By the Gifted Writer JOEL BENTON, ESQ.,
AUTHOR OF "EMERSON AS A POET," ETC., ETC.

Mr. Benton has been for about thirty years a most INTIMATE FRIEND OF MR. BARNUM AND FAMILY. His services as Author therefore, insure freshness, accuracy, excellence, and completeness far beyond any other work that has or may be issued

600 PAGES ELEGANTLY ILLUSTRATED.

The death of Phineas T. Barnum ends a career PERFECTLY UNIQUE in HUMAN HISTORY. There never was such a man before; there never will be such another. Scarcely excepting Lincoln and Grant; he was the BEST KNOWN AMERICAN of his time. He gave in his long career more innocent and instructive entertainment, more GENUINE MIRTH, more ACTUAL PLEASURE, to his fellow-men; than ANY OTHER MAN THAT EVER LIVED. For HALF A CENTURY his name has been a household word in every home in the land. To every American child his name has been a COMPEER of that of SANTA CLAUS HIMSELF.

Who would not wish to read the FASCINATING STORY OF HIS LIFE? Never was there another history so FULL of HUMOR, of ADVENTURE, of PICTURESQUE INCIDENTS, of EXTRAVAGANT ENTERPRISE. It is a record of the pleasures of a pleasure-seeking world for half a century! It is replete with AMUSING ANECDOTES, FUNNY PASSAGES, FELICITOUS JOKES, CAPTIVATING NARRATIVES, NOVEL EXPERIENCES, WONDERFUL as the TRAVELS of GULLIVER or the TALES of MUNCHAUSEN. It embodies a KEEN-WITTED YANKEE'S rules for MONEY MAKING by which he himself amassed a COLOSSAL FORTUNE. It abounds in shrewd sense, good advice, and kindly cheer to all the world.

This volume tells the whole story of this marvellous life; his STRUGGLING CHILDHOOD; the VICISSITUDES of EARLY YEARS; his FIRST SHOW; his FAMOUS MUSEUMS; his MENAGERIE and CIRCUS. It tells of JOICE HETH, his first great curiosity; of the MERMAID and the WOOLY HORSE; of TOM THUMB and COMMODORE NUTT; of JENNY LIND, whom he introduced to America; of his visits to the QUEEN of ENGLAND, the EMPEROR of FRANCE and other royal families; of JUMBO, the monster; of the SACRED WHITE ELEPHANT, CHINESE GIANT, &c., &c.

The author is enabled from his intimacy with Mr. Barnum and with the mass of correspondence &c. placed in his hands by Mr. Barnum, and by the family, to weave into this Biography a great deal of entirely new and original information, and to enrich it also with a generous variety of the thousand and one of Mr. Barnum's.

Practical Jokes, Novel Expedients, and Delicious Humor.

It presents many chapters of Barnum's life never yet laid before the public. It is splendidly illustrated with full-page plates prepared expressly for it, and is the book that all people of culture and all admirers of the great showman will desire to buy and read.

WARNING!! We understand that some publishers are attempting to put upon the Market an old book prepared apparently to advertise the "GREAT SHOW" and we believe given away in connection with it or sold at a very low price.

We hardly suppose anybody wants to buy knowingly such a book when they can get a choice new book, prepared by an able Author, as an eminently authentic and trustworthy biography of one of the greatest men of the present century.

BE SURE TO BUY THE GENUINE BOOK.

CONTENTS, STYLE AND PRICES.

This choice work is complete in one fine 12 mo. volume of about 600 pp., is finely illustrated with OVER THIRTY SPLENDID FULL PAGE PICTURES, and is printed on excellent paper made expressly for this book and is supplied to subscribers in handsome and durable bindings, as follows:

In Best English Cloth, with " half-tone" portrait of Barnum - - - - - $1.50
In Half Russia, Gilt Back and Edges, with beautiful " Photogravure " portrait of Barnum, 2.00
    Il Morocco, Elegant Gilt Edges, with   "   "   "   "   2.50

FIGURE 3.1. "The Unique Story of a Marvellous Life!!!," an advertisement in a canvassing book for a biography of P. T. Barnum by Joel Benton, offers a choice of bindings and illustration formats. American Antiquarian Society.

Most trade publishers also maintained subscription departments through which they offered expensive or heavily illustrated books, in some cases issued over an extended period in regular paper-covered parts that could later be returned to the publisher for binding. Around the turn of the century, many of these publishers also offered limited editions of their trade publications, often numbered and signed or printed on special paper, for subscription sale, as well as multivolume, collected editions of the works of popular authors. Houghton's heavily illustrated collected edition of Longfellow's *Poetical Works* was originally published serially in thirty paper-covered parts during 1879 and 1880 but was frequently reprinted and sold in two volumes in a variety of bindings (figure 3.2). Following Longfellow's death in 1882, a third volume of prose works and later poems was added to the set. In the following decade, the same firm began to issue multivolume sets of the collected works of its New England authors, often with new illustrations and editorial matter or with fugitive pieces collected for the first time. A prospectus for the "New Library Series American Authors" lists Emerson (in twelve volumes), Hawthorne (twenty-two volumes), Longfellow (eleven volumes), Lowell (sixteen volumes), Whittier (seven volumes), and Holmes (thirteen volumes). The heavily revised twenty-six-volume "New York Edition" of Henry James's *Novels and Tales*, published from 1907 to 1917 by Scribner of New York, had different sales arrangements: each volume was sold both in retail bookshops and by subscription in a variety of more expensive special limited editions. Through multivolume sets, trade publishers discovered that once a customer had "subscribed" to such a set, each volume could be delivered by mail rather than by an agent, relying on the customer's goodwill to submit payment for an enclosed invoice rather than on the agent's persistence.[18]

The postal system, which allowed publishers to reach customers directly without relying on retail bookshops, was another frequently utilized means of book selling. Advertising notices in catalogs and periodicals urged customers to order books directly by mail, often offering a discount on such orders. This practice, however, undermined the wholesale distribution system on which trade publishing chiefly relied. Editorials in *Publishers' Weekly* frequently decried mail orders, pointing out the contradictions and dangers to which it exposed the trade publishing system.[19]

Postal regulations also facilitated the sale of cheap "library" series that became popular during the late nineteenth century. These series utilized the government subsidy for second-class material, designed to encourage the circulation of newspapers and magazines. The postal laws required that books in these library series be dated, numbered, and published regularly in uniform style, thereby maintaining the appearance of serial publication. During the 1870s and

PROSPECTUS.

POEMS OF HENRY WADSWORTH LONGFELLOW.

R. LONGFELLOW'S Publishers, in recognition of the remarkable popularity which his Poems have gained throughout the world, have determined to prepare a new edition of these Poems in a style of typography and with a wealth of illustrations never before accorded to any poet. They do not propose merely to bring together a large number of pretty pictures, but to produce a work which, while attractive to the eye, shall be, in the character and quality of its illustrations, a fitting tribute to the genius and fame of the poet. It will contain more than

FIVE HUNDRED ILLUSTRATIONS

Consisting of landscapes, figure pieces, and ornamental designs, drawn and engraved on wood in the highest style of the art, *all new and expressly prepared for this edition*. The landscape views are actual transcripts from nature, and, like the ideal subjects and ornamental designs, have been entrusted to the best artists of America, who have cordially and unanimously coöperated in this effort to produce MR. LONGFELLOW'S Poems in a form worthy of the world-wide fame they enjoy. Among those who have furnished designs, each in his best and most characteristic manner, are the following: —

EDWIN A. ABBEY.	AUGUSTUS HOPPIN.
G. F. BARNES.	L. S. IPSEN.
GEORGE H. BOUGHTON.	EASTMAN JOHNSON.
J. APPLETON BROWN.	JOHN R. KEY.
F. S. CHURCH.	JOHN LAFARGE.
SAMUEL COLMAN.	HOMER MARTIN.
JESSIE CURTIS.	JERVIS MCENTEE.
F. O. C. DARLEY.	F. T. MERRILL.
J. O. DAVIDSON.	THOMAS MORAN.
JOHN W. EHNINGER.	GRANVILLE PERKINS.
MARY HALLOCK FOOTE.	CHARLES S. REINHART.
ALFRED FREDERICKS.	FRANK SCHELL.
G. GIBSON.	F. H. SHAPLEIGH.
W. H. GIBSON.	WALTER SHIRLAW.
R. SWAIN GIFFORD.	JAMES D. SMILLIE.
SANFORD R. GIFFORD.	A. R. WAUD.
WILLIAM J. HENNESSY.	WORTHINGTON WHITTREDGE.
D. C. HITCHCOCK.	THOMAS W. WOOD.
WINSLOW HOMER.	

The artistic supervision of the work has been entrusted to MR. A. V. S. ANTHONY, the well-known engraver, who in the rendering of the designs has secured the coöperation of the best American engravers.

A NEW STEEL PORTRAIT

Of MR. LONGFELLOW has been expressly engraved for this edition by MR. WILLIAM E. MARSHALL, from a photograph specially chosen by the author himself.

The Poems will be set in handsome and legible new type, adapted for the purpose, and the work will be printed upon sumptuous cream-tinted paper of the best quality used in modern book-making, manufactured with the greatest care by MESSRS. S. D. WARREN & CO. at their celebrated Cumberland Mills. The sub-titles of the Poems, under which the different volumes originally appeared, namely, *Voices of the Night, Birds of Passage, Tales of a Wayside Inn,* etc., are made the subjects of original and appropriate ornamental designs by MR. L. S. IPSEN. In short, this edition of MR. LONGFELLOW'S Poems will be, in accuracy of text, beauty of typography, excellence of paper, number and character of illustrations, and in mechanical execution, as nearly perfect as it can be made; so that every American may take pride in it as

A NATIONAL TRIBUTE

to a poet whom America delights to honor.

The work will be issued in Parts of large quarto form. Each Part will comprise thirty-two pages of text, combined with many illustrations, and will contain, in addition to the smaller illustrations, ONE OR MORE BEAUTIFUL FULL-PAGE PICTURES, the whole encased in a cover of unique and original design.

It will be sold exclusively by subscription, and will be completed in not less than Twenty-eight nor more than Thirty Parts, at Fifty Cents each, payable on delivery. No subscription will be received for less than the entire work, and neither canvassers nor deliverers are allowed to give credit or to collect money in advance. The Parts will be ready for delivery as follows: one each in May, June, July, and August, 1879, and two each subsequent month, beginning with September. The work will thus be completed in the autumn of 1880.

HOUGHTON, OSGOOD AND COMPANY, PUBLISHERS,
220 *DEVONSHIRE STREET, BOSTON.*
The Riverside Press, Cambridge.

FIGURE 3.2. A prospectus for an illustrated edition of the "Poems of Henry Wadsworth Longfellow," included as a back wrapper for a separately published part of *The Poetical Works of Henry Wadsworth Longfellow*, was retained and bound (Boston: Houghton, Osgood and Company, 1879). Henry Wadsworth Longfellow Collection (2001G-268F), by permission of the Houghton Library, Harvard University.

1880s a number of specialized firms began to offer such series as the Lakeside Library (Donnelly, Gasette & Lloyd) or the Seaside Library (George Munro) as a cheap source of reprinted fiction and other popular works, including joke books and sensational adventure or crime stories. Again, many trade publishers participated in this practice, most notably Harper Brothers with its Franklin Square Library. By 1888 it offered 600 titles, almost entirely English fiction, published weekly at a subscription cost of ten dollars per year; individual titles could also be purchased separately by mail for ten to twenty-five cents.

Technological developments had contributed to making such inexpensive prices possible: paper prices had dropped considerably with the development of efficient chemical methods of producing newsprint from wood pulp, and the use of fast cylinder and rotary presses—developed for magazine and newspaper production—also lowered the unit cost of the paper-covered, pamphlet-style library offerings. Most of the texts in these series were unprotected by copyright; their authors were either foreign or paid hack writers for fiction factories, so no royalties were paid. The extension of copyright protection to foreign works in 1891, however, jeopardized this means of publishing, which ended with changes in the postal regulations.[20]

A number of specialized publishing areas relied on alternative or specialized means of distribution that supplemented the dominant wholesale system. Sheet music, for example, was distributed alongside instruments in retail music stores; churches and other religious organizations distributed religious works; a specialized network of foreign-language book stores offered foreign-language works.[21] Again, many trade publishers participated in this trade, to greater or lesser extent, along with niche firms that specialized in it.

The enormous and lucrative trade in textbooks and other educational materials was particularly important with the increasing systematization and expansion of public education during this period. Local school boards often authorized special agents—not retail bookshops—to manage these sales. Most trade publishers maintained a range of textbooks as part of their lists, but they increasingly competed with firms specializing in the field. When the American Book Company incorporated in 1890, amalgamating four of the largest textbook publishers, the field became even more highly specialized, though it remains even today an important business for trade publishers.[22]

During the 1890s a number of new firms distinguished themselves by producing attractively designed editions of new literary works, as detailed by Megan Benton in chapter 9. These were heavily influenced by the aesthetics—both literary and graphic—of the arts-and-crafts movement, which in the book trades was dominated by William Morris, but also incorporated strains of japonisme and the poster arts styles popular in Paris. Most important were Copeland &

Day (1893-99), Lamson, Wolffe & Co. (1895-99), and Small, Maynard & Co. (1899-1906) in Boston; Stone & Kimball (1893-1906, later Herbert S. Stone & Co.) and Way & Williams (1895-98) in Chicago; and R. H. Russell & Son (1891-1906) in New York. These firms valued aesthetics over profits and were generally on the margins of the trade, usually catering to a select and mostly upper-class audience. The proprietors themselves were frequently the privileged inheritors of wealth: Herbert S. Stone, Ingalls Kimball, and W. B. Wolffe all became involved in publishing while they were students at Harvard College, from which Frederick Holland Day also graduated. Their output, though limited, was of impressive quality. These firms published many important literary and graphic works, including those of Bliss Carman, Stephen Crane, Hamlin Garland, Frederick Remington, and Walt Whitman, as well as American editions of works by Aubrey Beardsley, Max Beerbohm, and Oscar Wilde. From 1894 to 1898 Stone & Kimball published the influential literary and artistic periodical, the *Chap-Book*, and from 1894 to 1896 Copeland & Day was the American copublisher (with Mathews & Lane of London) of the *Yellow Book*. The attractively stylish books in which these firms specialized influenced the appearance of trade publications generally and was exploited more commercially by such niche firms as Thomas B. Mosher of Portland, Maine, and The Roycroft Shop of East Aurora, New York. Perhaps more importantly, however, these innovative publishers opened a market for cutting-edge and well-designed books, facilitating the twentieth-century emergence of such influential firms as Boni & Liveright, B. W. Huebsch, Mitchell Kennerley, and Alfred A. Knopf. They also pioneered the use of little magazines and the private press as major outlets for new modernist literature, discussed more fully in chapter 11 of this volume.[23]

Internationalization

With the failure of the net-pricing system, the problem of distribution persisted. Publishers were more successful, however, in dealing with the equally vexing problem of copyright. For most of the nineteenth century, American copyright law granted protection only to works by American citizens or authors residing in the United States. Publishers had no legally recognized claim on the works of foreign authors and simultaneously faced the impending expiration of copyright terms on many of the works by classic American authors. Publishers who specialized in republishing cheap and often garish editions of popular works quickly took advantage of the vast array of publicly available publications, distributing them through library series, department stores, and other nontrade retail outlets.

The lack of copyright protection for the works of foreign authors, which had always been an important part of the lists of all trade publishers, was particularly problematic. In the absence of legal recourse, trade publishers had established a set of informal conventions to regulate the rights in these works. This "courtesy of the trade" gave exclusive rights to the first firm to advertise the work of a foreign author as "in print," thus publicly announcing its intention to publish the work. These rights were held to be especially strong if payment had been made to the author or foreign publisher and extended to later works by that same author.

Courtesy of the trade proved to be remarkably serviceable, reflecting strong cooperation within the trade. By century's end, however, many nontrade publishers refused to honor it; even trade publishers frequently disputed the priority of announcements or claims to subsequent works. The need for formal copyright legislation had been debated since the 1830s, but only with the passage of the International Copyright Act in 1891 (commonly referred to as the "Chace Act") was equal legal protection extended to foreign works. Protectionist interests did, however, succeed in including the infamous "manufacturing clause," requiring that foreign works be produced in America. The Chace Act was subsequently superseded by the Copyright Code of 1909, but the manufacturing clause and other restrictive stipulations remained. As a result, the United States remained ineligible to participate in the Berne Convention, which it joined only in 1989.[24]

International copyright legislation signaled the growing complexity and internationalization of the book publishing business and was paralleled by other important developments. As Martha Woodmansee and Peter Jaszi point out in chapter 5, the right to publish a work was no longer deemed integral and whole, but rather consisted of many subsidiary rights: foreign publication, newspaper syndication, magazine serialization, translation, dramatization on stage and later screen, and so on. Specializing in managing these many rights, literary agents advised authors not only on the creation but, more importantly, on the marketing of their works, filling a new and increasingly important niche in the book trade.[25] The increasing internationalization of publishing in the United States and its concern with the import and export of books and exchange of rights led many trade firms to establish foreign offices. During these years, most offices were opened in London, although Canada's proximity and large English-reading audience also drew attention. This trend continued throughout the twentieth century as large, multinational media conglomerates came to dominate the American book trade.[26]

Book Production and Manufacturing, 1880–1940

By 1880 the major steps toward the industrialization of the production and manufacture of books had already taken place in the United States, but over subsequent decades the trend toward increased mechanization continued.[27] The many machines used in book production became larger, faster, and more complex; most books were produced in large, factory-like establishments; and laborers, both male and female, were increasingly viewed as doing work rather than practicing a craft. One example of this trend was the increasing use of cylinder presses for the manufacture of books as well as newspapers and magazines: these printing machines were large and expensive, requiring substantial outlays of capital, and were capable of printing at great speed large sheets of paper, which were fed into the press mechanically rather than by hand.

A major development of these years was the introduction and perfection of hot-metal composition machines, both Linotype and Monotype. A variety of cold-metal machines, using precast foundry type, had been in limited use since the 1850s but generally depended on hand labor for justification and distribution, whereas these new machines overcame that limitation by using specially designed matrices to cast new type as part of the composition process. The Linotype machine cast each line of text as a single slug after the matrices had been justified mechanically by means of wedge-shaped spacing bars; the matrices themselves were redistributed into a magazine for reuse as they were sorted by means of a pattern of teeth coded for each character. The Monotype system employed separate composing and casting machines to produce new type: the former machine produced a spool of punched paper tape that encoded the text, with the word spacing entered by its operator, line by line, as established by a mechanical calculator; the latter used the tape to position a matrix case containing a full set of matrices for a particular font over a mold in order to cast new type and spaces individually as the tape spooled through the machine.

These were complex machines consisting of many thousands of individual parts and were developed and improved during the final decades of the nineteenth century. Ottmar Mergenthaler of Baltimore was the chief inventor of the Linotype machine, but it was only with the adoption in 1889 of a system of producing matrices by electrotype (a system perfected by Linn Boyd Benton of Milwaukee) that he was able to produce his machine in quantity—by 1894 a couple of hundred machines were in use in the United States (figure 3.3).[28] The Monotype system was largely the work of Tolbert Lanston, who patented his machines in 1887 and made them widely available only after 1900. Both speeded the setting of text considerably over hand composition—the faster Linotype machine achieved a minimum speed of 3,000 ems per hour and, under good

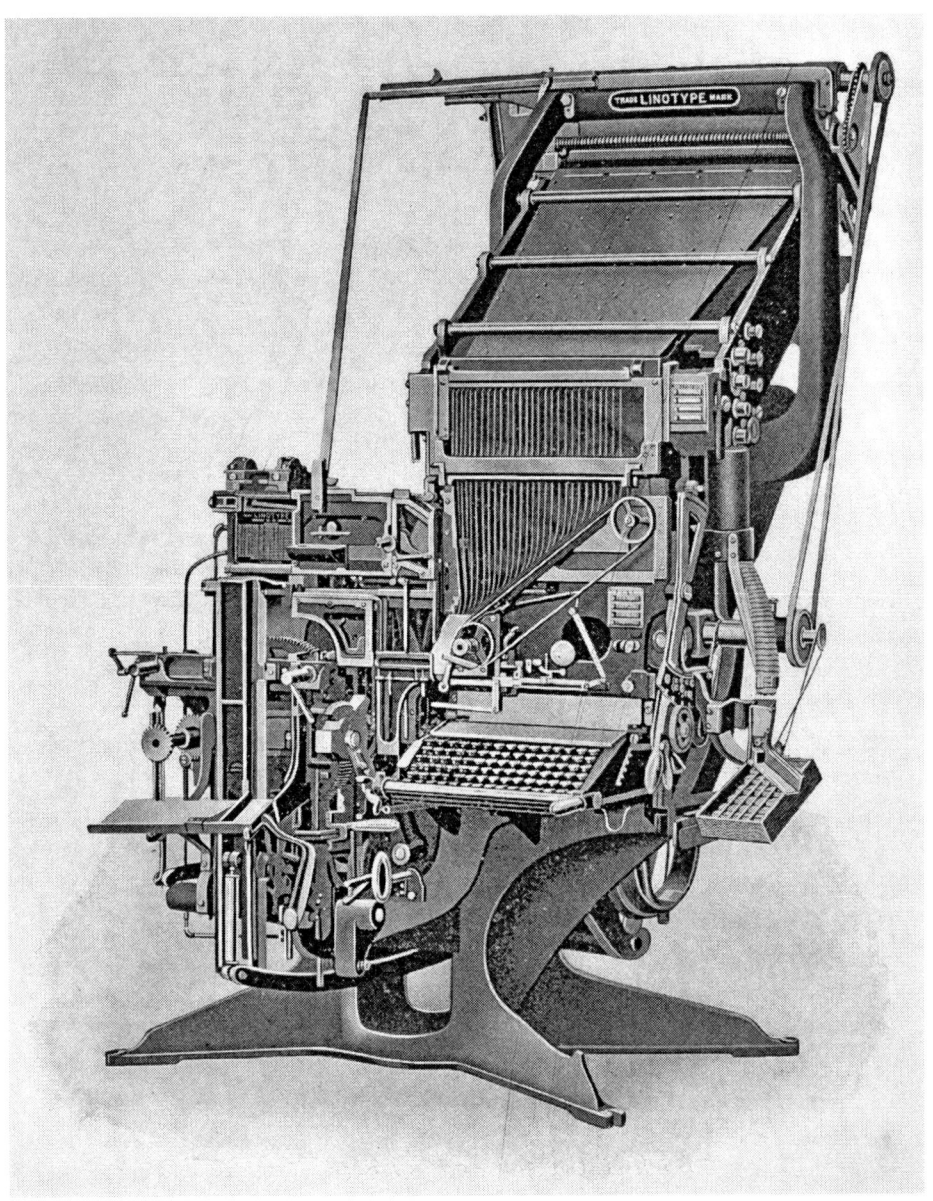

FIGURE 3.3. The quadruple magazine Linotype machine (Model 9) has "four interchangeable superimposed magazines, any of one of which can instantly be brought into operation and all of which are controlled from the standard Linotype keyboard of ninety keys." Lucien A. Legros and John Cameron Grant, *Typographical Printing-Surfaces: The Technology and Mechanism of Their Production* (London and New York: Longmans, Green and Co., 1916), plate 65. American Antiquarian Society.

conditions, an average of 4,000 to 5,000 ems by the beginning of the twentieth century.[29] The Linotype machine was first introduced in newspaper shops, where it became predominant, but both were increasingly also used for magazines and books in the new century (figure 3.4).

The incentive for the development of these machines came chiefly from the newspaper industry, where the need to reduce the time between submission of copy and production of printed sheets for distribution and sale had given traditional hand compositors a powerful position. Their union, the International Typographical Union, was one of the strongest in the United States and had long been influential in setting pay scales, working hours, and the distribution of work. The introduction of Linotype machines for the composition of newspapers threatened to eliminate the union's control of working conditions and led during the early years of the twentieth century to a series of bitter strikes and labor actions. The outcome was not only the widespread acceptance of a standard ten-hour working day but also an agreement that the union would be responsible for training apprentices in the use of this complicated new machine, which in effect allowed the International Typographical Union to maintain closed shops for much of the twentieth century.

The considerable investment required to develop these hot-metal composition machines was secured by the numerous patents that protected their new processes. The fact that they required the use of patented matrices limited the number of typefaces that could be set on them, but it also encouraged the development of many new proprietary type designs. Influenced by the ascendance of the arts-and-crafts movement, often associated with the work of William Morris, many of these were modern copies of Renaissance and other early type, but others were completely original, and the new situation led to the now familiar practice of identifying typefaces by a specific name. Many of the designers of these typefaces specialized in graphic design, a new profession that arose at the turn of the century supported by developments in the commercialization of the advertising industry.

Coincident with the emergence of the graphic designer in advertising, the book designer became a regular feature of twentieth-century book production, and many of the most influential—D. B. Updike, Bruce Rogers, Frederick W. Goudy, Beatrice Warde, and W. A. Dwiggins are only a few of the best-known early ones—are also remembered for the typefaces they designed, many of

FIGURE 3.4. Charles F. Hamilton of Worcester, Massachusetts, who owned and operated the first Monotype machine in central Massachusetts, kept very full records of the hours of its use, delays, and repairs. Charles Hamilton, Machine Composition Book, 1902–5, Charles Hamilton Papers, fol. vol. 5. American Antiquarian Society.

Keyboard. Caster.

1905

	Working h. m	Delays h. m	Repairs	No Copy	Oiling etc.	Work	Starting	Changing	Repairs	Delays Oiling etc.	Sorts & Melting
Dec. 1	5.50	2.30			.10	8.30	30				
2	3.20	5.10				8	30		.30		
3	7.	.50	.30		.10	8		1			
4	5.40	.10	2.30		.10	8.30	30				
5	7.15	.45	.20		.10	7	30		1.30		
	29.05	9.25	3.20		.40 41.50 42.30	40 h.	2 h.	1 h.	2 h.		
7	8				.30	5.15	30	45	2.30		
8	3.15	5.05			.10	2	30		6.30		
9	2.45	5.35			.10		30		8.30		
10		8.20	Caster Rep.		.10		30		8.30		
11	4.05	4.15			.10	7.45	30	45			
12	7.30	.50			.10 1.20	7.30	30	1			
	25.35	24.05			49.40 51.	22.30	3	2.30	26 h.		
14	4.55	3.25			.10	8.30	30				
15	8.20				.10	8.30	30				
16	8.05	15			.10	3.15					5.45
17	7.30	50			.10	7.15	30		1.15		
18	8.20				.10	8.30	30				
19	8	20			.10 1 50. 51	8.	30	30			
	45.10	4.50				44	2.30	30	1.15		5.45
21	7.50				40	8.15				45	
22	8.20				10	7.15	45			1	
23	7.40	40			10	3.45	45				4.30
24	8.05	15			10		45				8.15
26	8.20				10	3.30	1		1.30	3	
	40.15	55			1.20 41.10 42.30	22.45	3	15		3 15	15 45
28	7.10	25			55	8.	1				
29	8.15	5			10	3.15	1				4.45
30	8.20				10	4.15	45			30	3.30
31	6.95	45			1.0 1.25	8.15	45				
	31.20	1.15			32.35 34.25	23.45	3.30			30	8.15
Totals 26 days	171.25	40.30	3.20		5.45 221 h.	153 h.	14½ h.	4 h.	29½ h.	3¾ h.	29½ h.
						26 days – 234 hours					
	Total Comp. 390,313 ems					2551 ems per h. solid					
	2283 ems per h. solid										

which are still in use. This attention to appearance reflects another important development in the production of books at the time: a reduction in the cost of reproducing illustrations and other images. This has, in turn, signaled the major shift from the typographic to the graphic book that has characterized the twentieth century.

Traditionally, the cost of including illustrations in a book had added considerably to its expense, while at the same time increasing its appeal and salability. Many books published before the twentieth century did include illustrations, ranging in quality and cost from crude woodcuts printed in relief to expensive and elaborate inserted images that were reproduced by intaglio or chromolithography. The major cost in the preparation of illustrations was not usually their design, except in the case of the increasing number of those produced by recognized illustrators and artists whose work was widely sought after, but rather in the cost of preparing a medium for their reproduction, whether that consisted of relief wood engravings, intaglio plates, or the multiple stones required by chromolithography. In fact, many of the most famous illustrators of the nineteenth century—such as Winslow Homer—began as wood engravers, a necessary first step toward supporting their careers as artists.

This all changed with the emergence of photographic methods for the reproduction of images. From the 1850s American books had been illustrated with inserted photographs, but only later in the century were practical methods developed that employed photography as part of the process of reproducing images widely and inexpensively. A wide array of new photomechanical and photochemical techniques came to be used, though all shared the common method of using a photographic negative to transfer a design to a printing surface that had been treated with a photosensitive chemical. Once the exposed surface was further treated, the result was used to multiply the original image, whether by relief (e.g., process relief blocks), intaglio (e.g., photogravure), or lithography (e.g., collotype). Two subsequent developments followed: the use of the halftone technique, in which a finely etched screen was interposed between the design and photographic film in order to allow the resulting image to be reproduced with what appears to be continuous shading from black to white, and photographic color separation, in which colored photographic filter lenses were used to prepare multiple printing surfaces that, when used in what became the standard four-color process, could reproduce images displaying the full spectrum of color.

These developments occurred piecemeal over a number of years but were perfected during the final decades of the nineteenth century. The result was a marked change in the appearance and packaging of books, which increasingly were offered for sale inexpensively even when they were heavily illustrated. By the end of the century, it was not uncommon for some books to appear with endpapers illustrated with a design, illustration, or map that was specific to that work, something that would have been economically unfeasible earlier, and by the 1920s most trade books were offered to customers in colorful printed dust jackets that were intended to be preserved with the book permanently, bringing to an end the period of elaborate, artist-designed stamped bindings that had flourished at the end of the preceding century. By the 1930s some books were also being printed by photo-offset lithography, in which the text, set in type, was being reproduced as though the typographic text itself were an illustration. This last development allowed the easy, and inexpensive, integration of text with image, and by the end of the twentieth century had become the usual method used to print books.

A final innovation in the production of books was a feature of the first half of the twentieth century, though it is more difficult to characterize, as it does not involve the introduction of new machinery or methods. It is the result of the general increased scientific understanding of materials and processes, which in turn led to greater control and standardization of manufacturing practices. Thus, for example, on 19 June 1923 a conference of representative manufacturers, distributors, and users drafted a "Simplified Practice Recommendation R22, Paper" (subsequently revised on 27 September 1932 and accepted by the U.S. Bureau of Standards) that set standards for the sizes, qualities, quantity, and nomenclature of paper.[30] Whereas papermaking had—even after the introduction of papermaking machines and chemically treated wood pulp during the nineteenth century—remained as much a craft as a science, it now became regularized, and paper manufacturers and distributors were able to offer paper sample books, which had been virtually unknown earlier, that promised to deliver book paper identified by name in standard sizes of known quality and quantity. Similar developments are typical of many aspects of the book production industry, and if in 1880 books still shared at least some characteristics with those that had appeared during the preceding centuries, by 1940 they had become a thoroughly modern, and familiar, product.

CHAPTER 4

The Expansion of the National Book Trade System

James L. W. West III

. . .

For American publishers and booksellers, the period between 1920 and 1950 was a time of adjustment, transition, and expansion. Readily apparent by 1920 were the consequences of the failure to establish an American counterpart to the Net Book Agreement in Britain. Indeed, when American publishers' efforts to emulate the pricing agreements of the British trade collapsed in the wake of the Supreme Court's decision in the Macy's case, the U.S. trade turned to different measures for price maintenance and sought new ways of doing business.

Demographic and economic pressures affected American houses more deeply than their British counterparts. The American trade thus became more rough-and-tumble and front-list-oriented; it adopted a more pronounced gambling mentality and learned to expand through nontraditional channels of distribution and sales. American publishers became more commercial and readily tied themselves to other entertainment industries like theater, radio, and motion pictures. The book trade was constantly subject to market pressures. American publishers responded as businessmen in a large, popular democracy. Rather than imposing a British model on their book trade, American firms developed their own methods. These new practices were the foundation of American book publishing during the second half of the century.

Many of the houses founded during the 1910s and 1920s gained visibility and influence. Random House, Knopf, Liveright, Simon and Schuster, and Viking came to the fore; Harper, Appleton, Scribner, Putnam, and Holt, though losing ground, still controlled a considerable share of the book trade. Some of the new imprints came from modest beginnings. Random House developed from the Modern Library, a reprint line acquired by Bennett Cerf and Donald Klopfer from Horace Liveright in 1925.[1] Simon and Schuster's first publications in the late 1920s were softbound crossword-puzzle books, distributed through magazine and newspaper wholesalers.[2] These less prestigious publishing venues allowed the new houses to pursue fresh ideas about merchandising and distribution, ideas that brought books within convenient reach of nearly all American citizens by the 1940s.

Many of the newer imprints were headed by men of Jewish background, including Liveright, Cerf, Klopfer, Richard Simon, M. Lincoln Schuster, Alfred A. Knopf, B. W. Huebsch, Harold K. Guinzburg (of Viking Press), and Pascal Covici and Donald Friede (of Covici-Friede). The publishing world of the thirties and forties included many men of German or eastern European Jewish descent: Thomas Seltzer, Robert K. Haas, Leon Shimkin, Manuel Komroff, Harry Scherman, Maxwell Sackheim, George Braziller, Ben D. Zevin, William Targ, Jacob W. Greenberg, and Nat Wartels. Many prominent publishers, Jewish and gentile, were products not of Princeton, Harvard, or Yale, but rather of Columbia University. Among these were Knopf, Cerf, Klopfer, Simon, Schuster, Alfred Harcourt, Donald Brace, George Delacorte, Ian Ballantine, and Robert Giroux.[3]

An ethnic, urban background gave these newer publishers different viewpoints from those of their predecessors. They were less clubby, more liberal politically, more sympathetic to proletarian and minority authors, more interested in new European writers, and desirous of distributing books among all social classes, as Janice Radway shows in chapter 11 of this volume. The quantity and originality of literary works published by these newer publishers in the twenties and thirties is, in retrospect, astounding. In 1925 Liveright released Dreiser's *An American Tragedy* and Hemingway's *In Our Time*; Cerf and Klopfer produced influential works by William Faulkner, Eugene O'Neill, Gertrude Stein, and Sherwood Anderson. Cerf won a highly publicized court battle, allowing him to publish Joyce's *Ulysses* in 1933 and opening the way for greater frankness in fiction. The publications of Alfred and Blanche Knopf (including works by H. L. Mencken, Willa Cather, Dashiell Hammett, and Raymond Chandler) were widely praised for their handsome typography and well-designed bindings and book jackets.

Book Distribution: Expanding Readership

In his *Economic Survey of the Book Industry, 1930–1931*, O. H. Cheney urged publishers to utilize better methods of distribution.[4] This study, based on an extensive gathering of data about production and sales, was commissioned by the National Association of Book Publishers. Cheney's background in conventional business—not the book trade—made him an acerbic (and inadvertently humorous) critic of traditional publishing practices. He was particularly acidulous about whimsical, hunch-based publishing, calling it the "I-shot-an-arrow-in-the-air" approach. He described distribution in the United States as haphazard, citing inconsistent discount and return policies as damaging to both booksellers and publishers. Cheney called for more research on consumer tastes and greater efforts to cultivate dependable markets. He also advocated better record keeping and tighter control of cash flow. Publishers, said Cheney, needed to leave their New York offices more frequently to visit distributors and customers, talking with them and learning about their preferences and needs. Released at the beginning of the Great Depression, the study found receptive listeners in the book world, persons willing to experiment with new distribution methods, aim for broader markets, and pay more attention to consumers.

The most serious problem in American publishing, as Cheney and others recognized, was its ineffective distribution system. Independent bookshops alone were not sufficient for the task. There were too few of them, and they were often one-horse operations, poorly capitalized, and understocked. These bookshops depended on best-selling novels to attract patrons and were vulnerable to competition from other book outlets, such as remainder bins in larger retail stores. Small-scale booksellers had to diversify to survive, often offering magazines, prints, stationery, art supplies, and gift items. Some booksellers built customer loyalty by organizing neighborhood reading clubs and discussion groups, but these efforts were difficult to sustain. Small bookshops were the weak link in the system, ordering too little stock, carrying too many books on credit, and slowing sales and cash flow.

The Depression was not altogether detrimental for U.S. book publishing. While the rest of the economy floundered, most book firms held steady; some even grew and prospered. "During the Depression we were sitting in clover," recalled Cerf. "In fact, every year we went a little bit ahead, and there was never one when we went backward."[5] The only major firm to fail during the 1930s was Liveright, largely as a result of Horace Liveright's earlier gambles on best sellers and Broadway plays.[6] Some of the smaller houses experienced financial difficulties, but many were taken over by larger firms, providing new financial backing. Dodd acquired Duffield and Green in 1934, for example, and Putnam assumed control of Coward-McCann in 1936. The nature of the book business allowed publishing firms to survive slow economic periods, which often imposed a necessary discipline on the trade. Publishers had to restrict new publishing, reduce staff and overhead, milk the backlist, and wait for better times to arrive.

A general migration toward American cities during the first three decades of the twentieth century helped to create concentrated and relatively predictable book markets. By the 1930s urban areas housed more than half the population, public education had expanded, and leisure time had increased. Reaching established urban, middle-class markets became easier and cheaper, encouraging publishers to experiment with inexpensive books and new, more efficient printing technologies. Collective action, low overhead, and nontraditional sales methods allowed them to survive.

During World War II, the American public was hungry for information and entertainment, and the book market expanded tremendously. William Jovanovich remembered the war years as a boom period "simply because publishers were able to sell practically everything to war-workers, who had plenty of money and not much to spend it on."[7] Many best sellers were war books with titles like *Guadalcanal Diary* and *Thirty Seconds over Tokyo*; sales of conventional novels and escapist fiction were also strong. Paper shortages irritated publishers but deterred risky publishing and large print runs, forcing editors to project their sales figures more carefully. As a result, overproduction of new titles—long a damaging feature of the U.S. book trade—became less common. Prices remained stable, and publishers made money.

One of the most important developments during the 1940s was the establishment of the Council on Books in Wartime.[8] W. W. Norton, John Farrar, Malcolm Johnson, and other leading New York trade publishers began the council in 1942; it provided Armed Services Editions for American soldiers and Overseas Editions for inhabitants of liberated areas. These small paperbound volumes, secured by a single staple punched sideways through the spine, were designed to fit into the breast pocket of a military fatigue jacket. Nearly all of the texts were printed uncut, and the books were given away free. By the end of the war, more than 123 million had been printed and distributed, creating potential markets for American books all over the world. The Armed Services Editions also suggested the feasibility of mass paperback publishing (figure 4.1).

The demographic phenomena of the postwar period—the return of the servicemen, their college enrollment through the G.I. Bill, the invigoration of the U.S. economy, and the baby boom—maintained American publishers' prosperity through the 1940s. Burgeoning higher education especially stimulated demand for textbooks; publishers could expect an underpinning of support, year after year, from school and college classrooms. The American public's hunger for information and self-improvement supported publishing efforts in many fields, from encyclopedias to car-repair manuals, personal advice books to child-rearing guides, cookbooks to travel literature, etiquette books to political memoirs.

Book Clubs and Mail-Order Distribution

Mail-order book clubs grew significantly during the thirties and forties. Potential book-buyers were everywhere, especially in small towns and rural communities, but until 1925 there seemed to be no efficient way to reach them with advertising or to get books to them with dispatch. Shipping single copies to individual customers or to small bookshops was unprofitable—the handling

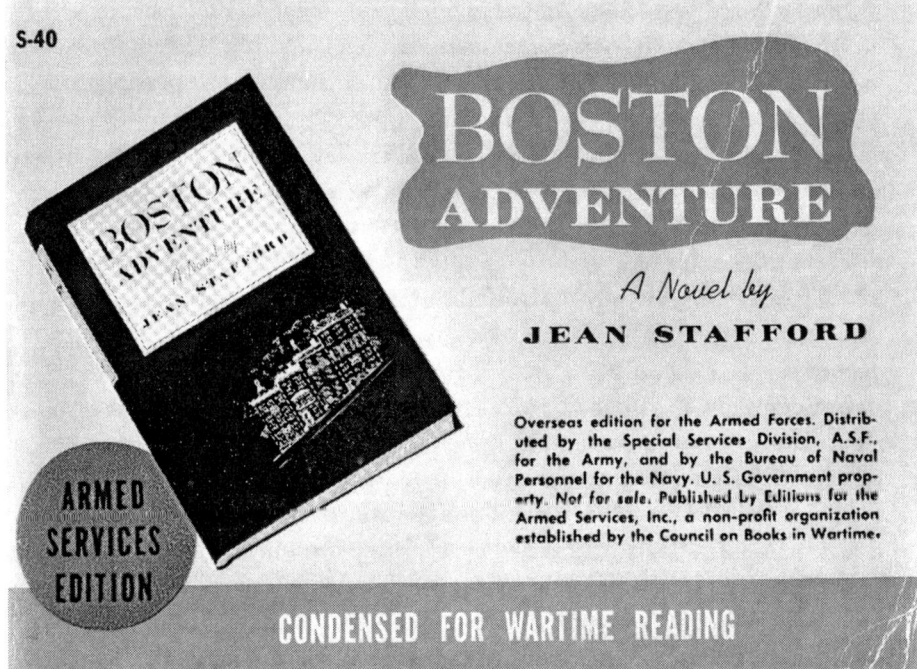

FIGURE 4.1. Through the Council on Books in Wartime, established by leading New York trade publishers in 1942, small paperbound volumes were made available for free distribution. This advertisement for the Armed Services Edition of Jean Stafford's *Boston Adventure* includes a photograph of the first edition published in 1944 by Harcourt, Brace and Company. Reproduced with the permission of Rare Books and Manuscripts, Special Collections Library, The Pennsylvania State University Libraries.

cost had to be charged against the return from a single book. Book club publishers realized that advertising in mass magazines could reach thousands of potential readers; the mail system then became a viable distribution vehicle, especially after the establishment of Rural Free Delivery, reaching customers in outlying areas. Sales costs could thus be spread over hundreds and even thousands of copies. Following this logic, Harry Scherman and Maxwell Sackheim began the Book-of-the-Month Club (BOMC) in 1926; in that same year Doubleday founded the Literary Guild. Both operations flourished, offering best sellers for reduced prices, giving bonus volumes to new subscribers, and recruiting members through widely circulated magazines.[9] Both clubs spawned imitators: smaller operations sprang up, specializing in history, crime fiction, cookbooks, children's literature, and other areas.

The Book-of-the-Month Club was the largest and most successful of these operations. In its first full year it reported net sales of more than $1,640,000 and net earnings, before taxes, of approximately $152,000. BOMC made steady gains through the 1930s, building a large subscription base, and the business was solidly established by the mid-1940s. In 1945 net sales for BOMC were just under $13,700,000 and net earnings just over $2,800,000. BOMC was a cultural phenomenon among the socially ambitious middle classes. Advertisements encouraged potential customers to question their literary sophistication and their reading habits. Had book buyers been left out of conversations for not having read the latest novel? Or were they ill-informed about current subjects? BOMC promised to remedy such shortcomings while boosting social status by providing books and conversational fodder. For the modernized and increasingly homogenized American bourgeoisie, this was a powerful appeal.

In its early years, BOMC chose its titles from books that were already published, printed, bound, and awaiting delivery to bookshops. As BOMC grew, it began to request more advance time, receiving texts in galley proofs, or even in manuscript. BOMC judges could thus pressure authors for prepublication revisions or cuts—authors received substantial payment for subsidiary rights in return. Most authors capitulated: Robert Trumbull, for example, made excisions in *The Raft*, and Ross Lockridge Jr. allowed bowdlerizations in *Raintree County*. In one of the most significant of these cases, Richard Wright made BOMC distribution possible by agreeing to eliminate the final section of a book he had entitled "American Hunger," replacing it with a new ending and retitling the book *Black Boy*. The result was less complex, more an indictment of southern racism than a revelation of Wright's involvement with the American communist movement.[10]

Trade publishers were ambivalent about book clubs, though they certainly welcomed the extra income from the sale of book club rights (usually divided equally between publisher and author). Such profits were almost effortless; publishers merely extended print runs to sell extra sheets to clubs or, later, leased printing plates to clubs, which would then manufacture their own sheets. But publishers suspected that they might be undercutting their own best-selling titles, trading high-volume sales at cut prices for almost as many individual sales at full retail rates. Independent bookshops resented the book clubs and put heavy pressure on publishers to boycott them. Bookshop owners feared that sales of the most popular titles—those that attracted buyers—would be usurped by book clubs, thus robbing them of dependable income and patronage. Book club advocates countered with claims that they targeted a different customer base from the one served by independent bookshops. Further, they argued, book clubs' huge promotional efforts actually stimulated sales of trade editions. Such issues generated considerable disagreement, but by the end of the 1950s they had become moot. The tremendous success of book clubs made resistance futile. Trade publishers learned to cooperate with clubs and, in so doing, expanded the audience for authors like Hemingway, Steinbeck, Cozzens, and O'Neill.

Paperback Publishing

The rebirth of paperback publishing—the "drugstore edition"—marked another major innovation in distribution. The American trade had experimented with low-priced paperbound books twice before, once from about 1840 to 1845 and again from around 1880 until 1893. These early paperback publishers, however, had cut prices to make quick profits, frequently pirating British texts. They wreaked havoc on the industry, wrecking the financial structure on which established trade publishers depended. Competition destroyed them eventually, but not before they damaged the book trade. Thus, when American publishers attempted softbound publishing a third time, they proceeded carefully.

Pocket Books, the first modern American paperback house, was founded in 1938 to emulate Penguin Books, an emerging success in England.[11] Robert de Graff, who began the Pocket Books imprint, had fourteen years of experience in the hardcover trade. His first twenty-five-cent edition was a proven title, Pearl Buck's *The Good Earth*; ten other titles followed, including the best sellers *Lost Horizon* by James Hilton and *Enough Rope* by Dorothy Parker. The Pocket Books concept was almost instantly successful: in its first seven months, some 1.5 million volumes were sold, mostly through such nontraditional outlets as drugstores, newsstands, and tobacco shops.

Unique distribution methods made early paperback publishing successful; the titles were distributed, usually by the American News Corporation, as if they were newspapers or popular magazines, not clothbound books. Paperbacks were marketed as impulse purchases, to be read and shared—or thrown away. Retailers stocked paperback titles for shorter periods, concentrating on currently popular books rather than backlist staples. Store owners, in fact, left title selection to the distributors, who delivered boxes of "hot" sellers and kept fresh titles on the revolving wire display racks. Paperbacks, sold in this way, quickly found audiences among middle-class readers: businessmen, travelers, housewives, teenagers, and eventually college students, to whom they were assigned as textbooks.

Numerous softcover houses developed as a consequence. Avon began operation in 1941, Dell and Popular Library the next year, New American Library two years later. In 1945 Ian and Betty Ballantine, who had been managing the Penguin imprint in the United States, left to found Bantam Books. Supported financially by Harper, Scribner, Random House, BOMC, and Little, Brown, Bantam's initial list included twenty titles. "In those days we simply had no returns at all," Betty Ballantine remembered. "The pipelines weren't filled."[12] While much of the list was genre fiction—westerns, whodunits, and light romances—softcover publishers also offered books by Mark Twain, F. Scott Fitzgerald, and John Steinbeck, as well as reprints of classic works from British and continental literatures. Grosset and Dunlap, a large reprint house, managed Bantam's distribution (see figure 4.2).

Paperback publishing suffered initially from a taint of commercialism caused partly by its humble sales outlets and partly by the lurid covers produced for many of its early titles. (Collectors today prize the misleading artwork on some of Hemingway's and Faulkner's early paperbacks.) Gradually, softcover houses became respectable, and authors began to appreciate the income from paperback rights—initially no more than $500 for a conventional novel but rising quickly to much larger sums: $35,000 for Norman Mailer's *The Naked and the Dead* in 1948, for example.[13] Respectable titles received less controversial artwork, and conventional bookshops began to stock paperbacks alongside traditional hardbacks. Paperback houses could respond quickly to the demand for popular new authors and to shifting tastes, while giving texts longer selling lives. In the late 1940s, for example, New American Library capitalized on William Faulkner's growing fame (from the success of the *Viking Portable Faulkner*) by promoting his paperback editions vigorously.[14]

The Subsidiary Rights Market

Book clubs and paperbacks reflected the great growth of the subsidiary rights market during this period. Authors, publishers, and literary agents discovered many new ways of exploiting ancillary literary rights for republication or adaptation to other media. Writing generated both initial income from first publication and sale and continuous income from various forms of recycling. This was not a new concept in American publishing: Longfellow, Emerson, and other nineteenth-century writers understood and practiced it, as did writers of the 1890s and early 1900s, including Frank Norris, William Dean Howells, and Mark Twain. In Norris's words, "The novelist—and one speaks now of the American—may sell the same work over many times."[15]

By the 1930s, however, in the wake of changing attitudes toward books and commodity-text publishing spurred by changes in copyright law (discussed by Martha Woodmansee and Peter Jaszi in the next chapter), such thinking was widespread in the trade. Works of literature were serialized or excerpted in newspapers and magazines before publication; they were adapted for the stage,

FIGURE 4.2. F. Scott Fitzgerald, *The Great Gatsby* (New York: Bantam Paperback ed., 1945). Courtesy Bantam Books, a division of Random House.

often generating significant income; cheap reprint publishers like Grosset and Dunlap, A. L. Burt, Blue Ribbon Books, and the Dollar Book Club leased the plates; and popular novels and stories were sold as "second serials" to large metropolitan newspapers, where daily installments appeared on the back pages of morning and afternoon editions.

The most significant source of subsidiary revenue, however, was Hollywood. Movie rights to popular novels could be extremely profitable. For example, Dreiser received $100,000 for *An American Tragedy*. Studios like MGM, Fox, RKO, Paramount, and Warner Brothers relied on New York representatives to closely monitor publishers' lists and buy up potentially lucrative material. Publishers angled for such sales, submitting novels in manuscript or galleys. Exposure through the cinema helped to spread the popularity of writers as diverse as Edith Wharton, Sinclair Lewis, Ernest Hemingway, Raymond Chandler, and Willard Huntington Wright (S. S. Van Dine). Even radio rights proved important: popular stories by authors such as Robert W. Chambers became radio scripts, and memorable characters — Dashiell Hammett's Sam Spade, the Continental Op, and the Thin Man, for example — became the leads in weekly radio serials.

Publishers and authors thus became more conscious of the value of subsidiary rights and more likely to negotiate vigorously for larger shares of the income they generated. Contracts during the thirties and forties reflect a new awareness of the worth of such rights; authors and publishers usually split the profits equally, though best-selling authors sometimes demanded and received a larger cut. The orchestrated publication of literary works, with various print incarnations and media translations feeding each other and prolonging sales runs for authors and publishers, was not yet a widespread practice in the literary marketplace. By the end of the century, however, publishers' boilerplate contracts routinely contained clauses covering "sub-rights" for toys, audiotapes, and T-shirts. The origins of such subsidiary activities lie in the 1930s and 1940s.

The Literary Agent

Such negotiations brought the literary agent to the forefront of the American publishing world.[16] Informal agents had existed since at least the 1820s in the United States, giving advice and small loans to authors and helping them in dealings with publishers. By the 1870s and 1880s, there were several literary agencies in New York — the Athenaeum Bureau of Literature, the New York Bureau of Literary Revision, and the Writer's Literary Bureau among them. The first truly successful full-time agent in America was Paul Revere Reynolds, who opened his business in New York in 1892.[17] Much of Reynolds's early activity involved international copyright; the 1891 Chace Act aimed to end overseas literary piracy, but its provisions were not altogether clear. Reynolds provided advice about publishing under the new law.

Publishers resented Reynolds and other early agents, despite their useful services, believing that they broke down friendly relations between authors and their publishers. There was some truth to the charge. Agents wanted to see mildly adversarial relationships between authors and publishers; mistrust on both sides helped to justify the agent's activities—and the 10 percent commission deducted from the author's payment. Publishers began to find it difficult to maintain a conventionally avuncular stance toward authors, who themselves learned to be more wary in contractual dealings.

In truth, though, American writers by the 1930s and 1940s had already become distanced from the publishing firms that manufactured and sold their work. Authors were insulated from publishers by editors, who were separated from book production by subordinates in other departments. Publishing was increasingly bureaucratized, and transforming manuscripts into salable literary goods required command of a specialized language and expertise. Agents thus aided writers by translating contracts, explaining royalty rates, revealing the mysteries of book manufacture, and functioning as go-betweens on such matters as dust-jacket design and advertising copy. Some agents even became virtual editors, offering advice on writing for national markets and sifting through manuscripts to find those suitable for particular magazines and book publishers.

Agents also became bankers and tax advisers, handling money for authors and sometimes advancing funds against unsold or unwritten work. Trade houses, in response, gave agents some of the small and less remunerative business of publishing—research chores, nickel-and-dime reprint rights, and lecture arrangements, for example—eventually blurring the line between agents and publishing-house editors. Authors learned to feel as much loyalty to their agents as they did to their editors and publishers; many authors, guided by their agents, spread their books among several publishing firms rather than staying with single houses for their entire careers. This often created copyright problems in later years when former publishers lost interest in early works they still controlled. It also virtually ended the long-standing practice of issuing collected editions of works by popular and productive writers toward the ends of their careers. The copyrights on those works were now often scattered among several competing imprints, and it was difficult to achieve cooperation on a collected series.

Conclusion

Large American publishing houses became more highly organized during the thirties and forties, resulting in greater task division and increased bureaucracy within most firms. Middle managers came into positions of authority; houses lost the early distinctiveness achieved by dominant founders with strong tastes and personalities. Firms founded in the nineteenth century ceased to publish their own house magazines and closed down their printing and binding plants, using jobbers instead. Sizable trade houses thus became more like one another, though individuals within those houses—talented editors such as Maxwell Perkins, Hiram Haydn, and Robert Giroux—were able to maintain individual imprints and lists.

The period between the 1920s and the 1940s in American book publishing was filled with expansion and experimentation. Especially significant were an array of new imprints and publishers, the emergence and rapid growth of paperback publishing and book clubs, the twin influences of the Depression and World War II, the postwar growth in economic capital, the expansion of secondary and higher education, and the willingness of publishers to develop new marketing and distribution strategies. Publishing firms were no longer recognizable expressions of individual tastes and styles; they increasingly became impersonal manufacturers and distributors of books. Literary agents appropriated considerable power and influence, particularly in the marketing of subsidiary rights; authors felt less closely tied to particular imprints and learned to negotiate literary contracts more astutely. Most of the major developments in American book publishing during the 1960s, and in the years that would follow, had their roots in the three decades just before midcentury.

CHAPTER 5

Copyright in Transition

Peter Jaszi and Martha Woodmansee

. . .

The first important treatise on American copyright, Eaton S. Drone's influential *A Treatise on the Law of Property in Intellectual Productions in Great Britain and the United States*, was published in Boston in 1879. In 1944 two New York lawbook publishers issued a standard survey of the subject for another generation: *The Law of Copyright and Literary Property* by Horace G. Ball.[1] A comparison of these volumes reveals that in the intervening decades the law of copyright in the United States had undergone a marked transformation. That transformation facilitated the emergence of the American book trade as an enterprise engaged in commercially oriented, large-scale, commodity-text publishing.[2]

The period from 1880 to 1940 was an eventful one in American copyright history. A series of important legislative actions culminated in the general revision of the copyright statute in 1909. In addition, the numbers of reported copyright decisions from the federal courts increased significantly. Finally, a specialized legal literature concerning copyright developed. This chapter examines the evolving infrastructure of legal doctrine that facilitated developments in the publishing industry. Significant changes in the law included the judicial articulation of the "work-for-hire" doctrine, the passage of legislation ushering in international copyright relations between the United States and the rest of the world, and the rise of the doctrine of "substantial similarity." All three developments contributed to the expansion and consolidation of the book trade by providing a firmer legal foundation for the effective assertion of publishers' claims to the literary productions of individual writers. Although these legal changes seem to have chiefly served publishers, their justification was rooted in appeals to the rights of "authors."

The rhetoric of authorship invoked in this body of law casts authors as individuals of superior talent, or genius, who break with tradition to create something new and unique, in a word, "original." This distinctly modern way of representing the craft of writing emerged in the course of the eighteenth century and gathered such force in Romantic poetic theory as to effectively efface the social or collaborative aspects of writing.

Many minds and hands contribute to the production of any given book. Until the mid-eighteenth century, the craft of writing was considered on a par with other aspects of book manufacture—papermaking, bookbinding, type founding, or typesetting.[3] The early modern writer was considered master of a body of accepted rules and techniques for manipulating traditional materials to achieve meanings and effects prescribed by the individual or institutional patron to whom he owed his livelihood. Rarely did he view himself, nor was he treated, as a privileged actor in the production process. In the early era of book manufacture, the writer was the person of least account in this process; for writers could be had cheap compared with paper, type, founders, and compositors—or for nothing, if they were being subsidized by a patron.

The emergence of the modern "author" depends on a cultural forgetting of these diverse interdependencies. In the poetics of writers of the Romantic period, the moment of composition is increasingly figured as the only genuinely creative moment in the process of book production, and the act of composition itself is increasingly figured as solitary and originary—as an act of inspired genius, rather than one involving mastery and a redeployment of inherited ideas and techniques, and as resulting in new, original works expressive of the unique genius of their maker.

Space does not permit exploration of the historical roots of this Romantic mystification of creative activity generally, and writing in particular. Our object is rather to call attention to its centrality in the body of doctrine that provided the legal infrastructure of the modern American publishing industry. This coincidence of rhetoric and result is far from unusual in the history of copyright generally. Since 1710 publishers have frequently found their interests well served by laws purporting to recognize the "natural rights" of authors.[4] Nor were the invocations of Romantic authorship in American copyright law during the period covered in this chapter without local historical precedent. In fact, what has been termed a "Lockean" notion of authorial entitlement has been a part of American copyright discourse from its beginnings.[5]

By the 1850s some doctrines of American copyright law were marked by this Lockean way of thinking if not yet by the fully mystified Romantic vision of the tribute due to genius that would develop later. For example, writers were absolutely entitled to claim the initial copyright in their personal works, even if those works had been created in connection with a salaried employment or on a special commission. And although it is generally said that U.S. law recognized no copyrights in the works of foreign authors before 1891, the reality was more complicated: foreigners could and did claim U.S. copyright on the basis of their residence in this country.

Other doctrines, however, displayed the influence of alternative (if not contradictory) "republican" or "utilitarian" approaches to rationalizing literary property that stressed the importance of promoting the public circulation of printed texts.[6] The vision of works of authorship as useful knowledge held sway where legal doctrines addressed the scope of rights in protected works; these were restrictively defined in deference to the value of promoting the flow of information: the narrower the definition of rights, the more broadly new versions of existing texts could be circulated without legal interference.

Each of these midcentury competing copyright doctrines in some way hindered the emergence of the market in commodity-texts, for in one way or another, they all limited a publisher's legal authority over a text. By 1880 significant rethinking of these and other core copyright doctrines was underway, and by 1940 copyright law had been substantially remade.

The Work-for-Hire Doctrine

In order for a market in "commodity-texts" to exist, copyrighted works must be freely alienable—that is, capable of being bought and sold without restriction like any other commodity in the market. In particular, legal conditions that support the allocation of rights in works to firms engaged in large-scale text production are required.[7] Ideally, this allocation of rights should be based on the operation of general "default rules" rather than fact-sensitive legal tests that require elaborate "case-by-case" application. At the beginning of the period in question, however, no such default rules existed.

"The mere fact of employment does not make the employer the absolute owner of the literary property created by the person employed," Drone noted in 1879. "Where there is no agreement or implied understanding that what is produced shall belong to the employer, it is clear that the latter acquires no title to the copyright. For the property is in the author, unless he has chosen to part with it."[8] In this view, the employer could enjoy rights in the work only by virtue of an express or implied contract with the individual author. Simultaneously, Drone acknowledged the possibility that "[a] case might arise where a writer follows so closely the directions given by his employer that the creation of the work may be due to the mind of the latter, and he may properly be regarded as the author."[9] Drone implies that in such a case, the deep logic of the Romantic conception of authorship, with its emphasis on the importance of mental or spiritual inspiration as distinct from mere artisanal labor, would justify awarding rights to a corporation rather than an individual creative worker. Though no such case was cited, Drone's suggestion was a fateful one: slightly less than a century later, the law would fully embrace the notion that employers were entitled to claim copyright when they served as "the motivating factors" behind the making of a copyrighted work and possessed the power to "direct and supervise" the creative work of their employees, even when they chose not to exercise it.[10] By 1940 U.S. law had made a substantial shift toward this eventual position.

Horace Ball marks the shift in a 1944 discussion of the legal status of the works of salaried employees: "[W]here an author is employed at a salary to write a text book, prepare a compilation or perform other literary labor in accordance with the terms of a contract with his employer, the literary property in the completed work belongs to the employer, who is entitled to copyright it."[11] The case-by-case factual inquiry into copyright ownership invoked by Drone in 1879 has been replaced by a generally applicable legal principle that awards copyright to the employer.

Although Ball does not describe the process by which this rule came to apply, Richard C. DeWolfe, writing in 1925, does: "The United States Supreme Court has quoted with approval the definition of author in Worcester's Dictionary: 'He to whom anything owes its origin; originator, maker, one who completes a work of science or literature.'" If the "originator" is the supervisor of the creation of the work, DeWolfe continues, and the creator is simply carrying out the instructions of the supervisor, then the supervisor is the author. This was embodied, he notes, in the 1909 Copyright Act in Section 62, in which an employer was recognized as author in the case of works made for hire.[12]

DeWolfe referenced two significant developments. One was the inclusion in the 1909 Copyright Act of the aforementioned Section 62; the other was the emergence in cases and commentaries of a new perspective on the employer-employee relationship that validated the allocation of rights provided in the statute by invoking the authorship construct.

Section 62 stated "[t]hat in the interpretation and construction of this Act . . . the word 'author' shall include an employer in the case of a work made for hire." This provision was made even more significant by the fact that Section 4 specified "[t]hat the works for which copyright may be secured under this Act shall include all the writings of an author." Thus the 1909 Copyright Act represents the first legislative recognition of the phenomenon of employed authorship; the operative concept, "work made for hire,"[13] had not previously appeared under that name in either statutory or case law. Curiously, there was no substantive discussion of this innovation recorded in the deliberations leading up to the 1909 legislation.[14] This silence, along with the failure of the statute itself to define the term "work made for hire," means that there is no direct evidence of the intended scope of the concept, or the original rationale supporting it.

The courts supplied the definition and the rationale in the first round of work-for-hire cases stretching from 1909 through 1940 (and beyond). Focusing on the legal position of the works of salaried employees, judges began to apply the doctrine with full force so as to deprive those employees of any claim of right in their literary productions. The ideological basis for such an application is highlighted, for example, in *National Cloak & Suit Co. v. Kaufman*,[15] where the court emphasized the organizing and directing role of the employer company in creating the catalog at issue. It cites, at length, the company's own description of its activities in assembling and underwriting a team of artists and writers who, together, accounted for what could be regarded as original in the publication. However gifted the *artists* may have been, in the eyes of the court the *company* that paid their salaries deserved to be considered the "effective cause" of their work and, accordingly, its "true" author. The work-for-hire doctrine may be viewed as a working out of the basic premises of the Romantic conception of authorship: inasmuch as an employer holds contractual power to assign tasks, it constitutes the "effective cause" of its employees' creative labor, and the product thereof constitutes a work "made for hire."[16] Through elaboration of the implications of Romantic ideology corporate legal authority over the work of individual creators was secured.

To recapitulate: at the beginning of our period, Lockean views of authorial entitlement militated against awarding rights in texts to employers. But the work-for-hire doctrine, as it evolved by the end of the period, successfully invoked the Romantic valorization of originary genius to rationalize the market in literary productions by "clearing title" on the productions of employed creators.[17] This development represented an essential step in the establishment of the commodity-text.

The Coming of International Copyright

The story of the United States' early notoriety as the foremost haven for international copyright piracy is too well known to require retelling here. Prior to 1891 most works of foreign authors were ineligible for copyright protection under U.S. law, although there were exceptions: as already noted, foreign authors could qualify for protection if they were "resident" in the United States, or if they wrote in collaboration with an American citizen in whose name the work could be registered.[18] Nonetheless, through most of the nineteenth century, unauthorized reprints of popular British books, which had the dual advantage of being available without royalties and of having been pretested in the British literary marketplace, were staples on the lists of most American publishing houses.[19]

Simon Nowell-Smith points out that inaction rather than inattention characterized the attitude of the U.S. Congress to the matter of international copyright in the second half of the century: "Between 1843, the year of Dickens' first visit to America when he talked of little else, and 1886, the year [of] the Berne Convention, no fewer than eleven international copyright bills were presented to the United States Congress only to fall by the wayside. A twelfth bill, Senator Chace's, hung fire until 1890; his name survives because the thirteenth bill, an unlucky thirteenth compromise between enlightenment and protectionism, signed by President Harrison in 1891, was substantially the same as Senator Chace's."[20] It is with the events of the intervening period—and, in particular, with the nature of the public discourse surrounding those events—that we are concerned.

In 1944 Horace Ball offered a bland retrospective account of the coming of international copyright. After noting that the Chace Act of 1891 extended the provisions of the copyright laws to citizens of nations that had granted those protections to American authors, Ball writes, "The reciprocity provision was added to the Copyright Law for the purpose of enabling the United States to negotiate or bargain for equal treatment in those countries for American authors. The intent of the amendatory sections one and two of the Act of 1891 was to make an all-inclusive grant of the benefits of the copyright statute to any author of a copyrightable work, though he be not a citizen or subject of a foreign state or nation, nor a citizen or resident of the United States."[21] Only the last sentence of this uninflected account describing the Chace Act's unconditional extension of copyright protection even to the works of stateless authors offers any suggestion that an ideological investment in Romantic "authorship" helped to shape the United States' entry into reciprocal copyright relations with other states.

That such ideological considerations were at work becomes clear, however, in Drone's account of what he considered the deplorable absence of such relations in the late 1870s. Drone begins by quoting, with approval, a congressional select committee report of 1837 that responded to a petition by British authors for international copyright protection. The committee states:

> That authors and inventors have, according to the practice among civilized nations, a property in the respective productions of their genius, is incontestable; and that this property should be protected as effectually as any other property is, by law, follows as a legitimate consequence. Authors and inventors are among the greatest benefactors of mankind. They are often dependent exclusively on their own mental labors for the means of subsistence; and are frequently, or from the nature of their pursuits or the constitution of their minds, incapable of applying that provident care to worldly affairs which other classes of society are in the habit of bestow-

ing. These considerations give additional strength to their just title to the protection of the law.²²

In sum, for the congressional committee, authors possess an inherent entitlement to copyright protection that no mere national boundary should be allowed to frustrate. Thus, international copyright relations are required as a matter of simple justice.

Drone then takes up the cause himself, elaborating the author-centric rhetoric of the congressional report while sounding the twin themes of inherent entitlement and the promotion of access to useful knowledge:

> This country is put to shame by the legislation of England and other foreign nations on this subject. The English laws, as far as they relate to foreign authors, show a comprehensive liberality, a broad, catholic spirit, not found in those of the United States . . . [I]n legislating "for the encouragement of learning" in Great Britain, Parliament has made no distinction between native and foreign authors. . . . No less liberal should be the United States. Her gates bearing the inscription *Tros Tyriusque mihi nullo discrimine agetur*, should be opened wide to the authors of all tongues, all races, all creeds. All countries should be one for noble men who labor, in whatever vineyard, for the advancement of knowledge and truth. Whoever shall move Congress to pass a law inviting authors, composers, and artists, of every nation under the sun, to send their treasures of learning, science and art to our shores, where they shall be protected, will deserve a monument more durable than brass.²³

Drone's articulation of a Romantic rationale for international copyright deserves consideration not only—or even in particular—because it was influential, but rather because it is representative of what emerged as the dominant theme in public discussions of the issue during the years immediately preceding the 1891 legislation. The emergence of authors' rights as a rallying cry in the 1880s in turn reflected a dramatic realignment of publishers' interests around American international copyright policy.

Throughout most of the nineteenth century, foreign and American authors had argued without success for change in U.S. law.²⁴ Unaided, however, they had been unable to mobilize the rhetoric of Romantic authorship to bring this about. Nor did the first Act of the Berne Convention for the Protection of Literary and Artistic Works, concluded in 1886, substantially alter congressional (or popular) opinion on the issue of international copyright in the United States, though it certainly added weight to the author-centered vision of legal rights.²⁵

Instead, the impetus for change came from another quarter. Had Drone's hypothetical monument to the triumphant champion of international copyright been erected, it surely would have portrayed publisher George Haven Putnam leading the forces of the American Publishers' Copyright League. It was the political and economic muscle of the elite publishing trade in the United States, represented by the league, that finally influenced Congress to pass long-delayed legislation on the conditions for international copyright. The campaign was justified, however, by reference to "authors' rights."

While the Putnam family had a long-term commitment to the cause of international copyright,[26] most of the members of the league were relatively recent converts.[27] Their conversion resulted from a shift in perceptions of self-interest. Increasingly, elite publishers faced competition from firms that utilized new technology to undersell them in the marketplace for cheap reprints of English novels. The prospect of international copyright, which once appeared as a costly legal imposition, began to look increasingly like a source of economic salvation: a mechanism by which elite firms, who could afford to license the copyrights of foreign authors, could mobilize copyright law to exclude competitors from the marketplace.[28] As Stephen Ladas wrote in 1938, "[f]or this reason, the most important publishers in America took their place at the head of the movement to secure protection to foreign authors."[29]

In 1889 the authors and publishers who favored international copyright joined forces with printers, who were (collectively) among the most politically powerful players in the American book trade. In that year, two national, male-dominated printers' organizations (the International Typographical Union and the Typothetae) joined the campaign, giving expression to members' newfound concerns that the spread of cheap reprint publishing threatened not only the livelihoods of individual printers but the very structure of their trade. In particular, they feared the increasing passage of work into the hands of low-paid, female, non-union workers.[30] The unions' alliance with the Publishers' Copyright League tipped the political scales decisively in favor of the enactment of international copyright legislation; it also affected the shape of the final legislation profoundly. As it finally emerged from Congress, the Chace Act included an unprecedented protectionist provision, the so-called Manufacturing Clause, which stipulated that a printed book could secure American copyright only if it were manufactured from type set in the United States or from plates made from such type.[31]

In its final form, the 1891 legislation extending protection to foreign works consolidated elite publishers' and printers' authority over the production and circulation of printed texts. Paradoxically, however, this was the outcome of a lobbying campaign conducted, for the most part, under the convenient banner of "authors' rights." Certainly, the Chace Act benefited foreign authors in the United States and (ultimately, if indirectly) American authors abroad. As so often has been the case in copyright history, however, the most immediate interests served by this enactment lay elsewhere. In effect, the rhetoric of Romantic authorship provided a means by which to justify new laws that safeguarded existing commercial interests and provided legal security for new developments in information commerce.

The Rise of "Substantial Similarity"

Today, perhaps the most valuable right possessed by many copyright owners is the exclusive right to prepare "derivative works" based on the copyrighted work.[32] This right gives the owners of copyright in a work of fiction, for example, the authority to negotiate for adaptations in various media: translations, abridgments, and dramatic and motion-picture versions. In the mid-nineteenth century, serious questions remained unresolved about the scope of the copyright monopoly — and the amount of legal control that copyright owners could claim over such follow-on uses. The uncertainty was exacerbated by a leading case in 1853, *Stowe v. Thomas*,[33] which held that a full and literal unauthorized German translation of *Uncle Tom's Cabin* did not infringe the copyright in Harriet Beecher Stowe's novel,[34] because legal protection attached only to the writer's formal expressive choices. In the court's view, the literal language that Stowe's labors had reaped from the fields of her imagination was entitled to protection, while the gleanings were free for all to take:

> By the publication of Mrs. Stowe's book, the creations of the genius and imagination of the author have become as much public property as those of Homer and Cervantes. . . . All her conceptions and inventions may be used and abused by imitators, playwrights and poetasters. . . . All that now remains is the copyright in her book: the exclusive right to print, reprint, and vend it, and those only can be called infringers of her rights, or pirates of her property, who are guilty of printing, publishing, importing or vending without her license, "copies of her book." A translation may, in loose phraseology, be called a transcript or copy of her thoughts or conceptions, but in no correct sense can it be called a copy of her book.[35]

In equating literal language with the aspects of authorial personality receiving legal protection, the decision honored the Lockean approach to copyright to a certain extent; clearly, however, it did not reflect a fully developed Romantic understanding of the rights owed to genius. As a result, the incomplete vision of authorial entitlement developed in the court's analysis easily gave way to the competing value of free information exchange.

Writing in 1879, at a moment when the Romantic conception of authorship had taken firmer hold on the legal imagination, Drone could barely contain his outrage at the *Stowe* decision and its failure to give authorial genius its due. In his view, that genius was a matter of far more than mere language: "Literary property . . . is not in the language alone; but in the matter of which language is merely a form of communication. It is in the substance, and not in the form alone. That which constitutes the essence and value of a literary composition, which represents the results of the author's labor and learning, may be capable of expression in more than one form of language significantly different from that of the original."[36] In Drone's commentary, the literal language of the written or printed text, which was the focus of legal protection under earlier copyright laws, is figured as merely incidental to the "essence and value" of the work. This essence is to be found in the thoughts and sentiments that reflect the creative personality of the author. The clear implication of Drone's vision is that all (or at least most) potential variants of which the author's inspired imaginative conceptions are capable should be embraced within the copyright. In practice this reimagining of the scope of protection proved at least as beneficial to authorized publishers as to authors themselves.[37]

By 1944 the notion of a "copy" was no longer limited to a literal reproduction of a text or some portion of the text; instead, the key term embraced what might be called a doctrine of "emotional equivalents." The "right to multiply copies" extended not only to new versions that are duplicates or near duplicates of the original, but also, in the words of Ball, to "any of the various modes in which the subject matter of any publication is appropriated, imitated or transferred, with evasive variations or colorable alterations." All of these, he states, "constitute copying."[38] Obviously, over time, an expansive—indeed transformative—change had occurred in the legal conceptualization of the "copy."

This transformation was mediated by the elaboration of a new doctrine, "substantial similarity," in judicial opinions and the writings of commentators, and the period from 1880 to 1940 was a crucial phase in this doctrinal development. Although the first intimations of such a doctrine can be found as early as 1850, in the case of *Jollie v. Jacques*,[39] it emerged as a significant formation in copyright law only in the latter years of the century.[40] In turn, discussions of substantial similarity were informed by a new kind of personalist view of authorial entitlement—a more expansive vision of the role of the individual creator, which resonated with the Romantic conception of authorship.

The relationship between the changing visions of authorship and the doctrine of substantial similarity appears clearly from the 1908 opinion in *Dam v. Kirke La Shelle Co.*, one of the first literary adaptation cases to discuss the doctrine at length.[41] The suit concerned the production of a play, *The Heir to the Hoorah*, that, it was alleged, was an unauthorized dramatization of a short story entitled "The Transmogrification of Dan." In finding for the plaintiff, Judge John R. Hazel compared the two works and found that the story was "substantially imitated" in the play, even though the dialogue and other aspects differed.

> No other play, drama, or literary production is called to my attention, and I have examined the exhibits in evidence, from which it may be ascertained that the subject of the author's composition, together with the various characters which give it prominence, was not original. It is true the dialogue of the drama is not in the words of the copyrighted story but its exact phraseology was not necessary to the adaptation of the plot or subject, or the portrayal of the different characters to the play. The actors in the play "The Heir to the Hoorah" portray or imitate the characters in the copyrighted story, and in addition thereto make use of incidents and situations which apparently give expression to the central theme or purpose of the author. Whatever of addition has been introduced in the play does not obscure or emasculate the central figure of the story, namely, the rejuvenate husband.[42]

Judge Hazel concludes that what has occurred in this case is a wrongful taking, notwithstanding the absence of literal similarity and the difference in medium between the two works involved.

In his opinion Hazel draws on Romantic ideology to define the "idea," "theme," and "purpose" of the story as reflections of the author's personality. He also invokes the value of "originality," which took on legal significance as a result of its valorization in literary discourse of the late eighteenth and nineteenth centuries. The dramatist is liable because his work is "substantially similar" to the copyrighted story—a similarity attributable not to any appropriation of words, phrases, or other formal features of the text, but rather to the inspired (or original) conception devised by the story's author, and the character(s) that embody that conception.

Although substantial similarity would take on an even more vivid Romantic coloration in years to come,[43] the fundamental link between the Romantic vision of the creative process and an expansive understanding of rights under copyright—and, in particular, of potential subsidiary rights—was in place as early as 1908. It would be carried over into, and flourish under, the new Copyright Act that emerged from the general legislative revision process in 1909.

Conclusion

The period between 1880 and 1940 saw rapid growth in the American book trade and the emergence of the kind of large-scale commodity-text publishing with which we are familiar today. Our aim has been to call attention to the important role played by Romantic ideology—by a vision of creative activity as essentially solitary and originary—in the evolution of some of the key legal arrangements needed to support and sustain this consolidation of the publishing trade.

CHAPTER 6

Diverging Paths
Books and Magazines in the Transition to Corporate Capitalism

Richard Ohmann

In the late nineteenth and early twentieth centuries, magazine publishers radically transformed the economics of their business, which then expanded far more rapidly than book publishing. Because the story is well known,[1] it will be abstracted only very briefly here before turning to the main task of this chapter, which is to consider relations between the two businesses and the two forms of print culture, especially from 1880 to 1910, when their differentiation was most intense. The focus here is on monthly magazines, which initially stood in close relationship to books.

Circulation, Price, and Advertising

In 1880 prestigious monthlies such as *Harper's* and the *Atlantic* sold for twenty-five or thirty-five cents an issue and attained modest circulations—probably no higher than 150,000—among cultivated and relatively affluent readers. Like the most successful women's monthlies (*Godey's Ladies' Book*, *Peterson's Magazine*, the *Delineator*), they carried little advertising, drawing revenue chiefly from subscriptions.

This landscape shifted suddenly in and after 1893, when a price war developed among three new general monthlies: *McClure's*, *Cosmopolitan*, and *Munsey's*. The latter was first to set a newsstand price of ten cents, selling subscriptions for a dollar a year. Its circulation rose from 40,000 in October of 1893 to 200,000 the following February. After reaching 500,000 in April, it increased steadily. *Cosmopolitan* and *McClure's*, matching *Munsey's* price, reached similar figures soon thereafter. The *Ladies' Home Journal* had already established a ten-cent price, but initially did not compete directly with more "general" magazines. By 1900 it became the first to attain a circulation of 1 million copies, and its content increasingly resembled that of the others.

At the *Journal*, publisher Cyrus Curtis and editor Edward Bok had gradually worked up a business practice that S. S. McClure, Frank Munsey, and John Brisben Walker (*Cosmopolitan*) more abruptly and somewhat desperately adopted during the panic and recession of 1893. Curtis and Bok worked to find and organize an audience of middle-class people with money enough to spend on brand name commodities but not well served by the elite monthlies; to meet and shape the cultural needs of that audience; to build unprecedented circulations across the United States; to sell advertising space to makers of brand name commodities at rates based on circulation; to sell the magazine at a price below its actual cost of production; and to make advertising the source of profit. In this way, magazine publishers actually changed their business: now their main "product" was not the physical magazine itself, but the interested attention of readers, sold en bloc through ad agencies to manufacturers, who were now the main customers.[2]

The change was timely, and the results striking: total U.S. circulation of monthly magazines rose from about 18 million in 1890 to 64 million in 1905, or nearly four magazines per month per American household, far outpacing weeklies, newspapers, or books. Magazine advertising revenues simultaneously burgeoned at a comparable rate, and the industry sustained vigorous growth through the 1920s.

House Magazines: Book Publishers' Organs

This dramatic expansion of the magazine industry changed its relation to book publishing and can best be understood by examining their relationship *before* the 1890s; most of the new magazines' direct antecedents were periodicals founded by book publishers. As early as 1842, New York publisher Appleton produced the *Home Book Circular*, a quarterly house periodical announcing new Appleton books that was free to booksellers. A year later it was replaced by a monthly, *Appleton's Literary Bulletin*, which reported on new books from many publishers in the United States and Europe.[3] Such catalog-like trade journals probably led other publishers to develop house monthlies. The most successful of these was *Harper's [New Monthly] Magazine*, originating in 1850. An obscure Boston publisher founded the *Atlantic Monthly* in 1857; Ticknor & Fields acquired it in 1859, and by 1873 it had come to Hurd & Houghton (later Houghton, Mifflin), where it remained until 1908. Its circulation rarely exceeded 50,000, but its cultural authority was enormous.[4] The *Century* followed a similar path in the 1880s, having begun as a house journal, *Scribner's Monthly*, in 1870. It passed to the Century Company in 1881, along with the premier children's monthly, *St. Nicholas*, and Century also began publishing books. In 1886 Charles Scribner's Sons started a second house journal, *Scrib-*

TABLE 6.1. Pages of book ads in publishers' monthly magazines, 1880–1890

	1880	1885	1890
Atlantic	9	25	12
Harper's	16	10	15

ner's Magazine, which rivaled the other elite monthlies until its demise in 1937. Other monthly magazines that bore the names of prominent publishing houses included *Putnam's Monthly*, *Lippincott's Magazine*, and *Appleton's Journal*. *St. Nicholas*, *Popular Science*, and *House Beautiful* were also essentially the creation of book publishers.

Several aims led book publishers to start or acquire magazines. Most obviously, monthlies were used for advertising. Representative single issues of the *Atlantic* and *Harper's*, taken at five-year intervals, contain many pages of ads for Houghton, Mifflin and Harper books, respectively (see table 6.1).

Each monthly magazine listed, described, and praised approximately 100 books and also gave prices and sample illustrations. The books were promoted as gifts and commended for their material qualities and cultural capital. Publishers also advertised through newspapers, billboards, and posters, but their own journals provided cheap and reliable access to an interested audience (figure 6.1).

A publisher's book list embodied its magazine's cultural values for two closely related reasons. First, book lists and magazines often featured the same texts and authors. From the outset, house magazine editors serialized or excerpted novels, memoirs, and travel narratives before they were published in books, believing that this would increase demand for these texts in book form. Appleton, Scribner, and others agreed. George Harrison Mifflin, on the other hand, believed that "periodical publication was far from essential for commercial success." He wrote to one novelist, "The truth is, strictly between us, that few people read serials in the magazines." *Atlantic* editor Horace Scudder disliked serialized novels but continued to print them in the nineties as "an essential feature." His successor Bliss Perry had similar views; when he omitted this "feature" in 1906, not a single reader registered an objection. Most publishers did, however, regard serialization as essential. For part of 1885, excerpts and serials of *Huckleberry Finn*, *The Bostonians*, and *The Rise of Silas Lapham* filled every fiction page in the *Century*. Authors frequently bargained for double publication; publishers like James R. Osgood with no magazines found serial outlets elsewhere for their authors. *Atlantic*, skeptical of such practices, gave *McClure's*

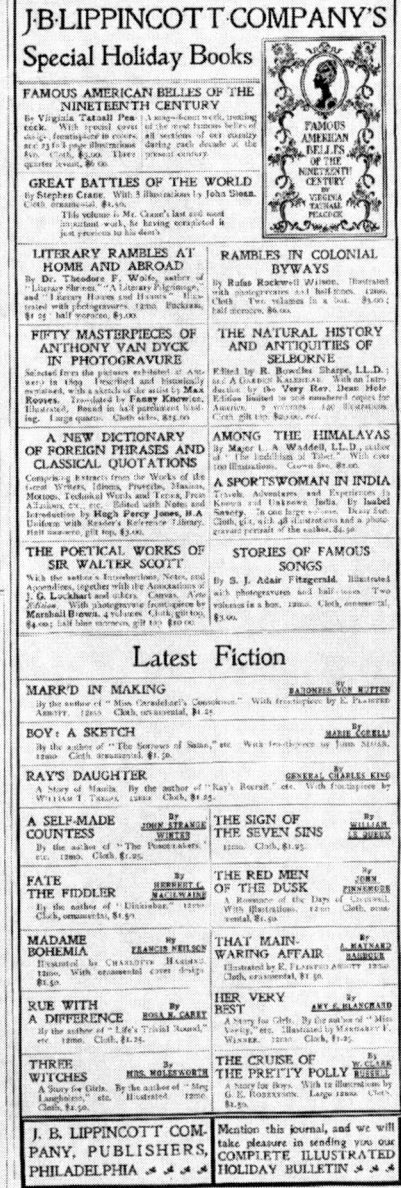

FIGURE 6.1. An advertisement for Philadelphia publisher J. B. Lippincott Company's Special Holiday Books makes a small concession to illustration by reproducing a book jacket in what is largely a list of new titles. *Harper's Weekly* 45 (8 December 1900): 1190. Courtesy of HarpWeek.

and the *Ladies' Home Journal* serial rights to Houghton, Mifflin books.[5] In short, literary monthlies and respectable book publishers organized cultural space around the same values—those of elite northeasterners.

Second, publishers from the outset subordinated magazines to the exigencies of the book business. Publishers appreciated profitable monthlies, but few were, and many, like the *North American Review*, regularly lost money. The *Atlantic* was rarely profitable but was maintained by Mifflin in the nineties for its prestige and its ability to attract new authors, often by accepting short stories or sketches early in their careers. Scribner's money-losing magazine was subsidized for similar reasons—the magazine provided authors "a vestibule to the House." Although some editors were fairly independent, journals clearly served the purposes of their parent houses. Bookmen founded the magazines, bought and sold them, paid for them out of book profits, and hired and fired editors. In the ideology of print culture as in its business relations, the book was dominant. Long before he became editor of the *Atlantic*, Horace Scudder saw that "the magazine carries [the publisher's] name like a flag everywhere it goes, and accustoms people to associating certain qualities with it; for the magazine rarely fails to symbolize the house from which it issues."[6]

The magazine was a *signifier*, not only of the house, whose "character and taste" it reflected, but of "certain qualities" identified both with the house and with a high level of culture. As Carl Kaestle and Janice Radway argue in chapter 1 of this volume, the bound book has generally been the form of print culture with "the highest authority and permanence." But not all books, even bound books, have claimed cultural dominance. In the United States after the Civil War, the ones that did often had British authors and were primarily those associated with the old reputable publishing names—Harper, Appleton, Putnam, Scribner, Dodd, Mead, Dutton, Houghton, Mifflin, Osgood, or Lippincott. Such gentlemanly publishers purported to have a greater interest in literature than in profit. Some sponsored general monthlies that reflected the "character" of their house and the "qualities" of elite book culture. The monthly genre connoted gentility, class prestige, Anglo-American roots, intellectual seriousness, and high culture. McClure, Walker, Munsey, Bok, and others sought to appropriate such connotations around 1890, downscaling them somewhat by trumpeting the vigor and worldliness of their new productions in contrast to the ascribed effeteness of the elite monthlies. Theirs was a business revolution, a cultural modulation. The mass-circulation magazine descended from the old book via the elite monthly.

Selling Books with Magazines

Admittedly, a variety of magazines existed from the eighteenth century onward, and some influenced the founders of the new monthlies. However, the older "general" monthly magazines not connected to publishing houses were frail enterprises, most of which died in the 1840s and 1850s; the most famous of them, the *Knickerbocker*, lasted only to 1865. The sectarianism and partisanship of religious and political journals disqualifies them as models: the popular monthlies aimed to identify their own work with the interests of society as a whole, building readerships assembled around middle-class views and ways of living. Advertisers simultaneously sought not to associate their products with sectarian polemics. Women's magazines achieved a suitable tone of middle-class respectability but had to expand beyond narrowly "feminine" concerns—as the *Journal* gradually did—in order to appeal to advertisers as family magazines. Finally, although cheap "story papers" suggested the possibility of advertising-based profits, they were too rude and were read by too many poor people. McClure and the others aptly sought to imitate and popularize the cultural form established by genteel book publishers.

The new entrepreneurs challenged and changed that form, but incorporated it into the new editorial mix. Book chat was a standard genre of cultural instruction; authors were profiled as celebrities alongside actresses and statesmen; the new visual display included halftones of writers and their homes. Magazine entrepreneurs also energetically serialized prepublication novels and other texts, negotiating with book houses and, incidentally, increasing authors' earnings. There were myriad connections between book and magazine publishing. Walker (*Cosmopolitan*) and Munsey issued books from their own presses. Frank Leslie and later his widow had long published books with their string of popular magazines. McClure, eager to compete with editors who could offer writers book *and* magazine publication, joined with Frank Doubleday to found Doubleday, McClure & Co. in 1897, and took over Harper and Brothers (at the request of J. P. Morgan, its new owner) when it failed in 1899, though both ventures were short-lived. Doubleday and Walter Hines Page also founded magazines (*World's Work* and *Country Life in America*) not to "symbolize the house" but to make money. Book publishers also contributed to the subfield of magazines *about* book culture. Dodd, Mead's 1894 American edition of the *Bookman* printed the first best-seller lists in 1895; Appleton's *Book Buyer* lasted forty years.

Commutation across these print genres was commonplace at the turn of the century. Pictorial dust jackets appeared regularly in the 1890s and became almost universal after 1900, intensifying the visual appeal of books to compete with magazines' monthly selection of pictorial cover designs. Halftone illustrations in books also increased, insinuating affinities with illustrated monthlies. Some publishers of cheap books even tried including ads. "Libraries" and series from the fiction "factories" (dime novels, Alger stories, Frank Merriwell, the Rover Boys) mirrored the periodicity and formulaic repetition of magazines.[7] Book clubs subsequently intervened to build a new kind of periodicity and cultural continuity.

Business practices, too, blurred boundaries in print culture. Through the 1890s, as noted in previous chapters, literary agents established the necessity of their services for authors and editors. Seeking the most profitable outlets for their clients, they further emphasized the commodity status of text (indeed, of talent), and thus its amenability to different manifestations in books, magazines, and newspapers as negotiated by agents. Newspapers, growing toward their twentieth-century formats through the 1880s and 1890s, increasingly included material (especially fiction) that also appeared in books and magazines. Syndication, earlier reserved for cheap filler texts, hastened this process. In the mid-1880s, several entrepreneurs began heavily syndicating newspaper publication of stories and novels. S. S. McClure became the runaway leader in this field; his syndicate—a predecessor and partial foundation of *McClure's Magazine*—provided mass urban readership for Robert Louis Stevenson, Rudyard Kipling, Thomas Hardy, Mark Twain, William Dean Howells, Hamlin Garland, and others.[8] Like literary agency, syndication intervened between author and editors, while distribution had similarly amalgamated print forms. The American News Company, formed in 1864, had by the 1890s virtually monopolized magazine distribution and amassed a large share of the wholesale book market. Both print formats jostled with newspapers at thousands of newsstands and other outlets, proclaiming the unity of the cultural field. Meanwhile, a much older practice, subscription publishing of books, continued to flourish, encompassing almost the whole production process by ensuring sales (through orders gathered by drummers), usually in advance of publication, or even before the text was written.[9]

Content: Production and Manipulation

Finally, book and magazine publishers were both taking aggressive roles in the actual generation of text. News magazine entrepreneurs frequently declined to wait decorously to choose among offered manuscripts. Instead, they chased after authors, sometimes creating assignments, suggesting ideas for articles, and planning a series to run over several issues before its content would be issued in book form. McClure called this "magazining." Organizers of fiction factories had long generated cheap books even more imperiously, reducing the writer to a pseudonymous hired hack who formulaically fleshed out the editor's outline, producing stories for loyal readers seeking dependable pleasures. Reputable publishers rarely utilized such methods, for their product's appeal rested on the ideology of an individual author and his or her artistic originality. But by the first decade of this century, these publishers, too, had progressed significantly toward the initiation of book ideas and the management of talent. In sum, magazine publishing strongly influenced its parent industry in the early twentieth century.

The magazine and book businesses, and to a lesser extent the newspaper business, collaborated in a long historical process of literary commodification, circulating texts "packaged" in different product categories. Regarding the new "commercial book," Radway suggests that it was less the old "unified volume conceived, penned, and edited by a single writer" than "an ephemeral apparition, that is, a temporary embodiment of cultural material in wide circulation at the time in other formats." The account here supports Kaestle and Radway's attempt to "conceptualize the world of print as an already functioning system in the twentieth century with many different points of entry or intervention."[10] Mass-circulation magazines were more economically dominant than their predecessors and helped diffuse reading habits associated with what Radway calls the "commercial book"—dime novels, for example—across a wider social spectrum. Turn-of-the-century observers undoubtedly felt that the privileged, older style of reading—the leisured, "gentlemanly exchange" of elite monthlies and their high literary culture—was under assault. The new editors favored a brisker, more personal, and more muscular style, promoting reading for awareness of the new, the timely, and the most progressive. Advance publicity for future issues generated anticipation and eager consumption similar to that engendered by advertisers of household goods.[11] Book publishers entered bidding wars for celebrity authors, enlarged their advertising campaigns, published material already "boomed" by magazines, and in general imitated new editorial methods. As a result, middle-class book reading tended more toward the hurried pace and social urgency fostered by magazines.

Within print culture, however, the book and magazine industries remained distinct. Competition for readers even prompted mutual antagonism. Despite cross-disciplinary literary synergy, the scarcity of leisure necessitates cultural choice. Even before the magazine revolution, Henry Holt worried that monthly magazines would "kill off" books, and indeed, growth in magazine readership in the 1890s far outpaced that of books, especially among new monthlies, not the old elite models economically tied to the book industry. These rival business groups competed for authors as well, driving up the price for serial rights and allowing leading authors to draw income primarily from magazines. Writers with wide appeal quickly became too costly for old book-and-magazine publishers: Horace Scudder of the *Atlantic* wrote Sarah Orne Jewett that he could no longer regularly afford her submissions, given that the "illustrated magazines . . . are like buyers in an auction room bidding hard against each other." The bidding wars intensified as new monthlies turned even the Harper magazines into money losers, thus hastening the bankruptcy of the venerable house.[12] *McClure's*, *Munsey's*, and their cohort bought and packaged their wares more efficiently than the older book publishers and their magazine subsidiaries, selling them to an expanded readership.

Business Problems, Business Solutions

This conceptualization, however, overlooks more profound changes in print culture and in the whole economic system, of which magazines' ascendance was an effect. New magazine publishers surpassed their genteel predecessors in making and distributing a familiar commodity, the "general" monthly magazine. Additionally, however, they joined with newspaper publishers in commodifying the audience's attention. They marketed this new product as a means of advertising other commercial goods: breakfast cereals, cleansers, toothpastes, canned goods, baby foods, soft drinks, cigarettes, typewriters, ready-made clothing, kitchen appliances, and a variety of household conveniences. These commodities were themselves novel, not in their basic qualities and uses, but in the way they were marketed.

Crucially, all came with brand names: Mellin's, Ivory, Uneeda Biscuit, Cream of Wheat, Quaker Oats, Campbell's, Welch's, Wrigley's, Coca-Cola, Swift, Armour, Gillette, Kodak, Arrow, 1847 Rogers Brothers; some remain familiar while others are long forgotten. Advertising seems nearly impossible without brand names and their accompanying trademarks. The National Biscuit Company's "Uneeda" was distinguished from the anonymous crackers scooped from grocers' barrels by its uniform packaging and an 1899 advertising campaign that established Uneeda's trademark and slogan. Such copy and iconography marked display ads in this period. Though a few products had long-standing commercial images, the National Biscuit Company's model became normative only toward the end of the nineteenth century. The number of registered trademarks rose from 121 in 1870 to more than 10,000 in 1906. This was a sales revolution, generated by broad economic forces (figure 6.2).

Between 1850 and 1900, American manufacturers greatly expanded industrial production and established the economic centrality of factories and cities. While they dominated the world they had made, their *control* was weak and

FIGURE 6.2. Typography, illustration, and white space were being used effectively in advertisements for consumer products other than books. *Harper's Weekly* 47 (5 July 1902): 886. Courtesy of HarpWeek.

disjointed. Despite possessing various stabilizing mechanisms (trusts, pools, gentlemen's agreements on pricing, and so on), individual enterprises remained volatile, bankruptcies abounded, profits gradually declined, and the boom-and-bust cycle spiraled uncontrollably. Severe depressions of the late nineteenth century generated social upheaval and intense labor conflict, especially in 1877, 1885–86, 1892, and 1894. Many observers feared anarchy or revolution. Populist movements and parties gained momentum and, in 1892 and 1896, electoral force.

The large, vertically integrated corporation was the structural solution pursued by leading capitalists.[13] These new giants gradually consolidated the entire process of production and distribution, from extraction of raw materials to final sales, minimizing the uncertainty of getting products to consumers. Previously, firms had concentrated on making the goods and relied on jobbers, wholesalers, and other middlemen to place them in stores. The new corporations sought to disempower such unreliable distribution agents. They built elaborate sales organizations within the corporate structure, using brand names, uniform packaging, and extensive advertising to ensure demand for their products. They wanted a customer who shopped for Ivory Soap or Quaker Oats, not one with generic needs.

Magazines: Advertising Modernity

Advertising agencies created desires, which assumed their modern form in the 1890s, providing a new business model for backward or uncertain corporations. Earlier, agents had essentially been brokers, providing local advertisers like department stores with space in newspapers. That practice continued, but modernizing agencies such as N. W. Ayer and J. Walter Thompson quickly expanded their services to give meaning to brand names, offering market research, copy writing, art, and design unique to each commodity. Advertising these items, "sold at grocers everywhere," required amassing a large, national audience of those willing and able to live efficient, modern lives, for whom new commodities would be both practical and symbolic.

The illustrated monthly magazine quickly filled such a role. Bok, McClure, Walker, Munsey, and others had differing goals and ideologies, but each flattered readers for their progressive ideas and worldly leadership, providing cultural maps of the social world in which they would meet their equals (face-to-face *and* through the pages of the magazine). Through the new halftone process they dazzled readers with art and photography. Their fiction fed dreams of individuality and merit, while a hundred or more pages of carefully crafted advertisements generated mass appeal for a stunning array of commodities. In monthly magazines, as in suburbs, universities, and the emerging network of professional, civic, and social organizations, the new professional-managerial class developed its self-awareness. Throughout the Progressive Era and after, these individuals politically tempered and legitimized corporate capitalism while they consolidated it economically.

Like advertising agents, and like the mail-order and department store merchandisers omitted here, magazine editors and publishers were far more than compliant errand boys for the captains of industry. Their business served their own purposes, not limited to profit making. Advertising was for them a means to establish both a cultural form and, usually, a fresh configuration of social and domestic life, a nation realigned on sensible, forward-looking principles. However one sorts out the complexities of historical agency in the transformation of American society, magazine publishers were integral to it.

The older elite monthlies participated only marginally in such affairs, and, for reasons that should now be clear, book publishers were hardly involved at all. They continued to make and sell the same commodities as always, in much the same ways. Nor *could* books easily have become vehicles for advertising about soap and cereal, even had publishers considered that possibility. Although series, cheap "libraries," and best sellers were successful and sold in large quantities, most books remained discrete commodities; readers might buy them or not, rarely with regard for previous purchases. "Brand loyalty" to authors was unsteady, and to publishers almost nonexistent. (One failed advertising slogan, "when in doubt, buy Scribner's," showed that publishers understood the problem.) Lacking secure and continuous control of an audience's attention, book publishers had nothing to offer the new corporations.

A New Era of Book Publishing

Publishers themselves rarely adopted new corporate forms like vertical integration. Some publishers had long tried to control their own raw materials (authors and texts), manufacturing plants, and distribution sites (bookstores). Such efforts faltered, however, amid the growing imperialism of other businesses. The "trade courtesy" practiced by older firms prohibited them from pilfering another publisher's authors. But such practices, like contract clauses giving a publisher first option on an author's next book, were often observed erratically. Some reputable publishers tried holding on to prized authors by contracting for all their output, as Harper and Brothers did with William Dean Howells in 1885 (at the enormous sum of $10,000 a year). Amid bidding wars and increased competition with popular monthlies at the end of the century, however, most such attempts failed. Publishers' ownership of production facilities was equally venerable. Nevertheless, although many publishers had begun as printers, the trend around 1900 was to separate printing from publishing; in 1914 just 18 percent of publishers ran their own presses.[14]

Regarding distribution, few book publishers were willing or able to adopt new merchandising strategies. Many still favored subscription and mail-order business over sales in retail stores. Indeed, they attempted to enforce standard markups, to fix prices, and to regulate their market just as manufacturers generally were abandoning such tactics in favor of the new corporate structure and the effort to ensure large sales by associating images of the good life with products such as gelatin and toothpaste.[15]

Publishers did increase their negligible advertising investments of the 1860s to perhaps $5 million annually by the end of the century and more in the next decade, remembered as the era of the "boomed book." Extravagant ad campaigns sought to sensationalize individual books, propelling them into best-sellerdom. A publisher might spend $10,000 on newspaper, magazine, direct-mail, billboard, and streetcar advertising for such a book, in addition to money spent by local dealers. The results were highly erratic. Numerous publishers admitted that they had no idea how to entice the public or make a book popular; many lamented that pressure from authors and competitors drove them to imperil profits in the attempt. After Houghton, Mifflin increased its advertising budget from $30,000 in 1881 to nearly $100,000 in 1900, Mifflin set out to study the effectiveness of such expenditures. His colleague Francis Garrison found no connection between ad costs and sales of a single book or yearly advertising budgets and gross Houghton, Mifflin sales. He concluded that the firm had "wasted" tens of thousands on advertising "for many years past." A $23,000 cutback followed this study, and 1900 remained the firm's peak advertising year for a long while.[16] Many houses found similar effects, causing the entire industry's commitment to publicity to decline by 1914.

Magazine Advertising: Learning the Trade

Repetition was a key principle in advertising, especially for products like safety razors and oatmeal. Books, however, remain popular only for a few weeks, if at all, and because name recognition does not necessarily carry over to the *next* book, advertising cannot insistently accrete meaning around the book-as-commodity. Advertisers in elite monthlies in 1900 sought to correlate successive campaigns by positioning a new book in a high-culture narrative: "the most important book he has written"; "remind one strongly of Poe's tales"; has the "qualities that made 'Q' famous"; and so on. Ads in the mass-circulation magazines chiefly concerned middlebrow books, highlighting the values they shared with other domestic accessories. Encyclopedias, definitive biographies of Napoleon, and nine-volume histories of the world would offer practical knowledge and give an impressive look to your living room at an astonishing bargain. While the *Atlantic* and its peers continued to carry ten to thirty pages of book ads (separated from soap and cereal ads), such advertisements nearly vanished from popular monthlies. Book publishers seemed to recognize their stark differences from businesses like Proctor and Gamble; advertising in *Ladies' Home Journal* would be pouring money down the drain. Proctor and Gamble sought to ensure that customers would ask specifically for Ivory Soap, but book advertising failed any such test: according to a 1901 survey, book retailers unanimously believed that the average customer came into the store not knowing what he or she intended to buy.[17]

Magazine entrepreneurs facilitated and fed on the corporate transformation of the U.S. economy; some, like Curtis, became large corporations. Book publishers continued to grapple with nineteenth-century uncertainties, including basic ones about the nature of their product, who owned it (because copyright laws remained confusing until 1909), who would pay for its production, and how its profits might be divided. Hustling, piracy, and cutthroat competition went forward alongside the genteel procedures of the old houses, with their reliance on authors' loyalty and the quaint idea that literary culture was not really part of the capitalist market. For reasons mainly beyond their control, dependable sales eluded the publishers. Four out of five new books lost money.

Until after the period covered by this volume, book publishers remained predominantly family firms. Two of the major houses, Harper and Appleton, failed in 1899–1900 amid frenetic mergers and corporate reorganization in other industries and the triumph of new magazines. J. P. Morgan aided in the rehabilitation of Harper and Brothers, providing financial support as it began to fail, but even Morgan's magic could not make publishing compatible with new capitalist arrangements. The industry stayed remarkably unconcentrated. Still a leader in 1914, Harper had less than 2 percent of total book sales among the 819 publishers listed by a Census Bureau report. The same report showed that the book industry accounted for one-fourth of 1 percent of all manufacturing value, down from 1 percent in 1850.[18] Magazines' success far outpaced that of books, further cutting into their profits. In short, magazines played a leading role in the corporate revolution, while books neither did nor could have. They became in effect a niche product until, in the 1960s and after, still another transformation brought them within the compass of the multinational corporation and the pursuit of media synergy, along with magazines, which by then had also become a niche product, pushed aside by radio and television.

CHAPTER 7

From Partisanship to Professionalism
The Transformation of the Daily Press

Richard L. Kaplan

· · ·

Throughout the nineteenth and into the early twentieth century, the daily newspaper was the dominant source of stories and information for most Americans. When Americans read, they picked up their local newspaper first. The press, in turn, characterized its central role in narrating American life as a service to democracy. Journalists proclaimed their ethical devotion to aiding the public—providing crucial information and analysis and enhancing public deliberation. The manner in which the press served the public, however, changed drastically between 1880 and 1920. Over time, daily papers altered what they judged appropriate public rhetoric, whom they considered a proper public speaker, and how they understood their reading public. This chapter describes the press's shifting democratic aspirations from the late nineteenth century into the first half of the twentieth.

For most of the nineteenth century, newspapers were purchased by the few, read by the well-to-do, and addressed to the elite. Despite its reputation as a democratic country with universal white, male suffrage, newspaper distribution in the United States remained a restricted affair. Until the 1870s circulation hovered between three and four daily papers for every ten households. In the waning years of the century, however, the press experienced a revolution that was both economic and political. From 1870 to 1910, the press rapidly expanded to reach many more Americans. This media growth was driven by innovations in printing technology, increasing advertising revenues, lower paper costs, and the drive for greater profits. By 1910 newspapers were full-scale incorporated companies, earning and spending millions of dollars, paying dividends to stockholders, and consolidating into extended media chains.[1]

The commercial expansion of the press was followed by a political revolution. Early twentieth-century newspapers rejected their past political heritage as noisy, argumentative, and partisan.[2] Instead, the U.S. press declared itself independent of all political attachments. Notwithstanding manifold behind-the-scenes connections to politicians and the persistence of hidden political sympathies, the newspapers' official rhetoric positioned them as beyond the fray of everyday politics. By transforming their official public mission, mainstream journalists renounced their authority to interject an explicit viewpoint into their reports. Reporters could no longer speak with the evaluative, aesthetic, or analytical intonations of a particular narrative voice. Thus, the news evolved from plural, politicized, competing perspectives to an impersonal, unified authoritative discourse. Modern journalism purported to supply an impartial, even "objective," account of America's daily triumphs and tragedies, acting as a neutral arbitrator in democracy's public debates.

The reconstruction of journalism's public ethic was propelled by broader political and economic transformations detailed in chapter 1 of this volume. Following the historian Alan Trachtenberg, we may label these the "incorporation of America," through which social decision making was often withdrawn from local economic and political control and concentrated in the administrative bureaucracies of corporations and the national state. Journalism's new public philosophy of objectivity both reacted to and reinforced these broader developments. This new professional ethic brought distinct gains but also severe limitations on the press's capacity to narrate critically the discourses, dramas, and dreams of public life.

The Nineteenth-Century Partisan Journal

The late nineteenth century in the United States, as in western Europe, was an age of mass political parties. In the early American republic, political parties had challenged the elite leadership by bringing the white, male masses into the electoral arena and granting them political influence. American voters in turn rewarded their parties with strong bonds of affection and loyalty. By the mid-nineteenth century, party identifications had been widely assimilated into family traditions and were handed down from generation to generation along ethnic lines. The parties forged competing national narratives, intermingling ethnic, class and regional identities into their visions.

Given their public legitimacy and their extensive control of governmental resources, the two dominant parties spoke as the central, if not exclusive, public voices on all issues of national import. Newspapers pledged allegiance to the Democrats or their opponents, first the Whigs, later the Republicans. Outside of the dominant parties, with their perpetual wrangling and polemics, there appeared to be no neutral space from which journalists could comment upon and observe American social life.[3]

Partisanship had deep ramifications for nineteenth-century journalism, permeating its highest ideals as well as its everyday practices. First and foremost, a newspaper was expected to endorse the party's "men and measures" without expressing any qualms or quibbles. Indeed, contravening important policy positions might bring censure, reader boycotts, or blazing bonfires of newspapers piled high.[4] Far from being an independent producer of information, the partisan paper was part and parcel of a public political community.

Newspapers built partisan identities through expressive rites of group loyalty. Such constructed ties of partisan solidarity, the editors thought, enhanced the party's prospects in its pursuit of electoral victory. For historians Michael McGerr and Michael Schudson, these expressive rituals defined nineteenth-century partisan journalism. In tandem with the broader political culture, the press enacted spectacular displays of party loyalty. These narratives of partisan commitment made parties seem a natural and salient part of American public life. According to McGerr, this emotional political style cultivated a communal culture that reached across class lines, engrossing the populace in political dramas and debates.[5]

Partisan papers showcased public debate even as they simplified it by stereotyping the issues and arguments. Throughout the last half of the nineteenth century, the majority of opinion columns, whether in election season or not, pleaded the party's cause and defended its policies.[6] Papers spoke not as external commentators, but as representatives of the political community. Editorials became part of an extended dialogue between local papers representing the two parties. The newspapers thus implied that two parties exhausted the relevant spectrum of political opinion, reinforcing the assumption of the broader political culture that parties were the only pertinent political speakers.

Because all journals were committed to one party or another, it was necessary to own or have influence at a paper to gain access to the public sphere. Indeed, to procure adequate public representation, the Democrats and later the Republicans launched an organ in every city and town. Parallel systems of partisan publicity flourished, with networks of papers exchanging, manufacturing, and reprinting partisan material.[7] Other views were neglected or derided; papers suppressed issues that conflicted with the party's agenda or potentially divided its electoral base. Republican newspapers refused to publicize views about alcohol prohibition, and both parties ignored or co-opted labor's demands.[8] Tied to parties, owned by the wealthy, and read by the upper third of the population, newspapers tended to disregard the interests of the mass of workers, the poor, and immigrants.[9]

Many Gilded Age critics condemned this simplified, emotional journalism as "inane" and "puerile"—a mockery of the republican public sphere. In the view of E. L. Godkin, a leading public intellectual of the day, partisan papers reinforced blind group loyalties at the expense of real public discussion.[10] As we shall see, such "Mugwump" criticisms of emphatic, public partisanship were eventually incorporated into a new Progressive public philosophy that advocated a restrained style, reflecting the perspective of corporate managers, professionals, and other members of the new middle classes. For the educated elite, the solution to class conflict was in disinterested, expert decision making rather than emotional, partisan advocacy. This approach derided the traditional, more participatory, political culture described by McGerr and resonated with the twentieth century's hierarchical culture of specialists and experts.[11]

Despite its pretensions, the partisan daily press never fully monopolized democracy's public arena. Both the genteel elite and a range of others bitterly criticized the impoverished public debate of the parties and their journals. Farmers joining the Populist movement and workers in the Knights of Labor believed that the dominant parties stymied proper public deliberation, benefiting the rich and the powerful. Myriad radical and alternative weeklies and monthlies publicized the concerns of African Americans, Native Americans, newly arrived immigrants, trade unions, women, and various protest movements. The alternative press stood as a constant reminder of what the dailies excluded. Indeed, as Sally Miller has detailed elsewhere in this volume, often the first accomplishment of an ethnic group or reform movement was to establish its own journal—its own public voice and proud presence in the contentious public arena.

Given the partisan press's emphatic, evaluative voice, the content of the Gilded Age newspaper appeared irredeemably slanted. It emerged from a specific political community and stood opposed to the news of its political foes. Indeed, these papers seemed to be crafted by the force of their editors' personalities. In the nostalgic accounts of the era, this was the last flowering of a personal journalism, before the arrival of complex bureaucracies and commercialized news corporations.[12] In reality, nineteenth-century news was a mass-produced affair, depending on an elaborate division of labor and contrived according to party interests.

Expanding the Readership of the Daily Press

In the years 1880 to 1910, the press rapidly expanded to incorporate the mass of Americans into its reading audience, through both the increasing circulation of the mainstream papers and the proliferation of more diverse dailies. Indeed, as cheap evening papers multiplied across the land, newspaper reading became a necessity for the average American. Price reduction and innovations in content—most notably the creation of "sensationalism"—were the key mechanisms used to attract the mass of literate Americans. Earlier, the press had been divided by political party affiliation but united in serving high-status readers. After 1880, as the press absorbed new social groups into its audience, that common cultural tone fractured into competing class aesthetics. In addition, the press's race for new subscribers carried myriad economic consequences, some foreseen, others hidden but portentous for journalism's highest ideals and everyday practices.

The chief problem for any *popular* press, as publishing magnate Edward Scripps observed, was price. In the 1870s, Scripps noted, newspapers cost four or five cents, a hefty share of a worker's average wage of a dollar a day. Indeed, he said, "newspapers were luxury items. . . . People to whom the humble nickel represented butter if not bread thought twice before buying a newspaper and then usually bought butter." Yearly subscriptions, which were much more common than street sales, ran from twelve to eighteen dollars per year. Consequently, price was a major barrier to the expansion of the newspaper audience.[13]

Media scholars have described the dynamic, novel economics that supposedly overcame this barrier to newspaper expansion and profits in the late nineteenth century. Harry Baehr Jr. wrote that the new journalism of Pulitzer and Hearst "was founded on cheap, mass circulation with advertising footing the bill."[14] According to Richard Ohmann, three interlinked processes explain the explosive growth in the mass market for periodicals in the 1890s. First, lower magazine prices stimulated a growing readership. This burgeoning circulation, in turn, produced expanded advertising revenue. Magazines then employed the newly generated funds (along with a reduction of the per unit costs of magazine production) to cut subscription prices further, sparking another increase in circulation.[15]

In the 1870s and early 1880s, however, two obstacles prevented newspapers from implementing such a dynamic economic program. On the one hand, the high cost of newsprint paper prohibited the creation of a cheap, mass-circulation newspaper.[16] For the press, paper stock constitutes the largest single source of "variable costs." And variable costs (i.e., costs that vary directly with the volume of production, such as ink or paper) were a disproportionate share of the costs of production.[17] With such a high ratio of variable to fixed costs, only limited economies of scale could be achieved through expanded production. In addition, since the Civil War escalating demand and a scarcity of cloth rags had driven paper costs skyward. Given such high prices for newsprint, reducing a paper's price in order to capture a larger audience might well have reduced profits.

Publisher James Scripps noted another difficulty confronting journalism in the postbellum era: "the advertising patronage of the country fell far short of the capacities of the papers to accommodate it." The abundance of available newspaper space, in the face of limited demand, allowed advertisers to dictate the terms of trade. Prices remained low and journals printed antiquated advertising with little hope of collecting the fees.[18] Confronting these barriers, publishers nationwide had scoffed at the possibility of issuing a cheap, popular paper.

These obstacles were first circumvented not by the giants of the New York publishing industry but by small entrepreneurs in the Midwest. These innovators launched a wave of cheap afternoon dailies in the booming industrial cities of Chicago, Cincinnati, Kansas City, Buffalo, and St. Louis, adopting an entirely different economic strategy to reach a mass audience. Scripps, founder of the *Detroit Evening News* in 1873, was a leader among these press entrepreneurs. In 1872 he outlined a new model for confronting the limitations of the market.[19] Instead of a dynamic model of publishing based upon a continued cycle of expanding production and popular consumption, Scripps proposed an all-around cutting of production costs. By implementing strict economies, he argued, publishers across the Midwest could revolutionize the urban news markets.

The key to the Detroit plan was reducing paper costs by decreasing paper size. At the time, all Detroit's papers were immense "blanket sheets" with each page spreading out to eight, nine, or ten columns of print. In contrast, Scripps issued his paper in a greatly reduced format, approximately one-sixth the size of other papers, with four pages measuring eighteen by twelve inches. In addition to saving on paper and printing costs, Scripps applied a general ascetic formula to his daily. The *Evening News*, he declared, had no need for "lavish expenditure for telegraphs and $35-a-week writing," which were "not appreciated by the common people whom we should seek for our constituency."[20]

In 1873 Scripps launched the *Detroit Evening News* on this basis. It cost two cents. Within three years, the *News* achieved success. Producing 17,000 copies daily, the *News* outsold all other Detroit papers. With profitability assured, Scripps followed his Detroit venture with papers in Cleveland, Cincinnati, St. Louis, and Buffalo. Meanwhile, other publishers such as Victor Lawson in Chicago and William Nelson in Kansas City established their own cheap afternoon sheets. Each was a short, scrappy bulletin paper, supplying an abbreviated but complete news report to urban working populations. The wave of newspaper growth across the United States between 1880 and 1910 largely rested on the expansion in number and circulation of these afternoon publications. Between 1870 and 1910 (the high-water mark for dailies in the United States), the number of sheets published jumped almost fourfold, from 574 to 2,600. By 1910 evening newspapers constituted 74 percent of the dailies and between 1880 and 1910 they made up 79 percent of the increase in papers.[21]

FIGURE 7.1. Workers are putting plates into presses before they start rolling. *New York Times*, Press Room, 1942. Prints & Photographs Division, FSA-OWI Collection, Library of Congress (LC-USW3-009062-E).

Throughout the Gilded Age, the U.S. population grew at a fierce rate, buoyed by the "second wave" of immigrants from southern and eastern Europe. The population in the five largest metropolises (after New York) more than doubled between 1880 and 1910 and newspapers more than matched the growth of the burgeoning population. In New York City, where four copies circulated for every ten inhabitants in 1870, the number increased to nine for every ten by 1910. In America's next five largest cities, circulation surged from about five copies per ten inhabitants to slightly more than one for every resident in 1910 (figure 7.1).[22] By the early twentieth century, buying and reading a paper was the normal routine, indeed a daily rite, among workers. In the early 1920s, Robert and Helen Lynd surveyed the consumption expenditures of blue-collar households in *Middletown*. One hundred percent subscribed to a daily journal.[23] Other studies in that decade report that "newspapers were by far the most common reading matter of young workers, followed by fiction magazines, the 'pulps.'"[24]

The near-universal reading of newspapers contrasted greatly with the consumption of magazines and books, which varied by education and social class. In surveys conducted in Hyde Park and North Evanston, Illinois, in 1928, more than 70 percent of those with only a grade school education had not read any books in the prior six months. Book consumption was concentrated among those with some college instruction. Those with lower levels of educational achievement, however, typically spent *more* time each day perusing the paper than those with more schooling. Among those with a high school education or less, about half devoted more than an hour a day to the leisurely inspection of the news, whereas only 15 percent of those with a college degree read newspapers so extensively (figure7.2).[25]

In the 1930s and 1940s, as radio became the principal home entertainment, a close scrutiny of the paper remained a required evening ritual. On average, readers devoted twenty minutes to their reading, with the radio supplying background noise.[26] Such habits persisted until the 1960s when newspaper consumption began a long-term, persistent decline among the middle and lower classes.[27] For the vast majority of Americans in the first half of the century, social reality—at least in its official narratives and rites—was defined and delivered by the daily paper.

Despite their innovations, the first cheap afternoon sheets of the 1870s and 1880s maintained the conservative business orientations of traditional nineteenth-century entrepreneurs. The *Detroit Evening News*, for example, was a family company, built with family capital, and staffed and controlled by Scripps siblings and cousins. The paper adopted a limited market niche perspective; instead of dynamically competing with existing publishers for a mass audience, it sought out those segments of the market previously unaddressed.[28] Some publishers distrusted dependence upon advertising and banking capital as a potential threat to the autonomy and purity of their enterprise. Pennypinching in production allowed their newspapers to subsist on an income of subscribers' pennies.

In the late 1880s seismic shifts in the economic landscape disturbed the static, ascetic financial strategies of the cheap dailies. Rocketing demand for advertising space and collapsing prices for paper stock compelled a reconstruction of the urban evening paper. These pressures for greater efficiency and consolida-

FIGURE 7.2. A newsstand displays foreign-language newspapers, 1941. Prints and Photographs Division, Library of Congress (LC-USF346-001359-Q-C).

tion reflected not so much the "natural" or internal evolution of the newspaper industry but rather the more general transformation of the U.S. economy into a mass-market, corporate-organized consumer society. Facing new economic realities, late nineteenth-century journalism ineluctably acceded to a commercial logic of audience maximization and market concentration. Newspapers aggressively pursued advertisers and audiences with new material, especially through the unprecedented use of violent, titillating, and scandalous stories and lurid illustrations that came to be known as "sensationalism." These shifts in practice created essential preconditions, if not sufficient motive, for newspapers' later departure from their avid partisanship of the nineteenth century.

At first, these economic changes were experienced as crises, not as opportunities for growth. At the Scripps papers in Michigan, for instance, managers feuded over the proper policy responses. In 1887 Edward Scripps, as chief managing officer of the Scripps chain, perspicaciously recognized the emerging opportunities for an aggressive newspaper. He quickly pursued his ideas in a series of investments and innovations. Publisher James Scripps, his brother, reacted in anger and consternation to this challenge to his traditional journalistic ideals and his newspapers' steady, if small, profits. In an exchange of letters, the brothers heatedly argued over Edward's proposed changes.[29] First, Edward pointed out to James: "The cost of paper is racing down hill. . . . I prophesy that very little paper will be sold during 1890, at a higher price than three cents. This means that the competition will require larger papers. . . . I believe that the time is shortly coming when the [*Cincinnati*] *Post* will print for a cent an eight page paper as big as the *News* is now."[30] Second, Edward reasoned that a massive increase in advertising justified expanding the newspaper's size and production facilities. On 30 May 1889, he wrote: "[Our *Detroit News* must] enlarge sufficient to monopolize the advertising business that can be gotten, [otherwise] some other papers will take it and over the profits grow rich and hence [become] a powerful competition for the *News*. . . . We have been leaving advertising out of the *News* at a rate of $1,000 a month. That money which advertisers are willing to spend in Detroit or at least a portion of it is going to *The Journal*, *The Free Press* and *The Tribune*, making them stronger financially and more fashioned for advertisers."[31]

In essence, Edward argued that collapsing newsprint prices and booming advertising revenues rendered the small, well-trimmed, penny paper of the 1870s irrelevant, even risky, in the contemporary news market. If the *Post* and the *News* did not expand to encompass a proliferating demand for advertising space, then rival journals would seize this potential revenue. These competitors would use the income to improve their product, increase their journal size, and reduce their prices—all potentially grabbing readers from the Scripps.

By and large, Edward Scripps correctly assessed the novel economic forces confronting the daily press in the late 1880s. These market pressures undermined the use of limited advertising and expensive paper stock and gave new meaning to the afternoon papers' strategy of a reduced price based on reduced costs. Advertising revenue at the Scripps *News* rose, rocketing from 38 percent of the gross profits in 1886 to 58 percent in 1889. U.S. census data similarly indicate that advertising as a proportion of all periodical income (including magazines) climbed steadily from 44 percent in 1879 to 60 percent in 1909.[32] Papers across the nation reported a sudden influx of advertising revenue. Even country dailies in the heart of Kansas, such as William Allen White's *Emporia Gazette*, shared in the riches as local merchants turned to advertising to fend off the appeals of big-city retailers and mail-order catalogs.[33]

This increase in ad linage rested on a massive rise in "display" advertising. Following the lead of Wanamaker's in Philadelphia, department stores in the 1880s began to use full-page ads to entice customers into their stores in large numbers. They strove to attract customers from throughout the streetcar city,

FIGURE 7.3. Reading the newspaper and sleeping are the primary occupations of the six "Bench Warmers, Union Sq.," 1908. George Grantham Bain Collection, Prints and Photographs Division, Library of Congress (LC-USZ62-71322).

creating high-volume sales.[34] Henceforth, advertising copy had to be changed daily and appear large enough to draw notice.[35] In the 1890s, Ohmann explains, this tactic of the retail trade was followed by a push for publicity by national brands, as the economy shifted from an era of family firms serving local markets to an era of corporate mass production on a national scale. The advertising boom that enriched newspapers was a key part of the corporations' strategy to expand sales.[36]

In place of the cheap, self-sufficient bulletin sheets serving a limited market niche, a new, dynamic newspaper flourished by hunting for ever more news and readers and, above all, through advertising. Advertising income underwrote production costs and spurred both price cuts and the addition of more pages packed with journalistic attractions. This burgeoning appetite for readers led to keen competition among papers and eventually to a saturated market.

By the 1890s the newspaper industry entered into a "mature stage," during which the growth in readership was accompanied more by rising circulations of existing papers than by the creation of new newspaper establishments. The requisite start-up costs grew rapidly, raising entry barriers. Increased competition for news required larger editorial staffs to cover local news and sports, as well as the purchase of wire services and syndicated features. Soaring circulation necessitated the acquisition of the newly invented typesetting machines and the latest model of the Hoe cylindrical printing press.[37]

With such large sums of capital potentially at risk, newspapers became a serious business. Market imperatives and the concerns of business managers weighed ever more heavily on the conduct of journalism.[38] At the same time, the number of readers needed to break even at competitive prices increased. New publishers had to struggle against the entrenched position of established papers before they could secure a large enough share of the market to return a profit.[39]

Because of heightened competition and rising production costs, newspapers sometimes struggled and failed, but more typically they were bought out by rival papers. Indeed, consolidation made increased economic sense once market barriers increased the probability that failed papers would not be replaced by new ones. Between 1879 and 1909, the absolute number of U.S. dailies continued its stunning rise to a peak of 2,600 in 1909. But thereafter newspapers dwindled to 2,441 dailies in 1919 and 2,080 by 1932. In the early 1900s, select metropolitan markets saw the onset of consolidation mania, initiated by calculating businessmen. The most famous, Frank Munsey, had already heaped up a sizable fortune in magazine publishing when in 1912 he "embarked on his career of cannibalizing the financially weaker New York newspapers."[40] One after another, Munsey purchased and then merged or folded the *New York Herald*, the *Evening Telegram*, the *Morning Sun* and the *Evening Sun*, and the *Globe* and *Commercial Advertiser*. New York City's population of papers increased to a remarkable 85 dailies in 1910, but the number dramatically declined thereafter. Similarly, in the nation's next five largest cities, newspapers grew from an average of sixteen per city in 1880 to twenty-three in 1910, and then commenced a permanent decline (figure 7.3).[41]

The survivors of this bloodbath were rewarded with a relatively secure market position and a steady, even rich, stream of profits. Not even the later onslaught of television would disturb the press's financial complacency. By the 1940s, James Baughman writes, "The typical mid-size city publishers no longer had a competitor or a prospect of one. . . . Big cities usually had two or more dailies, an evening and a morning rag, with publishers able to carve the market by class."[42] Thus, the central tendency of the twentieth-century press was growing oligopolistic dominance of each urban market. Financially secure newspapers were content to speak as the voice of the mainstream. Their editorials and news supported a politics of growth that assumed a harmony of interests among businesses' desire for unimpeded commercial development, the papers' greed for rising advertising revenues, and the public good of the community.[43]

The Impact of Advertising

A surfeit of advertising not only enriched the daily paper but also induced a reconstruction of the reigning notions of journalism. In Scripps's words, newspapers needed to be "fashioned for advertisers." E. L. Godkin suggested similarly that publishers began to "cower" before the power of advertisers. In fact, Godkin's pronouncement constituted standard criticism in the early 1900s. Progressive reformers often feared that concentrations of wealth and power would corrupt the public realm.[44] Yet, in truth, advertising worked in more subtle ways than many Americans suspected. Increasingly, the demands of commercial publicity infiltrated the press; the daily paper was transformed into a vehicle for the organization and administration of consumer markets. Newspapers packaged subscribers as much as they packaged news. In the process, the reader was no longer addressed only as citizen or engaged partisan but also as a customer, consumer, and passive spectator.[45]

To begin with, advertising promoted an expanded, more variegated newspaper—appending page after page in the hunt for customers. In the course of the eighties, for example, Pulitzer's *New York World* jumped from four to eight to fourteen pages, reaching sixteen in the nineties. More elite papers like the *New York Post* and the *New York Tribune* doubled their pages to eight while reducing their price to three cents.[46] Following Pulitzer's lead, other papers added such sections as sports, comics, and a woman's page, catering to an array of advertising interests and customers.[47]

The addition of book reviews as daily fare is a prime example of this rationalization of the press for advertisers' concerns. Elite journals such as the *New York Times*, the *New York Herald Tribune*, and the *Chicago Tribune* all created literary review supplements and published individual reviews. As described by Ellen Garvey in this volume, such literary sections burgeoned at the turn of the century in tandem with an increase in book advertising. Book reviews sought to entice the "better class" of readers, while creating one more showcase for elite goods. Their appearance helped to bifurcate the urban newspaper market into upscale and downscale papers, reflecting the drive to define sellable audiences. In his popular 1908 manual, Walter Scott advised advertisers: "If [an advertiser] wanted to reach the better classes, he would use the morning papers; if he wanted to reach the laboring class, he would employ the evening papers."[48]

With an increased assortment of topics, the newspaper became different things to different people, mimicking the consumer economy of which it was

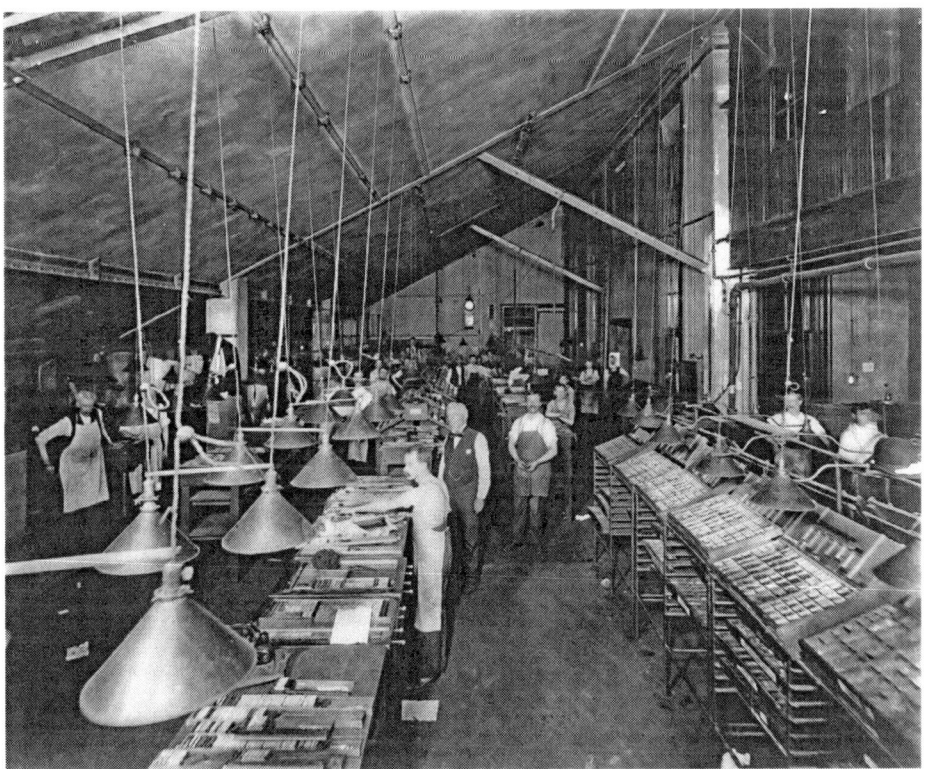

FIGURE 7.4. A supervisor inspects the *New York Herald* composing room and Linotype machines, 1902. George Grantham Bain Collection, Prints and Photographs Division, Library of Congress (LC-USZ62-54415).

both product and chief organ. Thus, journalism abandoned its nineteenth-century republican ideals of a unified community engaged in reasoned, political dialogue.[49] Instead, in the imagery of the new consumer society, the newspaper was described as a great big restaurant, filled with bustle and noise, and tantalizing its customers with a jumble of smells. Some likened the press to a "department store," or a "dime museum" filled with sights varied and bizarre.[50]

For turn-of-the-century social observers, nothing challenged the traditional republican political associations of the press as much as the new inclusion of women in the reading audience. Pulitzer, in particular, catered to women readers, whom he considered an attractive demographic draw for advertisers. Society and women's sections, 2.5 percent of the newspaper space early in the century, occupied 6.3 percent at century's end. Thus the Gilded Age press, like the department store, evolved into a new public space suitable for the promenading of middle-class women through its columns.[51]

In the end, as Paul Weaver argues, advertising shifted the very size and definition of the audience to which a journal was responsive. As advertising grew, readers' pennies no longer directly counted. Individual papers stopped emphasizing a core community of readers especially interested in the news or tied to a shared public identity. Instead, with their prices falling, "the media began to focus on the marginal customer, who, despite little interest in the news and little willingness to pay for it, was the building block of the ever-bigger audience sought—and paid for—by advertisers."[52] The papers' new financial foundations rested not on a community of political believers but on advertising that would entice readers through a heterogeneous mix of topics and narratives. Furthermore, the increasingly disparate content helped free the journal from the political demands of its readers. If a divisive political position offended some readers, other, perhaps more important, bases of subscriber loyalty could sustain their readership.

The economic transformation of the daily paper—from an expensive publication with a limited audience to a mass publication with a diverse readership—certainly affected the press's partisanship. In general, though, it weakened, rather than eliminated, the newspaper's public, formal links with parties. In the waning years of the century, journals continued to maintain party affiliations. Whether the elite *New York Times* or the popular *New York World*, U.S. dailies found that their public partisan identity continued to be economically advantageous (figure 7.4).

Sensationalism and Its Critics

The cheap evening dailies and the new journalism wrought by Pulitzer and Hearst employed shocking new contents and enticing garb to "dip into strata of newspaper readers which older editors had left untouched."[53] Turn-of-the-century cultural critics labeled the contents of these yellow sheets "sensationalism." They considered them a blemish upon, even a parody of, the "respectable" press. As the term implies, sensational content supposedly compelled a physical reaction from the reader—a surprise or a shock, more immediately felt than cognitive communication. In 1920, for instance, leading sociologist Robert E. Park declared that papers written for an expanded audience aimed "to thrill the crudest intelligence" and to stimulate "fundamental passions."[54] Various cultural critics argued over the years that sensationalist news entailed a corrupt commercial exploitation of the populace's degraded cultural sensibilities.[55] According to this view, a cultural industry supplied the masses with diverting spectacles and appeals to crude instincts, thus displacing critical reflection by the public. Corporate capital became the new cultural arbitrator, they suggest, destroying working-class cultural autonomy and preempting genteel cultural control. In catering to popular tastes, journalism was elevating a dangerous class perspective.[56]

Certainly, sensational news violated Victorian cultural sensibilities and was experienced as a pointless shock. Already in 1881, William Dean Howells revealed distaste for the violence of the news with its mélange of clashing front-page stories. In *A Modern Instance*, one of his genteel characters queries the entirely unrestrained, opportunistic journalist, Bartley Hubbard: "Why should I sup on all horrors of a railroad accident, and have bleeding fragments hashed up for me at breakfast? Why should my newspaper give me a succession of shocks to my nervous system, as I pass from column to column, and poultice me in between shocks with the nastiness of a distant or local scandal? You reply, because I like spice. But I don't. I am sick of spice." Indeed, the new journalism of the 1880s and 1890s heightened this distaste for "spice" and was blamed for various upper-class maladies. Echoing Howells's fears, George Beard depicted an epidemic of upper-class languor in his 1880 book, *American Nervousness*. He blamed the "periodical press," along with "the telegraph, sciences, steam power, and the mental activity of women."[57] All of these offered disturbing temptations and the breakdown of social boundaries, threatening the Victorian elite's precarious self-control. Newspapers entered daily into peaceful domestic settings, providing tragedies and travesties to be casually consumed with breakfast, jeopardizing the separation of the domestic haven from the public world of cutthroat bargaining, corrupt politics, and rough talk. Shrieking headlines of murder, mayhem, and divorce—favorites of the 1890s press—menaced the boundaries in which Victorian society had invested its social fortunes.[58]

The critics of sensationalism depict the populace as passive and culturally debased. Against this interpretation, it is necessary to juxtapose another view of the new journalism. Far from offering mere shock, thrill, or distraction, its appeal resided in its ability to portray American daily life in a manner that effectively captured the hopes and fears of its expanded, mass readership. In addition, its success was tied to its capacity to employ popular cultural forms that dramatically communicated to readers. Because this aesthetic, with its dramatic depictions, differed sharply from that of papers of the elite, it provoked consternation among them.[59]

Urban journalism has always tried to penetrate "the mysteries of the city," to publicize the metropole's disorders and dangers, to reveal "how the other half lives."[60] In making the city comprehensible and manageable, however, serious news and sensationalist news employed vastly different social philosophies to emplot their stories. The plots of the elite press entailed a bureaucratic logic of causality. The mass press mobilized an allegorical logic of melodrama. In both narrative strategies, journalism sought to illuminate the hidden ties that unite and explain phenomena. But while serious news supposedly delineated the broad, if abstract, social forces affecting society—paying most heed to official, powerful actors and institutions—sensationalist news started from the small and the personal. Popular journalism suggested that the broader social world was unknowable and uncontrollable; only the personal was comprehensible.

Sensationalism, says Roland Barthes, operates not through a comprehension of causes but a gasp of astonishment.[61] In a 1910 memo, Pulitzer outlined this very logic of popular journalism, listing what the *New York World* should publish: "What is original, distinctive, dramatic, romantic, thrilling, unique, curious, quaint, humorous, odd, apt to be talked about, without shocking good taste or lowering the general tone, good tone, and above all without impairing the confidence of the people in the truth of the stories or the character of the paper for reliability and scrupulousness."

Just as in the early "cinema of astonishment,"[62] an attitude of skeptical credulity and playfulness operated in the yellow press. Looking at an 1897 copy of the *World*, for instance, one finds such "marvelous," and astonishing stories as: "Baby Elephants at School"; "FIRE-HORSE SAVES A CHILD'S LIFE. With a Girl Nesting at His Feet He Refused to Respond to Gong's Call"; and "HER DREAM CAME TRUE. Mrs. Mueller Had Warning in Her Sleep that Her Place Would Be Robbed." Sensationalism's exaggeration, its carnivalesque hyperbole, its self-promotion, and indeed its fakery offended the restrained sensibilities of the elite press. But in the context of willing popular credulity, elite denunciations of sensationalism fell on deaf ears.

Popular journalism emphasized the personal while ignoring changing historical forces and social contexts. Given limited space to develop plot motifs, context, or character, the sensational news recounted the forever-true dramas of the little folks—stories of family, love, death, disaster, heroism, and villainy. The same 1897 issue of the *World* encompassed six separate articles under the banner headline: "Misfortune the Lot of These—The Tender Babe, Mother, Wife, and Father." The news provided melodramatic narratives of innocent people—families torn apart, babies injured—victimized while great political and economic powers pursued their predatory interests. The persistence of such melodramatic conventions, as Thomas Elsaesser suggests, reveals how popular culture registered the social fate of society's poor and despairing. Also, however, melodrama "resolutely refused to understand social change in other than private contexts and emotional terms."[63] For such scholars as Michael Denning, the growth of the sensationalist press's seemingly apolitical melodramatic tales displaced more distinctively working-class narrative traditions emphasizing capitalist villains and stalwart artisan heroes.[64] In truth, sensationalism did not so much end this cry of the oppressed heart as continued it in a veiled narrative form.

Sensationalism, always an unwelcome companion to the mainstream press, suffered an unnatural death. Born in the competitive struggle to attract a popular audience, and periodically revived in subsequent waves of tabloids, sensationalism's big daily papers had perished by the middle of the twentieth century. Consolidation in urban news markets brought respectability to the newspaper trade.[65]

Declarations of Press Independence

Throughout the nineteenth century, whether serious or sensationalist, the press remained largely partisan. At century's end, however, the power of parties to dominate the American public sphere began a precipitous decline. Two key episodes marked this toppling of parties: the critical election of 1896, and the antipartisan political reforms of the Progressive Era, 1904–19. Against this political backdrop, the U.S. press broke from all party ties and reformulated its role in American public life, proclaiming itself independent from all encumbering political affiliations.

At first, the presidential campaign of 1896 seemed to signal an upsurge in partisan fervor. William Jennings Bryan and the Populist Party captured the Democratic presidential nomination, ushering contentious new issues into the political arena and establishing the Democratic Party as the voice of protest and reform. Inequitable railroad rates, declining prices for agricultural goods, and a deflationary currency induced farmers to join the public debate. Soon the specific protest issues were overwhelmed by hysteria. The *Nation* declared, "Probably no man in civil life has succeeded in inspiring so much terror without taking life as Bryan." The Democratic candidate was repeatedly reviled from the platform as well as the pulpit while Democratic papers deserted the party en masse. Conservative elite dailies like the *New York Times* and the *Detroit Free Press* issued "declarations of independence." Even liberal, sensationalist journals like Pulitzer's *World* or Scripps's *Cincinnati Post* dumped the party. In New York City, only the heretical Hearst trumpeted Bryan's candidacy. At the campaign's close, Bryan remarked on the journalistic inequality between the two parties: "With all the newspapers of the country against us, our 6,500,000 votes is a vindication of which we have a right to be proud."[66]

The fallout from this election reinforced the press's flight from the Democrats. The emotional issues of the campaign fundamentally reshuffled the social coalitions underlying the two parties and disrupted long-standing party affiliations. Furthermore, the election so weakened the Democrats that everywhere but in the South they were demoted to a minority party. Elections became uncompetitive. Deprived of significant choice, voter participation dropped and continued to fall from 84 percent in 1896 until it reached its nadir in 1920 at 53 percent.[67]

Newspapers had bolted from parties before, notably in the exodus from the Republicans in 1872 and 1884. But after momentary apostasy, papers had always returned, usually humbled, to one political church or the other. In any case, bolting papers had maintained their right to express their opinions forcefully. In the early twentieth century, however, this open public partisanship came to a permanent end. As party competition and polemics turned into an extraneous sideshow, the Progressive movement attacked parties and their public legitimacy. Levying vociferous criticisms of "corrupt" "party machines," Progressives initiated reforms that undermined the parties' central role in political life: among these were primary elections, direct election of senators, nonpartisan ballots, and civil service reform.[68]

In this context of fading party power and a middle-class antipartisan ideology, newspapers severed their official links to the Democrats and Republicans. Publishers and editors drew upon the new political rationales of Progressive reformers to reconstruct journalism's public role. Progressive notions of "public service" and professional expertise became the rhetorical mainstay of journalism's occupational ideals and a defense against all external criticisms and pressures.[69] In the American Society of Newspaper Editors' 1923 Code of Ethics, the key words were factuality, independence, impartiality, and public service.[70] Amid widespread fears over monopolies, the ideal of public service challenged the idea that concentrations of journalistic power would advance private interests.[71] The press countered that monopolization of the public sphere was not employed for private goals. "Our policies in the conduct of the *News* are not private policies. . . . We have no ulterior motive, no private axe to grind," defensively wrote one publisher in 1915.[72] Journalism was purportedly devoted to the general community and was rewarded only for serving that public good. Furthermore, Progressive Era publishers asserted that professional expertise, not personal judgments or political motivations, would direct their news choices and interpretations.[73]

In the first half of the twentieth century, the press professed its independence and objectivity. Yet, as Michael Schudson argues in his chapter in this volume, journalists continued to cultivate alliances with leading politicians. Certainly journalists and politicians were permanent bedfellows, with news workers aiding and abetting their preferred causes as best they could. But commencing in the early 1900s, these connections were steadfastly denied and no longer a matter of publicly proclaimed allegiance.

Journalism's assertion of its objectivity represented a fundamentally reformulated claim of legitimacy after the previous century's justification on the basis of formal, demonstrative partisanship. Party papers had affirmed a right to political speech. In the twentieth century, publishers claimed to be above the wrangling of politics. The news, journalists asserted, is not part of the swirl of opinion and partisan bias.[74]

Newspapers' new "objectivity" resonated with a more general ideological development. Progressive Era political culture encouraged a segmentation of society into specialized domains for decision making. Just as progressive reformers claimed that social problems were a question of facts and technical solutions best left to impartial, informed experts, so early twentieth-century newspapers highlighted their own professional autonomy and supposed objectivity. The hope was that the growth of technical administrative procedures would reduce the public expression of conflict among classes and diverse social interests. Progressive Era professionalism aimed at eliminating the open, contentious, collective deliberations of politics.

In its purported public impartiality, the press supposedly did not operate as a platform for one dominant public voice but rather as a "channel" for a variety of speakers. Ideally, new voices could gain access to the press and thereby enter into democracy's public discussion. More often, guided by their technocratic ethic, the dailies did not so much expand their coverage of civil society's diverse opinions as continue to publicize the policies and pronouncements of "important" speakers from formal political institutions. In contrast to the past, however, newspapers now balanced their coverage between the two major parties. Wire service and hometown papers typically paired the statements of one party official with those of his opposite number.[75] Far from eliminating the influence of particular class interests, journalism's technocratic ideals took for granted the established hierarchy of power. Governmental and corporate power holders were taken as the embodiment of modern industrial society's functional rationality. Their pronouncements should be reported and their decisions respected, rather than probed and challenged.[76]

As the century progressed, the press moved beyond its role as effaced medium for elite speakers and assumed the task of summarizing, synthesizing, and interpreting world events. Journalism's independent power to provide its own analyses and interpretations, however, confronted severe limitations. Because of its professed disconnection from political power and claims to nonpartisanship, the early twentieth-century press lacked the authority to press its own interpretations against the pronouncements of other powers in the public sphere. In the face of controversy, the press inevitably retreated, deferring to "legitimate" public authorities and mainstream opinion.[77] In their 1920s study of Muncie,

Indiana, the Lynds remarked, "It is usually safe to predict that in any given controversy the two leading papers may be expected to support the United States in any cause, the business class rather than the working class, the Republican party against any other, but especially against any 'radical party.' "[78]

Romance of the Reporter/Romance of the Nation

While the reformed press derided both partisanship and sensationalism as a series of excessive, contrived stories, all news—high or low—depended upon plots and theories in order to organize its narrative material. In its modern incarnation, the news dispensed with the official narratives of parties and began to craft its own tales. In their new role as independent news professionals, however, the media hid their own active authorial hand in the interpretation of events. They accomplished this by relying upon society's shared and largely taken-for-granted norms and rules to define their interpretations. In the media's view, journalism became a flexible and apolitical profession; they celebrated its capacity to observe the facts without any ideological or moral blinders, all the while reproducing whatever prejudices were most predominant and convenient.

Reporters were the main protagonists of this new view. Refusing to recognize any theories or philosophies as governing their actions, reporters saw themselves as enacting the modern fantasy of a mobile eye: observing, absorbing, unaffected, and detached.

Indeed, twentieth-century journalism elevated the reporter as a new public hero with whom the mass audience could identify. The Victorian era had spawned the romance of the editor who dared to challenge the politics and the morality of the entire country, as in Horace Greeley's antislavery campaign. The twentieth century sponsored its own romance. The star of modern journalism was the adventurous reporter who fearlessly explored all corners of the globe, capturing every experience for the audience back home. Reporter James Creelman recalled only a moment's trepidation upon entering the innermost royal sanctum of the king of Korea. Then he quickly regained his composure, for "American journalism must invade the presence of the hermit monarch. . . . See his face, question him, weave his sorrows into some up-to-date political moral. The artificial majesty of kings, after all, counts for little before the leveling processes of modern newspaper power."[79]

H. L. Mencken recalled that by 1900 reporters held editorial writers, with all their moralizing cant, as beneath contempt. "The hero of our dreams was . . . Richard Harding Davis who was reputed to own twenty suits, or else James Creelman, who interviewed the pope." Journalists were men of action, not just moral pieties. Cub reporters such as Heywood Broun or Mencken might hope to emulate their glamour, independence, and pay.

In addition to these men of action, a second literary character gave a human face to the gray columns of print and countered somewhat journalism's claim to objectivity: the columnist. Authors like Walter Winchell on the Broadway beat, Eugene Fields and Peter Dunne in Chicago, Malcolm Bingay in Detroit, not to mention the daily sports writers, all wrote columns of wit, social observation, literary expression, and personal revelation, however limited. They added a recognizable human voice and personality to the functional technocratic machinery of the daily paper. In this manner, each paper crafted an individual personality and contrived an intimacy and a pseudocommunity for the mass audience amid the anonymous anomie of the city.

The glittering prominence of these journalist stars, however, obscured the unnoticed drudgery of the many. Writers on the order of Stephen Crane, Creelman, and Davis were recognized personalities and were granted by-lines to attract the newsstand reader; but the mass of news workers engaged in anonymous, poorly paid labor. The reporter usually worked as an employee, a paid laborer doing piecework, or as a professional and an expert, but rarely as a personality and star.[80] Most articles received no by-line until the 1940s.[81] With its emphasis on speed and topicality, the news devalued individual trademarks and personal aesthetic style. The reporter had little autonomy from the copy editor's quick blue pencil. In fact, the copy editor's excisions and corrections represented graphic lessons from management about how to write, about what the news was, and indeed about what was true and important about the social order. In the evening papers, especially Hearst's, some reporters never even returned to the office. Instead, they phoned in their harvest of facts to a special "rewrite man," talented in quickly assembling punchy stories.[82] Journalism was considered an education in social realities for the aspiring novelist; John Reed recalled that young writers at Yale were advised to "get in, get wise and get out." Otherwise, reporting could be only a "short and brutish" career.[83]

In Amy Kaplan's accounting, the ideal of the reporter as a detached observer for a voyeuristic public reached its peak in imperialist adventures abroad—specifically, in the Spanish-American War. Indeed, the war provided a central model for all U.S. reporting and represented a solution of sorts for the crisis of American liberal culture. As historian Richard Hofstadter noted, the war of 1898 grew out of a deep cultural crisis "that might be called the psychic crisis of the 1890s."[84] Marred first by an economic depression and then the stunning, savage battle between the Populists and establishment forces, the 1890s had been preceded by vast labor unrest. The resulting class conflict and the expansion of large-scale cartels and trusts called into question the liberal vision of a harmonious social order based on individual economic opportunity and striving.

War abroad, like the rising office of the "imperial" presidency, offered a new solution to these social divisions. In wars, at least in the best wars, the "good wars," there flourished the fantasy of a united nation, engaged in moral battle against a heinous foe. The Spanish-American War in particular achieved a popularity throughout the country even if Hearst's *Journal* and Pulitzer's *World* claimed proprietary rights to it.

Especially in the 1898 conflict, reporters often seized center stage in the war adventure and gave performances that were matched only by the histrionics of the publicity-hungry, future president, Theodore Roosevelt. The New York dailies decorated their war stories with portraits of their correspondents. Leading reporter Creelman, known for his bravery under fire, was depicted in news illustrations as leading a battle charge. In 1898's melodramatic scenario, the hero whether reporter or soldier—posed as the vigorous, virile defender of an innocent and vulnerable female (Cuba), who was threatened by a dark, despotic villain (Spain). Headlines in Hearst's *New York Journal* ran: "Does Our Flag Protect Women?—Indignities Practiced by Spanish Officials on Board American Vessels . . . Refined Young Women Stripped and Searched by Brutal Spaniards."[85]

The press was crucial to this dramatic performance, allowing the military spectacle to be enacted before an entranced domestic audience. Through vicarious participation in the army's forceful actions, the populace recovered the freedom it had lost as economic producers or citizens at home. War provided the opportunity for submerging internal division in an effort of collective sacrifice for the common good, a battle of regeneration for lost virtues and forgotten discipline. Attributes of the Cuban conflict enhanced its transmutation into an exciting, absorbing narrative for the mass public. What John Hay termed a "splendid little war" was more precisely a very convenient journalistic war; nearby and short, the war was a quick military success with "no defeats to sober the country, no long casualty lists to divert attention. Its history could be . . . called a glory story."[86]

In the minds of such Mugwump critics as E. L. Godkin, the histrionics of the yellow press were responsible for the 1898 war. Such a charge is disputed today, but at least there occurred a frightful collusion of interests. As Godkin averred, nothing sells papers like war. "War means daily sensation and excitement." Indeed, the potent mix of governmental propaganda, elite interests, and mass sentiment compelled the press to impose a nationalistic plot upon war news or else face losses in prestige and profits. With the nation (or the lives of "its boys") threatened, and its most "sacred" values at stake, the press had to abandon its detached tone. It had to rally the citizenry to the flag. "In the tumult of a great war," Godkin asserted, ". . . the rules of evidence are suspended by passion and anxiety."[87] In their reporting of war, and indeed of foreign affairs more generally, the press tended to reproduce simply and uncritically the government's spin and to suppress dissent.[88]

In each subsequent war of the twentieth century, critics repeated these charges of press collusion with the government. Walter Lippmann's famous 1922 volume *Public Opinion* coined the term "stereotype" to describe the patriotic fears and fantasies that plagued reporting during the Great War. For this distorted news, Lippmann blamed the mass public for living in a dream world. In his earlier 1920 study of the coverage of the Bolshevik Revolution in the *New York Times*, though, Lippmann indicted reporters and publishers for completely erroneous reporting.[89] The *Times*'s inaccuracies stemmed from its reliance on government and other sources, whose views matched the policy desires of the newspaper and those of the Wilson administration. During World War I, both the *New York Times* and the *Tribune*—leading elite papers that were crucial conduits of foreign correspondence—were rabidly patriotic.

In the end, the U.S. press's wartime reporting merely enacted on a broader world canvas the twentieth century's new paradigm of press and public-state relations. In this paradigm, print journalism stood as a supposedly independent mediator between government and people. Yet journalism's posture of disinterested impartiality, along with the technocratic reformulation of U.S. political institutions, deprived the press of any independent authority for interpreting the American drama. Divorced from the norms and viewpoints articulated by citizens in public debate, news reports depended for their credibility and salience upon how well they reiterated the facts and frames of leaders.

In sum, during the late nineteenth and early twentieth centuries, shifts in the politics and economics of journalism, as well as of the country more generally, combined to promote a fundamentally reformulated press. Almost every citizen was included in the journalistic republic of letters and supplied with the diversions, entertainment, and insights of mass journalistic narratives. In the process, however, the press recalibrated its professional ethic from partisanship to "objectivity" in an attempt to assure its continued public authority in narrating the nation's daily tragedies and triumphs. Nonetheless, because of the relatively weak state of debate in public life and the weaknesses of its own apolitical ethic, the press possessed limited means to fulfill its own democratic charge: to enhance critical, inclusive political debate in the American public sphere.

CHAPTER 8

Persistence of Vision
Partisan Journalism in the Mainstream Press

Michael Schudson

· · ·

In its most familiar form, the American newspaper is a business run for profit married to a political enterprise run for influence. In the late nineteenth century, the business side began to dominate the marriage. Even so, the newspaper's daily production was run by workers with their own literary, political or career aspirations and, in the half century after 1880, a growing identity as professional journalists. American news workers developed a sense of professionalism earlier and more thoroughly than their European counterparts, whose identity was more securely affixed to politics. In the United States, reporters developed a pride of craft and an esprit de corps independent of party inclinations. They proclaimed that they, and not the newspaper owners, were the moral custodians of the journalistic enterprise.

From the 1920s on, journalists increasingly claimed that the "objectivity" of their reporting justified their moral guardianship. The seriousness, even the solemnity, of this claim can be seen in a variety of expressions in the 1920s and 1930s. Raymond Clapper, a Washington correspondent for the United Press wire service, refused to register to vote when he moved to Chevy Chase, Maryland, in 1929 because he would have had to choose a party designation. He wanted, he wrote, to be "free to criticize either party without having the precinct chairman call and ask me why I was being disloyal to my party." On the same grounds, he refused to join any organizations that spoke out on political issues.[1] The refusal of partisan politics could become a steady opposition to all parties and politicians. H. L. Mencken explained his criticism of Calvin Coolidge this way: "I had no special animosity to him; he was simply the sitting President of the United States, and in all my life I don't recall ever writing in praise of a sitting President.... It was the business of a journalist, as I conceived it, to stand in a permanent Opposition."[2]

Most professional journalists defined their role less astringently, developing a more cool and detached view of news and politics. Edward McKernan, superintendent of the Eastern Division of the Associated Press, stressed the grave importance of factuality in the press. "I beg of you to remember this, for it is fundamental: The Associated Press never comments on the news."[3] Even publisher Joseph Pulitzer II criticized his paper, the *St. Louis Post-Dispatch* for injecting opinion in news columns, even though these supported his own opposition to President Roosevelt's Court-packing scheme. He feared that "readers, especially pro-Roosevelt and neutral readers, will lose confidence in our news columns if we continue the present policy."[4] The forces encouraging the professionalization of journalists and the commercial orientation of newspapers are analyzed in Richard Kaplan's chapter in this volume. This essay adds a qualification to these observations: that the newspaper's old involvement in political advocacy and political maneuvering survived in both old and novel forms.

The American newspaper in the first half of the twentieth century was in its salad days. It prospered with the growth of cities; it prospered with war; it prospered with America's growing international interests. There seemed little it could do except prosper. The newspaper's multifaceted nature allowed new functions to be added without altering its fundamental identity as daily provider of political news. It was a vehicle of advertising and local commerce, an expression of ego, ambition, and adventure for its proprietors, a vehicle of intra-urban communication through classified ads, a booster and voice of local and regional economic development, and a means of urban integration and Americanization for immigrants who used it as an organ of entertainment and an instrument of civic instruction. It could be all these things at once without contradiction and with minimal tension. Newspapers added sports coverage, women's pages, comics, crossword puzzles, and radio listings without diminishing or changing the primary news enterprise.

Despite all these new functions, the newspaper's traditional purpose of political education and political advocacy endured. Yet the modes of political advocacy changed; political advocacy could increasingly be maintained only sub rosa and in tension with norms of professionalism. Press and politics have remained intertwined in the twentieth century even as a professional ethic of nonpartisanship became ascendant.

Book publishing firms have long been judged according to their contributions to "art" or "culture." They have been known by the authors they publish or sometimes by the impressive sales they ring up. In contrast, newspaper publishers have generally been measured by their contributions to the quality of political discussion and their ability to publish a hot story a day, an hour, or even a minute ahead of their competitors. Their role in the society's informational circulatory system, therefore, is evidently different from that of book publishing. Their connection to democratic politics is more intimate and incessant. Democratic politics needs wordsmiths. There are speeches to be written, ideologies to be articulated, elites and masses to be informed. Democratic governments need eyes and ears, and, especially in foreign affairs, the well-informed correspondent is a treasure to be cultivated. In an age before the rise of the independent political consultant, journalists were often recruited for all of these roles. Publishers frequently went into publishing with political motives, but reporters and editors as often as not had political involvement thrust upon them. How did this happen, even as journalists routinely pledged their allegiance to objectivity?

What is at stake here for the history of print is simply this: the authority of the printed word takes on a variety of forms in different spheres of publishing. Print conveys authority, but it conveys many different kinds of authority. In the newspaper, it takes on a variety of forms even in the same publication. This happens in book publishing, too. For instance, in a work of fiction, the front matter that identifies author, publisher, and copyright speaks in one voice, the author's acknowledgments speak in another, and the fiction itself in a third. The naming of the publisher on the title page announces ownership of the work and, to insiders in the world of fiction, may suggest whether the work at hand is standard or experimental, the author at the beginning or at the height of a career, and the publication a notable or a routine event. In other genres, such as anthologies, the number of voices can multiply.

In a newspaper, the multiple voices are much more pronounced. The earliest newspapers in America, in the 1700s, had multiple authors. Colonial printers wrote very little of what they printed; their newspapers were a miscellany of pieces reprinted from other newspapers or books as well as letters from occasional, unpaid correspondents. Such multiple authorship was often muted, however. Not until the 1820s did newspaper proprietors routinely hire reporters. Only in the 1880s and 1890s did some reporters step into the limelight and claim authorship of what they wrote. The by-line that developed during the Civil War was the technical instrument of this change. But more important was the emergence of reporting as a self-conscious profession, an occupation whose members began to identify with and to write for one another as much as — or more than — for their own editors. In a word, a group of hired men (and a few women) began to claim authorship of the news institutions that employed them.[5]

Yet the publisher did not relinquish his voice. Instead, that voice migrated to the editorial page, where the publisher remained a political personage, an actor more than a commentator, exercising influence in addition to the rest of the newspaper. At the same time, especially in the 1920s and 1930s, the number of distinctive political voices in newspapers began to multiply as the syndicated political column came into its own. World events began to impinge more routinely on American life in this period, and ambitious American newspapers began to maintain foreign correspondents, reporters whose independent activities abroad sometimes provided them a distinctive voice and personal authority. Newspapers between 1880 and 1950 became conversation parlors, with multiple voices and multiple, simultaneous conversations. The press sought to maintain its cultural authority in part by sharing it more widely among its contributors—publisher, editor, reporter, columnist, and foreign correspondent.

Political Advocacy in Journalism

Most leading newspapers were staunchly partisan organs in the late nineteenth century, as Kaplan argues in the previous chapter. Editors and publishers were commonly and intimately intertwined with political elites. In Rhode Island, the statewide machine was even named after the state's leading newspaper because the "Journal Ring" included among its key members the editor of the *Providence Journal*.[6] In 1892 *New York Herald Tribune* publisher Whitelaw Reid was the Republican Party's candidate for vice president. Such connections continued into the twentieth century. Publishers continued to use their newspaper kingdoms to promote their favored parties, policies, or personal political advancement, despite much official rhetoric claiming "objectivity" and political neutrality as journalistic ideals. Publisher William Randolph Hearst ran successfully for Congress in 1902 and 1904, failed in his bid for Democratic presidential nomination in 1904, and ran unsuccessfully for governor in 1906 and mayor (of New York) in 1909. Reluctantly accepting the role of kingmaker rather than candidate, Hearst then bought the *Atlanta Georgian* to promote the candidacy of Champ Clark for the Democratic presidential nomination in 1912 and sent John Temple Graves, editor of the *New York American*, to Atlanta to set up the Clark campaign there.[7] His influence would grow later along with the reach of his growing chain of newspapers. In 1932 his antipathy to Al Smith led him to swing the California delegation at the Democratic National Convention to Franklin Delano Roosevelt, securing FDR's nomination.

The size of Hearst's ambition and his newspaper empire were both unusual, but it was commonplace for publishers to be in the thick of partisan political maneuvering. The *Nashville Tennessean* was the personal mouthpiece for Colonel Luke Lea, who was U.S. senator from 1911 to 1917; later, the paper was bought by Silliman Evans, a former Texas political reporter who had made his way to the chairmanship of Maryland Casualty Company and a position in the postmaster general's office under Roosevelt. His aim at the *Tennessean* was to create a southern exponent of the New Deal—in 1940 it was the only daily in the state to endorse Roosevelt's run for a third term.[8] Charles C. Carlin owned the *Alexandria Gazette* (Virginia), served in the U.S. Congress, managed A. Mitchell

Palmer's effort to win the Democratic nomination for president in 1920, and became Oscar Underwood's campaign manager in his 1924 presidential bid.[9] Robert W. Bingham, publisher of the *Louisville Courier-Journal* and *Louisville Times* received for his financial and editorial support of Franklin Roosevelt the ambassadorship to the United Kingdom from 1933 to 1937.[10]

For the publisher-editor in American politics, 1920 was a landmark year: in that year both the candidate of the Republican Party and the candidate of the Democratic Party for president of the United States were newspaper men. Warren G. Harding was the publisher and editor of the town paper of Marion, Ohio, while the Democratic candidate, James M. Cox, at the time Ohio's governor, was the publisher of the *Dayton Daily News*.[11]

Harding and Cox were not the last publishers to grace national tickets, though they were the last to take the top spot. In 1936 newspaperman Frank Knox sought the Republican presidential nomination but had to be satisfied with the vice-presidential line on the ticket. As publisher of the *Chicago Daily News*, Knox had been among the most outspoken critics of the New Deal.[12]

Every history of American journalism quotes Adolph Ochs's famous statement, upon taking over the *New York Times* in 1896, that the paper would give the news "impartially, without fear or favor, regardless of any party, sect or interest involved." Often omitted is the next paragraph of Ochs's statement, which laid out his commitment to sound money, tariff reform, low taxes, and limited government. Ochs took these principles seriously enough to march, along with top editors of his paper, in the parade for the "Gold Democratic" ticket in 1896.[13] There is a tendency to push "objectivity" back to the 1890s, or earlier; in reality, only later did it become an established practice and ideal.

Publisher Josephus Daniels, soon-to-be editor and publisher of the *Raleigh News and Observer*, wrote to a friend in 1894 that there was a "pressing need for a daily and weekly at Raleigh that will be an aggressive exponent of Democracy [i.e., the Democratic Party] free from factions and favoritism. I believe that, with the proper help, I can make such a paper—one that would be in touch with the democracy of every county in the commonwealth; one that would be open to all shades of opinion within the party; one that would be as broad as the principles of our party are lasting."[14] In his efforts to help find ways to disenfranchise blacks (who regularly voted Republican), Daniels traveled to Louisiana on behalf of the North Carolina Democratic Party to study voting practices.[15] His stalwart support of the Democrats won him a cabinet post under Wilson and the ambassadorship to Mexico under Franklin Roosevelt.

Over time, newspapers bought or founded for specifically political purposes became the exception rather than the rule. Still, such practices did occur, the most notable of which was perhaps the 1941 establishment of the *Chicago Sun*, designed to counter the isolationist influence of Colonel Robert R. McCormick's *Chicago Tribune*. Department store magnate Marshall Field agreed to underwrite the paper and received the personal blessing of President Franklin Roosevelt for doing so.[16]

The continuing interconnection between politics and journalism is evident not only in the political activities of publishers but in the continuing importance of the newspaper editorial page. Adolph Ochs considered dispensing with it when he took over the *New York Times* in 1896, but neither he nor his successors ever did so.[17] The Pulitzer Prizes from their beginning in 1917 have recognized editorial writing.

In the 1930s nearly all newspaper editorial pages endorsed a candidate for president (95 percent). This would decline later, but it was still at 80 percent in 1952.[18]

Editorial writers sometimes have had political careers of their own. Shortly after coming to New York in 1926 as editor of the *New York Evening World*, Claude Bowers, journalist and popular historian, was invited to a dinner with Robert Wagner, a Democratic politician then about to make his first (and successful) bid for the U.S. Senate. "I fell in love with Bob Wagner the moment I saw him," Bowers would later recall. Before the evening was over, Wagner asked Bowers to write his first speech as the Democratic candidate. Bowers, who would shortly be writing editorials in support of Wagner, did not hesitate. He wrote Wagner's first two speeches. Before the election, he ran daily editorials supporting Wagner—when no other newspaper in the city backed him. Three years later, Bowers nominated Wagner for his second term at the state Democratic convention.[19] Bowers would scarcely be the last editorial writer to try his hand at political speech writing while maintaining his journalistic post. Geoffrey Parsons, chief editorial writer for the *New York Herald Tribune*, for example, drafted the foreign affairs section of Wendell Willkie's 1940 acceptance speech.[20]

Publishers and editorial writers continued to play partisan political roles in the mainstream press, while journalism theorists urged reporters to take a nonpartisan neutral stance. However, many papers committed to a particular political outlook or the interests of a particular group made political advocacy part of their identity from top to bottom. Newspapers that served ethnic or religious communities were partisans on behalf of those communities. Advocacy characterized the subjects that parochial newspapers chose to cover and often the slant they took. Even more than in the mainstream press, publishers, editors, and reporters were often political advocates beyond the pages of their papers. For example, Carter Wesley, editor of the *Houston Informer*, submitted an amicus curiae brief to the Supreme Court in *Nixon v. Condon* (1932), an important case challenging the "white primary."[21] Robert Vann, a lawyer as well as editor and publisher of the *Pittsburgh Courier*, was actively involved in party politics in Pennsylvania, helping to promote the shift of black voters from the party of Lincoln to the party of Franklin Roosevelt—for which he was rewarded with a post in the attorney general's office in FDR's first term.[22]

While publishers, editors, and editorial writers took part in politics, a new set of voices emerged in the world of print—the syndicated political columnists. Originating in the 1920s with the work of David Lawrence, Mark Sullivan, Frank Kent, and Heywood Hale Broun, the political column was by the mid-1930s firmly established. By 1937 Walter Lippmann was syndicated in 155 newspapers, Arthur Brisbane in 180, David Lawrence in 150, and Frank Kent in 125. The *New Republic* observed in 1937 that "much of the influence once attached to the editorial page has passed over to the columnists."[23] Columnists' articles could be selectively dropped, or even altered, by subscribing newspapers, but the columns nonetheless provided new forms of authority within the newspaper.[24] Columnists were political actors as well as political commentators. Ernest K. Lindley, a *New York Herald Tribune* columnist, wrote campaign speeches for Roosevelt in 1932 and remained a close friend of the president while covering him in the White House. Eleanor Roosevelt herself became a columnist in 1935, and her "My Day" column was carried in 140 papers by 1940.[25]

The influence of the columnists was not only in what they wrote but in their central location in a network of Washington insiders. Joseph Alsop, a leading syndicated columnist, was a special case: he was Eleanor Roosevelt's cousin. Alsop, who favored a hard line against Hitler's Germany, sought in 1939 to write a long piece on the making of American foreign policy for the *Saturday Evening Post*, despite that publication's isolationist tendencies. Alsop approached Eleanor, seeking to interview the president for the story. He averred that he was "deeply in accord" with Roosevelt's foreign policy, that he would submit the finished story to Roosevelt before sending it to the editor, and that he would conceal the president's involvement in helping on the story, "for we wish to avoid like the plague any imputation of propaganda."[26] Rejected ultimately by the *Post*, the 30,000 word article was published as a book by Simon and Schuster.[27]

This was a different mode of political interaction—the use of news space or journalistic access to advance the candidacy, career, or policies of favored politicians. Walter Lippmann, the most honored and respected journalist of his day (which extended from the 1920s to the 1960s) operated in this fashion. He told presidential candidate Wendell Willkie in 1940 that his campaign would sink if he adopted a "1936 mentality" and longed for the pre–New Deal days.

Bitterness against the New Deal, Lippmann warned, would position Willkie as a reactionary. (Willkie, as his campaign continued to founder, moved further and further from Lippmann's counsel and Lippmann finally could not support either candidate.)[28]

Lippmann's commitment to an internationalist perspective was well known, so it was not surprising when, in 1940, Lord Lothian, British ambassador to the United States and an old friend, called Lippmann to the embassy and worked out with him a proposal to get around isolationist opposition to aiding the British by advocating a deal to trade destroyers to Britain in exchange for bases in the Western Hemisphere. Lippmann and Ernest Lindley of *Newsweek* urged General John J. Pershing, the octogenarian hero of World War I, to make the case to the public. Lippmann then worked with *Louisville Courier-Journal* editorial writer Herbert Agar to write Pershing's speech. When a reporter at the anti-interventionist *St. Louis Post-Dispatch* learned Lippmann wrote the speech, he threatened to expose what he judged a "plot to get America into the war" (a fair enough description) and to start a congressional investigation. Lippmann scotched this effort with a phone call to *Post-Dispatch* publisher, Joseph Pulitzer II, his summer-place neighbor on Mount Desert Island.[29]

Also in 1940, at the urging of Senator Claude Pepper, Lippmann sat down with presidential aide Benjamin Cohen and a Texas publisher, Charles Marsh, to draft a plan that became the basis for the Lend-Lease bill. Of course, he also endorsed Lend-Lease in his newspaper columns. In 1945 Lippmann and *New York Times* writer James Reston convinced the ambitious Republican senator Arthur Vandenberg that his isolationist leanings would not serve him well if he ever wanted to be president, which he clearly did. The two journalists wrote a speech for Vandenberg that he delivered in the Senate to great acclaim. Reston wrote in the *Times* that the speech was "wise" and "statesmanlike," and Lippmann likewise praised Vandenberg's turnabout in his column.[30]

In the politically tense year of 1940, Wendell Willkie seemed a particularly big draw for journalistic elites, not just Walter Lippmann, but a host of other columnists, editors, and publishers. The managing editor of *Fortune*, Russell "Mitch" Davenport, took a sabbatical to be Willkie's campaign manager and authored the speech nominating him at the Republican convention. Stanley Walker, the veteran *New York Herald Tribune* city editor, was a key figure in Willkie's inner campaign circle. John Cowles, publisher of the *Minneapolis Star*, and his brother Gardner Cowles Jr., publisher of the *Des Moines Register*, invited Willkie to test his appeal in St. Paul. When his speech went over well, the Cowles brothers put their weight behind him.[31] *Herald Tribune* columnist Dorothy Thompson, along with *Herald Tribune* publishers Helen and Ogden Reid, offered Willkie their support. Thompson would defect before the campaign was over, for which defection the Reids ultimately forced Thompson off the paper.[32]

This intimate involvement of columnists and reporters in partisan politics will seem to observers of journalism today to cross a line of propriety. It surely did not seem so to Walter Lippmann, a mandarin of the daily press who probably regarded himself, and certainly was regarded by others, as above the normal rules of the game. For Lippmann, in his position as the preeminent journalistic commentator in the country, giving private advice to public figures was, as his journalist friend Marquis Childs put it, "part of the responsibility that went with his privilege."[33] Childs himself held to the same ethic. General George Marshall discussed with him the pressures he felt to push for a hasty demobilization at the end of the war. According to Childs, Marshall asked for advice and received, not that, but a column urging orderly demobilization.[34]

It is no coincidence that Lippmann, Childs, and others exercised their influence most of all in foreign affairs. In foreign affairs, the expertise of correspondents was an irresistible asset to government officials, and this grew especially in the interwar years. Even before World War I, American reporters in China exercised some influence. According to one dyspeptic critic, they "strutted about as unofficial plenipotentiaries, offering advice—solicited and unsolicited—carrying official messages, negotiating, lobbying, criticizing, applauding and even occasionally writing."[35]

Foreign correspondence became a more significant element in the American press when World War I introduced American readers to the international world. In the 1920s, more newspapers deployed Americans full-time as foreign (meaning European) correspondents, and these men (and several notable women) were "among the few expert observers of international affairs whose information and opinions could be tapped not only by the general public but by American government officials and interested business and other leaders as well."[36] The new standing of the foreign correspondent was marked in journalism by the awarding of the first Pulitzer Prize in that category in 1929 (to Paul Mowrer of the *Chicago Daily News*); the popular recognition of the foreign correspondent was marked by best-selling books by leading correspondents, especially John Gunther's *Inside Europe* (1936), sixth-ranking nonfiction book for the year. Fifth-ranked was the autobiography of Negley Farson, another *Chicago Daily News* foreign correspondent. Gunther and others also made highly successful lecture tours during the 1930s. By the time Alfred Hitchcock made the film *Foreign Correspondent* in 1940, the small corps of correspondents had made a decisive mark on American politics.

Journalists were among those most involved in promoting a more internationalist and interventionist outlook in the years just before World War II. Indeed, this was the moment more than any other when reporters, columnists, editors, and publishers found a cause that overrode any sense of professional neutrality. In 1939 William Allen White of Kansas, the celebrated Republican editor of the *Emporia Gazette*, agreed to chair the Non-Partisan Committee for Peace through Revision of the Neutrality Law; his prominent support for a Democrat-supported measure, especially when he had originally supported the Neutrality Law in 1935, had considerable symbolic significance. Other journalists on the committee included publisher Frank Knox, *Nation* editor Freda Kirchwey, *San Francisco Chronicle* editor Chester Rowell, and *Birmingham News* editor John T. Graves. Henry R. Luce, publisher of *Time, Life*, and *Fortune*, was a major financial supporter of the committee as it set up local units in thirty states, distributed literature, and pressured Congress. When the law was successfully revised, making it easier for the United States to offer aid to Britain, White breathed a sigh of relief. "This was the first time I had ever had hold of a lever that controlled a national current," he wrote. "I had turned the juice on and off in Kansas many times for forty years and knew this switchboard fairly well. But I was so jittery, sitting before the big national switchboard that my mouth was dry and I kept licking my lips most of the time and batting my eyes."[37]

This was only the beginning for White. On 2 June 1940 Francis and Helen Miller convened a group of friends to move America into the war. Francis was an executive of the Council on Foreign Relations, and Helen, Washington correspondent for the *Economist* (London). The group drafted "A Summons to Speak Out" and circulated it among more than one hundred opinion leaders. Thirty finally signed the summons, a call to the nation to go to war. These included Herbert Agar, chief editorial writer of the *Louisville Courier-Journal*; Frank Kent, syndicated columnist from the *Baltimore Sun*; and Walter Millis, author and editorial writer for the *New York Herald Tribune*.

From the "Summons" group emerged an organization called the Century Group (and later the Fight for Freedom), dedicated to intervention in the war in Europe. Among its leaders were Ulric Bell, Washington correspondent for the *Louisville Courier-Journal*. His impressive Washington contacts made him a leading actor in the Century Group's efforts. If Bell was the practical man, Herbert Agar was a leading thinker for the group. He met several times with President Roosevelt in the summer of 1940 on behalf of the Century Group. Also involved were Geoffrey Parsons, chief editorial writer for the *Herald Tribune*; George Fielding Eliot, naval correspondent for the same paper; John Balderston, a journalist, playwright, and — beginning in the summer of 1940 — director of the pro-British "William Allen White News Service," to which the famous journalist had lent his name. Elmer Davis, CBS radio news commentator, and publisher Henry R. Luce were also involved.[38] Columnist Robert S.

Allen later joined in, as did CBS news correspondent Edmond Taylor.[39] Joseph Alsop was recruited to the Century Group at the *Louisville Courier-Journal* suite at the Democratic National Convention in 1940. He made use of his excellent British contacts to provide the Century Group with information on British matériel needs and their prospects for holding off the Nazis.[40]

Objectivity versus Partisanship

American journalists today typically pride themselves on their professional detachment. They proclaim loyalty to the news and to the truth, not to a candidate or a party. This does not mean they are necessarily naive about "objectivity." Indeed, the very idea of objectivity aroused critics almost as soon as it became an articulated ideal. By the 1930s journalists and journalism educators were calling for more interpretive and explanatory reporting, and this critique became more frequent after 1940. In 1948 *New York Times* reporter James Reston told the Associated Press Managing Editors' convention, "You cannot merely report the literal truth. You have to explain it."[41] The famous radio commentator, Elmer Davis, said in 1951, "This striving for objectivity was in its beginnings a good thing; but it went a little too far."[42]

Such criticism notwithstanding, journalists increasingly insisted that they were neutral observers of the battles of partisan politics. Reality proved more complicated. The cultural authority of newspapers derived only in part from the currency of objectivity. It came also from an institution seeking to modernize its authority in a variety of ways, maintaining its own central place in the culture by multiplying and diversifying the voices through which it spoke. Diverse forms of political advocacy, both open and hidden, reached dizzying heights in foreign affairs by 1940 when journalists weighed their commitment to professional norms against their sense of civic obligation and patriotic duty. This, along with the seductive quality of being insiders rather than observers of political change, meant that the call toward professional impartiality was sometimes trumped by other loyalties.

CHAPTER 9

Unruly Servants
Machines, Modernity, and the Printed Page

Megan Benton

"Typography is a servant," thundered eminent designer and artist T. M. Cleland in a 1940 speech aptly titled "Harsh Words." Typography's only job is a self-effacing one, he declared: to make an author's message clear. When instead the look of a printed page impudently calls attention to itself, he scorned, "it is just a bad servant," frolicking with new freedoms it is ill suited to enjoy. Cleland vowed to suppress those unruly and uppity tendencies of modern typography, "to put it in its place and make it behave like a decently trained servant."[1]

Cleland's contempt for splashy type styles and wayward layouts was more than a single man's campaign for tradition and social order. It was among the last great rhetorical blasts in a long struggle to define the role and nature of typography in modern America. The fundamental disagreement concerned the appropriate relationship between a text and its printed presentation, a relationship that many felt reflected the cultural status of the written word itself.

Reverberating throughout the debate, the metaphor of the servant echoed earlier, related misgivings about the impact of radical changes in the technology of printing. With full mechanization by the end of the nineteenth century, the printing industry wrestled with deep anxieties about the relative power of human printers and the new machines with which they worked. Many feared that mechanized production rendered the printed word as lifeless as the machines used to produce it. They worried that yielding typographic prerogatives to the machine would surrender the deeply human essence that kept human language alive on the page. Would human judgments and values control what the machines wrought, or would machine production dictate a new industrial typography featuring technology as the agent of modernity itself? Typographic leader and critic Carl Purington Rollins invoked politically and racially freighted language when he swore that, though he abhorred slavery, he would rather "that the machine should be my slave than my master." For Rollins, a socialist, the struggle to control print technology was a struggle to protect the very freedom and dignity of both typographers and the humanity they sought to preserve in printed form.²

This chapter explores the relationship between printing technology and notions of modernity in book and magazine publishing between 1880 and 1940. In this volatile era of social and cultural change, technology was pivotal in understanding the "modern." For some, welcoming new technologies registered affinity for modernity more broadly. For others, new technologies heightened an alienation from all that modernity encompassed, especially growing commercialism and democratized social and cultural institutions, including print culture. From this ideological tension, two ideologies emerged. One celebrated technology, hailing it as a servant that enabled breathtaking improvements in daily life and work. The other warily monitored technology, regarding it as a servant whose insidious inclination to "take over" must be rigorously held in check. The metaphor of servant and master—fraught with the language of obedience and authority—resonated throughout the struggle between humanistic and industrial values for control over the material and visual form of print in modern America.

Changes in Form, Changes in Content

After three centuries of relatively unchanging technology, the nineteenth-century printing industry witnessed a dizzying succession of transformations. Often, however, technological developments in one part of the production process created bottlenecks elsewhere. Early in the century, for example, new power-driven presses could print far faster than manually operated hand presses. Yet they could rarely be used at top speeds, because printers lacked plentiful supplies of inexpensive paper, which depended upon quantities of increasingly scarce rags. Only after midcentury, when chemicals and high heat were used to reduce wood chips to pulp, could machines in fact generate seemingly endless supplies of cheap paper.

Typesetting and image engraving—both heavily dependent on hand labor—were not mechanized until the 1880s. The relative slowness and expense of typesetting in particular had long limited output. By the end of the century there were more than 1,500 patents for varying gadgets to speed typesetting. Only 2 eventually prevailed, in part because they combined typecasting and typesetting in a single mechanical system.³ As Michael Winship has noted earlier in this volume, Ottmar Mergenthaler's 1884 Linotype machine was followed in 1887 by the Monotype, developed and patented by Tolbert Lanston. Both the Linotype and the Monotype had keyboard operations for assembling matrices, which were then filled with type metal to cast justified lines of type, the Linotype as

FIGURE 9.1. Linotype compositors were at work at the *New York World* in 1909. George Grantham Bain Collection, Prints and Photographs Division, Library of Congress (LC-USZ62-68002).

a single slug and the Monotype as individual letters. Both systems shortened composition time by substituting keyboard strokes for manual type assembly. They eliminated time spent justifying lines and distributing type after it had been printed or stereotyped, and they produced fresh, sharp-edged type for each new composition (figure 9.1).

The second great technological development of the 1880s was halftone engraving, also discussed by Winship, which offered a mechanical means both of making blocks or plates for relief printing and of reproducing continuous-tone images, like photographs. When placed against a sensitized plate and exposed to bright light through a piece of glass marked with a fine grid of crossed lines, a negative image could be preserved on the plate in a network of tiny dots that varied in size according to intensity. The areas of the plate that received no light were then chemically etched away, leaving the exposed areas as a raised surface of dots. From a reading distance the dots blended together to appear toned, as if printed in shades.[4]

By 1890, thanks to mechanical typesetting and halftones, every basic facet of print production could be mechanized. The most immediate consequences were economic. As machines provided cheaper material and required less labor, costs dropped and production rates rose. Publishing historian John Tebbel explains, for example, how the introduction of wood pulp and improvements in papermaking machinery dramatically reduced paper prices in the 1870s and 1880s, producing a flood of cheap books and periodicals. The two basic grades of paper, newsprint and "fine book," dropped from roughly twelve and seventeen cents per pound in 1870 to about three and seven cents per pound by 1889.[5] Prices fluctuated for a variety of reasons, but each time that machinery replaced human hand labor and preindustrial materials, costs and prices were further reduced.

Linotype predominated in newspaper and magazine production, though most book publishers initially preferred Monotype, which allowed some manual fine-tuning. As hand typesetters became familiar with the new equipment, they increased composition speed at least sixfold.[6] One contemporary critic marveled that a full-page halftone of "very fine quality" could be produced in a single afternoon for between $9 and $12, while a wood engraving of the same image would take an artist some three to four weeks to produce, costing the publisher more than $200.[7] The new technologies soon fueled a huge increase in the quantity of printed material, much of it pictorial.

The printed page of the late nineteenth century was thus strikingly different from its predecessor a century earlier. For example, paper made from wood pulp rather than rags tended to disintegrate or cockle when moist; printers thus abandoned their centuries-old practice of dampening paper before printing to increase its pliability and improve the quality of the impression. To remedy the often pale unevenness of printing on dry and sometimes brittle paper, leading American printer Theodore Low De Vinne began coating paper with a thin film of clay.[8] This produced smoother inking and sharper impressions, but it made the paper vaguely slick and glazed, unlike the slightly textured surfaces of paper made by hand from rags.

Similarly, machine-set type was particularly crude in its early years, marred by clumsy and erratic spacing and alignment. A practiced eye could readily distinguish a text composed by hand in foundry types from one composed on the Linotype. Furthermore, the few type styles available for machine composition were widely scorned as "perfunctory" and "mediocre . . . weak and ugly" by most typographic judges.[9] These familiar, commonplace types, known simply as "modern," produced a generic effect. Their serifs were particularly thin and angular, and their forms were light; short ascenders and descenders (the vertical strokes extending above or below the main body of a letter, as in b, d, p, and y) allowed for tighter lines. While scores of new ornamented and decorative display typefaces flourished in the nineteenth century, text typefaces received little design attention. "Modern" types evolved merely as debased copies of the neoclassical types on which they were modeled, types that had been in vogue in Europe at the start of the nineteenth century.

Most striking, halftone reproductions of photographs looked distinctly different from the wood engravings that preceded them, spurring new notions about the role and appearance of images on the printed page. Because photographs offered images that seemed immediate and exact, neither mediated nor interpreted by an artist, they aptly served the informational and timely purposes of newspapers and magazines. Although more halftones began to appear in books after the turn of the century, book illustration witnessed a resurgence of openly interpretive, graphic woodcuts and engravings in the early decades of the century.[10]

The new technologies not only produced printed matter less expensively and more quickly than ever before but also rendered work that was materially and aesthetically new, prompting questions about the consequences of those material differences. Although some unequivocally favored economy over aesthetic considerations, most sensed that progress in production quantity had outpaced or even stifled progress in typographic quality.

Concerns focused first on functional considerations—legibility, durability, and general suitability of form to purpose—but soon became more complicated. Many questioned whether the machines that set the parameters for production speed, volume, and economy should similarly define the aesthetic nature of modern print. Would the traditional humanness of print, emanating from minute variations inherent in preindustrial hand processes, be replaced by a new industrial aesthetic? Should machine-made goods be evaluated by new machine-based criteria of beauty, clarity, and effectiveness? Many responded with adversarial fervor. Carl Rollins remained adamant that "the more we rely on these inhuman machines the less scope we offer to man's soul."[11] Human or machine: which would subordinate the other?

The language of servitude and mastery betrayed troubling ambiguities about hierarchy and control in the world of modern American print. A text's presentation intrinsically determines what is perceived; however slight or seemingly innocent the typographical filter, it subtly shapes the interpretive environment in which readers encounter content. Power over *how* print was produced conferred some measure of control over *what* was produced.[12]

Two Typographies

Evidence of this tacit struggle for control—technological and aesthetic—often appeared on the page itself. Attitudes toward the role of technology in print crystallized into opposing design ideologies that quickly marked the poles of a spectrum on which much of the publishing and typographic community arranged itself throughout the twentieth century.

Advocates of technology celebrated the new ethos of a "machine civilization," arguing that by replacing workers, machines freed humans from difficult, dangerous, or tedious servitude. "Only by perfecting the machine can mankind escape from slavery," declared Thomas Edison in 1926. "Not until we substitute motors for muscles will intellectual progress be possible."[13]

Modernists believed that machine-made goods should reflect the modern technology that produced them. Although they recognized the poor aesthetic quality of most nineteenth-century machine printing, they blamed the conventional preindustrial forms on which it was based rather than the technology itself. The chief tenets of typographic modernism were formulated at the Bauhaus school of design in Germany. Its leading spokesman was the brash and brilliant Jan Tschichold, whose 1928 *Die Neue Typographie* called for a radically new, iconoclastic aesthetic that mirrored key traits of modern industrialization: streamlined speed, simplicity, standardization, precision, economy. New typography, Tschichold announced, "allows us for the first time to meet the demands of our age for purity, clarity, fitness for purpose, and totality."[14]

Proposing a new machine aesthetic, modernists defied traditional typography. Their radically asymmetric layouts shifted white space from the edges to the interior of the page, while the only ornaments were a few bold geometric forms. Modernism's most dramatic effect was its reliance on sans serif types and photographic images; these new visual features signaled modernism's allegiance to purpose and clarity, emphasizing universal, "pure," and precise forms more than individual distinctiveness rooted in subjective notions of beauty inflected by historical and nationalistic values.

Typographic modernism emerged from the acute political, social, and cultural climate of Germany and central Europe between the wars. Because the culture of mainstream publishing and commercial circuits in the United States shared few of those tensions, modernist ideologies rarely resonated with American printers or their clients. Only a few copies of Tschichold's manifesto, displaying the stark typographic reforms he espoused, ever circulated in the United States, and an English translation was not published until 1994. Although the American typographic community was abuzz with modernism's startling design assertions by the 1930s, only a small minority of designers embraced, or even really recognized, modernism's larger claims about the radical new nature and needs of modern life.

Chicago designer and critic Douglas McMurtrie came closest. In 1929 he published *modern typography and layout*, a treatise that modeled the new design it championed (figure 9.2). The following year, McMurtrie argued in *Publishers' Weekly* that modernism offered an astute and empathetic interpretation of twentieth-century life in America as well as in Europe. "The leaders in the modernistic movement in typography have discerned in the modern age the spirit of movement. In this they are absolutely right," he declared. "This is not a contemplative age. We no longer walk through life—we are borne along on vehicles, both spiritual and material. . . . If there is anything that the new typography must express, in order to express the modern age at all, it is motion."[15]

To most American printers and publishers, motion meant progress, not revolution. It evoked the energy of growth and construction; new eras in travel, communication, and urbanization; and rising national preeminence, both political and economic. While European modernism subtly challenged many powerful corporate and government interests (and eventually was suppressed by the Nazis), American typographic modernism—in distinct contrast to its more complex and politically radical literary and artistic cognates—came to embody the entrepreneurial, industrial enterprise underpinning prosperity and progress. European modernists saw the machine as a radical political and social engine; American modernists celebrated machinery as the agent of commercial plenitude and prowess.

Boston printer Jim Clarke urged typographers to convey the motion of progress in their designs. His 1933 article, "Modernism Has Come to Stay: Dump the Classics in the 'Hell-Box,'" proclaimed that "we're living in an Age of Speed, and typography and printing must keep up with this speed or lose their old right to leadership."[16] To illustrate his point, Clarke overhauled his earlier pen-and-ink advertisement for Raymond & Whitcomb, "America's oldest travel company." Resting comfortably upon a center axis, the original ad sported archaic pilcrows, or paragraph markers, and was composed primarily in a decorative antique italic with swash characters, giving the text an air of leisurely, classical refinement.

As a convert to modernism, however, Clarke declared this ad a failure: "It is static, today, and will not get the desired attention." His modern version was laid out asymmetrically on a geometric grid (figure 9.3), featuring a bold mechanically derived typeface. He replaced the earlier advertisement's elegant travelers waiting beside a train with a sleek locomotive hurtling across the page. Clarke insisted that the powerful machine with its suggestions of speed and motion could "do the job" of attracting readers.

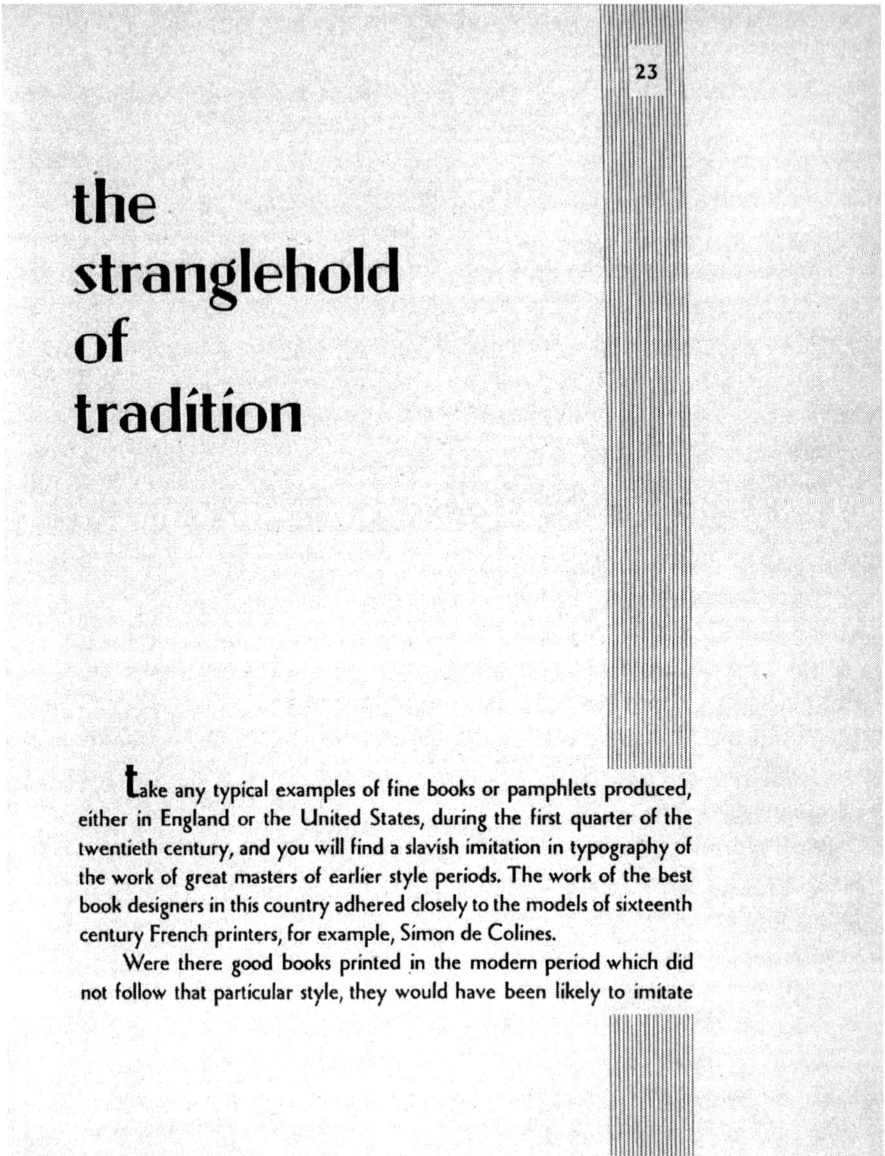

the stranglehold of tradition

take any typical examples of fine books or pamphlets produced, either in England or the United States, during the first quarter of the twentieth century, and you will find a slavish imitation in typography of the work of great masters of earlier style periods. The work of the best book designers in this country adhered closely to the models of sixteenth century French printers, for example, Simon de Colines.

Were there good books printed in the modern period which did not follow that particular style, they would have been likely to imitate

FIGURE 9.2. "the stranglehold of tradition," a chapter opening from Douglas C. McMurtrie's *modern typography and layout* (Chicago: Eyncourt Press, 1929), 23, illustrates the modernist sensibility in typography and design for which he was an advocate. Red ink is used for the vertical line.

Not everyone appreciated the growing centrality of machinery in American life and work, however. Many pointed out that, although machinery arguably "freed" workers from the tedium of their labor, it also eliminated skilled jobs. While hand compositors had been responsible for most design decisions regarding type size and style, line length, use of italics and decorative faces, and so on, by 1894, when nearly 40 percent of the nation's typesetting positions had been eliminated,[17] those who remained became machine operators. Given typographic instructions by supervisors, modern typesetters simply input—keyboarded—the text and ensured that "output"—composed type—was fast and smooth. Rollins complained in 1935 that keeping machines running smoothly diverted printers' attention from the comeliness of design. Typographic values, he asserted, had simply capitulated to the machine's capacities.[18]

Rollins spoke for a loosely defined community of traditionalists who resisted the ascendancy of machinery on both aesthetic and ideological grounds. Influenced by the arts-and-crafts-inflected "private press" movement in England, led by William Morris's Kelmscott Press in the 1890s, traditionalists maintained that only the human hand could produce ideal printing.[19] Although they readily conceded that handcraft production was not feasible for most modern printing needs, they believed that its aesthetic qualities should inspire printers to coax the best possible work from the machines.

The reverence for craft technology spawned a new typographic aesthetic rooted in the primacy of human skill and judgment. The generation's foremost professional printer and typographic expert, Daniel Berkeley Updike, was among the first Americans to heed Morris's call for a rehumanized typography. Working at Houghton Mifflin's prestigious Riverside Press in Boston and then his own Merrymount Press, Updike produced several influential books in Morris's dramatic, archaic style. Even after shedding the heavy medievalism of his English mentor, Updike remained committed to standards of design and production that were humanistic, not mechanistic. Those standards required high-quality, enduring materials and attention to beauty as well as clarity. Updike relied on hand composition well into the 1920s, partly because the faces available for machine composition did not meet his standards. His and others' insistence that the "subtle manipulation" needed for the finest work was possible only by hand spurred significant refinements in machine composition technologies.[20]

Traditionalists' call for printers to reclaim mastery of their tools, including power-driven machinery, meant a new emphasis on design. Before printers could exercise their own typographic judgments and tastes, however, they needed a greater variety of types available for machine composition. In the push for new types, traditionalists not surprisingly turned to the work of great preindustrial European printers for models, reviving both the spirit and the style

Travel with RAYMOND-WHITCOMB

—the oldest *American* travel company

IN 1879 — *when* RUTHERFORD B. HAYES *was president of these United States — and the railroads across the continent were still new — and the few trans-Atlantic steamers still carried clouds of sail —* RAYMOND-WHITCOMB *was founded.*

¶ *In the half century that has followed* RAYMOND-WHITCOMB *has had an important part in making the United States a nation of travelers. Often it has had a pioneer part.*

¶ *There were* RAYMOND-WHITCOMB *tours to California when a trip to the Pacific coast was still an adventure —* RAYMOND-WHITCOMB *tours to Alaska and the National Parks when both were practically unknown —* RAYMOND-WHITCOMB *tours to Europe when to go abroad was front page news.*

¶ RAYMOND-WHITCOMB *ran some of the first pleasure cruises on record. They invented Land Cruises — the most perfect form of travel on land. They perfected independent travel in America, in Europe, and even in South America and the Far East.*

This half century of unrivalled experience is at the service of every traveler who wishes it. Call on the nearest RAYMOND-WHITCOMB office in person, by telephone or by mail.

RAYMOND & WHITCOMB COMPANY

Executive Offices: 145 TREMONT STREET, BOSTON, MASSACHUSETTS

NEW YORK   PHILADELPHIA   CHICAGO   LOS ANGELES   SAN FRANCISCO

I set this several years ago in the classical manner. It is static, today, and will not get the desired attention

FIGURE 9.3. Two advertisements by Jim Clarke offer a comparison between a traditional, symmetrical layout (*above*) and a modernist alternative (*opposite*). A bold typeface and a sleek locomotive suggest a more streamlined pace than the old-fashioned steam engine and waiting top-hatted and crinoline-skirted passengers. Jim Clarke, "Modernism Has Come to Stay: Dump the Classics in the 'Hell-Box,'" *Direct Advertising* 19 (Fall 1933): 25.

TRAVEL

with RAYMOND-WHITCOMB

oldest American travel company

RAYMOND-WHITCOMB was founded in 1879 — when Rutherford B. Hayes was president of the United States — and the railroads across the continent were still new — and the few trans-Atlantic steamers still carried clouds of sail. In the half century that has followed, Raymond-Whitcomb has had an important part in making the United States a nation of travelers. Often it has had a pioneer part.

RAYMOND-WHITCOMB conducted tours to California when a trip to the Pacific coast was still an adventure — Raymond-Whitcomb conducted tours to Alaska and the National Parks when both were practically unknown — Raymond-Whitcomb conducted tours to Europe when to go abroad was front page news.

RAYMOND-WHITCOMB ran some of the first pleasure cruises on record. They invented Land Cruises — the most perfect form of travel on land. They perfected independent travel in America, in Europe, and even in South America and the Far East.

This half century of unrivalled experience is at the service of every traveler who wishes it. Call on the nearest Raymond-Whitcomb office in person, by telephone or by mail.

RAYMOND & WHITCOMB CO.

Executive Offices: 145 Tremont Street, Boston

New York   Philadelphia   Chicago   Los Angeles   San Francisco

I have reset Raymond & Whitcomb ad in the modern manner. It is dynamic and will do the job — Jim Clarke of that work and adapting it for twentieth-century purposes. Amid a flurry of historical research, the era's landmark work of typographic scholarship was Updike's own two-volume *Printing Types: Their History, Forms, and Use: A Study in Survivals* (1922).[21]

The Monotype Corporation led the way in "putting design first," its publicist Beatrice Warde boasted in 1929, issuing "faithful reproductions of the finest typefaces of various definite periods in the history of printing."[22] After roughly a century of relative stagnation in text type design (neglected in the Victorian exuberance for ornamental types), a new generation of artists and typographers launched a virtual renaissance of new typefaces. Most were either inspired by or directly resurrected from the pages of old books cloistered in elite libraries, immortalizing the great printers of the past—Jenson, Aldus, Garamond, Caslon, Baskerville, Bodoni. Revived in the 1920s and 1930s, these typefaces remain the cornerstones of classic typographic style.

By 1930 the unprecedented palette of new types available for machine composition meant ample opportunities for creative style and interpretation, granting printers greater professional responsibility, authority, and privilege. As Warde reassured her readers, "the machine must always be completely dominated by and must be subservient to the individual creative designer."[23]

This dramatic new array of typographic choices left most printers both exhilarated and intimidated. Updike and other traditionalists offered copious guidance on how to work with them effectively and appropriately. One hallmark axiom was to match the spirit of the type and layout with the character of the text to be printed. For "serious" or straightforward texts, which demanded thoughtful reading undistracted by typographic flair or novelty, a calm and familiar look was recommended. Updike insisted that good typography's aim was not to deny the fast-paced character of the modern age (as modernists charged) but to counterbalance it, restoring order, beauty, and peace to the printed page. Modernists "mistake eccentricity for emancipation," he chided in 1937. "We do not want printing to surprise but to soothe us."[24] Exemplifying the point, the sober, traditional typography of his *Printing Types* was as monumental and impeccably dignified as the treatise itself (figure 9.4). Most

FIGURE 9.4. The distinguished Boston printer, typographer, and typographic historian of the late nineteenth and early twentieth centuries Daniel Berkeley Updike was also a highly successful book designer. His advocacy of dignified traditional typography offered American book designers an understanding of the variety of resources available to them. His classic book, based on a series of lectures given at Harvard between 1910 and 1916, was first published in 1922. Title page. Daniel Berkeley Updike, *Printing Types: Their History, Forms, and Use: A Study in Survivals*, 2nd ed. (Cambridge, Mass.: Harvard University Press, 1937). Copyright 1922 by Harvard University Press.

PRINTING TYPES

THEIR HISTORY, FORMS, AND USE

A STUDY IN SURVIVALS

BY

DANIEL BERKELEY UPDIKE

WITH ILLUSTRATIONS

*"Nunca han tenido, ni tienen las artes otros
enemigos que los ignorantes"*

VOLUME I

SECOND EDITION

CAMBRIDGE
HARVARD UNIVERSITY PRESS
LONDON: HUMPHREY MILFORD
OXFORD UNIVERSITY PRESS
1937

twentieth-century American book designers similarly used the new panoply of historically inspired typefaces to safely ground trade book design in pre-Victorian principles of symmetry and balance.

The defining precepts of modernism and traditionalism were thus clearly distinct: modernists sought a radically new typography that would privilege the timeless universal over the particular, while traditionalists strove to reconnect typography to its preindustrial, printer-as-designer heritage. In practice, however, the work of most printers and designers reflected influences of both notions. Just as American modernism signaled prosperity and progress more than revolutionary change, traditional typography was not necessarily staid or conservative, nor was it slavish in its adherence to historical models.

In fact, traditionalists produced much of the era's most fresh and lively typography, in part because they drew from the modernist "look" as readily as from any other model. Paradoxically, the sudden wealth of machine-produced new typefaces enabled *personality* to emerge as traditionalism's chief typographic value; a few designers' styles became as distinctive and marketable as a brand name. Books published by Alfred Knopf, for example, were as admired for their striking design as for their literary merit. Knopf's leading designer, W. A. Dwiggins, brought a deft art deco touch to the books' covers and title pages that was undeniably modern, yet deeply humanistic in its calligraphic flair and use of old-style, serifed letterforms. While the books' texts, often composed in the serifed Caledonia typeface Dwiggins designed, were clearly traditional in their typography, the more commercial elements of cover and title page sported a fresh contemporary feel well suited to the modern literary texts they presented.

Technology and the Masses

A strong link between technology and mass audiences lay at the core of the typographic debate between modernist and traditional values. Mechanized production increased the availability and affordability of print, fueling bold visions of "mass" numbers of readers and potential readers. Even so, expanded print production hardly ensured universal distribution of cheap print. While machines could generate remarkable quantities of low-cost print at unprecedented speeds, doing so was not always pragmatic. Publishing is, after all, a commercial business. Production had to be scaled not to maximum possible output but to likely avenues for distribution and sales. The mass potential of print was thus determined as much by commercial opportunities as by new production capacities.

In general, magazine publishers readily exploited new machine-derived opportunities for expansion, while book publishers were more wary of "cheapening" the perceived nature of their books along with their cost. This divergence was partly pragmatic. As Richard Ohmann describes elsewhere in this volume, magazines could expand their production in ways that books simply could not. The vast circulation of the great "general" magazines that emerged in the 1890s was driven not by subscriptions but by advertising, an economic model that was fundamentally unworkable for books. Except perhaps for the Bible and a few reference or educational texts, books had never been a truly mass commodity. Only the most spectacular best sellers of the nineteenth century had yearly sales that approached some magazines' monthly circulation. Book buyers' consumption patterns were more enigmatic than formulaic; even to publishers, book purchasing seemed erratic and inscrutable. Books offered advertisers none of the lure of the new national-circulation general magazines.

Advertising was also unpopular with many key players in the mainstream American book trade, as Ellen Garvey points out in chapter 10. Anxieties about advertising reflected larger anxieties about books and their relation to mass culture. To many, books represented a set of cultural values that resisted the new ethos of the mass market. For them, books signified leisurely, extended, private intellectual and imaginative engagement with an author's thoughts. Books were to be havens from, not venues for, commercial crowd-forming.

Mass production seemed to threaten the traditional nature of books. Cheap, standardized goods appealing to the widest possible audience, and vigorously promoted as such, struck many as anathema to the life of the mind and the spirit. Fearing that mass-produced books might lead to mass-produced ideas, beliefs, and tastes, they argued that mass production exalted the mediocre and the vulgar. "When a book cost money," a *New York Evening Mail* editorial noted wistfully in 1880, "it was something to be preserved with care, and guarded and cherished as a thing of value." If carelessly made in vast quantities, it is "likely to be regarded like a newspaper—skimmed over and forgotten."

Although many periodicals addressed small specialized clienteles and some book publishers courted huge readerships, for the most part the extent of potential readership differentiated books from magazines. Their respective typographies often reflected this critical interdependence of mass production and commercial scope—the degree of technological "presence" in a publication's visual form registered not only its aesthetic values but its commercial energies. The design of a publication, then, revealed assumptions, or ambitions, about the size and cultural values of its readership.

Broadly speaking, the more a publication courted large audiences, the more it openly embraced machine technology. Eager to embody the spirit and style of modernity, popular magazines showcased the technologies that allowed the latest stories, articles, and advertisements, all copiously illustrated, to arrive at newsstands across America every few weeks. Editors proudly described the new coated papers, Linotype composition, halftone technology, and huge, lightning-fast presses, reassuring readers that their modern magazine was the "full realization of nineteenth-century business and industrial genius."[25]

Popular magazines provided a natural outlet for the peculiarly American modernist typographic theory that crystallized in the 1920s, for they shared its assertions about fast-paced modern life. Visually and textually, magazines shifted from page to page, inviting what Ellen Garvey calls a "moment-by-moment multiple focus."[26] One navigated a magazine by glance and by scan, pausing to read texts that were often brief and fragmented, laced from page to page through an array of images and tableaux of consumer advertisements. This setting epitomized movement and change, providing snapshots of information or interest. Photographs offered a sense of timely, unmediated intimacy with their subjects. Asymmetric arrangements and bold sans serif types were perfect accoutrements: both captured attention as unconventional innovations, and both made it easier to read in short, streamlined bursts. The entire look and feel of magazines aligned them and their readers with the latest forms of social, cultural, and technological progress, with all that was new and modern in American lives.

If modernist typography found its natural venue in popular magazines, with their emphasis on the ever-changing contemporary pulse of a wide reading public, at the other end of the spectrum traditionalism served the relatively serious and timeless needs of the smaller community of book readers. Most book pages were designed to offer a restful retreat from the bustling pace of modernity. Traditional typographic values of mainstream twentieth-century book publishing sought to efface any hint of modern technology in the look of the page. As Warde famously declared in 1932, typography *to be read* should strive to be as "invisible" as the finest crystal goblet.[27] Shaping books in explicit contrast to magazines, traditionalist typography sought to create a quiet, undisturbed communion between reader and author in an environment of classical conventions ostensibly rendered transparent by centuries of familiarity.

Whose Servant? Producers or Consumers

The struggle over whether technology should be showcased or subordinated revealed not only a tension between the producers of books and the producers of magazines but a potential gulf between the producers of books—authors, publishers, printers—and their readers. Technological changes highlighted the broader question of whose interests typography should serve. The answers evoked vague but unsettling notions of cultural hierarchy. In traditionalist book design, the ethic of invisibility meant that typography was expected to accede to the authority of the text. Good design, wrote critic Paul Johnston, must "invite" readers into a text, create a comfortable atmosphere into which they might settle, then, "like a toastmaster who has introduced a speaker, take a back seat."[28] Good book design aimed to privilege not merely a particular author's message but the larger cultural prerogatives of the book itself.

Transparency, though, was not innate to traditional design. Preindustrial typefaces resurrected from rare books were hardly "invisible" to untrained twentieth-century eyes. By restoring historically informed elegance and decorum to the printed page, traditionalists subtly reinforced a sense of typographic etiquette intended to discipline and instruct readers as much as to enrich their experience. Adopting an elite and historicized publishing practice, Knopf's books, for example, concluded with a colophon, or statement describing particulars of design and production, to foster knowledgeable appreciation of the text type's history. Traditional design was neither invisible nor disinterested; it taught readers to approach texts with new codes of deferential respect. Like protocols for visiting an art museum or attending an opera, traditional typography urged readers to redignify, and at times even sacralize, the cultural experience of reading a book.[29]

Mistrustful of the cultural and aesthetic values of mass production, book typography generally resisted modern commercial tendencies to "capitulate" to popular tastes. Such tendencies were epitomized by the growing prominence of images in magazines. As early as 1893, shortly after halftone technology had spurred the growth in printed imagery, one writer scorned that the masses' "growing aversion to reading and increasing fondness for labor-saving and thought-saving graphic representation" signaled not the march of progress but a "reversion to barbarism." The ancient belief that images promote illiteracy and ignorance was reiterated in 1938 in an essay by J. L. Brown contemptuously titled "Picture Magazines and Morons." "Since the majority won't or can't read," Brown asserted, pictures sated their basest appetites. "Hordes of people who never ruffle the pages of a book devour with fierce interest the pictures of sex and death which the tabloids print as news."[30]

Books, however, fostered leisurely, immersed, and thoughtful reading, not quick, fragmented perusal of ideas or information. In mainstream book typography, interference with the reader's full engagement was usually construed as inappropriate, inept, or, worse, subversive. Although illustrations featured heavily in reference texts and deluxe editions, they usually appeared in more general books only as occasional vignettes. Such illustrations were more typically drawings or engravings—both because they imparted an artistic, handcrafted allure and because they did not require the coated papers strongly associated with magazines and halftone photography. Halftone photographs were used most frequently in textbooks, scientific works, and nonfiction "coffee table" books.

In contrast, magazines constructed themselves as the reader's sympathetic servant. They developed what Ohmann describes as "affectionate, personal, you-directed prose," transporting readers into an important and exciting world of things they wanted and needed to know about. As Frank Munsey suggested in 1897, even advertising "served" readers by helping to "keep readers in touch with progress." Only through such advertisements could readers keep pace with "this age of invention, of mechanical perfection."[31]

Magazines' willingness to cater to readers' ostensible demands was underscored typographically. They moved to the modern cultural beat, but never left their readers behind, tempering their march to accommodate the pace of readers. In 1930, for example, *Vanity Fair* reverted to using initial capital letters in headings after experimenting for five issues without them. While modern typography was "compulsory for any magazine that pretends at all to a place in the modern parade," the editors conceded that the magazine should press no innovation until readers could appreciate it. In typography as elsewhere, *Vanity Fair* remained readers' "very obedient servant."[32]

Like its contemporaries, *Vanity Fair* promoted a modernism that signaled more than popular fashion. Asymmetric layouts, bold streamlined typefaces, and abundant photography tacitly hailed the triumph of a dynamic, new, uniquely twentieth-century style. Lowercase composition was particularly emblematic of this subtly antiauthoritarian stance. When writer Ford Madox Ford's literary magazine, *the transatlantic review*, dropped capital letters in its name to underscore its modernist values, indignant members of a local ladies' club burned copies featuring the new design. "They took it to be equivalent to advocating the decapitation of monarchs," he wryly concluded.[33] For *Vanity Fair*, *the transatlantic review*, and other publications, modernist typography positioned them as fresh, forward-looking alternatives to traditional cultural hierarchies.

Such vague impudence—breaking rules to declare them irrelevant—infuriated traditionalists like Tom Cleland, whose 1940 "Harsh Words" declared that modernist typography is about as "new as the neu in neurosis." "The order of the day, it seems, is disorder."[34] Cleland's words were harsh because he knew that modernism was as engrained in American typography as the indelible commercialism of print culture itself. He understood that the real tension had been less between modernist and traditional aesthetic ideologies than between the commercial and the cultural environments, and their attendant associations with popular and elite audiences.[35]

By 1940 mechanized production was no longer the issue in typography; machines produced both styles with equal aplomb. Inextricably linked to the thriving commercial world through which modern America navigated, most magazines were readily defined by that world, in form as clearly as in content. Book publishers faced a trickier negotiation. They were engaged in a commercial business of selling products that offered ostensible refuge—or at least a few moments' pause—from that fast-paced modern commercial climate. They resolved the paradox through a combination of typographic compromise and rhetorical finesse. Mirroring the doubleness of books' nature, the typography of text typically remained soberly conventional, rooted in traditional principles of "invisible" deference to the authority of content. To ensure that those texts would survive as a modern commodity, though, publishers literally wrapped them in a cover or jacket usually designed to be as visible and alluring as possible. Spanning the entire typographic spectrum, from ultramodern to deeply archaic, designs of those public elements were often blithely unconnected to the books' interior design. Thus, a book's exterior design strove to thrust it into the bustling marketplace, while its interior typography sought to anchor it in an environment of calm timelessness.

. . .

In sum, by the end of the nineteenth century, the fully mechanized production of print affected not only the price and plenitude of printed matter but also its material and visual form. Such aesthetic changes subtly but significantly also altered the role and cultural nature of print. Technological breakthroughs enabled the production of new materials and styles for both types and images, rendering design an interpretive tool and intensifying the emblematic function of print. As the twentieth century progressed, and both the book and magazine publishing industries settled into recognizably modern patterns, production and design developed a palette of typographic styles that reflect a spectrum of cultural tastes and values. Those styles have become part of what we read when we encounter a printed book or magazine.

CHAPTER 10

Ambivalent Advertising
Books, Prestige, and the Circulation of Publicity

Ellen Gruber Garvey

When publishers advertised, they generally had one of two goals. They could reach out to sell books to the many who rarely or never bought them. Or they could market particular books to the minuscule number of Americans who regularly purchased hardbound books. Until the 1920s, the old-line publishers largely targeted existing readerships and the bookshops that supplied them. Other publishers, including those specializing in cheap reprints, pirated editions, and popular formula fiction, reached out to patrons of newsstands and stationery stores, and tried mail-order campaigns and subscription sales.

Reprint and mail-order publishers certainly supplied books to more Americans than bookstores, but their readers were considered culturally marginal by the taste makers and gatekeepers who read the elite magazines and circulated judgments on contemporary literary standards. Yet different publishing strategies were sometimes used for the same titles—either because different publishers pirated the same English editions, or because cheap publishers reprinted works of old-line publishers. Thus, the value of more expensive books did not rest merely on their texts.

As Richard Ohmann's article in this volume explains, the old-line publishers traded in cultural clout and works of individual genius, while the cheap edition purveyors sold entertainment to the masses. When they used advertising, old-line publishers asserted the superiority of their books over the works available on newsstands, tried to consolidate their reputation, and attempted to defend higher prices as a symbol of value.

Prestige and Books' Peculiar Relationship to Advertising

Advertising became increasingly significant and visible in the United States from the 1890s on, as manufacturers sought national markets for their goods, as new kinds of goods came on the market, and as new promotional media such as advertising-dependent magazines, billboards, and eventually radio increased in prominence. While newsstand and mail-order publishers used posters and mass-circulation magazine ads, old-line publishers eschewed these new forms and techniques for two reasons. First, the established publishers believed that marketing books amid products like soap (a favorite comparison) would destroy books' prestige. Second, significant differences in the way books and the new mass-produced goods were manufactured, distributed, and sold meant that, while advertising a book could increase its sale, it might also cut too deeply into its profit margin to be worthwhile.

Discussion of how and whether to advertise books turned on an unstated question: what *is* a book? Is it the physical object, whether a saddle-stitched pamphlet or bound in expensive leather or cloth? Or is it the text in whatever form it takes? Is it the subject matter that the text "contains"? Is it the literary qualities that might be addressed in a review? Is it the entertainment or education that the book supplies? Or is it the emotions and sensations felt by the reader? And where did this prestige that publishers valued reside? Would it be destroyed if the book were marketed to the wrong people?

The answers to these questions shifted over time. Trade publishers initially seemed to agree that they were selling the object: the printed text, its binding, and illustrations. For later publishers, the physical book became secondary to its impact, the access it offered to different or heightened emotional states. Publishers also asserted that reading their books would make book buyers successful by allowing them to participate intelligently in important discussions of the day.

Before the early twentieth century, old-line publishers advertised little. Without the protection of an international copyright law, many believed that advertising was not profitable, for other publishers could simply step in and reap the rewards.[1] Even after the International Copyright Act of 1891, resistance to advertising continued. Given the difference between books and other goods, publishers wondered whether advertising was useless or even harmful. As Walter Hines Page of Doubleday and Page noted, "The book is a commodity. Yet the moment it is treated as a mere commodity it takes severe revenge on its author and its publisher."[2] Too frankly acknowledging commodity status threatened the prestige that old-line publishers considered essential to success. Prestige could not be bought outright; it could only be traded or invested for greater prestige. If accompanied by prestige, however, money invested in promotion could increase both cash and cachet, which could be rolled over into future profits and cultural influence for the author and the publisher. Bold advertising announced the commodity status of a book, an attempt to produce money with money. Prestige differentiated the products of old-line publishers from the cheap editions, reprints, and pirated works of publishers who advertised in posters, eye-catching window displays, and newspaper ads.

A Natural Circle of Readers

For the most part, before the 1920s, the restrained advertising of old-line publishers reflected both their prestige and their belief in the natural limits of book readership. Henry Houghton of Houghton Mifflin, for example, thought the real work of publicity was complete "when knowledge of a book was brought immediately to the attention of the person who might naturally be interested." Such publishers advertised merely by collecting names of probable book buyers and by placing subdued notices of renowned authors' new books or related works inside other books or in any magazines that the publisher controlled. Specialized catalogs, carefully classified publication lists, and book reviews provided exposure for their books.[3] Old-line publishers shaped book reviews through their ownership of flagship magazines, generating publicity indirectly. Magazines, in turn, established the conventions for book reviewing in newspapers and other magazines. Thus, reviews were restricted to works available in bookstores. (This convention remained in place well into the twentieth century, with the *New York Times Book Review*, for example, rarely reviewing paperback originals that were typically sold in venues other than bookstores.) The "natural circle" of readers was bounded by class, taste, and education and excluded the buyers of cheap reprints.

The concept of a natural circle of readers also reflected the sense of community shared by old-line publishers and the buyers of their books. This community granted publishers the authority to judge manuscripts, while the readers' supposed unwillingness to respond to advertising demonstrated their own discernment. J. B. and George Haven Putnam declared that "no amount of advertising" could help a book that had received only fair reviews or had not attracted attention on its own. Books could not "be crammed down the throat of the public like Mrs. Winslow's Soothing Syrup."[4] When ads generated greater sales, to old-line publishers it meant that people beyond the "natural" community of book readers had entered the gate. When hard-cover best sellers and extensive advertising became more important, these publishers chafed at serving those beyond their gated community.

Old-line publishers maintained that books *were* different from other commodities, as Richard Ohmann points out. They continually compared advertising each title separately to a soap company producing and promoting an entirely new product each week. Old-line publishers believed that each work was unique; its handcrafted distinctiveness was part of its attraction. But no publisher could profitably advertise each title. Less genteel publishers whose product was more standardized could promote multiple works of a prolific writer like Horatio Alger in a single ad or develop sets of books like the Seaside Library, the Library of Popular Fiction, or Beadle and Adams' Half Dime Library, and thus avoid the waste of advertising single titles.[5] Mail-order book outfits similarly relied on advertising to sell books by the shelf. In the 1920s publishers like E. Haldeman-Julius standardized production and offered lists of works like his Little Blue Books to be bought cheaply in bulk. Subscription publishers supported the efforts of their traveling salespeople with advertising leaflets and broadsides as well. Beginning in 1926 book clubs provided a reliable monthly source of entertainment and education. For old-line publishers, however, each new title remained a new product.

Book distribution was also different for old-line publishers. Soap manufacturers advertising their products in the new world of the 1890s knew that consumers inspired by their ads could buy a bar in a nearby store—no correspondence or orders were necessary. But there were far fewer bookstores than grocery stores, and many readers lived far from them. Trade publishers therefore advertised their firms' addresses for direct sales decades longer than did other industries. Emphasizing mail-order sales too strongly, however, risked antagonizing the retailers on whom they depended. Books could not, in other words, be easily treated as nationally distributed products like soap.

The Ad and Its Audiences

Until 1920 or so, old-line publishers advertised trade books—fiction and general nonfiction sold in retail stores—with restrained announcements, perhaps quoting from a review or an endorsement. Their primary function was to encode information for several key audiences. Publishers such as Scribner's and Harper's both published magazines, which they used to inform potential buyers of their newly published books, described as for sale by booksellers or by mail order. That the book was advertised alerted booksellers that the publisher considered the book important and so should be stocked (figure 10.1). Such ads also addressed writers. Walter Hines Page asserted in 1905 that "much book advertising is done not with much hope of selling the book, but chiefly to impress writers with the publisher's energy and generosity."[6] Given the narrow parameters of the traditional publishing scene, the author's friends were likely to be among the "natural circle" of book buyers. Upon viewing ads like those in *Scribner's*, these readers might reassure authors of their books' publicity. Ideally, the soothed authors would then remain with their publishers, who would be thus assured of additional books with increasing sales. Presumably, such publicity would encourage other authors to sign up with a publisher who had a reputation as an advertiser.

These ads also addressed other publishers, thereby protecting and enhancing

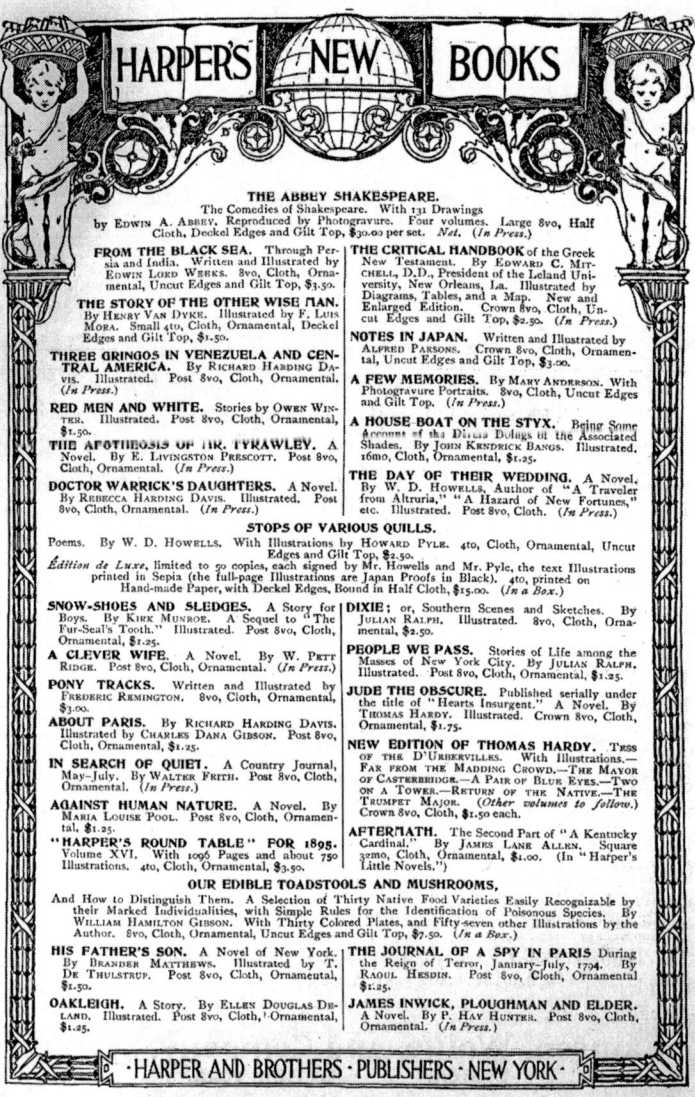

FIGURE 10.1. Publishers, including Scribner's and Harper's, published magazines such as Dodd, Mead's *Bookman*, offering a venue for extensive advertisements for newly published books in addition to literary articles and poetry. "Harper's New Books," *Bookman* 2, no. 6 (February 1896): iii. American Antiquarian Society.

the publisher's professional reputation. Advertising demonstrated a publisher's prosperity and staked out its presence in the select community that advertised in elite magazines. This inner circle of publishers and the ring of authors around them were the primary audiences for the cultivation and display of what was sometimes known as reputation, sometimes goodwill, but usually described in more hushed and reverent terms. As one publisher explained in 1913, "Though it is an axiom that few books are bought because of their imprint, nevertheless a house's sales involve mysteriously but importantly the very tissue and repute of the house. . . . [G]ood will . . . has many times more reality in publishing than in most other businesses. Next to its list, this mysterious quality is by far the publisher's most precious possession."[7]

"Good will" was more precious in relationships with other publishers and authors than in direct retail sales. It differentiated the old-line publishers' product from that of reprint houses and pirates. Even after the new copyright regulations diminished piracy, and therefore reduced the need for "trade courtesy"—respecting one another's investment in a book—this concept remained important to older houses. Trade courtesy protected each firm's investment by preventing other publishers from poaching on their authors and thus also limited pay to authors. This gentlemanly stance worked only if supported by publishers whose interests were aligned as members of a community upholding these practices for one another's good. The nineteenth-century publishing industry was famously clubby. Publishers socialized with one another, even literally sharing in a loving cup engraved with the names of Harper, Scribner, Holt, and Putnam.[8]

This sense of community is reflected in *Publishers' Weekly*, the industry trade journal addressed chiefly to booksellers. Its nineteenth-century ads, in which the industry reinforced and recirculated its self-image, closely resembled restrained book ads in elite magazines. By contrast, the several trade magazines addressed to news dealers are far wilder. Full-page ads contained enticing pictures of dime-novelist Laura Jean Libbey (figure 10.2). Others offered product tie-ins such as cigars, chewing tobacco, and soft drinks named after books. An 1894 ad was headed "Chew, Read, Smoke, or Drink 'Sweet Silence'" and promised, "Every news-dealer can make big money and increase their trade by handling it." Such an ad would have been inconceivable in *Publishers' Weekly* of the same decade.[9]

Restrained advertising visually depicted publishers' commitment to the meaning and worth of books. The publishing industry even developed terminology to distinguish itself from other industries. Publishers' trade symbols, for instance, in use since the mid-nineteenth century, were not called "trademarks" or "logos," but "colophons." Their advertising departments were often called

FIGURE 10.2. A trade journal advertisement for *Lovers Once but Strangers Now* is illustrated with a photograph of a sultry Laura Jean Libbey, author of some eighty novels. *American Bookseller*, 15 September 1890, 217. American Antiquarian Society.

"sales promotion" or "publicity" departments. Even the cozy term "house" seemed less commercially oriented than "company."

Nineteenth-century advertisements also addressed serious book buyers. Detailing specialized minutiae—12mo or 8vo, morocco or half calf—evoked a community of book connoisseurs. Even those who could not understand these terms were assured the assistance of capable publishing houses in selecting books as enduring objects. This reverential focus on the book's binding, size, and type is a telling reminder that nineteenth-century trade publishers were advertising first and foremost the physical book. It further highlighted the contrast between the products of the old-line houses and the cheap paper-covered reprints and libraries of the more commercial houses.

Booksellers were likely to favor books issued by reputable firms. However, a house's reputation rarely influenced readers directly, for few noticed who published what titles. The cultivation of reputations did not create a brand name, except for those readers who occupied significant gate-keeping roles as critics, academics, and librarians. A strong reputation among academics, however, did benefit other, often more profitable parts of the firm's business. A textbook salesman for Harcourt Brace noted that his young company's "image of success, compounded of Sinclair Lewis' *Main Street* . . . Lytton Strachey['s] . . . *Eminent Victorians* and *Queen Victoria*, and E. M. Forster's . . . *Passage to India* . . . meant that a salesman who walked into the office of a college teacher of literature or history or other humanity and said he was from Harcourt Brace found a ready hearing and a favorable attitude."[10]

The publisher's name might also signal its link to its flagship magazine and that magazine's own publicity. Magazines were less restrained in promoting themselves and their contents, and publicity spilled over to books. As Ohmann argues in this volume, magazines issued by book publishers were initially intended to support and fuel the book business by enticing authors with increased publishing opportunities and by publicizing the house's achievements to readers.

Publication of fiction in magazines bolstered an author's reputation and book sales. An 1890s ad might remind readers that a book offered stories or a novel they had read in the magazine. Although publishers often feared that cheap book editions of works would cut into the sale of more expensive ones, they found that serialization increased rather than stifled sales, inspiring readers to purchase a complete copy in permanent form. The book condensations in *Reader's Digest* that began in the 1930s similarly publicized and generated best sellers.[11] Although from the 1880s on general magazines increasingly competed with books for readers' money and leisure time, publication of a specific work within a magazine stimulated its sale as a book. The book form itself was apparently important to many readers.

The New Print Media and the Ad Boom

Changes in other print media in the 1890s both challenged publishers' sales strategies and showed them how to reach new markets. Earlier tactics merely increased awareness of a new book among its natural audience. From the exponential growth of magazines and their subscription lists in the 1890s publishers realized that middle-class readership was not as finite as they had supposed. Readership evidently responded to prices and publicity. Although the new print media dwarfed book sales, they inspired publishers to reconceptualize their wares. New publishers experimented with larger advertising investments, trying out poster campaigns and advertisements in mass-circulation publications. More conservative, established publishers also dabbled in new approaches to advertising.

Mass-market magazines and newspapers guided readers in negotiating middle-class life. They became a mechanism for circulating information and expertise. Publishers learned both to feed information to the system and to draw publicity from it. In response to the new media's focus on timeliness and topicality, publishers used public relations techniques to market books as subject matter. Increasingly advertising their gate-keeping expertise rather than their books' physical qualities, they emphasized how essential their books were for participating in the important conversations of the day.

Book publishers' interactions with the new print media took varied forms. Authors were treated as celebrities in small-circulation literary magazines—among them the *Critic* (initially independent but published in the 1900s by Putnam) and the *Bookman* (Dodd, Mead)—and in columns in the new large-circulation magazines unconnected to the book industry such as *Munsey's*. These developing circuits of publicity reflected the media's interest in itself. They featured literary gossip about authors, their books, sources, publication plans, and monetary success. Mass-circulation magazines like *Ladies' Home Journal* publicized the royalties received by their authors, thereby kindling interest in both the magazine and the book with its insider knowledge. Publishers learned that awareness of a book could increase sales, and thus sought to buy such notice directly through advertising.

The advertising boom itself was initiated by several new publishers outside of the traditional centers of publishing. They often had roots in the stationery trade. In 1898 Bowen-Merrill (later Bobbs-Merrill) of Indianapolis bought full-page ads for *When Knighthood Was in Flower* and then *Alice of Old Vincennes*, both promoting the books and boasting of their considerable sales. Bowen-Merrill ran ads in metropolitan dailies and small local papers around the country but also utilized old-line book routes by advertising in the literary magazines.[12]

New approaches to advertising enabled new and smaller firms to compete with old-line publishers for space in bookstores, the front line of book sales. Old-line publishers responded with new efforts to target confirmed book buyers and recruit suitable new buyers. Some strategies underscored reputation and dignity. For instance, when old-line publishers tried placing prestige-enhancing artistic posters in bookstores, they were such aesthetic successes that they were swept off by collectors or put aside by clerks for favorite customers. Thus they were of little use as advertising.[13] Publishers eventually supplied bookstores with less overtly artistic posters for window and in-store use.

Within the bookstore, certain aspects of the physical book itself functioned as sales aids. The printed cloth cover of the 1890s and the even more colorful dust jacket of the 1900s and 1910s increased visual appeal. Dust jackets added blurbs and endorsements from advance reviews but were criticized for imposing advertising on the customer and interfering with the enduring value of the book. Thus, while jackets' posterlike appeal made them attractive to booksellers, many readers as well as libraries automatically removed and discarded the jackets for decades. Nonetheless, pressure to compete with other colorful books in the store meant that nearly all publishers soon issued dust jackets. Conventions of jacket art and later paperback covers soon ensured that readers could tell a good deal about a book from its cover.

New publishers moved posters beyond in-store display. At least one stationer-turned-publisher, Caro M. Clark, took to billboards, selling a quarter of a million copies of the tedious, folksy novel *Quincy Adams Sawyer* on the strength of the campaign. A bill posters' trade journal noted with satisfaction that posters had been crucial to the novel's success, for the book had neither the backing of an old and reliable house nor an author's popularity to recommend it to the reading public.[14]

Older publishers eschewed the shortcuts inherent in these new advertising methods. Walter Hines Page complained that a writer "writes a story (let us call it a story, though it be a mild mush of mustard, warranted to redden the faded cheeks of sickly sentimentality) which, for some reason that nobody can explain, has the same possibility of popularity as Salvation Soap. A saponaceous publisher puts it out; he advertises it in his soapy way; people buy it—sometimes 200–300,000 of them." The success of such works compelled publishers to gamble on promoting similar works.[15] Even Clark ultimately conceded that, despite her success, book publishing was a very chancy business.

The flash-in-the-pan success of books like *Quincy Adams Sawyer* deepened the older publishers' dislike of broad advertising. Such successes undermined their belief in the natural development of literary reputation, founded on the renown of good publishing houses, the recognition of literary standards, and

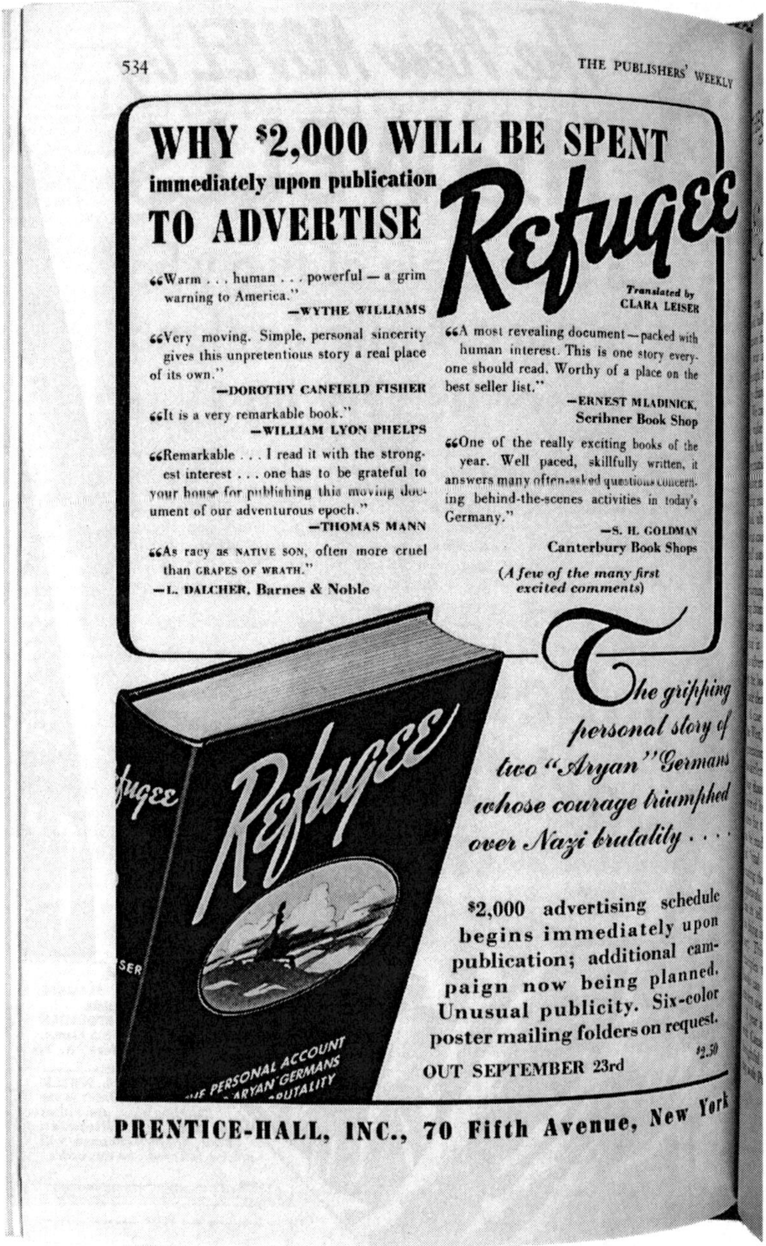

FIGURE 10.3. Prentice-Hall's advertisement for *Refugee* in *Publishers' Weekly* 130 (24 August 1940): 534 illustrated the book and trumpeted the timeliness of the story. Comparable to other publishers' advertisements to the trade, it announced the amount of money to be spent on the advertising campaign launched on behalf of the book. American Antiquarian Society.

FIGURE 10.4. A poster advertising John Ford's film of John Steinbeck's *The Grapes of Wrath* gestured toward the book by naming the author and including an illustration of the book with its dust jacket. Photograph by Rudolf Burckhardt, used by permission of the Estate of Rudy Burkhardt; *The Grapes of Wrath* © 1940 by Twentieth Century Fox. All rights reserved.

the existence of a small circle of readers tutored in tastes like their own. Nonetheless, the boom whetted appetites for greater sales even among old-line publishers, which now competed more directly with the new publishers than with dime-novel and reprint newsstand sales. Thus, established publishers increased their advertising budgets in the early twentieth century, discovering that heavy advertising of individual titles increased their *sales* tremendously, though often not their profits, given the high cost of single-title advertising (figure 10.3).

New media far outsold books and magazines in the early twentieth century but opened publicity possibilities for individual titles. Hollywood boosted sales of works that had been adapted for film by advertising the title itself with more extensive and expensive campaigns than any book publisher could attempt. Movie posters often borrowed the prestige of the physical book by including an inset of the book's cover, further promoting that image (figure 10.4). Bookstore displays then borrowed the glamour of the movies, linking books, movies, and movie stars. Radio also significantly shifted the marketing emphasis from books as handsome objects to books as producers of emotion or as contact with attractive personalities.

Mail-Order Books and Marketing Emotion

Mail-order bookselling, however, was the strategy that first sold the reading experience and its transformative qualities rather than the book as an object. In this, mail-order companies learned from the advertising of other commodities, avoiding the problems of single-book advertising by selling sets, whether of a single author's works or varied titles offered in a uniform binding, and issued in installments. Initially, advertising for sets echoed earlier prestige marketing of the book as physical object, but they also invited readers to join the bandwagon of readers by touting the number of sets sold. Mail-order advertisers did not assume that their readers were already part of a book-buying coterie; thus, they eschewed the limited old-line magazines and took double-page spreads in the *Saturday Evening Post* and other high-circulation magazines. Coupon response and test ads taught these publishers that a focus on the book as object was not the most successful strategy. As a result, they moved on to other angles.

Some mail-order book ads appealed to the reader's desire for education or achievement. From 1909 through the 1920s, promotion of Collier's Harvard Classics, also known as Charles W. Eliot's Five-Foot Shelf of Books, foregrounded a reader's potential benefits from owning and reading the books. Indeed, the ads stressed that the collection could furnish a liberal education (figure 10.5).[16]

Other ads invited personal identification and emotional connection to books.[17] Helen Woodward, a mail-order copywriter, reported that when ads promoting O. Henry's literary qualities or number of sets sold failed to attract buyers to a 1913 collection of his works, she touted instead the affective experience the reader could expect from the stories. Her most successful advertisement showed a girl with tears running down her face seated on a pile of books, looking at a photograph. The caption was "Finish This Story for Yourself." Woodward explained that, "As briefly as possible I gave a little outline of the beginning of a story, arousing the reader's curiosity as to how it ended."[18]

Such a sample of style and plot had helped magazine serializations and story publications succeed before in promoting books, but Woodward's ads combined a "to-be-continued" line with a picture that merged the story's heroine with a deeply moved reader. This approach, which Woodward called using "human interest" to sell books, established a personal connection with the reader. One of her O. Henry ads failed when it was headed "After Twenty Years," but succeeded when it was titled "If This Happened on Your Wedding Night."[19] De-

FIGURE 10.5. Advertisement for "Dr. Eliot's Five-Foot Shelf of Books, The Harvard Classics," inviting readers to acquire the fifty-volume set of books selected by Harvard president Charles Eliot to provide a thorough, liberal education. The bindings bear the Harvard seal. *Collier's Magazine*, 28 May 1910, 35.

spite the power of an affective appeal, trade book publishers were slow to adopt it. The new, overtly commercial Simon and Schuster, however, enthusiastically embraced it in the 1920s, in what was mocked as its "windswept" copy.

Best Sellers

The initial advertising boom in trade publishing around 1900, though brief, initiated a lasting expansion of newspaper coverage of books, as book review sections and supplements gained prominence. After a halting beginning in 1896, the *New York Times Saturday Review of Literature*, for example, expanded and became a Sunday supplement in 1911. Some newspapers claimed that the book supplements were not profitable themselves but were useful because they attracted upper-middle-class readers coveted by other advertisers. Book reviews and book advertising were attractive enough to newspapers that a syndicate founded in 1912 supplied book reviews and sketches of literary figures to newspapers around the country, with the advertising end of the business managed by Sinclair Lewis.[20] These new publications suggested that readers should know what everyone else was reading. Promulgating the sense that everyone was reading a book became an important selling technique. After printed dust jackets became standard in the 1910s, publishers would sometimes offer booksellers extra jackets of a particular title to wrap around other similarly sized books; displays thus created the illusion that the bookstore had stocked hundreds of copies of the title being promoted.

The best-seller list further broadcast those claims. The list began in the United States in the 1895 American version of *Bookman* magazine, mirroring the London *Bookman*'s practice of running such a list, compiled from reports of bookstores—but not newsstands—in sixteen cities.[21] *Publishers' Weekly*, the *New York Times Book Review*, and others soon developed their own best-seller lists. Even if customers did not use the best-seller roster as their shopping list, booksellers heavily stocked and prominently displayed the listed titles. These books could be confidently recommended, and such recommendations influenced buyers. Therefore booksellers who reported their sales to the *Bookman*, *Publishers' Weekly*, or the *New York Times* had an incentive to distort their reports to get rid of overstock.[22] Despite long-standing criticism of their inaccuracies, the lists remained popular with editors and publishers in part because they provided a sure source of advertising copy.

The best-seller lists, like other publishing institutions, drew lines demarcating cultural influence. They raised some categories of books to cultural visibility and importance, promoting them in conversation while rendering others invisible. The lists generally excluded reprints and staple sellers such as dictionaries, the Bible, and cookbooks. They excluded textbooks sold in bookstores, which might have had a significantly larger sale than trade books over time, and they entirely ignored mail-order and book club sales. Thus, they defined a narrow field of books as worthy of literary discussion. The lists' focus on sales within a short period served the era's interest in timeliness. Consistent with a focus on "print in motion," lists of the year's best sellers simply compounded the monthly lists, rather than announcing which books had sold the most copies in a year or longer.

Lists alerted booksellers that particular titles were likely to be in demand, and thereby helped to create that demand. In his 1930-31 report for the National Association of Book Publishers, O. H. Cheney complained of the "spell" of bestsellerdom that the book industry was under. "[T]he phrase is, of course, a tribute to the theory that book buyers are sheep. . . . The belief on which best-sellerism is based is that a book buyer, as soon as he is told that a book is a best-seller, will immediately want to join the thousands—or hundreds of thousands—of the inner circle of readers of the book." Declaring a book a best seller increased word-of-mouth advertising as well: "As soon as everybody thinks that everybody else has read it—or should read it—a best-seller gets talked about—and talk leads to the ringing of the cash register," groused Cheney.[23] Readers were anxious to keep up with others and develop the necessary cultural expertise to succeed in a nation with an increasingly rapid flow of information. Although best-seller lists inspired much talk among culture critics about the degradations of mere popularity, they became a new form of gate keeping, facilitating a book's entry into desirable conversation.

Public Relations

Public relations experts developed complex synergies among different media and further redefined the book. They recognized that newspapers, magazines, and other media were hungry for "content," and they learned to re-present books in a media-ready fashion. They planted stories, fostered events, and spurred news coverage related to books. In the process, a book's subject matter became a transferable commodity. Public relations pioneer Edward Bernays shifted emphasis away from the qualities of a book that might attract a potential reviewer and focused instead on the author's expertise, standing, or personality, or the book's value as news or a special feature. He developed this technique as a theatrical promoter. In one early foray, he publicized a play based on *Daddy Long Legs*, a novel written as letters from an orphan to her benefactor, by helping to form college "Daddy Long Legs" societies to sponsor orphans, and encouraging newspapers to write about those societies. Such subject-matter angles connected the potential customer's interests and concerns with the novel and play.[24] Fiction became enmeshed with issues found in it, making it difficult to discuss the issue without reference to the book, and making the book a natural segue to the issue. In other words, the book was not to be appreciated primarily for its literary or even for its affective qualities but as an essential source of information on a subject important to knowledgeable people.

The public relations approach made publishers reach into the rest of the newspaper through news or items with "journalistic value" derived from the book's "selling points."[25] Books' difference from other commodities had heretofore seemed to stifle their promotion. Book publishers had half-proudly complained that books could not be sold like other commodities because each title was a unique product, suggesting that books were prestigious products of individual genius. But Bernays turned this on its head, taking advantage of the novelty of each title. Soap had no news value, but a book's content did. Public relations could inexpensively leverage editors' demand for media content into publicity for books.

Word-of-Mouth Advertising

Although advertising and journalistic promotion of books became common in the 1920s, many publishers remained ambivalent, fearing that the readers attracted by such tactics were inferior or sheeplike. *Conversation* about a book, as prompted by reviews and literary periodicals, seemed different, a more genuine measure of a book's worth among publishers, critics, and the readers they saw as peers. As late as 1950, Charles F. Bound summarized decades of industry consensus in seeing "large book sales primarily [as] the result of favorable word-of-mouth promotion."[26]

Publishers valorized word-of-mouth promotion for its connection to the values of the past—to the idea that books' significance and sales transcended commerce and were produced by the interest of a discerning community of readers. Yet as they tried to spark a word-of-mouth promotion, they turned to books as subject matter and as affective experience. Like the best-seller list, word-of-mouth advertising created a bandwagon effect. Alfred Harcourt explained that he promoted Sinclair Lewis's *Main Street* among salesmen by using the main character as a foil for talking about a topic dear to the hearts of the salesmen: strategies for reaching the small-town woman. He sent free copies to people who would enter that conversation and whose occupation created a constant need for new subject matter to chat about with customers.

Once a book was started, he found, "all you have to do is remind people of the title—you do not have to argue with them, their friends are all arguing about it."[27] Word of mouth became the gold standard, the benchmark of book promotion and the test of a book's virtue. The idea was so accepted by 1940 that even an advertising agency promoting paid ads for books boasted that its campaigns would stir word-of-mouth publicity, not sales. Paid advertising, too, referred to it, as did book columns and syndicated pages in magazines, with titles like "Books They're Talking About."[28] In 1925, for example, Little, Brown announced in *Publishers' Weekly* that "'Word of Mouth' advertising has carried this fine novel into nation-wide popularity. . . . Discriminating readers everywhere are telling their friends that *Soundings* is a novel they *must* read."[29] Authors' lectures similarly sparked conversation and sales. On the National Town Hall authors' lecture circuit, publishers augmented this effect by arranging study groups before the talks and sales after them.[30]

Radio

Book columns might be called "Books They're Talking About," but radio could actually present such talk. Hungry for content, fledgling radio stations attempted to simulate as well as stimulate word of mouth by being conversational.[31] Paid ads, puffs, and word of mouth mingled more thoroughly on the radio, and sales were augmented significantly as a result.

When radio broadcasts began in the early 1920s, publishers first feared them as yet another rival for readers' attention but soon began to use them to promote books. Frederick Melcher of *Publishers' Weekly* began the trend with a 1922 radio talk show entitled "Great Books Are Life Teachers."[32] By the mid-1940s, more than fifty programs were partially or entirely concerned with books.[33] Publishers were excited about the huge audiences suddenly available. They fashioned shows in an inviting and popularized form to captivate consumers who might otherwise change the station.[34] Book show speakers cultivated an informal, conversational style, as if speaking to listeners in living room easy chairs rather than lecture halls or auditoriums. The reviews themselves were often perfunctory. As with other commodities promoted by celebrities, what counted was the projected personality of the speaker. The chatty, conversational style increased the popularity of both the programs and the books. In 1930, ten publishers and a book bindery sponsored "The Early Bookworm," the first nationwide book-review program, with Alexander Woollcott, a powerful theater critic, as its reviewer. The bindery distributed booklets called "Radio Book Chat" to booksellers and listeners, full of "interesting and personal material about the authors."[35] The radio show and its supporting publicity materials amplified and standardized word-of-mouth advertising and bookstore advice.

Woollcott's opinions were wildly influential. As *Literary Digest* explained, "he had only to mention that he had gone 'quietly mad' over a book to have the country go mad too."[36] Listeners responded to his intimate, emotional, enthusiastic approach to books, conveyed via wit rather than explanation or critique. Personality and the semblance of personal conversation were paramount.

Radio thus drew listeners into vicarious conversations about reading. Woollcott's approach assured listeners that the same emotions by which he had been transported were also available to them. Even if the average listener could not attend opening nights and meet Woollcott's celebrity friends, he or she could join in the more democratic experience of reading the same book. Radio convinced listeners that important people really were talking about particular books; only by reading them could they join such conversations in their own communities.

Conclusion

By 1940 segments of the book industry that in the 1880s had seemed to belong to different species were sometimes hard to tell apart. In the 1880s there had been a clear distinction between the old-line publishers, whose marketplace strategies relied on asserting their products' prestige, and newer-style, more commercially oriented houses. Where traditional publishers focused their sights on bookstores and readers who already patronized them, other segments of the industry generally ignored prestige, seeking profits through newsstands, stationery stores, mail-order campaigns, and traveling salespeople. In the 1880s the prestige group had relied on limited, restrained advertising, reinscribing its reputation while highlighting the status of each book as a unique artifact. The second group was already primed to seek out sales and profits directly, without generating prestige. It increasingly utilized new advertising techniques and venues, first to market its capacity to entertain and later to position its books as vehicles for emotional transport or self-improvement. By the 1930s, however, bankruptcies among the old-line houses and significant developments in other media industries had shifted the terrain, leaving little distinction in advertising strategies between prestige-based houses and the others.

New publishers who straddled the old division eagerly used new media to promote book ownership as a means of access to the information, arguments, and emotional experiences required for participation in important conversations of the day. Publishers transformed and refocused earlier high-prestige approaches. Knopf, for example, targeted readers' interest in the literary qualities of a book, but acknowledged the fact that some new customers might lack the skills associated with that older, natural circle of readers. One of its campaigns addressed readers who would appreciate a writer like Thomas Mann yet might need guidance in approaching his difficult text. Knopf obliged by supplying a helpful booklet with *The Magic Mountain*.[37] Although book buyers were still a minority of Americans in 1940, publishers saw a larger potential audience for their wares, and they sought a place for books in the commercial world of mass media.

Section III

The Social Uses of Print

Introduction

Carl F. Kaestle and Janice A. Radway

. . .

Section II of this volume focused on the mainstream publishing trades — the publishers, the printers, the editors, the advertisers, and others who produced the nation's most highly regarded or most popular books, the best-selling magazines, and the big-city newspapers. The essays in that section demonstrate profound ferment and expansion in those enterprises. During our period, these publications reached wider audiences. More people gained a high school education, and print became more ubiquitous in their lives. It would seem that mainstream publications had the potential to gather more people into a shared national culture. As we shall see, however, the very same processes of declining prices and increasing access to publishing also promoted the proliferation of diversity in print production.

This section moves outward from the mainstream publications to examine the diverse social uses of print and does so in two dimensions. First, there were whole *sectors* other than commercial publishing, including government, religious, and academic publishers, that often operated under different motives, economic circumstances, publishing practices, and distribution methods. Most important, they were not in a pure market situation. They enjoyed certain subsidies.[1] In the academic world, for example, the full costs of print production were often not borne by the readers. University presses and academic journals were subsidized by universities and by government grants to research libraries. In the religious sector, churches often subsidized publishing ventures from general revenues and distributed many materials at a loss or without charge. Governments — especially the federal government — were prodigious producers of print. Well known for its regulatory, legislative, and bureaucratic use of paper, the federal government also published influential works on exploration, history, and science, as Charles Seavey's chapter details. Recognizing that there was widespread activity outside the commercial sector complicates our picture of the history of print in salutary ways.

The second dimension of diversity lies in the social uses of print by distinct *groups* in the society, as when radical politicians, or Hispanic Americans, or

Swedish immigrants used print to transmit traditions, news, and other forms of shared culture.

Groups with the capacity to disseminate print could either consolidate or differentiate their memberships; what were the trends across our period? Did the culture of print offer such increasing opportunity for both distinctiveness and assimilation that both grew apace, in a seeming paradox? Indeed, it did, but it is no paradox. It is a complex issue, and some of the most interesting work of the chapters in this section address it in fascinating ways. In the case of Jewish print culture, for example, Jonathan Sarna explains that the attempt to reconcile and unify the factions and ethnic groups within American Jewry was an explicit goal of the Jewish Publication Society, a goal that failed. It succeeded instead in creating an American claim to excellence in Jewish literary and scholarly achievement. And yet, he writes, there was some growing sense, fostered by the Jewish newspapers and other publications, of being a part of a Jewish "community" in the United States.

In some cases, then, one sees both tendencies at work. In other cases, scholars try to sort out the tendency or function that seems dominant. In the case of American Protestants, William Vance Trollinger Jr., concludes that proliferation and diversity were the central direction for Protestant print culture between 1880 and 1940, reflecting the waning influence of the moderate old-line Protestant denominations and the thriving diversity of sects seen earlier as being on the margins. Una Cadegan sees more evidence of consolidation in Catholic publishing, but, she judges, it was not achieved through rule-governed authority so much as by persuasion and negotiation.

In the case of the foreign-language press of European ethnic groups in America, the sociologist Robert Park long ago established the thesis that the tendency was always toward assimilation, as most papers emphasized American citizenship and economic participation and made the transition to language.[2] This thesis has become the central problematic in the history of the immigrant press. Nicolás Kanellos rejects the Park model for the Hispanic press in America, especially that segment that he rightly calls the "native" Hispanic press, representing a history not of immigrants but of people incorporated into the United States on their own territory through war and imperialism, leading to deep feelings of injustice over land, influence in the government, and economic subordination. Sally Miller also criticizes the Park model, in her case, for the very groups about whom Park was writing, European immigrants. Miller puts more emphasis on cultural maintenance and less on assimilation. More important, she makes generalizations across groups that tend to predict whether a given group's focus and attention will be on the American society or on the group's native home, predictions depending on whether the political situation in the home country is turbulent or placid or whether large numbers of the immigrant group expect to return to the homeland.

Whatever the mixture of assimilation and cultural maintenance, access was increasingly possible for distinct groups to use print. The very developments that supported national consolidation—cheaper print matter distributed faster and more widely—also allowed easier access to those outside the mainstream. As Kanellos notes, technology brought not only the equipment for printing to the Southwest but also cheaper paper and faster transportation. Hispanic presses flourished. In that turn-of-the-century nightmare of oppression and violence against African Americans, James Danky writes, their local print cultures took off, finally getting traction from access, education, and training in the print trades. The National Association for the Advancement of Colored People began its journal the *Crisis*, and the *Chicago Defender* became a national paper.

Some groups used this access to demand recognition and respect. In doing so, they sometimes criticized the status quo. Other groups attempted to develop alternative views, purposes, and communities. These bristling uses of print prompted mainstream elites to try to control publishing, to reassert order when the flurry of new contending ideas seemed to threaten. They could do this in a variety of ways; some strategies, like immigration restriction, were not aimed at print matter. Others were, however. School reformers promoted attendance at public schools, where students would find a bland, Anglo-oriented curriculum and learn common American legends and narratives. Protestant groups continued proselytizing through print matter, even as Catholic and Jewish publications proliferated. Some Americans attempted to achieve hegemony and rectitude through the censorship of print matter. As Paul S. Boyer documents in his chapter, formal efforts to censor printed materials grew weaker as the twentieth century progressed and the Gilded Age consensus on moral strictures eroded. To treat the decline of formal censorship as a triumph of progressive open-mindedness would be to overlook all the informal means by which print was also governed; but as Boyer demonstrates, the trend was indeed toward a loosening of the reins.

Other factors worked against the restoration of order in print. The organizational diversity of the academic research world, writes Marcel LaFollette, meant that "no single set of gatekeepers could inhibit information flow." There were pockets of control, created through the organization of disciplines and peer review within the fields. But there was too much diversity, too much freedom, and too much zest for discovery to discipline academic research. Generating all this motion was a new concept of learning. In this view, knowledge was evolving, cumulative, subject to constant revision. Both LaFollette and Janice Radway place central emphasis on the rise of the academic journal, based on just this premise. Journals appeared regularly, reporting ongoing research and revision. They were not repositories of knowledge so much as essays on theories and evidence, *print in motion*.

Nor did one have to be down-and-out to be oppositional. Debate and disagreement were embedded in the research universities' raison d'être. Alienation, too, developed within the professional literary sphere. Radway writes about the advent of the literary author as avowed social critic, beginning with William Dean Howells's depiction of ordinary people and their problems, then moving on to the openly critical realist and modernist writers of subsequent decades. Expanded access to the literary sphere by women, blacks, working-class writers, and immigrants also helped to decouple literary stature from the status quo and from a celebration of a unified America. Academia bred social criticism among social scientists as well, once they took as part of their mission the solution to glaring social problems. Of course, they do not all look politically progressive in retrospect, but their enterprise was in constant motion, their commitment was to change, diversity, and argument.

Janice Radway's essay lays down a broad base for the essays that follow in this section. She also pursues in more detail the arguments sketched in this introduction, arguments and conclusions that are central findings of this volume.

CHAPTER 11

Learned and Literary Print Cultures in an Age of Professionalization and Diversification

Janice A. Radway

. . .

An Introductory Overview

In 1936 Henry Seidel Canby, editor of the *Saturday Review of Literature* and chief judge at the Book-of-the-Month Club, published a thoughtful memoir about academic life, entitled *Alma Mater: The Gothic Age of the American College*. His book took stock of how changing definitions of learning had altered American society and assessed the impact of the modern college, asking "what it was, what it did to us, [and] what powerful hands it laid upon the United States of our generation."[1] Canby warned that he was not writing about "that larger organization of professional schools, service bureaus, and organs of scholarship, called a university."[2] Nevertheless, his elegiac account is dogged by the figure of the modern research university and the changing definitions of learning it promoted. Canby acknowledged that the college of 1910 was a different institution from that of 1870 because the years between witnessed "the triumph of applied science, the breakdown of stereotyped religion, the defeat of the classics in American education, and the dramatic appearance, full blown, of American confidence in our own scholarship and our own literature."[3] These developments that altered the American college so irrevocably were connected most intimately with the appearance of the American research university in the years between 1870 and 1915.

The history of the American university is traditionally connected to specialization, professionalization, and the rise of corporate capitalism, but as this chapter demonstrates, it is connected as well to the changing cultures of print that developed during this period. The forms of learned culture that emerged slowly in the late nineteenth century reflected changes in writing and reading practices and altered information distribution networks as much as shifting epistemologies, subject matter, and goals. Although traditional, bound books maintained their role in learned culture, especially in the disciplines termed "the humanities," ever more specialized cultures of higher learning increasingly advanced through regularized journal publication.

Journals proliferated in part because learning lost some of its association with the mastery of settled tradition, especially at research universities where the sciences had a major impact. Traditionally conceptualized as a process of inductive reasoning from established principles, scientific study was increasingly associated with empirical investigation and the timely publication of new research results. As learning was imagined more frequently as a dynamic practice continually generating new, more accurate information, demand for additional outlets to publicize that information grew.[4]

This gradual reconception of learning also affected methods for teaching received literary traditions. As Canby observed, "Scholars in literature who called themselves scientific began to dominate the graduate schools and extend their influence into the sacred precincts of the undergraduate college. Applying the technique of scientific research to language, they revealed an evolution with laws of its own the discovery of which was a noble extension of knowledge."[5] As modern language study supplanted the classical curriculum, philology and literary history grew in importance and the emerging discipline of English generated its own specialized journals as well.

Such a shift did not go unchallenged, however. Self-described "generalists" such as Canby—most clustered in the colleges—championed an alternative model of learning known as "the liberal arts ideal." Its advocates opposed research specialization and sought to cultivate character and intellect rather than the utility of the new. In the ensuing protracted struggle over cultural and intellectual authority, the college-affiliated humanists and generalists allied themselves with an emergent class of "literary" writers who committed themselves to defending fiction writing and literature more generally as essential knowledge of "the real." Together, they pitted literary language and aesthetic perception against scientific "truth," and dismissed the philologists' histories and linguistic analyses for disregarding the aesthetic complexities of literature.

In this context, American literary realism, naturalism, and modernism developed as relatively autonomous aesthetic movements. To be sure, they were responding to the increasing commercialism of American life as well as to the growing prestige of the sciences, with their utilitarian forms of thought. However, given their effort to assert the value of "literary" reading and writing practices in contrast to those pursued by university scholars in the sciences and the humanities, these literary movements ought to be seen as well as competing efforts by another professionalizing elite to articulate its claims to cultural authority.[6] In fact, by the end of the century, a distinct career path had been defined for aspiring writers of "serious" literature who were expected to publish in the most respected literary monthlies or with a few well-established publishers. Portrayed as a professional as well as a celebrity, the literary "author" became recognizable as an identifiable social figure whose "genius" and presumed endurance was constituted in opposition to the supposed commercialism of hacks and lady writers and to the purported technicism and obsessional specializations of university-based academics.[7]

Despite the foregrounding of such oppositions, modes of writing for publication actually proliferated as the widening distribution of literacy and the commercially motivated exploration of new markets produced an ever more varied print world. Access to publication opened up to more people from non-elite backgrounds as well as to those who used print for purposes other than the learned or the literary.[8] Because social relationships were complicated by class, ethnic, gender, and race differences and attenuated by geographic distance, Americans increasingly turned to print to articulate identities and affiliations of various kinds and to constitute social communities around mutual interest rather than geographic proximity.

The resulting explosion of print challenged previous definitions of the literary, rendering it more catholic, more fluid, and more diverse. Self-proclaimed arbiters of the aesthetic responded, seeking to reorder the chaos by cordoning off what they called "literature" from everything else through the rhetoric of brow levels. Popular literary taste was branded as the "low" to literature's "high," demonstrating with the allusion to phrenology that a social cartography was being overlaid upon an aesthetic one. This racist biological innuendo defamed the literary tastes of many, including women, working people, immigrants, and African Americans.[9]

The rhetoric of brow levels caught on because it seemed to capture something of the reification of class difference that impressed itself upon nearly everyone in the United States of the period, including cultural commentators such as Jacob Riis and Thorstein Veblen. It also appeared to describe loose configurations of authors, publishers, writing practices, and modes of book production that seemed to coalesce in the years after 1880, including a self-consciously "literary" constellation, and another more broadly oriented mode targeting the taste of the "masses." Despite the imprecision of tracing boundaries between literary territories and the fact that these realms were never as pure as either their critics or their defenders opined, a third category of the "middlebrow" emerged in the early decades of the twentieth century. By then, resort to this apparent hierarchical cartography had broadened and become habitual, regardless of its accuracy.[10]

Even in the face of such literary policing, differently focused, sometimes specialized writing and publishing practices proliferated. Some of these crossed the supposed high-low divide as they concerned themselves simultaneously with aesthetic and other issues. For example, although the literary modernists who clustered in New York around 1910 are commonly considered an avant-garde, aesthetic elite, some involved themselves in working-class issues, thereby seeking to create forms at once literary and political and oriented to a broader readership. African Americans, too, took up literary modes but within the context of a broader range of writing and publishing practices designed to contest dominant ways of "knowing" the Negro. The printed materials that resulted were issued in a range of formats targeting interested readers with varied education and income levels. Women writers, radicals, working-class writers, and a variety of immigrants, too, including Asian Americans and Latinos, developed rich literatures, both fictional and not, that explored issues of concern to them, effectively contributing to the production of new ways of not only constituting identity but also targeting readers. Indeed, as complex literacy and education increased, as U.S. society became more diverse, and as more profit could be made from publication and print, proliferating writing, publishing, and reading networks contributed to the "explosion of language" and the "riot of words" that characterized this period in the United States.[11]

Cultures of Learning in the Age of the University

Universities, Research, and the Pursuit of the New

Any narrative seeking to explain the transformation of learned culture between 1880 and 1915 risks oversimplification by arranging coincident developments into a causal sequence. Nonetheless, the literature on the American research university has made plausible arguments for the significance of several determining agents. These include the German model of higher education, the outmoded college curriculum, the growing success of science and its ability to meet the needs of American business and manufacturing, the rise of technically oriented and utilitarian forms of knowledge, the impact of specialization, and the development of modern professionalism.[12] Between 1880 and 1915 these developments transformed previously local and avocational circles of learning into increasingly organized systems of professional knowledge production.[13]

While the liberal arts college cultivated mental discipline and character by familiarizing undergraduates with received knowledge in literature, moral philosophy or natural science, research universities, land-grant agricultural schools, and technical research institutes focused enthusiastically on the generation and communication of new knowledge. Faculty increasingly devoted themselves to the business of research and the reading and writing that supported it, defining their primary academic relationships as those with their specialist peers. Seeking association with scholars with similar interests, they formulated new social and communication networks that became essential to university life. Disciplines, departments, professional associations and societies, and specialized journals and university presses were all installed as critical components of learned culture during these years.[14]

Although research and its emerging writing and reading practices soon had far-reaching influence on business and government, this changed culture of learning was commonly associated with the development of research universities. The founding of the Johns Hopkins University in 1876 looms large in this narrative. Modeled on German university training, Hopkins became the inspiration for the reorientation of graduate research training in the United States.[15] Still, other institutions also had an impact on the reorientation of higher education around the practice of research, especially land-grant colleges and universities that developed in the years following the passage of the 1862 Morrill Act.[16] Additionally, technical schools and research programs sponsored by the federal government—such as those at the U.S. Department of Agriculture, the Geological Survey, and the Bureau of Ethnology—and by philanthropic foundations and industrial enterprises all began to exert pressure on older conceptions of learning.[17]

Land-grant colleges and universities were noted early on for promulgating the assumption that learning should have utilitarian benefits. The Morrill Act required that institutional recipients of federal funds offer agricultural and mechanical education to the people of their states. This promoted an institutional focus on agricultural research, providing advice on legislative programs, and pioneering extension courses to foster ongoing education.[18] The University of Wisconsin, for example, sought to train a diverse student body for a range of practical and politically oriented vocations. At the same time, President Charles Van Hise sought to extend the university's outreach beyond the campus, calling it "the Wisconsin Idea." Indeed, in a 1909 magazine article publicizing Van Hise's success, Lincoln Steffens celebrated Wisconsin for its willingness "to teach anybody—anything—anywhere," and touted the university's "machine shops, model dairy farms, a Housekeeper's Conference, and other examples of grass-roots utility."[19] Like Wisconsin, other land-grant institutions created extension services and issued numerous publications of their own, including agricultural reports, information handbooks, and pamphlets on topics ranging from home economics to the proper way to plant corn. These publications demonstrated the value of the knowledge generated by their research faculties.

Together, the research model and the service ideal challenged older understandings of learning as the profession of a stable body of truths, canons, and traditions. Learning came to mean as well the pursuit of a highly specialized body of constantly improving knowledge about a particular fraction of the world through the mastery of a specialized set of techniques for apprehending it.[20] Even a Latinist, William Gardner Hale, embraced this ideology of the new, insisting that "It is to the *discoverers*, in far greater measure than to the transmitters, that the world is under obligation."[21]

As many research-oriented university professors placed less emphasis on face-to-face teaching than their counterparts in liberal arts colleges, they developed new forms of transmitting information. In fact, it became ever more important to communicate with peers about common pursuits and, crucially, to disseminate information about research findings to the lay population from whom financial support had to be drawn. Increasingly, these practices were integrated, albeit informally. While researchers communicated with each other through specialized scholarly journals and the presentation of research results at annual conferences, they communicated with the broader public through popularized accounts of their research in magazines and in trade books designed for the educated, general reader.[22] Indeed as print networks proliferated and the demand for content increased, publishing needs in the wider literary world helped to underwrite the cultural legitimacy of the new research culture within the precincts of the learned.

The Business of Knowledge Production and Transmission

The sciences emerged as powerful forces at this time in part because a new "investigative temper" promoted the importance of evidence and displayed an intensified faith that the "gold of reality" would be revealed through the investigation of "the unique, nugget-like fact."[23] Consolidating their authority by promising to create utilitarian methods for addressing the most pressing problems of a rapidly incorporating society, the sciences further augmented their standing by capitalizing on the practice of specialization. As research scientists moved to differentiate their fields theoretically and methodologically from each other, they created autonomous departments, professional societies, specialized journals, and their own forms of credentialing. By disciplining their work and that of the graduate specialists they sought to train, they professionalized thought, transforming it slowly into a business — the business of knowledge production.[24] The university, in turn, evolved as a complex corporation with semiautonomous departments coordinated and managed at different levels for different purposes. Not surprisingly, university presidents viewed corporate executives as kindred leaders and promoted the image of their research faculty as scholarly professionals.

The role played by Johns Hopkins in this history is too familiar to rehearse here.[25] Still, it is worth noting that, at its creation, the university was conceived as a collection of scholars who "should have the ability and the leisure too, to add something by their *writings and discoveries* to the world's stock of literature and science."[26] As founder Daniel Coit Gilman moved to institutionalize graduate education in the United States, Hopkins pioneered in the forging of intricate connections between altered definitions of learning, new institutional forms, reconfigured social relations, and particular publication practices.

When Gilman set out to hire Hopkins's first scientists, the American research community was small. As Daniel Kevles has pointed out, only "about thirty chemists, twenty physicists, and probably still fewer mathematicians pursued and published research with any regularity" in the United States in the 1870s. Because of a dearth of outlets as well, most had to publish abroad.[27] In order to establish Hopkins's credentials as an institution, and in direct competition with the Europeans, Gilman encouraged his faculty to assume vanguard positions in their respective disciplines by establishing their own *American* journals to lay claim to the priority of their findings.[28] Indeed, only a few months after Hopkins was created, Gilman financed a group of mathematicians led by J. J. Sylvester to form the *American Journal of Pure and Applied Mathematics*, which published its first issue "under university auspices" in 1878. He also encouraged Ira Remsen of the chemistry department and faculty in other fields to create specialized journals that would publish in a timely fashion.[29] Ultimately, Gilman reported with satisfaction to the trustees that "Publication has been encouraged . . . when necessary through agencies of our own. . . . We have hoped in this way to extend the usefulness of this foundation far beyond the company of those whom we constantly instruct."[30]

Gilman further underwrote research work, consolidated the legitimacy of his faculty, and contributed to the association of learning with what was new when he encouraged the creation of associations to support the formation of diversified publishing networks. He supported creation of the Philological Association, the Historical Association, and the Mathematical Conference, all of which fostered paper presentations in fields not treated in the curriculum, thereby contributing to the creation of new objects of knowledge and even new departments.[31] Imitation of these forms of publicity and association spread beyond Baltimore and fostered lines of affiliation among similarly trained peers scattered across a small number of institutions clustered mostly along the east and west coasts and in the upper Midwest.[32]

As Roger Geiger has argued, the pace of academic professionalization picked up additional speed in the decade 1880–90. In addition to the Modern Language Association and the American Historical Association, the Society for Biblical Literature and Exegesis, the American Society of Naturalists, the American Economic Association, the American Mathematical Society, the American Academy of Political and Social Science, and the American Society of Zoologists all were founded during these years.[33] They were followed in the 1890s by the American Chemical Society, the American Psychological Association, the Botanical Society of America, the American Physical Society, the Astronomical and Astrophysical Society of America, and the American Society for Microbiology.[34] Nearly all of these disciplinary organizations sponsored nationally oriented, regularly appearing publications. Although for a time, some of them retained a catholic focus and an orientation to a generally educated public, increasingly they published technically complex research for a small group of similarly trained peers.

Although there is as yet no comprehensive history of the scholarly journal in the United States, Marcel LaFollette's essay in this volume gives it significant attention. Journals published by national scholarly associations accepted research articles and were often funded by subscription fees and membership dues. They were joined by department-based journals seeking to publicize the results of local faculty research. In the years between 1880 and 1906, for instance, Chicago funded twelve such journals, Harvard eight, Columbia six, Cornell five, and the University of California four (see table 11.1).[35] Although subsidized temporarily by their university sponsors, few department journals achieved financial independence or longevity because most American university departments could not produce the amount of high-quality research necessary to fill the pages of a regularly appearing publication. Many were discontinued. By 1906 scholarly publication in the United States was dominated by a vast array of specialized, association-sponsored journals. Still, like the very different, mass-market magazines that developed simultaneously, these research publications emphasized their periodicity and timeliness. As such, they, too, were characteristic products of an era marked by the formalizing properties of incorporation and its demand for regularity and efficiency in the circulation of up-to-date information to a range of different audiences.[36]

The proliferation of these scholarly publications challenged the preeminence of the bound book as the principle technology for the generation and circulation of learned culture. Hugh Hawkins notes for instance that though it possessed a remarkable collection of periodicals in its early years (1,000 serials by 1889), the library at Hopkins had only one-tenth of the books claimed by Harvard.[37] Inasmuch as the period under investigation here might be deemed the high-water mark of book culture in the United States, so too must it be seen as the era when the book was increasingly challenged by other print forms, especially those emphasizing periodicity and timeliness.

TABLE 11.1. Principal scholarly publications of research universities, 1906

University	Publication	Date of first publication
University of California	*Publications in American Archaeology and Ethnology*	1903
	Publications in Classical Philology	1904
	Publications in Botany	1902
	Publications in Zoology	1902
University of Chicago	*Studies in Classical Philology*	1895
	Economic Studies	1895
	American Journal of Sociology	1896
	American Journal of Semitic Languages and Literature	1884/92
	American Journal of Theology	1897
	Astrophysical Journal	1882/95
	Biblical World	1883/93
	Classical Philology	1906
	Journal of Geology	1893
	Journal of Political Economy	1892
	Modern Philology	1903
	The School Review	1893
Columbia University	*Studies in History, Economics and Public Law*	1891
	Political Science Quarterly	1886
	Columbia University Contributions to Philosophy and Psychology	1884
	Columbia University Biological Series	1894
	Columbia University Geological Series	1906
	Columbia University Studies in Romance Philology and Literature	1902
Cornell University	*Studies in Classical Philology*	1887
	Cornell Studies in Philosophy	1900
	Philosophical Review	1892
	Physical Review	1893
	Journal of Physical Chemistry	1896
Harvard University	*Harvard Historical Studies*	1896
	Harvard Studies in Classical Philology	1890
	Studies and Notes in Philology and Literature	1892
	Harvard Oriental Series	1891
	Harvard Psychological Studies	1903
	Quarterly Journal of Economics	1886
	Harvard Law Review	1887
	Annals of Mathematics	1889
University of Illinois	*Journal of English and Germanic Philology*	1897/1906

TABLE 11.1. (*continued*)

University	Publication	Date of First Publication
Johns Hopkins University	*American Journal of Mathematics*	1878
	American Journal of Philology	1880
	American Chemical Journal	1879
	JHU Studies in Historical and Political Science	1883
	Modern Language Notes	1886
	Beiträge zur Assyriologie und vergleichenden semitischen Sprachwissenschaft	1890
Massachusetts Institute of Technology	*Technological Quarterly*	1887
University of Michigan	*Michigan Law Review*	1902
University of Minnesota	none	
University of Pennsylvania	*Astronomical Series*	1895
	Contributions from the Zoological Laboratory	1893
	Series in Philology and Literature	1891
	Series in Political Economy and Public Law	1885
Princeton University	irregular publications in geology, psychology, and philosophy	
Stanford University	occasional monographs	
University of Wisconsin	*Economics, Political Science and History Series*	1894
	Philology and Literature Series	1898
	Science Series	1894
Yale University	*Yale Psychological Studies*	1892
	Yale Studies in English	1898
	Yale Law Journal	1891

Source: Roger Geiger, *To Advance Knowledge: The Growth of American Research Universities, 1900–1940* (New York: Oxford University Press, 1986). Used by permission.

This is not to say that book publication was outmoded in the academic world. Bound books still carried a significant amount of prestige, and many researchers sought to present their work in the expansive and extended format made possible by the traditional codex book. In fact, the very years that saw the proliferation of scholarly periodicals also saw the development of the first American university presses at Cornell and Johns Hopkins. By the time the University of Chicago was organized in 1893, a university press was incorporated as one of the four major divisions of the institution because its president ranked publication equal to research and teaching.³⁸ California, Pennsylvania, Notre Dame, Sewanee, Howard, Columbia, Northwestern, North Carolina, Stanford, Princeton, Yale, and Harvard followed suit, all organizing presses by 1919.³⁹ Most were relatively small operations designed for publication and targeted circulation rather than for profit making or mass appeal. Distribution was largely carried out through gift and exchange, a practice that helped augment the collections at many university libraries but failed to achieve distribution beyond small scholarly communities.⁴⁰ Indeed early university presses tended to issue bulletins, reports, monographs, and series of scholarly books that would never have been published by the trade. California boasted twenty-three different monograph series by 1913, including titles in geology, entomology, archaeology, and philology. Despite this proliferation and diversification, university publications have always constituted a very small portion of American book publishing.⁴¹

As universities fostered more research and published more books and periodicals, it became necessary to find tools to facilitate access to the knowledge thereby produced. American libraries, once understood primarily as repositories, increasingly focused on augmenting book circulation and use.⁴² With Melvil Dewey's 1876 creation of the first modern classification system for books, a system that was both open-ended and capable of fostering book searches by subject as well as by title or author, libraries slowly reoriented themselves around service to their patrons.⁴³ Designed specifically to incorporate new publications, the modern library catalog further emphasized the contemporaneity and innovation that had come to define higher learning. Indeed it might be said that the card catalog and the specialized, regularly appearing journal were critical material embodiments of the business of modern knowledge production.⁴⁴

Print Culture and the Age of the Expert

In tracking the relation between changed cultures of learning and print production, special note should be taken of the fact that the growing importance of scientific research substantially affected fields of inquiry that soon would be grouped as the "social sciences." Those fields in particular contributed significantly to the legitimacy and cultural authority of the professional expert. Oriented simultaneously to the standards of their research peers and to the demands of a lay population, new experts in psychology, economics, and political science as well as in other areas accessed clients not only in face-to-face situations but through the mediating agency of print production. Consequently, social science experts developed a major presence in the country's fast-developing mass and middlebrow print culture.

Dorothy Ross has argued that the social sciences first "began to take root as separate, academic, and scientific disciplines" as religious control of the colleges waned after the Civil War.[45] Previously formal examination of social life had been carried out primarily by professors of moral and mental philosophy exploring the nature of moral behavior in a world ordered by God. By the 1870s, these authorities were joined by new kinds of experts who delivered practical social services or who engaged in political, social, economic, and educational reform within their emergent disciplines, all of which were deeply affected by new European modes of evolutionary and historicist thought.[46] Ross suggests that the attraction to these new theories was produced by a "crisis" among intellectuals brought on by "declining religious authority, growing urban problems, and the prolonged depression and labor conflict of the 1870s."[47]

The social sciences gained further traction by throwing themselves into the characteristically modern business of professionalization, generating new departmental configurations, graduate programs, journals, and professional associations.[48] As part of their raison d'être, they offered their professional expertise to the expanding middle classes, who were less inclined to identify with the values and leadership of an older elite. As Ross suggests, "the middle class public turned from the moral advice of the clergy to the expert advice of the university social scientists, from the old elite's conception of society as hierarchically ordered by virtue to the new elite's conception of society as a meritocracy, hierarchically ordered by competence."[49]

The growth in prestige of the social sciences and the concomitant rise to prominence of the professional expert was likewise made possible by the adoption of elaborate credentialing procedures including formal training, forms of apprenticeship, and peer review. Publication was as central to this professional regime as it was in the natural sciences. Within the social sciences, however, journals and monographs deliberately sought to address not only their peers but also policy makers and officials who utilized their expert testimony before investigatory and regulatory commissions.[50] Significantly, too, these new-style social scientists offered their services as "experts" to popular magazines such as *McClure's*, the *Saturday Evening Post*, and *Munsey's* that developed in the 1880s and 1890s and reached their heyday during the Progressive Era. As Christopher Wilson and Richard Ohmann have shown, these magazines were significantly different from the older, more literary monthlies associated with traditional elites.[51] They offered their broader middle-class audience more nonfiction, including popularized science; interviews with experts, specialists, and celebrities; self-help articles; and muckraking investigations. In doing so, they functioned symbiotically with the apparatus of scholarly print production to establish the public credibility of the professional expert. In translating material originally created for professionalized and specialized audiences, the magazines run by Bok, McClure, and Munsey enhanced the prestige of the new social sciences by creating public awareness of the specialized knowledge they could offer municipalities, government bureaucracies, schools, businesses, and other public institutions. They were essential, then, to the establishment of the client base of the professional expert and to public support for the new higher learning.

The Humanities, the Pursuit of Culture, and the Consolidation of a New Elite

The classical disciplines were also affected by the scientific research ideal and the search for empirically determined "truth," as a new group of philological specialists trained in Germany raised historical questions about the genealogy of languages. These were the men decried by Canby, who noted in *Alma Mater*, "Accuracy in little things was the new virtue, and we were encouraged to believe that the world was more in need of correct texts, exact dates, and a knowledge of sources, than of estimates, appreciations, and opinions which, however just, were not scientific because they could not be proved."[52] Because many shared Canby's disdain for the new "scientific" bent in higher learning, the very idea of "the humanities" emerged in response to the growing dominance of the natural sciences in the university context and to the competition with social sciences for resources and prestige.

In his justly famous essay, "The Plural Organized Worlds of the Humanities," Laurence Veysey acknowledges that while the university was the central institution affecting the humanities in this period, museums, libraries, archives, orchestras, voluntary associations, reading groups, and study circles also proliferated beyond university walls.[53] Indeed, many historians have sought to explain the general explosion of cultural activity that took place between 1880 and 1925. Most agree with Veysey's argument that burgeoning cultural activity helped to consolidate and unify a changing elite class.[54]

After the Civil War, a new national class of manufacturers, industrialists, and financiers began to consolidate wealth and power, challenging the status of an older elite composed mainly of a socially homogeneous and interconnected group of merchant families in the northeastern cities.[55] This new bourgeois class was especially anxious to demonstrate its claim to leadership and its superiority over a fast-expanding and restive working class of immigrants, former slaves, transplanted farmers, and women. Many of the latter groups were making vigorous efforts to mobilize print culture in their own interests by generating and circulating among themselves alternative forms of information and different views about what should count as "knowledge." The emergent bourgeois class turned to culture as a means to insist on its genealogical relation to older elites and as a way to mark its members as different from the "masses" teeming into cities, whom they associated with the labor unrest of the 1870s.

In aspiring to appear as cultivated as the older elites, the members of this new bourgeois class sought to educate their children at the nation's best schools. They also organized and endowed libraries, colleges, universities, art museums, and concert orchestras. As their wives improved themselves in reading groups and literary societies, they moved to furnish their homes with books, literary magazines, and paintings garnered sometimes from abroad.[56] Culture, as Thorstein Veblen would soon note, became a highly valued commodity in the final decades of the nineteenth century.[57] As it did, an elaborate and variegated literature of justification developed both in literary precincts and within the academic context. Writers examined the transformative powers of what was variously called "liberal culture," "the liberal arts," and, in the academic context, "the humanities."[58]

In its academic form, this literature of defense took issue not simply with the forces of cultural degradation, typified often by mass-produced literature written by women, but also with the new, research-based culture of the scientifically oriented universities. Over time, the academic defenders of liberal culture helped to deepen the categorical divide between the disciplines. As Gilman commented in 1903: "Earth and man, nature and the supernatural, letters and science, the humanities and the realities, are the current terms of contrast between the two groups and there are no signs that these distinctions will ever vanish."[59]

The disciplinary divide, in fact, was much discussed in print circles. The nation's revered literary monthlies and respected publishing houses devoted thousands of pages to the discussion of the fate of higher learning in what was clearly becoming the age of the university. Many defenders of liberal culture in the colleges and universities came from elite social backgrounds and had close ties to the literary establishments in Boston and New York.[60] This connection gave them easy access to the pages of the literary monthlies and publishers like Houghton Mifflin, Scribner's, Harper's, and Macmillan. Men like Brander Matthews, Henry Van Dyke, Hiram Corson, and Bliss Perry produced critiques of the new research ideal that were angry and dismissive. In their view, utilitarian research was just another excrescence of the business-oriented civilization that had taken over America and degraded its art and culture in the pursuit of profit.

The advocates of liberal culture acknowledged their ties to the older mental-discipline curriculum, believing that higher education could cultivate "character" and devotion to higher ideals. As Gerald Graff has observed, they were "spokesmen for the missionary view of literature they inherited from Arnold, Ruskin and other Victorian apostles of culture."[61] Defenders of liberal culture further claimed aesthetic study was inherently connected to the dominant moral and social norms of the day. Although they paid lip service to the value of democracy, they were also decidedly Anglophilic and believed, finally, in an aristocracy of taste. They were appalled by the burgeoning mass-produced literature of the period and by the cheap and shallow trappings of culture available in reproductions and magazine illustrations.[62]

Stressing breadth rather than specialization, contemplation and meditation rather than utilitarianism, and things of the spirit rather than of the material world, advocates of liberal culture such as Charles Eliot Norton vigorously defended the liberal culture curriculum in the colleges and at places such as Yale and Harvard. In addition, men such as Hiram Corson opposed the adaptation of scientific methods to the study of literature. In *The Aims of Literary Study*, published by Macmillan in 1896, Corson claimed that "Little or no vital knowledge of the language is imparted by these means, and whatever susceptibility to literature any student might otherwise have, is more or less deadened by petty details, grammatical, philological, and other, and irrelevant matters of every kind, which drink up all the sap of the mind."[63] Instead, literary education should be about appreciation and judgment, anchored in the attentive reading of original texts made available in anthologies produced by a textbook industry beginning to turn its attention to the needs of colleges and universities.[64]

It is important to point out here that, although academic literary generalists recommended residual Victorian norms and aesthetic ideologies, they also styled themselves cultural critics and associated themselves with the notion of literature as salvific. In fact, they were closely allied both ideologically and socially with the writers, editors, and publishers of what would later be called "genteel" literary culture.[65] That culture was dominated by men such as William Dean Howells, Richard Watson Gilder, and George William Curtis, who, though successful and powerful in the world of letters, were also deeply critical of the trajectory of American society. Alan Trachtenberg has suggested that, together with the academic generalists, and despite their bourgeois social status, the literary men of Howells's generation constituted the first group of American writers to understand themselves as alienated.[66] Building on the ideological work of Arnold, Ruskin, Carlyle, and, in America, Emerson, this first generation of American literary professionals crafted for themselves a complex and sometimes contradictory social role in a society that troubled them deeply.[67] In doing so, they laid the groundwork for the subsequent emergence of an even more dissident group, the literary and cultural avant-garde that began to appear after 1910.

Cultures of the Literary in an Age of Diversification

Professionalizing the High Literary

The literary men of William Dean Howells's generation saw themselves as defenders of higher things, as the conscience of a nation that had mistakenly turned its attention to the mendacious world of business. At the same time, they wrote critically of the new mass culture and lamented higher education's neglect of things of the spirit. Indeed the French term *intellectuel* would be adopted in the United States by the turn of the century, naming the new cultural figure made possible by the literary practice of Howells and his peers.[68] The intellectual was a professional thinker, a literary, social, and political critic, a revered denizen of the world of arts and letters. And that world, increasingly, construed itself as an alternative to business values as well as to the scientific realm of technical expertise. Ironically, then, the cultural activity that helped to unify the new bourgeois elite also produced a public discourse of critique installed in the very heart of the country's developing literary culture.

In fact, a distinctly marked, high-literary sphere emerged gradually during the decades after the Civil War. Centered initially in Boston, it would gravitate later to New York City. This sphere was the product of an alliance between the belletristic branch of the publishing industry and the Boston bourgeoisie, as has been documented extensively by Nancy Glazener.[69] In practical terms, it arose from a set of interlocking institutional, social, and aesthetic relations that joined prominent publishing houses such as Ticknor & Fields and Houghton, Mifflin with influential literary journals, a particular collection of editors and writers who circulated among those magazines, and a small but highly influential and socially prominent readership. Although the *Atlantic Monthly* and its two most influential editors, Howells and James T. Fields, are often considered at the head of this culture, scholars have shown recently that a number of New York magazines, including *Harper's Monthly* and the *Century*, contributed significantly to the *Atlantic*'s cultural project. The *Atlantic* group, as Glazener has labeled it, consolidated its power through the 1870s and 1880s by self-consciously addressing an educated national audience.

The *Atlantic* group's members offered "Literature" as the secular equivalent of religion, providing an alternative to the utilitarianism and instrumentalism that so distressed them. Championing art and learning as the proper route to moral salvation and the achievement of a more refined sensibility, the editors and writers of this group construed the idea of "serious literature" in opposition to the sentimental "effusions" of domestic fiction and the "sensational" tales of dime novels. In the 1890s they railed against popular magazines such as *Munsey's*, *Cosmopolitan*, and the *Saturday Evening Post* for embedding fiction and poems among ads for soap and crackers and fawning articles about new business and entertainment celebrities, thereby revealing their commercial orientation. This bald admission of commercial aim was anathema to the literary men.

In effect, the men of the *Atlantic* group understood themselves to be engaged in a civilizing mission. They believed that reading, as a moral and civic activity, would unite the increasingly diverse American citizenry on the basis of the higher values represented in literature. Thus, as part of their critique of business values, some argued that "distinction" should be extended democratically through the larger population. Such an ideological orientation even enabled a few, including Howells himself, to profess sincere sympathy for laborers and the labor movement. Howells went so far as to decry the trial and conviction of the anarchists purportedly responsible for the 1886 Haymarket bombing in Chicago that killed a policeman. Despite the political sympathies of individuals, however, the writing activities of the *Atlantic* group as a whole institutionalized the writer as a professional, regularized and stabilized his (rarely her) audience, and provided a kind of sinecure for creativity and critique. Accordingly, in the words of Richard Brodhead, these men and the print outlets they dominated created "the same high or distinguished zone in the literary realm that the classical museum or symphony orchestra produced in art or music, a strongly demarcated high-status arena for high-artistic practice."[70] In effect, their work served to consolidate the cultural "leadership" of the bourgeois class by working to incorporate others into its intellectual purview.[71]

This project was pursued explicitly in the extensive critical reviews carried by the monthlies, nearly all of which took great pains to distinguish "serious" literature from the merely sensational or sentimental. At the same time, the pedagogical project of the *Atlantic* group was carried out further by the very literary forms and genres the group adopted. In fact, both regionalist and realist fiction, the forms championed by Howells and his colleagues, addressed the effects of the social cataclysms of the late nineteenth century. Though their goal was to render realistically the lives and speech of ordinary people, regionalist and realist novels also taught their bourgeois readers how to construe such figures as "fascinating" rather than threatening.[72]

Regionalist writers like Edward Eggleston, Sarah Orne Jewett, Mary Noailles Murfree, and Mary Wilkins Freeman accomplished this linguistically by subordinating carefully rendered dialect forms to the capacious, judicious, "literary" prose of an educated narrator. Analogously, realist fiction like that penned by Howells himself or even by Henry James or Mark Twain presented itself as neutrally unsentimental and therefore "objective," depicting the true lives and suffering of ordinary people facing contemporary problems. In each case, Glazener explains, "the lowness or the ordinariness of the materials of realism . . . becomes the precondition for the transforming artistry of the realist writer and testifies to the sophisticated perceptiveness of the realist reader by extension."[73] This commanding perspective conferred power and legitimacy on both narrator and reader. It also exposed bourgeois readers—increasingly isolated in the new suburbs—to social diversity in a way that was manageable rather than frightening. The dispassionate recording eye of the realist satisfied the bourgeois reader's curiosity about new forms of urban life while the regionalist's ethnographic rendering of distant precincts eulogized quaint customs at the moment they were disappearing. Both practices managed these tasks by endowing readers with the linguistic and conceptual means to feel superior to all that was different.[74]

In effect, the new high-literary zone produced another form of professional expertise. The authority of the serious regionalist, realist, or naturalist was predicated on the ability to render in print the "really real."[75] And though such readers were presumed to be educated, the genre assumed that they still needed expert enlightenment about realities that were not obvious.[76] What the final effect was on readers is difficult to tell; but the accounts of scholars like Glazener and Kaplan suggest that by offering their middle-class readers knowledge of the socially marginal and subordinated, these new high-literary professionals functioned like the new social scientists, revealing truths about social netherworlds and psychological depths.[77] Their critique of business and the dominant new understanding of learning notwithstanding, in their writing practices this first alienated generation of literary intellectuals may well have inadvertently augmented the growing status of the learned expert and reinforced the social hierarchies and uneven distribution of knowledge upon which that status was predicated.

Expanded Access to the Literary Sphere

The *Atlantic* group's literary practices had additional contradictory effects, however. Despite legitimating bourgeois perspectives, this first real literary establishment in the United States also altered what Brodhead has identified as "the terms of literary access." During the last decades of the century, authors who were published in the pages of the literary monthlies were generally more diverse in social origin and educational background than earlier writers. This was possible because the sketchlike and formulaic nature of the realist genre required little in the way of literary sophistication but depended on knowledge of "cultural backwaters" and unfamiliar locales. As Brodhead notes, "in this respect regionalism made the experience of the socially marginalized into a literary asset, and so made marginality itself a positive authorial advantage."[78]

All of this was possible because educational access was broadening. As shown in chapter 2, both literacy and school enrollment were increasing significantly just before the turn of the century and considerable efforts were being made to open higher education to women and to African Americans.[79] For increasing numbers of people then, the realization of personhood was more intricately stitched to the practices of print culture, whether through reading or writing. As innovations in printing, publication, and distribution technologies further increased the outlets for literary matter, more individuals imagined themselves contributing to newspapers and magazines. From this enlarged pool of writers serving a more variegated print world emerged a more diverse group aspiring to write in what they perceived to be "literary" ways. When some of this material was accepted for publication by established publishing houses and the monthlies associated with them, the very definition of the literary was challenged if not altered significantly.

Virtually every writer in the pantheon now associated with naturalism apprenticed with essays in the columns of fast-multiplying newspapers and then went on to write for the monthlies: Charles Chesnutt, Stephen Crane, Theodore Dreiser, Frank Norris, Jack London, Ambrose Bierce, Kate Chopin, and Abraham Cahan. For entrepreneurs, such as S. S. McClure, Edward Bok, or Cyrus Curtis, the sudden accessibility of a mass audience made publishing look like a good business opportunity.[80] More than 1,000 foreign-language periodicals were founded in the United States by 1897.[81] Still others sought access to specialized newspapers and magazines to express a particular political mission, to serve a targeted population, or simply to converse with people who shared their interests. The committed editors of prominent African American newspapers like the *New York Age* (T. Thomas Fortune), the *Chicago Defender* (Robert S. Abbott), or the *Crisis* (W. E. B. Du Bois), native-born and expatriate Hispanic writers and journalists such as Néstor Ponce de León, Adolfo Carillo, and Ricardo Flores Magón, and even the publishers of technical journals like *Plumber's Trade Journal*, *Advertising News*, or *Philatelic Monthly* served these aspirations.[82]

Many of these new outlets, especially those associated with the fast-developing business and trade press, did nothing to challenge dominant values or the beliefs articulated by the new knowledge classes. However, some contributors used print to raise more radical questions than those posed by America's first alienated literary professionals. Indeed, the very railroads, telegraph lines, and pages upon pages of printed matter that brought news of urban culture, political developments, and literary and artistic trends to regions around the country, enabled readers and writers to imagine themselves gaining access, speaking up, and producing significant change. Many such individuals felt drawn to fast-changing cities like Chicago, Milwaukee, Cincinnati, St. Louis, San Francisco, and even places like Spokane, Washington; Cleveland, Ohio; and Rochester, New York. In all of them, socialists, anarchists, radicals of different sorts, artists, and intellectuals cultivated pockets of dissident thought, seeking both to reach and to create communities of the like-minded through print.[83]

Radical and Alternative Print Cultures

Radical print cultures and alternative publishing networks proliferated during the years that witnessed the transformation of higher education and the professionalization and diversification of the literary sphere. The outpouring was so large, so varied, and couched in so many different languages that it is difficult to summarize developments even briefly. A significant portion of radical writing appeared in the immigrant press, especially in German-language newspapers. Scholars have noted, in fact, that from 1880 to the turn of the century, at least two-thirds of all foreign-language newspapers in the country were in German and furthermore that, between 1870 and 1902, more than 120 German language radical periodicals were founded, including citywide labor papers, union papers, and papers of socialist and anarchist groups.[84]

But radical thought appeared in English as well and in many different print formats. Frederic Jaher notes, for instance, that, "beginning in the 1870s and multiplying in number through the 1880s and early 1890s hundreds of economic novels appeared," responding to the economic unrest of the period. "By 1888," he continues, "the year in which Edward Bellamy's utopian novel, *Looking Backward* was first published by William Ticknor, fourteen other utopias, eleven fiction, had already been written in the United States since the Civil War."[85]

Dissident thought in English ran the political gamut and appeared in vehicles located in cities scattered across the nation. Deliberately abjuring the mass-market magazine strategy of relying on corporate advertising, these papers and their publishers generally cobbled together funds from dedicated individuals, collective publishing societies, and even from union dues. Many lasted no more than a few years, but significant numbers of them persevered, driven by the commitment of their contributors, some of whom worked for long periods without pay. These publishing ventures, which generally offered a mix of economic and political news, organizational information, history, opinion, and even some self-consciously "literary" material, were so important to the left political movement in the United States that Joseph R. Conlin has remarked that "it is by no means frivolous to suggest that the movements, parties, factions, and tendencies that make up American radical history were actually subsidiary to their organs."[86]

Among the early standouts of the radical press was the socialist paper, the *Appeal to Reason*, which was first published in Kansas City in 1895 by J. A. Wayland and later moved to Girard, Kansas. An "[e]rstwhile real estate speculator and utopian colonizer," according to Paul Buhle, Wayland "carried the message of the violated social contract to the Plain states' small independent or tenant farmers, the free-thinking petty merchants, the railroad machinists, schoolteachers and minister's wives."[87] In fact, Wayland was so successful as a socialist evangelical that *Appeal to Reason* became one of America's best selling political weeklies and eventually achieved a circulation of 750,000 by 1913.[88] According to John Graham, editor of an important collection of its offerings, *Appeal to Reason* even managed printings of single-issue papers during certain elections that reached as high as 4.1 million copies.[89]

In addition to political news and commentary, *Appeal to Reason* included cartoons as well as poetry and fiction. Those literary offerings were international in origin, direct and accessible enough to be understood by readers with a range of literacies, and generally celebratory of working-class life.[90] Sinclair Lewis's *The Jungle* was first serialized in the *Appeal*, which also published work by Bellamy and Howells. When the weekly ceased publication in 1922, its project of working-class cultural education was carried on by one of its editors, E. Haldeman-Julius, who created the Little Blue Books. These 3½ by 5 inch books—priced between five to twenty-five cents—made the classics available to a readership that could ill afford traditional, bound volumes. Haldeman-Julius was proud to have Fordized literature. It is estimated that "over the next forty years an estimated five hundred million bluebooks appeared under two thousand different titles."[91]

Another significant radical publishing venture took shape in the city of Chicago in the 1880s—by then, the "headquarters and center of western literature, book-making, and all the kindred arts" and the nation's second most important publishing center.[92] Organized for the most part in support of the socialist cause, Charles H. Kerr & Company issued a range of pamphlets, soft and hardcover books, and several influential periodicals. Founded by Charles Hope Kerr, the son of a University of Wisconsin professor of Greek who taught at the university and lectured in its extension service, the younger Kerr's publishing operation was decidedly not-for-profit. It sought rather to use a range of print vehicles to create a viable alternative public sphere and to educate workers about the social and economic forces affecting their lives. Often unable to generate advertising revenue and disinclined to rely on it even when it could, the house depended for its success on creative financing measures, subscription sales—a specialty of the Chicago book trade—and the cooperation and collaboration of a host of dedicated individuals.

In addition to the *International Socialist Review* (1900–18), Kerr published the radical Unitarian weekly *Unity* (1886–93), two populist monthlies *New Occasions* (1893–96) and the *New Time* (1896–98), and a range of books that included translations of the most significant works of Marxist socialism. In fact, according to a historian of the house, Allen Ruff, Kerr's company "became the most significant English-language publisher and exporter of Marxism in the world between 1900 and 1925."[93] Through all of these ventures, Kerr and his collaborators maintained an international perspective and published critiques of capitalism that were global in nature. The Kerr firm's heyday was from the 1880s into the 1920s, and, although its effectiveness was curtailed by state and U.S. government censorship efforts during World War I, it continued to issue materials well into the second half of the twentieth century.

In the years prior to World War I, the radical press and alternative publishing ventures burgeoned throughout the United States, both in fast-expanding urban areas and in small out-of-the-way places.[94] Much of this publishing activity was traditionally political in nature as Socialists, Communists, Anarchists, Wobblies, and a host of others elbowed their way into print seeking to advance their causes by informing the like-minded and hoping to convert the still unsure. But the publicity and influence promised by print was appealing to many other nonconforming groups as well, including intellectuals of various sorts, literary radicals and avant-garde artists, and even the "sex radicals," discussed by Joanne Passet and Christine Stansell, who participated in a movement that began before the Civil War but continued well into our period.[95] As Passet has pointed out, in many ways the sex radical movement was synonymous with its press. One participated in the movement by founding and supporting relevant periodicals, by recruiting new subscribers, by ordering books and pamphlets, by reading certain key texts, and by contributing to defense funds when editors found their ideas and publications censored.[96]

Of course, print did not displace oppositional political organization or alternative social movement during this period. It did, however, develop as an integral part of proliferating challenges to the status quo, challenges fostered by a rapidly expanding, increasingly mobile, and diversifying population. Nowhere was this more evident than in New York City, with its special cacophony of fast-moving traffic, multiple languages, diverse politics, and countless forms of new communication that drew vast numbers of people into the city's cultural orbit. In New York, as Christine Stansell has shown, "a booming print culture, the spread of advertising, and the compression of polylingual populations . . .

touch[ed] off an explosion of language."[97] These conditions also contributed to the production of significant unrest in the literary field as writers of many different sorts with different agendas sought to redefine what counted as the literary.

Remaking Literature for the Modern Era

Drawn to the Lower East Side for its roiling political discussions, familiarity with European intellectual developments, and its famous nightlife, new-style literary aspirants like Dreiser and Crane and later Max Eastman, Waldo Frank, and Randolph Bourne mingled with the immigrants who poured into New York between 1890 and 1910. Seeking to escape what was then lamented as the "standardization" of American life, they talked ceaselessly of contemporary intellectual, political, and aesthetic developments. In their painting, writing, music, and politics, they questioned older pieties. "There was," according to Eastman, "a sense of universal revolt and regeneration, of the just-before-dawn of a new day in American art and literature and living-of-life as well as in politics."[98]

Many of these erstwhile literary bohemians congregated in and around Greenwich Village, conversing with the resident Jewish socialist and anarchist intellectuals who were involved in the creation of a significant Yiddish press and the ongoing production of New York's vibrant socialist print culture. These immigrant intellectuals introduced their American followers to the works of Freud, Nietzsche, Hegel, Bergson, Gorky, Tolstoy, Chernyshevsky, and others. Drawn thereby into an international literary and artistic culture that was critical of the instrumentalism and market orientation that its proponents associated with capitalism and modern business culture, Greenwich Village intellectuals and their followers together began to explore new subjects and alternate ways of writing. As they did so, many, though not all, clashed with the expectations of traditional publishing houses and their aging periodicals. Over time, they formed new networks of writers, editors, publishers, and readers interested in a range of experimental literary work, including that which challenged traditional sexual mores. As they did so, they also generated a host of new political journals and "little magazines" open to dissident forms of thought.

A short list of some of the periodical titles that appeared between 1910 and 1915 alone conveys the intellectual vibrancy not only of New York but of other American cities such as Chicago and San Francisco during these years: the *Masses* (New York, 1910); *Poetry* (Chicago, 1912); the *Smart Set* (New York, 1913); the *New Republic* (New York, 1914); the *Little Review* (Chicago, 1914); the *Seven Arts* (New York, 1916). Although each of these magazines had its distinct agenda, most shared the assumption expressed by Herbert Croly, founder of the *New Republic*, that "social improvement was an intellectual and cultural problem, not a merely political or technical one."⁹⁹ The *New Republic* would subsequently break rank with some of the more radical intellectuals over World War I, but in its early years, like the more literary "little magazines," it sought to explore how cultural life might regenerate the political and social life of the nation.¹⁰⁰ In that effort, these magazines introduced Americans to the works of Carl Sandburg, Vachel Lindsay, T. S. Eliot, Wallace Stevens, Marianne Moore, and Ezra Pound, who once advised Harriet Monroe as she was organizing *Poetry* that, "If one is going to print opinions the public agrees with, what is the use of printing them at all?" "Publish the best poetry directed toward the broadening and development of the Art of Poetry," he told her, "and 'TO HELL WITH HARPERS AND THE MAGAZINE TOUCH.'"¹⁰¹

World War I painfully compromised the dream that, for a time, animated the "little renaissance" in New York and in the bohemian quarters of other cities. Increased censorship and a general wariness of radical ideas made it harder to believe in the possibility of a society in which artists and writers would lead the way into a future.¹⁰² When Margaret Lawrence and Jane Heap serialized installments of James Joyce's *Ulysses* in the *Little Review*, for instance, from 1918 to 1920, issue after issue was seized by government authorities and eventually Lawrence and Heap were charged with purveying obscenity through the mail.¹⁰³ Still, the radicals, intellectuals, and bohemians who flourished during the first two decades of the twentieth century laid the institutional and intellectual groundwork for a cultural formation that would develop swiftly after the war. That formation united a new generation of literary men, the adventurous publishing houses they created, and a host of writers who were familiar with the revolutionary aesthetic movements of the continent like futurism, cubism, constructivism, and symbolism and who were determined to transform American writing into something more challenging, more aesthetically rigorous, more "modern."

American literary modernism was a richly complex, contradictory formation whose full history cannot be told here.¹⁰⁴ Still, it is essential to note that this key aesthetic development of the twentieth century was made possible not only by the writers themselves but also by the publishers and editors who nurtured their work, helped to hone it, and worked tirelessly to introduce it to a sometimes inhospitable American audience. The years between the two world wars saw the rise to prominence of a new group of publishers who challenged the cultural dominance of family firms like Harper's and Scribner's and even more recently established companies like Holt and Doubleday. As James West notes in chapter 4, a preponderance of these newer publishing houses were organized by German Jewish immigrants, many of whom who had been educated at Columbia University and who were familiar with the literary developments in Europe. Bristling at genteel literary strictures about what could be represented and how, publishers such as B. W. Huebsch, Alfred A. Knopf, Mitchell Kennerly, Alfred Harcourt, Horace Liveright, Albert Boni, and Bennett Cerf organized their ventures in the hope of renovating not only American writing but American culture more generally.

When Alfred A. Knopf, whose house had been founded in 1915 and who boasted one of the most prestigious lists in all of publishing, announced the 1923 creation of *American Mercury* (to be edited by H. L. Mencken from Knopf's own offices), he was giving voice to a perspective that also underwrote his book publishing practices and was shared at least in part by many of the men of this new publishing cohort:

> The aim of the *American Mercury* will be to offer a comprehensive picture, critically presented, of the entire American scene. It will not confine itself to the fine arts; in addition, there will be constant consideration of American politics, American governmental problems, American industrial and social relations, and American science. The point of view that it will seek to maintain will be that of the civilized minority. It will strive, at all times, to avoid succumbing to the current platitudes, and one of its fundamental purposes will be to discover and develop writers in all fields competent to attack those platitudes in a realistic and effective manner.[105]

In that spirit, Knopf himself published Katherine Mansfield, Willa Cather, Floyd Dell, Carl Van Vechten, Sigrid Unset, André Gide, and Thomas Mann. B. W. Huebsch prided himself on having introduced Sherwood Anderson, D. H. Lawrence, and James Joyce to Americans. He also published Thorstein Veblen, Anton Chekhov, and Maxim Gorky. Alfred Harcourt published John Maynard Keynes, Sinclair Lewis, Dorothy Canfield, Carl Sandburg, and E. M. Forster. Horace Liveright brought out Dreiser's *An American Tragedy* and was instrumental in the introduction of the work of Ernest Hemingway and William Faulkner to American readers.[106]

Together, these men were willing to publish avant-garde and experimental fiction as well as nonfiction that took on difficult issues of the moment, whether social, political, or cultural. As Paul Boyer writes in this volume, they were also willing to resist the censorship of the Comstock laws. Some were more radical in their personal politics than others but, generally, these new-style publishers were committed to the idea that the literary arts broadly conceived were necessary to producing a democratic social life in America.

In tracing the connection between literary modernism and the publishing apparatus that made it possible, it is important to avoid excessive romanticizing of the revolutionary motives of men such as Knopf, Harcourt, Cerf, or Charles Scribner II, who presided over the family firm's most celebrated years when Maxwell Perkins shepherded the major works of F. Scott Fitzgerald, Thomas Wolfe, and others into the American literary arena. However much these men championed the work of an aesthetic avant-garde, they also entered the publishing business to generate an audience for their writers and to make a profit for themselves. In fact, the very same promoters of modernist fiction arranged for its printing in beautifully designed modern editions and used some of the most up-to-date marketing methods to sell their books. And, as scholars, including Lawrence Rainey, Jennifer Wicke, Joyce Wexler, Michael Levenson, and Catherine Turner, have demonstrated, they were oftentimes joined in this by the very writers who constituted their work in opposition to the commercialism, instrumentalism, and utilitarianism of the market.[107] In fact, modernist writing was a complicated practice. At once anticommercial and yet heavily invested in the desire to sell, both disdainful and desirous of an audience, it was deeply critical of the society that nurtured it and yet, like it, was thoroughly commercialized and commodified.

Understandably, then, the various modernisms that competed for attention during these years were highly controversial. They generated passionate debate among critical authorities and the readers they addressed, a fact that underscored the diversity of the ever-expanding literary sphere that, during the twenties, also witnessed the rise to prominence of middlebrow institutions like the Literary Guild and the Book-of-the-Month Club; the flourishing of a culture of best sellers; the maturing of literatures written by African Americans, women, and a range of ethnic minorities; and the proliferation of a pulp literature targeting a mass audience. While the establishment of an American literary avant-garde was often associated with the further reification of the divide between the highbrow and the lowbrow, the literary scene that developed in the twenties and into the thirties was far more fluid, more contentious, and thus more fractured than is implied by the familiar dichotomy.

Still, while some modernist fiction sold well, especially after men such as Knopf, Scribner, Harcourt, and Cerf learned to associate their titles with readers' desires to appear cultured and "up-to-date," a good deal of modernist literature remained highly experimental in form, intensely allusive to global literary traditions, and linguistically idiosyncratic. It therefore demanded, for the most part, an educated or at least culturally informed reader because it was notoriously difficult to read. As a consequence, modern writers were frequently attacked for being deliberately obscure and their work was said to appeal only to a small coterie. At the same time, because many modernist novels were much more candid about sex and employed colloquial slang, they were frequently charged with being ugly, sordid, or merely fraudulent.

Critics debated the relative merits of modernist titles versus those more traditional in form and accessible in language in the flourishing literary press of the period, that is, in the pages of the *Nation*, the *New Republic*, the *Saturday Review of Literature*, the *New Yorker*, the *Bookman*, and *New York Herald Tribune Books*.[108] This ephemeral criticism was augmented by a burgeoning, book-length criticism that sought to assess more formally the meaning of contemporary American literature. Written by reviewers, critics, and prominent academics (who had begun to take notice of contemporary writing), much of this criticism was skeptical about the merits of modernist experimentation. In his 1930 analysis of *The New American Literature*, for instance, Fred Lewis Pattee spoke for many when he observed that the "'modern school' of novels that were 'overloaded with sex, with coarseness, with the logic of futility' reflected 'a generation debauched by war.'"[109] In discussing the work of Ernest Hemingway, he noted that Hemingway had "deliberately violated every canon of the old handbooks and even the elementary rules of grammar." Pattee further warned, "The real artist does not flaunt himself, nor pose, nor perform bad-boy tricks for sensation in the presence of dignity, nor does he deliberately place strangeness and sex uncleanness and grotesque newness among his leading artistic canons."[110] Middlebrow authorities like Stuart Sherman, Irita Van Doren, John Erskine, and even Book-of-the-Month Club judge Henry Seidel Canby, who tended to be more adventurous than some, added their voices to those calling for a more fully accessible literature acceptable to the "general reader."[111]

Still, modernist writers continued to write, their titles sold (sometimes in substantial numbers), and slowly they began to build a readership attentive to the aesthetic and intellectual pleasures of modernist form. Among their most vocal supporters were H. L. Mencken, Van Wyck Brooks, and especially Edmund Wilson and Malcolm Cowley, who, in two widely read books, *Axel's Castle: A Study in the Imaginative Literature of 1870–1930* (Scribner's, 1936) and *After the Great Tradition: American Writers since 1910* (W. W. Norton, 1937), made a strong case for the aesthetic centrality of this new literary movement.

Then, in the thirties and the forties in the university context, a new criticism began to appear that was related to the writings of these early champions of literary modernism but focused less on judgment and questions of value and more on interpretation and the determination of meaning.[112] Pitched quite explicitly against the concerns of the now well-established research specialists in academic literary studies, what became known as the New Criticism was associated with the introduction of contemporary writing and American literature into the university curriculum. It was also attuned to the problem of how to teach a difficult and richly ambiguous literature to a growing population of undergraduates who did not have deep familiarity with the classical literary tradition. First fully articulated as a critical program by Cleanth Brooks in *Modern Poetry and the Tradition*, published in 1939 by the University of North Carolina Press, New Criticism and the literature that was its inspiration made a strong bid for both academic and cultural legitimacy that same year when Henry Holt published what would become a highly influential textbook, *Understanding Poetry: An Anthology for College Students*.

It should be underscored here that the controversies surrounding the arrival and maturation of literary modernism were exacerbated by the unrest that characterized the literary field from the years around the turn of the century well into the 1930s. In part because of the field's expansion and its more thoroughgoing commercialization, in part because of the extension of more advanced literacy throughout the population with the growth of high schools and colleges, and in part because of significant immigration around the turn of the century, greater opportunities presented themselves to an even more diverse pool of potential writers than that from which regionalist and realist writers were drawn in the 1880s and 1890s. Women, African Americans, Yiddish and Jewish writers, Asian Americans, and other ethnic, working-class, and socialist writers all made their bid to define the literary in these years. Some of their poetry and prose situated itself well within aesthetic movements of the period and was perceived to be part of regionalist, realist, and even modernist trends. Some of it, however, was based on quite different understandings of the literary and its social function as writers struggled to articulate new identities and used their fiction, poetry, essays, and criticism to appeal to readers whom they perceived to be in need of writing that addressed concerns not seen either in mainstream print culture or even in most dissident and avant-garde publications. "New Women" and the "New Negro" made their literary presence increasingly well known, for example, in the years just before and then after the turn of the century.

New Literatures for Emergent Audiences and Coalescing Communities

As with literary modernism, this is not the place to tell the history of literature written by women or people of color during our period. However, it is worth noting how the changes documented in this volume enabled previously marginalized populations to create print forms that offered new identities, new communities, and new ways of knowing. The same set of economic, social, and cultural pressures that helped to create universities and academic print culture as well as mass-produced literature, middlebrow culture, and the high-literary zone also produced new institutions of higher learning designed to educate women and African Americans. And those institutions facilitated the entrance of their students into the myriad arenas of a professionalizing society, including the broadly literary zones of print culture.[113]

Following the Civil War, doors were opened to women by a range of institutions of higher learning, including some land-grant state universities and the new, single-sex women's colleges.[114] Female enrollment increased significantly at both kinds of institutions during the 1880s and 1890s because bourgeois families were more willing to grant their daughters access to higher education. Although the founders of the women's colleges frequently had to respond to fears that higher education would "unsex" women, they managed, nonetheless, to persevere in their mission. By the time M. Carey Thomas was installed as president of Bryn Mawr College in 1893, attitudes had changed enough to enable her to model the institution after "the standards, curriculum, and scholarship" of the research-oriented Johns Hopkins.[115] Overall, the women's colleges pioneered in hiring female faculties, in promoting leadership opportunities for women, and, in some cases, in curriculum reform. They stressed the modern languages more than the ancient, organized some of the first classes in American literature ever taught in the United States, and concentrated significant resources in the teaching of the biological sciences.[116]

A significant number of the graduates of Mount Holyoke, Smith, Wellesley, Vassar, Bryn Mawr, Radcliffe, and Barnard left those institutions with the desire to engage actively in the public world of work and to live lives different from those of their mothers. Some, like Jane Addams and the Hamilton sisters discussed by Barbara Sicherman, sought access to traditional professions and prepared themselves for careers in social work, medicine, or teaching.[117] Others, like M. Carey Thomas and her circle of friends, built upon their adolescent reading by experimenting with nontraditional gender identities and by questioning the near universal assumption that women ought to marry.[118] Others married but participated in the club movement that drew large numbers of middle-class women (white and African American alike) into various forms of literacy work including book discussions, the preparation and presentation of research papers, and the founding and administration of local libraries. Others went into settlement house work with immigrant and working-class women.[119] These pursuits of educated women of the early twentieth century allowed them to explore new forms of economic independence, homosocial relationships with other women, different forms of femininity, and new uses of knowledge and literacy.[120]

"New Women," it seemed, were everywhere. As Anne Ruggles Gere has noted, "Between 1890 and 1920 numerous writers devoted considerable energy to defining, criticizing, and poking fun at the 'new woman,' a journalistic encapsulation of changes in women's views and expectations."[121] When women responded, seeking some measure of control over their own representation, a cultural struggle ensued over the proper definition of womanhood. Some of this writing was polemical; some of it was expository or pedagogical; a fair portion of it was poetic and fictional because in fiction and poetry women could exercise imaginative freedom and construct new models for themselves and their daughters. The new women's literature produced over the next twenty to thirty years raised fundamental questions about virtually every aspect of women's role in society.

Building on women's regionalist writing of the 1870s and 1880s, writers like Ellen Glasgow, Chopin, Cather, Edith Wharton, Gertrude Stein, Josephine Herbst, Nella Larson, Jesse Redmon Fauset, Tilly Lerner Olsen, and Meridel Le Seur imagined women who grappled with things other than romance or the pleasures of domesticity. As they envisioned new lives for women or attempted to portray their problems honestly, they explored sexuality as well as work and economic independence. Their stories often circled about questions of agency and choice for women as they complicated the traditional marriage plot and portrayed women struggling to act on their own behalf.

Because the notion of female independence was so threatening, some of these writers suffered greatly at the hands of nervous publishers, skeptical editors, and hostile reviewers. Chopin was devastated by the reaction to her novel, *The Awakening*;[122] Cather bristled at the reviews that labeled her a novelist of "small things";[123] and Stein decided to pursue her own highly original version of the literary life abroad.[124] Still, these early pioneers pressed on in their quest to demonstrate that women, too, far from being popular scribblers, could actually be literary artists of the first order.

It is difficult to trace the concrete effects of this writing upon the readers of books like *My Antonia*, *O! Pioneers*, *The Awakening*, or *Barren Ground*. It seems likely, though, that by endowing female characters with self-knowledge and a measure of agency, they inspired younger women to think beyond constricting gender roles and to imagine new social and cultural arenas for female achievement. The younger generation of women who succeeded these pioneers, including Mary Heaton Vorse, Neith Boyce, Susan Glaspell, Mabel Dodge, Margaret Lawrence, Nella Larsen, Jesse Redmon Fauset, H.D. (Hilda Doolittle), and Marianne Moore, participated actively in the emergence of early modernism.[125] Together, these two cohorts of literary women produced the first sustained body of American fictional work devoted to exploring the relationship between gender, subjectivity, and, in some cases, race. Many years later, that work would be revived and used anew to challenge what passed for conventional knowledge about women, gender, race, life, and work.

It might be argued that between 1880 and 1915, African Americans faced even more daunting challenges than did white women in their quest to be heard in the public domain. Literacy, generally denied to slaves, increased dramatically among freed persons following emancipation. In the 1880s and 1890s, however, blacks faced a campaign of repression through disenfranchisement, segregation, brutality, and murder. Meanwhile, learned culture often constructed African Americans as a "problem"—a pathological object for study by white experts. Two of the new disciplinary domains, sociology and anthropology, asserted their legitimacy on the basis of their ability to offer knowledge of alien populations to those who aimed to help or control them. Although whites offered African Americans modest educational opportunities during this period, many were designed to channel blacks into industrial, domestic, and service work. Against such oppression, African Americans began to elaborate their own visions of education and sought access to the world of print to contest the claims of those who would wield the pen and other instruments of knowledge production against them.

Virtually all of the early black colleges were private institutions established with the assistance of philanthropic organizations, both white and black. Most were founded by patrons who saw in Negro education an extension of abolitionist work and a means to achieve racial equality in civil and political life. Accordingly, they aimed to prepare individual men and women of character to lead a program of racial uplift. Henry L. Morehouse, of the American Baptist Home Mission Society, was the first to describe this projected leadership group as "the talented tenth" who should be educated and "trained to analyze and to generalize," producing "thoroughly disciplined minds."[126]

Early efforts at Negro education sought to duplicate the curriculum of New England academies and colleges. They were challenged, however, by the contemporaneous development of another view of how to educate former slaves. A model of "industrial education" first championed by white philanthropist and educator Samuel Chapman Armstrong was implemented at Hampton Normal and Agricultural Institute in 1868. Tuskegee Normal and Industrial Institute subsequently copied this model in 1881, where Chapman's prize student, Booker T. Washington, sought to follow his mentor's ideas. Later, white philanthropists seized upon the Hampton-Tuskegee model as the ideal way to prepare a supposedly inferior race for its naturally subordinate place in the new industrial order.

Booker T. Washington's famous 1895 speech defending the Hampton-

Tuskegee model generated vociferous debate within the ranks of a growing black intelligentsia. Some wished to pursue industrial education, gradualism, and accommodation to white society. Others, termed "radicals" by August Meier, were more interested in educating the "talented tenth" to lead in the agitation for civil and political rights and to explore the possibilities of integration.[127] Many followed the leadership of W. E. B. Du Bois who argued that the kind of education promoted by Washington and his allies undersold black Americans by rendering them socially and economically inferior.

The bitter debate over education that followed the discussion between Washington and Du Bois was carried out in the pages of the black newspapers and magazines that proliferated during this period, as James Danky shows in chapter 17. African American print culture expanded significantly in the years after 1880 not only because general literacy increased among blacks but also because thirty-four institutions had been established by 1900 devoted exclusively to offering college-level training to African Americans. By 1900, 2,000 black Americans had graduated from institutions of higher learning.[128] These developments helped to create a growing group of black readers, writers, editors, and publishers who sought access to print in order to articulate a more confident, differently racialized identity. In print they explored alternatives to the view of blacks as mentally inferior then being disseminated by white publishing houses like Grosset and Dunlap, which issued Thomas Dixon's *The Clansman* (1905) and some university presses like Columbia, which issued Howard Odum's 1910 book, *Social and Mental Traits of the Negro: A Study of Race Traits, Tendencies and Prospects*.[129]

Racist views like these were actively contested not only by entrants in the world of print but also by a whole new generation of African American teachers and their students, including the growing ranks of educated, middle-class black clubwomen who, as Elizabeth McHenry shows in chapter 25, were deeply involved in establishing the first libraries in African American communities. Nearly as important as the schools in encouraging literacy and reading among black Americans, these institutions sought to acquaint their patrons not only with the dominant forms of knowledge produced by whites but also with what was then called "race literature."[130]

First defined by Victoria Earle Matthews as "all the writings emanating from a distinct class . . . a general collection of what has been written by the men and women of that Race: History, Biographies, Scientific Treatises, Sermons, Addresses, Novels, Poems, Books of Travel, miscellaneous essays and the contributions to magazines and newspapers,"[131] race literature came to mean books by, for, and about people of color. Although some notable books in this genre were published by white-owned houses, including George Washington Williams's *History of the Negro Race in America from 1619 to 1880* (G. P. Putnam's Sons, 1883) and Du Bois's own *The Souls of Black Folk* (A. C. McClurg Co., 1903), most of this literature was issued by the book-publishing units of black cultural, professional, civil rights, social welfare, and educational institutions.[132]

In the period after 1880 four important black national organizations were founded, all with their own research and publishing departments that strove to issue materials that would treat the lives of African Americans in a nonracist manner. The American Negro Academy (1897), the National Association for the Advancement of Colored People (1910), the National Urban League (1911), and the Association for the Study of Negro Life and History (1915) all addressed the demand for pamphlets, journals, and books about the history and achievements of Africans and African Americans. Atlanta University Press, as well, began publishing in 1896, issuing not only informational materials designed to garner students and philanthropic support for the university but also more scholarly studies, including a number of dense and detailed sociological reports on the condition of Negroes in the South.[133] Similarly, the Negro Year Book Publishing Company was organized at Tuskegee in 1910 to document the progress of black Americans. According to Donald Joyce, "The Negro Yearbook was the most comprehensive source of facts and statistics on the Black American to appear in the first four decades of the twentieth century."[134]

In seeking to counter racist writing, these and other print establishments provided venues for the work of a new cohort of highly literate, better-trained African American authors.[135] Dickson Bruce Jr. estimates that 80 percent of the writers who published between 1877 and 1915 held professional positions as ministers, educators, physicians, or attorneys. Most were college-educated, two-thirds of them at black colleges, and most labored in relative obscurity.[136] While it is true that Paul Lawrence Dunbar was eventually championed by Howells and published in *Harper's* and by Dodd, Mead and that Charles Chesnutt's work appeared in the *Atlantic*, for the most part, as James Danky emphasizes in his essay, black men and women were published by the African American press. Still, some sought to reach not only black audiences but whites as well.[137] An 1892 conference of African American authors noted the failure of black writing to "make its way among our white fellow-citizens to anything like a desirable extent, and not even to a degree which our literary merit deserves."[138]

When the predominant religious periodicals proved too limited in what they would publish, African American intellectuals founded magazines like the *Colored American Magazine*, *Voice of the Negro*, *Alexander's Magazine*, and *Howard's American Magazine*, all of which published a broader range of literary writing, including poetry, by black authors. Although the audiences they reached were small, Bruce argues that, as the main outlet for the amateurs who dominated African American literary activity at this time, these magazines were "the chief arbiters of taste in Black literary life."[139] Together with the printing establishments of the black cultural, political, and social organizations, these and other black-owned periodicals like the *Crisis*, the official organ of the NAACP, managed to create what Meier has termed "the social and intellectual origins of the New Negro."[140] The works written and published by these African American pioneers in the four decades around the turn of the century contested harmful stereotypes about blacks and sought to document the character of African American life. In doing so, they helped create new subjects who, though they might strive for middle-class respectability and for acceptance by whites, also began to think of themselves as people with a distinct racial identity and culture worthy of defense.

Perhaps most influential within this new intellectual formation was Du Bois — teacher, scholar, activist, novelist, and, for twenty-five years, the editor of the *Crisis*. Du Bois pursued his goal of contesting the dominant ways of objectifying the Negro through the many different channels of print culture, including journalism, critical essays, sociological studies, and fiction. In doing so, he helped to forge alternative ways of knowing *as* an African American, that is, as "an American, a Negro, two souls, two thoughts, two unreconciled strivings, two warring ideas in one dark body."[141] Over time, as his biographer, David Levering Lewis has shown, Du Bois attempted to balance a longing for national citizenship with the sense that only the development of a keenly critical, indeed revolutionary, black subject might make that possible.[142]

Although he produced a highly varied, rigorous, and profoundly radical corpus of work in that effort and sought to address many different audiences on his own, it is important to note here that Du Bois also exerted his influence as an editor by enabling the work of like-minded others. He worked closely, for instance, with Fauset, the literary editor of the *Crisis*, to publish a broad range of "race literature." During its most influential years, 1919–26, the *Crisis* regularly reviewed books by young African American writers, many of whom would come to be associated with what at the time was referred to as "the New Negro movement" or "the Negro Renassiance."[143] Arna Bontemps, Langston Hughes, Countee Cullen, and Jean Toomer, for instance, all were published early on by the *Crisis*.

Despite the central role played by the *Crisis* and the importance more generally of print culture within the African American community, for the most part, black-owned publishing establishments were not the houses that issued most of the poetry and prose associated with the Renaissance. As Harold Cruse, Nathan Huggins, David Levering Lewis, Houston Baker, Anne Elizabeth Carroll, and

Cherene Sherrard-Johnson have shown, the literary and aesthetic movement encouraged by Charles S. Johnson, Alain Locke, James Weldon Johnson, Fauset, Walter White, and Casper Holstein depended heavily on the patronage of white publishers and editors like Carl Van Vechten, H. L. Mencken, Horace Liveright, Max Eastman, and Charles and Albert Boni, men who were dubbed "Negrotarians" by Zora Neale Hurston.[144]

In the 1920s white literary culture discovered that the African American was a salable commodity as a symbol of raw, uncultivated nature. As Lewis has put it, "if the factory was dehumanizing, the campus and office stultifying, and the great corporations predaceous, the Afro-American—excluded from factory, campus, office, and corporation—was the perfect symbol of cultural innocence and regeneration."[145] Although the patronage born of this kind of racialized romanticism was warily welcomed by Harlem's just-developing literary scene because it enabled writers like Fauset, Toomer, and Cullen, to appear in book-length form, it was also viewed critically for the way in which it trafficked too often in familiar stereotypes of the Negro as exotic, sexualized, and unusually physical. In fact, literary historians of the movement have suggested that despite its most earnest intentions, the patronage of the progressive wing of the white literary establishment worked as a kind of "benevolent censor, politely but pervasively setting the outer limits of its creative boundaries."[146]

Despite their compunctions, black writers of this period submitted to white patronage in part because there was not a large enough audience within the black community to support their work. But they also participated in their own cultivation by leading literary lights within the white publishing establishment because they longed to be accepted as equals on their literary merits alone, as serious writers rather than as mere representatives of their race. Still, despite the fact that their work was not rooted organically in the wider black community (in fact, Harlem itself was becoming a slum during the very period when the Renaissance flourished) and often gave voice most insistently to their concerns as middle-class black intellectuals, their work raised radical questions about the arbitrariness of race as well as about the undeniable and extended effects of its near universal mobilization within American culture.[147] In doing so, the writers of the New Negro Renaissance produced a body of work that proclaimed the entry of African Americans into the high-literary field and thereby moved to break the association between Negroes, the body, and sensation. In seeking to attest to the intellect and aesthetic sensibility of the "New Negro," this body of work strove to constitute new forms of subjectivity for people of color, forms that would be protested by some as too white and appreciated by others as the result of a sustained effort to articulate the humanity and particularity of black Americans in the face of persistent white racism.

A New Cultural Formation Takes Shape

After the stock market crash of 1929, a more working-class-oriented black literature developed as part of the flourishing of a literary left. As Michael Denning has recently demonstrated (building on the earlier work of Daniel Aaron and others), a new generation of "plebeian artists and intellectuals who had grown up in the immigrant and black working class neighborhoods of the modernist metropolis" began to produce a diverse body of literature in the 1930s that took the lives of laborers, immigrants, blacks, women, and other outsiders as its principal subject.[148] Building on their education within the public schools and by the socialist, immigrant, and foreign-language print cultures that flourished in American cities in the 1920s and 1930s, these writers published stories and poems in "little magazines" such as *Blast, Anvil, Dynamo, Broom, Partisan Review, Left Front, Challenge,* and Mike Gold's *New Masses*. They authored ghetto pastorals, tales of unemployed drifters, racial romances, gangster stories, novels about labor struggles and craftwork like stonecutting and bricklaying, migrant narratives, and even a Marxist literary criticism, which, for a time, had an enormous impact on debates about the nature of American literature in the contemporary press.

This was possible because in the 1930s what had previously been censored as radical or outside the mainstream became acceptable forms of thought as a new cultural formation took shape in the wake of the continuing industrialization of labor and its extended impact on the social, political, and cultural life of the nation. Writers like Anya Yezierska, Mike Gold, Claude Mackay, Richard Wright, Tillie Lerner Olsen, Nelson Algren, Meridel Le Seur, Chester Himes, Ralph Ellison, Grace Lumpkin, Mari Tomasi, H. T. Tsiang, Pearl Chang, Harriet Arnow, Ernesto Galarza, John Steinbeck, Carlos Bulosan, and John Dos Passos, among a host of others, wrestled with familiar literary genres, with narrative conventions, and with the very definition of what constituted a story in order to narrate the significance of lives rendered monotonous by poverty and mind-numbing labor. They were published, for the most part, by the major houses of the period because, as Denning has so vigorously argued, the "Age of the CIO" (Congress of Industrial Organizations) and "the laboring of American culture" created what was referred to at the time as the "Cultural Front," that is, a new cultural formation willing to explore the consequences of transformations in the racial and sexual organization of labor, in gender relations, in household formations, and in the very nature of social life itself.

Although these subjects were taken up within the many precincts of left literary culture, they were also explored in the images and stories purveyed by a whole new cultural apparatus as well, that is, the culture industry of leisure and entertainment built on the new technologies of motion pictures, recorded sound, and broadcasting. These industrialized technologies and the corporate financing and advertising networks that supported them provided the culture industries access to audiences significantly larger than anything addressed by print culture's best-selling books or its most widely circulated newspapers and magazines. In the years to come, the novel, the poem, and the short story would be challenged as the preeminent forms through which American culture thought imaginatively about its past and its future by film melodramas, adventure tales, and biopics as well as by radio and television dramas and sitcoms. The cultures of the learned and the literary would continue to exercise their dominant hold on the intellectual life of the nation even into the second half of the twentieth century. But after the brief interlude represented by the Cultural Front, they would be challenged. A visual and leisure culture had risen to prominence, offering its own, sometimes differently pitched, stories and pleasures to a mass audience that, over time, turned less frequently to lettered, print culture for imaginative and informational forms addressing its principal concerns, desires, worries, and anxieties about the future. That, however, is a story for the next volume in this series.

CHAPTER 12

Crafting a Communications Infrastructure
Scientific and Technical Publishing in the United States

Marcel Chotkowski LaFollette

. . .

In the twentieth century, as American science, engineering, and medicine grew to maturity, a complex, interconnected communications system, involving books and journals, commercial publishing firms, and nonprofit professional associations, developed alongside the research organizations to support the dissemination of knowledge. The system's products fit no single model, ranging from slender theoretical essays on physics and elaborate astronomical charts to detailed engineering handbooks, from medical treatises to best sellers about evolution and atomic energy. Textbooks synthesized the state of knowledge in a field and trundled on through the years in revised editions. Reference books served as indispensable research tools, telling where to locate a certain star, how a chemical reacts to heat, or precise values for logarithms.

These publications were manufactured similarly to other products of American publishers. Their professional functions, however, were unique: validating status and the status quo, establishing credit and priority, defining and defending intellectual boundaries, and formalizing evolving technical standards. With the exception of books aimed at popular audiences, the authors usually were the same specialists who validated, evaluated, and then bought and consumed the content. Every researcher was expected to participate in the publishing system not only as reader and author but also occasionally as reviewer, editor, or adviser.

Each entity in this communications infrastructure—commercial publishers, nonprofit university presses, professional associations, and government agencies—operated independently and set its own policies, procedures, and goals, yet all accepted the practitioners' standards for evaluating intellectual quality. This arrangement structurally reinforced scientists' control over the content vital to their work, without requiring them to assume the financial or managerial responsibility for publication and distribution. Scientists served as advisers to publishers. Laboratories, research corporations, or government agencies, not individuals, generally underwrote book production. And the publishers indulged scientists' penchant for continual revisions by issuing multiple editions of essential texts for fields experiencing dramatic intellectual growth. Scientists, engineers, and medical researchers shaped the system to satisfy their craving for "good" (i.e., accurate and timely) information. They encouraged the proliferation of outlets to accommodate all those who wanted to publish, despite defending the preeminence of accredited expertise and quality control.

During this same period, the modern scientific periodical, the "journal," acquired much of its current identity and importance. Issued sometimes weekly, sometimes as annual volumes, these publications were assembled with the same care as traditional bound books, but at an accelerated production schedule, and they were treated with equal status in the knowledge system. Starting in the nineteenth century, technical publishers frequently produced both books and journals.

As formal modes of content evaluation (i.e., "peer review") evolved among journals, those standards began to influence editorial selection within book publishing, although rarely to the same degree as in the journals. Within commercial, technical book publishing, economic considerations were never completely subordinated to intellectual ones; only for technical books published by university presses were such arguments routinely allowed to outweigh high cost. In every sector, the decision to publish took account of an author's reputation and expertise, intellectual trends within disciplines, and shifts in techniques and theoretical schools lest the publishers alienate or lose touch with the customers on whom their survival depended. Numerous sources of funding contributed to the vast growth in technical publishing during the twentieth century, including subsidies from industrial laboratories, a university system that encouraged research and publication, and a growing system of government grants that treated publication as an appropriate and necessary research activity.

Wartime posed varied challenges to technical publishers. During World War I, the disruption of European outlets left U.S. publishers struggling to fill the gap for vital reference works heretofore produced abroad. During World War II, publishers cooperated in both government-imposed and voluntary censorship of sensitive material. They also quickly produced hundreds of thousands of books in special editions for technical training schools. After 1945 these same publishers would move nimbly to capitalize on the Cold War expansion of the research system.

In addition to professional texts and journals, during the 1930s trade publishers produced more popular and middlebrow literature directed at general audiences. These books sought to satisfy Americans' curiosity about all sorts of new theories and technologies. Although this popular literature clearly derived its authority and significance from technical experts, it represented an independent product for most publishers, who could tap the new profession of science journalism for the authors of such books.

This chapter assembles what is known about scientific, medical, and engineering book publishing during a critical period of definition and expansion. Because journal articles, rather than books, have been the principal arenas for intellectual debate within disciplines, especially from 1900 on, any history of this communications system must also take into account the co-dependent relationship between these types of publication.[1]

It is especially interesting to consider the formative history of this publishing sector from the perspective of a time when scientists' primary communications venues have begun to shift from print-based to electronic formats. These changes have prompted many publishers and scientific groups to take a fresh look at the purposes, standards, and allocation of costs for such communication, aspects that are rooted in its history. This chapter describes how, in the first half of the twentieth century, researchers in all fields cooperated with willing and opportunistic publishers to construct a system that would accommodate to their own professional goals and requirements.

A Favorable Climate in the New World

Although by the late nineteenth century Americans were making significant global contributions to science, Europeans were still setting the standards for its diffusion. Technical books published originally in the United States were likely to be eclipsed by their European cousins; American publishers tended to favor British scientists; and, until the 1870s, few specialized journals were published in the United States.[2] The imprimatur of European publication remained essential to building one's professional reputation in science, medicine, and engineering.

Independence blossomed first in fields related to human health. In 1870 the chairman of the American Medical Association's Committee on Medical Literature praised the "growing improvement in native American publications" and the "decreasing dependence upon foreign literature."[3] By 1879, 135 health-related journals were published in the United States, the most in any country, and Henry Charles Lea of Philadelphia was, according to John Tebbel, "the largest publisher of medical, surgical, and scientific books in the world."[4]

Publishers specializing in engineering and technology also experienced dramatic growth around this time. David Van Nostrand had created his own imprint in 1848; and, although its early business depended on imported texts, by the 1880s the Van Nostrand firm carried a substantial list of original publications in mining, metallurgy, and similar topics.[5] From *Van Nostrand's Engi-*

neering Magazine (established in 1869) came the Van Nostrand Science Series, pocket-sized volumes that eventually numbered 127 and remained in print until 1920.[6] Each season's catalog mapped new areas of growth: Van Nostrand's 1889 catalog listed 19 new works on pure and applied chemistry; by 1910 there were 100. Its nearest rival, John Wiley and Sons (founded in 1807 as a general publisher), began offering "scientific circulars" in five engineering fields during the 1880s; by 1910 its list was predominantly science (largely chemistry) and engineering, with many U.S. authors.[7] After the Civil War, editor Edward L. Youmans initiated Appleton's International Scientific Series, a subscription set that capitalized on the reputations of European scientists and by 1900 included 100 volumes.[8] In response, Henry Holt & Co. founded its American Science Series directed at "students and general readers," which featured U.S. authors.[9]

As Janice Radway argues in the previous chapter, the establishment of academic institutions emphasizing research, such as Johns Hopkins University (1876) and Stanford University (1891), reinforced the professionalization of expertise in science, medicine, and engineering in the United States.[10] The *Physical Review*, for example, was founded in 1893 and published for Cornell University by the commercial firm Macmillan, thanks to a subsidy from the university trustees; more than one-quarter of its articles were written by Cornell physicists before it eventually became the official journal of the American Physical Society in 1899.[11]

As science grew more epistemological and specialized, researchers sought both new outlets for their work and better ways to monitor developments in their fields. Once those interested in a topic reached critical mass, they tended to found an organization (e.g., American Society of Naturalists, 1883; American Psychological Association, 1892; Astronomical and Astrophysical Society of America, 1899) and create some type of journal.[12]

Journals were scientists' principal venue for dissemination of their work to peers. In scientific and technical publishing, an intimate but informal relationship also existed between periodicals and books, in their social and intellectual impact on each field as well as their overlapping content. Journals signaled the birth of fields and theoretical approaches: as new topics arose, new periodicals were established and textbooks followed. A journal, Daniel Kevles notes, gave a discipline the "institutional instruments necessary to set standards of quality in research on a national scale."[13] As a result, the development of journals played a significant role during the twentieth century in the formalization of evaluation systems for technical content—the processes and standards we characterize today as "peer review."[14]

The subsidies for editing, production, and circulation costs of periodicals could be a source of contention because journal publication required long-term organizational commitments and investments greater than those needed to publish a book. In many instances, journals strained an association's coffers; in others, however, it expanded them. Although the American Medical Association (AMA) had existed since 1847, Elizabeth Knoll observes, it was the *Journal of the American Medical Association* (*JAMA*) that "put the AMA on the map."[15] *JAMA* began in 1883 with a circulation of 3,500 and "fair advertising patronage"; by 1898 circulation had grown to 11,270, exceeding AMA membership by more than 3,000.[16] By the late 1940s, *JAMA* and the other AMA specialty journals "were the main — almost the only — source of AMA income . . . and over 70 percent of the organization's payroll went to people who worked for the editor."[17]

Most journals concentrated on a topic or field. Only a few attempted to cover the broad landscape of the American scientific community, the most notable of these being *Science*, now owned by the American Association for the Advancement of Science (AAAS). *Science* was established in the 1880s, independent of the association, and suffered financial instability until ownership was transferred in 1895 to noted psychologist James McKeen Cattell. Cattell edited *Science* as the AAAS's official publication for fifty years, until AAAS repurchased it from his estate.[18] By promoting meeting reports, book reviews, letters, and other discussions of scientific activities, *Science* linked researchers across fields and institutional environments. Rapid publication, such as an article on the Wright brothers' "flying experiments at Kitty Hawk" published within weeks of the event, helped to fuel excitement and pride in American innovation.[19]

To oversee operations and set policy for their journals, scientific associations began in the late nineteenth and early twentieth centuries to set up publication committees or sections. Some of these operations eventually evolved into full-scale presses, issuing books, transactions, reference manuals, and monographs as well as periodicals. An 1892 merger made the American Chemical Society one of the largest U.S. publishing operations in chemistry and a successful competitor with established commercial firms. Other scientific societies chose to establish partnerships with commercial publishers to produce, market, and distribute their publications, gaining them editorial subsidies or a percentage of sales while retaining control of the content. No matter who published a journal or monograph series, the disciplines appointed — or, at the least, anointed — the editors. Many publishers welcomed such arrangements because journals provided space to advertise their books to targeted audiences and to capitalize on the imprimatur of the association.

In consequence, both books and journals were essential to technical publishers. Each journal issue resembled a small paperbound anthology, its articles selected from a pool of submitted manuscripts according to technical criteria rather than literary merit or profitability. Compared to journal issues, books may have seemed to possess greater physical permanence but researchers often treated their journals like books, shelving them for ready reference. A journal article could also accumulate as much prestige as some books. During the 1930s, physicist Hans Bethe took two years to synthesize current knowledge about nuclear phenomena into three articles for *Physical Review*; Kevles writes that at the time "Bethe's bible" could be "found on the desk of virtually every nuclear physicist in the United States."[20]

Expanding Markets and Increasing Profits

By 1900 Americans were building scientific research facilities that rivaled those in Europe.[21] Until then, such research had received only minor direct support from the U.S. government or commercial sources. Now, philanthropic groups such as the Rockefeller Foundation awarded grants to researchers at the start of investigations, in "contrast to the usual practice of rewarding researchers, if at all, at the termination of their work," and also supported preparation of publications.[22] More scientists, laboratories, and research projects meant more publications of all types. Estimates of the number of scientific and technical journals worldwide in 1900 range from 9,000 to 10,000, but all observers agree the subsequent growth was probably exponential; between 1900 and 1920, the number doubled.[23] No longitudinal quantitative analysis has looked at scientific and technical books published in the United States for the period 1880-1940, or tracked changes in fields and specialties; but selected studies indicate that growth here, too, was significant and steady. *Publishers' Weekly* figures show that around 1905 trade books on science, medicine, and technology began to constitute at least 10 percent of all new books published in the United States; Herbert Bloch's analysis of *Publishers' Weekly* categories for "science," "medicine," and "technical books" showed that together they constituted more than 12 percent of *all* new books and editions published between 1920 and 1940; by 1935 they represented 16 to 17 percent.[24]

Analysis of the acquisitions lists of technical libraries highlights other important changes that occurred in that time. Beginning in 1908, the Applied Science Department of the Pratt Institute Free Library in New York prepared a list of new technical books in its collection, a compilation widely regarded as a "best books" rating.[25] These lists show U.S. technical publishers slowly taking business away from European sources: in 1908, 40 percent of that library's new titles had been issued by non-U.S. publishers, but by 1919 that figure had dropped to 21 percent. The lists also show the emerging dominance of four major U.S. publishers: 40 percent of the titles listed were published by either Van Nostrand, Wiley, McGraw-Hill, or the U.S. subsidiary of the British publisher Macmillan.²⁶ University presses gained only one place per year through 1919, although the range of other publishers—correspondence schools, professional societies, manufacturing firms, journals, and government—foreshadowed the diversification that would occur in subsequent decades.

Measures of vitality extend beyond a publisher's new books to the dynamic nature of their backlists. Tebbel argues that, at the turn of the century, scientific and technical publishing "required a love of the subject on the part of the publisher and faith in the growth of a technological society," in part because the decision to publish frequently entailed a long-term commitment to revision.²⁷ "In fiction and general literature," the head of Van Nostrand explained, "a great book once published endures for its lifetime without change" and can stay on the backlist forever, while the technical book "must be revised periodically ... and each revision necessitates new plates, usually new cuts, and in an overwhelming number of instances entirely new composition."²⁸ William Osler's 1892 classic *Principles and Practices of Medicine* was in its sixth edition by 1905, with press runs of 105,000, but each revision required the recasting of plates for hundreds of pages.²⁹ First edition sales were relatively small: "A technical book that sold in excess of 5000 copies a year was a bonanza ... ," the "equivalent of a trade best seller."³⁰ Once a book gained acceptance, however, it required constant revision to remain competitive; a new edition might require total rewriting if the field was changing rapidly, demonstrating the dynamic nature of technical publishers' backlists. Most technical books had "lives" of two to fifteen years, depending on the field.³¹ One of Wiley's stars, for example, was *Elements of Electricity* (1911) by MIT professor William Henry Timbie; four editions of this work sold 263,553 copies alone.³² Thomas E. French's *A Manual of Engineering Drawing*, first published by McGraw-Hill in 1911, sold 1.5 million copies in eight editions through 1953.³³ When the New York Public Library listed its holdings in "engineering, industrial arts and trades" in 1913, all the titles had been published since 1906 or were editions of works considered definitive. The vitality of a subject is reflected in the proportion of revised editions: of the 276 electrical engineering books listed, for example, 18 percent were revised; of 75 in metallurgy, 23 percent; but in the fledgling field of aeronautics, only 7 percent.³⁴ Later library lists routinely recommended technical titles in their fifteenth or twentieth editions.

When texts that were successful went into multiple editions, they began to outlive their authors, and so, when death or incapacity prevented the original author from completing subsequent revisions, a suitably prestigious replacement editor was appointed. When Osler's *Principles and Practices*, for example, reached its twenty-first edition in 1984, its editors were an illustrious group of medical researchers, many of whom had been born after the book was first published.

Production of technical books continued to grow after World War I. For three decades following the conflict, Van Nostrand's chemistry list nearly doubled, to almost 200 titles, and the books themselves grew in size. One classic text, *Standard Methods of Chemical Analysis* by Wilfred Welday Scott, was first published in 1917 in a single 850-page volume, then divided into two volumes and issued as a third edition in 1922; the fifth edition, in 1939, was 2,700 pages in length.[35]

To market such rapidly changing stock, publishers needed to maintain close relationships with their customers as well as their authors. In the 1880s many firms began to dispatch "travelers" to colleges and universities who peddled books, built relationships with thriving academic departments, and recruited manuscripts from faculty.[36] As late as 1930, even members of the Wiley family regularly participated in such promotional trips, although (unlike his employees) the head of the firm, Major Wiley, toured in a chauffeur-driven Pierce-Arrow.[37]

Another innovation attempted to transfer economic risk "from the reader to the publisher."[38] Before "on approval" policies were introduced, the technical book buyer had to search dull catalogs and either open an account at every publisher or submit cash. When more "flamboyant" advertising circulars offered to send books for a period of "free examination," according to publisher Edward M. Crane, "the tempo of mail-order selling quickened enormously."[39] By the end of World War I, most firms had eschewed direct circulation and adopted this "no risk" sales method.[40]

Knowledge fueled the system, encouraging the scientific enterprise to grow. More authors and more readers meant more sales. Commercial and nonprofit presses flourished hand in hand with research groups in universities. At the turn of the century, "no publisher . . . had . . . a specially organized department to secure manuscripts in the college field and to promote the sale of the resulting books," but by 1938 publisher Frederick S. Croft could point to "at least a score" of these and to a booming technical market.[41]

The Rise of University Presses

The initial decision to publish a scientific book is, by tradition, justified by its perceived significance and importance to the advancement of knowledge. Nevertheless, social significance and profit potential ultimately play a role. As McGraw-Hill executive James Stacy Thompson explained, the technical publisher can seek advice on "the accuracy, up-to-dateness, comprehensiveness, and pedagogical quality of a manuscript," but "he alone must make up his mind as to whether the venture is feasible."[42]

The mission statements of university presses founded in the late nineteenth and early twentieth centuries touted a loftier ideal—that selection was governed by intellectual criteria alone, driven by "considerations of quality" rather than of "market or popularity."[43] Such presses have often claimed that without them, "the determination of what is published would be entirely in the hands of the commercial publishing houses," implying that diversity and quality of content might suffer.[44] But university presses are also appendages of their sponsoring institutions. Initially, most university-owned presses accepted only the work of their own faculty.[45] Exclusionary policies such as that of the University of Chicago were eventually abandoned, however, and presses were directed to encourage manuscripts from scholars outside their home universities.[46]

Few American university presses concentrated on the natural and physical sciences to the same extent as either commercial publishers or the publishing divisions of scientific associations.[47] As late as 1948, only 14 percent of university press books published in the United States were on natural science topics.[48] One notable exception is the MIT Press (created in 1932 as the Technology Press): five years after its founding, MIT and Wiley established a plan of "cooperative publishing" that lasted until 1962, whereby the commercial publisher manufactured and sold most of the manuscripts prepared by MIT.[49] Such arrangements were not unusual. By the late 1930s, the University of Chicago Press had engaged in a series of contracts with ten different commercial publishers for promotion and distribution of its publications.[50]

Most university presses were administrative departments or separate corporations controlled by the faculty; in a few cases, such as at Fisk University, the institution underwrote, edited, and published books under its imprint but employed subcontractors to carry out this work.[51] Whatever the managerial arrangement, faculty committees, university officials, and trustees were able to influence editorial decisions and to encourage a "noncommercial" approach. Although university presses undertook some complex, lengthy, and expensive projects of high scholarly quality, they left much of the field of technical publishing to the private sector.[52]

By 1935 only around 11 percent of all new titles in science, medicine, and technology were published by university presses.[53] According to Chester Kerr, during the 1930s, university presses began paying more attention to serving audiences outside academe, with books designed to link "the specialist with the educated layman," and Joseph Brandt claimed that "university presses were among the earliest to translate for the layman the tremendous progress made" in science, citing Chicago's publication in 1926 of *The Nature of the World*.[54] Although originally designed as a freshman survey text, the trade edition of that collaborative work sold more than 70,000 copies and was named by the American Library Association as one of its "Forty Notable Books of 1926."

Extenuating Circumstances

Technical publishing in the early twentieth century is distinguished by four particular features, each of which contributed to the health of the research system. First, the commitment to multiple, revised editions construed a technical book as part of an evolving research enterprise rather than a declaration that knowledge is unalterable. Second, the close relationship between journals and books allowed journals to evaluate and validate ideas, trends, and reputations in a field as well as to stabilize markets for a firm's books. Third, the system's organizational diversity guaranteed that no single type of publisher dominated, no single set of gatekeepers could inhibit information flow.

Scientists encouraged the development of these aspects of a concatenated system, parallel to the research enterprise itself but institutionally and financially separate from it. They exploited all opportunities to disseminate their work, cultivating multiple rather than exclusive relationships with commercial as well as nonprofit publishers. The list of publications by geneticist Thomas Hunt Morgan typifies the range of such interactions.[55] Macmillan published his *Regeneration* in 1901. Between 1910 and 1915, he coauthored *The Mechanism of Mendelian Heredity* (Henry Holt & Co., 1915; revised in 1923), published one other volume on genetics with Columbia University Press, fifty journal articles on genetics, and many other articles on other subjects, some of which appeared in the popular press. Between 1915 and 1930, he published two more books on genetics (one with Lippincott, the other with a university press); *Critique of the Theory of Evolution* (Princeton University Press, 1916) was revised and republished in 1925; he authored or coauthored another fifty articles on genetics; with his research group he wrote and published an essential laboratory manual (*Laboratory Directions for an Elementary Course in Genetics* [Henry Holt & Co., 1923]); and he served on the editorial boards of several journals.

The fourth important aspect was that, for most technical books and journals, the intended consumers were the same group of people who produced and evaluated the work. As a result, the content and presentation of technical books tended to reflect each expert community's own standards for credibility, originality, and independence. Throughout much of the twentieth century, scientists maintained close control of their knowledge systems, determining who was published, accepted, rewarded, or marginalized. This insularity also encouraged development of an attitude within the research communities whereby scientists claimed ownership of their publication outlets, perceiving the journals and monograph series as "theirs," even though the intellectual property may have been produced, sold, and copyrighted by the publishers, who bore the financial risk of market failure and reaped much of the profit.

Cooperative Publishing and Intellectual Tool Kits

By the 1920s firms such as Wiley, Van Nostrand, and McGraw-Hill built their business on aggressive solicitation of manuscripts. Publishers' representatives and editors traveled "into the offices and laboratories of the professors on campuses from Boston to LA, from Maine to Oregon," recruiting consulting editors, series editors, technical consultants, and authors: "If a prominent teacher, a recognized authority in his field, decided he would like to write a book for McGraw-Hill, they would say, 'Why not a whole series? You be the editor. You help us plan a list of books needed in your field. Suggest names for the best authorship, and give us general advice on manuscripts and possible sales.'"[56]

For publishers, long-term relationships with the experts who acted as "outside editors" was a source of pride.[57] On occasion, a successful manual or handbook series that began as a single-authored text became, in subsequent editions, the product of an editorial board, representing a significant change from publishing patterns in the past.[58] In the mid-1920s, when Russell L. Cecil, professor of clinical medicine at Cornell Medical School, concluded that a single-authored textbook in medicine was no longer feasible, he assembled a group of collaborators for the "Cecil" *Textbook of Medicine*; its seven subsequent editions "probably secured more than 90 percent of all medical textbook use in the English-speaking world" and was translated into a dozen languages.[59] When biochemist J. Murray Luck created the *Annual Review of Biochemistry* in 1932, the relevant literature was scattered throughout biochemical, physiological, and chemical journals. Luck compiled the information and classified it by field, producing annual "comprehensive appraisals" written by leading biochemists; this format was imitated in other fields.[60]

Cooperative publishing became the rule. Crane estimated that, beginning in the 1920s, "possibly 60 percent, perhaps even 75 percent" of Van Nostrand's books were "projected and planned in office conferences."[61] In 1925 McGraw-Hill convened its own team of experts to plan an extensive series in chemical engineering; their suggestions resulted in dozens of texts and reference books, including the comprehensive *Chemical Engineers' Handbook* (first published in 1934).[62] Other publishers established formal relationships with technical firms or industrial laboratories. Van Nostrand initiated a series with Bell Telephone Laboratories engineers in 1925 that survived into the 1950s, and Wiley had similar arrangements in 1932 with the General Electric Company and, in the late 1940s, with Westinghouse.[63] Such ventures provided access to creditable expertise, explicit endorsement, and assured sales.

For major reference works, success and longevity demanded teamwork. Although they are often neglected in publishing histories, these handbooks, manuals, charts, and indexes are among the most important parts of a researcher's intellectual tool kit, as "indispensable as dictionaries" and found in every laboratory and office. Such works were not mere lists or tables of facts and numbers; they classified knowledge within each field and required high levels of accuracy and authentication.[64] Many had prestigious editorial boards, and publishers sought the imprimatur of scientific association endorsement.

Some of these reference tools were highly profitable; others required creative subsidies to survive. One of Wiley's turn-of-the-century innovations was "pocket-sized" editions of its standard engineering texts; these sold so well that they evolved into a comprehensive handbook series.[65] The first in the series, William H. Searles's *Field Engineering* (1880) was "still going strong" in 1960 in its twenty-sixth edition.[66] When World War I inhibited scientists' access to one essential reference work published in Germany, the American Chemical Society formed a group to publish the *International Critical Tables*.[67] The National Research Council underwrote all the editorial expenses, and some 300 scientists cooperated to produce seven large volumes, printed in four languages, with two index volumes, which were then published by McGraw-Hill and proved to be a financial as well as public relations success.[68]

Increased collaborative research also spurred a rise in multiauthored publications.[69] The U.S. government's expanding role in conducting as well as financing research and the success of industrial research laboratories in physics, chemistry, engineering, and medicine played a role in this surge of knowledge. Agencies such as the Public Health Service not only employed scientists (who then had research to write about) but also spurred public interest in science — and belief in its importance.

This is not to say that single-authored technical texts disappeared. The relationship between author and publisher, however, especially for textbook projects, grew more interactive. In the mid-1930s, for example, Harcourt Brace's high school department "got a foothold in science" when executive James M. Reid heard from a sales representative about an Ohio biology teacher who was unsatisfied with the available high school textbooks and so had written and mimeographed her own materials.[70] Reid then persuaded her to work with them to create a suitable new book. The resulting text, *Exploring Biology* by Ella Thea Smith, introduced innovative features like unit-problem organization (each unit opening with a "dramatic episode" from the history of biology) and a "technical vocabulary" list of 496 terms classified for specific grade levels.[71] The book also went "all out in teaching evolution" at a time when many texts avoided using the word altogether or used only synonyms such as "development," though Harcourt Brace knew that it risked losing many state adoptions in the South and West.[72] Upon publication in 1938, *Exploring Biology* proved to be such a sensible text that it was adopted even in bastions of antievolutionism. It went through at least six successful editions, second in sales only to the Holt biology text by Moon and Mann (later Moon, Mann, and Otto) through the 1940s and 1950s.

Explaining Science to the Public

Expanding knowledge production created the demand for new outlets of diffusion and stimulated public interest in the science behind the innovations. Sewing machines, typewriters, automobiles, and radios all created new markets for manuals, handbooks, and how-to texts, as salesmen, customers, and repair personnel tried to understand each new device's design and operation.[73] *Popular Mechanics*, the best-known technical consumer magazine, began in 1907 to provide practical translations for "technically minded homeowners and homemakers."[74] To its founder, Henry Haven Windsor, "'mechanics' meant not only the nuts and bolts of machinery, but also 'the way the world works.'"[75] A burst of popular interest in science had occurred in the mid-nineteenth century — manifest in lecture tours by prominent British and American scientists and in magazines such as *Scientific American* (1845) and *National Geographic Magazine* (1886) — but these efforts were overshadowed by the wave of popularization in the early twentieth century, producing periodicals such as *Scientific Monthly* (1915).[76]

"Popularized" books and magazines interpreted science for those who were not experts, responding to audience demand and to the experts' desires to explain, interpret, and promote their work to others (see figure 12.1).[77] The im-

FIGURE 12.1. (*opposite*) These popular representations of science in the 1920s by Will Andrews for the Star Series of nonfiction books referenced both science's laboratory creativity and its practical application for industrial operations. Albert E. Wiggam's *The New Decalogue of Science* (Garden City, N.Y.: Garden City Publishing Co., 1922) proposed "ten commandments" for scientific work, outlining moral and ethical frameworks for coping with the discoveries of "new biology." In *Science Remaking the World* (Garden City, N.Y.: Garden City Publishing Co., 1923), noted scientists described how advances in chemistry, biology, and public health assisted the economy as well as improved home gardens and even "our daily bread." Editors Otis W. Caldwell and Edwin E. Slosson (whose first name was misspelled on the jacket) had trained to be scientists but switched careers to become science popularizers.

pulse to "evangelize" about the scientific way of life, or to persuade others of science's importance, was strong.[78] The Progressive Era had linked research with economic progress and social improvement, shown science's relevance to "personal interest and payoff for each consumer," and piqued audience interest in what lay behind the discoveries; World War I had demonstrated science's military and strategic importance.[79] Americans were eager to learn more.

A critical factor in the increase of popularization in the United States during the interwar years was the establishment in 1921 of a not-for-profit organization, Science Service, by wealthy newspaper owner E. W. Scripps and biologist William E. Ritter.[80] Scripps had become convinced that "working the spirit and substance of science into the community mind" would be in the national interest but that scientists needed guidance to break free of a tendency to write their books "at each other . . . using such big words and such technical language that the average man, even if he attempts to read their books, can't understand what they say or what it is all about."[81] The organization endowed by Scripps sought to bridge the gap between the scientific establishment and the pragmatic world of publishing by selling syndicated news products, brokering scientists' popular book manuscripts to other publishers, and, through its success, creating a "demand" for scientific matter generally. The approval of scientists lent the organization prestige and authority; their direct involvement as trustees, news sources, and authors gave the Science Service journalists access to the latest research and helped to ensure the accuracy and authenticity of the products.[82]

The news coverage given to Albert Einstein and Marie Curie and sensational events like the John T. Scopes antievolution trial in 1925 contributed to enhanced public interest in all of science.[83] Another factor in increased popularization was that scientific associations began to use popular books in their publicity campaigns and to encourage news coverage of their meetings. Chemists sensitive to the negative images prompted by the use of chemical weapons during World War I embarked on aggressive efforts to educate the public. In 1925 the Chemical Foundation placed a full-page advertisement in the *New York Times Book Review* offering for sale, at a nominal price, six books on "The Progress—The Romance—The Necessity of Chemistry!"[84] The Foundation donated 20,000 sets to schools and public libraries, and sales of one volume exceeded 100,000 within a year.[85] Other chemistry associations subsidized popular books throughout the 1930s, such as the lavishly produced *Man in a Chemical World* (Scribner's, 1937) to celebrate the tercentenary of the U.S. chemical industry. (See figures 12.2 and 12.3.)

The market for popular science was not as stable or predictable as the academic one, however. For example, when Van Nostrand decided to capitalize on budding interest in building radio sets, it handpicked a group of experts to

MAN
IN A
CHEMICAL WORLD

THE SERVICE OF CHEMICAL INDUSTRY

By

A. Cressy Morrison

CHARLES SCRIBNER'S SONS · NEW YORK
CHARLES SCRIBNER'S SONS·LTD·LONDON
1937

FIGURE 12.2. During the 1920s and 1930s, the chemical industry and the chemistry associations engaged in significant public outreach through books and similar popular media. A. Cressy Morrison, *Man in a Chemical World* (New York: Charles Scribner's Sons, 1937), a lavishly produced and illustrated book prepared for the American Chemical Industries Tercentenary, offered a celebratory view of chemistry's achievements and declared resoundingly that "Nature is the great chemist." The title echoed contemporary assumptions about gender and science, and the book's illustrations served to reinforce that message.

FIGURE 12.3. In his illustrations for Morrison, *Man in a Chemical World*, Leon Soderston provides dramatic portrayals of the thinking, creative scientist (*above*) and the practical scientist (*opposite*) concerned with knowledge application, both of which echoed themes found in American popular science throughout the twentieth century.

conduct a symposium early in 1922 and create a "publishable manuscript in two weeks."[86] The complete manuscript went to the printer on 1 March, and bound books were delivered on 18 April. By 15 May more than 20,000 copies of *Radio Phone Receiving* (1922) had been sold. Then the warm spring weather brought static, for which no effective screening devices were yet available. People became bored with the poor reception on their homemade sets and by July the publisher was selling only five copies per month. The book thus had an effective sales life of about thirty days.[87] Scientific encyclopedias and compendia represented more reliable products, such as Van Nostrand's successful nine-volume *Library of Modern Science* (1920), edited by scientists E. E. Slosson, Harrison Howe, and Matthew Luckiesh, or the sixteen-volume *Popular Science Library* ("A Complete Education in a Single Set") published in 1923 by P. F. Collier & Son, sold with a ten-year "loose-leaf revision service" to keep subscribers abreast of the latest discoveries.[88]

The popular books were published primarily by commercial firms. By including these works on their lists alongside professional texts and by asking prominent scientists or engineers to endorse them, publishers attempted to infuse the books with credibility and authority by association, even though the authors were not necessarily scientists and the content was not routinely subjected to the same rigorous technical review as the professional books. The publishing of popular science books appears to have followed a pattern similar to that of magazine articles where professional writers eventually began to dominate as authors.[89] Ronald Tobey argues that as scientists received less professional credit for writing popular magazine articles, their inclination to participate in print popularization diminished.[90] Because this change occurred at the same time as the development of professional science journalism, there was a critical mass of writers eager to fill the gap and serve as interpreters of science.

One measure of the growing audience for accessible science books was the establishment of the Scientific Book Club in 1921. Its founders, a group of scientists, said they had been "besought persistently by associates, students and friends for information about the newest scientific books."[91] Advertisements for the club in the 1930s assured potential members that the advisory board and editorial committee (which included such eminent scientists as Kirtley F. Mather and Arthur Holly Compton) "do the preliminary work of discovering the books most worth your while." In 1946 this club was purchased by Henry Holt and Company and renamed the Science Book Club.[92]

Another measure was the inclusion of science on "best books" lists that identified those works considered essential or recommended reading for middle-class Americans. During the 1920s and 1930s, Asa Don Dickinson, librarian of the University of Pennsylvania, compiled and scored recommendations from dozens of such lists, "selected by a consensus of expert opinion as most worthy of the attention of intelligent American readers."[93] Science books rarely made the top of Dickinson's compilations, but they were always present (e.g., 19 of the 400 "best books of the decade 1926–1935" were on science, as were 13 of the 400 chosen for the decade 1936–1945). Books on science-related topics also appeared on best-seller lists.[94] Writer Paul de Kruif, who helped Sinclair Lewis with *Arrowsmith* (1925), the best-selling novel about a scientist, published his own nonfiction best seller, *Microbe Hunters*, in the following year (figure 12.4).[95] *Scribner's Monthly* serialized Michael Pupin's autobiography (from September 1922 through January 1923) as promotion for publication of the complete version, *From Immigrant to Inventor*, by Charles Scribner's Sons in 1923. Eve Curie's biography of her mother Marie appeared in eight parts in the *Saturday Evening Post* during 1937, and the book version (*Madame Curie*, Doubleday Doran, 1938) was one of the best sellers of its day.

As late as the 1920s, most authors of best-selling popular science books in the United States were not American, a lingering reflection of the prestige of European science.[96] Two famous best sellers, J. Arthur Thompson's *Outline of Science* (Putnam, 1922) and Lancelot T. Hogben's *Mathematics for the Million* (Norton, 1937), were first published in England. By the 1930s and early 1940s, however, lists of recommended and best-selling books on all subjects, including science, displayed a "steadily increasing proportion of American titles."[97]

From the 1920s to the 1940s there was also a modest but notable increase in books that made or answered criticism of the social and economic impacts of science. Albert E. Wiggam's best seller *The New Decalogue of Science* (Garden City Publishing Co., Inc., 1922), for example, commented on ethical questions raised by advances in biology. Endorsed on the book jacket by such luminaries as the biologist Raymond Pearl of Johns Hopkins, the text featured "the stern warning and high commands" that the author believed it was "the duty and the privilege of the scientist . . . in this day and age to utter." Public debates over evolution, the interpretation of fossil discoveries, the meaning of "uncertainty," and the implications of the development of atomic energy were waged in books written by both scientists and nonscientists.

By the 1940s, popularized science had become less dependent on the organized scientific community. Readers' interests ranged from astronomy to invertebrates, from the engineering of automobiles to the chemistry of photography, and publishers rushed to fill the demand.[98] Although publishers still courted scientists' endorsements, the jacket statements were akin to window dressing. Americans did not need scientists' approval to become excited about the latest discovery of dinosaur bones or permission to put technical information to use.[99] If the reward systems in science did not encourage scientists to engage in

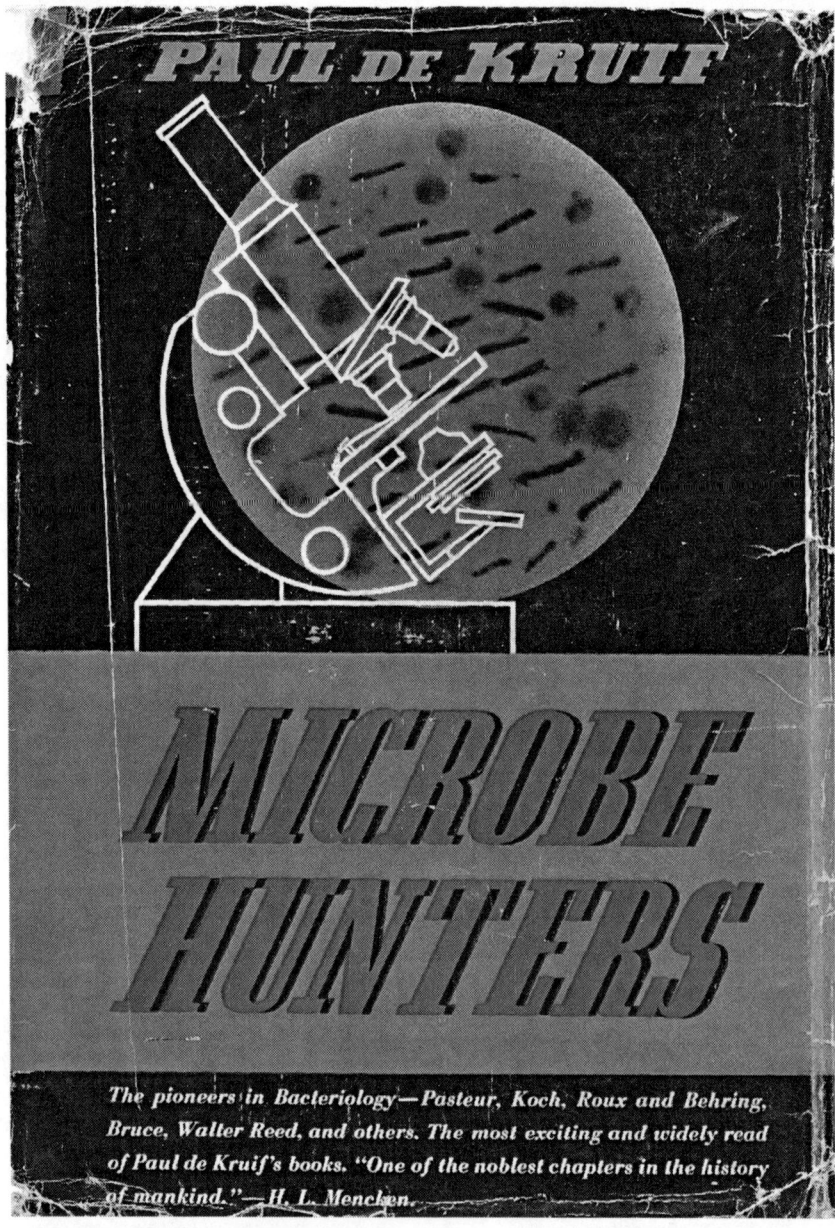

FIGURE 12.4. Paul De Kruif's *Microbe Hunters* (New York: Harcourt, Brace and Company, 1926), an inside story of the pioneers in bacteriology, attracted enthusiastic endorsements from famous scientists and literary figures such as H. L. Mencken and newspaper editor William Allen White. The success of De Kruif's books, which turned laboratories into the sites of adventure and drama, demonstrated that popular science could be not only technically accurate but also well written and accessible to general readers.

popularization, then that created opportunities for science writers and further loosened experts' control over the content and tone of popular science.[100]

American Science Claims Center Stage and Copes with Censorship

The technological exhibits of the New York World's Fair of 1939 attempted to capture science fiction's long imagined "World of Tomorrow." American science had escaped Europe's shadow, and young scientists "no longer felt the need to study abroad."[101] In 1935 a prominent European scientist told the *New York Times* that "Today scientific publications from the United States are awaited with an impatience and curiosity inspired by those of no other country."[102] Basic and applied research flourished in all fields. Because delays in publication slowed the dissemination of new ideas, journals expanded or split into new journals to accommodate additional material. The pages of the *Physical Review* more than doubled during the 1920s (to around 3,800 annually), and it became a biweekly publication in 1929.[103] Between 1920 and 1950, journals such as *American Mathematical Monthly*, *Chemistry*, and *Journal of Experimental Psychology* grew linearly, each publishing more than 500 pages per year by the mid-1930s.

The explosive growth of these publications reflected both the dynamism of research in this period and scientists' innate impulse to communicate with their peers. In the 1930s, physicists accustomed to the free flow of information faced a particularly difficult dilemma: indiscriminate communication about their discoveries in nuclear physics might assist Nazi weapons research.[104] Many publishers, in fact, began voluntary self-censorship in the late 1930s, and a few individuals deliberately delayed publishing their work on fission.[105] Once war began, the National Academy of Sciences–National Research Council Joint Advisory Committee on Scientific Publications reviewed material in nuclear physics, electronics, and medicine prior to publication but left initial submission of material "suspected of having military potential" to the discretion of editors and publishers.[106] In 1941, months before Pearl Harbor, the U.S. government imposed an embargo on the export of textbooks, technical books, and handbooks to Japan after publishers reported receiving suspiciously large orders from Japanese customers.[107] When war was declared, all items published in the United States became subject to rules established by the Office on Censorship, and the export of any technical book or journal required its approval.[108]

Despite paper shortages and preoccupied scientists, the war energized technical publishing. Although many scholarly periodicals suspended operations between 1941 and 1945, scientific journals continued publication because of their perceived relevance to the war effort.[109] The *Physical Review*, for example, reduced its publication schedule during the war, appearing monthly rather than bimonthly between 1942 and 1945 and notably decreasing the number of articles per volume, announcing on the front page of the January 1942 issue that this was because of "the occupation of many physicists with national defense research."[110]

The publishing industry benefited from campaigns promoting reading at home and among service personnel, as well as the increased demand for technical information.[111] The Council on Books in Wartime, established by U.S. publishers in 1942, asserted that "books were weapons" and stated as one of its primary aims the efficient provision of technical information.[112] "Everyone was going to school ... to adapt their profession to wartime uses," and government needed all types of special books, "refresher books, mathematical texts, books on mechanical or topographical drawing," as well as those describing the fundamentals of new instruments and weapons.[113] The entire country had been turned into a "university of war," with "courses of study drawn from every technological field," James Stacy Thompson of McGraw-Hill noted in 1942.[114] Appropriations for the Engineering and Science Management War Training program, for example, soared from $9 million in 1940 to $30 million in 1942, and each trainee required books, manuals, and teaching materials.[115] By the end of 1942, McGraw-Hill alone had published 167 books for such courses, often written, assembled, and printed "in record time."[116] When the need for a new aeronautical training text was announced, Macmillan responded by "transforming 6,000 pages of manuscript into a complete series of eighteen volumes" in just thirty-eight days.[117] Major publishers reported devoting between 50 and 80 percent of their efforts to war-related publications.[118] "Ordinary marketing channels overflowed," and even department stores were enlisted: In 1942 R. H. Macy in New York carried between 2,000 and 3,000 technical books, five times its normal business.[119] By May 1942 Wiley recorded a 30 percent increase in new retail accounts (some bookstores reported scientific-industrial sales up 35 to 60 percent), and even sales of such classics as Timbie's *Elements of Electricity* (Wiley, 1911) had a notable surge when "the U.S. Signal Corps called for more men with a knowledge of electrical fundamentals."[120]

During the war, the United States and Great Britain cooperated in a massive effort to obtain and microfilm foreign scientific and technical periodicals; the reprint firm Edwards Brothers was established in 1943 to publish photo-offset paper copies under a license from the U.S. Alien Property Custodian, which had impounded copyrights of the periodicals.[121] "Vast numbers" of German and Japanese technical reports were also accumulated through intelligence operations.[122] When the lid of secrecy was finally lifted, release of this confiscated material—and declassification of government research reports—helped to fuel a scientific and technical publishing boom.[123]

Postwar Realities and Opportunities

In August 1945 publishers faced the immediate challenge of dealing with mountains of material previously restricted, including impounded foreign publications. The market for technical material, "primed" by the same training programs the publishers had been assisting, left people eager for explanations of the new source of energy used in the atomic bombs. The day following the explosion at Hiroshima, McGraw-Hill executives established an editorial committee on atomic energy; employees familiar with nuclear physics would "keep in close touch with developments in the whole broad field of atomic energy and its applications" and serve as "the source of authentic information for every editor to draw upon."[124] As a result, in September 1945 every McGraw-Hill publication carried an eight-page insert, "The Atom—New Source of Energy," which explained fission "in simple, nontechnical language with simplified drawings" and was later distributed to colleges and universities as a textbook supplement.[125]

Princeton University Press fulfilled a different type of information need by publishing in 1945 the "Smyth Report," entitled *Atomic Energy for Military Purposes: The Official Report on the Development of the Atomic Bomb under the Auspices of the United States Government, 1940–1945*. Its author, Henry DeWolf Smyth (1898-1986), was chairman of the Princeton physics department; as a principal consultant to the Manhattan Project, he had been asked to produce its official report. Although the manuscript had been rejected by a commercial publisher and was printed initially by the U.S. Government Printing Office, Princeton undertook republication as a public service. "The ultimate responsibility for our nation's policy rests on its citizens and they can discharge such responsibilities wisely only if they are informed," Smyth wrote in the preface. In fact, demand was so great that by 1 November 1945, the book was already in its fifth printing. His Princeton colleague, chemist Hugh Stott Taylor (1890-1974), later recalled that the Smyth Report was "that rare bird in University Press lists, a sound scholarly book that became a best-seller . . . more than ten readers bought the Press edition for every purchaser of the government issue. It was one of few books to be published with copyright but with the unexpected announcement 'Reproduction in whole or in part authorized and permitted.'"[126] Popular books explaining atomic energy came out within weeks of the war's end, dramatically exemplified by Pocket Book's publication in August 1945 of *The Atomic Age Opens!* Many books—such as David Dietz's *Atomic Energy in the Coming Era* (1945) and the Maurice Sendak–illustrated *Atomics for the Millions* (1947) — sought to combat growing public fears with technical information.[127]

Federal policies initially encouraged such openness. It was argued that rapid declassification would stimulate new science and technology industries and assist postwar economic recovery. This contention was articulated best in the most influential science policy book of the postwar period, Vannevar Bush's *Science — The Endless Frontier* (1945). "Publication Should Be Encouraged," it advised: "We should get this scientific material to scientists everywhere with great promptness, and at as low a price as is consistent with suitable format."[128] In the late 1940s, scientists lobbied vigorously for public policies that would place few restrictions on their communications infrastructure. To some extent, the American scientific community was seeking to return to prewar conditions; but its rationale was unashamedly self-interested — the more open the system, the more easily each scientist's own work and publications could be disseminated and put to use.

Even before V-J Day, President Harry S. Truman signed executive orders designed to speed this distribution. Two new entities, the Publication Board and the Office of Technical Services, worked with the Library of Congress Photoduplication Service to make available tens of thousands of scientific and technical reports created by the U.S. Office of Scientific Research and Development.[129] The number of reports made available through this service soared quickly — from 8,391 in 1945 to 18,622 in 1946. By 1947 the U.S. Patent Office was processing over 300,000 confiscated Japanese reports for inclusion in the Office of Technical Services system.[130] In 1949 a new Science Division was created at the Library of Congress, and by 1954 one-fifth of the total loans made by the Library of Congress were in the classes of science, technology, agriculture, or medicine; the requests in pure science had almost doubled from those of the previous year.[131] The library was also receiving 25,000 serials in science and technology, representing about one-half of all then published worldwide.[132]

Dissemination of scientific and technical material was not without limitation. On the very day that wartime voluntary censorship of the press was lifted, the War Department declared that everyone connected with the Manhattan Project must "continue to comply with present security regulations" and all citizens should keep discussion of the subject "within the limits of information disclosed in official releases."[133] When General Leslie Groves reportedly refused to allow use of photographs of devices at Oak Ridge that had already been described in the Smyth Report, *Popular Science Monthly* "dramatized this situation by leaving blank spaces in an article on atomic medicine in its issue for May, 1946."[134] As Cold War tensions grew, careful identification of what was subject to security restrictions became commonplace.

War, then, had represented only a brief "diversion" for technical publishing. As Derek J. de Solla Price observes, "once science had recovered," researchers began to publish at the same exponential rate as before.[135] Commercial book and journal publishers, university presses, scientific associations, governments, laboratories, and institutes all contributed to an expanding communications system. This concatenated infrastructure was a legacy of the period 1880 to 1940. Each link in the infrastructure was separate and separable, each independent yet related: the system drew its strength and efficiency from the interconnections. After World War II, observers no longer wondered whether American scientists were publishing enough or were being overshadowed by foreign experts. Instead, they routinely spoke of "information overload" and a "superabundance of literature." What individual readers bemoaned as "too many" books and articles, the technical publishers now saw as an unprecedented opportunity for growth. In the decades following, those organizations profited significantly from the scientists' encouragement of unregulated expansion and the belief that open access to scientific and technical knowledge was an American birthright.

CHAPTER 13

The Government as Publisher

Charles A. Seavey with Caroline F. Sloat

. . .

The federal government is one of the hidden phenomena of the book world. The publishing industry does not track sales or distribution of government items, but when we turn to the government's own figures on its publishing activities, we discover a world of print vigorously in motion, increasing in scope, volume, and speed. Beginning as a modest effort to record the proceedings of the U.S. Congress, government publishing grew to a prodigious volume by the end of the nineteenth century. In fiscal year 1895-96, for example, the United States Government Printing Office (USGPO) produced, bound, and delivered 1,255,454 volumes, requiring 5,457 tons of paper, 490 tons of binder boards, and 51,600 sheepskins.[1]

Print runs of single publications were sizable, sometimes exceeding 100,000.[2] The purposes of government documents by this time had extended far beyond the actions of the Congress. Descriptions of government-sponsored explorations facilitated westward expansion during the nineteenth century. Many a wagon train went West with a copy of John C. Frémont's 1845 *Report of the Exploring Expedition to Rocky Mountains in 1842, and to Oregon and North California in 1843–44* (and map) within reach of the wagon master.[3] Government publications either stimulated or settled many scientific controversies of the late nineteenth century. Farmers used government information to improve crop production. Social scientists made extensive use of data collected and published by the government. The U.S. government had become (and still is) the largest publisher in the world. This chapter briefly reviews some of the highlights prior to 1880 and then focuses on some important changes in the organization and practices of the government's printing activities from 1880 to 1940.

Government Publishing: Informing the Populace

America's founders frequently argued that participants in a democracy must be both educated and informed. In 1822 James Madison wrote to his friend W. T. Barry: "A popular government without popular information, or the means of acquiring it, is but a prologue to a farce, or a tragedy, or perhaps both. Knowledge will forever govern ignorance; and a people who mean to be their own governors must arm themselves with the power which knowledge gives."[4]

Although an informed populace was one of the implicit cornerstones of the republic, the government only gradually developed into a major publisher. The Constitution requires Congress to keep a journal and make it available but beyond that is silent on the topic of publicly available information. In a nation wary of central government and new taxes, support for an extensive government publishing function, like the support for free public education and libraries, came very gradually.

By 1850, however, most states in the Northeast and the Midwest had established free elementary schools. After the Civil War, two institutions of literacy came into their own: the free public high school and the public lending library. Their diffusion was uneven by region, class, and race, but their growing presence among America's institutions sparked demands for more access and much rhetoric about the need for an informed citizenry. Similarly, the idea of an organized distribution system for government information developed gradually over the course of the nineteenth century. The Congress expressed a need for the government to inform citizens about the activities of the three branches of the federal government in 1813.[5] A major milestone was the establishment of the Government Printing Office in 1861. By the 1870s, just before our period began, Congress had established that the USGPO, not private contractors, would print all government documents.[6]

Publishing historian John Tebbel wrote that "the rapid growth of the United States government as a publisher" was "one of the most striking and little noticed developments in publishing" between 1865 and 1919.[7] In part, this expansion of government publishing paralleled and was spurred by the proliferation of government agencies. Between 1789 and 1909, roughly 1,000 "Departments, Bureaus, Divisions, Offices, Commissions, [and] Committees" existed within the federal government. Not all of these agencies existed simultaneously, however; many came and went, like the Mexican Boundary Survey that existed from 1882 until 1896, or the Alaskan Boundary Tribunal of 1903. Other agencies were renamed or, like the Army Corps of Topographical Engineers, were absorbed into a larger agency. Nonetheless, all of these agencies published material worthy of note in the *Checklist of United States Public Documents*.[8] Some of those agencies were strictly administrative in nature—the Commissioners of the District of Columbia, for instance. Others, perhaps two-thirds of all the agencies listed in the *Checklist*, disseminated information to the general public or some special reading public outside of Washington, D.C., as part of their basic mission. The government created the Department of Agriculture during the Civil War, followed by the U.S. Weather Bureau in 1870, the Bureau of Commercial Fisheries in 1871, and the Coast and Geodetic Survey in 1878—an expansion of functions, information, reports, and research that continued into our period.

Contemporaneous with the founding of the USGPO was the Morrill Land Grant Act of 1861, which encouraged the founding of colleges and research universities (discussed in chapter 11 of this volume by Janice Radway). As colleges and universities provided a cadre of technically trained workers, business and government both relied heavily upon them and on the research and statistics they generated for the new corporate industrial world. Congress used such material in its legislative functions; executive branch departments were also involved in policy making and administration, in areas such as agriculture, education, mining, engineering, and libraries. As a result, the government report as a genre, argues Oz Frankel, eventually succeeded the political pamphlet. "The report supplemented (and at a certain point replaced) the pamphlet as the archetypical political genre, signifying the bureaucratization of public life and the early stages of expert culture."[9] Frankel argues further that the proliferation of printed government reports resulted in something he calls, "print statism," that is, a "field of communication between the state and its constituencies," implicating the government and the legislature in the scrutiny and control of both its citizens and the disenfranchised.[10]

Having opted for a government monopoly on government printing, the Congress had to upgrade the facilities progressively. After electric lights were installed in the printing plant in 1882, a new building was constructed between 1899 and 1903. A description of this seven-story building suggests the scope of the operation by the opening of the twentieth century:

> The first floor of the building is occupied by the press and roller divisions; the second floor by a portion of the folding division and the supervising and clerical force of the office; the third floor by the folding division; the fourth floor by the bindery; the fifth and sixth floors by typographical and proof divisions; and the seventh floor by the divisions devoted to job work, and the electrotype and stereotype foundry.... A pneumatic tube system for the rapid transmission of copy and proof to the various portions of the office has been installed, and is in successful operation.... In the loft of the building are located ventilating fans, operated by electricity, and the machinery for operating the carriers in the pneumatic tubes, the power being also furnished by electric motors. Provision has been made for eight elevators for passenger service, four freight elevators, one sidewalk elevator, and two form elevators.[11]

A year later, Congress authorized USGPO to update its printing equipment by purchasing forty-six double magazine typesetting machines from the Mergenthaler Linotype Company and twenty-eight additional typesetting machines from Lanston Monotype Company. As occurred in private industry, these purchases roused anxieties among the typesetting laborers. Printing had become a big business in an age of quickly evolving technology.

A Decentralized System of Publishing

While the printing at USGPO was centralized, the editorial and publishing processes were not. Thus, any discussion of government publishing must consider the roles played by the individual agencies. While the USGPO printed massive quantities of material, it was not a publisher, that is, it did not initiate the projects, make publishing decisions, identify the audiences, or write and edit the texts. USGPO was only a contract printer and distributor. The other processes, and the budget for them, lay in the individual government agencies. Publishing practices varied greatly from agency to agency, reflecting different missions, different emphases on public relations, and different views of their constituencies outside of Washington, D.C. To understand the nuances of this history, one would have to look at many agencies individually, which is beyond the scope of this chapter.

One development that had an effect across many agencies was the changing nature of the relationship between the executive and legislative branches of government. From 1789 through the early part of the twentieth century, Congress issued most government publications. Executive branch material was largely published as reports *to* Congress; most executive agency material was presented and bibliographically organized as congressional publications until the first quarter of the twentieth century. From 1820 through 1870, each Congress published an average of fifty-two volumes. Starting with the Forty-sixth Congress in 1880, the output climbed sharply. By the Sixty-first Congress (1909–11) the output reached 512 volumes. Subsequently, however, executive agencies began to decrease the amount published through Congress, and by the Seventy-sixth Congress of 1939–41, the congressional total had fallen to 253 volumes. The period 1880–1940 averaged 310 volumes per Congress, peaking just before World War I. Since that time, the executive branch agencies have published material largely independently, not as congressional reports—hence the declining number of congressional volumes. The growth of congressional publishing after 1880, however, clearly demonstrates government expansion, even as the individual agencies started publishing their own departmental editions.

Although the USGPO is the center of federal *printing*, federal *publishing* is highly decentralized. In effect, each government agency is an independent publishing house, all contracting to the same printer. In theory, the Congressional

Joint Committee on Printing oversaw all federal publication from 1846 until the end of the twentieth century. In practice, the committee's attention and influence has varied across time. It created the USGPO in 1861 and oversaw the large-scale reforms passed by Congress in 1895, but it never provided a focal point for policy or guidance on federal publishing efforts.

The structure of federal publication developed by 1896 existed until late in the twentieth century. Most of the actual printing had begun shifting from private to public enterprise with the establishment of the USGPO in 1861. In 1873 responsibility for the *Congressional Record* and the *Statutes at Large*, the official compilation of laws passed in each congressional session, changed from private publishers to the federal government. An 1895 law codified the distribution and depository system, established a sales program, and provided for the first time indexing services for USGPO output. No further fundamental changes to the USGPO were legislated until well after 1940.

It would seem, then, that by 1900 the federal government not only was publishing and printing its reports but was promoting their use. However, the legislation of 1895 also inadvertently made access to government publications difficult for the average library user. By then, all federal documents were being distributed to about 700 libraries designated as depositories across the country; but the bibliographic control system initiated by GPO and adapted by libraries for government publications hindered rather than helped citizens trying to use them. A complicated classification scheme that did not mesh with existing library systems by and large precluded integration of these government publications into the card catalogs of the nation's libraries. Only with the development of on-line systems in the latter third of the twentieth century did true bibliographic integration become possible.

Publishing Diversity: From Legislation to Exploration

Government publications of the late nineteenth and early twentieth centuries fell into several different categories. The first included "the business of government," including the *Congressional Record* and its predecessors, other material generated by the legislative process, laws, treaties, and agency annual reports — the daily grist from the governmental mill.

A second large category of government publications involved the production and dissemination of statistical information about the United States with data drawn from a range of official sources. In 1878, for instance, the government initiated publication of an annual series, *Statistical Abstract of the United States*, which drew on the work of increasing numbers of government staff devoted to the business of numbers tracking and compilation. Formally, this report was a production of the Treasury Department, presented to the Speaker of the House of Representatives, and, by action of the House, referred to the Committee on Ways and Means, which then ordered its printing.

Once the compilation and publication of this series of statistics was under way, its detail and complexity expanded decade by decade. The subjects covered in 169 tables of closely printed columns in the 1882 issue of the *Statistical Abstracts* included, for example, finance, coinage, commerce, immigration, shipping, the postal service, population, railroads, agriculture, and coal and iron mining.[12] Although the preparation of the twenty-third number (in 1900) was still a task of the Treasury Department, by then it was credited to the department's own Bureau of Statistics. Twenty years later, with its contents even more extensive, the participation of many more individuals with specified responsibilities was acknowledged. By that point, series production had shifted to the Bureau of Foreign and Domestic Commerce lodged within the Department of Commerce, then directed by Herbert Hoover. The editor of these commerce reports headed a team of nearly fifty departments gathering data about various commodities and technical matters and utilizing input organized geographically, some of which had been contributed by local chambers of commerce and some by foreign offices. Statistics were then being collected about new processes and commodities, such as automation, chemical and electrical equipment, and petroleum, alongside products with a longer history, such as agricultural implements, hides and leather, paper, and textiles.[13]

The Census Bureau also generated large quantities of statistical information that had to be printed by the government. Space does not allow discussion of the full range of census material generated, compiled, and printed during our period, but a few strategically chosen examples can give a sense of how its reach and impact grew. The 1880 census, for instance, included so many questions and covered so many new geographic entities that it took almost a full decade to tabulate and publish the results.[14] Despite such delays, however, public interest in this sort of information grew, and, as a result, government staff responded by collecting some of the information in specialized, targeted studies of the nation's population.

The massive 1904 report *Negroes in the United States* was one such compilation based on data gathered for the twelfth census.[15] Instead of sending interested inquirers the twelve quarto volumes reporting the census, or even the published abstract, staff brought together information scattered throughout the report in order "to bring out more clearly the meaning of the statistics regarding the present conditions or the recent changes of the negro population." Particular attention was paid to the analysis of "the figures on occupations" for which "much use has been made of the Special Report on Occupations." Contributors included the chief statistician of the Census Bureau, William Chamberlin Hunt, who adapted tables from the 1900 census; Walter Francis Willcox, professor of geology at Cornell University, who compiled statistics relating to agriculture; and W. E. B. Du Bois, professor of economics and history at Atlanta University, who provided a specially commissioned section on the Negro farmer.[16]

This early special report was followed by a series of monographs on religious demographics in the United States, which ran from 1906 until the 1930s.[17] In 1910 the Labor Department's Bureau of Labor Statistics began publishing the Women in Industry series, including the nineteen-volume *Report on Condition of Woman and Child Wage Earners in the United States*.[18] Subsequently, in 1920, *The New Position of Women in American Industry* appeared.[19] During the Depression, the Census Bureau broadened the scope of its investigations even further, producing such works as the 1935 *Potential Earning Power of Southern Mountaineer Handicraft*.[20] By 1940 publication of U.S. census data required a more than 30 percent increase in the number of volumes published than had been necessary for the 1880 census.

A third large group of government publications recorded American expansion into, and exploitation of, the trans-Appalachian West. When Thomas Jefferson authorized Lewis and Clark's expedition, the federal government involved itself in exploring, settling, and inventorying the resources of the continent. Although the government's goals for westward expansion were largely political and economic, scientific research was also considered important. Before the Civil War, in fact, Congress had called for some sixty volumes providing scientific exploration and maps of the new American territories. This emphasis on the West continued after the war as the sale of western land was, until 1913, the chief source of federal revenue. Arguably, the reports of western exploration were needed to demonstrate the economic potential of the lands being explored. Still, the ad hoc scientific content of those early explorations continued in the post–Civil War era until the number of federal agencies with officially mandated scientific missions increased dramatically. (See figure 13.1.)

A fourth group of publications reflected the government's growing involvement in science and technology more generally. With respect to the West, after 1880 science benefited from a shift in federal interest from exploration to economic exploitation of newly acquired lands. Although these studies always contained a component of pure science, mineral extraction and agricultural improvements were the main thrusts of government activity. Beginning in the 1880s, then, geological survey maps of mineral resources had direct economic motivations. Similarly, after the establishment of the Department of Agriculture as a cabinet level office in 1889, its publications were aimed at translating basic research into usable technology capable of increasing crop production. From

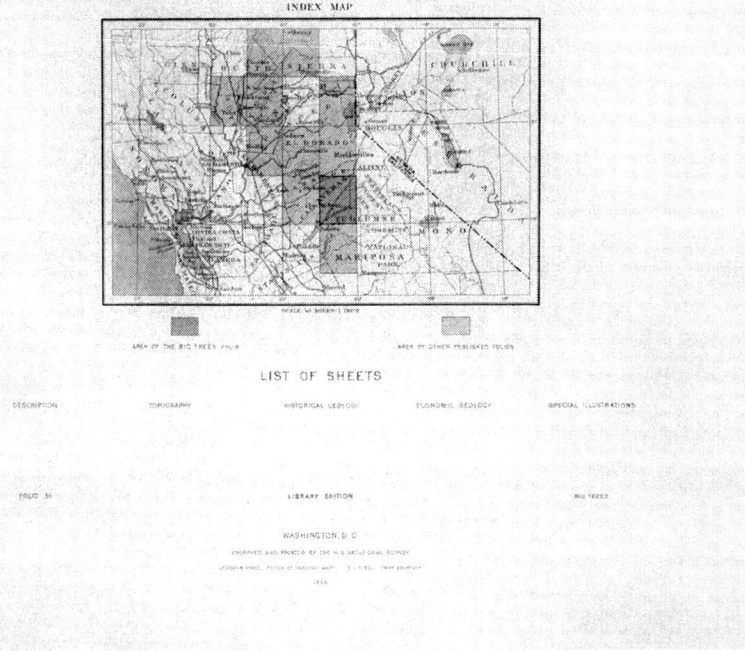

FIGURE 13.1. George F. Becker et al., *Big Trees Folio*, fol. 51 of *Geologic Atlas of the United States* (Washington, D.C.: Government Printing Office, 1898), cover. American Antiquarian Society.

its inception, the Agriculture Department was deeply involved in what came to be called extension work. Economic motivation was not limited to geology and agriculture, however. Created in 1901, the National Bureau of Standards was placed within the Department of Commerce, demonstrating the union of science and business.

In the latter part of the nineteenth century, the federal government was involved in nearly every area of scientific investigation, as Marcel Chotkowski LaFollette shows in chapter 12. Many eminent scientists moved easily between government service and the academy, and their publications encompassed both the official and the popular. The paleontologist Othniel Charles Marsh (1831-99) worked for both Yale and the U.S. Geological Survey. His great rival, Edward Drinker Cope (1840-97), taught at Haverford College and also did substantial field research with the Geological Survey in the 1870s before returning to teach at the University of Pennsylvania. His book, *The Vertebrata of the Tertiary Formations of the West*, popularly known as "Cope's Bible," was in fact a volume of the final report of the Geological Survey.[21] John Wesley Powell was a professor at Illinois Wesleyan University when he made his first federally funded explorations of the Grand Canyon in 1867 and became a full-time government employee in 1879. Powell's government funded expeditions are heavily documented. His official report, *Explorations of the Colorado River of the West and Its Tributaries*, was published by the Smithsonian Institution in 1875.[22] He had used some of the material previously in a series for *Scribner's Monthly Magazine* (1874), which generated the funding for the expedition. Later, he repackaged the whole project in *Canyons of the Colorado*, published commercially in 1895.[23] Although not everyone was as aggressive as Powell, the lack of copyright on government publications promoted such multiple uses of textual material. Powell eventually became the second director of the U.S. Geological Survey in 1881, serving until he resigned in 1894 to pursue his own interests in ethnography. Having also founded the Bureau of Ethnology in 1879, he would head it until his death.

As the century waned, government agencies were involved in scientific investigations—and hence scientific publication—in a number of fields ranging from physical sciences like geology to social sciences like anthropology. They also produced basic data that could be used across many academic disciplines. Beginning in 1882, for instance, a series of U.S. Geological Survey monographs helped establish the dominant paradigm of worldwide geologic thinking for the next fifty years. Clarence Dutton's *Tertiary History of the Grand Cañon District* of 1882 was a landmark of American science that invented what we now call geomorphology.[24] William Morris Davis of Harvard carried the work further, illustrating the rapidly increasing interchange between government and university science. Davis published with both the Geological Survey and the National Academy of Sciences, incorporating the basic work of Dutton, Powell, and Grove Karl Gilbert of the survey into the dominant American and European conceptual approach to geology. Davis was the first to offer holistic theories about geologic processes. Written in the 1880s and 1890s, Davis's work and that of the Geological Survey coincided in this seminal approach to geology, although Davis later moved further into theory and, as well, into the pedagogy of teaching the earth sciences.

The social sciences benefited significantly from government publishing. As research universities proliferated toward the end of the nineteenth century and into the twentieth, distinct social science disciplines became ever more articulated and differentiated. Simultaneously, the government increasingly gathered and published information that became raw material for academic research. The Bureau of American Ethnology, for example, which existed from 1879 to 1965, produced a huge literature fundamental to the study of Native Americans. Even today, many publications remain standard works, including Franz Boas and John R. Swanton's 1911 article on the Siouan (Dakota) language in the *Handbook of American Indian Languages*.[25] Other bureau publications, such as Victor Mindeleff's "A Study of Pueblo Architecture: Tusayan and Cibola" of 1891,[26] or Jesse Walter Fewkes's monograph on Hopi *kachinas* of 1903 contained illustrations, often in color, of Native Americans.[27] Monograph reprints of Mindeleff's and Fewkes's works are common today, but have color reproductions far inferior to those in the originals (figure 13.2).

. . .

The discipline of history, too, was profoundly affected by the growing availability of printed documents, records, and statistics relating to the history of the United States. Although the publication of historical records was only a minor part of the government publications program, it was a visible one and one in which the historical profession itself played a significant role. For example, the first volume of the long-anticipated project, *The War of the Rebellion: A Compilation of the Official Records of the Union and Confederate Armies*, was published in 1880.[28] By the time the project was published in 1902, it amounted to seventy volumes in 128 parts, including an index. This project had been undertaken after a comparable documentary project covering the Revolutionary era had foundered. *American Archives*, under the editorship of Peter Force, was thought to have wasted time and resources reprinting work already in print. To avoid such problems, the Civil War volume's editor, Robert N. Scott, wisely involved individuals who had fought with the Confederate army and then relied on their cooperation to select material judiciously.[29]

FIGURE 13.2. Department of the Interior, *Excavation and Repair of Sun Temple, Mesa Verde National Park* (Washington, D.C.: Government Printing Office, 1916).

During this same period at the end of the nineteenth century, Frederick Jackson Turner and many of his colleagues in the historical profession became engaged in writing a new kind of history, that of the West and the South, about which the government was actively producing large quantities of information. Indeed, Turner made much of a short passage appearing in the *Bulletin of the Superintendent of the Census* for 1890 that commented on maps prepared to illustrate that unsettled land in the West was rapidly disappearing. The census report noted: "Up to and including 1880 the country had a frontier of settlement, but at present the unsettled area has been so broken into by isolated bodies of settlement that there can hardly be said to be a frontier line. In the discussion of its extent, its westward movement, etc., it can not, therefore, any longer have a place in the census reports."[30]

"These significant words" caught the eye of Turner, then a youthful assistant professor of history at the University of Wisconsin, while he was preparing a talk for presentation at a meeting of members of the American Historical Association to be held in Chicago during the Columbian Exposition. At the time, the association was still in its earliest years of operation and its reports appeared as publications of the USGPO.[31] Turner used this particular passage as the opening statement of "The Significance of the Frontier in American History," a project he had been trying out and refining in his public lectures and seminars at the University of Wisconsin during the academic year preceding the delivery of the formal address. In that address, he declared, "This brief official statement marks the closing of a great historic movement."[32]

Although his remarks did not create much of a stir on the evening of 22 July 1893, or in newspapers issued immediately afterwards, when his full text was included in the association's annual report, what became known as "the Turner thesis" began to exert an effect on the history profession that would last for many years. The influence of Turner's work, along with that of other historians who shared his interests and belief that the American Historical Association neglected the Western region in its conferences and publications, led eventually to the 1907 creation of a competitor association, the Mississippi Valley Historical Association (forerunner of the Organization of American Historians), designed to promote the history of the South and the West.

Impact of the Great Depression

The Great Depression—an economic catastrophe that threw millions out of work and caused enormous social upheaval—fundamentally changed the nature of the federal government and federal publishing as well.

The Agriculture Department, particularly after its elevation to cabinet status in 1889, was deeply involved in extension work. Organizationally the department was, and still is, complex, with numerous subagencies with shifting names and responsibilities. For the period 1923-53, the "lead" agency for extension was the Extension Service. Yet actual extension work and publication was not limited to the lead agency but rather spread across the entire department.

The annual *Yearbook of Agriculture*, for instance, begun in 1894, was actually published by the secretary's office and contained "an appendix designed to serve as a handbook of useful information for the farmer."[33] One article appearing in a section of the volume entitled, "Know Your Markets," identified its targeted audience and economic purpose with the question, "Do you want to sell your potato crops?"[34] By the late 1930s, however, the *Yearbook* had begun to reflect the political impulses of the Roosevelt administration with titles like the 1938 *Soils and Men* and the 1939 *Food and Life*. It might be said that the Agriculture Department constituted one large extension service. *The Monthly Catalog of United States Government Publications* for January 1939, for instance, takes eighteen pages to list and briefly cite the department's publications and its twenty subagencies. Most of those publications were aimed at farmers or the consumers of farm products. The Dairy Industry Bureau, for instance, put out a ten-page bulletin on *Care of Milk Utensils on Farms*,[35] and the Extension Service weighed in with *Home Economics Extension Objectives as They Relate to the Training of Extension Workers*.[36]

Oddly enough, the well-known federal publishing program of the Depression era, the Federal Writers' Project, established in 1935 as part of the Works Progress Administration, produced only *one* volume actually published by the government. Created to employ authors and other people associated with the publishing industry, the Federal Writers' Project was a federal-state cooperative venture that eventually employed more than 6,000 people over time. It eventually produced more than 3,800 publications, but because the project was cooperative in nature, most publications were produced by the cooperating states or by other publishers.[37] The notable exception was *Washington, City and Capital*, part of the famous American Guide Series for each state.[38] Other books in the American Guide Series, such as *New Mexico: A Guide to the Colorful State*, were not published by the federal government at all.[39]

The government was clearly the driving force behind the Federal Writers' Project, and, as we have seen, was ultimately responsible for a great many publications. Technically, however, most of its publications cannot be described bibliographically as government documents.

Similarly, although the Farm Security Administration produced *the* iconographic image of the Great Depression, its relationship to government publication is difficult to summarize. Like many Roosevelt administration innova-

FIGURE 13.3. This iconic photograph, now known as "Migrant Mother and Children," was taken by Dorothea Lange for the Farm Security Administration and originally titled "Destitute peapickers in California, a thirty-two year old mother of seven children." Circa 1936. Prints and Photographs Division, Library of Congress (LC-USZ62-107705.)

tions, it was aimed at putting people, in this case photographers, to work. The images produced by Dorothea Lange, Walker Evans, and Gordon Parks (among many others) are regarded today as among the finest American photographs ever taken. The archival remains of that photographic work are largely in the Library of Congress or the National Archives. Original publication of many of the images, however, is difficult to trace. Many were widely reproduced in the popular press, and there is no adequate inventory. The bibliographic record (WorldCat) largely identifies current archival holdings, not original publications. As with publications of the Federal Writers' Project, any book emerging from the Farm Security Administration was generally not published by the government. Hence Dorothea Lange's *An American Exodus: A Record of Human Erosion* of 1939 was published by a commercial firm, although the photographs were all produced for the government (figure 13.3).[40]

The Farm Security Administration also started stretching the definition of "publication." The agency produced at least two documentary films, *The River* and *The Plow That Broke the Plains*, today regarded as classics of the genre. The films are somewhat outside the scope of this essay but do foreshadow later debates as to what, exactly, constitutes a government "publication."

During the Great Depression, the government became directly involved with the citizenry in ways undreamed of even ten years previously. If the extension activities of the Agriculture Department and other agencies were aimed at increasing productivity, it can be argued that the Federal Writers' Project and the Farm Security Administration had a more ideological bent. Government involvement was intended to acknowledge poverty while lending the condition sufficient dignity to be worthy of support, not scorn. In essence, the government was using the power of publication to make clear the *human* side of the Depression and to create an atmosphere that lent itself to cooperation and not agitation. In the same way that the government had "sold" the American West in the previous century, attempts to alleviate the effects of the Depression are visible in government publications.

A Nation of Print

This chapter only briefly suggests the scope of American civilization investigated by the federal government and discusses only a small portion of the vast number of publications documenting those investigations during this period of rapid expansion. Unlike Mindeleff's "Pueblo Architecture" or Lange's photography, most government publications were not visual treasures. Furthermore, for every example of inspired prose like Dutton's *Tertiary History*, there were thousands of pieces of writing that were mundane at best, turgid at worst. As a possible lens through which to view the nature of American civilization, however, federal publishing offers much to the book historian and interested reader. Publications reported on the topic at hand, while giving evidence of the government's current priorities. Arguably, government publications provide profiles of the policies and the philosophies of that government, as well as the larger social forces that influenced such publishing activities. For all their plainness and awkwardness of access, government publications are primary sources of the relationship between science, the government, and the public sphere in the United States.

CHAPTER 14

Gilded-Age Consensus, Repressive Campaigns, and Gradual Liberalization
The Shifting Rhythms of Book Censorship

Paul S. Boyer
. . .

Censorship, the regulation of the printed word and other forms of communication, derives from the Latin noun *censor*, the Roman census takers whose duties gradually encompassed the oversight of public morals. This chapter examines such moral oversight in an American context between 1880 and 1940.

Whereas First Amendment scholars and legal historians typically regard censorship as legal restraint or the threat thereof, cultural historians often expand the term to encompass numerous processes governing the flow of print material to the public. Since Gutenberg's day, every society has employed formal and informal means to oversee and regulate its print culture. From the Gilded Age to the Eisenhower era, America was no exception. Among the many forms of "censorship" are pressure from advertisers, the day-to-day practice of editorial selection, the acquisition preferences of teachers, school boards, and librarians, and marketing decisions by bookstores and magazine dealers. Authors also practiced self-censorship, assessing the cultural climate of the moment. These were far more important, cumulatively, than formal legal censorship in determining access to print material. Thus, while this essay focuses on censorship as a legal phenomenon, it will also consider the larger array of cultural and social processes that control the movement of the written word from the author to the page to the reader.

"The Genteel Tradition"

As has been documented earlier in this volume (see the chapters by Winship and Radway, in particular) American book publishing in the 1880s was dominated by a few old-line companies: Harper's; Appleton's; Charles Scribner's Sons; Dodd, Mead; and E. P. Dutton in New York; Little, Brown; and Houghton Mifflin in Boston.[1] Led by successive generations of native-born Protestants educated at elite colleges, these firms helped shape the nation's literary standards. They did so not only through the books they published (or refused to publish), but also through their literary magazines, such as *Atlantic*, *Harper's*, *Century*, *Putnam's*, *Scribner's*, and *Lippincott's*, where books were reviewed and novels serialized.

The publishers maintained close ties with their authors and with major newspapers such as the *New York Evening Post*, *Boston Evening Transcript*, and *Chicago Tribune*. At the local level, ministers, booksellers, librarians, and newspaper editors—indeed, many Americans of all social classes—identified with the values of the powerful publishing houses. These values comprise what the philosopher George Santayana would in 1911 call "the genteel tradition." As historian Donald Sheehan summarizes, "The leading publishers of the Gilded Age were a reasonably homogeneous group which took pride in its conservatism. As pillars of the church and guardians of the family, they were as steadfastly traditional in their personal ideals as in their public convictions."[2]

This conservative outlook centered on assumptions regarding proper print material. Throughout the nineteenth century, the open discussion of sex had become increasingly taboo for the expanding middle classes in Europe and America, and definitions of the obscene had grown steadily more restrictive. This attitude (sometimes called "pecksniffery," after a character in Charles Dickens's 1844 novel *Martin Chuzzlewit*) contrasted starkly with earlier conventions. European literature had long been rich in bawdiness, vulgarity, and ribaldry, from Chaucer to Shakespeare, Richardson, and Balzac. In America, Benjamin Franklin's *Autobiography* included his youthful sexual adventures. By the 1870s and 1880s, however, in both England and America, a far stricter code determined what was publishable. Urbanization, capitalist expansion, the rise of the middle class, and the spread of evangelicalism helped shape a culture of uplift, optimism, aspiration, and moral oversight, and, indirectly, a stricter view of literary propriety.

These years also saw the spread of literacy and public schools, and consequently an expanded market for children's and family literature. Female readers increasingly influenced publishers' calculations.[3] Racy books and bawdy tales once savored by gentlemen in their libraries were now deemed inappropriate for pious middle-class men and women, not to mention their children. Thomas Bowdler of Edinburgh, whose expurgated *Family Shakespeare* had appeared as early as 1818, posed a test for printed material that would long endure: "[Can it] with propriety be read aloud in a family[?] . . . Will it cause the innocent to blush?"[4]

The genteel literary code was designed not for censorship per se but for moral and spiritual uplift. The purpose of literature, like the Sunday sermon, it was assumed, was to induce people to reject the sordid and aspire to higher ideals. Thus, disapproval met any work that wallowed in base behavior or social conflict, portrayed humanity's lustier side, or exposed the underside of slum life, even if it did not violate explicit sexual taboos.[5]

Excising Impropriety

Among elite publishers, the genteel code entirely governed literary production. Authors, usually sharing publishers' social background, understood the prevailing standards. Should an author overstep the bounds, editors intervened. Noticing the sentence, "A painted girl glanced at him as he moved away," editor Henry Mills Alden of *Harper's Magazine* quickly wielded his blue pencil. William Dean Howells expunged all profanity from Mark Twain's *Life on the Mississippi* before serializing it in the *Atlantic Monthly* in 1883. Hence, an angry steamboat officer could only explode "dash-dash-dash-*dashed.*"[6]

Howells found the tables turned in 1885, when he submitted his novel *The Rise of Silas Lapham* to be serialized in the *Century Magazine*. Editor Richard Watson Gilder objected to a passage in which a wealthy Bostonian wonders nervously why the city's poor do not dynamite the mansions of Beacon Hill while their owners are on vacation. Howells revised the incendiary passage, demonstrating that the genteel code encompassed not only sexual impropriety but also material deemed politically or socially dangerous as well.[7]

If a book that violated the genteel code somehow appeared in print, a phalanx of reviewers, booksellers, and librarians stood ready to condemn it or restrict its circulation. The rules of propriety also applied to anthologies and standard editions of the classics. Bawdy or erotic poems or portions of poems disappeared from anthologies; sexually explicit passages in Chaucer, Shakespeare, Swift, or Defoe were silently expunged or altered.[8] Dictionary publishers also conformed, rarely including terms for sexual organs or sexual behavior in nineteenth-century dictionaries; profanity, vulgarisms, and expletives were absent entirely.

Walt Whitman was the one major American writer at the time to openly flout the genteel code. Whitman's sensual, homoerotic verse, coupled with his unquestioned genius, confounded the literary establishment. His *Leaves of Grass*, first published in 1855, was rejected by most booksellers in the 1870s and 1880s.[9] This is not to imply, however, that the genteel code operated at every level of print culture. Literary erotica and pornography had long circulated clandestinely, as did the occasional sub rosa production of an established contemporary author, such as Mark Twain's ribald classic *Conversation, As It Was by the Social Fireside in the Time of the Tudors*. Despite this literary shadow world and the troublesome Whitman, the larger pattern is clear: by the 1880s, a strict code of propriety ruled respectable American book publishing and print culture. As Noel Perrin has observed, this code was enforced in a "quiet and business-like" fashion that rarely drew comment. When Henry Mills Alden omitted an entire chapter from a *Harper's* serialization of Henry James's translation of an Alphonse Daudet novel, he explained that he was only following the "usual rule in such a case."[10]

Beyond the Code

Of course, print culture extended beyond this elite nexus of leading publishers, critics, booksellers, and editors, creating a more complex picture. The tabloid press, dime novels, and mass magazines such as the *National Police Gazette* survived into the 1880s. The *Police Gazette* featured lurid crime stories infused with sex and risqué lithographs of scantily clad women (figure 14.1). At the outer fringes of the print world, trading cards, cigar-box illustrations, and cigarette-package premiums portrayed alluring women in exotic or suggestive poses (figure 14.2).

Even the more raffish publications, though, were closely monitored and exercised some self-censorship. Crime magazines and dime novels were routinely denounced as vulgar and sensational, but they avoided out-and-out obscenity or blatant violations of the code. Despite their sex and violence, even these melodramatic stories typically ended moralistically, with criminals, prostitutes, and other shady characters suffering for their misdeeds. In 1896, responding to persistent criticism, the dime-novel publisher Street & Smith launched a new adventure series by "Burt L. Standish" (Gilbert Patten). The hero, Frank Merriwell, was a moral paragon. As Patten later wrote, the very name symbolized "the chief characteristics I desired my hero to have—*Frank* for frankness, *merry* for a happy disposition, *well* for health and abounding vitality." The series reflected "the doctrine of a clean mind and healthy body."[11] Belatedly, even the dime novels had embraced the genteel code.

The Heavy Hand of the Law

Behind the phalanx of institutional forces upholding the code of propriety lay the ultimate line of defense: legal censorship. Despite the First Amendment's guarantee of press freedom, the courts had consistently excluded obscenity from constitutional protection. Congress made this explicit in 1873 when it amended the postal code to prohibit the mailing of "obscene," "lewd," or "lascivious" books or other printed matter.

FIGURE 14.1. "The Tattooing Freak—What an energetic journalist discovered in relation to this latest and most grotesque caprice of feminine fashion through the connivance of the tattoo-artiste" describes the cover illustration on this weekly crime magazine. *National Police Gazette* 35, no. 112 (15 November 1879).

FIGURE 14.2. A tobacco label depicts a southern lady holding a fan, with the Virginia emblem and motto, "Sic Semper Tyrannis" depicted at center. The Belle of Virginia was one of the brands manufactured by David Dunlop of Petersburg, Virginia. This chromolithograph was produced by A. Hoen and Company of Richmond, one of many printers that supplied the tobacco industry. The Baltimore firm opened its plant in Richmond in 1876, remaining in operation until 1981. Circa 1880. 34.7 cm by 15.9 cm. American Antiquarian Society. Gift of Vincent Golden.

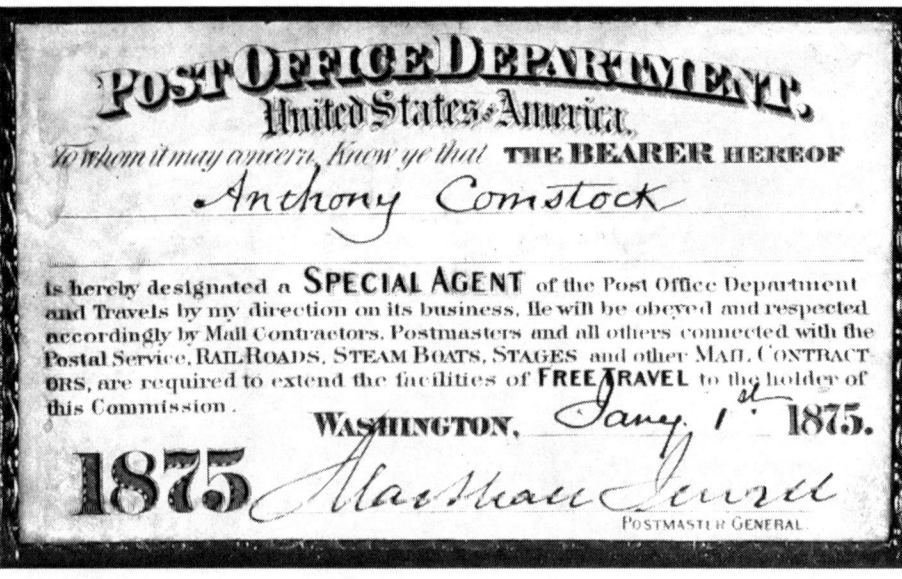

FIGURE 14.3. Anthony Comstock's 1875 appointment as a special agent (subsequently an inspector) for the Post Office Department gave him special power and national scope for his investigations.

The legal definition of obscenity generally accepted from the 1870s to the 1930s (though with growing reservations) was formulated by a British jurist, Alexander Cockburn, in the 1868 case *Queen v. Hicklin*: "The test of obscenity is this, whether the tendency of the matter charged as obscenity is to deprave and corrupt those whose minds are open to such immoral influences, and into whose hands a publication of this sort may fall."[12] The *Hicklin* test cast a very broad net. In addition to the obscenity that Cockburn so capaciously defined in 1868, politically suspect material could fall afoul of the censors as well. Although censors between 1880 and 1940 were predominantly concerned with obscenity, publications deemed politically dangerous faced significant repressive efforts during national crises.

Antivice societies in many cities assisted the courts in enforcing the ban on obscene publications. The New York Society for the Suppression of Vice arose in 1872. Its leader, Anthony Comstock, helped secure passage of the 1873 federal obscenity law and was appointed a special post-office investigator (figure 14.3). Although such organizations later attracted ridicule, they initially enjoyed good press and elite support. The New York Society, regularly listed in the *New York Charities Directory*, counted among its backers bankers J. P. Morgan and Morris K. Jesup; copper magnate William E. Dodge; and soap baron Samuel Colgate.[13]

Obscenity laws and antivice societies were additional links in an informal but elaborate network of guardians of the genteel code, extending from leading publishers and editors to local bookstores, churches, libraries, and school committees. "[T]he whole movement stands upon a firm basis in the approval of the best people . . . ," declared the Boston-based Watch and Ward Society in 1899; "it has public sentiment behind it, which is heavier than any penalty of law."[14]

Given this consensus, the courts and vice societies in the 1870s and 1880s had little need to monitor established book publishers and literary magazines. None of the eight thousand novels issued by mainstream houses in the 1880s is known to have run afoul of the law. Among established authors, only Balzac and Tolstoy, both foreigners, faced legal censorship. In 1885 Comstock successfully prosecuted an obscure New Jersey publisher who had issued an edition of Balzac's *Droll Stories*. In 1890 the postmaster general banned Tolstoy's *Kreutzer Sonata*, a novel about prostitution. Despite Tolstoy's reformist intent, the *New York Times* condemned the novel; New York City police commissioner Theodore Roosevelt called Tolstoy a "sexual and moral pervert."[15] Even crime magazines and dime novels typically faced condemnation rather than prosecution. In *Traps for the Young* (1883), Comstock lambasted dime novels for infusing youthful minds with "lawlessness and licentiousness" but tacitly conceded that they were not legally actionable. Parents, he declared, must protect children from such "putrid" publications.[16]

Legal censorship was initially reserved for sexually explicit drawings and photographs, publications with titles like *The Lustful Turk* and *The Stag-Party*, and ephemera such as erotic playing cards.[17] Comstock and moral guardians in other cities encouraged authorities to target also the occasional unexpurgated Ovid, Rabelais, or Boccaccio, as well as sex reformers like Ezra H. Heywood, author of *Cupid's Yokes*. Those who promoted illegal lotteries or mailed condoms, diaphragms, or pamphlets discussing contraception or abortion—all considered obscene by the cultural establishment—were also prosecuted. America's cultural and moral leaders (largely indistinguishable in these years), including the major book publishers, initially approved these efforts.[18] Millions of ordinary Americans added their support to the cause of decency and propriety.

When postal and customs censorship cases did reach the courts (most were handled administratively), the prosecutors enjoyed a conviction rate of well over 90 percent. In 1879 the Watch and Ward Society secured the signatures of 300 "leading citizens" on a petition calling for the suppression of "degrading" (but not hitherto actionable) publications such as the *Police Gazette*. Subsequently, in 1885, the Massachusetts legislature outlawed the display or sale to minors of periodicals featuring "criminal news, police reports, or accounts of criminal deeds, or pictures and stories of lust and crime," resulting in the prosecution of several Boston-area news dealers.[19]

A New Code: Propriety in the Twentieth Century

By the 1890s, however, sweeping social and cultural changes were undermining the genteel code and the assumptions justifying literary censorship. Immigration was changing the demographics of the nation. Amid the depression of 1893-96, new currents of social thought challenged the presumption that elite status was granted by a kind of divine right. Darwinism and the scientific worldview, coupled with the rise of critical biblical scholarship, encouraged religious skepticism and weakened the moral absolutism and cultural idealism of the Gilded Age. Further, science's growing cultural authority diminished that accorded to works of the imagination (and thus their power to corrupt). Feminists like Charlotte Perkins Gilman, meanwhile, challenged stereotypes of female fragility and vulnerability that had further buttressed the genteel code.

New intellectual and cultural currents were also stirring in Europe: the naturalism of Flaubert and Zola; Nietzsche's philosophic challenges to Christian morality; Ibsen's dramas probing middle-class social conventions; Shaw's plays skewering whole herds of Victorian sacred cows; the fin-de-siècle vogue of fashionable decadence. The paintings of Cézanne, Van Gogh, and Gauguin, extending the Impressionists' aesthetic revolution, disoriented those accustomed to realistic and sentimental genre canvases.

Awareness of these trends quickly crossed the Atlantic, unsettling the engrained assumption that literature and art existed solely to reinforce moral idealism and religious faith. The New York literary and art magazine the *Chap-Book* (1894-98) reflected this new consciousness in its fin-de-siècle tone of worldly sophistication. The naturalist aesthetic emerged from a group of diverse, younger American writers that included Stephen Crane, Theodore Dreiser, and Abraham Cahan in New York, Frank Norris and Jack London in San Francisco, and Kate Chopin in New Orleans. Even when these younger writers did not violate specific taboos, their deterministic fictional worlds — in which human beings are driven to pursue their ambitions and desires — challenged the idealism of the genteel tradition.

Modernity and Cultural Turbulence

Although new mass magazines such as *Cosmopolitan* (founded 1886) and the *Ladies' Home Journal* under editor E. W. Bok (1889-1919) observed the genteel code, their pages displayed a flood of alluring advertising that introduced readers to consumption and material abundance. As Richard Brodhead has noted, the values of these advertiser-driven magazines are mirrored in the acquisitive, materialist urban culture of novels like Dreiser's *Sister Carrie*, further challenging the genteel culture's aura of high-minded idealism and uplift.[20]

The tides of modernism inevitably affected the world of print culture. The line between acceptable and unacceptable began to blur, leaving mainstream publishers and the literary establishment—with an occasional intervention by the courts—to struggle with new cultural forces and shifting literary standards. The shocks of this process of reorientation would reverberate for decades.[21]

A few examples suggest the cultural turbulence of the 1890s. The firestorm of criticism surrounding Kate Chopin's candid depiction of female sexual frustration in *The Awakening* (1899) effectively ended her career. Earlier in the decade, journalist Stephen Crane chronicled the descent of a New York slum girl into prostitution in *Maggie, a Girl of the Streets*. The manuscript's theme and milieu clearly violated the genteel code, and every publisher Crane approached, including Harper's and Century, rejected it. Crane himself published his novella pseudonymously in 1893. Appleton's reissued an expurgated edition only after Crane's success with *The Red Badge of Courage* in 1895. "I have carefully plugged at the words which hurt," Crane wrote his editor; "[T]he book wears quite a new aspect." The *Library Journal* denounced even this purified version for "imbruted vulgarity," underscoring the cultural volatility of the decade.[22]

Theodore Dreiser's first novel, *Sister Carrie*, was initially accepted in 1900 by Walter Hines Page of Doubleday, Page & Co. But even this new publisher, poised between the traditional and the modern, had second thoughts about the social-climbing heroine's two illicit relationships and success as a music-hall performer. Thus, the firm printed only some 500 copies, not all of which were bound. The book was not advertised (though some review copies were distributed), and only 227 copies were sold. Only when Dreiser's reputation grew (and the code of literary propriety evolved) was *Sister Carrie* truly "published."[23]

The Dawn of a New Era

The pace of change accelerated after 1900. In New York's Greenwich Village, political radicals and avant-garde writers flouted prevailing sexual and cultural conventions. *The Smart Set*, edited by Henry L. Mencken and George Jean Nathan after 1914, mocked Victorian proprieties. Little magazines like Harriet Monroe's *Poetry* (1912) and Margaret Anderson's *Little Review* (1914), and the socialist *Masses* under editor Max Eastman (1913–17), espoused aesthetic and political radicalism. As the iconoclastic work of Nietzsche, Ibsen, and Shaw reached American readers, the 1913 Armory Show in New York introduced artistic modernism.[24]

As the cultural revolution proceeded, print material once deemed inappropriate was increasingly published by established houses or eager newcomers. After Charles Scribner refused U.S. rights to Arnold Bennett's *The Old Wives' Tale* in 1908 for its "unpleasant and sordid details," George H. Doran published the English best seller in America, selling 100,000 copies in three years.[25]

While some found the breakup of the old order exhilarating, others clung to familiar stability and assurance. Princeton English professor (and Presbyterian minister) Henry Van Dyke could still proclaim in 1905: "The only enduring literature is that which recognizes the moral conflict as the supreme interest of life, and the message of Christianity as the only real promise of victory." As late as 1916, ruthlessly expurgated anthologies like Harvard English professor William A. Neilson's *Chief British Poets of the Fourteenth and Fifteenth Centuries* were still being published.[26]

Legal Battles for Censorship

In this unsettled cultural environment, more controversies involving openly published works by well-known authors found their way into the courts. A production of Shaw's play about prostitution, *Mrs. Warren's Profession*, was legally closed in New Haven in 1905. In 1915 Theodore Dreiser's autobiographical novel *The "Genius,"* which deals somewhat openly with sex, was withdrawn by the New York branch of a prominent British publisher, John Lane Company, when the New York Vice Society threatened prosecution. In the same year, Elinor Glyn's best-selling *Three Weeks*, chronicling an idyllic Venetian love affair between an English youth and a mysterious Russian noblewoman, was prosecuted in Boston by the Watch and Ward Society and deemed obscene. Publications promoting radical political and social thought were also indicted; the postal authorities banned a 1913 issue of *The Call*, a socialist weekly, for featuring an article about venereal disease by birth-control advocate Margaret Sanger. In 1914 Sanger fled to England to escape federal prosecution for distributing by mail her socialist journal *Woman Rebel*, which advocated legalized contraception and denounced capitalism.[27]

But victory for the censors was becoming increasingly problematic. Comstock's 1905 effort to suppress *Mrs. Warren's Profession* in New York City failed, after which postal officials terminated his thirty-year appointment as a special agent.[28] Also unsuccessful was Comstock's 1913 complaint against Daniel Carson Goodman's *Hagar Revelly*, a reformist novel about a young working woman who becomes her boss's mistress out of economic necessity. The publisher was Mitchell Kennerley, a young Britisher of advanced views who had recently immigrated to New York. The jury acquitted Kennerley after a federal judge, Learned Hand, criticized the venerable *Hicklin* test as a "mid-Victorian" relic unrelated to "the understanding and morality of the present time."

Nevertheless, despite (or because of) the pace of cultural change, the antivice societies retained substantial public support, media approval, and elite backing. Adopting the language of progressivism, censorship advocates likened purifying the moral environment to other reformers' efforts to improve factory and slum conditions. In 1903 a Boston social worker praised the Watch and Ward Society—"a sort of Moral Board of Health"—for its "profound contribution to the work of every uplifting agency" in the city.[29] And a speaker at the 1906 National Conference of Charities and Correction praised the battle against "salacious literature" as a worthy part of the struggle for social betterment in urban-industrial America.

Wartime Trends

America's entry into war in 1917 engendered a spirit of political conformity and moral purification on the home front. The Progressive Era antiprostitution campaign intensified, targeting red-light districts near military bases. The Prohibition movement surged to victory with ratification of the Eighteenth Amendment. John S. Sumner, Comstock's successor, went to France as a YMCA worker, upholding what the Vice Society called America's "reputation for high ideals and moral greatness."[30]

Fervent patriotism and moral zealotry strengthened censorship of perceived political as well as moral menaces. The Trading-with-the-Enemy Act, the 1917 Espionage Act, and the 1918 Sedition Amendment targeted speeches, printed matter, and imported publications that jeopardized the war effort. Those who employed "disloyal, profane, scurrilous, or abusive language" about the United States government, the Constitution, the flag, or military forces were subject to heavy fines or imprisonment. Under these draconian measures (and similar state laws), books were suppressed, while antiwar and radical periodicals lost mail privileges, effectively silencing them. The socialist leader Victor Berger received a twenty-year prison sentence (later commuted) for publishing antiwar articles in his *Milwaukee Leader*. Postal authorities seized the October 1917 issue of Margaret Anderson's *Little Review* for an innocuous story by Wyndham Lewis describing a British draftee's seduction of a young woman. Lewis's real offense was his pacifism. In 1918 postal officials declared Andreas Latzko's antiwar novel *Men in War*, published by a recently established New York firm, Boni

& Liveright, nonmailable.³¹ In wartime the line between political and moral censorship was often blurred. As Margaret Anderson and Margaret Sanger both learned, publications that were politically *and* culturally radical were doubly vulnerable.

Ironically, two 1919 Supreme Court cases upholding this wartime censorship elicited pronouncements by Justice Oliver Wendell Holmes Jr., that would later be employed to good effect by free-speech advocates. Although *Abrams v. the United States* found the Sedition Amendment constitutional, Holmes argued eloquently in dissent that free societies require press freedom. In *Schenck v. United States*, Holmes's majority opinion upheld Schenck's conviction under the Espionage Act on the grounds that his published attacks on the draft had posed a "clear and present danger" to the war effort. Civil liberties lawyers later used these words to *defend* threatened publications that did *not* pose a "clear and present danger" to the nation.³²

The shifting balance between moral and political censorship, so sharply highlighted during World War I, raises the question of censorship's varying focus in different eras. Presumably, censorship targets the greatest perceived threat. Amid the urban expansion, growing cultural diversity, and new intellectual currents that challenged conventional social mores in the later nineteenth and early twentieth centuries, morally "obscene" works faced the greatest criticism. Between 1910 and 1920, however, as socialists gained electoral strength, the Bolsheviks took power in Russia, and Woodrow Wilson led the nation into war, the emphasis shifted to political censorship. While obscenity remained an issue, works that espoused radical political ideologies or threatened support for the war were deemed especially dangerous. Such politically directed censorship had characterized other eras of political crisis, resulting, for example, in the Alien and Sedition Acts of 1798, an effort to muzzle Jeffersonian supporters of the French Revolution, in the Lincoln Administration's attempts to silence northern antiwar opinion during the Civil War, and in the purging of the U.S. Information Agency's overseas libraries of suspected leftist writers' works during the anticommunist hysteria of the early 1950s.

The 1920s: A Clash of Ideals

The culture wars continued in the 1920s, as the focus of censorship shifted back to social and sexual behavior. Widespread revulsion against exalted idealism and enforced conformity, especially among the young, accelerated the repudiation of the genteel code already underway before the war. Famously disillusioned postwar writers like John Dos Passos, Eugene O'Neill, Sinclair Lewis, Ernest Hemingway, and F. Scott Fitzgerald epitomized the radically altered outlook. Simultaneously, however, millions of Americans longed to return to clearcut moral and cultural standards. For them, censorship seemed a legitimate last resort for defending threatened standards from the forces of disintegration and chaos.[33]

The book publishing world itself was transformed by growing numbers of newcomers—many of recent immigrant origins, as discussed by James West and Janice Radway earlier in this volume In some cases, established houses came into the hands of younger family members who proved far less conservative than their elders. Young George Palmer Putnam, for example, played such a role at the venerable G. P. Putnam's Sons in the 1920s. Eager, brash, and undaunted by the genteel code, these newcomers shook up a stodgy industry, courted unknown writers, tested the limits of the acceptable, and changed American book publishing forever.[34]

The resulting outpouring of books broke old taboos while reflecting a broader range of cultural and ethnic voices. H. L. Mencken's magazine *American Mercury* (1924), published by Knopf, championed the new writers and derided the old guard (see figure 14.4). Long-suppressed classics resurfaced. Daniel Defoe's *Moll Flanders* (1722) was issued in at least three new editions in 1924.[35]

Dismayed by these trends and emboldened by coercive wartime sentiments, John Sumner targeted numerous postwar publications for censorship in New York City. Among these were James Branch Cabell's *Jurgen* (Robert McBride & Co.), a fable full of labored phallic symbolism; D. H. Lawrence's *Women in Love* (Thomas Seltzer, Inc.); Arthur Schnitzler's *Casanova's Homecoming* (Thomas Seltzer, Inc.); Robert Keable's *Simon Called Peter* (Dutton), a novel about a promiscuous Baptist minister; and a reissue of a translation of Petronius's *Satyricon* (Boni & Liveright). Amid waves of publicity and manifestos by anticensorship "emergency committees," no publishers were convicted. Despite their earlier defense of Comstock and the genteel code, the *New York Times*, the *Nation*, and other periodicals now criticized censorship efforts.[36] A "Clean Books League" led by John Ford, an Irish American Catholic and state supreme court judge, campaigned from 1923 to 1925 for a tightening of New York's obscenity law, but again to no avail.[37] Some publishers even exploited censorship prosecution for publicity. Covici-Friede, another new house, trumpeting Sumner's failed prosecution of Radcliffe Hall's lesbian-themed novel, *The Well of Loneliness*, sold 100,000 copies. Anticensorship lawyers like Arthur Garfield Hays and Morris Ernst of the American Civil Liberties Union became celebrities.

But the culture wars, and hence the censorship efforts, continued. In 1921 John Sumner successfully prosecuted *Little Review* for publishing an erotic excerpt from James Joyce's work-in-progress *Ulysses* (figure 14.5). In 1928 Alfred A. Knopf withdrew as the U.S. publisher of *The Well of Loneliness* after

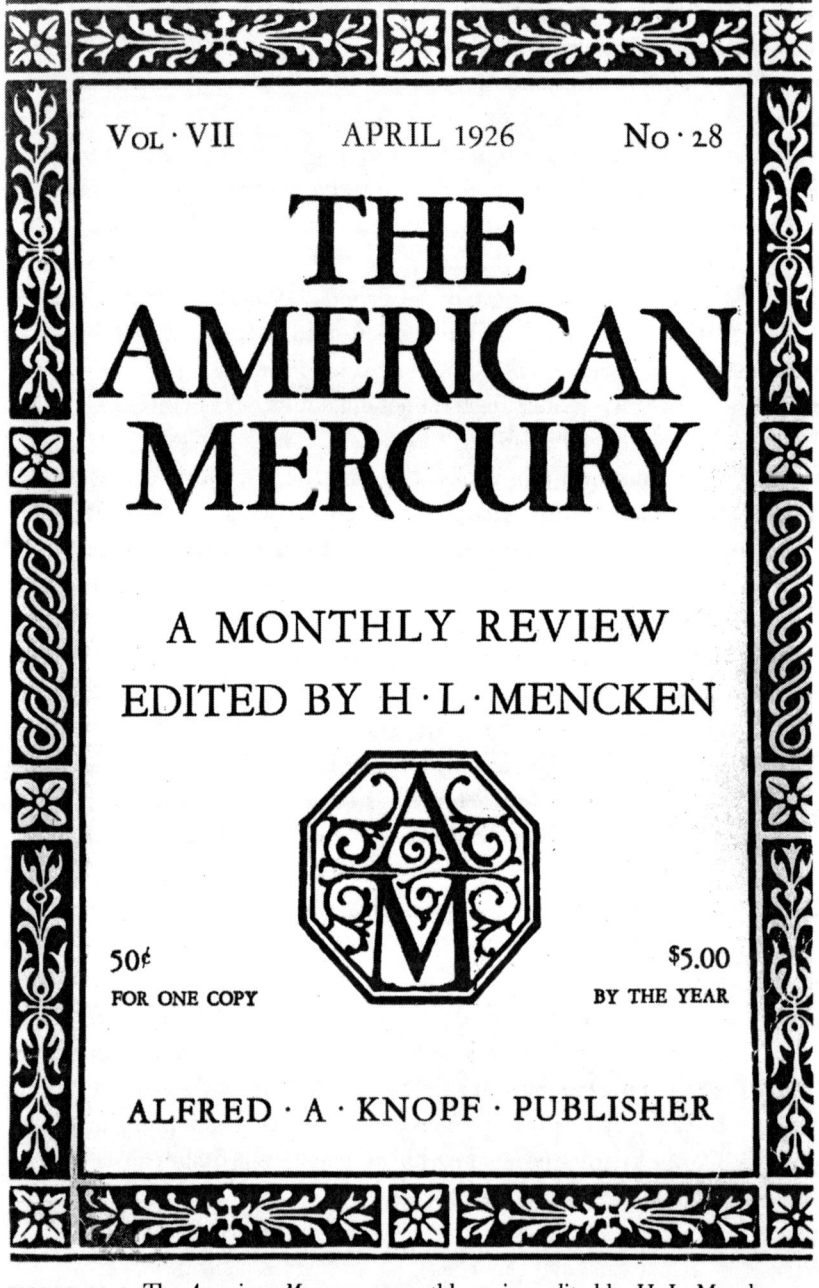

FIGURE 14.4. The *American Mercury*, a monthly review edited by H. L. Mencken, as noted on its cover, offered a varied bill of fare ranging from jazz to the ballads of the Old West and reporting on cultural activity across the country. The April 1926 issue (vol. 7, no. 28) included Herbert Asbury's story, "Hatrack," about a small-town prostitute. The New England Watch and Ward Society's attempt to suppress this issue in Boston triggered a highly publicized censorship confrontation.

The AMERICAN MERCURY

VOLUME VII   April 1926   NUMBER 28

TABLE OF CONTENTS

THE ANATOMY OF JAZZ	Henry Osborne Osgood	385
HALSTED	Fielding H. Garrison	396
BALLADS OF THE OLD WEST	Stanley Vestal	402
THE RETREAT FROM UTOPIA	Harold MacGrath	404
THE UNIONS LOSE SAN FRANCISCO	David Warren Ryder	412
EDITORIAL		418
THE METHODISTS	James D. Bernard	421
AMERICANA		433
INDIANA	Samuel W. Tait, Jr.	440
LITERARY LADIES OF THE SOUTH	Isaac Goldberg	448
THE ARTS AND SCIENCES:		
Sentimentality	John McClure	453
The Cancer Problem	E. S. Pickering	455
HORSES	James Stevens	458
IOWA TAKES TO LITERATURE	Josephine Herbst	466
JOURNALISM IN TEXAS	Chester T. Crowell	471
HATRACK	Herbert Asbury	479
THE LIBERATOR (*A Story*)	L. M. Hussey	484
CLINICAL NOTES	George Jean Nathan	492
NOTES AND QUERIES		495
THE THEATRE	George Jean Nathan	500
THE LIBRARY	H. L. Mencken	506
THE AMERICAN MERCURY AUTHORS		511
INDEX TO VOLUME VII		512
EDITORIAL NOTES		xxvi
CHECK LIST OF NEW BOOKS		xxxvi

Unsolicited manuscripts not accompanied by stamped and addressed envelopes will not be returned and the Editors will not enter into correspondence about them. Manuscripts should be addressed to The Editors and not to individuals. All accepted contributions are paid for on acceptance, without reference to the date of publication. The whole contents of this magazine are protected by copyright and must not be reprinted without permission.

Published monthly at 50 cents a copy. Annual subscription, $5.00; Canadian subscription, $5.50; foreign subscription, $6.00. . . . The American Mercury, Inc., publishers. Publication office, Federal and 19th streets, Camden, N. J. Editorial and general offices, 730 Fifth avenue, New York. . . . Printed in the United States. Copyright, 1926, by The American Mercury, Inc. . . . Entered as second class matter January 4, 1924, at the post office at Camden, N. J., under the Act of March 3, 1879. Published monthly on the 25th. Five weeks' advance notice required for change of subscribers' addresses.

Alfred A. Knopf, *Publisher*
H. L. Mencken, *Editor*
George Jean Nathan, *Contributing Editor*

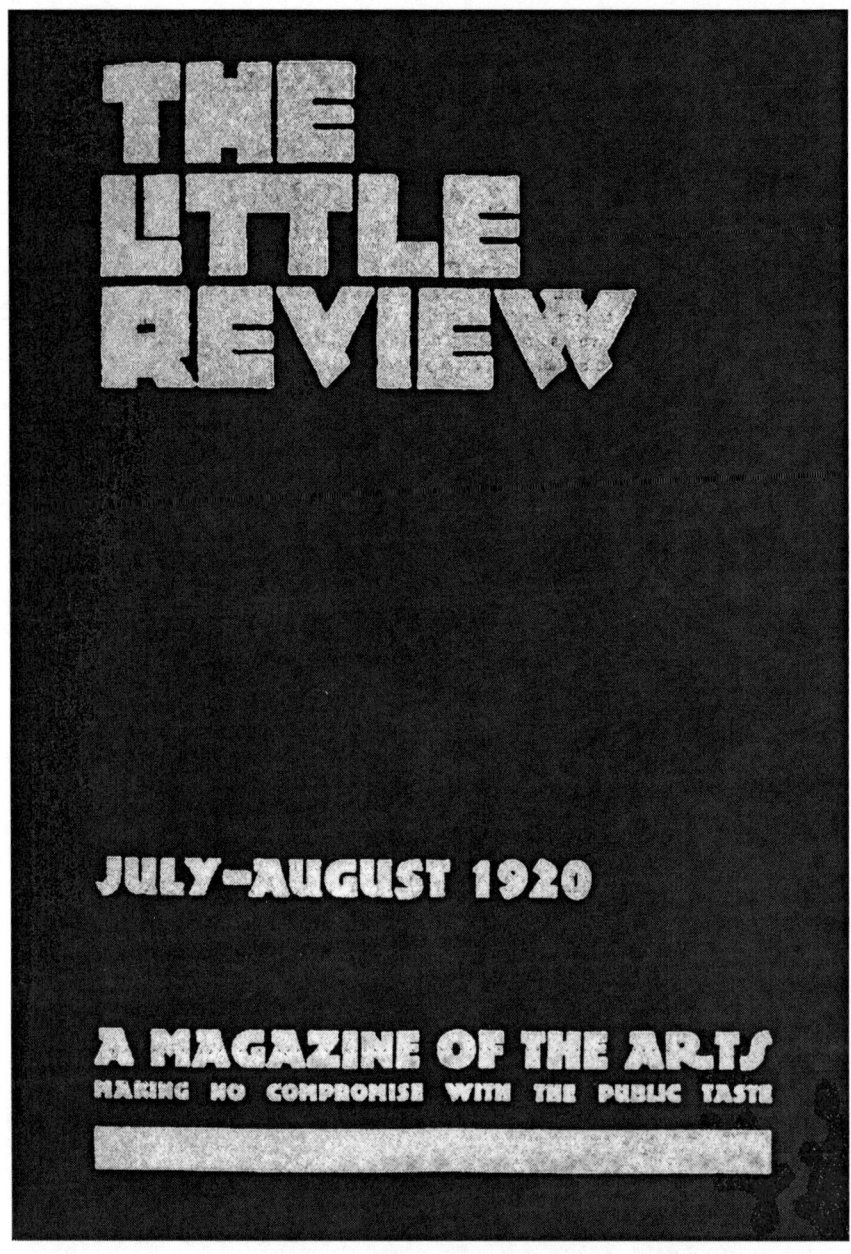

FIGURE 14.5. The *Little Review*, which described itself on its cover as "A Magazine of the arts making no compromise with the public taste," is representative of publications in which political radicals and avant-garde writers flouted prevailing sexual and cultural conventions; an example is the serialization of James Joyce's *Ulysses*, a section of which is listed on the contents page in the issue of July–August 1920 (vol. 7, no. 2).

THE LITTLE REVIEW

VOL. VII   JULY-AUGUST   No. 2

CONTENTS

Photograph of James Joyce	
Magic	Mary Butts
Genius	
Fluctuation	Anthony Wrynn
Soil	
Mother	Djuna Barnes
Drawing	Stuart Davis
Chanson on Petit Hypertrophique	John Rodker
Four Chronological Poems	Malcolm Cowley
Black Umbrellas	Ben Hecht
In the Country	Robert Reiss
Poems	Else von Freytag-Loringhoven
Study	Charles Ellis
Discussion:	
"The Public Taste"	
"Dada"	
May Sinclair in the "English Review"	
"The Modest Woman"	
Arrested Movement	Jerome Blum
Ulysses (Episode XIII concluded)	James Joyce
A New Testament (XI and XII)	Sherwood Anderson
The Reader Critic	

Subscription price, payable in advance, in the United States and Territories, $2.50 per year; Single copy, 25c; Canada, $2.75; Foreign, $3.00. Published monthly and copyrighted, 1920, by Margaret C. Anderson.
Manuscripts must be submitted at author's risk, with return postage.
Entered as second class matter March 16, 1917, at the Post Office at New York, N. Y., under the act of March 3, 1879.

MARGARET C. ANDERSON, Publisher
27 West Eighth Street, New York, N. Y.
Foreign Office: 43 Belsize Park Gardens, London, N. W. 3

British authorities successfully prosecuted the novel, leaving the bolder Covici-Friede to face Sumner's attacks.[38]

Defending Censorship

Censorship retained support even in the book world. Conservative organizations such as the American Booksellers Association, the American Library Association, the Authors' League of America, and the trade journal *Publishers' Weekly* rarely protested censorship in the 1920s, and indeed sometimes denounced the publishers and authors who did. Such popular writers as Hamlin Garland, Edwin Markham, Lloyd C. Douglas, Gene Stratton Porter, Booth Tarkington, and Mary Roberts Rinehart, as well as conservative literary critics and academics like Paul Elmer More and Yale's William Lyon Phelps, publicly lamented the erosion of the genteel code and even defended censorship. Exploiting these fissures in the literary and publishing worlds, Sumner implored "decent authors" and "the fine old publishing houses" to join him in defense of literary purity. A veiled nativist and even anti-Semitic tone sometimes crept into these attacks, though few went so far as the 1924 Watch and Ward speaker who called on the "Christian Forces of America" to launch a "Holy War" against the alien degenerates who were polluting American literature.[39]

Boston became a major battleground in the 1920s censorship wars.[40] This reflected a convergence of outlook between, on the one hand, a Protestant elite and middle class that had long supported the Watch and Ward Society and, on the other, a working-class immigrant population, heavily Irish Catholic, that rallied behind the repeated calls for literary purity in the diocesan weekly *The Pilot*, reinforced by the Vatican's 1927 denunciation of immoral literature. In 1915, facing this formidable alliance, the Boston booksellers' association had granted the Watch and Ward Society de facto control over which books could and could not be sold in Boston.

This arrangement highlights the strength of censorship sentiment in the 1920s *within* the print-culture world. The Boston booksellers' association was dominated by Richard F. Fuller, a deep-dyed conservative who fully supported the Watch and Ward Society. "Some of the bookleggers [*sic*] have slipped thru the lines and there is where you have got to have a strong organization that will hold them in line," Fuller declared at the American Booksellers Association's 1923 convention. A Boston librarian, addressing the American Library Association in 1924, fully agreed. "For ten years," she asserted, the collaboration between the Watch and Ward and the city's booksellers "has kept the worst books . . . out of the bookstores."

The Boston police department in 1926 launched its own clean-books campaign, warning bookstores of recently published works whose sale could lead to prosecution. These included Percy Marks's novel about postwar college life, *The Plastic Age* (Century Co., 1924); Frances Newman's *The Hard-Boiled Virgin* (Boni & Liveright, 1926); and Ernest Pascal's *The Marriage Bed* (Harcourt Brace, 1927). Although *Publishers' Weekly* initially dismissed the matter as insignificant, the reaction sharpened when Sinclair Lewis's *Elmer Gantry* (Harcourt Brace, 1927) and Theodore Dreiser's *An American Tragedy* (Liveright, 1927) were added to the list. Boston's booksellers, newspapers, and librarians all denounced the police censorship. Editors at Little, Brown and Co., and the *Atlantic Monthly* followed suit, as did *Publishers' Weekly*, the *New York Times*, and other national periodicals. "Banned in Boston" became a national byword.

The conflict took on class and ethnic dimensions, with overtones of intellectual condescension, as censorship opponents ridiculed Boston's police and immigrant population. In 1926 the New England Watch and Ward Society—ridiculed the previous year in an article titled "Keeping the Puritans Pure"—pressured bookstores to ban the April issue of Henry L. Mencken's *American Mercury* magazine, popular with college students and the avant-garde, for a story called "Hatrack," about a small-town prostitute publicly pilloried but privately patronized by the town's elite. Advised by his publisher, Alfred A. Knopf, and his lawyer, civil-liberties attorney Arthur Garfield Hays, Mencken went to Boston and, in a nationally publicized confrontation on Boston Common, defiantly sold a copy of the offending issue to a Watch and Ward official. Five thousand supporters, including many Harvard students, cheered him on. He was duly arrested, but a judge quickly dismissed the charges and denounced the Watch and Ward Society, securing Mencken's reputation as a battler against censorship and a champion of intellectual freedom. At a 1929 anticensorship rally in Boston, Clarence Darrow, Arthur Garfield Hays, Morris Ernst, Harvard historian Arthur Schlesinger Sr., and others deliberately aimed to make Boston a laughingstock. Effective in the long run, this strategy backfired in the short run, as a jury of working-class Bostonians upheld the ban on *An American Tragedy*.

Nevertheless, the tide was shifting, even in Boston. In October 1929 a Watch and Ward agent using an assumed name trapped a respected Cambridge bookseller into selling him a copy of D. H. Lawrence's *Lady Chatterley's Lover* (1928) and then filed a police complaint. Although a superior court found the book obscene, the Watch and Ward Society was widely condemned. In 1930 the Massachusetts legislature liberalized and modified various restrictive features of the state's obscenity statute.[41]

The celebrated censorship battles of the 1920s erupted at a moment of cultural transition, as an already-weakened genteel code finally gave way to a more permissive standard. By the decade's end, the culturally dominant view of what could legally and appropriately appear in print had shifted radically. As attorney Morris Ernst wrote in 1930, "In recent years *there has not been a single instance* where a book generally accepted by the public, the press, literary critics, and the reading public, and the community at large, and openly dealt with by the publishers and the book trade, was ultimately condemned by the courts."[42]

Censorship: A Cultural Practice

The cultural wars of the 1920s also remind us that censorship can take many different forms. Public librarians of the twenties acted as censors when they chose not to acquire a controversial new novel or not to subscribe to a radical periodical. School boards, school librarians, textbook commissions, and even state legislators acted as censors when they barred textbooks or other works considered objectionable. In 1925 the Tennessee legislature outlawed the teaching of evolution in the state's public schools. Prodded by the American Civil Liberties Union, high school biology teacher John Scopes challenged the law by reading his students a summary of Darwin's theory from a contemporary science textbook. In a trial that turned into a media extravaganza, Scopes was convicted, but the conviction was later overturned on a technicality.

The Scopes trial highlights the deeper sources of the censorship impulse, as embattled defenders of threatened values and a besieged social order rallied to defend themselves. In the Scopes trial, William Jennings Bryan passionately defended censorship, emotionally voicing the fear that evolutionists, public-school teachers, and big-city textbook publishers were turning children against their parents and their parents' religious beliefs.

Between 1930 and 1955, a series of federal court decisions ratified the cultural revolution of the preceding decades and extended First Amendment protection to works unquestionably obscene by 1880s standards and in some cases still banned in the 1920s. In 1930 federal judge Augustus N. Hand reversed a lower-court obscenity finding against Mary Ware Dennett's *The Sex Side of Life*, a booklet offering straightforward sexual information for young people. That same year, Congress included in the Smoot-Hawley tariff a provision mandating judicial review of all censorship rulings by the Customs Bureau and extending special protection to works of "literary or scientific merit."[43]

This provision laid the groundwork for *United States v. One Book Called "Ulysses"* (1933), a watershed case permitting legal importation of James Joyce's novel. Rejecting the *Hicklin* rule, Judge John Woolsey held that the legal test of obscenity must be a work's effect upon persons of "average sex instincts" (rather than children or the particularly susceptible). Books were to be judged in their entirety, not by isolated words or passages. The word, "fuck" was allowed to remain in *Ulysses*, despite its long-standing status as prima facie evidence of a work's legal obscenity. Dismissing the once-powerful genteel code, Woolsey observed: "The words which are criticized as dirty are old Saxon words known to almost all men and, I venture, to many women, and are such words as would be naturally and habitually used, I believe, by the types of folks whose life, physical and mental, Joyce is seeking to describe." When the U.S. Court of Appeals upheld Woolsey's ruling in 1934, Bennett Cerf of Random House (who, with Morris Ernst, had initiated the test case) published the first U.S. edition of *Ulysses*.[44]

Conclusion

Censorship remained a real threat for publishers beyond the period covered by this volume. The Massachusetts Supreme Court found Lillian Smith's *Strange Fruit* and Erskine Caldwell's *God's Little Acre* obscene in 1945 and 1950. In 1946 the New York Supreme Court imposed a ban on the sale of Edmund Wilson's sexually explicit *Memoirs of Hecate County* under that state's obscenity statute.[45] But the long-term trend was clear. In 1949 Judge Curtis Bok of the Pennsylvania Supreme Court dismissed obscenity indictments against a whole set of recent novels, including *God's Little Acre*, William Faulkner's *Sanctuary*, and James T. Farrell's *Studs Lonigan* trilogy, applying Justice Holmes's "clear-and-present-danger" test.[46]

The U.S. Supreme Court addressed the obscenity issue in 1957 in two linked cases: *United States v. Roth* and *Alberts v. California*. In these cases, the Court significantly extended First Amendment protection of the printed word, adopting a flexible, socially based definition: a work was legally obscene if "to the average person, applying contemporary community standards, the dominant theme of the material taken as a whole appeals to prurient interests."[47] The *Roth/Alberts* decisions became the cornerstone of post–World War II obscenity law in the United States, capping the long process by which the censorship powers of the state were increasingly circumscribed.

The history of print censorship, however, is not simply a triumphalist narrative of inexorable progress toward ever greater freedom. Repressive impulses wax and wane, reflecting larger political and cultural dynamics. Nor was the decline of censorship from 1900 through the 1950s solely a triumph of First Amendment libertarians over benighted pecksniffs. The cultural processes of censorship battles were, and are, highly complex. For example, the decline in censorship pressures on books and periodicals coincided with the emergence of radio, the movies, phonograph recordings, and, beyond our period, television. The advent of these new communications technologies not only raised new censorship issues but also invites speculation that the censors' interest in print culture may have diminished in part because print was coming to seem less influential in an age of burgeoning electronic media.

Still larger cultural processes that unfolded in these years affected attitudes toward censorship as well. The twentieth century saw the emergence of a consumer-based, advertiser-driven mass culture that placed a high premium on pleasure and titillation. This culture partially supplanted earlier principles of restraint, spiritual aspiration, social uplift, and elite moral oversight of society. The implications of this shift are obvious: the once culturally integrated system for monitoring and controlling print culture gradually came to be viewed as an anachronistic impediment to the operations of a mass culture based not on repression and moral idealism but on consumption and material gratification.

Whatever the reasons, the overall trajectory of American print censorship between 1880 and 1940 is clear. In 1880 print culture was rigidly circumscribed by a strict moral code enforced by a dominant cultural elite, by public opinion, and ultimately by the threat of prosecution. The boundaries of acceptability steadily expanded. By the 1940s Anthony Comstock seemed a quaint and remote figure, and the phrase "Banned in Boston" evoked only nostalgia for a distant era. Nevertheless, understanding the history of print culture in modern America requires a firm grasp of the half-century process that pulverized a once-powerful genteel code and vastly extended First Amendment protection of the printed word.

CHAPTER 15

Distinctive Media

The European Ethnic Press in the United States

Sally M. Miller

. . .

Between 1880 and 1920, millions of immigrants from Europe joined the American population and faced special challenges regarding print culture. As the volume of immigration grew, more immigrants came from southern and eastern Europe (13 percent of all immigrants in 1882, 81 percent in 1907) than from northern and western Europe.[1] On the whole these newcomers were poorer, less educated, and more culturally different from the natives than the predominantly British, Scandinavian, and German immigrants of the pre–Civil War era.

Forming new diasporas, they sought to develop their own print media to communicate with each other, to keep in touch with their homelands, to interpret American institutions and politics in the language of their group, and to begin the task of adapting their identities to their new situation. Several earlier immigrant groups in the United States had developed an ethnic press, including the Germans in the British colonial period. Now, in this period when immigration increased rapidly and the number of substantial immigrant groups in the United States proliferated, many new groups had sufficient numbers and a leadership with skills and capital to establish presses.[2]

Sociologist Robert Park's classic 1922 study, *The Immigrant Press and Its Control*, emphasized that these newspapers were commercial, that is, they provided a livelihood for their staff, they carried advertising, and they competed for subscribers. Of course, they were also cultural institutions, providing information, opinions, and advice about the homeland and the United States.[3] As many scholars of the ethnic press have observed, these presses served simultaneously to assimilate their readers into American life and to sustain the group's heritage, language, and customs, and these contrasting functions intertwined in interesting ways. Finally, these papers reflected and articulated internal divisions over politics or religion within groups, helping to shape their readers' sense of group identity and the issues surrounding it.[4]

These presses evolved over time, both in the individual histories of single publishing ventures and in their collective history as the publishing activities of a given ethnic group. Marion Marzolf formulated a stage model for this evolution. In the first phase, small groups struggled to provide institutions like newspapers, and sometimes traditional allies had to cooperate—Danes and Norwegians, for example, or Russians and Serbs. In the "pioneer" stage, groups attempted to establish their own presses, despite experiencing instability. Next, for those that survived there might be a period of stability when the group and its press flourished. Finally, for many ethnic presses, there followed a period of decline, as their groups dispersed, leaving behind many of the institutions significant in the pioneer stage. Nonetheless, argued Marzolf, some presses adapted and survived "as long as there [was] a shred of ethnic distinctiveness to enjoy."[5]

The newspapers of diverse groups were remarkably similar in the types of coverage they offered.[6] By featuring news of special interest to their groups, the ethnic papers made themselves attractive supplements to the mainstream papers, even for those among their subscribers who could read English. Lists of those recently arriving from or returning to the homeland attracted readers, as did ethnic interpretations of mainstream news. Lacking capital and reporters, ethnic papers freely copied news from each other and from metropolitan papers. Letters to the editor were often heated and divisive, especially in the early years of a group's history in the United States. The ethnic papers also included a substantial amount of fiction, both excerpts drawn from their national literatures and from world literature, and reader-authored poems and stories. Much space was devoted to the group's social calendar, which publicized and chronicled community events. Advertisements for neighborhood businesses appeared in most newspapers, as well as classified listings, sometimes used by readers attempting to find long-lost relatives and friends, among other functions. Indeed, in several regards, these papers could be considered neighborhood papers, even when their circulation was regional or national. Whereas metropolitan dailies attempted to provide all the current news, ethnic papers reported only the stories most relevant to their ethnic groups.[7] The interactive nature of these papers, whether through letters to the editor, personalized classifieds, or readers' contributions of fiction and poetry, linked readers and editors. The most famous of many such features was the "Bintel Brief," an advice column compiled by Abraham Cahan, in the *Forverts*.[8] As community papers, the ethnic press also served as a booster, covering group activities, spotlighting individuals' achievements, and publicizing the political and economic advances of the group as a whole.[9]

Many ethnic papers operated within a tightly focused frame of reference that determined what news to include and what editorial stands to take. Michael P. Mulcrone demonstrated this phenomenon in the case of the Irish press, which was pervasively Anglophobic, concerned, for example, with any heightened influence of Anglo-Saxon institutions in the United States.[10] An urgent nationalism pervaded the papers published by Polish and other eastern European immigrants whose homelands lacked independence. Groups subjugated to the Ottoman Empire before World War I, as seen in Syrian Arabic-language newspapers in the United States, had similarly nationalistic views. As Jonathan Sarna indicates in chapter 19, the Jewish press in America, whether publishing in German, Yiddish, Judeo-Spanish (Ladino), or English, was fundamentally concerned with defending the well-being of Jews throughout the world. Although these papers also had some Americanizing functions as well, they were more essentially community newspapers, in the geographically expansive sense of the word "community."

The Scope of the Ethnic Press

How many ethnic newspapers were published during our period is not known with any precision, but historians agree that the number of foreign-language newspapers reached nearly 800 by 1884.[11] Because American newspaper directories tended to include only mainstream papers, such records are not useful for determining the scope of foreign-language or other marginal presses, including the African American, Native American, or counterculture newspapers. By 1900 the number of foreign-language newspapers is estimated to have exceeded 1,100, and by 1917 it passed 1,300, the likely peak of such newspaper publication. In 1924 the United States placed severe restrictions on immigration, and by 1930 the number of ethnic or foreign-language newspapers declined to about 1,000.[12]

Although the early ethnic papers worked at the margins, facing high failure rates, some attained impressive longevity, especially when supported by other immigrant institutions such as mutual aid societies, unions, or political parties. Indeed, some lasted for a century or more, for example, *Den Danske Pioneer* (Danish Pioneer), the New York *Staats-Zeitung* (Public News), *Il Progresso Italo-American* (Italian American Progress), and *Forverts* (Jewish Daily Forward). Those that survived evolved as their readers changed, eschewing their educational role in assimilation, celebrating ethnic traditions, and publishing wholly or partly in English. The general trend after 1920, however, was the decline of the ethnic press as a whole.

The impact of the ethnic press cannot be estimated from circulation figures. We know from qualitative sources that papers were shared and often read aloud to individuals or groups. Literacy levels varied by nationality, religious traditions, and gender, but immigrants arriving after 1880 were less likely to be literate in their own language than earlier immigrants because of the limited educational opportunities in their homelands. Even for those with low literacy skills, though, the ethnic press served a function. The ethnic papers circulated in their neighborhoods and provided information and viewpoints that were then transmitted orally, informing them of news, cultural activities, developments in the home country, and other useful information. The ethnic press, then, was an institution through which immigrants organized their lives and structured their communities.

The ethnic press even served to stabilize and standardize a group's language. Some immigrants were from ethnic regions only beginning to form a single nation, and they spoke diverse dialects. The ethnic press provided the first generation of immigrants with a stable, common version of the language. At the same time, many challenges had to be overcome. For example, insufficient type plagued operations for several groups, as diverse as Norwegians, Jews, and Arabs. The Arabic-language newspaper *Al-Huda* had to be set by hand until 1910, when an Arabic language Linotype was secured through the intervention of the U.S. ambassador in Istanbul. For papers using Cyrillic characters or requiring various diacritical marks, the lack of characters required improvisation. For example, the first Slovene-language newspapers, *Amerikanski Slovenec* (American Slovene, New York, 1891) and *Glas Naroda* (People's Voice, Chicago, 1892) were printed in Czech plants that already had type with diacritical marks.[13]

Some technological and transportation advances were of particular importance to the ethnic press. Late nineteenth-century developments in telegraphy and oceangoing travel enabled international news to travel faster, while the transcontinental railroads aided in the distribution and delivery of newspapers, a boon to ethnic presses trying to reach a selective audience that might be geographically dispersed. Also, as for the larger mainstream newspapers, high-speed presses, cheaper newsprint, typesetting machinery, and news-gathering services increased profitability and made publishing somewhat more economically viable for hard-pressed ethnic presses.[14] Case studies of the press in several groups highlight similarities and differences among them.[15]

The German Press

The German press was the largest of the ethnic presses. More Germans immigrated to the United States than any other nationality — 6 million by the middle of the twentieth century — and they published an estimated 5,000 periodicals of various types during their long history on this continent. Their newspapers, appearing in every location with a sizable German population, expressed anything

FIGURE 15.1. Founded in 1812, the German-language *Allentown Friedens-Bote* survived until 1916. Shown is the New Year's issue with verse greetings, 4 January 1888. American Antiquarian Society.

but a monolithic perspective. German-speakers represented different regions, religious persuasions, classes, and dialects (figure 15.1).[16]

Typically Republican in its allegiance, the German press opposed and belittled the growing temperance movement and its successor, the prohibition movement, for contradicting the freedoms promised by the Bill of Rights. German newspapers also shared a virtual consensus in condemning the burgeoning women's rights movement and the suffrage movement that emerged from it. However, the confidence of the German community, as reflected in these publications, was upset in 1890 when Wisconsin and then Illinois prohibited the use of non-English languages in public schools, which had become a common practice in many communities.[17] Defending this practice led to perhaps the greatest unity of the German press in this period.

The German-language labor press expanded dramatically at the end of the nineteenth century. As an organized labor movement developed in the United States, many German Americans became union officers, organizers, and rank-

and-file members. German-speaking unions were commonplace. Accordingly, German-language labor newspapers were prominent in all metropolitan areas from New York to San Francisco. Among them, Marxist sheets were not unusual. Some labor newspapers spawned printing companies, issuing newspapers, election campaign broadsides, and union circulars, an example of which is the Milwaukee firm that published the *Wisconsin Vorwaerts* (Forward) and the *Milwaukee Leader*. Other German newspaper firms published German-language Sunday School readers, hymnals, and devotional materials.

More than 120 German-language labor newspapers were published between 1870 and 1900. By the 1890s the growth of the German-language press had reached its zenith.[18] The New York *Staats-Zeitung* enjoyed a circulation of 90,000, the largest among German-language newspapers anywhere in the world. In 1892–93 the number of general circulation, German-language periodicals peaked at about 800 (a figure that includes magazines), and as late as 1910 German presses still produced seventy daily newspapers. In the short run, the German press appeared stable. Its newspapers, like American papers in general, were by the twentieth century seldom merely expressions of personal or partisan journalism, and many enjoyed commercial or institutional ties. They had become less vitriolic in editorial tone and in their competition with one another. Community activities became central fare, including cultural and literary supplements. Their celebration of the group life of Germans in the United States became a central focus.[19] The stability of these institutions would, however, be utterly destroyed in the second decade of the twentieth century. Immigration had slowed after the unification of the German empire, and increasingly the German American community was native-born. American intervention in World War I, opposed by virtually all German Americans, effectively obliterated their ethnic press, due to anti-German sentiment and specific government actions designed to suppress the foreign-language press.

The Norwegian Press

The Norwegian press in the United States was considerably smaller than its German counterpart, but the clustered settlement pattern of the 800,000 Norwegians in the upper Midwest allowed them to develop fully functioning immigrant communities. The Norwegians of Illinois, Wisconsin, Minnesota, Iowa, and the Dakotas had begun to immigrate to this country, most choosing rural locations, in the 1840s and 1850s. Their first newspaper, the weekly *Nordlyset* (Northern Light), was established in 1847 in rural Wisconsin, lasting almost four years. By the 1860s, a few papers, most especially the Chicago-based *Skandinaven*, had regional readership and national influence, circulating via the mails. Language similarities allowed Danes and Swedes to read Norwegian papers as well. The most vibrant era of Norwegian newspaper publishing occurred in the three decades from the mid-1870s to 1905. High literacy among Norwegians made possible a dynamic newspaper world with very active letters-to-the-editor sections.

The Norwegian press was as quick as the German to immerse itself in American political and social issues. While offering its readers basic civics lessons, even printing Norwegian translations of the federal and state constitutions, it introduced subscribers to American public concerns, frequently criticizing capitalism and the conditions it spawned. Simultaneously it reinforced Norwegians' linguistic and cultural bonds.[20] In the late nineteenth century, the Norwegian American press was often Republican in alignment but some papers sympathized with third-party movements such as the Populist Party, the Progressive Party, and the Nonpartisan League. Typically they supported the temperance movement, given its popularity within the Norwegian American community, and applauded the leadership of Norwegian American congressional representative Andrew Volstead and other countrymen in the Prohibition Party. The newspapers debated women's rights and the suffrage movement, mirroring English-language press efforts to introduce features addressed to women readers, even issuing some women's monthlies (one of which attained a circulation of 75,000). Possible American involvement in World War I greatly concerned the Norwegian press as it did others; some papers favored the noninterventionist policies of Senator Robert La Follette. While these newspapers eventually supported the American war effort, they were placed on the defensive when public opinion turned against foreign-language use as a whole.[21]

German and Norwegian newspapers in the United States offer comparable pictures within their respective linguistic and cultural worlds. Promoting their heritages, they discussed American economic and social developments and took positions on selected electoral issues with as much interest as the English-language press. Indeed, the German and Norwegian papers for many decades demonstrated no hesitancy in expressing their opinions. While the German press was more internally divided by religion, ideology, and class than its Norwegian counterpart, it was usually cohesive on major policy issues.

The following survey of other ethnic presses highlights further similarities and differences. Decades after the arrival of groups from northern and western Europe, immigrants from eastern Europe began to settle in the United States. They left behind political upheaval and socioeconomic changes. Polyglot empires of the area were often highly volatile, breeding nationalism and riveting the attention of the immigrants residing in this country on events in their home societies. Indeed, a generation after the German American press had turned much of its attention away from the fatherland, Old World events were the central concern of eastern Europeans and their newspapers in the United States. Indeed, these presses gave little space to American events.

The Polish Press

The large influx of Polish immigrants to the United States began in the 1870s, and by 1924 2 million Poles and their children resided in this country. They had settled mainly in metropolitan areas like Chicago, Milwaukee, Detroit, Buffalo, Pittsburgh, and Cleveland, as well as in mining towns. Their exposure to education prior to immigration typically was less than that of Germans or Norwegians, but they had the same need for information. Thus, not surprisingly, the 1870s and especially the 1880s witnessed a significant development of a Polish press. With the publication of the Milwaukee-based *Kuryer Polski* (Polish Courier) in 1888, the Poles had their first daily newspaper, and within two years, a second, *Dziennik Chicagoski* (Chicago Daily News). Polish-language newspapers were frequently the offshoots of clerical or fraternal associations. Over the next four decades, Poles produced at least nineteen dailies and sixty-seven weeklies, exclusive of special interest publications.

Like the community it served, the Polish press was deeply divided between religious and secular, nationalist and socialist. These conflicts shaped Polish America. From the church perspective, Catholicism was the foundation of the Polish community in the United States. The secularists maintained that the keystone of Polish community life should be a group heritage that was not religiously defined. Clerics favored an independent Poland with Catholicism as its state religion, while their opponents were avid nationalists who did not believe that an autonomous Poland should be a Catholic state. The starkness of the divisions between the two sides can be glimpsed through the fact that when the Milwaukee newspaper, the nationalist *Kuryer Polski*, instigated a campaign to divest control of education from the clergy, the Wisconsin church hierarchy banned the newspaper. Amid such debates, neither camp gave much attention to concerns such as the emergence of corporate capitalism or American overseas acquisitions. The secular press became consumed with the possibility of an independent Poland, using this goal to shape its editorial pages and news content. One student of the Polish press has argued that it was not until the 1930s that this press developed interest in American matters.[22]

World War I marked a great watershed for all aspects of Polish life. Initially, the press disagreed as to which side's victory would strengthen the possibility of an independent Poland. Once the United States intervened, however, Polish Americans and their newspapers avidly supported the allied war effort. The

Paris Peace Conference followed the war, redrawing the map of central and eastern Europe. The Polish American press covered the conference in minute detail, making recommendations to President Woodrow Wilson and the other negotiators. Following the establishment of the Polish republic, the press maintained a running commentary on Polish politics, but increased its attention to issues of Polish life in the United States.[23]

The Slovak Press

Other eastern European immigrants, though fewer in number, reflected and even magnified the early Polish pattern in their own newspapers. Their concern for issues confronting their countries-of-origin and lack of involvement in American matters exceed that of the Polish American press. Moreover, many of these immigrants did not intend to remain in the United States, and their sense of impermanence precluded the development of an early interest in American affairs. The Slovaks, for example, arrived in the United States in small numbers at the end of the nineteenth century. A half million Slovaks eventually scattered across the eastern states, struggling to maintain their Old World identity. Their press, which dates from 1889, grappled with the issues of Slovak nationalism and independence, their relationship to the Czechs — with whom circumstances often tied them together — and their limited loyalty to the king of Hungary, the Hapsburg emperor, Franz Joseph. Reflecting these various connections and allegiances, their first paper, *Amerikanszko-Szlovenszke Noviny* (American-Slovak News), was printed in a Slovak dialect in Magyar orthography, and its editor favored Slovakia remaining within the Dual Monarchy. The next editor changed both print and editorial policy, printing the paper in a different Slovak dialect and endorsing Slovak autonomy. As Slovak papers proliferated, the substantial church-sponsored component of the press favored continued ties to Hungary. The most successful Slovak newspaper, *Slovák v Amerike* (Slovak in America), published from 1889 to the present, promoted the goal of an independent Slovakia. Slovaks, fragmented not only by politics but also by religion — Roman Catholic, Lutheran, Calvinist, and Greek Orthodox — remained seriously divided after World War I, far more than Polish Americans. When the Paris Peace Conference established Czechoslovakia, Slovak nationalists continued their drive for a state of their own. Under the circumstances, the Slovak press in the United States demonstrated very little interest in American politics, focusing instead on unresolved nationalistic questions.[24]

The Greek Press

Another group further reinforces this picture of the eastern European presses. The Greek press in the United States, dating from 1892, was also caught up in the politics of the homeland and paid relatively little attention to American life. Its readers, fewer than half a million sprinkled thinly across the United States, were divided heatedly between monarchist-conservatives and republican-liberals. The newspapers informed their readers about Greek political and military news, including wars with Turkey and expansionist activities in the Balkans. Some editors hoped that a revived Byzantine Empire would successfully replace the Ottoman Empire, but by the mid-1930s — with the permanent reestablishment of the Greek monarchy and the resulting stability and moderation of Greek politics — the Greek American community and its newspapers became less concerned with Greek politics. By 1936 the two major Greek dailies in the United States focused more on American politics. *Ethnikos Keryx* (National Herald) and the *Atlantis*, both in New York, split over support for Franklin Delano Roosevelt and the New Deal.[25] Unsettled homelands — where politics are volatile, intrigues loom large, and issues enflame nationalistic fervor — simply cannot spawn a diaspora unaffected by those passions. Only people whose homeland has attained some stability and internal peace can thoroughly immerse themselves in their new societies, or so these findings suggest.

World War I and the Immigrant Press

Of all the events that affected American ethnic groups, World War I had the greatest impact. After 1915, Germans and immigrants of virtually all national backgrounds found themselves the object of suspicion and were pressured to Americanize to prove their loyalty to the United States. Even Scandinavian Americans whose homelands were uninvolved in the war faced legislation that impinged upon their use of native languages. Irish Americans had to fend off government probes because of their hostility to the English. Croatians and others with traditional ties to the Central Powers also suffered.

Vulnerable to the waves of wartime hysteria, Congress and the federal government adopted policies suppressing speech critical of the war against Germany by enacting restrictions on foreign-language publications. Those that accepted money to publish antiwar advertisements on the eve of America's entry into the Great War were specifically singled out for criticism by the Congress. Under the Trading with the Enemy Act of 1917, publishers of foreign-language articles about the war were required to file English translations of articles about international events or government policies with local postmasters before pub-

FIGURE 15.2. Newspapers published in a language other than English became suspect after the United States entry into World War I in 1917, when Congress responded with legislation requiring translations and official review of political content. This issue of *Svoboda*, published in Jersey City, New Jersey, 17 February 1918, was described in English on its masthead as the "Official organ of Ukrainian National Association," but Cyrillic fonts were used to present news and opinion. American Antiquarian Society.

lication. This self-censorship of the press proved too costly for foreign-language newspapers—many of them were forced to close down, while others failed by losing readers fearful of being perceived as less than "100 percent American." Still others lost their mailing privileges because they were viewed as critics of U.S. government policy. Some editors were charged with disloyalty under the Espionage, Sedition, or the Trading with the Enemy acts or were even interned as enemy aliens.

The use of a language other than English had begun to concern the American public, as well as local and state governments, even before the war (figure 15.2). During the war, state-level Councils of Defense—whose stipulations lacked the force of law but were widely adopted—intensified earlier campaigns for English-only instruction in public schools. Language limitations continued after the war until a Supreme Court decision in 1923 ended such restrictions.[26] The German American experience was, of course, the most dramatic. The group became the scapegoat for the country's first major involvement in an overseas war. Its press, except for its socialist newspapers, gave nearly unilateral support for the German war effort when the war began in August 1914. As the United States began to move away from its official neutrality policy, and especially when President Wilson initiated a so-called preparedness campaign in 1916, many German American newspapers began to censor their own views. With the declaration of war against Germany in April 1917, these papers avowed their loyalty to the United States but nonetheless were hampered by the various wartime laws. Many lost subscribers and advertisers, and some ceased publication. The German American press experienced a debacle from which it never recovered. During and after the war, the press as a whole shrank in readership, and many newspapers merged or simply went out of business. Its numbers in 1920 were fewer than half of what they had been in 1910.[27]

The Decline of the Ethnic Press in the United States

The particular circumstances of the German press's demise notwithstanding, decline soon overtook the ethnic press in general. A chastened foreign-language press remained dynamic in the first postwar decade, but strong assimilationist pressures continued. Public suspicion of foreign-language users, combined with the drastic restriction of immigration in the early 1920s, diminished the pool of potential readers. Meanwhile, literacy in Old World languages and interest in the ethnic press lessened with second and third immigrant generations, even when its papers were published in English. Although in 1940 more than 1,000 newspapers and periodicals in thirty-eight languages were still published in the United States, the interwar experience suggested to some the imminent extinction of the ethnic press.[28] Such predictions proved to be erroneous. Decades later, with the entrance of millions of immigrants as a result of World War II, the Cold War, and a wide reopening of the door on immigration in the 1960s, the foreign-language press expanded and experienced a renaissance, manifested more and more in Asian languages rather than in European ones.

The ethnic press in the United States was a vehicle by which groups gained access to the printed word. Newly arrived, marginal peoples in American society lacked access to the increasingly powerful and consolidating world of print culture. Simultaneously, they needed to raise their own voices as alternative perspectives to the dominant culture. Initially lacking influence on metropolitan dailies, immigrant groups of all backgrounds developed print cultures of their own and expressed their own viewpoints. Most had limited experience with print culture prior to their arrival in the United States, but in order to foster group identity, strengthen their cultural heritage, and communicate with each other and the larger society, a vibrant ethnic press arose and thrived. Inexpensive newspapers and magazines provided outlets for these groups at the same time that mainstream print culture became more standardized and encompassing.

Aided by the information presented by the ethnic press and its perceptions of group interests, people increasingly participated in American electoral activities, deciding between the two major parties and supporting or rejecting a changing line-up of third parties. Although many ethnic presses opposed legislation that might negatively affect their group or conflict with their traditions, most took positions on major American issues, if sometimes circumspectly, and scrutinized American foreign policy and its possible impact on ancestral homelands. Thus, the ethnic press was an important agency through which groups attempted to shape their own futures.

CHAPTER 16

Exiles, Immigrants, and Natives
Hispanic Print Culture in What Became the Mainland of the United States

Nicolás Kanellos

. . .

Histories of the United States rarely describe Hispanic people's initial introduction of Western culture to lands that would eventually become the United States. Yet the integration of the Hispanic contribution into the history of the United States is long overdue. Its absence or minimization is even more regrettable because many allegedly Anglo-American institutions and values were first introduced and used by Hispanic people — Spaniards, Hispanicized Africans and Amerindians, mestizos, and mulattoes. For better or worse, Spain was the first country to disseminate Western culture in the New World.[1]

With his Florida travel diaries of 1513 Juan Ponce de León first introduced written European language into the area that would become the mainland United States. Ponce de León's exploration marked the beginning of keeping civil, military, and ecclesiastical records that became commonplace in Hispanic America. Written culture not only facilitated record keeping, correspondence, and the development of commerce but also fostered the first written studies of the flora and fauna of these uncharted lands. Print made possible the writing of laws for governance and commercial exploitation as well as the maintenance of official written history of Hispanic culture in these lands.

Numerous other explorers, missionaries, and colonists followed, including Alvar Núñez Cabeza de Vaca, the first anthropologist and ethnographer of the New World. He documented his eight years of observations and experiences among the Indians in his book, *La Relación* (The Account), published in Spain in 1542, the first book of "American" literature written in a European language.[2] Other chroniclers, memoirists, playwrights, and poets subsequently came to Florida and the area that would become the southwestern United States.

Books were imported soon thereafter, first authorized for Mexico in 1525. Juan Pablos (Giovanni Paoli) introduced the printing press in Mexico City in 1539, and began publishing newspapers there in 1541. By the end of the sixteenth century, nine presses were functioning in the capital of New Spain. Literate culture spread northward through New Spain and into lands that the United States would capture through conquest, annexation, and purchase by the mid-nineteenth century.

Many institutions of literacy—including schools, universities, libraries, archives, and courts—were first introduced to North America by Hispanics. During the colonial period, Spain founded twenty-six universities in the Americas, in addition to numerous theological seminaries. During the seventeenth century, the University of Mexico achieved great distinction in the Americas, for its contributions in canon law, theology, medicine, and the Aztec and Otomí languages.[3]

The first schools in what would become the continental United States were established by 1600 in Spanish Catholic missions in present-day Florida and Georgia. As Spanish and Hispanicized people settled in the Southwest, mission schools were also introduced there. Elementary schools in missions and convents taught Spanish children reading, writing, arithmetic, and religion. Later, the mission schools also taught children of Indians and mestizos. The mission education system was central to the very creation of the mestizo population of the Americas. Attempts to convert and acculturate Amerindians relied upon the introduction of literate culture. While mission schools existed throughout the Spanish colonies, public education was not consistently promoted until the nineteenth century.[4]

Initially, then, Hispanic print culture was introduced in North America to facilitate Spain's colonial administration. Later, writing and publication facilitated the colonial subjects' separation from Spain, allowing Hispanic native culture to develop its own distinctive history. During the Mexican period of government, the missions were secularized, and the responsibility for education shifted into the hands of a liberal government struggling to establish a democracy.[5] Among the liberal initiatives in 1834 and following years was the authorization of printing presses into the frontier areas of California and New Mexico. The first New Mexican press was operated by Father Antonio José Martínez, who printed catechisms, law books, and textbooks as well as New Mexico's first newspaper, *El Crepúsculo* (Dawn), beginning in 1835. The printing press had already made its way into Texas in 1813 as part of the movement for Mexico's independence from Spain. Thus, considerable efforts to establish a literate Hispanic population had been implemented before northern Mexico was incorporated as "territories" of the United States.

Hispanics settling in the thirteen British colonies also had access to Spanish print matter. In the mid-seventeenth century, Sephardic Jews established the first Spanish-speaking communities in the Northeast of what would become the United States. They were followed by other Hispanics from Spain, New Spain, and the Caribbean who, by the 1790s, were printing and publishing books in the Spanish language, mainly in New York City and Philadelphia, but also in Spanish Louisiana. By the 1800s numerous publishing houses issued not only political and commercial books but also original creative literature written principally by Cuban and Spanish immigrants and political refugees. Among the first books written and published by Hispanics in the United States, beginning with Giral de Pino's *New Spanish Grammar* in 1795, were textbooks, Spanish readers, and anthologies, reflective of two cultures coming more and more in contact with each other in the early republic. This educational publishing activity soon blossomed into an industry that issued grammars, Spanish-English dictionaries, and textbooks that would support Spanish language and literature.

Beyond religious and educational publications, Hispanic literate culture in the United States had roots in trade and politics. The first Spanish-language newspapers published in the United States were *El Misisipi* (1808) in New Orleans and *La Gaceta de Texas* (Texas Gazette) (1813) in Nacogdoches, Texas. Others followed in Florida, Philadelphia, New York, and elsewhere. Despite the existence of Spanish-language book publishing during the nineteenth century, the newspaper was the principal publishing enterprise in Hispanic communities in the United States and northern Mexico. Hundreds of newspapers carried news of commerce and politics as well as poetry, serialized novels, stories, essays, and opinion from both the pens of local writers and the reprinted works of the most highly regarded Hispanic writers and intellectuals.

When northern Mexico and Louisiana were incorporated into the United States, this journalistic and intellectual discourse intensified. The newspapers attempted to preserve the Spanish language and Hispanic culture in territories and states where Hispanic residents were becoming rapidly outnumbered by Anglo and European migrants. The newspapers became the libraries of the small towns in New Mexico, the *defensores* (defenders) of Hispanic rights in the large cities, and often the only Spanish-language text for those learning to read and write Spanish in rural areas. Many of the more successful newspapers grew into publishing houses by the beginning of the twentieth century.

Hispanic newspapers in the United States, unlike those in Mexico City, Madrid, or Havana, had the additional function of protecting and preserving the Catholic religion within a cultural environment dominated by Protestantism. Quite often, too, Hispanic-owned newspapers offered alternative views, challenging those published in the English-language press, especially as concerned their own communities and homelands. By the beginning of the nineteenth century, Hispanic print culture had diversified, developing three viewpoints that have characterized U.S. Hispanic culture to the present: those of the exile, the immigrant, and the native. In considering each of these separately, we see both how they sometimes blended and sometimes competed and why one of these functions, that of the native voice, distinguished the Hispanic press from the typical print culture of European immigrant groups discussed by Sally Miller in the preceding chapter.

Hispanic Print Culture in Exile

Hispanic exiles first began book and periodical publication in New Orleans, Philadelphia, and New York. They established the model of the Hispanic exile community producing publications to be shipped or smuggled back into their homelands or distributed among other expatriate communities in the United States and abroad. The raison d'être of the exile press was to influence life and politics in the homeland—providing information and opinion about the homeland, changing or solidifying opinion about politics in the *patria*, assisting in raising funds to overthrow the current regime, and providing the ideological base for that overthrow. Over time, as their communities became more permanent in the United States and the return to the homeland was no longer feasible or of interest, the Hispanic exile press faded or blended into either the Hispanic immigrant press or the Hispanic native press.

The Hispanic exile press in the United States chronicled some of the great moments in the political history of the Hispanic world, including the independence movements of the Spanish American colonies, the Mexican Revolution, the Cuban Revolution, and numerous other struggles to establish democracy in Spanish America. Hundreds of thousands of political refugees fled to the United States as a result of these struggles, seeking democracy and freedom of expression, and joining the large communities of Spanish-speakers that had developed there through immigration and territorial expansion. Thus, the refugees found familiar societies where they could conduct business and eke out a livelihood while abetting change in the lands to which they hoped to return.

The first political books printed by the exile press were written by Spanish citizens protesting Napoleon's installation of a puppet government in Spain. The earliest of these were printed by American printers, such as John Mowry and Mathew Carey. By 1822, however, Hispanics began operating their own presses and publishing houses. One of the first was Vicente Rocafuerte in Philadelphia; by 1823 New York too had Hispanic presses. The books printed in Philadelphia were designed to export American liberalism to Spanish America during the second decade of the nineteenth century. These included translations of the U.S. Constitution, works by Thomas Jefferson and John Quincy Adams, biographies of the Founding Fathers, and speeches by Daniel Webster, Edward Everett, and other political thinkers. Also printed were attacks on

Spanish despotism, including publications by Bartolomé de las Casas detailing Spanish atrocities visited on the Amerindians during the periods of conquest and colonization.[6]

The longest lasting independence movement in the Hemisphere was that of Spain's Caribbean colonies, Cuba and Puerto Rico. Much of their independence struggle was plotted, funded, and written about from U.S. shores. One of Cuba's first and most illustrious exiles was the philosopher-priest Félix Varela, who founded *El Habanero* (Havanian) newspaper in Philadelphia in 1824 and moved it to New York in 1825. *El Habanero* openly militated for Cuban independence from Spain, setting a precedent for Cubans and Puerto Ricans who published in exile and circulated their works in their home islands.[7]

For the most part, the expatriate journalists and writers founded and wrote for Spanish-language periodicals. Some worked for bilingual newspapers, hoping to influence Anglo-American public opinion and U.S. government policy regarding Cuba and Puerto Rico. Very few of the exiles found work in the English-language press, except as translators. One notable exception was Miguel Teurbe Tolón, a pioneer of Hispanic journalism who in the 1850s worked as an editor for Latin America on the *New York Herald*. Teurbe Tolón also helped to promote the broader literary activities of Hispanics in exile. His pioneering 1856 anthology, *El laúd del desterrado* (Exile's Lute), is believed to be the first anthology of exile literature published in the United States.[8]

Many important Cuban and Puerto Rican intellectuals published books and wrote for newspapers between the 1830s and the outbreak of the Spanish-American War in 1898. Néstor Ponce de León, the Havana editor and literary figure who was forced into exile in 1869, promptly founded a press in New York. He also coauthored in English, with José Ignacio Rodríguez, *The Book of Blood*, which aimed to influence the U.S. government to intervene against Spain by detailing the barbaric treatment of Cubans by the Spanish. By the mid-1870s, Ponce's press was publishing a wide variety of books in Spanish, not just political tracts but technical dictionaries, histories of Cuba, biographies, medical and legal books, novels, and books of poetry, including those by the most celebrated Cuban poet of the time, the exiled José María Heredia. Ponce also printed some of the leading Spanish-language periodicals in New York, was proprietor of the most important Hispanic bookstore in the Northeast, and in 1887, along with José Martí and Colombian immigrant Santiago Pérez Triana, founded the influential literary club, Sociedad Literaria Hispano-Americana de Nueva York.[9]

Puerto Rican intellectuals joined the expatriate Cubans in establishing revolutionary clubs and supporting publications. In addition to writers, two craftsmen were essential to the cause of Puerto Rican revolutionary journalism: typesetters Francisco Gonzalo "Pachín" Marín and Sotero Figueroa. Marín brought his influential newspaper *El Postillón* (Postilion) from Puerto Rico, where it had been suppressed by the Spanish authorities, to New York in 1889. In his New York printshop Marín published his paper, as well as books and broadsides for the Cuban and Puerto Rican expatriate communities. His shop became a meeting place for intellectuals, literary figures, and political leaders. A poet in his own right, Marín published two foundational volumes of his own verse: *Romances* and *En la arena* (In the Sand).

Thanks to these printer-publishers and many others, hundreds of books and pamphlets were issued in New York and distributed to expatriate communities throughout the United States and in various Spanish-American republics, as well as in Cuba and Puerto Rico. Within the four years preceding the Spanish-American War, eighty titles on Cuba alone poured forth from the exile press, located mainly in New York, but also in Tampa, Key West, Philadelphia, and abroad.[10] According to Fornet, some of these titles were issued in printings of 5,000 and 10,000 copies. When considered together with the countless periodicals produced by expatriates, this outpouring demonstrates not only the passion and intensity of the discourse but also the centrality of the printed word in these communities.

Meanwhile, the virtually open southern border of the United States allowed Mexican expatriates to establish their press with relative ease. They simply crossed the border and joined the long-standing Mexican-origin communities of the Southwest. The Mexican exile press movement began around 1885, when the Porfirio Díaz regime in Mexico became so repressive that scores of publishers and editors were forced north into exile. Publishers like Adolfo Carrillo, who had opposed Díaz, crossed the border, hoping to smuggle their papers back into Mexico. Carrillo ended up in San Francisco, where he established *La Republica* (Republic) in 1885. Other exile papers followed: *El Mundo* (World, Brownsville) in 1885, *El Monitor Democrático* (Democratic Monitor, San Antonio), and *La Voz de Juárez* (Voice of Juárez, Laredo) in 1889.[11]

By 1900 the most important Mexican revolutionary journalist and ideologue, Ricardo Flores Magón (1873–1922), had launched his newspaper *Regeneración* in Mexico City and was promptly jailed. After four more stints behind bars, Flores Magón went into exile in the United States. In 1904 he began publishing *Regeneración* in San Antonio,[12] moving the paper to St. Louis in 1905, to Canada in 1906, and to Los Angeles in 1908. Throughout these years, the Flores Magón brothers used every possible subterfuge to smuggle their newspapers back into Mexico, where they were distributed to sympathizers throughout the country (figure 16.1).[13]

Ricardo Flores Magón was a major leader in the movement to overthrow the Díaz regime, founding the Liberal Reformist Association in 1901. Moreover, he

FIGURE 16.1. Ricardo Flores Magón (1873–1922), a Socialist newspaper publisher, was a leader in the Mexican Revolution. He was frequently arrested for what he wrote by both the Mexican and U.S. governments, which wished to silence the presentation of views highly critical of them.

wedded his ideas about revolution in Mexico to the struggle of working people in the United States, strengthening his newspapers' popularity among Mexican American laborers engaged in unionizing efforts in the United States. Pursued by Díaz's agents in San Antonio, Ricardo and his brother Enrique fled to St. Louis but continued to correspond with organizations across the Southwest that spread their revolutionary ideology. Numerous Spanish-language periodicals in the Southwest thus echoed the ideas of Flores Magón. Among the most interesting of these newspapers were those that articulated labor and women's issues as social changes that should be implemented with the triumph of the revolution. These included Teresa Villarreal's *El Obrero* (Worker, 1909), Isidra T. de Cárdenas's *La Voz de la Mujer* (Woman's Voice, 1907 [figure 16.2]), and Blanca de Moncaleano's *Pluma Roja* (Red Pen, 1913–15).[14]

The Mexican exile press continued to flourish into the 1930s, with weekly newspapers and publishing houses taking sides in the revolution and issuing political tracts. Novels depicting the Mexican Revolution also flourished. In the 1920s and 1930s, however, the exile press was by no means as uniformly liberal as it had been prior to the outbreak of the revolution. On the contrary, a new exile press developed, founded largely by conservatives dislodged from Mexico by the socialist revolution. Many came with financial resources and business acumen. Some founded newspapers to serve the rapidly expanding numbers of economic refugees, and their newspapers eventually became the backbone of an immigrant rather than an exile press, as their entrepreneurial spirit overtook the earlier exiles' commitment to political change in the homeland.

The Cristero War (1926–29), resulting from government persecution of the Catholic Church, produced a new wave of political refugees. They founded newspapers and publishing houses to attack the Mexican government and to serve the needs of the religious community in exile. Prominent examples include Bishop Vera y Zuria's *¡Viva Cristo Rey en la hora de suprema angustia!* (Long Live Christ the King in the Hour of Supreme Anguish) in El Paso (1928) and *La Esperanza* (Hope, 1924) in Los Angeles. Because Cristero refugees also influenced many Mexican exile publications, the already conservative counterrevolutionary papers focused on religious persecution in Mexico and the atrocities committed by the socialist government. A spate of books appeared defending the church and decrying abuse of the clergy in Mexico. More importantly in the long run, a Hispanic religious publishing industry, issuing books and periodicals in both languages, emerged in El Paso, where it still functions today.

The next large wave of Hispanic political refugees came from across the Atlantic: the liberals defeated by Spanish fascism in the 1930s. The Spanish expatriates quickly established their own exile press in Depression-era Hispanic communities that were hotbeds for union and socialist organizing. From Manhattan

La Voz De La Mujer

● SEMANARIO LIBERAL DE COMBATE ●
Defensor de los Derechos del Pueblo y Enemigo de las Tiranías.

La mujer forma parte integrante de la gran familia humana; luego tiene el deber y el derecho de exigir y luchar por la Dignificación de su Patria

AÑO I.   EL PASO, TEXAS, SEPTIEMBRE 6 DE 1907.   NÚM. 9

LABOR DE FÍGAROS.

El flagelo de nuestra fusta ha sangrado los escamosos morrillos de la burguesía altanera. Nuestras rebeldías no han conocido valladar que contenga las justas iras emanadas contra el sistema atentatorio con que los impunes sueñan en reivindicar su historia de oprobio; por que, impotentes para combatir con razonamientos, son tenaces, también para reicidir, enfangados en el estercolero que les sirve de lecho.

Á nuestra mesa de redacción nos llegan distintas quejas de los atentados que cometen en la ín aula de los contrabandos los bandidos caciques investidos de autoridad.

El primer fustazo que nuestro semanario asestó al contrabandista en funciones de Jefe Poíl tico, Silvano Montemayor, lo hizo convertirse en réptil, se enroscó, y dió un chillido; le robó a nuestro papelero unos ejemplares y lo amagó con hos pedarlo en el *hotel de su propiedad*, si volvía a vender "La Voz de la Mujer." Nuestra protesta cargó sobre el cacique vulgar, castigando su insolencia como lo merecía.

Un Castrado ascendido y cornamentado ha tomado a su eh cargo molestar a los abonados y repartidores de nuestro periódico, amagándolos con cárcel ¿Con qué derecho lo hace este Musa?

¡Tales son los méritos de los bandidos de uniforme!

Hoy nos visita una nueva querella: Un paquidermo que *ruge* de cobrador en el mercado de C. Juárez, y de eunuco de antesala, se opone a viva fuerza á que circule "La Voz de la Mujer," en la cafrería donde cree tener, en simil el derecho de usufructo.

Éste estulto cuadrúpedo no está conforme con andar en cuatro remos, sino que, persiste en escarbar con la trompa.

La impudicia de tales moluscos los congestiona, padecen sonambulismo y sueñan en el exterminio de la prensa independiente. ¡Falsa creencia! para que los ideales mueran, se necesita destrozarnos, ya que odiados somos; sólo que ese odio nos eleva por que prueba nuestra honradez, desde el momento en que los tiranos no nos estiman. Por esto los flagelamos para despertar su encone, seguras de que si sucumbimos debe ser levantando ámpula; nuestra vacante será substituida con nuevas energías, con plumas viriles empapadas en luz febea.

Nuestros caractéres están enteramente trocados: nosotras, rebeldes, ellos serviles; nosotras honradas, ellos bandidos; nuestro medio no es el de ellos; el espíritu de rebeldía tonifica nuestros cerebros y es el talismán que nos hace prepotentes en los azares políticos, en la cruenta lucha que sostenemos con los burgueses; somos pobres y la pobreza es maga cuando va emparejada con honradez y abnegación; porque en los mayores infortunios, el porvenir nos sonríe, nos da fuerza y nos acaricia. Esto no pasa con los tiranos criminales: su existencia es mezquina y ruin; sus espíritus siempre están emponsoñados por el crimen y la maldad; sus morbosos y enfermisos cerebros a diario se sienten atacados por la misma ruindad que los deprime; no tienen convicciones propias y viven en continuo asecho de victimas que aseguran sus camonjías; sus almas siempre sarnosas sólo piensan en el mal; jamás se preocupan por nada loable.

¡Horrible torcedor para los tiranos, pensar en dia de las represalias! ¡La hora suena, innecesorable y justiciera contra los autores de tanto crimen! ¡Oidlo, bien, tiranos y bandidos y si es que lo olvidáis, nosotras os lo recordaremos!

¡Vivid tranquilos!

DEFUNCION.

En San Antonio, Texas, rindió tributo á la Natraleza el rebelde liberal Aurelio N. Flores, dejando un vacío en las filas liberales.

¡La muerte se engalanó al apoderarse de alma tan noble! El Partido Liberal perdió un valiente luchador. ¡Paz á sus resto! ¡Consuelo á sus deudos!

FIGURE 16.2. The Spanish-language weekly *La Voz de la Mujer*, published in El Paso, Texas, by Isidra T. de Cárdenas, was one of a few but significant feminist publications of the Mexican revolutionary movement published in the United States.

and Brooklyn alone issued *España Libre* (Free Spain, 1939-77), *España Nueva* (New Spain, 1923-42), *España Republicana* (Republican Spain, 1931-35), and several others. Many of the Hispanic labor and socialist organizations also published newspapers, such as *El Obrero* (Worker, 1931-32), that supported the Republican cause, as did the long-running anarchist paper, *Cultura Proletaria* (Proletarian Culture, 1910-59).[15] In these papers the exile press blended with the Hispanic immigrant press.

The Immigrant Press

By the mid-nineteenth century, Hispanic immigrants had created Spanish-language periodicals to serve their enclaves, maintaining a connection with the homeland while helping the immigrants to adjust to a new society and culture. The Hispanic immigrant press shared many of the characteristics that Robert Park identified in 1922: using the language of the homeland; serving a population united by that language, irrespective of national origin; interpreting events from their particular point of view; and furthering nationalism.[16] According to Park, the immigrant press provided a population in transition with news and interpretation and facilitated its adjustment to the new society while maintaining a link with the old. Underlying Park's scholarship, however, as well as that of many early students of immigration, were the concepts of the American dream and the melting pot, the notions that the immigrants came to find a better life and a better culture, and that soon they or their descendants would become Americans and they would no longer need an immigrant press.

Resistance to assimilation, however, has characterized the Hispanic immigrant press from the nineteenth century to the present. The advice of Corpus Christi's *El Horizonte* (Horizon, 1879-80) to its Mexican readership on 24 March 1880 was typical of many immigrant publications: do not become citizens of the United States because there is so much prejudice and persecution here that "we shall always be foreigners in the United States and they will always consider us as such."

In addition to the functions that Park articulated, the immigrant press played an important role in the defense of the community. Hispanic newspapers were especially sensitive to racism and abuse of immigrant rights. Almost all of the Hispanic immigrant newspapers announced on their mastheads or in editorials their role in protecting the community. Some led campaigns to desegregate schools, movie houses, and other facilities or to construct alternative institutions for the Hispanic community's use. Contrary to Park's prognosis, Hispanic groups in the United States have displayed a persistent ethnicity, while fresh immigration from Spanish-speaking countries, almost a steady flow since the founding of the United States to the present, has kept the initial purposes of the Hispanic press vital. Some immigrant newspapers, however, have evolved to serve multiple Hispanic groups. English-language or bilingual periodicals that served ethnic-minority interests rather than immigrant ones gradually became more available to the children of immigrants.

Important Immigrant Publishers

In the mid-nineteenth century, when large Hispanic immigrant communities began to form, immigrant newspapers were founded to serve the burgeoning community of immigrants from northern Mexico and throughout the Hispanic world. Many were drawn to the San Francisco Bay Area by the Gold Rush and collateral industrial and commercial development. From the 1850s through the 1870s, in fact, San Francisco supported the largest number, the longest running, and the most financially successful Spanish-language newspapers in the United States. The owners and editors of these papers included immigrants from Spain, Chile, Colombia, and Mexico. The largest of these was *El Eco del Pacífico* (Echo of the Pacific), which had grown out of a Spanish-language page of the French-language newspaper *L'Echo du Pacifique* (Echo of the Pacific) and had become independent in 1856.[17]

The San Francisco Hispanic press covered news of various homelands, ranging from Spain to Chile, Central America, and Mexico. They reported closely on the French intervention in Mexico, and various newspapers supported fundraising events for the war effort and aid for widows and orphans. In addition, they worked with the local Junta Patriótica Mexicana (Mexican Patriotic Committee), printing entire speeches made at the junta's meetings. The newspapers defended the Hispanic *colonia*, or colony, in California, denouncing discrimination and abuse of Hispanic workers. Hispanic readers in California were acutely aware of racial issues in the United States and sided with the North during the Civil War, which also was extensively covered in the newspapers.

Although San Francisco's Hispanic population had been the state's largest in the nineteenth century, more refugees fled to Los Angeles after the revolution of 1910. Thus, in the twentieth century, Los Angeles, along with San Antonio and New York, supported some of the most important Spanish-language daily newspapers, periodicals that began as immigrant newspapers. Between 1910 and 1924, some half million Mexican immigrants settled in the United States; Los Angeles and San Antonio were their most popular destinations. In these two cities, an entrepreneurial class of refugees established businesses of all types—from tortilla factories to Hispanic theaters. Through mutual aid societies, churches, theaters, and newspapers, they were able to disseminate a nationalistic ideology that promoted the solidarity and insularity of their community. Between 1910 and the Depression, the flood of Mexican workers into both cities spurred the founding of numerous Spanish-language newspapers, more than in any other city in the United States.

El Heraldo de México (Herald of Mexico), founded in Los Angeles in 1915 by owner Juan de Heras and publisher Cesar F. Marburg, has been called a "people's newspaper" because of its focus on and importance to the Mexican immigrant worker in Los Angeles.[18] It often proclaimed its working-class identity and its Mexican nationalism. Its publishing house issued in 1928 the first novel narrated from the perspective of a Mexican working-class immigrant, Daniel Venegas's *Las aventuras de Don Chipote o Cuando los pericos mamen* (*The Adventures of Don Chipote or, When Parrots Breast Feed*). With a circulation of more than 4,000, *El Heraldo de México* was the most popular Mexican newspaper at this time.[19] Like many other Hispanic immigrant newspapers, it devoted the largest proportion of its coverage to news of the homeland, followed by news directly affecting the immigrants in the United States, including news and advertisements that would be of interest to working-class immigrants. Its most important social role was defending Mexican immigrants, devoting considerable space to combating discrimination, mistreatment, and exploitation of immigrant labor. In 1919 *El Heraldo de México* attempted to organize Mexican laborers into an association, the Liga Protectiva Mexicana de California (Mexican Protective League of California), in order to protect their rights and further their interests.[20]

Defense of civil and human rights also extended to protecting Mexican immigrants from the influence of Anglo-American culture and Protestantism. Many publishers, editorialists, and columnists promoted the idea of a "*México de afuera*" or a Mexican colony existing outside of Mexico, in which individuals were called upon to maintain the Spanish language, keep the Catholic faith, and insulate their children from what community leaders perceived as the low moral standards of Anglo-Americans. Basic to this belief system was the idea of an imminent return to Mexico when the hostilities of the revolution were over. Mexican national culture was to be preserved while in exile in the midst of iniquitous Anglo Protestants, whose culture was aggressively degrading even while discriminating against Hispanics. The ideology was expressed by cultural elites, many of whom were the political and religious refugees from the revolution. They represented the most conservative segment of society in Mexico; in the United States, they exerted cultural and economic leadership in all phases of life, providing a conservative bedrock for Mexican American culture for decades to come.

One of the most powerful of these figures was Ignacio E. Lozano, founder and operator of the two most powerful and well-distributed daily newspapers: San Antonio's *La Prensa* (The Press), founded in 1913, and Los Angeles's *La Opinión* (Opinion), founded in 1926 and still publishing today. Lozano, from a successful business family in northern Mexico, relocated to San Antonio in 1908 in search of business opportunities; there he opened a bookstore and gradually learned the newspaper business while working first for San Antonio's *El Noticiero* (News) and later *El Imparcial de Texas* (Impartial Texan).[21] With the business training and experience that he received in Mexico, Lozano contributed professionalism and business acumen to Hispanic journalism in the United States. He hired well-trained journalists, beginning with his appointment of Teodoro Torres, the "Father of Mexican Journalism," to edit *La Prensa*. The ideas of men such as Torres and Lozano reached thousands not only in San Antonio but throughout the Southwest, Midwest, and northern Mexico through a vast distribution system that included newsstand sales, home delivery, and mail. *La Prensa* also established a network of correspondents who regularly issued reports on current events and cultural activities in Mexican communities as far away as Chicago, Detroit, and New York. Unlike the publishers of many other Hispanic immigrant newspapers, Lozano sought also to serve the long-standing Mexican American population in the Southwest and bring it within the "México de afuera" ideology. Many of the immigrants never moved back to Mexico, however, and their children became United States citizens. *La Prensa* thus became an ethnic minority publication, providing ideological and political analysis of the post–World War II Mexican American civil rights movement. According to Rubén Munguía, a printer, publisher, and writer himself, *La Prensa*, a conservative paper, awakened the liberal thinking of men who organized vibrant, aggressive organizations, such as the Knights of America, the Sons of America, and the League of United Latin American Citizens (LULAC).[22]

La Prensa did not survive to see the Chicano movement of the 1960s, the civil rights movement that promoted a cultural nationalism of its own. San Antonio did not continue to attract a steady or large enough stream of immigrants to sustain the newspaper, and English had become the dominant media language among the younger generation. In its day, though, *La Prensa* was indeed influential. Lozano and many of his prominent writers and editorialists became leaders of their communities, and San Antonio became the publishing center for Hispanics in the Southwest, housing more Spanish-language publishing houses, including the Casa Editorial Lozano, Viola Novelty Company, and Whitt Publishing, than any other city in the United States. Each of these firms published and imported books and printed catalogs for mail order. Lozano and Viola Novelty, which were connected to newspapers, also published book listings in their parent newspapers, *La Prensa*, *La Opinión*, and the satirical *El Fandango*. Those associated with bookstores, such as Lozano, Quiroga, and Librería Espanola, of course, had a ready sales outlet. Among the San Antonio publishers' offerings was everything from secretaries' manuals to exiles' autobiographies. The Librería de Quiroga seems to have dedicated itself to supplying the leisure reading for housewives, especially those of the middle class, with such sentimental fare as María del Pilar Sinues's novel *El amor de los amores* (The Love of Loves) and Harriet Beecher Stowe's *La cabaña de Tom* (*Uncle Tom's Cabin*).

Almost all of these houses published novels of the Mexican Revolution, as numerous expatriate intellectuals fictionalized their personal experiences of the revolutionary whirlwind. One of the first to establish this genre was the now classic work, Mariano Azuela's *Los de abajo* (The Underdogs, 1915), which was first published as a serialized novel in an El Paso newspaper. However, the majority of these novels were issued from San Antonio.

In the Northeast, large daily and weekly newspapers flourished, and they also published books, as did small, ephemeral presses. In 1913, Jose Campubrí founded *La Prensa* (The Press) in New York City to serve the community of mostly Spanish and Cuban immigrants in and around Manhattan's 14th Street; little did he know then that *La Prensa* would become the nation's longest-running Spanish language daily newspaper. It survived because it was able to expand and adapt to the needs of new Spanish-speaking immigrants, especially the Puerto Ricans who migrated en masse during and after World War II, forming the largest Hispanic group in the city. In 1948 *El Diario de Nueva York* (New York Daily) was founded by Dominican immigrant Porfirio Domenici, specifically appealing to the Puerto Rican community and giving *La Prensa* competition for this growing readership.[23] Over the years, *El Diario de Nueva York* conducted many campaigns and programs on behalf of the Puerto Rican community. It published exposés of the abuse and mistreatment of Puerto Ricans in migrant farm labor camps on the East Coast and of the phantom labor unions and labor racketeering that were bleeding funds from poor Puerto Ricans.[24]

We see, then, in *El Diario*'s persistent and strenuous assertion of the interests of the Hispanic community in New York the reverse of the model proposed by Robert Park earlier in the century. Park proposed that immigrant presses had contrasting purposes: they maintained the group's culture while at the same time assisting the process of assimilating to the mainstream Anglo culture. Assimilation, Park believed, would ultimately predominate as maintenance declined. In the Hispanic press of New York and elsewhere, however, we see the adjusting function subordinated to the protecting function, a trend that persisted for many decades.

The Labor Press

Another factor that kept Hispanic print culture vital across the decades was the labor press. While Hispanic workers shared some interests with the general labor movement, they also experienced pervasive discrimination as a distinct group. Historically, the Hispanic labor unions and their periodicals were created by and for Latinos working in very specific industries—industries often associated with their native cultures or old-country backgrounds: cigar rolling, mining and agriculture, cattle ranching, copper mining, and fruit harvesting.[25]

One of the first, largest, and most significant industries to rely almost exclusively on Hispanic labor was the cigar-manufacturing industry, with factories in Key West, Tampa, New York, and San Antonio, among other locations. In 1886 the first transfer of a whole industry from Latin America to the United States began when Spanish and Cuban entrepreneurs acquired Florida swampland near Tampa and built a cigar-producing town, Ybor City. By 1900 there were about 150 cigar factories in West Tampa and Ybor City.[26] However, the cigar company owners were unable to escape the labor unrest that was endemic to the industry in Cuba. Indeed, the greater freedom of expression afforded on U.S. soil allowed the cigar workers to organize more openly and to publish periodicals more extensively. The cigar workers formed the strongest Hispanic unions in the United States and struck in 1899, 1901, 1910, 1920, and 1931.[27]

Workers in the cigar crafts obtained high levels of informal education through the institution of the *lector*, a person selected and paid by the workers to read to them throughout their laborious workday rolling cigars. This led to the politicization of workers, as the *lectores* would read from world literature, national authors, and, of course, newspapers and magazines. Ambrosio Fornet summarized the importance of the *lector*, an institution brought from Cuba and Puerto Rico: "The Reading was the first attempt at extending books to the masses for solely educational and recreational reasons. Among the privileged classes, the book had always been a sumptuous object and, ultimately, an instrument of domination or lucre; the proletariat converted it into an instrument of self-education, using it only to advance itself ideologically and culturally."[28]

The roots of the Cuban American labor press are thus found in the tobacco workers' tradition and its publications. Cuban tobacco workers in Tampa established their first labor newspaper, *La Federación* (Federation, 1899), as the official organ of their union. Other union newspapers in Tampa came and went in the drumbeat of labor activism and radical perspectives.[29]

In New York, Hispanic laborers, including the cigar workers, transformed the existing revolutionary press to serve the needs of the labor movement. At the end of the nineteenth century, New York received a large influx of Spanish working-class immigrants; they joined their fellow Spanish speakers in Harlem, 14th Street, and Brooklyn and participated in raising working-class consciousness through such newspapers as *El Despertar* (Awakening, 1891–1912) and *Cultura Proletaria* (*Proletarian Culture*, 1910–59), the longest lasting Hispanic anarchist periodical published in the United States.[30] Puerto Ricans early on established their own labor and radical press in such organs as *La Mísera* (Miserable One, 1901) and, much later, *Vida Obrera* (Workers' Life, 1930–32).

High-Culture Print Production

While labor periodicals served the immigrant working-class, Hispanic elites in the United States and its territories felt the need to reproduce the cultural refinement that was the product of their education and breeding in the homeland. Some high-quality periodicals, like the New York monthly *El Americano* (American, 1892), retained the newspaper format, but primarily published literature and commentary, along with illustrations. Others resembled Anglo-American cultural magazines published at the turn of the century, such as *Harper's Magazine* and *Cosmopolitan*. Their distinctive function, however, was to provide the Hispanic immigrant community of the United States with an international cultural map, for they drew selections from writers of prose and poetry from Spain and Spanish America as well as from the United States.

Pan-Hispanism and hemispheric integration formed the basis of *El Americano*'s ideological stance. Because of its offerings, it had a circulation overseas as well as in the United States. From within a similarly internationalist perspective developed the most important illustrated Hispanic magazine, *La Revista Ilustrada de Nueva York* (Illustrated Review, 1882), which, at a subscription price of $3.00, explicitly targeted middle- and upper-class educated Hispanics in the United States and abroad. Despite its generally positive stance on American civilization, the magazine nevertheless called for pan-Hispanic resistance to the expansion of the American empire during a time of U.S. intervention in Spanish America. Thus, despite its elitism, *La Revista* felt it had to protect language, culture, and Hispanic interests just as the working-class Hispanic newspapers did.

The Native Hispanic Press

Lubomyr Wynar and Anna T. Wynar have argued that the ethnic press in the United States functions dynamically to reconcile assimilation with cultural maintenance and distinctive group interests. Thus, "as it promotes the full and equal participation of the ethnic community within the larger order, at the same time it encourages retention of the distinctiveness that differentiates the community from the dominant society."³¹ This analysis relies on the premise that the ethnic press evolves from an immigrant press. A press built on immigration, however, differs substantially from one that develops out of the colonialism and racial oppression experienced by a nonmigrant population. Such doctrines as Manifest Destiny and the Spanish Black Legend subjected Hispanics to more than a century of "racialization."³² The Mexicans of the Southwest, the Hispanics in Florida and Louisiana, the Panamanians in the Canal Zone and in Panama itself, and the Puerto Ricans in the Caribbean were either conquered or incorporated into the United States through territorial expansion and then treated as colonial subjects. In many ways, Cubans and Dominicans also developed as peoples under United States colonial rule during the twentieth century. The subsequent migration and immigration of these peoples to the continental United States was incidental to the colonization of their homelands by the United States. Their cultural and political perspective on life in the United States was thus substantially different from that of most European immigrant groups. The Hispanic native or ethnic minority perspective developed first among Hispanics already residing in the Southwest when the United States appropriated their homelands from Mexico, shaping Hispanic attitudes toward civil and political rights. Their ethnic-minority or native press was cognizant of the minority status of its readers within U.S. society and culture. While acknowledging immigrant readership and interests, and while maintaining an international perspective, the press mainly concerned itself with its readers' lives in the United States. Unlike the immigrant press, it did not have one foot in the home country and one in the United States.

Many of the Hispanic newspapers, books, and other publications that appeared after 1848 fostered the view of Hispanics as an ethnic minority within the United States. The sudden conversion of the Mexican population to colonial status in the newly acquired territories of California, New Mexico, and Texas made their publications sounding boards for Hispanic rights, first as colonials and later as "racialized" citizens of the United States. After the introduction of the printing press to California and New Mexico in 1834, Spanish-language newspapers began to appear in the northern provinces of Mexico: for example, Santa Fe's *El Crepusculo de la Libertad* (Dawn of Liberty) and Taos's *El Crepusculo* (Dawn, 1835).

In Texas, numerous newspapers had been publishing bilingually since just before the proclamation of the Texas Republic in 1836.³³ In New Mexico, Anglo newspaper owners found that publishing in Spanish was a necessity because the vast majority of the inhabitants of the territory were Spanish speakers. The American presence in New Mexico and California increased during the outbreak of the Mexican War in 1846, and many newspapers began publishing bilingually there. Later, states and local governments in California subsidized newspaper publication of laws in Spanish, as the state constitution required that laws be issued in both languages.[34] This initial motivation developed into a profitable enterprise once the Spanish-language market was identified and cultivated. Indeed, the Spanish-language section of the *Los Angeles Star* grew into *La Estrella de Los Angeles* and then a separate newspaper: *El Clamor Público* (Public Clamor, 1855–59). Across California, the Anglo-established press was often a bilingual institution. Despite this, only about 12 percent of the journalists employed by the bilingual newspapers were Hispanics.[35] Félix Gutiérrez has seen this imbalance as typical of the colonial condition of Hispanics in the Southwest: "the conquering group establishes media for the conquered group, but then controls the media by restricting employment opportunities, establishing a dual labor market, controlling the context of the news, and delivering even that news a week later to members of the conquered group."[36]

Even Spanish-language newspapers that were published independently by Hispanics were often dependent on the Anglo economic and political structures. Some Hispanic publishers survived only by working within the system, not attacking it for breaches of Hispanic civil rights. Other Spanish-language newspapers, from California to Texas, were affiliated with the Anglo-dominated political parties. Gutiérrez thus concludes that attempts were made to harness the Spanish-language press and utilize it as an instrument of social control."[37]

As we have seen, however, many other Spanish-language publishers survived despite their critical, pan-Hispanic, international perspective. Furthermore, despite the apparent dependence of Hispanic publishing on the Anglo-American establishment, the availability of Anglo-American technology and equipment brought presses to Hispanics as never before, facilitating the founding of Spanish-language newspapers to serve the native Hispanic population.

Many of these presses also issued books. Although Spanish books had been printed from the earliest introduction of the printing press in 1834, the arrival of the railroad in the territories in the 1880s and 1890s dramatically increased access to machinery and technology as well as to better means of distribution. The last third of the century thus saw an explosion of independent Spanish-language publishing by Hispanics. Enhanced technology and transportation did not always have a standardizing effect on publishing. In this case, for a considerable time, it enhanced diversity and distinctive voices.

During this period, books containing native Hispanic literature helped to develop a sense of ethnic and regional identity for Hispanics in the Southwest. Autobiographies, memoirs, and novels appeared, addressing Hispanics' sense of usurpation and subordination, felt as a loss of patrimony and a fear of persecution as a racial minority in the United States. One of the earliest of these was the *Personal Memoirs of John N. Seguín*, written in English in 1858 by an embattled political figure of the Texas Republic. It was still a steady seller in the late nineteenth century. Seguín expressed great disillusionment in the transformation of Texas by Anglo-Americans.³⁸ In 1872 María Amparo Ruiz de Burton published the first novel written in English by a Hispanic of the United States. *Who Would Have Thought It?* satirized the dominant U.S. myths of American exceptionalism, egalitarianism, and consensus.³⁹

After the turn of the century, Mexican immigration to the Southwest increased, as did Puerto Rican, Cuban, and Spanish immigration to the Northeast. The viability of native Hispanic publishing ventures receded as immigrant culture overwhelmed the native Hispanic perspective. While many European ethnic groups moved from immigrant status to native status in the United States, the Hispanic population shifted during this period from a largely native population to a largely immigrant one. Certainly native writing persisted and laid the foundation for the bilingual, bicultural citizenry of later decades, but most often native authors either self-published or worked through the immigrant newspapers and publishing houses.

Hispanic Print Culture in Different Settings

By examining four different locations — three states and the city of New York — we can further contextualize the evolution of native Hispanic print culture.

New Mexico

Because it drew fewer Anglo settlers and entrepreneurs than California and Texas — and because of its vastly larger initial Hispanic population — New Mexico's Hispanics maintained a demographic majority in the late nineteenth and early twentieth centuries, and New Mexico was the first territory to develop a widespread independent native Hispanic press. The Nuevomexicanos were able to hold onto more lands, property, and institutions than the Hispanics of California and Texas. Control of their own newspapers and publications was essential for the development of Nuevomexicano identity and self-determination. Hispanic intellectuals and community leaders wanted to control their own destiny and preserve their own language and culture while enjoying the benefits and rights of statehood. But the Nuevomexicanos immediately realized the dangers of Anglo-American cultural, economic, and political encroachment on New Mexico. According to A. Gabriel Meléndez, many of these leaders believed that through newspapers the native population could learn to protect its rights and merit statehood.⁴⁰

In the 1880s, following the arrival of the railroad, native Hispanic journalism increased dramatically in New Mexico. By the 1890s some thirty-five Spanish-language newspapers were being published.[41] The English-language and bilingual newspapers were left to serve an elite that was mostly English-speaking, while the Spanish-language papers served the Hispanic majority. By 1891 native Hispanic journalism had become so widespread that a newspaper association was founded, La Prensa Asociada Hispanoamericana, to set up a network of correspondents, to share resources and to facilitate reprinting items from each member newspaper in a type of informal syndication. By 1900 every settlement along the Rio Grande corridor had a Spanish-language newspaper.[42] Thus, in a few short decades, the Hispanic writers and publishers of what had been a backwater province under Mexico and a frontier colony under the United States had been transformed into intellectuals and activists utilizing printing and transportation technology. They were taking the lead in ushering their community into the twentieth century and statehood.

How and why did this occur? The new technology that Nuevomexicanos adopted did not represent fundamental cultural change; rather, it empowered long held and deeply felt cultural expressions. The creation of formal institutions of education in the territory was also critically empowering. Meléndez and others credit the Catholic Church for establishing schools within the territory, not only at the primary and secondary levels but, more importantly, at the college level to train the Hispanic leadership in New Mexico.[43] Many of the Hispanic newspaper owners and editors were educated at the parochial schools, and then graduated from one of the three Catholic colleges: St. Michael's College (Colegio de San Miguel) in Santa Fe, or Lorreto Academy or the Jesuit College, both in Las Vegas. Included among the pioneers of Catholic education in the territory was the Reverend Donato M. Gasparri, an Italian Jesuit who headed the New Mexico Colorado Mission. He founded the Catholic press in New Mexico and was the first editor of the long-lasting *La Revista Católica* (Catholic Magazine, 1875–1962), which he issued from the Jesuit College that he founded in Las Vegas (figure 16.3).

The young professionals entering journalism in the 1880s and 1890s thus had access to both higher education and new communication technologies. They also carried with them, according to Meléndez, "a sense of mission and urgency fostered by the social, racial and political contentions of their age. . . . Educated in the classics, inspired in the power of the press, seasoned in the copy room, they were driven by the imperative to raise their voices in opposition to the suppression of their culture and language, and as they did so, this generation began to assert its civic, cultural, and human rights as never before."[44]

Meléndez documents how the Nuevomexicano journalists constructed their

REVISTA CATOLICA.

Se publica todas las semanas, en Las Vegas, N. M.

Año X.   27 de Enero de 1884.   **Núm. 4.**

SUMARIO.

Crónica General.—Sucesos Patrios: Fiestas movibles de 1884; Calendario de la Semana.—El Amable Jesus.—Actualidades.—Extravagancia en los funerales.—Evangelio [ilegible].—Progreso del Catolicismo en Nueva York.—Unirse y Obrar.—Diócesis que nos hacen falta.—Un asilo de huérfanos.—La embajada francesa cerca del Vaticano.—Contra la fiebre amarilla.—Primer libro de español.—Los fenómenos actuales.—Los Neo-Mejicanos.—Noticias de la Agricultura.—Neron.—Lo Huérfano.—[ilegible] para [ilegible] el vino picado.—El Arroyo (poesía).—"Quien al cielo escupe"...

CRONICA GENERAL.

Incendio del "Moteznuma Hotel."—El dia 17 del corriente, mientras los numerosos huéspedes del "Moteznuma Hotel" de Hot Springs, estaban esperando el tan deseado toque de la campana, que había de llamarles al comedor, viéronse precisados á correr á todo escape hácia afuera para poder salvar su vida. Pues á las doce precisamente se declaró en aquel magnífico edificio un incendio tan terrible, que en menos de una hora lo redujo todo á escombros y cenizas. Las pérdidas se evalúan en $250,000, de los que solo $100,000 estaban asegurados. Ya se piensa en edificar otro Hotel aun más suntuoso que el primero.

Felices encuentros.—Un misionero que volvió de la Guyana á Europa por motivo de salud, visitaba últimamente la Exposicion de Amsterdam. Pronto se detiene asombrado al oir el alegre grito: "¡Hé aquí nuestro Padre!" Este grito salia de un grupo de sus antiguos feligreses que vinieron á arrodillarse á sus piés, asegurándole que permanecerian siempre fieles á las promesas de su bautismo. En la misma Exposicion otro Misionero encontró á varios Chinos católicos. Un tercero al dirigirse á la Iglesia de Amsterdam pasó cerca de dos turcos católicos, que arrodillados en el suelo esperaban la hora de la Misa.

El célebre Abd-el-Kader.—Ese famoso jefe árabe ha fallecido en Damasco á la edad de setenta y seis años. Siendo Emir de dicha villa, él dispensó toda su proteccion á los Cristianos durante las horribles jornadas de Julio 15 1860. Hizo de su misma casa un asilo para cuantos quisieran refugiarse en ella, y así logró salvar entre otros á unos á los Padres Lazaristas y á las Hermanas de la Caridad. Cuando casó la carnicería, sus jinetes escoltaron hasta Beirut á los mil quinientos cristianos que arrancó á la muerte.

"Las Siervas de los pobres."—La Superiora de las Canosianas ó *Siervas de los Pobres* de Hong-Kong escribe lo siguiente: "Las 170 niñas de nuestro asilo de huérfanos nos dan mucho consuelo. Todo el día lo pasan en varios ejercicios, y muestran mucha aficion al trabajo. Las clases de niñas externas son muy frecuentadas. Tenemos tambien abierta una escuela para niñas ciegas, muy numerosas en China. Sus progresos han sido tales, que han podido presentar al público labores exquisitos de aguja, flores, en-

ejes, etc., todo lo cual sirve para mejorar la situacion de estas desgraciadas."

Un tesoro debajo del agua.—Un abogado de Nueva York está tratando de recuperar del fondo de las aguas del estrecho de Hell-Gate, el tesoro que, se dice, contiene el buque Hussar, el cual se fué á pique en 1780. Venía dicho buque de Inglaterra con un millon de libras esterlinas para pagar el ejército inglés que entónces ocupaba á Nueva York. Cuéntase que se fueron tambien al fondo 70 prisioneros Americanos encadenados en el entrepuente.

El frio en Nueva York.—Dicen las *Novedades*: "Dos dias llevamos de un frio que nos hace imaginar que nos hemos acercado al Polo. El resultado es que los transeuntes andan por las calles con presteza extraordinaria. Hay frotamiento de manos, chapoteamiento de piés, y hasta pellizcos de orejas y narices, esos dos termómetros del cuerpo humano, y el *ichiske*, descienden á los estómagos para sacar organizarse tal vez á los cascos. El termómetro bajó á los 9 grados sin que se haya el menor indicio de cuánto subirá."

Noticias del Japon.—Escribe desde Kobé la Superiora de la Congregacion del Santo Niño Jesus: "La familia que el Señor me sigue confiando crece en número y en edad, y por consiguiente las obligaciones se multiplican cada dia. Me siento felicísima con mi familia de pequeñuelos, y por nada al mundo quisiera separarme de ellos. Lo único que me da pena es que á veces me veo obligada á rehusar nuevas peticiones. Nuestros limitados recursos no nos permiten recibirlas en tan gran número como desearíamos. No siempre tengo bastante valor para despacharlas, y un dia una, un dia otra, se va aumentando sensiblemente su número."

¡Si no se hubiese hecho fraile!—El finado Zenon Baroux, habiendo hecho su testamento, dejó en depósito á la ciudad de Baltimore la suma de $80,000, con el fin de entregarlos á su hermano Frank, caso que este hubiese cumplido con la condicion necesaria, de que no seria jamás sacerdote católico. Ahora bien Frank ha entrado en la Compañía de Jesus, y en vista de que tarde ó temprano será ordenado de sacerdote, el Juez Fisher ha fallado, desde luego que los $80,000 se deben á la ciudad de Baltimore.

Futura Catedral.—Un despacho de Lóndres, con fecha 12 de Enero, anuncia que los Católicos de Inglaterra han concluido ir reglas para empezar la construccion de una nueva Catedral en Westminster que costará más de medio millon de libras esterlinas. Los planos aprobados son semejantes á la "Notta Korcha" de Viena.

El Colegio americano de la Inmaculada Concepcion en Lovaina, Bélgica, acaba de enviar diez y siete nuevos misioneros á varias diócesis de los Estados Unidos.—A la diócesis de Saint Paul, Minn., el

---

FIGURE 16.3. *Revista Católica*, founded by the Italian Jesuit Donato M. Gasparri, was published from 1875 to 1962. Along with a publishing house of the same name also begun by Gasparri, the periodical flourished for many years as the only Spanish-language Catholic weekly in the Western Hemisphere.

own "national" culture, which consisted of preserving the Spanish language, formulating a version of history, and developing their own literature, all of which would foster self-confidence and pride as they entered the Union. These leaders were a cohesive corps of native historians, creative writers, and publishers. The development of the New Mexican Hispanic press, a *native* press, thus followed a very different pattern from that of New York's Hispanic press, which attracted publishers, writers, and journalists who were trained abroad and who saw themselves as exiles or immigrants.

The cultural nationalism of these native journalists sprang from the necessity to defend their community from the cultural, economic, and political encroachments and denigration of outsiders. They turned the tables on the Anglo-Americans, championing their own high culture and Catholic religion over the low morality, vicious opportunism, and hypocrisy they saw among the Protestant interlopers.

One publication stands out in its furthering of the ethnic nationalist goals of the Nuevomexicanos: the *Revista Ilustrada* (Illustrated Review), published by Camilo Padilla in Santa Fe from 1917 to about 1931. The *Revista Ilustrada* was ahead of its time in identifying and furthering a Hispanic ethnic minority culture in the United States. In addition to publishing poetry, stories, and history, often with illustrations, the magazine allowed Nuevomexicano intellectuals to ponder the fate of their culture. Among the collaborators were such notables as Nuevomexicano historian Benjamin M. Read, poet and novelist Eusebio Chacón, and linguist and professor Aurelio M. Espinosa. The *Revista Ilustrada* championed Spanish language and Hispanic culture, advertising books of European and Latin American literature in Spanish that could be bought directly from the magazine.[45] As Meléndez asserts, the promotion of a "national" literature and a "national" history by these editors and writers demonstrates that as early as the late nineteenth century the Nuevomexicanos were seeing themselves as a national minority of the United States.

Camilo Padilla's death in 1933 symbolizes the end of this dynamic period in New Mexico Hispanic publishing. Statehood achieved, the forces of cultural homogenization, coupled with the demographic ascendancy of the Anglo-American population made it increasingly difficult to sustain Spanish-language publishing in New Mexico. As Meléndez writes,

> By the 1930s the social authority to determine what was suitable and appropriate learning for both native and nonnative peoples in New Mexico ... had passed into the hands of a growing community of recently emigrated Anglo-American educators, authors, historians, ethnographers, editors, and a sundry group of cultural do-gooders, who, for all their love

of Southwestern subjects, remained tied to the print culture of the eastern United States; that is to say, they operated as agents of a "circuit of communications" that privileged Euro-American observations and ideas over those of regional and ethnic communities.[46]

The Public Education Law of 1894 made English the language of instruction in the public schools, and after statehood, the expansion of public education further accelerated the displacement of Spanish as a public language. The Depression likewise took its toll on a Hispanic publishing industry that was already competing with larger publishing enterprises in the East as well as locally.

California

Different economic and demographic conditions produced a sharply contrasting history in California. Soon after the Gold Rush and statehood in 1850, the native Hispanic population of California became overwhelmed by an influx of Anglo-Americans and was quickly converted to minority status.[47] During the post–Civil War years, in-migration of Anglos increased dramatically. With the arrival of the railroads, the breaking up of the Californio ranches, and the rapid capitalist development of the economy, the native population was rapidly transformed into a proletariat. The Californios and Hispanicized Indians were displaced from farms and ranches and were assimilated into the new economy as laborers on the railroads, in mines, and in the fields.

Still, there were newspapers owned by native Hispanic publishers, and an ethnic minority consciousness began to develop.[48] When Francisco P. Ramírez took the Spanish section from the *Los Angeles Star* and founded a separate newspaper, *El Clamor Público* (Public Clamor, 1855–59), he spread awareness that Hispanics in California were being treated as a separate race from the Euro-American newcomers.[49] Even the wealthy Californios who had collaborated in the Yankee takeover saw their wealth and power diminish under statehood. *El Clamor Público* also attempted to present an image of educated refinement, demonstrating the high level of civilization achieved by Hispanics. This was in part a defensive reaction to the negative propaganda of Manifest Destiny, which had cast Mexicans and other Hispanics as barbarians incapable of developing their lands and the natural resources of the West, thus justifying the Anglos in taking their lands. Despite its staunch counterarguments, *El Clamor Público* maintained strong ties to the Anglo-American business community in Los Angeles. Ramírez strongly supported the learning of English, not just for business, but also for protecting the Californios' rights.[50] However, his indignation became greater as it became clear that the Constitution he loved so much would not protect the civil and property rights of the Californios.

Ramírez was one of the first Mexican American journalists of the West and Southwest to use the press to establish a native perspective, forging a different strategy from those employed by native Hispanic editors in neighboring New Mexico. In the decades after statehood was established, *El Clamor Público* and most of the other Spanish-language newspapers of California insisted on integration into the American education and political system and promoted learning the English language for survival. In doing so, they created a bicultural version of an ethnic minority identity.[51]

In California, as in Texas, refugees from the Mexican Revolution of 1910 overwhelmed the native populations. The large immigrant daily newspapers, such as *El Heraldo de México*, *La Prensa*, and *La Opinión*, focused on the needs of the new immigrants, even while developing Hispanic native issues and culture. The effect was to subsume native Hispanic interests in the immigrant press. Nevertheless, as the community matured and evolved into a Hispanic culture of the United States, many immigrant newspapers returned to the earlier stance, thinking of their readership as a national ethnic minority, not as immigrants who would either assimilate or return to Mexico. By the time of the Depression and World War II, while more and more Hispanic publications were issued in English, a new generation saw itself portrayed as a permanent community in their pages. This new consciousness existed side by side with immigrant and exile publications.

One California periodical that combined integrationist themes and ethnic pride was the *Mexican Voice* (1938?–44), a publication of the Mexican American movement and the product of youths who had either been born or raised in the United States. The *Mexican Voice* promoted citizenship, upward mobility through education, and active participation in civil and cultural activities outside the barrio.[52] While hesitant to acknowledge racism as a factor hindering success, the magazine did promote pride in the pre-Colombian background and in Mexican *mestizaje* (mixed Spanish and Amerindian heritage). This was accomplished in part by publishing brief biographies of high-achieving Mexican Americans in Southern California.

The ideas expressed in the *Mexican Voice* resembled those expressed by the Mexican American civil rights organization, the League of United Latin American Citizens. Although the Mexican American movement and the Chicano movement are often contrasted, the English-language periodicals formed a vital link to the attitudes of the Chicano movement, which produced a flowering of politically committed newspapers and magazines and even scholarly journals based at California's universities in the 1960s and 1970s.

Texas

From Texas statehood in 1850 through the period of intense Mexican immigration in the twentieth century, newspapers serving Texas Mexicans assumed active roles in defining Mexican American identity. Such newspapers as San Antonio's *El Regidor* (Regent, 1888-1916) saw the protection of Texas Mexicans' rights as their duty, but it was the journalist Catarino Garza who made their civil rights a crusade. Born on the border in 1859, Garza worked on newspapers in Laredo, Eagle Pass, Corpus Christi, and San Antonio. In the Brownsville-Eagle Pass area, he became involved in local politics and published two newspapers, *El Comercio Mexicano* (Mexican Commerce, 1886-?) and *El Libre Pensador* (Free Thinker, 1890-99), which "criticized the violence, usurpation, and manipulation suffered by Mexican Americans."[53] In the late 1880s, Garza became more militant and struck out at authorities on both sides of the border with a band of followers. Texas Rangers eventually broke up his raiders, and Garza fled in 1892 to New Orleans and from there to Panama, where he was reportedly killed fighting for Panamanian independence.[54] Garza's exploits were followed in detail in the Spanish-language newspapers of the Southwest, helping feelings about exploitation and dispossession to coalesce among the Mexican American population. This process was enhanced by the reprinting of Garza's articles in newspapers throughout the Southwest.

Another influential newspaper along the border was Laredo's *La Crónica* (Chronicle). Its editor, Nicasio Idar, argued for many liberal causes, including the establishment of Mexican schools for children in Texas as an alternative to the segregated public schools. *La Crónica* decried everything from racism and segregation in public institutions to negative stereotypes in Anglo plays and films.

In Texas, the process of Mexican Americanization, that is, establishing a firm identity as a U.S. ethnic minority, gave rise to the two most important national civil rights organizations: the League of United Latin American Citizens and the American G.I. Forum. Founded in 1929, LULAC's members were at first mostly middle-class Mexican Americans, and American citizenship was required. Early on, segregation and unfairness in the judicial system were its primary concerns. Various local chapters had their own newsletters, but the organization's main periodical was *LULAC News* (1931-79), published monthly in English and Spanish for national distribution. The American G.I. Forum was founded in Corpus Christi by World War II veterans to protect the civil rights of Mexican American veterans. The forum's periodical was the *Forumeer*. The organization became actively involved in electoral politics and created a voting bloc within the Democratic Party, which, some experts believe, won the 1962 presidential election for John F. Kennedy.[55]

Newspapers and civil rights periodicals were not the only publications representing the evolving native Hispanic perspective in the Southwest. Although no publishing houses consistently issued books from that perspective—mainly because the Mexican immigrant press dominated the discourse—individual Mexican American writers self-published their works or successfully printed them through newspapers and immigrant publishers. These books, as well as *LULAC News* and the *Forumeer*, were predecessors of the Chicano movement publications that were issued in the 1960s and early 1970s. They reinforced the entitlement of Mexican Americans as citizens of the United States to the rights and benefits of American society, without racial, class, or linguistic discrimination, while expressing great faith in the American Constitution, Congress, and the judicial system to remedy discrimination and injustice.

New York

New York has been the principal U.S. port of entry for immigrants from Europe and the Caribbean and has been a center for immigrant publishing and culture. A native Hispanic identity did develop there, although under quite different circumstances. *Gráfico*, a typical immigrant newspaper serving Puerto Ricans and Cubans in East Harlem, emphasized the American citizenship of its readers and demanded their constitutional rights. The Jones Act of 1917 extended automatic citizenship to Puerto Ricans, so they did not have to acculturate or assimilate to become citizens.

During the Depression, New York did not experience the massive repatriation of Hispanics that occurred in the Southwest. Indeed, hard economic times in Puerto Rico brought even more immigrants to the city, a trend that intensified during World War II as northeastern manufacturing and service industries experienced labor shortages and recruited heavily in Puerto Rico. The massive influx of Puerto Ricans during and just after the war deepened the community's identity as a native citizenry. Local newspapers urged community members to organize politically and vote. The tone and goals of such a native Hispanic consciousness—viewing Hispanic Americans as a permanent minority with citizens' rights, a culture to be protected, and alliances to be made—is different from the transitional preoccupations of the immigrant press.

In the late 1920s, a league was formed in New York City to increase the power of the Hispanic community by unifying its diverse organizations. Among the very specific goals of the Liga Puertorriqueña e Hispana (the Puerto Rican and Hispanic League) were representing the community to various authorities, working for the economic and social betterment of the Puerto Ricans, and propagating the vote.[56] The Liga founded a periodical in 1927 entitled the *Boletín Oficial de la Liga Puertorriqueña e Hispana*, which functioned as a community newspaper and included essays and cultural items as well as news.[57]

Other publications developed native Hispanic stances, some of them fleeting, others long-standing. *Pueblos Hispanos: Seminario Progresista* (Hispanic Peoples: Progressive Weekly, 1943-44) was affiliated with both the Puerto Rican Nationalist Party and the Communist Party of America. While encouraging political involvement in the Democratic Party by Hispanic citizens and openly endorsing the reelection of FDR, *Pueblos Hispanos* promoted Puerto Rican independence from the United States and, as its name suggested, Pan-Hispanism and the integration of Latin America. Edited by the Puerto Rican poet and Communist Party activist Juan Antonio Corretjer, the newspaper ran weekly columns on politics and culture in Russia as well as on socialist movements around the globe, and covered Puerto Rican politics on the island and in New York in detail. It may seem paradoxical that *Pueblos Hispanos* was concerned with safeguarding the civil rights of Puerto Ricans in New York while advocating the island's separation from the United States. But this confidence in the safeguards of freedom of the press, freedom of expression, and the right to organize dissenting political parties only underlines the confidence that the editors and community had in their status as American citizens. They were exercising their rights fully and openly, assuming stances missing in immigrant newspapers.

Conclusion

New York's *Pueblo Hispanos* stands at the radical end of a continuum of native Hispanic newspapers and periodicals. These publications demanded their readers' rights, not a process of earning acceptance. They urged political participation, while emphasizing the minority status of their readers and the injustices inherent in that status. There were Hispanic exile publications and immigrant publications during this period, but the most salient and permanent publishing legacy of the years from the 1880s to the 1940s was the development and expression of a native Hispanic viewpoint.

CHAPTER 17

Reading, Writing, and Resisting
African American Print Culture

James P. Danky
. . .

"The *Colored Citizen* continues to gain friends," Charles Hunter wrote encouragingly in April 1878 to the editor of the *Colored Citizen*, a four-month-old newspaper published in Fort Scott, Kansas, some 300 miles west of his home in St. Louis, Missouri. "Our mutual friend Emanuel Davis, the popular Morgan Street barber, says he can't keep shop without it. I am about to take a trip up the country in Illinois among the farmers, and as a great many of the colored people over there are anxious to learn all they can about Kansas and emigration, I shall present the Citizen to them as the means of obtaining the desired information."[1]

These few lines reveal much about African American print culture during the first decades following emancipation: the interconnectedness of black people on the frontier; the diffusion of printed information through community spaces where print matter was shared; and the value of the printed word as a source of "desired information" about emigration. The Fort Scott paper, and many others like it, provided a national black forum that informed politics, shaped organizations, and aroused public opinion around such issues as assimilation, emigration, and education.

The influence of the African American press is often acknowledged in the historical literature, but until recently, few publications had examined African American history from the perspective of the press, and there has been little curiosity about its readership.[2] Regional, religious, gender, generational, and class differences, which shaped and were shaped by racism and segregation, created a richly varied African American culture and an equally diverse black print culture. This chapter examines the attainment of mass literacy and the development of a vibrant print culture among African Americans in the seventy-five years following emancipation.

Today, little evidence remains of the 2,700 African American papers published between 1827 and 1950.[3] At its height, the power of the African American press was immense, though it was never the sole print source for black Americans. Many read white newspapers, and generations of black students studied Webster's blue-backed speller and *McGuffey's Reader*. For African American writers, however, gaining access to this dominant print culture was more difficult; the few who did so frequently had to depend on white-owned publishing houses for distribution. Publishing in black newspapers like the Fort Scott *Colored Citizen* and with black-owned publishing companies, such as the National Baptist Publishing Board, African American writers could better ensure that they communicated with their intended audience. The African American press offered a powerful counternarrative to the dominant press, providing shelter from white interference and the burdens of racial representation and oversimplification, allowing space to communicate the richness and complexity of African American life. "Those who would honestly seek to know the Negro must read his papers," wrote Robert Kerlin in 1919. "It is in them that the Negro speaks out with freedom, with sincerity, with justice to himself, for there he speaks as a Negro to Negroes, and he is aware that the white people do not so much as know of the existence of this paper."[4]

While an individual life cannot illustrate the entire history of African American print culture for the period 1880-1940, it is tempting to use W. E. B. Du Bois as such an example. Born in Great Barrington, Massachusetts, in 1868, just three years after Appomattox, he lived until 1963, the year of the great civil rights march on Washington. Beginning with his first published piece—a letter to the editor of T. Thomas Fortune's *New York Globe* in 1883—Du Bois helped to create African American print as author, editor, and publisher.[5] Education, especially reading, was his "ticket out of Railroad Street," the poor area of Great Barrington where his mother lived with her fatherless children because it was close to school.[6] Du Bois was the quintessential man of print. As an editor, a role that began with his high school paper and continued throughout his long life, print was never far from his mind. From the outset, he understood the interpretive and transformative power of the printed word. From his pen flowed a torrent of articles, books, essays, letters, edited works, and more—all aimed, specifically or generally, at achieving justice and racial equality. He earned a Ph.D. at Harvard (1895) and taught economics and history at Atlanta University from 1897 to 1910, when he became founder and editor of the *Crisis*, the journal of the nascent National Association for the Advancement of Colored People.

Du Bois's interests ranged widely. In the 1920s he supported the creation of *Brownie's Book*, a children's counterpoint to the *Crisis*; and in 1940 he promoted a new scholarly journal, *Phylon: The Atlanta University Review of Race and Culture*. The latter emerged from Du Bois's lifelong ambition to harness social science to the betterment of African American life. *Phylon* was an outgrowth of his work at Atlanta University Publications, where Du Bois had served as editor in the 1890s, and from similar efforts at Hampton and Tuskegee. These annual publications used the latest academic research to discuss themes such as health, religion, crime, and urban life. They addressed multiple audiences, not only showcasing black academic achievement but also presenting useful information that might improve the quality of daily life for black people. Amid global tumult, Du Bois, together with scholars like E. Franklin Frazier and poets like Langston Hughes, used print to enlighten and lead African Americans toward a new and better world. Without doubt, he was a giant.[7]

Yet no single voice within the black press ever unified all readers. A central theme of the African American press was its efforts to challenge white supremacy; but black writers, publishers, and readers approached this challenge in different ways. Forthright criticism, particularly regarding lynching, segregation, and sex, could be extremely dangerous. Authors' and editors' stances ranged from acquiescent to dissident. Rivalries emerged between competing black newspapers, religious bodies, educational institutions, and civil rights groups, suggesting the importance of the issues at stake. Emigration, education, assimilation, and black nationalism were but some of the concerns that fostered continuing debate.

What, then, is African American print culture? How did differences of region, class, generation, and gender affect print production and consumption among African Americans? How and in what ways was print produced and used differently among black and white Americans? How was African American print culture informed by the dissident culture that manifested itself in everyday conversation, jokes, stories, and folklore? These are some of the questions that animate the history of African American publishing and reading.

Beginnings

With the end of the Civil War in 1865, millions of former slaves struggled to secure the long-withheld fruits of their labor. Beyond access to land, education, and the courts, they sought literacy and ways to communicate through print. Even during the war, black soldiers had petitioned for regimental schools. Following the war, adults and children studied together in makeshift schools after a day's work in the fields. Ex-slaves used literacy to read the Bible, to scrutinize contracts with landlords, to write letters to the press and government, and to locate family members. Though former slaves welcomed the educational efforts of the Union army, the federal Freedmen's Bureau, and northern missionary societies, they were quick to organize their own schools staffed by black teachers.[8]

Literacy was the crucial foundation for African American print culture. A minority of the African American population was literate for most of the nineteenth century, but those who could read often read to those who could not, thus extending print to a larger audience. Shared reading at meetings, barbershops, work breaks, church socials, and similar informal gatherings provided critical community information, interpretation, and collective education for African Americans. The father of black history, Carter G. Woodson, recalled reading Virginia newspapers to his father in the 1890s, and later reading to groups of miners in West Virginia who, though they could not read, subscribed to black weeklies and northern dailies. All this had an impact. In 1860 only about 5 percent of African Americans could read. By 1880 literacy had risen to 30 percent and by 1920 to 77 percent.[9]

In much the same way, the rise of higher education facilitated print production by African Americans. In 1867 Howard University of Washington, D.C., was incorporated as part of the Freedmen's Bureau. The following year, Hampton Normal and Agricultural Institute opened in Virginia. Hampton and its Alabama protégé, the Tuskegee Institute, became nationally recognized models of industrial education, a curriculum that trained students in hygiene, "practical morals," and hard work. Although both institutions were primarily concerned with training teachers, many students came to learn skilled trades. These schools were sharply criticized by later African American leaders who favored a classical curriculum such as was taught at Howard, Fisk, and Atlanta Universities. Among the eighty-five black colleges founded between 1865 and 1885, industrial education, which afforded some valuable opportunities for training in printing, was the dominant model.[10]

Still, even the best-trained black graduates found it nearly impossible to obtain work in the printing trades. Lewis Henry Douglass, a son of Frederick Douglass, had learned printing in the office of his father's paper, the *North Star*, before enlisting in the Union army. In 1866, the same year that he served on a prestigious black delegation charged with interviewing President Andrew Johnson, Lewis was refused employment as a printer because of his race. After relocating to Colorado, he was denied union membership because he was a "colored man." Back in Washington, he obtained work as a compositor for the Government Printing Office but was again blocked from membership in the union local. In his address "We Are Not Yet Quite Free," Frederick Douglass spoke passionately of his son's crushing dilemma of being "denounced for not being a member of a Printer's Union by the very men who would not permit him to join such [a] union."[11]

Religious publishing remained the most established, stable, and prolific venue for aspiring printers and publishers following the Civil War. The Bible was the most commonly read book throughout the nineteenth century. It was distributed to African Americans by white organizations like the American Bible Society and by black religious groups. Likewise, hymnals and spiritual guides were the most common pamphlets. Some of the earliest black-owned book publishing companies were founded in the Northeast and affiliated with the African Methodist Episcopal Church. Toward the end of the nineteenth century, the hub of the black religious publishing industry shifted southward. By 1896 Nashville was headquarters to the A.M.E. Sunday School Union and Publishing House and the National Baptist Publishing Board. The latter allowed African Americans to develop their own Sunday School literature, because the white American Baptist Publication society refused to accept material from black authors. Within its first two years, under the direction of the Reverend R. H. Boyd of San Antonio, the house organized its own printing shop with modern equipment and an editorial staff overseeing several Sunday School periodicals. As with other religious publishers, independence from white creditors, philanthropists, and printers allowed the National Baptist Publishing Board to produce important secular works in addition to religious texts. By its second decade, the board was publishing works on theology, parliamentary procedure, denominational histories, law commentaries, comic poetry, and science.[12]

Outside the religious sphere, it remained extremely difficult for black writers to gain access to publishing, particularly for books. One notable exception was George Washington Williams, whose two-volume *History of the Negro Race from 1619–1880* was published by G. P. Putnam in New York in 1883. Born in 1849 in Pennsylvania, Williams lived a life of adventure and accomplishment as a Union soldier, pastor, attorney, judge advocate, state representative, newspaper publisher, editor, and public speaker. The man whom Du Bois called "the greatest historian of the race"[13] passed away at the age of forty-one during his investigation and exposé of racial exploitation in the Belgian Congo.

African American elocutionists, many of whom were women, played a central role in bringing literature, national political debates, and inspiration for social change to a mass black audience during Reconstruction. One of the first was prolific author and eloquent speaker Frances Ellen Watkins Harper. Born to free parents in Maryland in 1825, she published her first collection of verse in 1845. Her novel *Iola Leroy* (1892) was probably the best-selling novel by a black author in the nineteenth century. A speaker on the northern abolition circuit before the Civil War, Harper afterward traveled and lectured throughout the South. Other prominent black elocutionists included Hallie Quinn Brown, Ednorah Nahar, Alice Franklin, and Henrietta Vinton Davis. Davis made her debut on the public stage in 1883, reciting Shakespeare in Washington, D.C. She toured the nation with her own theater company and became the most famous African American actress of the nineteenth century.[14]

If it was difficult for African American authors to gain access to white publishers, it was nearly impossible for African American publishers to acquire contracts with popular white authors or to enter the mainstream of print distribution. An exception was William Henry Lee, cofounder of the Chicago publishing company Laird & Lee, who refused to respond to allegations that he was of "mixed blood." He made a small fortune in the book trade, publishing a novel by Émile Zola and William T. Stead's *If Christ Came to Chicago*.[15]

More often than books, however, it was newspapers that provided outlets for black writers and editors. Consider the brothers William and James Eagleson, editors of the *Fort Scott Colored Citizen*, and their entry into careers in printing. William had learned the newspaper trade working as a printer's devil in Tennessee at the end of the Civil War. In a small shop, this could include setting the type, operating and cleaning the press, sweeping up, and running errands. In the early 1870s, William moved with his family to Missouri, tried farming, quickly grew frustrated, and decided to try the real estate business in Fort Scott.[16] Instead, in January 1878, with an old press, an assortment of secondhand type, and the help of his brother, he published the first weekly issue of the *Colored Citizen*.[17]

The front page of the *Citizen*, like most papers of its day, was largely filled with advertising—for rail travel and patent medicines, local dry goods stores and land agents, as well as laundry, blacksmith, and attorney services. Though a few of these businesses were black-owned, the majority were not. As Julius Thompson notes, the black press depended on advertising dollars from outside the black community, and this impeded its efforts to get black views "published and distributed to the world."[18]

Half of the typical four-page weekly African American paper was "boilerplate," printed with stereotyped plates subsidized by advertisers. These pages carried national and regional news, serialized stories and poetry, and didactic information on farming and housekeeping, all written, presumably, by white authors. Papers also ran home health remedies, simple recipes, and science columns that described earthquakes one week and kangaroos the next. In addition to this mass-produced fare, the editors of the *Colored Citizen* contributed their own wit and wisdom on all manner of topics, from preventing fence post rot to personal behavior and etiquette.[19]

The *Colored Citizen* directed much of its advice to African Americans who wanted to escape southern sharecropping, deepening indebtedness, Jim Crow laws, and the Ku Klux Klan. The editorial pages of the *Citizen* from the summers of 1878 and 1879 provide a window on African American print consumption and readers' reciprocal influence on print culture. Subscription orders and letters flowed in from across the nation. So many letters arrived from "our colored friends throughout the southern states" that the paper responded with a series of instructive articles, beginning with "Where to Locate—Where Good Homes Can be Purchased for a Trifle, Surrounded by Thriving Towns and Larger Cities—Come to Southern Kansas." Specific instructions on where to buy land (listing counties along the railroad lines) and explanations of land purchasing plans and credit followed.[20] A southern exodus was beginning, and print played a crucial communications role.

As with white newspapers, African American newspapers of the late nineteenth century were generally short-lived. One notable exception is the *Christian Recorder*, which began publication in 1852 and is still published today. The *Colored Citizen*, more typical of black periodicals, lasted only a few years, publishing its last issue on 10 January 1880. The paper had burned bright and hot in its brief existence, providing both the tools for making a new life and a forum for protest and resistance against segregation and disenfranchisement.[21]

Like the *Colored Citizen* many newspapers announced their racial identity: the *Colored Visitor* (Logansport, Indiana), the *Afro-American Advance* (Minneapolis and St. Paul, Minnesota), and the *Negro American* (Birmingham, Alabama). By the early twentieth century, most states had African American newspapers, though many existed only briefly. Those published in big cities like New York, Chicago, and Los Angeles served a growing urban black population, but towns and smaller cities also had black-oriented papers, as in Nicodemus, Kansas (*Nicodemus Cyclone*), Kankakee, Illinois (*Progressive Era*), and Bookertee, Oklahoma (*Bookertee Searchlight*).

Advertising and subscriptions were the primary source of revenue for newspapers during this era, but many papers also relied on external support from religious organizations and emerging civil rights organizations. Booker T. Washington's influence and patronage created a deep division within the black press. Critics accused papers subsidized by the "Tuskegee Machine" of conceding to Washington's stance of accommodation and his brand of industrial education. One noted competitor who became a casualty was J. Max Barber, editor of the weekly *Voice of the Negro of Atlanta* (1904–5), who frequently criticized the Wizard of Tuskegee. Washington chased off Barber's advertisers and pressured his publishers to remove him as editor, forcing him into a career in dentistry.[22]

T. Thomas Fortune, the North's most prominent "race man," whose *New York Age* (1887–1960) presaged the more radical *Chicago Defender* and *Pittsburgh Courier*, managed to obtain Washington's support while maintaining his editorial independence. After attending a Freedmen's Bureau school in Florida and studying briefly at Howard University, Fortune moved to Jacksonville where he learned the printing trade. His newspaper career began in Washington where he was employed by a black newspaper, the *People's Advocate*. In 1879 he moved to New York City and became a partner in *Rumor*, a weekly tabloid. Fortune's commitment to full political, economic, and social equality for African Americans strongly shaped his paper, variously titled the *Globe* (1882–84), the *New York Freeman* (1884–87), and finally the *New York Age*.[23]

Fortune also collaborated with other turn-of-the-century activists, including Memphis newspaper publisher and editor Ida B. Wells-Barnett. Wells-Barnett began her journalism career at age twenty-five when she became part owner and editor of a secular paper, the Memphis weekly *Free Speech*.[24] In the first year, she increased the number of subscribers from 1,500 to 4,000 by canvassing the Delta for new subscribers. Writing as "Iola," she published editorials condemning the dismal conditions of colored schools and denouncing lynching, which became her lifetime crusade. When, in 1892, whites murdered three black co-owners of a successful grocery store, Wells-Barnett attacked the rationale for lynch law—the "old thread-bare lie that Negro men assault White women." In response, a mob ransacked the *Free Speech* offices. Wells-Barnett, who was in Philadelphia at the time, was unable to return to Memphis; but she capitalized on her temporary exile by working with Fortune and his partner Jerome B. Peterson to expose the false pretenses of "lynch law" in the columns of the *New York Age*. The following year she coauthored a pamphlet, *The Reason Why the Colored American Is Not in the World's Columbian Exposition*. It celebrated the accomplishments of African Americans and castigated white Americans for "barbarism and race hate."[25] Ida Wells-Barnett settled in Chicago, where she continued her distinguished career in journalism and social reform.

The "New Negro" and the Efflorescence of African American Print Culture

On 21 January 1896, in the wake of Booker T. Washington's Atlanta Exposition address, and just four months before the Supreme Court upheld racial segregation in *Plessy v. Ferguson*, John M. Henderson presented a paper on education entitled "The New Negro" to the Bethel Literary Association of Washington, D.C. The term had appeared several months earlier in a *Cleveland Gazette* editorial to describe black men and women of "education, refinement and money." In 1900 Fannie Barrier Williams, Booker T. Washington, and N. B. Woods coedited *The New Negro for a New Century: An Accurate and Up-to-Date Record of the Upward Struggles of the Negro Race*, a richly illustrated record of the accomplishments of black people in their first generation of freedom.[26]

The final years of the nineteenth century and the first decades of the twentieth, however, were dark years for African Americans. Lynching peaked in the 1890s, when the number of documented cases often surpassed 100 annually.

Mass lynchings, or "race riots," claimed hundreds of African American lives, from the massacre in Wilmington, North Carolina (1898), through the destruction of African American neighborhoods in Tulsa, Oklahoma (1921). Such extralegal violence was but the popular expression of strengthened legal, institutionalized, racial exploitation and discrimination. After *Plessy v. Ferguson* (1896), increasingly elaborate codes of racial segregation in transportation, schools, hospitals, parks, and even cemeteries became fixed in law. Similar racial strictures also prevailed by custom in many northern states. Social separation belied the economic interdependence of whites and blacks. Low-wage African American agricultural and domestic labor was essential to the southern (and national) economic structure; both labor unions and employers systematically excluded African Americans from skilled jobs. Compounding these economic hardships, by 1908 the ex-Confederate states had disenfranchised almost all black voters through literacy tests, poll taxes, and the all-white primary. As if the devastation of Reconstruction had not been convincing enough, the outrageous theories of white supremacy propounded by scientists such as Charles B. Davenport of New York and sociologist Edward A. Ross of the University of Wisconsin were powerful evidence for African Americans that in order to achieve political, cultural, and social self-determination, literacy alone would not suffice.

Thus, during this period of unprecedented need, when northern whites joined ex-Confederates in embracing new "scientific proofs" of black racial inferiority, African American print culture blossomed and flourished. Skilled printers trained at black colleges and a few high schools such as Armstrong Manual Training School in Washington, D.C., armed with newly acquired equipment, helped to provide unprecedented access to print. The number of African Americans whose primary occupation was bookbinding rose from 66 in 1890 and 86 in 1900 to 278 in 1910. An astonishing 43 percent of these bookbinders were women. Among "printers" and "lithographers," 2,244 African Americans were employed in 1910, up from 944 in 1890. Union discrimination against black workers continued to limit access to these occupations; many African Americans involved with print held additional jobs, in or out of the printing trades. It was not uncommon for one person to serve as publisher, editor, and typesetter. Publishing was closely intertwined with printing for many African Americans, given their precarious economic prospects. Alliances with the Republican Party in some places, however, provided subsidies to blacks in the form of contract printing, ads for candidates, or the publication of campaign newspapers.[27]

With the dawn of the twentieth century, publishing became a more profitable and efficient business. Improvements in printing technology permitted better text and graphics at lower cost, which in turn meant that more readers could be reached with every dollar spent. Founding a newspaper was still a risky business, but after 1900 more African Americans were able to enter the printing trades. It was imperative that black people mount their own defense and tell their own stories. To do this required, ideally, that they gain control at every stage: writing, printing, shipping, selling, reading, and responding. Through African American print culture, black readers and writers confronted spurious race science, social Darwinism, racial stereotyping, and the continual linkage of "Negro" with "Problem" in the progressive white press.

"To aid, by publications, vindication of the race from vicious assaults" was one of five foundational articles set forth by the American Negro Academy, one of the first national black cultural associations. At their first meeting in 1897, participants discussed the need to respond to and refute racist scholarship in print. The academy published several of its papers and one book, *The Negro in American History*, a text written by the organization's founder, the Reverend Alexander Crummell.[28] It was a good beginning, and more soon followed.

After earning a Ph.D. from Harvard in 1912, Carter G. Woodson founded a constellation of African American cultural institutions, including the Association for the Study of Negro Life and History (1915), the *Journal of Negro History* (1916), and Associated Publishers, incorporated in 1921. He also produced specialized pamphlets such as *152 Important Events and Dates in Negro History* as a means of reaching a nonacademic African American audience. Reaching this broader audience required personal commitment, start-up capital, and subsidies to keep the presses rolling. Woodson acquired a loan from an insurance company to pay for the publication of his first book, borrowed against his own life insurance policy to pay printing costs for the first issue of the *Journal of Negro History*, won grants from the Carnegie and the Rockefeller foundations to subsidize research, and sought funds from the General Education Board to hire a field worker to sell books and subscriptions to the *Negro History Bulletin* door to door. The poet-critic Sterling Brown (1901–89) declared that Woodson, "probably more than any other single figure, has encouraged a Negro audience to buy books by Negroes about Negro life and history."[29]

Although developed by the North Carolina Mutual Provident Association to supplement and support sales of life insurance, the *Durham Negro Observer* targeted a broad audience with a variety of issues. Its maiden issue appeared in June 1903. Editor Irwin Buchanan was blunt in stating the paper's mission: "We scan papers of other races and find we can't get honorable mention unless we play leading roles as 'chicken thief', 'rapist', 'murderer', 'bad nigger'. We read too much about the dark side. . . . We have come to let you know that there is hope."[30] Through the *Observer*, and later the *Weekly Review* and the *Whetstone*, the leaders of North Carolina Mutual utilized print for communicating with their employees and policyholders. Beyond building their own business, these publications encouraged black self-improvement, especially through developing institutions such as churches and community groups.[31]

As the black middle class emerged, the number of professional associations that issued their own publications increased. The funeral industry, for example, produced the *Colored Embalmer* (Chicago, 1927-32), and the *Progressive Negro Funeral Director* (Atlanta, 1939-?). Teachers, like many other black professionals, were excluded from both white schools and white teachers' associations, so they formed their own groups and founded their own publications, such as the *Colored Teacher* (Wilberforce, Ohio, 1916-?), the *Texas Standard* (Teachers State Association of Texas, 1927-?), and the *Explorer* (Pennsylvania Association of Teachers of Colored Children, 1939-?). Similar developments in the fields of law and medicine further emphasized the ties between individual advancement and community responsibility.

African American women's struggles assumed unprecedented visibility in the years 1890-1920. Many black intellectuals labeled this period "the Woman's Era." Nonetheless, despite higher living standards and a more comfortable niche than those black women who labored as sharecroppers or domestics, middle-class black women activists lacked the security enjoyed by white middle-class women. Black women had a long, hard row to hoe, and they knew it. Public figures such as Nannie H. Boroughs, Anna J. Cooper, Mary Church Terrell, and Fannie Barrier Williams used the press tirelessly to push for social change and racial justice.[32]

Women were at the forefront of the 1901 National Baptist campaign, which vowed to "provide literature capable of keeping the identity and increasing the pride of the rising generation or they must be entirely overshadowed by the dominant race of this country." Between 1900 and 1903, more than 13 million copies of pamphlets and booklets were put into circulation. In the next decade, the million-member Woman's Convention of the National Baptists produced a wealth of tract literature intended to cultivate self-respect, cleanliness, hard work, sexual purity, and piety. The pamphlets bore straightforward titles: *Ten Things the Negro Needs*, *Take a Bath First*, *Anti-Hanging Out Committee*, and *How to Get Rid of Bed Bugs*.[33]

An explosion of black magazines also provided new venues for women writers and editors. Advanced print technology and cheaper postage rates fueled a four-fold jump in the number of periodicals, which increased nationwide from 700 to 3,300 between 1865 and 1885. At the turn of the century, churches, clubs, and civil rights groups sponsored many African American periodicals, particularly those with substantial circulation. The *A.M.E. Church Review* (revived in 1884) and the *National Baptist Union Review* (1899), for example, are still in print. In 1894 Josephine St. Pierre Ruffin and her daughter Florida founded the *Women's Era*, which was essential in organizing the National Association of Colored Women (NACW). In 1897 the more conservative *National Association Notes*, edited by Margaret Murray Washington, became the official organ of the NACW. A reputation for radicalism appeared to enhance the circulation of the *Colored American Magazine* (1900-9), edited by Pauline Hopkins, and *Voice of the Negro* (1904-7) edited by J. Max Barber, each with a circulation of 15,000 copies. Despite these more assertive voices, protest in black periodicals was usually implicit, combating racial inferiority through celebration of black middle-class achievements. College and higher education, for example, were staple subjects of debate, while discussion of the terrible condition of black elementary and secondary education—dilapidated buildings, overcrowding, unequal tax support, and a lack of high schools—hardly ever appeared.[34]

New civil rights organizations were also important producers of African American print culture. The National Association for the Advancement of Colored People (NAACP) was founded in 1910, followed by the National Urban League in 1911. Under the direction of Du Bois and the literary editorship of Jessie Fauset, the NAACP journal the *Crisis: A Journal of the Darker Races* reached a circulation of approximately 100,000 by 1919. The NAACP also published a variety of books, ranging from *A Child's Story of Dunbar* (1913) to *Thirty Years of Lynching* (1919). The National Urban League began publishing *Opportunity* in 1923 and four years later issued its first book, *Ebony and Topaz*, an anthology edited by Charles S. Johnson.

Academic publishers were another small but important group of black print institutions. Drawing on conference presentations from 1896 through 1918, Atlanta University Publications issued a collection of influential monographs including *The Negro Artisan*, *The College-Bred Negro*, and *The Negro in Business*. *The Negro Yearbook*, published from 1912 to 1952 at the Tuskegee Institute, covered various facets of the African American experience: sports, music, fraternal organizations, Pan-Africanism, and lynching. The first volume, priced at twenty-five cents, sold out immediately. *The Yearbook* was so successful that within its first three years, it doubled in size and tripled the number of copies printed.[35]

Mass distribution was a major obstacle for black publishers. Sutton E. Griggs, a prolific novelist and publisher who sought to unite and inspire the masses of black people, sold his books door to door, on the campuses of black schools, and to workers on their lunch breaks. Griggs later founded Orion Publishing Company in Nashville, through which he published four novels: *Overshadowed* (1901), *Unfettered* (1902), *The Hindered Hand* (1905), and *Pointing the Way* (1908). "Though virtually unknown to White American readers," writes literary scholar Hugh Gloster, "[Griggs's] novels were probably more popular among the rank and file of Negroes than the fiction of Chesnutt and Dunbar."[36]

Depressed agricultural conditions and racial tensions in the South at the onset of the Great War (1914) pushed many African Americans northward, beginning what came to be called the Great Migration. The rise and reach of northern black newspapers also helped to fuel this demographic shift, touting job opportunities and the blessings of a new life in industrial cities above the Mason-Dixon line. Central among these papers was the *Chicago Defender*, which, except for the Bible, was probably the most influential publication in Afro-America. Founded in 1905 by Robert S. Abbott, the *Defender* gained power through its aggressive stance in combating racism. Like so many other publishers, Abbott learned the printing trade at the Hampton Institute. Barred from a legal career by racial discrimination, he began publishing the newspaper out of his home, selling it door to door. Within a few years, the *Defender* editors recruited railroad porters to bring them out-of-town papers, and, in turn, to distribute the *Defender* nationwide (see figures 17.1, 17.2).[37]

Targeting the "masses" rather than the New Negro "classes," the *Defender* quickly distinguished itself from other African American papers of the time, and it became the main source of printed information about the North (and especially Chicago) for most African Americans living in the South. Thousands of people wrote to the *Defender* asking about jobs, housing, and societal conditions in Chicago and other cities in the Midwest. Some simply expressed a longing to escape their lives in the South: "Dear Sir: I thought you might help me in Some way either personally or through your influence, is why I am worrying you for which I beg pardon. . . . My greatest desire is to leave for a better place but am unable to raise the money. I can write short stories all of which potray [sic] negro characters . . . can also write poems . . . these things will never profit me anything here in Natchez. Kindly let me hear from you. . . ."[38] The *Defender* responded by posting job opportunities, providing information about train schedules, and even organizing clubs to ease the transition to urban life.[39]

True, the *Defender* also attracted its mass audience with a steady stream of lurid stories about corruption, scandal, vice, gambling, and other crimes. It offered more than mere sensationalism, however. Abbott serialized Carter G. Woodson's *The Negro in Our History* and Charles Chestnutt's *The House behind the Cedars*,[40] and the paper's editorials resonated powerfully with its readers when attacking racial segregation and lynching—topics that were rarely covered by black-operated papers in the South. Exemplifying the *Defender*'s style was Abbott's famed editorial "When the Mob Comes and You Must Die, Take at Least One with You." Such fiery pronouncements did not endear the *Defender* to whites in either the South or the North. Its critics sometimes accused the

FIGURE 17.1. Flora Sengstack, mother of Robert S. Abbott, who founded the *Chicago Defender* in 1905, holds one of the first newspapers printed in 1921. The *Defender* moved in 1920 into a former Jewish synagogue on Chicago's South Side. Courtesy of the *Chicago Defender*.

FIGURE 17.2. A newsboy hawks the *Chicago Defender*, 1942. Photograph by Jack Delano, Prints & Photographs Division, FSA/OWI Collection, Library of Congress (LC-USF34-9058C).

paper of "rabble rousing" or "inciting to violence." The *Defender* was repeatedly censored and banned in the South. But the most outspoken and courageous black newspaper editors intended not only to inform and galvanize their readers; their mission was to create a record for posterity, to resist the erasure of black memory from American history. So successful was its mix of yellow journalism, self-help, and racial pride that by 1920 the *Defender* was the best-selling African American newspaper in the nation. Thanks in large part to the railroad porters, two-thirds of its 280,000-plus issues circulated outside Chicago.[41]

Struggles in the Promised Land: Beyond World War I and the Northern Migration

World War I marked a major change in the lives of all Americans and particularly for African Americans. In search of new opportunities, many migrated from the rural South in search of jobs in the industrializing North or military service. Wartime mobilization drew 500,000 black southerners to northern cities in search of higher-paying work and greater personal freedom. Editors of northern black newspapers responded to wartime propaganda stressing democracy and freedom by noting the irony that the black community lacked equity before the law. In response to President Wilson's declaration that the "world must be made safe for democracy," the *Cincinnati Union* changed its banner to "While making the world Safe for Democracy, why not make the U.S. Safe from Lynching, Disfranchisement, [and] 'Jim Crow Cars'?" The private reaction of one government censor was to lament that "these colored editors have a certain talent for spreading a seditious feeling without uttering anything actually seditious." He singled out New York's *Amsterdam News* as having "a peculiar talent for saying the most fervently patriotic things in the most unpatriotic manner."[42] More than 400,000 African Americans served in the racially segregated U.S. Army, and when they returned home, these veterans expected to enjoy the benefits of democracy.

Marcus Garvey (1887–1940), who arrived in the United States in 1916, having been encouraged by Booker T. Washington to undertake a lecture tour to raise funds for a school in Jamaica modeled on Tuskegee Institute, soon discerned a role for himself in promoting black racial pride and dignity. Garvey was born in Jamaica, where he had trained as a printer and worked for a time at the government printing office. His real goals, however, were to become a public activist through journalism and oratory. He arrived in the United States after spending time in London, where he had discovered and read Booker T. Washington's memoir, *Up From Slavery*, and in Jamaica, where he established the Universal Negro Improvement Association (UNIA) in 1914. Attempting to establish him-

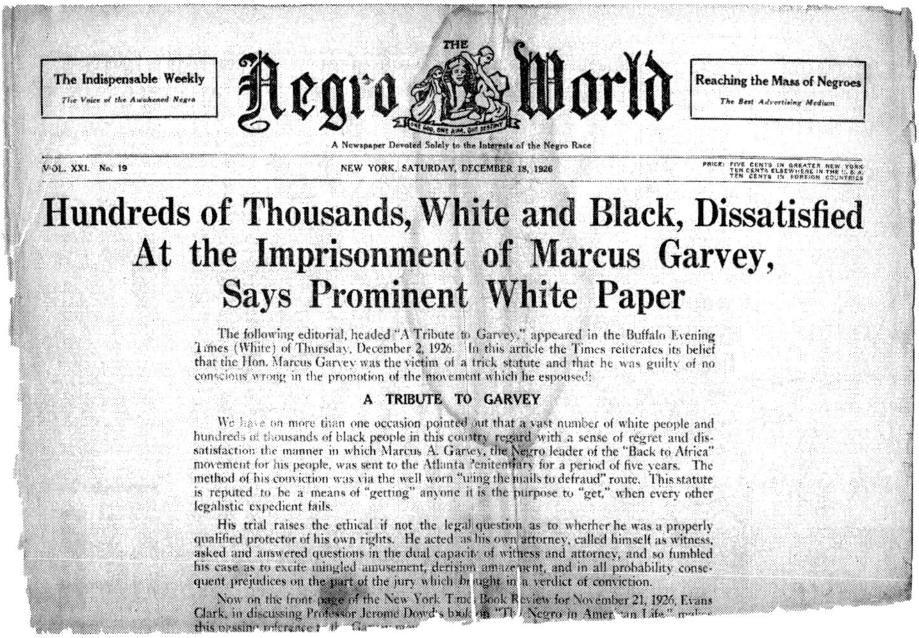

The Indispensable Weekly
The Voice of the Awakened Negro

THE
Negro World

Reaching the Mass of Negroes
The Best Advertising Medium

A Newspaper Devoted Solely to the Interests of the Negro Race

VOL. XXI. No. 19 NEW YORK, SATURDAY, DECEMBER 18, 1926

Hundreds of Thousands, White and Black, Dissatisfied At the Imprisonment of Marcus Garvey, Says Prominent White Paper

The following editorial, headed "A Tribute to Garvey," appeared in the Buffalo Evening Times (White) of Thursday, December 2, 1926. In this article the Times reiterates its belief that the Hon. Marcus Garvey was the victim of a trick statute and that he was guilty of no conscious wrong in the promotion of the movement which he espoused:

A TRIBUTE TO GARVEY

We have on more than one occasion pointed out that a vast number of white people and hundreds of thousands of black people in this country regard with a sense of regret and dissatisfaction the manner in which Marcus A. Garvey, the Negro leader of the "Back to Africa" movement for his people, was sent to the Atlanta Penitentiary for a period of five years. The method of his conviction was via the well worn "using the mails to defraud" route. This statute is reputed to be a means of "getting" anyone it is the purpose to "get," when every other legalistic expedient fails.

His trial raises the ethical if not the legal question as to whether he was a properly qualified protector of his own rights. He acted as his own attorney, called himself as witness, asked and answered questions in the dual capacity of witness and attorney, and so fumbled his case as to excite mingled amusement, derision amazement, and in all probability consequent prejudices on the part of the jury which brought in a verdict of conviction.

Now on the front page of the New York Times Book Review for November 21, 1926, Evans Clark, in discussing Professor Jerome Dowd's book on "The Negro in American Life" ...

FIGURE 17.3. *Negro World* 21, no. 19 (18 December 1926). Thomas Harvey Papers, Manuscript, Archives, and Rare Book Library, Emory University.

self in the United States during the upheaval of the Great War, Garvey founded a branch of UNIA and preached racial pride and dignity from Lafayette Hall in Harlem and other venues. He also began publishing the *Negro World* (1918–33), the UNIA paper (figure 17.3).

Rather than providing prescriptions for Victorian respectability, Garvey's *Negro World* lauded the historic splendor of African civilizations and the possibility of economic strength through pan-African unity. Sections printed in Spanish and French were introduced in 1923 and 1924, and the page, "Our Women and What They Think" edited by Amy Jacques Garvey, appeared from 1924 to 1927. By various means, the paper was distributed all over the world. A generation later, Kenya's first president, Jomo Kenyatta, noted its impact, recalling how "in 1921, Kenya nationalists, unable to read, would gather around Garvey's newspaper, the *Negro World*, and listen to an article two or three times. Then they would run various ways through the forest, careful to repeat the whole, which they had memorized, to Africans hungry for some doctrines which lifted themselves from the servile consciousness in which Africans lived." In 1923 T. Thomas Fortune took over as editor, holding that position until his death in 1927. At its height, the circulation of *Negro World* reached 200,000 a week.[43]

Not all black papers achieved such popularity. The impact of Cyril Valentine Briggs's *Crusader*, for example, cannot compare with Abbott's *Chicago Defender* or Garvey's *Negro World*. But as Frederick Detweiler primly observed in 1922, the *Crusader*, a radical New York weekly founded in 1918, had become the leading publication among a "small group of Negro magazines in New York making an impression quite out of proportion to their numbers . . . [and which] looks from its safe distance on Russia with pleasure and even mentions socialism rather approvingly." Postal inspectors were much less tolerant of Briggs's politics, summarized by his editorial declaration, "If to fight for one's rights is to be Bolshevist, then we are Bolshevists and let them make the most of it!" They repeatedly detained copies of the *Crusader* sent through the mail. Detweiler, for his part, was troubled by the *Crusader*'s espousal of working-class unity in tandem with black nationalism, and indeed, Briggs was purged from the Communist Party in 1941 for his "Negro nationalist way of thinking." Briggs never represented a majority position among African Americans, but his revolutionary vision of economic equality and racial nationalism seemed prophetic to activists of the 1960s such as Robert F. Williams, who appropriated the title *Crusader* for the weekly newsletter of his radical NAACP chapter in Monroe, North Carolina.[44]

Although the Harlem Renaissance is the best-known African American literary movement in American history, its reputation overestimates its impact among African Americans. White publishers, not black, issued the fifty or sixty novels produced during the Renaissance, marketing them mainly to a white audience, obscuring the continuing utility and vitality of black-controlled publications to African Americans. White control of production deeply frustrated many writers of the Renaissance. Langston Hughes detested the cover of his first book, *Weary Blues* (1926), which depicted a grotesque caricature of a black man. Lawrence Reddick later took Hughes to task for the "disgraceful" cover of *Shakespeare in Harlem*, published by Alfred Knopf, which depicted an outstretched hand holding a wishing bone "and the inevitable dice cubes." Reddick also skewered Harper & Brothers' blurb for Arna Bontemps' *Golden Slippers: An Anthology of Negro Poetry for Young Readers*, in which the publisher had gushed, "the genius of the Negro spirit—gay, childlike, with its note of smiling melancholy—is captured in these lyrics." That, Reddick, retorted, sounded like "twaddle" from some "sociologist at the University of Mississippi."[45]

By the 1930s, as never before, African American authors, publishers, scholars, and intellectuals refused to dine on scraps and crumbs from the white folks' table. The *Journal of Negro Education* (1932–present) and the *Quarterly Review of Higher Education among Negroes* (1933–69) introduced vital public forums for discussion and criticism of the dominant press and white-produced printed material. Scholars assessed the derogatory racial attitudes reflected in college textbooks, surveyed recent literature on the Negro, and reviewed children's literature dealing with African American life. Studies published in these periodicals pointedly questioned the assumptions of white supremacy diffused in everyday print, pointing out how history textbooks justified slavery, condemned the "excesses" of Reconstruction, and generally sympathized with "the unhappy fate of the White folk."[46]

During the Depression, many poor, young African American men wrote and produced their own publications as they labored within the camps established by the Civilian Conservation Corps, created in 1933 as part of President Roosevelt's New Deal. Although the majority of the editors were white, the staff of the newspapers produced in these racially segregated camps was black.[47] The 134 surviving black camp newsletters bear titles that reflect black culture at the time, such as the *Dunbarite* of Vandalia, Ohio, commemorating the literary figure Paul Lawrence Dunbar, and, *Hi-De-Hi-De-Ho* of Anderson, South Carolina, evoking a hit from Cab Calloway's band. As the addresses of their newsletters indicate—for example, the *Oil Rambler* of Smackover, Arkansas; the *Vesuvius Lake Ledger* of Pedro, Ohio; and the *Monthly Yuccan* of Kaweah, California— some African American volunteers in the Civilian Conservation Corps found themselves transported to rural work sites distant from their homes.[48] In the pages of such publications, young African Americans—far from home, sometimes feeling friendless and lonely—used print to give expression to their lives and to leave their mark on history.

The decade of the 1940s marked an apex of black print culture not seen again until the Black Arts Movement of the 1960s. Yet, by the advent of World War II the dialectic of decline was already quietly at work. Marcus Garvey's dynamic career had ended badly. In 1925 he had been convicted of mail fraud; two years later, his sentence commuted by President Coolidge, he left the United States for good. In May 1940, convalescing from a stroke that had left him paralyzed on one side, sixty-year-old Garvey was shocked to read a headline in the Chicago *Defender*: "Marcus Garvey Dies in London, Lost Wealth and Prestige before Death," followed by a two-page laundry list of Garvey's failures. A few weeks later, after several days spent reading his own obituaries and the flood of condolence telegrams that arrived at his home, the founder of the largest mass movement of African Americans collapsed and died.[49]

Garvey's passing presaged the end of an era. Television and the civil rights movement would transform the world of black print. Over the past sixty years, the demographic foundation of African American life had also changed dramatically. In 1880 Africans Americans were concentrated in the southern states, and they were a people new to the world of print as readers as well as producers.

By 1940, thanks to the Great Migration that the Chicago *Defender* did so much to promote, there was an important black presence in nearly every state of the union. This growth and shift in black demography dramatically transformed major cities like New York, Chicago, Pittsburgh, Detroit, and St. Louis. Black workers had become a major component of America's industrial work force and of labor unions in every sector.

Black Americans created a rich, vibrant print culture. Black newspapers recorded the details of daily life; and black poets and playwrights wrought meaning from five centuries of struggle and achievement. Perhaps most important, African Americans in every walk of life used the printed word to inform and enrich their lives and to determine their destinies in new ways.

CHAPTER 18

An Outpouring of "Faithful" Words
Protestant Publishing in the United States

William Vance Trollinger Jr.

. . .

Central to Protestant doctrine is the conviction that religious authority rests in Scripture alone. "Sola Scriptura" notwithstanding, Protestantism was and is more than simply a religion of the Word. It is a religion of many words, those that are preached, prayed, sung, and — of special interest to this volume — words that are printed. Nowhere have more Protestant words been printed than in the United States. Optimistically evangelical, American Protestants have relied upon the written word to convert people, to inspire individuals to higher callings, and to effect moral behavior. From their first settlements, Protestants poured forth a stream of religious publications. Between 1880 and 1940, they inundated the American landscape with Bibles, hymnals, tracts, Sunday School lessons, novels, and nonfiction books.

Despite this deluge, the historiography of Protestant printing is quite limited. In 1963 Martin E. Marty lamented that a "sustained analysis of the religious press in America has long been overdue," especially that of the Protestant press, which, despite its prodigious output, was "invisible" to scholars.[1] This chapter seeks to give the subject more visibility by providing a general picture of Protestant publishing in the United States between 1880 and 1940 and by suggesting some key themes. Understanding the history of the book in these years requires careful analysis of Protestant publishing. This essay offers a simple but consistently overlooked conclusion: including the religious press in the history of American print culture dramatically changes the landscape.

The Protestant Establishment

American Protestantism's cultural hegemony was increasingly challenged between 1880 and 1940. This is not to say that "mainline" Protestants lost their cultural clout; as William Hutchison has noted, the influence of the Protestant establishment lasted into the late twentieth century.[2] Nevertheless, these seven decades mark America's substantial transformation from a Protestant nation to a religiously diverse nation. This shift largely reflects the massive immigration of Catholics, Eastern Orthodox, and Jews from southern and eastern Europe to the United States in the late nineteenth and early twentieth centuries. Darwinism, historical biblical criticism, and other intellectual challenges also threatened the foundations of Protestant orthodoxy. Accelerating urbanization exacerbated the process, contributing to Protestants' belief that traditional moral standards were eroding.[3]

In the first half of the nineteenth century, several Protestant publications in eastern coastal cities had operated as daily papers, providing both religious and nonreligious news. As the secular press expanded in the second half of the nineteenth century, however, the Protestant press retreated from the news field. By the end of the nineteenth century, the typical Protestant periodical was a weekly or monthly magazine produced by a particular denomination or denominational subgroup, focusing on issues relevant to the group. This "denominationalization" process accelerated in the first half of the twentieth century.[4]

In 1963 Martin E. Marty argued that the Protestant press had failed "to cope with [the] pluralism and secularity" of twentieth-century America, the unfortunate result being an array of magazines that limited themselves to the "self-nurture of a [specific] denomination."[5] Marty's point is well taken, but we should not discount the importance of Protestant denominational publishing. As Marty and other historians of American religion have observed, denominations — self-supporting religious organizations that were neither established churches nor dissenting sects, and that were equal competitors under the law — are unique to American Protestantism.[6] Although some observers argue that a postdenominational age began in the late twentieth century, denominations were undoubtedly the organizational structure for American Protestantism between 1880 and 1940, and they were a critical locus of identity for American Protestants. Weekly and monthly periodicals played a crucial role in these organizations, providing the "vital link" in "disseminating denominational news" and "reinforc[ing] the common goals of the body."[7]

Virtually every Protestant body in America published denominational magazines.[8] The 1915 *Federal Council Year Book* listed 91 Protestant denominations and 389 denominational periodicals.[9] Methodists alone printed 69 journals; the major black Methodist denominations were responsible for 13 of these, including the *Allenite*, the *Christian Recorder*, and *Star of Zion*. Some denominations, especially the Lutherans, needed to publish in a variety of languages for a variety of ethnic groups. Some denominations also produced an array of state and regional journals, for example, the Episcopalians. Still, many of these journals aspired to reach both within and beyond their group, and across the nation. Even the smallest religious bodies published periodicals. The Christadelphians, with 1,500 members, put out the *Christadelphian Advocate*; the General Church of the New Jerusalem, 1,213 communicants, produced *New Church Life*; and, the Church of God, Adventist, 600 members strong, published two periodicals: the *Restitution* and the *Restitution Herald*.

A Plethora of Print

Twenty-five years later the situation was even more muddled. According to the 1941 Federal Council's *Yearbook of American Churches*, there were 430 periodicals produced by 140 denominations.[10] To some extent this increase reflects more complete data, as periodicals produced by groups such as the Mormons were now included in the count. Much of the real increase, however, was generated by newer denominations established after the 1915 report, including the International Church of the Foursquare Gospel, established in 1927, with 16,147 members and five periodicals; the Church of God (Cleveland, Tenn.), established in 1923, with 17,612 members and four periodicals; and, the Church of Revelation, established in 1930 with 520 members and one periodical.

Although an accurate tally of denominational periodicals is largely impracticable, counting readership is an even greater challenge. The standard source for circulation data in this era is *N. W. Ayer and Son's Directory of Newspapers and Periodicals*. Established in 1880 as a reference tool for advertisers, the Ayer directory included a separate section on religious publications. Focusing on "regional" religious magazines that accepted advertising, the directory overlooked numerous other religious periodicals. Moreover, many listed periodicals failed to provide circulation figures. Thus, Ayer undoubtedly underestimated religious periodical circulation. Nonetheless, the numbers are still striking: according to the directory, Protestant periodical circulation peaked in 1909 at 12,770,937, dipped to 5,916,912 at the Depression's height in 1933, and then rose again to 8,157,656 in 1943. Rough calculations indicate that denominational periodicals accounted for 80 to 90 percent of total circulation.[11]

Between 1880 and 1940, then, American denominational periodicals and readers were abundant. The mainline churches (Congregational, Disciples of Christ, Episcopal, Methodist, Northern Baptist, Presbyterian, and United Lutheran) were unquestionably the most powerful contemporary publication machines.[12] As the twentieth century progressed, their share of the publishing field rapidly diminished. In 1915 the Federal Council *Year Book* reported that 51 percent of Protestant periodicals were published by mainline denominations; by 1940 only about 25 percent were mainline. As Dennis Voskuil has suggested, some of this reduction is explained by the elimination of weaker journals and the reduced need for foreign-language periodicals. Moreover, the Ayers' data suggest that despite declining numbers of publications, mainline denominational journals circulated to more readers than journals produced by other denominations.[13]

Nevertheless, by the mid-twentieth century the increasingly bureaucratized denominations at the center of American Protestantism were not as energetically concerned with their periodicals as in earlier days. Generally speaking, the more marginal the sect, the more important the publishing enterprise, and the more frenzied the publishing activity. Some of this fervor emerged from the intense desire of many sectarian groups to convert others to their understanding of truth. In part this was a matter of survival: for nontraditional groups at odds with the religious and cultural mainstream, creating and maintaining communities of believers was essential; periodicals were indispensable to this effort. Publishing also established religious legitimacy: religious groups with magazines were marked as worthy of respect and attention.

Denominational Publishing and New Protestant Movements

The press was vitally important for African American denominations. In the Colored (now Christian) Episcopal Church, ministers not only preached the gospel and administered the sacraments but were also "obligated by the [denominational] law" to secure "cash" subscriptions to the CME's *Christian Index*.[14] The African Methodist Episcopal Church's *Christian Recorder*, contrary to the general trend among Protestant periodicals, continued throughout our period to summarize for subscribers "the principal events in the secular world" and to document "notes of racial progress." It provided discussions of issues pertinent for African Americans, as well as denominational updates, reports from member churches, sermons, and Sunday School lessons. The *Christian Recorder* not only served as the key link between the African Methodist Episcopal Church and its socially marginalized membership but also countered the racism of the mainstream press, which rendered the African American community invisible.[15]

Radically decentralized Protestant groups further demonstrate the importance of the press in structurally unifying religious communities. Growing out of the nineteenth-century Restoration movement, the Churches of Christ were fiercely congregational, vehemently resisting any denominational label. Nevertheless, an informal organizational structure emerged, in which editors of journals such as *Firm Foundation* and *Gospel Advocate* became, in the words of historian Richard Hughes, "the functional equivalent of bishops," defining theological orthodoxy and establishing the mission for members of the Churches of Christ. Unlike some of their mainline counterparts, these periodicals were not official denominational publications routinely sent out to all members. The editors were thus, in Hughes's words, "democratically chosen" in that "their power was only as great as the length of their circulation lists."[16]

Periodicals also played a crucial role in advancing new movements that emerged within American Protestantism during these years, especially Pentecostalism, fundamentalism, and the holiness movement. These all utilized myriad weekly and monthly magazines, often locally or regionally based, to spread their particular religious message. This often required a wide variety of content; the *Moody Monthly* delivered large doses of fundamentalist theology and also Bible study materials, Sunday School lessons, and devotional materials. These periodicals frequently devoted space to fundamentalist battles or holiness meetings or Pentecostal revivals elsewhere in America, connecting their widely dispersed, often isolated adherents to a larger body of believers. Aggressive magazine editors utilized this sense of belonging for strategic purposes. In the 1920s and 1930s, William Bell Riley used his *Pilot* to create a fundamentalist empire in the upper Midwest, and Pentecostal revivalist Aimée Semple McPherson's *Bridal Call* welded her followers into a constituency supportive of her ministry (see figure 18.1).[17]

Paul Tinlin has proposed that the number and popularity of Pentecostal magazines "suggest that people widely stereotyped at worst as illiterate and at best as little concerned with the printed page in fact invested heavily in print media and were fundamentally shaped as a people by the printed word."[18] For groups at or beyond the definitional edge of Protestantism, the importance of the press for survival, recruitment, and legitimacy was even more pronounced. In 1941 Seventh-day Adventists were publishing fourteen periodicals; the Jehovah's Witnesses had one magazine, the *Watchtower*, with a global circulation of more than 1 million by the 1940s. The Mormons produced a number of publications, including one daily newspaper (*Deseret News*) that in the late nineteenth century fiercely defended the legitimacy of the Mormon experiment in Utah, including the practice of polygamy.[19]

The Protestant Press: A Fractured Whole

Considering the entire Protestant press between 1880 and 1940, one finds little evidence of consolidation. As the century progressed, some periodicals were combined within mainline denominations. In general, however, the Protestant press in these years largely resisted the consolidation occurring in the secular press. This is not surprising given the vigorous diversity of both the Prot-

FIGURE 18.1. Sister Aimée (Aimée Semple McPherson) preaches to her followers in 1938. *Los Angeles Examiner* Collection, Regional History Collection, University of Southern California.

estant press and American Protestantism at large. Holiness, Christadelphian, Pentecostal, and restorationist publications, for example, varied in theological content, and they were produced and read by strikingly disparate communities. In short, diversity was the rule in Protestant periodicals.[20]

While periodicals were the crown jewels of denominational publishing, they were not the only printed material denominations produced. Survival as a cohesive denomination required an enormous amount and array of publications, most of which were even more invisible to the outside observer than the denominational periodicals. The Methodists were most impressive in this regard, producing a cascade of hymnals, Sunday School and Vacation Bible School materials, evangelistic tracts, and a variety of devotional and other religious books and booklets. They employed a vast array of editors, printers, publishers, and salespeople to aggressively ensure that their captive adherents were surrounded by Methodist publications.[21]

Even small denominations like the Mennonites produced a surprising number of publications. Between 1908 and 1945, the Mennonite Publishing House released 262 books and pamphlets, including such distinctively Mennonite publications as *Can Christians Fight?* and *Martyrs' Mirror*.[22] An even more striking example is the Church of God (Anderson, Indiana), a holiness denomination originating with preacher and editor Daniel Warner in the 1880s. As Colleen McDannell has detailed, Warner's Church of God was maintained not by "a set of doctrines and rituals but [by] a publishing company." Between 1881 and 1915, the Golden Trumpet Company was run by workers who lived communally, earned no wages, and devoted their time and energies to promoting their particular understanding of Christian truth. As McDannell observes, "while the communal life eventually died when the business expanded . . . the faith commitments of the workers survived." Early Golden Trumpet works included books, tracts, songbooks, and a periodical, as well as a variety of cards, paper mottos, and postcards. By the 1930s they were producing placemats, lamps, key chains, mirrors, and other products, all of which were imprinted with Bible verses, pious phrases, or religious pictures.[23]

Of course, as with periodicals, those groups at or beyond the Protestant border were most eager to publish books and pamphlets. This was especially true of groups whose sacred or near-sacred text was not the Bible, as with the Mormons' *Book of Mormon*, *Doctrines and Covenants*, and *The Pearl of Great Price*. Distributing these texts to believers and potential believers was a critical venture. The Seventh-day Adventists also produced various publications by visionary Ellen White, most notably *The Great Controversy between Christ and Satan: The Conflict of the Ages in the Christian Dispensation* (1884). The Christian Scientists had Mary Baker Eddy's *Science and Health*, claimed in 1950 to be second only to the Bible in all-time sales: "This volume has gone through hundreds of editions, comprising several million copies, bought by individuals all over the world."[24]

Broader Movements in Print

This chapter has focused thus far on Protestant publishing within particular faith communities. Indeed, most Protestant publishing between 1880 and 1940 was denominationally based. Beyond such boundaries, however, Protestant publishers produced numerous works more visible to the general public and more connected to the larger culture. That was certainly the case with the Disciples of Christ magazine, *Christian Century*. Established in 1884 as *Christian Oracle*, it was renamed in 1900 to envisage the enduring strength of Christianity for the coming 100 years. Despite this optimism, insolvency was a constant threat until 1908, when Disciples minister Charles Clayton Morrison purchased the magazine at auction. Morrison edited *Christian Century* until 1947, aggressively stripping the periodical of its denominational bias. His "undenominational weekly" emphasized Protestant unity and the social gospel while engaging larger cultural issues. Morrison's magazine gradually became the voice of the Protestant establishment. As a later editor suggested, under Morrison's leadership *Christian Century* became the "most influential Protestant magazine" in America.[25] By the mid-twentieth century, *Christian Century* was often the sole Protestant magazine carried in public and college libraries; to the academy and the media, it was generally the *only* voice of American Protestantism.[26] Yet, for the public more generally, there were other influential nondenominational publications.

Christian Century's circulation never exceeded 40,000, while the *Christian Herald*, a nondenominational New York periodical circulated 250,000 copies in 1910, and perhaps more than 400,000 at midcentury. Theologically conservative and thoroughly moralistic, the *Christian Herald* promoted what Marty wittily called "the theology of the *Reader's Digest*," possibly explaining its lack of attention from scholars.[27] Nonetheless, *Christian Herald* more truly represented American Protestantism than any other periodical at the time.

Adapting the Bible

Most nondenominational Protestant publishing involved books, most importantly, of course, the Bible. Here the metaphor of a flood of "faithful" words seems most appropriate. There were about 487 English editions of the Bible and its various components published in the United States between 1880 and 1940.

When one subtracts Catholic, Orthodox, and Jewish editions the tally comes to approximately 450.[28]

From the founding of the colonies, the King James Bible held sway among American Protestants. This changed in 1881 when the long-awaited Revised Version of the New Testament was published amid great fanfare. In a front-page story, the *New York Evening Post* proclaimed that the appearance of the Revised Version—considered to be the most accurate version of the Bible ever produced—would prove to be "among the great events of the nineteenth century."[29] The *Chicago Tribune* and the *Chicago Times* went so far as to print the complete New Testament, pirating the text from the authorized publishers. The *Tribune*'s New Testament sold more than 100,000 copies; 3 million copies of the bound edition were eventually sold. Such fanfare was repeated in 1885 with the release of the entire Revised Bible, which also had stunning sales, though no newspaper reprinted all sixty-six books.[30]

The revision was produced by a committee of British and American scholars who viewed its creation as a great ecumenical and evangelistic opportunity. They failed, however, to reconcile the fact that some Protestants would perceive their efforts as alteration or distortion of the biblical text in the service of a liberal theological agenda. Critics like C. I. Scofield called for allegiance to the King James Version.[31] Scofield, a Dallas minister, was involved in the prophecy and Bible conference movement that swept through American Protestantism in the late nineteenth and early twentieth centuries.[32] Seeking to emphasize a literalistic and dispensational premillennialist understanding of the Bible, Scofield developed a King James edition that was filled with premillennialist notations and an extensive system of cross-referencing. Issued in 1909 by Oxford University Press, the Scofield Reference Bible quickly became a publishing phenomenon, the Bible of choice among fundamentalists and other conservative Protestant groups (see figure 18.2). As a result, dispensational premillennialist beliefs spread like wildfire among Protestants; many devotees came to see Scofield's annotations as part of the biblical text itself.[33]

The Scofield Reference Bible highlights an important point. American Protestantism was (and is) a bewildering panoply of faith communities sharing a sacred text but approaching it in a variety of ways. Thus, like Scofield, many individuals produced Bible editions to fit their community's particular theologies and needs. Numerous denominational ministers produced Bibles with accompanying notes to advance their interpretation; one holiness minister began his edition of the Bible with a greeting to "the Holiness People in All Lands." In Baptist Bibles and those produced by other believers in adult baptism, the Greek word "baptizo" was translated as "immerse" instead of "baptize."[34]

Even more dramatic was Joseph Smith's Bible. The Mormon prophet's "trans-in thee: for thy merchants were the great men of the earth; for by thy *a*sorceries were all nations deceived. 24 And in her was found the *b*blood of prophets, and of saints, and of all that were slain upon the earth.

CHAPTER 19.

(Parenthetical: the four alleluias of the glorified saints. Cf. Rev. 17. 1-7; 18. 1-8.)

AND after these things I heard a great *c*voice of much people in heaven, saying, Alleluia; *d*Salvation, and glory, and *e*honour, and power, unto the Lord our God: 2 For true and righteous *are* his judgments: for he hath judged the great *f*whore, which did corrupt the earth with her fornication, and hath *g*avenged the blood of his servants at her hand. 3 And again they said, *h*Alleluia. And her *i*smoke rose up for ever and ever. 4 And the four and twenty *j*elders and the four *k*beasts fell down and worshipped God that sat on the throne, saying, Amen; Alleluia. 5 And a *l*voice came out of the throne, saying, *m*Praise our God, all ye his servants, and ye that fear him, both small and great. 6 And I heard as it were the voice of a great multitude, and as the voice of many waters, and as the voice of mighty *n*thunderings, saying, Alleluia: for the Lord God omnipotent reigneth.

The marriage of the Lamb.

7 Let us be glad and rejoice, and give honour to him: for the marriage of the Lamb is come, and his [1]wife hath made herself ready. 8 And to her *p*was granted that she should be arrayed in fine linen, clean and white: for the fine linen is the [2]*q*righteousness of saints.

A.D. 96.
a Cf. Nah. 3. 4.
b Rev. 17. 6.
c Rev. 18. 20; 11. 15.
d the salvation. See Rom. 1. 16, note.
e power of our God.
f Rev. 17. 1.
g Cf. Rev. 6. 10; cf. Lk. 18. 7, 8.
h v. 1.
i Cf. Rev. 18. 9, 18; cf. Mk. 9. 48.
j Elders. Tit. 1. 5-9.
k living creatures.
l Cf. Rev. 18. 4.
m Cf. Psa. 134. 1.
n Cf. Ex. 20. 18.
o Bride (of Christ). vs. 6-8; Rev. 21. 9. (John 3. 29; Rev. 19. 6-8.)
p Cf. 1 Cor. 15. 10.
q righteousnesses. Righteousness (garment). (Gen. 3. 21.)
r Cf. Lk. 14. 15.
s Inspiration. Rev. 21. 5. (Ex. 4. 15; Rev. 22. 19.)
t Cf. Heb. 1. 14.
u Cf. Eph. 1. 9, 10; cf. 1 Pet. 1. 10-12.
v Contra, Rev. 6. 2; cf. Psa. 45. 4; contra, Mt. 21. 2-5.
w Christ (Second Advent). vs. 11-21; Rev. 20. 4-6. (Deut. 30. 3; Acts 1. 9-11.)
x Cf. Rev. 3. 7.
y Rev. 1. 14.
z diadems.
a Cf. vs. 13, 16; cf. Mt. 11. 27; cf. 1 Tim. 6. 16.
b Cf. Isa. 63. 2, 3.
c v. 21; cf. Rev. 1. 16; cf. 2 Thes. 2. 8.
d Rev. 14. 20; Isa. 63. 3, 6; cf. Mt. 21. 43.
e Rev. 17. 14; 1. 5.
f mid-heaven.

9 And he saith unto me, Write, *r*Blessed *are* they which are called unto the marriage supper of the Lamb. And he saith unto me, *s*These are the true sayings of God. 10 And I fell at his feet to worship him. And he said unto me, See *thou do it* not: I am thy *t*fellowservant, and of thy brethren that have the testimony of Jesus: worship God: for the *u*testimony of Jesus is the spirit of prophecy.

The second coming of Christ in glory. (Cf. Mt. 24. 16-30.)

11 And I [3]saw heaven opened, and behold a *v*white horse; and *w*he that sat upon him *was* called *x*Faithful and True, and in righteousness he doth judge and make war. 12 His *y*eyes *were* as a flame of fire, and on his head *were* many *z*crowns; and he had a name written, *a*that no man knew, but he himself. 13 And he *was* clothed with a vesture *b*dipped in blood: and his name is called The Word of God. 14 And the armies *which* were in heaven followed him upon white horses, clothed in fine linen, white and clean. 15 And out of his mouth goeth a *c*sharp sword, that with it he should smite the nations: and he shall rule them with a rod of iron: and *d*he treadeth the winepress of the fierceness and wrath of Almighty God. 16 And he hath on *his* vesture and on his thigh a name written, *e*KING OF KINGS, AND LORD OF LORDS.

The battle of Armageddon (Rev. 16. 14; 19. 17, note).

17 And I saw an angel standing in the sun; and he cried with a loud voice, saying to all the fowls that fly in *f*the midst of heaven, *4*Come and

---

[1] The "Lamb's wife" here is the "bride" (Rev. 21. 9), the Church, identified with the "heavenly Jerusalem" (Heb. 12. 22, 23), and to be distinguished from Israel, the adulterous and repudiated "wife" of Jehovah, yet to be restored (Isa. 54. 1-10; Hos. 2. 1-17), who is identified with the earth (Hos. 2. 23). A forgiven and restored *wife* could not be called either a *virgin* (2 Cor. 11. 2, 3), or a *bride*.

[2] The garment in Scripture is a symbol of righteousness. In the bad ethical sense it symbolizes self-righteousness (e.g. Isa. 64. 6; see Phil. 3. 6-8, the best that a moral and religious man under law could do). In the good ethical sense the garment symbolizes "the righteousness of God . . . upon all them that believe." See Rom. 3. 21, *note*.

[3] The vision is of the departure from heaven of Christ and the saints and angels preparatory to the catastrophe in which Gentile world-power, headed up in the Beast, is smitten by the "stone cut out without hands" (Dan. 2. 34, 35).

[4] Armageddon (the ancient hill and valley of Megiddo, west of Jordan in the plain of Jezreel) is the appointed place for the beginning of the great battle in which the

FIGURE 18.2. The Scofield Reference Bible (1909) was an annotated version of the King James Bible presenting a fundamentalist, premillennialist understanding of the Bible. This opening presents the text and annotations for the nineteenth chapter of the book of Revelation. University of Dayton.

lation" was developed between 1830 and 1833 but was not published until 1867. It was repeatedly published in the following decades, with a "corrected edition" released in 1944. As Philip Barlow has observed, Smith sought to bring the King James Bible into "line with the insights of his revelation and understanding." The result was the Inspired Version, containing 3,410 verses that differed from their King James counterparts. Smith, in keeping with his personal experience of having seen God, changed John 1:18 from "No man hath seen God at any time; the only begotten Son, which is in the bosom of the Father, he hath declared him" to "And no man hath seen God at any time, except that he hath borne record of the Son; for except it is through him no man can be saved."[35]

Portending future biblical scholarship, Elizabeth Cady Stanton and others published the Woman's Bible in the late 1890s, including scriptural selections along with commentary supporting a feminist understanding of the Bible. There were Masonic editions with attached Masonic materials, as well as "numeric Bibles" appealing to those Protestants seeking additional evidence of the Bible's divine origins by suggesting that biblical text is based on a mathematical code. Some editions were clearly produced by a community of one, including the 1922 version by Johannes Greber, who made use of an unusual editorial method: "In the rare instances in which a text pronounced correct by the divine spirits can be found in none of the manuscripts available today, I have used the text as it was given to me by those spirits."[36]

As Harold Scanlin observes, these numerous editions of the Bible "are testimony to a vigorous and variegated history of religion in America."[37] Religious diversity alone does not explain the flood of Bibles, however. There was also the market. As R. Laurence Moore observed in his masterful work, *Selling God*, mid-nineteenth-century publishers discovered the economic benefits of "repackaging" the Bible.[38] By 1900 commercialization had produced an astounding variety of Bibles that only expanded as the twentieth century progressed. Even their covers were diverse; a Bible sheathed in "protective" gilt metal and stamped with the phrase, "May God Bless You," was marketed to World War II soldiers, though it proved to be no protection against bullets. There were Bibles supplemented with timelines, maps, and other materials. Some seemed to contain everything: the M. R. Gately Company's 1880 edition included not only "100,000 Marginal References and Readings . . . Embellished with Nearly Two Thousand Illustrative Engravings," but also a "History of the Translation of the English Bible," a "Description of Israelite Tabernacles," a "History of the Books of the Bible," a "Map of the Holy Land . . . and maps of Jerusalem," a "Household Dictionary of the Bible," and, at the end, a "Family Record, Index, Concordance, Metrical Psalms, and Portrait Album." Some Bibles used colored type: the first "red letter" New Testament, with the words of Jesus in red type, appeared in 1899. The Marked Bible (1928) offered "the Themes of Salvation [Red], The Holy Spirit [Green], Temporal Blessings [Brown], Prophetic Subjects [Purple]." There was also the "Self-Pronouncing Bible" to aid in reading Biblical names and places, the "Runner's Bible" for "him who runs," and the "World's Smallest Bible . . . with imitation leather cover" for, presumably, the collector of religious miniatures.[39]

By the late nineteenth century, commercial publishers—including Harper's, Thomas Nelson, and J. B. Lippincott—were clearly aware of the profits to be made from publishing Bibles. The competition could be very intense: as John Tebbel observed, 1920s "publishers vied with each other to make improvements of every kind, in type, paper, sewing, and binding." In flush times and in depression, in peace and in war—the Bible, in all its forms, sold.[40]

Nonprofit Publishing

Despite this vigorous commercial traffic in Bibles, there were several nonprofit, primarily Protestant groups that sought to increase the distribution of Bibles. The Pocket Testament League, established in New York in 1916, encouraged people to carry the Bible with them everywhere, reading from it daily. More famous was the Christian Commercial Travellers Association, organized in 1899 by a group of Beaver Dam, Wisconsin, businessmen concerned with "the religious life of commercial men who spent long periods away from home." Better known as "the Gideons," they began placing Bibles in hotels throughout America. Just three years later, the Gideons placed an order for 100,000 Bibles from Thomas Nelson and Sons, whose presses ran nonstop for two months to fill the request.[41]

The Pocket Testament League and the Gideons continued and expanded the efforts of older organizations like the American Tract Society and the American Bible Society. From its founding in 1816 through most of the nineteenth century, the American Bible Society dominated the printing of Bibles in the United States, distributing free and paid copies.[42] By the late nineteenth century, unable to match rapidly improving technologies employed by commercial printers, the society reduced its printing efforts and stopped printing Bibles altogether in 1922. In 106 years, the American Bible Society had printed more than 76 million Bibles.[43] Even after 1922, it continued to distribute Bibles, particularly during wartime. Distribution of Bibles to American soldiers was so complete in the Spanish-American War that, according to John Tebbel, Spanish troops reported that "a copy of a gospel or a Testament could be found on the body of nearly every dead, wounded, or captured [American] soldier." For some, like General Toral, this was "evidence of 'the deep-rooted hypocrisy existing in the American nation.'" World War I was a much greater challenge for the American Bible Society, but it succeeded in providing chaplains and Young Men's Christian Association representatives with almost 5 million pocket-sized New Testaments—with khaki or navy blue covers—for distribution. The society provided only Protestant New Testaments, though, refusing the Paulist Press's offer to provide Douay New Testaments for Catholic soldiers. By World War II, however, the American Bible Society belatedly accepted that America was now religiously pluralist: the 7,420,910 volumes it provided during that war included Douay New Testaments for Catholics and Old Testament selections for Jews.[44] In World War II the drive to supply military personnel with Bibles was accelerated when it was reported that Eddie Rickenbacker and his crew survived twenty-one days adrift at sea because they had a New Testament to read. The result was a crusade to equip every lifeboat with a waterproof Bible: one airman reported that "I have been ordered not to pack these rafts until a New Testament goes in each one of them."[45]

In times of war, Bibles were more than Scripture to read in lifeboats or foxholes. The Bible has long had a central place in American civil religion. It is a source of ideas about America's place in the world—America as the New Israel, with a special covenant with God—and a tangible sign of the linkage between God and the American nation, as demonstrated by its use in political ceremonies like presidential inaugurations. Such linkages are often emphasized in wartime, as with the Wilson administration's portrayal of America's World War I involvement as a divinely mandated crusade. Thus, not surprisingly, New York City saw a huge public celebration in 1917 when the press released the first 100,000 New Testaments for American soldiers. As Creighton Lacy recounts, the celebration was replete with "martial music, patriotic anthems, abundant speeches, and 'the most beautiful silk American flags' that John Wanamaker's store . . . could provide"; the ceremony culminated with the "token presentation [of Bibles] . . . to representatives of the Y.M.C.A. and the Army and Navy."[46]

Beyond the Bible

Despite the Bible's secure dominance in American civil religion and culture, *Publishers' Weekly* reports that about 37,000 other religious books were published in the United States between 1880 and 1940, more than 600 per year on average. These numbers, imprecise and problematic, do not allow for confident generalizations. In some regards, however, production of religious books seemed to follow trends in book publishing more generally. Only during the Great Depression was there an exceptionally precipitous decline in the publication of religious books. According to *Publishers' Weekly* annual reports, religious books were usually between second and fourth in new titles, behind fiction and in close competition with children's books. Accurate sales figures are harder to determine, but the Census Bureau reported that 42,999,266 religious books were sold in 1945, constituting about 10 percent of total book sales in the United States that year.[47]

While numerous denominationally affiliated publishers poured forth books, pamphlets, and tracts, there were some nondenominational Protestant presses that intentionally sought a more general reading public. These presses included Thomas Nelson, William Eerdmans, and, most notably in these years, Fleming Revell. Revell's sister was married to the famous evangelist, Dwight Moody, whose sermons and other writings Revell began publishing in the 1870s. Moody's works served as a solid foundation, and Revell soon expanded his efforts, moving his headquarters from Chicago to New York. By 1900, to quote one scholar, Revell's "energetic program of publishing, importing, and distributing evangelical books, tracts, and periodicals made his the most important commercial religious publishing house in America," remaining as such into the middle of the twentieth century.[48]

As with Bibles, "religious" publishers were not the sole purveyors of other religious literature. The demand for religious publications lured many trade presses into the field. This trend accelerated in the 1920s, when Harper's, Doubleday, Macmillan, and Holt, perceiving an increased interest in religious topics, all established separate religious departments. In that same decade, a Religious Bookstore Group and the Religious Book Club were founded. *Publishers' Weekly* established its annual Religious Book Issue, while interested publishers established Religious Book Week.[49] "Religious" publishers and "nonreligious" publishers utilized comparable marketing devices.[50] Religious books produced by general trade presses clearly demonstrate such overlap. There were "best sellers," including the steady stream of religious fiction, from Lew Wallace's *Ben-Hur: A Tale of the Christ* (Harper, 1880) to Harold Bell Wright's *The Shepherd of the Hills* (Appleton-Century-Crofts, 1907) to Lloyd Douglas's *The Robe* (Houghton, Mifflin, 1942) (see figure 18.3). The most popular was probably *In His Steps* (1898), not properly copyrighted by author Charles Sheldon and thus released by at least sixteen different publishers, with very little money going to Sheldon.[51]

Even more significant was religious nonfiction, including Giovanni Papini's *The Life of Christ* (Harcourt Brace, 1923), Bruce Barton's *The Man Nobody Knows* (Bobbs-Merrill, 1925), and his follow-up, *The Book Nobody Knows* (Bobbs-Merrill, 1926). The two Barton volumes were second and third on the 1926 best-seller list for nonfiction, not surprising given that between 1900 and 1950 the majority of nonfiction best sellers were religious in nature. Most sig-

FIGURE 18.3. Facing pages in Lew Wallace's *Ben-Hur: A Tale of the Christ* (New York and London: Harper & Brothers, 1899) shows the frontispiece and title page. The staged photograph of Ben-Hur is an early use of this method of illustration, added to an edition of popular religious fiction issued some twenty years after its initial publication. University of Dayton.

nificant, however, was the flood of devotional, inspirational, and "Christian living" books put out by nonreligious publishers, most of which have escaped the attention of print historians.[52]

Printed Devotion:
Understanding the Impact of the Protestant Press

Differentiating religious from nonreligious publishers was (and remains) extremely difficult. Of course, trade presses that specialized in religious books sought to reach the broadest possible audience, and thus they resembled nondenominational publishers more than the denominational houses that concentrated primarily on their own particular religious communities. American Protestant publishing might best be understood as a spectrum ranging from more sectarian to less sectarian, with much greater diversity among sectarian publishers, and with trade presses and nondenominational publishers on the opposite pole.

The question still remains, When does print cease to be classifiable as Protestant, or as religious? Examining the history of Protestant publishing in the United States seems to require a bounded understanding of religious and "secular" publishing. Given the ubiquity of Protestantism in American culture between 1880 and 1940, however, establishing such a boundary is a daunting intellectual task. This is particularly true in light of Joan Shelley Rubin's fascinating discussion of how early twentieth-century mainline Protestant groups deliberately appropriated all sorts of ostensibly nonreligious reading material—particularly poetry—for use in worship services, summer camps, and devotional exercises. Regarding a 1926 collection of popular poetry, Rubin asks, when "campers chanted Longfellow or Ezra Pound before quiet meditation, taps, and a benediction seeking the blessing of the Great Camp Director, was *Magic Ring* an example of religious or secular publishing?"[59]

Distinguishing between religious and nonreligious print may indeed be important, but a definitive answer is not feasible. Even if we confine our attention only to publications that are clearly religious, by the most restrictive definition, the amount of reading material is huge—from periodicals to pamphlets to fiction and nonfiction books to Sunday School lessons to devotional aids to Bibles, and more. Here, then, is the central argument of this essay: American print culture between 1880 and 1940 cannot be fully understood without taking account of the staggering quantity and variety of Protestant reading material produced in these years. Yet how will the inclusion of Protestant publishing change our understanding of print culture in the United States? Three possibilities can be explored. First, the full range of Protestant publications includes a good deal of printed material that was not driven or shaped by the market. Most religious periodicals were heavily subsidized by their producers, who sought to create and sustain group identity and cohesion while finding converts to their understanding of the truth. Although the ever-expanding market may have somewhat affected these publications, and while groups did compete for followers in a market of religious ideas, religious periodicals generally resisted and stood apart from the trend of increasingly commercialized print. Protestant groups' determined efforts to distribute the Bible further elucidate the importance of Protestant publishing in a broader understanding of American print culture. While some Bible publishers had commercial motives, the market alone cannot explain the Gideons or the American Bible Society.

The Bible itself suggests a second way in which our understanding of American print culture might change. That is, to include Protestant publishing in the history of the book in America requires that the Bible have a central place in the narrative—as a category unto itself. Given the Bible's enduring ubiquity in American culture, no history of the book that neglects it is adequate. The Bible must be considered as a commercial product, as a cultural icon, and as a material object. It has been used liturgically by churches, devotionally by individuals, and collectively by that most popular form of book club, the Bible study.

This discussion of the Bible suggests a third way in which full inclusion of Protestant publishing can inform the history of the book in America. Individuals and small groups who read the Bible or other devotional literature did not (and do not) do so to gather information; instead, they often read slowly, meditatively, prayerfully—perhaps hoping for consolation or inspiration or spiritual insight. A person reading the *New York Times* and a person reading the Psalms were engaging in very different activities. Fully incorporating religious publications into the history of print culture thus requires full attention to different modes of reading, particularly reading as a devotional and contemplative exercise.

Such analysis merely scratches the surface. There is much left unknown about Protestant publishing in the years between 1880 and 1940. This, however, is certain: full consciousness of Protestant (and religious) publishing in all of its forms will fundamentally enrich our understanding of print culture in America.

CHAPTER 19

Two Ambitious Goals
American Jewish Publishing in the United States

Jonathan D. Sarna

. . .

A Great Day in Philadelphia Judaism

According to New York's leading Jewish newspaper, Sunday, 3 June 1888, was "a great day in Philadelphia Judaism." About 100 rabbinic and lay leaders from around the country — "the leading intellectual minds among the Hebrews" — gathered to create what became the Jewish Publication Society of America. A thirteen-page circular, published a few months later, appealed for "generous sympathy, active encouragement and liberal support" of the new organization. "We have given to the world the book, most wonderful in the effect it has produced on great masses in all climes and times," the circular declared. It expressed the hope that "Israel in America" would "proudly claim its literary period, as did our ancestors aforetime in Spain, in Poland and in modern Germany."[1]

The reference to earlier centers of Jewish culture hints at the new publication society's grand objective: creating a new Jewish cultural center in America to succeed that in Germany, which, it was alleged, had stagnated amid "a revival of mediaeval prejudices." Nineteenth-century students of Jewish history, following Nahman Krochmal, believed that centers of Jewry experienced a natural cycle of growth and decline. The decay of one center stimulated the rise of another elsewhere. Themselves the children of German immigrants, these scholars believed that the late nineteenth-century rise of German anti-Semitism signaled the end of cultural progress in their former homeland. "It befits us as free citizens of the noblest of countries," they announced, "to take it up in their stead." The Jewish Publication Society was to be a key agent in this cultural revolution. Blending American patriotism with concern for the welfare of fellow Jews, the society's founders looked to publish books that would prepare American Jewry to assume the burden of Jewish cultural leadership and announce to the world that the American Jewish community had arrived.[2]

An additional objective also underlay the creation of the Jewish Publication Society: the aim of integrating a fractious American Jewry into a nationwide community bound together by a common culture of print. More than 200,000 Jews from various countries had crossed to America's shores in the 1880s, nearly doubling the Jewish community's size. It would double again just ten years later. This massive in-migration, coupled with burgeoning intrareligious conflict, underscored for American Jewish leaders the importance of organizing and systematizing Jewish communal life, goals closely parallel to contemporary progressive reformers' hopes for American society as a whole. The Jewish Publication Society, as part of this effort, appealed to "all Jews of every shade of belief," and professed to favor "no special views and . . . no particular party." It sought to encourage "many men of many minds" to "work harmoniously together to one common end."[3]

These two ambitious goals—to forge a new Jewish cultural center in America and to integrate American Jewry into a nationwide community bound together by a common culture of print—highlight the central themes of American Jewish publishing from the late nineteenth to the mid-twentieth century (see figures 19.1, 19.2). The print output of the American Jewish community multiplied many times over during these years, keeping pace with burgeoning Jewish population growth and resulting in a torrent of books, magazines, and newspapers published in as many as five different languages: English, Hebrew, German, Yiddish, and Ladino (Judeo-Spanish). The American Jewish community became culturally self-sufficient at this time, and after years of competition came to succeed Europe as the unofficial center of the Jewish diaspora, a status tragically confirmed by the Holocaust.

Much to the disappointment of the communal elite, however, American Jews never fully united. Even as improvements in communication strengthened ties among American Jews, the forces of social, economic, political and religious diversification impeded the creation of a common group culture. As a result, the much-heralded Jewish Publication Society, for all that it sought to appeal to every Jew, became in the end just one of many competing voices in American Jewish public life, while Jewish publishing became ever more complex and variegated. Books and periodicals appeared in different languages, reflected different ideologies, and attracted different audiences. Instead of uniting American Jews, print media represented all that divided them.

Forward from Backwardness

For centuries, the North American Jewish community was stigmatized as being culturally backward. Rabbi Isaac Mayer Wise, the leader of nineteenth-century Reform Judaism in the United States, recalled that when he arrived in New York in 1846 he found "but three men in private life who possessed any Jewish or any

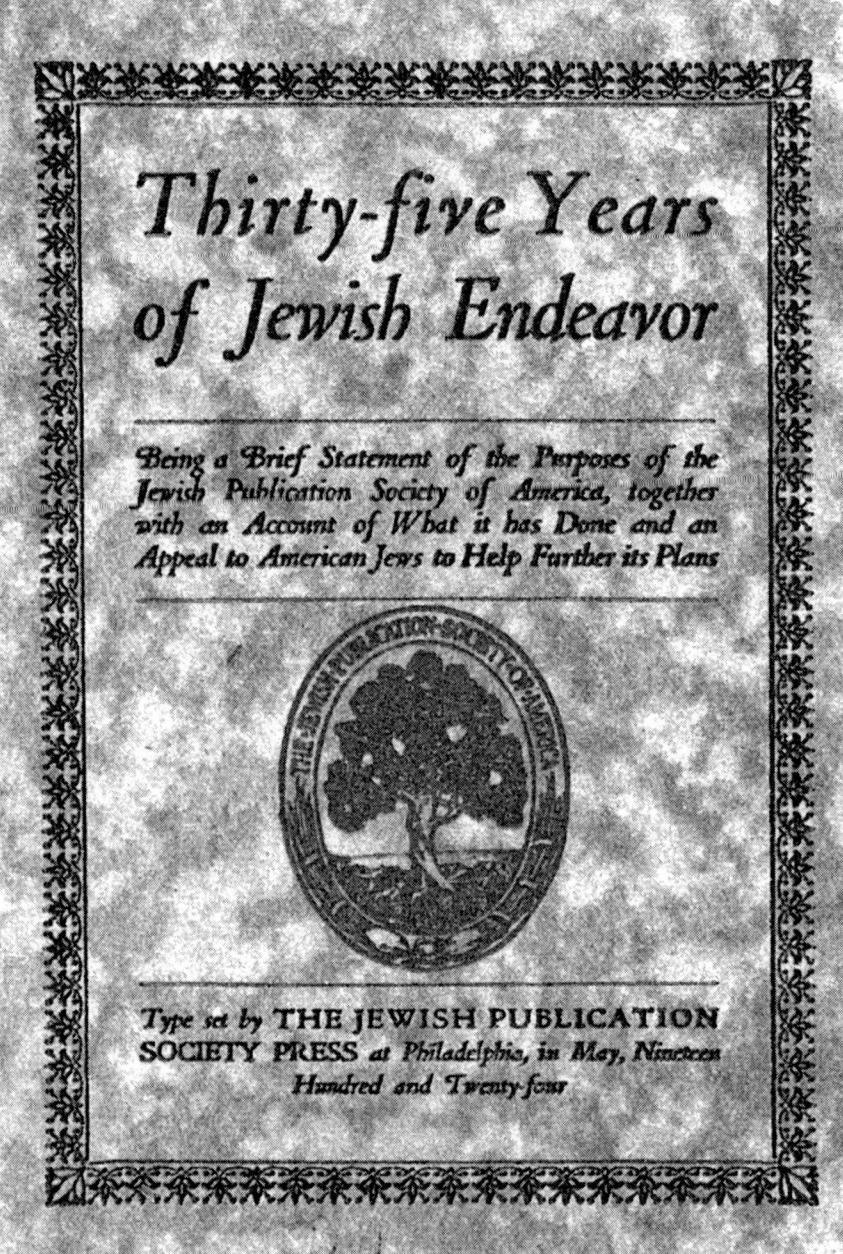

FIGURE 19.1. For its thirty-fifth anniversary, in 1924, the Jewish Publication Society issued this collectors' volume setting forth its goals and accomplishments and appealing for funds. The volume also reprinted, in miniature, the title pages of every book published by the JPS since 1888.

△
This
little
volume
of which
250 copies
have been prin-
ted especially for
the friends of the So-
ciety contains the title-
pages of over one hundred
and twenty books issued by
the Society of which over 1,500,000 copies have been distributed   The following are the names of the authors of these
publications [the names printed in Italics are no longer among the living, may their memories be a blessing.
The living, may they be encouraged to produce more
books to the greater glory of God and our people]:
I. Abrahams, C. Adler, E. Adler, *L. Adler*, *G.*
Aguilar, Ahad Ha'am, N. Bentwich, H. Bern-
stein, W. Canfield, I. Cohen, S. W. Cooper,
A. Darmesteter, I. Davidson, Nina Davis,
M. Davitt, *L. N. Dembitz*, *E. Deutsch*,
S. M. Dubnow, H. Friedenwald, H.
Frank, U. Frank, L. Ginzberg, M. Gold-
smith, S. Gordon, R. Gottheil, *H. Graetz*,
Julius H. Greenstone, *B. Halper*, E. Harris,
I. Husik, *H. Iliowizi*, A. S. Isaacs, *J. Jacobs*,
G. Karpeles, K. Kohler, I. Kraft, Jacob Lazarre,
M. Lazarus, E. Levinger, M. Liber, *K. Magnus*,
Henry Malter, M. L. Margolis, S. Miller, M. Misch,
S. H. Mosenthal, S. Oppenheim, Louis Pendleton,
I. L. Perez, David Philipson, P. M. Raskin, M. Radin,
Jacob S. Raisin, A. B. Rhine, *Esther J. Ruskay*, *Solomon*
Schechter, *L. Schnabel*, Harry Schneiderman, N. Soluschz,
Emily Solis-Cohen, *Judah*
Steinberg, Henrietta
Szold, *M. Wolfenstein*,
Yehoash, D. Yellin,
Israel Zangwill
Henry Zirndorf,
and others.
▽ ▽ ▽
▽ ▽
▽

FIGURE 19.2. This colophon from the thirty-fifth anniversary volume, in the shape of a Jewish star, boasts that the Jewish Publication Society had distributed more than 1.5 million volumes since its inception. Note that the list of authors includes European as well as American names, men and women alike.

Talmudical learning . . . ignorance swayed the scepter, and darkness ruled."⁴ Cyrus Adler, then the librarian of the Smithsonian Institution, complained as late as 1894 that American Jewry had "no libraries, no publications and no independent scholars."⁵ The dearth of Jewish book learning and book publishing prompted nineteenth-century European rabbis to describe America as a *treifene medina*, an "unkosher land."⁶

The two leading American Jewish religious leaders of the nineteenth century, Isaac Leeser (1806-68) of Philadelphia and Isaac Mayer Wise (1819-1900) of Cincinnati, labored to combat this sorry situation. Concerned about the lack of quality in Jewish education and eager to strengthen Jewish religious life—one as a proponent of Americanized Orthodoxy and the other of Americanized Reform—both men mounted vigorous publication programs. Between them, they wrote, translated, and edited almost 150 different works. These included three of the community's foremost periodicals: Leeser's *The Occident and American Jewish Advocate* (1843-69), Wise's *Israelite* (founded in 1854 and renamed the *American Israelite* in 1874), and, in German, *Die Deborah* (1855-1902).⁷ Amid the democratization of print culture, the burgeoning growth of Christian religious journalism, and the manifest success in America of "books, tracts and publications of all kinds," Leeser and Wise looked to the printed word to achieve two central objectives that Leeser had articulated back in 1845: first, to provide American Jews with "a knowledge of their faith" and, second, to arm them with the "proper weapons to defend . . . against the assaults of proselyte-makers on the one side and of infidels on the other."⁸ Jewish education and communal defense have remained central objectives of American Jewish print culture ever since.

Jewish newspapers—those of Leeser, Wise, and others—dominated American Jewish cultural life in the nineteenth century. They were not the "grand engine of a burgeoning . . . culture" that evangelical newspapers are reputed to have been.⁹ They did, however, play a vital role in shaping the very notion of a national Jewish culture and community. They served as a prime source of ingroup news and information, provided a forum for religious education and debate, and functioned as the hub of a communications web linking Jews from one end of the country to the other. By the 1860s Jewish newspapers published in New York, Philadelphia, Cincinnati, and San Francisco reached hundreds of communities, some of them places where only a single Jew resided.¹⁰ They transmitted a broad range of national, international, and local news, as well as polemics, homiletics and apologetics, serious scholarship, popular fiction, and helpful advice. Monthlies, like Leeser's *Occident* and David Einhorn's German-language *Sinai*, targeted a more elite audience than the more family-oriented weeklies, but such selectivity was tempered by their dependence on subscribers and advertisers for survival. Despite their different appeals, newspapers also projected a broad vision of American Jewish life, promoting among their far-flung readers a sense of community and group identity. These feelings of fellowship, mutuality, and interdependence transcended narrow limits and taught Jews to identify with the national community of "American Israelites."

Nineteenth-century American Jews also produced books—several thousand of them—but most were institutional documents (constitutions and reports), lectures and sermons, textbooks, prayer books, translations, and imports. Henry Frank, a Jewish immigrant from Bavaria, and later his son, Leopold, issued more than fifty volumes beginning in 1848-49. Isaac Mayer Wise's brother-in-law founded Bloch & Co (later Bloch Publishing Company) in Cincinnati in 1854, producing more than 150 volumes. Dozens of other printers, Jewish and non-Jewish alike, also produced books of Jewish interest.[11] Most of these volumes, however, lacked serious editing and required significant publishing subsidies. Compared to Germany, the center of Jewish scholarship and culture, the American Jewish community's literary output was embarrassingly small. American Jews imported far more cultural material than they created independently, and very little of what they did produce was deemed worthy of export.

Multiplication and Division

In the late nineteenth century, as America's Jewish population expanded, its cultural productivity kept pace. Robert Singerman's comprehensive bibliography of Judaica Americana published to 1900 makes it possible to track these changes.[12] The gross number of publications listed decade by decade (including everything from Christian conversionist literature and tracts about Jews to institutional documents, prospectus sheets, and broadsides) demonstrates slow, steady growth, followed by rapid expansion in the 1880s and 1890s (table 19.1).

During this time period, the quality of American publications pertaining to Jews also improved, as evidenced by the appearance of such volumes as *Statistics of the Jews of the United States* (1880) compiled by William B. Hackenberg, Isaac M. Wise's *History of the Hebrews' Second Commonwealth* (1880), Emma Lazarus's *Songs of a Semite* (1882), Moses Mielziner's *The Jewish Law of Marriage and Divorce in Ancient and Modern Times, and Its Relation to the Law of the State* (1884), and the first parts of Marcus Jastrow's monumental *A Dictionary of the Targumim, the Talmud Babli and Yerushalmi, and the Midrashic Literature* (1886-1993).

Yet, as the American Jewish community grew larger, the cultural ties that bound it together frayed. Generational, social, religious, and class cleavages de-

TABLE 19.1. Jewish publications by decade, 1850-1899

1850–59	507
1860–69	565
1870–79	659
1880–89	1,046
1890–99	2,017

veloped: natives versus immigrants, Germans versus East Europeans, Reform versus Orthodox, rich versus poor. Jewish newspapers proliferated and became more locally oriented at this time—hardly a surprise given the local character of American journalism generally—and this only accentuated divisiveness, for the newspapers now offered local instead of national perspectives on events, and their focus narrowed. Language too became a divisive factor in American Jewish life. Jews now spoke an array of different languages, including English, German, Ladino, and especially Yiddish, but they no longer shared a common language.

In this transitional era, Jewish leaders looked to books as a source of salvation. A traditional symbol of unity among Jews, books also historically brought status both to the individuals who wrote them and to the communities that produced and owned them. Communities that published quality books and boasted great libraries were elevated in their own eyes and in the eyes of world Jewry.[13] The American Jewish community, having grown almost overnight into one of the five largest in the world, coveted precisely that status. The Jewish Publication Society and numerous other book-related projects promised to fulfill that desire while simultaneously unifying American Jews.

American Jewish Culture Emerges

America emerged as a cultural center of world Jewry between 1900 and 1920, just as the nation's impact on global issues began to intensify and diversify. Freed from dependence on Europe for great books and new ideas, both native and immigrant Jews experienced an unprecedented sense of cultural independence. They now knew that they could produce great books themselves. No longer did they feel compelled to turn to Europe as a source of legitimation; increasingly, if somewhat begrudgingly, Europeans came to recognize their contributions.[14]

Two early twentieth-century events heralded American Jewry's "arrival." The first was the publication of volume one of the *Jewish Encyclopedia* in 1901. Initiated in 1898 by the European immigrant writer Isidore Singer, the encyclopedia

(12 volumes, 1901–6) sated the long-standing desire for a synthesis of all Jewish knowledge, traditional and modern, including the fruits of the nineteenth-century German-based Jewish scholarly movement known as *Wissenschaft des Judenthums*. Hundreds of Jewish scholars from around the world participated in the undertaking, which was centered in New York and largely overseen by American scholars. Previous European attempts to produce such an encyclopedia in other languages had failed, making the symbolic significance of the American undertaking all the more potent. The publication of the *Jewish Encyclopedia* marked a rite of passage in American Jewish life. Historian Shuly Rubin Schwartz writes that it became "the symbol par excellence of the emerging cultural and intellectual independence of American Jewry." It signified both that Jewish cultural authority was passing to the New World and that the language of Jewish scholarly discourse was shifting to English. "To America, and not unto us, is the glory of the new house," wrote Anglo-Jewish scholar Israel Abrahams in a glowing review of volume one. "America, once a quantity to be neglected in matters Judaic, is here the main factor." The Hungarian Jewish scholar Wilhelm Bacher went so far as to crown New York as the new "center of Jewish scholarship."[15]

In 1902 the arrival in the United States of one of the world's foremost Jewish scholars, Solomon Schechter, seemed to confirm this judgment. He left England for New York to assume the helm of the newly reorganized Jewish Theological Seminary of America, reinforcing the great cultural transition and the new ascendancy of American Jewry. Schechter's goal was to transform the Jewish Theological Seminary into a European-style Jewish research institution, "a center of Jewish *Wissenschaft* [scientific scholarship] pure and simple."[16] To this end, he appointed a faculty of young, European-trained Jewish scholars committed to joining him in leading American Jewry from the wilderness of insignificance into the promised land of Jewish cultural renown. "Jewish learning in this country . . . will be American in language, in scope, in method, and yet be distinctively Jewish in essence,"[17] one of those scholars, Israel Friedlaender, grandly predicted in 1914. Refusing to pay obeisance to German centrality in the field of Jewish studies, the scholars of the new seminary moved to place the distinctive stamp of their new American homeland on the Jewish scholarly map. They produced great works of original scholarship and proudly published them in English, a symbolic expression of their cultural independence and new language loyalty.[18]

The books issued by the Jewish Publication Society, while geared to a more popular audience, also reflected these goals. In the 1890s their most important publications were still American adaptations of European volumes. To Lady Katie Magnus's *Outlines of Jewish History* (1890), for example, the society added chapters discussing American Jewish history. It also improved the English and added a book-length index to the British edition of Heinrich Graetz's multivolume *History of the Jews* (1891–98). By the 1910s, in contrast, the most important Jewish Publication Society books were original works by authors living in America, including *The Legends of the Jews* by Louis Ginzberg (1909–13)[19] and *Zionism* by Richard Gottheil (1914). Its most significant work was *The Holy Scriptures*, a new Jewish translation of the Bible overseen by the American scholar, Max Margolis.[20] This volume—which remained the standard English translation of the Jewish Bible for more than half a century—carried an announcement of American Jewry's cultural emergence right up front in its preface:

> [W]e have grown under Providence both in numbers and in importance, so that we constitute now the greatest section of Israel living in a single country outside of Russia. We are only following in the footsteps of our great predecessors when, with the growth of our numbers, we have applied ourselves to the sacred task of preparing a new translation of the Bible into the English language, which, unless all signs fail, is to become the current speech of the majority of the children of Israel.[21]

Even the books published by eastern European Orthodox Jewish immigrants demonstrated an appreciation of the American Jewish community's new status. Menahem Blondheim shows that in the nineteenth century these Hebrew-language books usually carried approbations (*haskamot*) from rabbis in eastern Europe; the only rabbi practicing in America who was deemed significant enough to endorse a book was New York's chief rabbi, Jacob Joseph. By the first quarter of the twentieth century, however, the number of approbations from American Orthodox rabbis rose sharply. More than half of the Orthodox works that Blondheim examined between 1902 and 1925 carried endorsements *only* from Orthodox rabbis practicing in America; almost 70 percent were endorsed by at least one. What this means, Blondheim persuasively indicates, is that the source of legitimation for the immigrant Orthodox shifted to America in the twentieth century. Their books, like those produced by the Jewish Publication Society and by the scholars of the Jewish Theological Seminary, bespoke American Jewry's coming of age.[22]

"A Great Library Is Indispensable"

Cultural independence, of course, did not depend solely on the publication of books. A Jewish cultural center with high-level scholarship also required world-class Jewish libraries. In America, these emerged early in the twentieth century.

Energetic Jewish book dealers like Ephraim Deinard traveled the world assembling and importing large collections of Judaica, while bibliophilic Jewish philanthropists like Mayer Sulzberger and Jacob Schiff purchased these collections for American libraries.[23] In 1904 Sulzberger donated his own private library, assembled in large part with Deinard's help, to the Jewish Theological Seminary. He aimed to make the seminary "the centre for original work in the science of Judaism, to which end the acquisition of a great library is indispensable." This hope was soon realized as the seminary became "the greatest Jewish library in the world in Jewish hands"—an easy boast to make since in Europe, the greatest publicly available Judaica collections (like those of the Bodleian Library at Oxford or the British Museum) were under government auspices.[24] Beginning about 1910, Cincinnati's Hebrew Union College library began to "gather and preserve every procurable literary record of the Jewish past," competing with the seminary. A timely visit to Europe just after World War I secured some 18,000 rare items, following which the library grew rapidly.[25]

Munificent Jewish donations allowed American Jewish libraries to proliferate under government and university auspices at this time. Deinard's goal was "to establish [Jewish] libraries in all the leading cities of our land," and his collections were purchased for the Judaica Division of the New York Public Library (established in 1898), the University of California at Berkeley, the Library of Congress (which established its Semitic Division, later the Hebraic Section, in 1914), and Harvard University. Meanwhile, in 1915, George Alexander Kohut donated most of his father's 5,000-volume Judaica library to Yale.[26] Significantly, the major Judaica collections in these and several other public and university libraries were segregated from the general collections in their establishment, maintenance, and classification. For all that Jewish scholarship had achieved a place on the shelves of America's great libraries, Jewish books—like American Jews themselves—were still far from fully integrated into the mainstream.

The Schiff Library of Jewish Classics

All of these themes—American Jewry's cultural emergence, the quest to unite Jews around a common culture of print, the effort to strengthen Jewish education and Jewish religious life, and the relationship between Jewish and non-Jewish books—came together in one of the most ambitious American Jewish publication projects of the early twentieth century: the Schiff Library of Jewish Classics. Amid great fanfare, the Jewish Publication Society announced in 1915 that it would produce twenty-five volumes of carefully edited postbiblical Jewish classics with texts, translations, and scholarly notes. The model here was James Loeb's 1910 Loeb Classical Library, standard scholarly editions of the great works of Greek and Latin authors. Jacob Schiff, who funded the Jewish project and for whom it was posthumously named, was Loeb's brother-in-law. According to legend, his wife had suggested that he "do for the Jewish classics what Jimmie is doing for the Greek and Roman," and he agreed.[27] The cultural and religious symbolism, expressed in each case through book sponsorship, could scarcely have been more transparent. Loeb, an assimilated Jew craving social acceptance, attached his name to the central literary canon of Western civilization, one that excluded all of the great Jewish cultural works written in Hebrew, Aramaic, and Arabic. Schiff, a proud Jew who scorned assimilation, attached *his* name to the very works that his brother-in-law excluded. Where the Loeb Classics implied that Jews kowtowed to Western civilization, the Schiff Classics were designed to demonstrate the opposite—that Jews had a rich classical literature of their own.[28]

The Schiff series also demonstrated that painstaking textual scholarship— "the collation and accurate edition of . . . original sources and documents"— could now be accomplished by Jewish scholars working in America. Schechter considered this kind of research—a legacy both of German historicism and of the European Jewish enlightenment—central to the study of Judaism. It combined modern methods with age-old values, evoked a traditional Jewish concern for textual accuracy, and provided all Jews with a common core of reliable cultural works and a joint basis for study and reflection. Two decades earlier, such textual scholarship was largely impossible in America; the requisite books and manuscripts lay across the ocean. Now, the country's newly created Judaica library collections changed all that. The Schiff Classics demonstrated that in textual scholarship too, American Jewry had arrived.[29]

Hebrew Printing from Old World to New

The Schiff Classics project also established America as a significant center of Hebrew printing. Until World War I, American presses had limited Hebrew printing capabilities. Demand was low, and Hebrew books could be printed at lower costs in Europe or Palestine.[30] The kind of high quality printing the Jewish Publication Society demanded for its classics simply could not be found in the New World. When the war cut America off from quality Hebrew printing and destroyed some of Europe's most famous Hebrew presses, the pitfalls of such dependency became readily apparent. In response, the society decided to acquire its own high-quality Hebrew press: a pair of European-manufactured Monotype machines with duplex keyboards. Inaugurated in 1921, the new press was managed by Moses Alperovich, a former employee of the highly prestigious and now destroyed Romm Press of Vilna. He embodied the cultural transfer from Europe to America represented by the press and the classics series as a whole. Under the management of Maurice Jacobs at the society and then after 1950 as an independent venture under Jacobs's name, the press became one of the world's foremost printers of Hebraica and Judaica. Through books and printing it reenacted a perennial pattern in Jewish history, creating a new cultural center from the ruins of the old.[31]

Two Visions of Jewish Publishing

Despite its symbolic and substantive achievements, the Schiff Classics project ultimately failed. Sixteen of the twenty-five originally scheduled works were canceled before they appeared. The classics proved too highbrow for most readers: they neither united American Jewry around a common cultural canon nor broadened the corpus of "Western civilization" to include Jewish works. The series did, however, highlight a growing chasm within the American Jewish community concerning the meaning and purpose of Jewish books. The Jewish Publication Society's idealistic and somewhat elitist vision of cultural stewardship saw books as instruments for elevating, integrating, and transforming the American Jewish community. By contrast, the more popular mass vision judged books largely on the basis of their sales potential, usefulness, and enjoyment value.

Bloch Publishing symbolized the more pragmatic approach; its mission and mode of operations effectively represented everything that the Jewish Publication Society was not. Where the society was idealistic, Bloch was utilitarian; reputedly, publisher Charles Bloch "considered favorably any manuscript which in his judgment would yield him a profit." Like such American firms as Scribner and Putnam, but unlike the society, Bloch was both a publisher and a bookseller. It produced and sold a wide range of Jewish books—its own and others—in several languages, as well as textbooks and religious articles. It eschewed the society's selectivity, acting instead "as literary midwife for scholarly, semi-scholarly and popular books" alike. Indeed, Bloch sought to embrace *all* Jewish books. Its sales bulletin—for many years the most reliable listing of Jewish books in print—presumed that the Jewish community broke down into a medley of different brow levels, tastes, ideologies, and religious movements, each with distinctive book needs of its own.[32]

A Segmented Community

More-specialized Jewish publishers also emerged at this time. The most important of these was the Hebrew Publishing Company (established in 1901), whose immigrant and Orthodox clientele read Hebrew and spoke Yiddish. As a publisher and a bookseller, Hebrew Publishing produced and sold everything from effusive greeting cards and romantic sheet music to educational textbooks and pious religious texts, including highly profitable Bibles and prayer books. It helped its customers navigate their way between the Old World and the New, offering familiar devotional literature, pirated from Europe, alongside Yiddish-English dictionaries and highly touted self-help books designed to socialize and uplift those who sought to get ahead. Books such as *Harkavy's American Letter Writer with Useful Information and a Treatise on Book Keeping [in] English and Yiddish* (1902), *Ollendorff's Method to Acquire a Thorough Knowledge of the English Language without the Aid of a Teacher* (1909), and Tashrak [I. J. Zevin]'s *Etikette* (1912) were perennial best sellers. They buttress Daniel Soyer's claim that Americanization was not just a passive process, but that immigrants "exercised a high degree of agency in their growing identification with American society."[33] The press also published Yiddish classics and translations into Yiddish of secular classics like Chekhov, Goethe, Tolstoy, and Jules Verne. Books of high and low culture, religious works and secular ones all found willing readers within the immigrant community, and all were therefore issued by the Hebrew Publishing Company. Given the divisions and segmentations in the immigrant community, Hebrew Publishing reached out in various directions simultaneously.[34]

During the interwar years, these communal divisions sharpened. The end of mass immigration, burgeoning generational and religious conflicts, the growth of universalist, nationalist, and revolutionary ideologies, the rise of anti-Semitism, and, of course, the inevitable impact of social, cultural, political, and economic forces operating within American society at large shook the foundations of American Jewry. Books and periodicals, far from drawing the community together, both reflected and fueled these divisions. By World War II, a procommunist Yiddish Cultural Association and an anticommunist Central Yiddish Cultural Organization were both publishing significant books in Yiddish; there were also Reform, Conservative, and Orthodox Jewish publishers, Zionist and Hebraist publishers, several scholarly publishers, and assorted publishers of textbooks for Jewish schoolchildren.[35]

Periodicals proliferated even more broadly, spurred in part by demands from professional groups for journals of their own. In 1900 there were four English-language national Jewish periodicals: one for "young people" (*Young Israel*), one for "the Jewish Religious School and Home" (*Helpful Thoughts*), one for Hebrew Union College students and alumni (*Hebrew Union College Journal*), and one, the *Menorah*, the official organ of the Jewish fraternal organization, B'nai B'rith. By 1940 there were more than fifty such periodicals serving such diverse groups as agricultural Jews (*Jewish Farmer*), Jewish communal workers (*Jewish Social Service Quarterly*), Jewish educators (*Jewish Teacher*), and Zionist Jewish Women (*Pioneer Woman*). Astonishingly, five of these journals—*Hebrew Union College Annual, Historia Judaica, Jewish Quarterly Review, Jewish Social Studies*, and the *Journal of Jewish Bibliography*—devoted themselves exclusively to Jewish scholarship.[36] This represented a sea change from the turn of the century when there were no such forums in America at all. By the 1940s Jewish scholars in America—like so many other community subgroups—were communicating more and more with one another and less and less with the community at large.

Unity through Books

Despite such evident fragmentation, however, the ideal of American Jewish "unity through books" continued to inspire leading Jews. The "book" remained an important Jewish cultural icon and being characterized as "the people of the book" still distinguished Jews from their neighbors. As a result, efforts through the medium of books to "bring Jews back together again" persisted throughout the twentieth century. In 1918, for example, the short-lived "Kehillah of New York City," the overarching communal organization of New York Jews established in 1909, published a 1,600-page *Jewish Communal Register* described as the first "comprehensive interpretation" of the city's Jewish communal life. Based on an exhaustive demographic, economic, and institutional survey, the volume attempted—within the covers of a single book—to bind together the many variegated segments of New York Jewry. This figurative "binding," the Kehillah hoped, would facilitate the achievement of its ultimate goal: a "well-ordered, well-organized Jewish community." The preface made the nexus between the book and the goal abundantly clear:

> What, then, is the first duty of those who would bring order out of chaos in the communal life of the Jews in New York City? What is the immediate obligation of those who are eager to point the way for a sound and constructive policy of Jewish communal development in the years to come? Their first task, it would seem, is to help the community to know itself as it is at present. To perform this indispensable service for the Jews of New York City, "The Jewish Communal Register" has been projected and published.... It will help the individual Jew and the Jewish Community to see themselves as they really are in relation to each other, and will thus be the first step to a full realization of Jewish life in this city.[37]

The *American Jewish Year Book*, published annually after 1899, promoted itself in a similar vein. Longtime editor Harry Schneiderman wrote in 1948 that this annual record of events and trends in American and world Jewish life was designed to serve "as a force for the promotion of the homogeneity of the Jewish community of the United States." The *Year Book*, he believed, was itself an agent of change, working, among other things, to "keep alive and to nurture in the hearts of American Jews that sense of kinship and common destiny which has inspired our community worthily to fill the role of big brother to our overseas brethren."[38]

Epilogue: Holocaust and Revival

The destruction of European Jewry in World War II—the brutal murder of scholars and writers, the burning and looting of libraries, the rack and ruin of established presses—brought together the two themes that had dominated the history of the Jewish book in America since the late nineteenth century. Even before the horrors of the Nazi regime were fully known, the Holocaust demonstrated for American Jews that they had become, in the words of historian Jacob Rader Marcus writing in 1941, "the heart of . . . Jewish life": "Almost everywhere Jewish books are being destroyed. Almost nowhere outside the United States are they being printed. The Jewish Publication Society is the only surviving literary medium of mass instruction west of Jerusalem. . . . Jewish culture and civilization and leadership are shifting rapidly to these shores."[39] Indeed, with the last remaining Jewish presses in continental Europe destroyed or shut down, only those in England, Palestine, and the Americas remained. The Jewish Publication Society took this as a challenge. "Our press," Maurice Jacobs declared, "is ready to assume its greater responsibility. . . . The record of the scholarly presses of Europe can and will be duplicated and perhaps surpassed in the scholarly Press of Philadelphia."[40]

Suddenly burdened with the mantle of Jewish cultural leadership, American Jewry again looked to books to bring them together. The prayer book produced by the National Jewish Welfare Board for Jewish soldiers in the American armed forces reflected this quest for unity. Composed of sections from Reform, Conservative, and Orthodox liturgies, the volume received the endorsement of all three branches of Judaism and hundreds of thousands of copies were printed.[41] The Jewish Book Council, founded in 1942 and subsequently (1944) sponsored by the National Jewish Welfare Board reflected this same quest for harmony. An outgrowth of Jewish Book Week (later book month), initiated by librarian Fanny Goldstein in 1925, the Book Council sought to spark "a Jewish renaissance in America" in response to the destruction of Jewish communities in Europe. To this end, it stressed its "impartiality as regards denominational loyalties" and promoted all manner of books in English, Hebrew, and Yiddish "to infuse in both young and old the traditional ardent zeal for Jewish knowledge." It looked to Jewish books in general—though not in this case to any one book in particular—to unite Jews and to help them, as one rabbi put it, "to understand better the creative Jewish spirit and the creators of Jewish values."[42]

In the wake of the war, the "American Jewish revival" produced a torrent of new books. The great Jewish historian Salo Baron thought that he saw "incontestable signs" in 1947 "not only of a general cultural awakening, but of a certain eagerness of the Jewish public to pioneer in the unexplored realms of a modern culture which would be both Jewish and American, and to find some new and unprecedented spiritual and intellectual approaches to the Jewish position in the modern world."[43] Given these goals, most of the Jewish books appearing at this time—upward of 70 percent—were understandably published under non-Jewish auspices by trade publishers and university presses. Jewish books, like Jews themselves, could finally become mainstream. Indeed, in the 1940s, university presses alone produced twice as many Jewish books as did the Jewish Publication Society; by the 1960s, they would publish five times as many.[44]

This mainstreaming of Jewish books posed no small challenge to Jewish publishers, especially the Jewish Publication Society, which saw its once formidable role diminished. More fundamentally, the move challenged the central aims of Jewish publishing: the twin goals of promoting America as a center of Jewish cultural life and of binding American Jews into a community shaped by a shared culture of print. By 1950 the first of these goals was already accomplished; only Israel rivaled America for Jewish cultural dominance. The second goal, meanwhile, proved illusory; American Jews remained divided. Postwar Jewish publishing was most successful when books focused on particular subgroups such as women, children, spiritual seekers, and the Orthodox. As the entry of Jewish books into the mainstream indicated, the more important postwar story lay elsewhere—in the increasingly vital role played by Jews within American culture as a whole.

CHAPTER 20

Running the Ancient Ark by Steam
Catholic Publishing

Una M. Cadegan
. . .

In an 1868 *Atlantic Monthly* sketch of prolific Catholic publisher Isaac Hecker, biographer James Parton noted that Catholics were "adopting, one after another, all our Protestant plans and expedients . . . putting American machinery into the ancient ark, and getting ready to run her by steam."[1] U.S. Catholics wholeheartedly embraced some aspects of modernity but defiantly rejected others. Parton's metaphor captures the spirit of Catholic publishing that extended far beyond Hecker's efforts.

In 1880 the Roman Catholic Church in the United States was still mission territory and would be until 1908. Its membership, estimated to have been more than 6 million in 1880, had risen to 10 million by 1900 and 21.5 million by 1940. In 1880 many Catholics had little formal education; these immigrants and their children scrabbled for access to prosperity and respectability. The Roman Catholic Church had only begun to develop a national self-consciousness. Yet, despite the increasing Protestant-Catholic hostilities of the mid-nineteenth century, the eighty U.S. bishops and a handful of other church leaders attending the Third Plenary Council, held in Baltimore from 9 November to 7 December 1884, emphasized their hope that there could be "no antagonism" between American and Catholic identity, for nowhere else could a Catholic "breathe more freely that atmosphere of Divine truth which alone can make him free."[2] By 1940, after more than a century of nativist opposition, defensive self-definition, and upward mobility, Roman Catholics in the United States were on the verge of being the most affluent American subgroup, confident in the compatibility of their Catholic and American identities.

Changes in Catholic publishing over the course of this period both contributed to and exemplified U.S. Catholicism's movement from an immigrant mission church to a substantially assimilated subculture.[3] The history of Catholic publishing in these years sounds in many ways like the broader story of American publishing—expansion, consolidation, capitalization, and professionalization. Understanding the distinctiveness of this particular story, however, requires looking both at the places where it overlaps with dominant trends and at the institutional and ideological factors that shape its interaction with those trends.

This essay highlights two aspects of Catholic culture related to books and reading between 1880 and 1940: the connection between material objects and the printed word, and the role of authority in shaping both the institutional aspects and the content of Catholic publishing. It also emphasizes how, in their tumultuous but thriving print culture, U.S. Catholics adopted technically and organizationally advanced processes in the pursuit of religious and cultural goals that were, in the eyes of their contemporaries, perceived as largely antimodern.

The dramatic growth of the Catholic community between 1880 and 1940 was coupled with a constant need to define and defend itself as both Catholic *and* American. Consequently, Catholicism was understood both as a religion—that is, a set of ideas or beliefs and practices—and as a way of life, a culture characterized by its sacramentality, which maintained the belief that everything in the world was potentially revelatory of God's grace. Books and print culture more generally were enmeshed in a densely sacramental fabric of which they were both producer and product. Books were ritual objects and means of grace (the Word made flesh) and were thus sacramental artifacts. Simultaneously, as means of instruction and dissemination, they helped create the culture that produced them (see figure 20.1). Print culture reinforced the clear structure of Catholic authority while giving believers road maps to navigate the individualizing landscape of contemporary American culture. Catholic print culture reflected the heterogeneity of a multiethnic, rapidly growing church; at the same time, its shared elements revealed the community's perceived obligations across the generations.

The Declining Mission Church: 1880–1908

Many landmarks in Catholic publishing history antedate the Civil War—the founding of newspapers, periodicals, and tract societies; Catholic versions of the Bible; and the recognition of Catholic devotional markets by religious and secular publishers alike. Until nearly the end of the nineteenth century, however, newspapers dominated the print culture of Catholic readers.

Catholic newspapers both proliferated and consolidated between 1880 and 1920, spurred in part by the decree of the Third Plenary Council that each diocese should have its own newspaper. As the Catholic population grew and new dioceses were established, the number of Catholic newspapers, mostly weeklies, thereby increased steadily for more than half a century. Other factors re-

FIGURE 20.1. The gilded binding suggests the elegant production of this elaborate volume of more than one thousand pages. Richly illustrated in color, it contains chapters on Catholic doctrine, the life and teaching of Christ, devotions to the blessed mother Mary, and historical material about the church, including portraits and biographies of Catholic bishops in the United States and Canada. Francis DeLigney, S.J., the Abbé Orsinia, and John Gilmary Shea, *Catholic Gems; or, Treasures of the Church; A Repository of Catholic Instruction and Devotion* (New York: Office of Catholic Publications, 1887). 26 by 21.6 cm. College of the Holy Cross.

inforced the consolidation and nationalization of Catholic newspapers. After 1920, when American Catholicism began to lose its immigrant orientation, Catholic papers whose primary appeal had been to audiences eager for political news of a home country (particularly Ireland) were no longer as popular as they once had been. Failing Catholic newspapers were often purchased (either outright or with controlling interest) by individual dioceses, both to document diocesan activities and to present "the Catholic position" on issues about which the faithful needed to be informed.

By about 1920, then, newspapers were increasingly likely to be under the direct control of the diocesan hierarchy, which underwrote the cost of production and the means of distribution. For these reasons, the survival of these periodicals was ensured, but not without a price. Some Catholic journalists lamented that freedom of the press was curtailed,[4] but others recast the argument and lauded the distinctive contribution of the Catholic press to American Catholic freedom. From this perspective, the aim of newspapers was not "to compete with the secular dailies" but "to offset the worldliness of the general press and at the same time to acquaint their readers with the great amount of the news of their Church that is entirely lacking or dealt with only summarily in the general papers."[5] Newspapers thus evolved from being perhaps the most unfettered of Catholic print media to the one most religiously partisan, charged primarily with protection and communication of orthodoxy.

Magazines and other periodicals grew in relative importance during this period, while newspapers, with some important exceptions, diminished.[6] In 1880 forty-six Catholic newspapers and ten Catholic magazines existed; in 1900, seventy-three newspapers and eighty-two magazines existed. As with other elements of the Catholic press, many of its magazines were intended to be Catholic versions of secular or Protestant efforts. The best known of these was Isaac Hecker's *Catholic World* (figure 20.2). Intended as the Catholic equivalent of *Harper's* or the *Atlantic*, *Catholic World* was a review of art and culture, targeted at a middle-class audience with leisure and money to spare (when the first issue appeared in April 1865, the price of a subscription was five dollars). *Catholic World*, published by the Paulist Fathers continuously until the 1970s, was one of several periodicals (including *Ave Maria* and *Messenger of the Sacred Heart*) that established the "successful formula" of family appeal and religious devotions.[7] This appeal was directed to the middle-class family, the ideal toward which many Catholics aspired in late Victorian America.[8]

Magazines were more likely than newspapers to be published by religious orders and congregations, for whom publishing was an apostolate—that is, a part of their religious mission rather than a profit-making venture. As a result, funding and sustaining their ventures were constant struggles, particularly in

FIGURE 20.2. *Catholic World* was launched to compete with secular publications. The contents of volume 71, no. 421 (1900) included articles on religious subjects or general topics from a Catholic perspective, as well as notices of new books, dominated by, but not limited to Catholic studies. The frontispiece portrait of John Henry, Cardinal Newman points to an article in the middle of the volume; a discussion of "Modern Science and the Catholic Faith" opens the issue of April 1900.

view of the practice of giving away publications. The study of Catholic publishing is complicated by the general practice of counting both the number of paid subscriptions and the number of free copies when reporting the circulation of magazines and other religious literature. For example, the highest-volume Catholic publishers in the nineteenth century were the Catholic Publications Society, which gave away thousands of pamphlets, and the publishers of the magazine *Columbia*, a copy of which was sent (and still is) to every member of the Knights of Columbus.[9]

At the end of the nineteenth century and in the early twentieth century, both newspapers and magazines demonstrated a distinctively Catholic configuration of social relations that affected Catholic print culture. Many, if not most, publishing enterprises involved both lay people and members of religious orders or congregations; any officially Catholic enterprise was also subject to hierarchical authority.[10] The influence of the hierarchy was undoubtedly real and inescapable; the nineteenth-century church was more centralized and more sensitive to Vatican influence than it had been for centuries. However, close control—of the press or almost anything else—was simply impossible in the United States, even had it been considered desirable by all members of the hierarchy. The existence of an identifiable central authority offers such a clear point of contrast with other American religious subcultures that it is easy to overestimate the efficiency of such control.

That said, bishops greatly influenced what was published by and for Catholics.[11] Several of the decrees promulgated by the Third Plenary Council would stimulate new opportunities for Catholic publishing. For example, on the subject "Of books and newspapers," it was stated that "While objectionable writings are to be condemned, Catholics should oppose them also by orthodox newspapers and books." New markets were stimulated by reaffirming the decree of the 1866 council requiring each parish to establish a school (thus expanding the market for textbooks), and calling for the creation of a uniform catechism for religious instruction and emphasizing the importance of "Good Reading" and "The Catholic Press" for "The Christian Home."[12] However, the influence of bishops was not a simple matter of decree and obedience; it interacted with lay cooperation, initiative, and resistance.

Most major Catholic book publishers of the late nineteenth century were owned by families of European descent—immigrants with some experience in printing, bookbinding, or bookselling who established their own firm in the United States, such as Dennis and James Sadlier, or were branches of European firms like that of Benziger Brothers and F. Pustet.[13] By 1880 the largest concentration of Catholic publishers in the country was housed on Barclay Street in New York City.[14]

Lay-owned Catholic publishers produced a variety of printed religious material—Bibles, prayer books, spiritual reading, devotional guides, catechisms, missals, official liturgical texts, and textbooks as well as histories, poetry, and fiction. For example, an 1893 bibliography of Catholic publishing includes a translation of *The Secret of Sanctity according to St. Francis de Sales*, a gynecological handbook, manuals for members of devotional societies, books on the mass, and the fifth edition of *May Blossoms in Honor of the Blessed Mother of God, by an S.J.*[15] This array suggests the variety of contexts in which print was believed to be crucial to Catholic life and worship. Official liturgical rites were translated and duplicated in missals that allowed the laity to follow the Latin of the mass in their own languages and to supplement it with other prayers. In his 1863 *Guide to Young Catholic Women* (in its twenty-ninth printing in 1893),

Paulist George Deshon wrote: "It is a simple matter to attend at Mass. You come to worship God and to pray. No particular way of doing so is laid down. . . . Some say the Rosary, and occupy their minds with good thoughts while they do so. Others have a book with prayers for Mass, which they follow; all this is very well."[16] All aspects of life, from worship and private prayer to professional practice, were supported and supplemented with Catholic print materials.

Throughout the nineteenth century and well into the twentieth, devotional literature was a mainstay of Catholic publishing. These materials were published for use in prayer outside the official worship of the Roman Catholic Church, for either private individual prayer or devotional practice. Catholic publishers capitalized on the sustained success of titles like Thomas à Kempis's *Imitation of Christ*, Francis de Sales's *Introduction to a Devout Life*, and Butler's *Lives of the Saints*.[17] Ann Taves's study, *The Household of Faith: Roman Catholic Devotions in Mid-Nineteenth Century America*, examines with great methodological astuteness the role of devotional publications in the mid-nineteenth century, identifying important changes in mass-printing techniques, increasing educational levels among Catholic laity, and a focus on the household as the most important locus of religious faith.[18] Such factors only intensified after 1880, as the Catholic middle class expanded.

Devotional literature demonstrates the distinctive interplay of religious authority, market forces, and individual readers' preferences within Catholic print culture. The large quantities published reflect high demand among readers. At the same time, devotional publication was subject to forces other than the market. The contrast between clerical ownership of diocesan newspapers and lay publishing houses might suggest that one was thoroughly under ecclesiastical control and the other entirely free of it. For publishers actively seeking a Catholic audience or market, however, whether for the purpose of evangelization or profit, ecclesiastical authority was nonetheless a consideration. Canon law required that any religious text or sacred image directed at a Catholic audience be reviewed by "competent ecclesiastical authority" and found to be free of any conflict with Catholic doctrine. This procedure, referred to as *censura praevia* because the review took place before publication, was denoted by the *imprimatur* (Latin for "it may be printed") of a bishop on the obverse of the title page. The Counter-Reformation Catholic Church, fearful of the rapid spread of Protestant ideas made possible by the printing press, originally sought to censor and approve of *all* works for public use. That ambition, not surprisingly, had evaporated by the mid-sixteenth century; nineteenth-century American bishops had no way of *requiring* publishers to obtain such approval. However, because Catholics were forbidden to read certain categories of text published without the imprimatur, one presumes that publishers actively sought the goodwill of this large market and complied with censorship procedures accordingly (see figure 20.3). Advertisements often touted ecclesiastical approval of a particular text as a selling point.

As with most legal aspects of Catholic polity, use of the imprimatur was neater in the pages of canon law than in practice. The spread of new devotions usually outpaced the process of approval; bishops often waited to see the impact of a particular devotion before approving either its practice or its associated printed materials.[19] This variable application of prior censorship demonstrates the frequent fluctuations in ecclesiastical authority. Catholic print culture was in a constant, distinctive process of renegotiation, sometimes coerced, sometimes freely engaged.

Equally distinctive was the Catholic cultural configuration of the relationship between printed texts and material objects. Virtually every devotion had both material and print components. The best known was the rosary, in which the string of beads was accompanied by a meditation on a series of fifteen "Mysteries," incidents from the lives of Christ and Mary that were elaborated in hundreds of publications (see figure 20.4). Other devotions included the same combination of ritual object and printed prayers or directions: statues, pictures, or medals could be supplemented by specially written and approved prayers and meditations.[20] The connection between the word and the object was, for Catholic worship, organic and inextricable.

The majority of leading Catholic publishers also manufactured or distributed religious goods, including altar furnishings and linen, rosaries, scapulars, communion wafers, statues, medals, prints of religious images, and other objects of the extensive paraphernalia that bespoke and reinforced the devotionalism, domesticity, and consumerism of late nineteenth-century Catholic life. The assets of his father's business listed by P. J. Kenedy on 17 January 1866 included gilt prayer books, plain prayer books, slate pencils, catechisms, scapulars, religious pictures, stationery, and beads.[21]

This association derived partly from financial necessity, with sales of religious goods supplementing less-profitable publishing enterprises. A publishing venture that attempted to survive on its own was greeted with sympathy and skepticism. The connection between print and religious goods was more than merely pragmatic, however. As Colleen McDannell has pointed out, nineteenth-century Catholic piety differed from Protestant piety primarily in its dependence on material artifacts and visual images: "What the Protestants did through reading, the Catholics did through seeing."[22] Protestant print culture focused primarily on the Bible; for Catholics, the Bible was always part of a constellation that included an altar, bread and wine, and probably also an assortment of candles, bells, oil, ashes, incense, water, a crucifix, or palm branches.

FIGURE 20.3. A mimeographed notice pasted inside the front cover of the 1902 edition of *The Downfall* by Emile Zola (New York: P. F. Collier and Son, © 1902) reminded Catholic students that the title was on the Index of Forbidden Books and permission was required to read it. Roesch (formerly Albert Emmanuel) Library, University of Dayton.

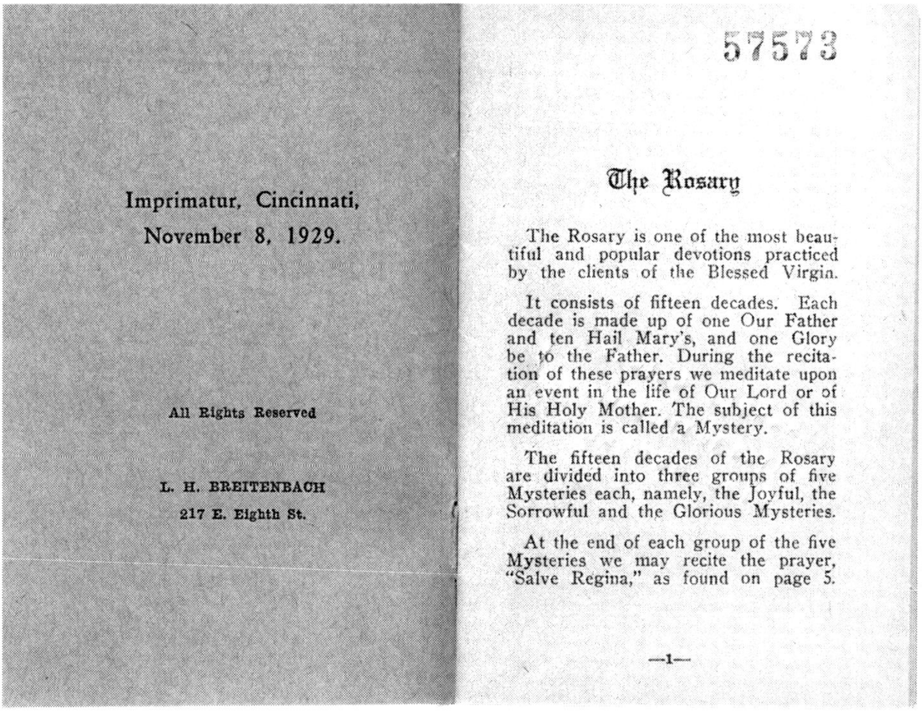

Imprimatur, Cincinnati,
November 8, 1929.

All Rights Reserved

L. H. BREITENBACH
217 E. Eighth St.

57573

The Rosary

The Rosary is one of the most beautiful and popular devotions practiced by the clients of the Blessed Virgin.

It consists of fifteen decades. Each decade is made up of one Our Father and ten Hail Mary's, and one Glory be to the Father. During the recitation of these prayers we meditate upon an event in the life of Our Lord or of His Holy Mother. The subject of this meditation is called a Mystery.

The fifteen decades of the Rosary are divided into three groups of five Mysteries each, namely, the Joyful, the Sorrowful and the Glorious Mysteries.

At the end of each group of the five Mysteries we may recite the prayer, "Salve Regina," as found on page 5.

—1—

FIGURE 20.4. *The Rosary Made Easier* (Archdiocese of Cincinnati, 1929). From the pamphlet collection of the Marian Library, University of Dayton.

Sometimes the association between word and object is strikingly explicit: in his widely reprinted advice book for young women in domestic service, Deshon insists that even if a young woman cannot read, she should "not be cast down on that account. . . . There is one beautiful book, at least, we can read; and that is the Crucifix," which contains "fountains of knowledge and true wisdom." In addition, the rosary is "another lovely book you have that you can read, though you never learned a letter of the alphabet."[23]

In The Mainstream, Not of It: 1908–1940

The first two decades of the twentieth century were a genuine turning point in U.S. Catholic history. The removal of the U.S. church from mission status in 1908 foregrounded a sense of national identity that was intensified by the experience of the First World War. Extensive participation in the war effort validated Catholics' legitimacy as Americans, as did rising educational and economic status. Not only did a significant number of Catholic Americans serve in the armed forces in the Great War, but to coordinate its participation in the war effort the church organized the National Catholic War Council. Reorganized and made permanent after the war as the National Catholic Welfare Conference, it did more than any other structure to establish a national Catholic presence and self-awareness in an increasingly corporate, highly organized society.[24]

Postwar restrictions on immigration stabilized the Catholic population, promoting nationalism and the growth of an increasingly assimilated, educated, and professional laity. Before 1880, Catholic publishing efforts tended to focus on poor and uneducated recent immigrants; by the late nineteenth century, Catholic family publications had a more middle-class tone. After World War I the audience for Catholic publishing consisted increasingly of economically successful, native-born Americans. The press thus shifted focus from the protection of an immigrant faith to a conscious awareness of the varying needs of a maturing community.

The sense of solidity and confidence that came from economic prosperity and from manifest patriotism was nonetheless accompanied by a persistent sense of difference, sometimes proud, sometimes defensive. Significant numbers of U.S. Catholics remained antagonistic to American culture, either because they perceived persistent attacks on the church or because they sought salvation from a degraded modern American society in the stability and teachings of the church.

Historian Philip Gleason characterizes the middle years of the twentieth century as a time when U.S. Catholics were actively engaged in "the search for unity." This notion resonates with the apparent ideological unity of the Catholic press. While historians of U.S. Catholicism have exposed the limits of such unity, it was an explicitly articulated goal between 1920 and 1960.[25] This is not to say that divisions among Catholics did not exist—far from it. Rather, Catholic cultural work was centrally concerned with wresting unity out of disagreement, disharmony, dissonance, and disarray. The press was a major contributor to this work.[26]

Old Wine in New Bottles

In the early decades of the twentieth century, the Catholic press adopted most of the centralizing and professionalizing strategies of the general press. Attrition rates for new periodicals, for example, declined dramatically between 1900 and 1936.[27] A Catholic Press Association was formally established in 1911 to facilitate communication nationally. The National Catholic Welfare Conference, the policy agency of the American bishops, established a news service in 1919 to provide wire reports on national and global Catholic news items to Catholic publications.[28] In addition, Catholic universities began to include journalism among the professional courses and programs that proliferated after 1900.[29] These efforts to formalize standards and centralize organizations reflect the growing national self-consciousness of increasingly well-educated Catholics, as well as national trends beyond the Catholic community.

This self-consciousness was not seeking mere assimilation, however. The Catholic press adopted increasingly modern methods to achieve seemingly premodern goals. Catholic publishing espoused both the need for resources to prevail against the antireligious and dehumanizing aspects of modernity and the need for Catholicism to engage the modern world, proclaiming the sacredness of reality and the existence of eternal truth. The self-conscious use of modern, professionalized methods to achieve at least partially countermodern ends is visible in two major publishing efforts of the early twentieth century: the catechism and the *Catholic Encyclopedia*.

At the turn of the century, most existing catechisms had been prepared hurriedly to meet the Third Plenary Council's call for a uniform national explication of doctrine, to be used in religious education.[30] After 1894, though, the catechism market began to change, especially after Pope Pius X's *Quam singulari*, the 1910 decree that lowered the approved age for first communion (previously between twelve and fourteen) to the "age of reason," somewhere around age seven. The 1884 catechism, even in subsequent editions, was an impractical tool. Its questions and answers about doctrine and practice were far too difficult for the seven-year-olds preparing for first communion. The 1910 papal decree promoted a stronger market awareness that resulted in a proliferation of catechism texts. Innovations included not only cosmetic changes such as cover color and illustrations but also pedagogical changes—glossaries for each chapter, graded texts, simpler language for younger children—and theological considerations such as topic arrangement based on the liturgical year or the addition of scriptural support and justification for the catechism's doctrinal content. The U.S. bishops, still committed to the goal of a universal text, in the mid-1930s once again authorized a revision; this five-year, widely consultative process was conducted with an eye to professional expertise, not just theological and ecclesiastical authority. The resulting 1941 *Baltimore Catechism* was informed by a growing awareness of contemporary pedagogical research and cognitive psychology. Central to the folklore of Catholic childhood in post–World War II America, it was seen by many in the generation after the Second Vatican Council as theologically conservative. Originally, however, it reflected the appropriation of techniques and ideas very much in the contemporary publishing mainstream.

A similar interplay of modern forms for traditional purposes characterized the production of the fifteen-volume *Catholic Encyclopedia* between 1907 and 1914. Born out of dissatisfaction with the treatment of Catholic subjects in secular encyclopedias, it sought to rectify errors and explain Catholic doctrine and history while presenting Catholic views on contemporary topics such as socialism and psychotherapy. Reflecting the simultaneously confident and yet defensive posture of American Catholics, the editors stated that they were "fully aware that there is no specifically Catholic science, that mathematics, chemistry, physiology and other branches of human knowledge are neither Catholic, Jewish, nor Protestant; but, when it is commonly asserted that Catholic principles are an obstacle to scientific research, it seems not only proper but needful to register what and how much Catholics have contributed to every department of knowledge."[31]

Examining relatively discrete enterprises such as the catechism and the *Encyclopedia* reveals crucial aspects of Catholic publishing in this period, but it can obscure some of the tensions the "search for unity" generated. A number of fault lines existed: liberal-conservative, lay-clerical, Eastern-Midwestern, Irish-German, male-female, religious order–diocesan hierarchy. Each was reflected in some dimension of the press. Devotional literature, for example, reveals that the more demonstrative and emotional aspects of Catholic piety were associated with recent immigrants, the working class, and women; assimilation and the pursuit of success fostered a more upper-class, more "Protestant" demeanor and aesthetic.[32]

Theology, taste, and class are deeply intertwined here. While sentimental piety and emotional excess were often deplored, even the most Brahmin of Catholics would not dismiss devotions entirely.[33] At the same time, much of Catholic publishing—magazines, elementary school textbooks, scholarly periodicals, and weekly newspapers—aimed at "elevating" the taste of the Catholic reading public by presenting European traditions of high culture as the rightful heritage of American Catholics. The fourth in a series of *Ideal Catholic Readers*, for example, by "A Sister of St. Joseph," included reproductions of works by Michelangelo, Raphael, and Doré. Textbooks also reconstructed U.S. history to include Catholic contributions and introduced the particularities of Catholic theological and material culture. The *Ideal Catholic Reader*'s first lesson, "The Young Missionaries," was followed by a new-word list that included "Xavier" and "cassock" along with "delightful," "interesting," and "astonishment."[34]

Catholic magazines of the period also reflect the desire to educate Catholics in European culture while seeking respect for Catholics as a group. Although the varying styles and cultural messages of different periodicals revealed the class distinctions among American Catholics, the editors also worked diligently to overcome these barriers through religion.

This desire to "Catholicize" high culture and make it available and attractive to Catholics is evident in a series of efforts to launch "quality" journals. *Catholic World* was joined in the twentieth century by two influential publications, *America* and *Commonweal*, the names of which do not reveal their religious affiliation. Founded in 1909 by a group of Jesuits, *America* was explicitly a review of politics, art, and culture from "the" Catholic perspective, notwithstanding the secular reach of its title. "The object . . . of this Review," the editors wrote in the first issue, is "to supply in one central publication a record of Catholic achievement and a defense of Catholic doctrine, built up by skilful hands in every region of the globe." Its mission was not solely intramural; non-Catholics, the editors asserted, "are . . . eager to have us exert our proper influence in the national and social life" by contributing to public discussion of important contemporary issues.[35]

Fifteen years later, editor Michael Williams and a group of lay people displayed similar confidence in launching *Commonweal*, asserting that "the conserving and regenerative forces of the fountain head of Christian tradition, experience and culture" could address "the problems that today all men of good will are seeking to solve." They viewed this duty as not only spiritual and moral but patriotic; the aim was not the advancement of the church but "the betterment, the happiness, and the peace of the American people."[36]

The ambitions of *America* and *Commonweal* reflect the growing confidence of the Catholic community. The theological imperative of sustaining Catholicism by providing Catholics with abundant information now widened to a cultural imperative to make the Catholic voice heard in the public realm. They knew that the world was modern and modernizing; *America* was launched as a weekly to replace its predecessor, the monthly *Messenger*, arguing that "The march of events is too rapid"[37] to be covered only monthly.

Apparently, some readers used the magazines to broach Catholic questions with non-Catholic neighbors. The editor of *America* received a letter in 1928 asking him to refrain from criticizing U.S. policy in Mexico, because the correspondent's "Protestant friends will read *America* but won't read the *Messenger of the Sacred Heart*."[38] The *Messenger of the Sacred Heart* was aimed at a popular audience, more explicitly devotional, and thus presumably less attractive to a Protestant reader. The contrast between *America* and the *Messenger* exemplifies a divide between high-culture Catholic journals and popular Catholic magazines. The latter, aimed at families and emphasizing devotion and pastoral concerns over cultural ones, circulated more widely than the former. One of the most popular twentieth-century devotional magazines is *Our Sunday Visitor*, founded in 1912. At first glance, *Our Sunday Visitor*'s differences from *America* and *Commonweal* are more apparent than its similarities to them. Its tone was sectarian and populist rather than urbane, and it focused intensely on antisocialism and on answering anti-Catholic attacks and misunderstandings. The first issue included headlines announcing "The Church Law of Annual Confession and Communion Strongest Basis of Society," "A Whole Army of Protestants Think That the Blessed Virgin Mary Should be Honored" and "Socialism's Foundation Shattered."[39] Despite the belligerent tone and the absence of a smooth East Coast cosmopolitan veneer, the magazine's subtitle for years was "The Harmonizer."

The differences in style and taste between *Our Sunday Visitor* on the one hand and *America* and *Commonweal* on the other reflect real class differences within U.S. Catholicism. However, the missions of the high-culture and the more pastoral periodicals overlap in ways that might at first be unclear. For example, each of these periodicals aimed to "create a taste for Catholic reading," but while *Our Sunday Visitor* did so by cultivating wholesomeness, *America*'s editors pursued artistic complexity. Nonetheless, despite striving to be "cosmopolitan," *America*'s "animating principle" remained "loyalty to the Holy See and profound respect for the wishes and views of the Catholic Hierarchy." Even if this was a gesture of goodwill or preemptive defense, it reflects an awareness that *America*'s readers belonged to a larger whole.[40] Culturally, the Catholic press often melded various brow levels. Simultaneously divided and longing for unity, Catholic leadership lamented both the taste of the Catholic reading public and the failure of the laity to read the Catholic books being provided for them.

This imperative of unity is visible also in Catholic scholarly enterprises, particularly during the first half of the twentieth century. The outpouring of historical scholarship on American Catholicism owes its existence largely to one person, John Gilmary Shea (1826–92), a layman who dedicated his life to documenting early American Catholic history before the records of its existence disappeared. He produced, among hundreds of other works, a massive *History of the Catholic Church in the United States*, by far the most ambitious such effort in the nineteenth century.[41] The succeeding generation of scholars often invoked Shea's legacy as they pursued the history of U.S. Catholicism with the same zeal for both unearthing sources and honoring the Church.[42]

Catholic publishing sought to demonstrate and advance Catholic unity not only within the United States but internationally as well. The first half of the twentieth century marked the "Catholic Revival" or "renaissance," a resurgence of scholarly and artistic activity in Europe that demonstrated to American Catholics the power and responsibility of Catholicism to speak to the modern world. Usually dated from the work of John Henry Newman, the revival encompassed writers from England (Hillaire Belloc and G. K. Chesterton), France

(Georges Bernanos, Leon Bloy, Paul Claudel, Jacques Maritain, and François Mauriac), and Spain (José María Gironella).

The revival's presence in the United States was established largely through the efforts of the English publishing house of Sheed and Ward, which opened a U.S. branch in 1933. The 1930s generally were an era of renewed vigor for Catholic book publishing—Bruce Publishing in Milwaukee and Newman Press were both established, while Prentice-Hall and McGraw-Hill added "Catholic lines." Like so many other Catholic publishers, Sheed and Ward's profits were rather shaky, but the operation had its greatest success in the United States, publishing works by Bloy, Mauriac, and Claudel in its first year.[43] Other major figures of the revival, such as philosopher Jacques Maritain and medieval philosopher-historian Etienne Gilson, were published by secular presses.

The philosophical and historical work of writers like Maritain and Gilson might seem to belie claims about the negotiation of unity within and through Catholic publishing efforts. On the contrary, the achievements of the Catholic Revival generated a distinctive sense of group pride and solidarity across class lines. Pastoral periodicals such as *Our Sunday Visitor* and *Ave Maria* claimed writers such as Chesterton and Maritain with at least as much glee as *America* and *Commonweal* did. Although the percentage of readers reading any of the authors of the revival cannot be determined, they nonetheless represented an ideal for U.S. Catholic achievement. If contemporary European Catholic authors could produce great literature, then the tradition could speak to the modern world. American Catholicism was thus challenged to nurture authors who could speak with equal skill and authority.

The Legacy

Culturally, Catholic publishing from 1880 to 1940 appears as it did to many of its contemporaries—foreign, premodern, and un-American. Financially, technologically, and organizationally, on the other hand, it was rather mainstream—technologically innovative, pragmatically commercial. Most successful Catholic publishers congratulated themselves and were regularly congratulated not only on the content and quality of their publications but also on the business savvy with which they were produced. The knowledge of advertising and marketing of John Noll, founder of *Our Sunday Visitor*, as well as his ability to seize the advantageous moment, ensured the success of that magazine as much as Noll's ability at religious commentary.

The *Catholic Encyclopedia* was published independently and funded through subscriptions and lay investments. This fact is remarked on in virtually every account of the *Encyclopedia*'s genesis, with a satisfaction that seems to match that taken in the work's scholarly quality. Several decades later, writers and media figures such as Daniel A. Lord, S.J. (1888-1955) and Fulton J. Sheen (1895-1979) were running the ancient ark, no longer by steam, but by rocket fuel. They used modern technology and public relations—Sheen is more famous for his television show than his writing; Lord wrote prodigiously and produced public pageants, musical plays, and radio broadcasts.[44] One contemporary lauded Lord as "a Shakespeare gone Chautauqua"; another as the "Flo Ziegfeld of the cloister."[45] Despite the surface of *Romanità* apparent in their midcentury clerical garb, Catholic literary entrepreneurs like Lord, Sheen, Noll, or Francis X. Talbot of *America* had at least as much in common with Americans like Louis B. Mayer or Henry Ford as they did with Pius XI.

Recognizing both aspects of Catholic publishing is difficult but necessary if we wish to understand the details in their full complexity. This essay has highlighted multiple cases; many more remain. For example, Catholic women formed reading circles in the late nineteenth century. Recognizing the benefits of the Chautauqua system, they established a Catholic version to provide young Catholics with a "more advanced plan of Catholic reading."[46] Catholics published *Catholic Digest* in order to capitalize on the popularity of the *Reader's Digest* with accessible excerpts from Catholic periodicals.[47] A group of Catholics with very different politics followed similar instincts in founding the *Catholic Worker*. They infused the passion for economic and social justice that characterized the *Daily Worker* with transcendent devotion, simultaneously developing within the upwardly mobile Catholic community an awareness of the suffering of the poor. Catholics also established a separate Book-of-the-Month Club, through which they hoped to supply books that "are cultural and artistic, that have a popular appeal, and that are, above all, expressive of the Catholic ideal, tradition and philosophy."[48] Through a complicated dance of imitation and appropriation, Catholic publishers sought to bring all aspects of life within the religiocultural boundaries of Catholicism. This interplay of confidence and vigilance distinctively configured the most transcendent and the most mundane of Catholic publishing ventures.

Section IV

Readers and Reading

Part A
Institutions

Introduction

Carl F. Kaestle and Janice A. Radway

We noted in chapter 1 of this volume that attention to the reader is now a cardinal priority of studies in the history of print. Chapter 2 employed that priority in looking at sites of reading in 1880. The intervening chapters have given intermittent attention to readers. In this section we turn our attention centrally to readers and the institutions of literacy. It is now a widely stated premise of print culture studies that text takes on meaning only in the presence of a reader. There are, however, often intermediaries negotiating this process of interpretation. Parents, peers, teachers, and others initiate reading opportunities, encourage readers, and in various ways shape the reader's interpretation of text.

Sometimes this mediation is institutional, and some institutions indeed are devoted centrally to literacy, that is, they select, develop standards for, promote, and dispense some body of reading matter. Schools, libraries, literary clubs, book clubs, government agencies, and literacy training programs come to mind. We have chosen two institutions—schools and libraries—that carried a great deal of weight in organizing and presenting American literate culture to readers, young and old. Two particular versions of these institutions—the public high school and the public lending library—came of age in our period, resulting in much more widespread exposure to publicly approved culture than had earlier been the case. It seems that all societies have attempted to define and control culture in some ways, especially for activities that are funded by the government. The United States was no exception.

The elementary and secondary school curriculum offered history training based in the British colonial experience in America, widening into a narrative of an expanding Protestant, republican, capitalist society. Similarly, the schools offered literature focused on the canon of English and American writers and devoted themselves both to defining quality in literature and to fostering moral values and character. To get to that curriculum, children (or adults) first had to learn basic skills, such as fundamental literacy and numeracy, as well as some factual and conceptual basis for understanding science. Once students were equipped with these skills, however, their future direction was not always predictable. If one trains people to read the Bible, they can also read pornography or seditious literature; and if one trains women to read in order that they may learn their place, they may also learn that they can aspire to others'. These are the Janus faces of literacy. All literacy training programs have an explicit or implicit cultural and ideological aspect, but that does not guarantee that readers accept it in whole or in part. Furthermore, there is a process of negotiation between institutions and their clients. As Wayne Wiegand writes in his essay on public libraries, librarians had to bend somewhat to the reading demands of their users.

The consequences of having a particular narrative and set of values embedded in the school curriculum or the local library were not trivial. For many students the diverse uses of literacy they experienced outside of the public schools, within their religious, ethnic, or racial group, were different from those of the school or the library. By their omission, those diverse uses of literacy were defined as external to the official American culture. Public schools did not attend to Orthodox Judaism, to the poetry of Langston Hughes, to foreign languages other than French and German, to Latino politics, or to many other aspects of the larger enterprises of literacy in the United States. The inroads of cultural diversity in the schools during our period were slight.

For some students, the lesson may have been twofold: not only was the curriculum of Shakespeare, Longfellow, and "our Puritan forefathers" not *about* them, but it was also not meant *for* them. The schools appeared to be inviting all students to learn to appreciate and benefit from the study of the most highly approved English literature and from the historical narratives of New England's unfolding. Indeed, many students presumably did so. But it is also plausible that the message for others was that Shakespeare's work made no connection with their lives but was the badge of someone else's cultural capital. This hypothesis has its analog in Magali Sarfatti Larson's observation about professionalization, that in order to have a profession, a group had to have secrets accessible only to them, but that in order for the public to *recognize* the expertise and value of the profession, the professional group had to reveal just enough of its secrets so that the public knew about them.[1] In order to have a profession, in other words, the general public had to value your expertise; by analogy, to have cultural capital, the general public had to recognize the value, if not the appeal, of the culture defined as superior. In our period, when culture was becoming more stratified and high culture was becoming more "sacralized," the public schools assisted in reinforcing the hierarchy of culture.[2] Libraries also had impulses to control the content and moral purpose of their stock in trade, but because library participation was entirely voluntary, and because patrons of libraries could choose their own reading material and interpret it on their own, that is, because the library's cultural teaching was more implicit than explicit, librarians had a harder time keeping the cultural message focused.

We selected one aspect of schooling and two aspects of libraries to explore in this section on the institutions of literacy. First, regarding the schools, Richard Venezky examines the teaching of reading, asking how it was influenced by mainstream cultural values, by the textbook trade, and, intermittently and imperfectly, by research on reading. On the one hand, reading texts seemed bland. This resulted principally because of the particular features of the textbook market, a subfield in the commercial publishing sector, which was not only seasonal but national. Success depended upon gaining sales in all regions and types of school districts. Thus, the impetus to avoid offending anyone was great. As a result, reading textbooks were influenced by that salient, profound shift in the American economy during our period: the shift to national markets, driven by improved transportation and communication and increased productivity. Given the resulting national character of the textbook market, the consequence in this case was a bland, homogenized product.

On the other hand, the reading texts carried definite social messages about behavior, gender, race, and other matters. Venezky attends not only to the "manifest" but also to the "latent" reading curriculum. As with the ideas about the functions of literature as cultural capital, Venezky also concludes that as analytically interesting as this subject may be, for the most part we can only speculate about the nature of educators' social control motives.

Working against schools' tendency to proclaim social messages, perhaps, was a profound shift in the reading curriculum and in the way people consequently learned to read: the shift from an emphasis on rhetoric and elocution to silent reading. This seems consistent with a society in which print was proliferating and diversifying, in which readers had to read fast to keep up and had to choose what to read among endless choices. It was during our period, after all, in the 1920s, that Henry Luce invented *Time Magazine*, designed to cut through the plethora of choices, saving "time" by summarizing all the news.

Public libraries, fledgling institutions at the beginning of our period, also wrestled with how to define and accomplish their social mission. Wiegand addresses their agenda—to bring the "best" reading to the most people at the least cost. Their determination to define the "best" reading, however, ran into trouble when the public demanded popular fiction as its main reading fare. Undaunted, librarians set out to create a profession, as did so many others in this great age of consolidation and organization. Still, as Wiegand argues, library participation was voluntary, and professional librarians disagreed about the wisdom of imposing particular kinds of approved literature on readers. As a consequence, the history of the public library illustrates the considerable power of readers in the process of defining this institution of literacy. And we should note the role of the public library, often called the "circulating" library, in increasing the free access to books and increasing the circulation of print in society.

Phyllis Dain explores the history of an altogether different type of library, the great research libraries, which also came into their own in our period. These huge, comprehensive collections partook of both the historic mission of great libraries as the repositories of the world's accumulated knowledge and the newer concepts of learning as evolving, constantly changing in the face of new research. In the latter role, they were in tune with the invention, in our period, of the research universities. They were also influenced by trends documented elsewhere in this volume: increasing access to print and the increasing speed of print's circulation. Research libraries were dynamic, always growing. Unlike the great libraries of Europe, America's major libraries allowed patrons to walk around the stacks. Their printed catalogs were displaced by the expandable card catalog designed to accommodate fast changing collections. Dain details these and other institutional consequences of the common historical generalization that large libraries underwent a transformation "from storehouse to workshop." Again, whatever the imperfect institutional implementation of these priorities, print was in motion, and the institutions of literacy had to deal with that reality.

CHAPTER 21

From McGuffey to Dick and Jane
Reading Textbooks

Richard L. Venezky with Carl F. Kaestle

Most children learn to read in school, with the help of a reading textbook. Nineteenth-century educators in the United States called these books "primers," indicating their primary, introductory nature; by the mid-twentieth century, they were called, in similar fashion, "basal readers," suggesting their basic or foundational function. Reading textbooks both introduced children to the process of reading and were a vehicle for moral and social training, an introduction to literature, and the occasion for teachers to instill a love of reading in schoolchildren.

The books came in series, a book for each grade or age level. Because almost every elementary school student in the nation needed a reading textbook, they were the basis of a big business. This chapter looks at the influence of educators and the influence of publishers on the striking changes in reading textbooks that occurred during the period between 1880 and 1940.

Reading Textbooks in 1880

William Holmes McGuffey, the nineteenth-century's most famous author of reading texts, died in 1879, the same year that the seventh edition of his successful textbook series appeared. *McGuffey's Readers* continued to sell in large numbers in the early years of our period; but other competitors quickly sprang up. One of the best sellers among these was *Appleton's School Readers*. Its au-

---

Richard Venezky's untimely death in June 2004 prevented the collaborative revision of this article. Carl Kaestle assumed responsibility for that revision. This was a labor of love; Dick Venezky was a distinguished expert on reading, one of the premier historians of reading instruction, and a charming bon vivant. The initial scholarship and the basic concepts are Venezky's; some additional arguments and research details have been added, in addition to stylistic changes. Kaestle gratefully acknowledges the research assistance of Ani Mukherji and Thomas Jundt, graduate students at Brown University in, respectively, American Civilization and History, but he assumes responsibility for any errors of fact or interpretation.

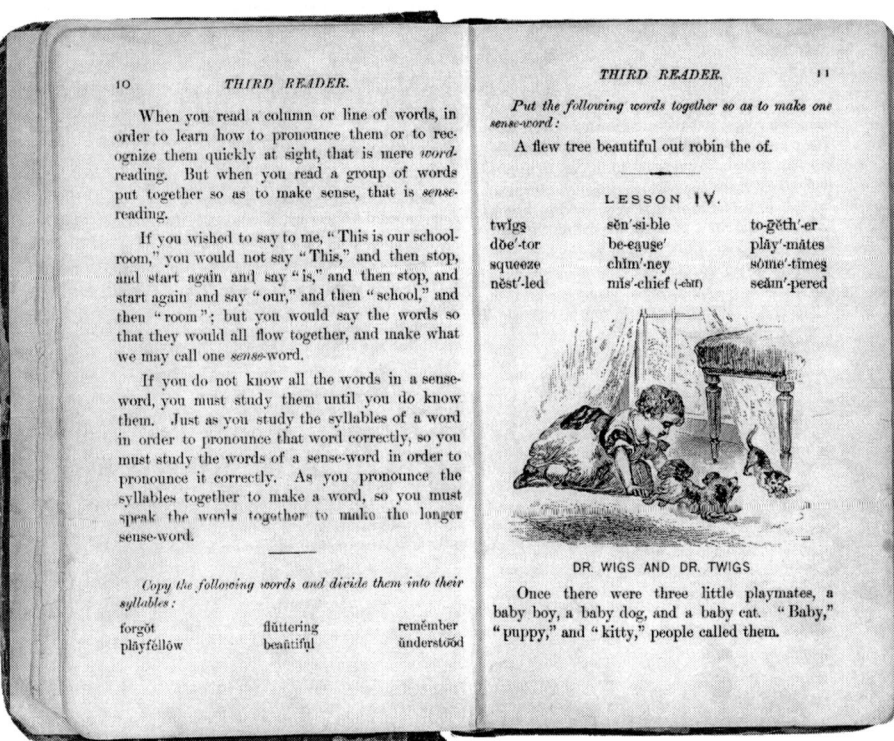

FIGURE 21.1. William T. Harris, Andrew J. Rickoff, and Mark Bailey, *Appleton's School Readers: The Third Reader* (New York: American Book Company, 1877), 10–11. Department of Special Collections, Spencer Research Library, University of Kansas Libraries.

thors were a star-studded team, including William Torrey Harris, an internationally recognized Hegelian scholar who had established the first public system of kindergartens during his tenure as superintendent of schools in St. Louis. Rounding out the trio were Andrew J. Rickoff, nationally recognized for reforms he instituted as superintendent of the Cleveland public schools; and Mark Bailey, an instructor at Yale and the author of several textbooks on elocution and reading.[1]

Appleton's Third Reader illustrates the characteristics of this typical series. Like its companion volumes, the *Third Reader* was a triumph of the phonic method (see figure 21.1). The authors promised that by mastering the "power of letters" and syllabication, students would learn to pronounce even the most difficult words from their spelling.[2] Mark Bailey contributed nine supplementary pieces on "How to Read." Like most other authors of the time, Bailey believed that reading was fundamentally an oral activity, akin to elocution. Bailey's advice for reading provided no strategies for obtaining meaning; rather, the student was introduced to the mysteries of syllables, pronunciation, intonation, and other mechanics. The textbook's seventy-one reading selections were short—averaging about 400 words each—and they were meant to be read aloud. Black-and-white illustrations adorned one of every five or six pages. Vocabulary was carefully controlled to present a range of difficulty, peaking with relatively arcane words like *guileless, sentinels,* and *languidly.*

McGuffey's and *Appleton's* stories had strong moral overtones. They often depicted the less pleasant realities of life, especially the dire consequences of undisciplined or immoral behavior. One story in *Appleton's* depicts a hero named Carl, running through the woods chasing butterflies and becoming very warm. He reaches a spring and sees a sign that says "Rest in the shade before you drink," but, of course, he is very thirsty, so he gulps down some water. Barely able to make it home, he is sick for several days, requiring a visit from a doctor. Carl's father says: "I think you will not again act so foolishly," and Carl answers that he will never "drink cold water when I am very warm."[3] *McGuffey's* tells the story of ten-year-old James Brown, who played hooky from school and fell in with idle boys. They took a boat out to sea. A severe storm came up; the boat capsized and they thrashed around in the water terrified, until they were rescued by some sailors. As a consequence, the text says, "James became regular at school . . . and learned to obey his parents perfectly."

In these tales about the less pleasant realities of life, animals abounded—bears, monkeys, sparrows, swallows, mice, toads, and more. In one *Appleton's* story, a merry brown thrush sings about her five eggs hidden in a cherry tree but warns that the joy won't last "unless we're as good as can be."[4] A second depicts a boy helping a chick to prematurely peck its way out of its egg, only to have the chick die by the next day. Reflecting on the bird's ill fate, Johnny surmises that "perhaps it would have grown up a wicked chicken, and broken its mamma's heart."[5]

Both *Appleton's* and *McGuffey's Readers* provided character education through brief moral tales. They also shared two core assumptions: first, that reading was an oral activity and, second, that phonics—sounding out words using knowledge of the sounds of the individual letters—provided the essential tools for learning to read.[6]

Social Change and the Reading Textbook

Despite these continuities between *McGuffey's* and *Appleton's* reading texts, forces were gathering that would change the purposes and methods of reading instruction during our period. As chapter 1 of this volume emphasized, faster communication and transportation fostered a national economy; industrialization spurred immigration and urbanization. Between 1893 and 1896, a serious depression further intensified the stress of daily life in America, spawning not just anxiety and poverty but various reform movements, including some education-oriented programs that addressed the expansion and diversification of the student population. Rapid population growth in the early twentieth century, coupled with changing economic roles for youth, sharply increased school enrollment in general and the proportion of the population attending high school in particular. Students stayed in school longer and attended more days each year. The percentage of five- to nineteen-year-olds enrolled in schools increased from 58 in 1880 to 75 by 1940, and literacy expanded apace.[7]

Mechanization, legislation, and unionization gradually reduced industrial child labor, and a rising standard of living allowed more families to bear the opportunity costs of withholding their children from the labor market. Commercial jobs for both men and women increasingly required high school training. The percentage of seventeen-year-olds graduating from high school increased from 2.5 in 1880 to 49.0 in 1940.[8]

These changes in the school population in turn had interesting and complicated effects on both educational theory and the textbook industry. This chapter unravels the impact of these changes upon reading instruction and on the reading textbook, one of the most ubiquitous pieces of print culture in our history.

Progressive Education and the Reading Text

Educators were intensely aware of the demographic changes transforming their schools, and they produced many contending ideas about what schools should do in response. The so-called progressive education movement encompassed a variety of contrasting, even contradictory, reforms. While child-centered reformers attended more to the students' interests and general development, social efficiency advocates sought to train students directly for different roles in an industrial society. Despite their divergent ideals, these two major Progressive Era reform groups adopted surprisingly similar approaches to reading instruction. They joined in three important departures from the methods and content of *McGuffey's* and *Appleton's Readers*: a shift to silent reading rather than reading aloud; a shift to the "whole word" method of reading rather than phonics; and a gradual softening of the moral messages of reading texts, culminating ultimately in the unceasingly harmonious and bland society of "Dick and Jane" in 1942.[9]

The wing of the progressive education reform movement associated with John Dewey urged close attention to the child's interests and motivations and to the processes by which children think. One of its early proponents was Colonel Francis Parker of Chicago, who advocated a loving, child-centered classroom. Studying German approaches to reading instruction, Parker encountered the whole-word method, which seemed far superior to the more mechanical phonics method of sounding out words. As superintendent of schools in Quincy, Massachusetts, he had implemented this innovation and received very positive publicity. The whole-word method emphasized comprehension and context. It had been proposed as an alternative to phonics as early as the 1840s, but it had not gained mainstream status by the beginning of our period in 1880.[10] Its popularity spread along with the child-centered progressive education movement, which, though most salient in small private schools and experimental units within the public schools, championed various educational practices that diffused more broadly into regular public school classrooms. The whole-word method of reading instruction was one of these.[11]

The second, competing wing of educational reform in the Progressive Era was more readily adopted by burgeoning public schools. It focused on providing efficient instruction through different curricula for different children.[12] Edward L. Thorndike, a prominent social efficiency advocate and psychologist at Columbia's Teachers College, provided a learning theory for this approach to reform. He called it "connectionism." This early version of behaviorism emphasized the use of rewards or punishments to reinforce or weaken the bonds between a given stimulus and a given response. Despite his rather mechanical view of children's learning, Thorndike, like the child-centered progressives, emphasized the importance of comprehension and thus favored the whole-word method of reading instruction. His 1917 study, *Reading as Reasoning*, helped popularize the idea of reading as thinking.[13]

Like Progressive Era organizational theorists and industrial managers who touted efficiency for greater productivity and higher profits, Thorndike recognized the need for efficiency in American schools to prepare children for jobs in American industries. Many curriculum theorists and school administrators took up the theme. Unlike the often slow and clumsy method of recitation, they thought, silent reading was much more attuned to these ideals. Silent reading, like the whole-word method, promoted both efficiency and comprehension. As one expert remarked, "many children may gain more from ten minutes spent in independent silent reading than they would in a twenty-minute oral-reading recitation period."[14] Reading instruction thus underwent parallel shifts from elocution to silent reading and from phonics to whole-word recognition.

The shift to silent reading also had its roots in the waning of the traditions of public speaking. In the mid-nineteenth century, almost every reading series had stressed elocution; one reader in each series was usually devoted entirely to this subject. Before reading tests were developed (ca. 1915–18), teachers could evaluate reading performance only through oral recitation. Lingering illiteracy—especially among the older population—also justified oral reading instruction because children were often required to read aloud newspapers and other print materials to illiterate family members. In addition, multihour sermons, lectures, and debates were popular forms of both entertainment and education, making elocution a revered skill through at least the first three-quarters of the nineteenth century.

The grand style of oratory so popular in the early nineteenth century began to wane after the Civil War, perhaps as part of a larger rejection of the emotional issues associated with mid-nineteenth-century politics and the war. By the end of the century, reading textbooks rarely featured oral reading but occasionally remembered its virtues. D. C. Heath's *Fifth Reader*, for example, argued that, "Good oral reading need not be one of the lost arts, though it requires careful training and much practice."[15] Nonetheless, although the popularity of elocution was fading by the turn of the century among educational experts, it took two more decades for silent reading to triumph across the nation's schoolrooms. According to William H. Appleton, his firm sold a million copies of *Webster's Speller* in 1880, almost 100 years after its initial publication.[16] And many schools, particularly in rural areas, retained the *McGuffey's Readers* in the early twentieth century. Silent reading was explicitly featured in numerous reading programs issued in the 1920s, including *The Silent Readers* and *The Silent Reading Hour*.[17] Each invoked selected aspects of the reading research literature to establish the virtues of silent reading, although the most convincing argument was simply that silent reading had become the dominant mode of reading outside of school, for adults as well as for children. Modern society seemed to require it. Furthermore, the impetus toward silent reading gained momentum in large public schools of the 1910s and 1920s, where "efficiency" and testing were valued, making the evaluation of individual oral performance less feasible and less attractive.[18]

By the late 1920s oral reading may have been a lost cause—witness this plaintive comment in a 1928 reader: "The current tendency to identify silent reading entirely with the gathering of information is unfortunate. Most home reading of all sorts nowadays is silent. The first impression of a poem, however, might well be gained through the ear. . . . When dealing with plays, poems, speeches, the dramatic scenes in stories, and occasional highly significant or charmingly written prose passages, oral reading is of course in place."[19] By the 1930s most reading instruction programs relegated oral reading to the beginning grades, and some even suggested that silent reading be featured from the start.

Shifts in reading instruction were rarely based on strong evidence during our period. A leading reading researcher lamented in 1931 that "There had been little experimental work since the publication of Huey's *Psychology and Pedagogy of Reading* [1908]."[20] Throughout our period, reading experts relied mostly on theory, instinct, and practical experience to justify silent reading and whole-word instruction. In retrospect, the shift from oral to silent reading appears to have begun with the decline of oratory and was reinforced by the waning of other adult oral reading. With or without a research base, prominent reading experts of the 1920s like Charles Judd and Guy Buswell advocated silent reading in the 1920s and beyond, to support progressive principles of efficiency and comprehension.

By the 1940s both the whole-word method and silent reading were pedagogical mainstays in reading instruction. This trend mainly reflects the preference of Progressive Era educators for comprehension and meaning. The publishers went along with their education experts but were not quiescent on some other matters.

The Textbook Publishing Trade

Expanding school enrollments made textbook publishing a large and growing industry after the Civil War. As in the meatpacking, steel, and oil industries, the textbook industry witnessed various mergers and acquisitions. Most notably, in 1890 several textbook publishers merged to form the American Book Company (ABC), a conglomerate that soon dominated the textbook market (see figure 21.2). Incorporated in the state of New Jersey in 1890, ABC encompassed all of the school publications of Ivison, Blakeman, & Co., D. Appleton & Co., and Van Antwerp, Bragg & Co., plus some school publications of A. S. Barnes and Harper Brothers.

Over the following decade, this large trust acquired at least ten other textbook publishers. ABC was often justly accused of the same corrupt practices and monopolistic activities in which Standard Oil, Northern Securities, and Swift engaged.[21] The *Chicago Daily Inter-Ocean* editorialized on 1 April 1923 that the history of the American Book Company was "honey-combed with crime, and its continued power is a menace to the public good."[22] In *The Goslings: A Study of the American Schools* (1924), Upton Sinclair claimed that early in the twentieth century "the American Book Company controlled 90 per cent of the [school textbook] business, and everywhere its name was synonymous with corruption."[23] The most common corrupt practice was bribing local school boards or state textbook adoption committees to adopt a given ABC text series. Reacting to such charges and to new state antitrust laws, ABC performed various legal maneuvers to avoid indictment. In 1908 it reorganized as a New York corporation and divested itself of its subsidiaries. This failed to ward off antitrust charges

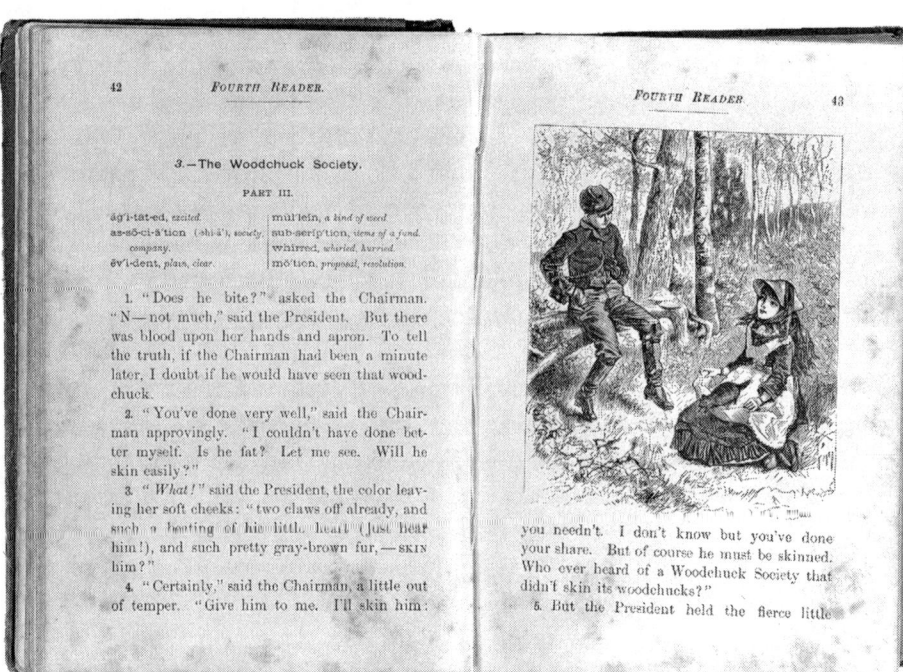

FIGURE 21.2. [William Swinton], "The Woodchuck Society," *Swinton's Fourth Reader* (New York, Cincinnati, and Chicago: American Book Company, circa 1883), 42–43. Department of Special Collections, Spencer Research Library, University of Kansas Libraries.

brought by the state of Texas in the same year, but those were settled out of court with little impact on corporate profits.

Reflecting on the tactics and reputation of the American Book Company in 1947, its vice president argued that rampant corruption existed in the book business long before the amalgamation of ABC. He noted, for example, that in 1881 the state of Kansas had seventy-eight active textbook publishers competing for the state's orders. "Nothing short of manslaughter was excluded" as a tactic, he quipped. However, he argued, "let us be fair. The schoolbook business was no worse than any other competitive business of that day—only a bit more colorful and zestful." To survive, he said, the American Book Company merely followed contemporary business practices.[24]

Despite the power of ABC, the textbook trade remained competitive. Although several major textbook publishers not associated with ABC experienced financial difficulties in the boom-and-bust economic cycles of the late 1800s and early 1900s, many others, including Ginn, D. C. Heath, Henry Holt, and Silver Burdett, continued to operate profitably.[25] Moreover, even if there had been no

American Book Company dominating the market, textbook sales would have been concentrated in a relatively small number of large firms. The textbook business required houses that could operate nationwide and could update their offerings regularly to meet the increasingly complex adoption regulations of major metropolitan areas and states. By 1940 ABC was no longer the colossus that it had been at its inception. Formidable competitors in the market for reading textbooks included Ginn; Heath; Silver Burdett; Allyn & Bacon; Scott, Foresman; and Row, Peterson.

Some smaller firms also gained national attention in textbook publishing by developing a niche and the sales capacity to handle state adoption systems. Houghton Mifflin, for example, specialized in reading texts, literature texts, and some history books. In its early years, during the 1880s, Houghton Mifflin's education department capitalized on the parent firm's eminence as a publisher of literary classics to produce fifteen-cent paperback sets of classics for schools. By 1930 millions of copies had been sold. As silent reading became increasingly well established, Houghton Mifflin modified its books to meet that demand. It also adapted texts to help prepare students for the newly introduced College Entrance Examination Board exams. When states began to play a larger role in textbook adoptions, Houghton Mifflin established various branch offices of its Education Department: Chicago in 1895, San Francisco in 1921, Dallas in 1927, and Atlanta in 1930.

During these years, the field of education became more separate and professionalized on university campuses. Schools of education with research faculty emerged, and teachers colleges sprouted around the country. Seeing a potential market for books about teaching, Houghton Mifflin in 1909 began on its accustomed literary turf by reprinting a work by Ralph Waldo Emerson and publishing another by Charles W. Eliot. But soon the firm hired Ellwood Cubberley, the dean of the School of Education at Stanford and one of the most influential educationists of his day, to develop its list of new books for teachers.[26]

Textbooks, unlike most forms of print, were not marketed through bookstores or regional distributors but directly to schools. Given the low, per-copy profit margins and the seasonal sales patterns of textbooks, bookstores rarely stocked them. Furthermore, when adopting textbooks, school districts and states not only negotiated prices and delivery schedules but also often requested that publishers provide supplemental support, such as training teachers how to use new textbooks and new methods in the classroom. Bookstores were not staffed to meet such demands.

National marketing of a reading series required not only a large sales force but also a selection of readings that were acceptable in all of the country's diverse regions. Certain kinds of readings had to be avoided. For example, although Lincoln's *Gettysburg Address* was recognized by the end of the nineteenth century as one of the masterpieces of English oratory, it appeared in few school readers prior to the 1920s because its inclusion limited sales in the South. Publishers also avoided pieces that extolled the virtues of particular regions, like the frontier or seacoast. Reading texts tended to be bland and homogeneous because they were designed for broad acceptance. Rather than striving to provide distinctive content or cheaper prices, publishers sought to distinguish their reading series from their competitors' by developing supplementary components — workbooks, wall charts, flash cards, and teachers' guides — and by ensuring that their materials and methods were in tune with those advocated by leading reading experts at university schools of education.

Reading texts in this period reflected both trends in the textbook industry and developments in the organization of the education profession. Like soap and cereal, textbooks were sold on a national scale, though they sold only once a year, in very large volume. This peculiar commercial rhythm distinguished their markets not only from soap and cereal but also from other sorts of books. This affected the politics of textbook sales and the production of textbook content: reading texts became blander and more uniform as all the publishers moved toward the inoffensive, avoiding the local, the colorful, and the controversial.

While these developments were occurring in the textbook industry, the development of the education profession affected who the experts were. After 1900 educational policy much less frequently involved the eminent generalists who had earlier participated in discussions about elementary and secondary education, people such as William Torrey Harris, not only a prominent school administrator and reformer but also an active and respected philosopher; and Charles Eliot, president of Harvard University, long active in the National Education Association, and chair of the National Education Association's famous "Committee of Ten," which recommended standards for college preparatory work. By the 1920s the authority to pronounce on elementary and secondary education was located in schools of education. Trends in reading instruction, therefore, were in the hands of professors of education, who researched and lectured on the teaching of reading. This does not mean that reading practices were more effective or less effective, but that the locus of control had shifted to a new education establishment.

The Authors of Reading Textbooks

The effect of this shift can be seen in the authorship of basal readers. Many nineteenth-century authors like William Holmes McGuffey wrote reading texts as sole author. *Appleton's Readers*, however, anticipating the future trend in

1880, convened a team of prestigious educators as coauthors. By the 1890s publishers' general practice was to hire a team of authors, and not, as in the case of *Appleton's*, two eminent scholarly education reformers paired with a professor of rhetoric from a university English department, but rather a mixture of professors of education and classroom teachers who specialized in reading curriculum. Furthermore, during the 1920s the proportions in this mixture shifted increasingly to favor education professors. Teams of authors were still chosen for the appeal of their prestige in the eyes of textbook adoption committees, but the basis for that prestige had changed. Two of Thorndike's students, for example, became leaders in the reading business. Arthur Gates was a professor of education at Teachers College, Columbia, an expert on children's vocabularies, and an authority on the construction of basal readers. William Gray, a professor of education at the University of Chicago, became a leading reading researcher and, in the 1940s, produced that great monument of mid-twentieth-century print culture, the Curriculum Foundation Series, popularly known as "Dick and Jane."[27]

From 1880 until World War I, males and females were equally likely to be senior authors of reading series, a contrast to the earlier nineteenth century.[28] However, as publishers turned increasingly to senior faculty at schools of education for their lead authors, fewer women were available for selection because almost all faculty members were male. Women continued to appear as second and third authors after this time, usually as representatives of school districts or of teacher training programs.

Professors tended to be of Anglo-American background, so racial and ethnic diversity among the new impresarios of reading texts was also lacking, though this was certainly not a new trend in the period from 1880 to 1940. A list of leading authors suggests the Anglo-American bias in this, as in so many aspects of corporate and academic life in the United States: Gray, Gates, Stickney, Pollard, Elson, and Sprague.[29] Despite the dramatic social and economic changes occurring between 1880 and 1940, then, the Anglo-American identities and perspectives of reading textbook authors remained constant.

The professionalization of authority in the education field and the large scale of the textbook industry combined to encourage the widespread diffusion of the pedagogy preferred by education professors reared in theories of the progressive education movement. Both the child-centered thrust and the social efficiency thrust of progressive education led to a shift to silent reading and an emphasis on comprehension, not phonics. The national and cyclical nature of the textbook market acted to encourage books that were bland in order to be uncontroversial.

The Evolution of Textbook Content

The goals of a text can sometimes be gleaned from explicit statements in the book. Other purposes may be inferred from the "latent" curriculum: the symbols, the selection and omission of topics, and other implicit messages. In 1880 beginning reading instruction was designed to equip young people for adult reading, to give them good values as citizens and as workers, and to introduce them to good literature. This third goal had developed in the latter half of the nineteenth century and remained constant throughout our period. It had several supporting motives. Reading teachers took as their province the English language, regarding literary expression as the most sophisticated application of the skills they taught. Thus, rudimentary reading instruction merged neatly into literary study in the middle and upper grades. Great literature encouraged students to develop good language skills, aesthetic appreciation, and a love of reading, while simultaneously reinforcing the centrality of Anglo-American traditions and accomplishments as the basis for an assimilative school culture.

The use of beginning reading texts for the presentation of social values and moral principles is a complicated matter. Reading textbooks provided a logical and convenient mechanism by which to present the idealized image of America that educators and many other adults wanted children to adopt. Some observers, however, have argued that schoolbooks' portrayals of democracy, social relations, and social merit were often disguised justifications for inequality and covert instruments by which to subordinate American newcomers and the working class more generally. Evidence for this argument draws on analysis of both the explicit curriculum of readers and the implicit or "latent" curriculum. The argument that textbook producers intended to assimilate and subordinate a diverse population is partly a matter of conjecture and partly a matter of focusing on educators' explicit statements about social goals, which were often quite straightforward about the need for class stability and assimilation into an Anglo-American culture.[30]

While motives of social stability and social control may have been constant, the particular values expressed in textbooks were not, and there is some research on this topic. Ruth Miller Elson examined the latent content of textbooks published during the nineteenth century, tracing, among other themes, the denigration of minorities, particularly Catholics, Jews, and African Americans. By the last two decades of the nineteenth century, textbooks had adopted an emphasis on material gain. The movement toward art, literature, and scholarship at the end of the nineteenth century still required a practical justification. Describing education in terms of men of business, Elson wrote: "The concepts of American culture presented in his schoolbooks would prepare him for a life devoted to the pursuit of material success and a perfected character, but a life in which intellectual and artistic achievements would seem important only when they could be made to serve some 'useful' purpose."[31]

Supporting this conclusion about material gain are the findings of Richard de Charms and Gerald Moeller, who sampled American readers from 1800 to 1950 and scaled them according to their presentation of achievement imagery, which rose steadily from 1800 until the period 1880–1900, then steadily declined. The authors concluded that the shape of this curve reflected a shift in American society around 1890 from a Protestant ethic that stressed individual thrift, hard work, and competition, to a social ethic emphasizing the group as the main source of an individual's creativity and belongingness as his ultimate need.[32]

De Charms and Moeller also found that moral teaching, defined as implicit or explicit statements of moral judgments, declined steadily from 1810 until 1950, with the largest drops occurring in the periods between 1850 and 1870 and 1910 and 1930. Given the other shifts that occurred in late nineteenth-century American society, there is at least general support for the de Charms and Moeller conclusions, which raise an issue of where such changes originate and how. The simplest answer is that the stories in the school readers were extracted from the broader body of children's literature, diffusing the cultural shift into the curriculum. Before the end of the nineteenth century the popularity of the Oliver Optic and Horatio Alger stories, which had emphasized earnest hard work and pluck, began to decline. According to Bernard Wishy, stories for children changed drastically around 1880. What followed was the golden age of children's literature, led by authors like Robert Louis Stevenson, Beatrix Potter, L. Frank Baum, and Howard Pyle. Adventure stories abounded, eschewing heavy moral overtones for engagement of the child's imagination.[33] By the advent of the Curriculum Foundation Series in 1942, preaching was totally removed from school readers. And children, who had been portrayed in late nineteenth-century reading texts as individuals—succeeding, behaving well or ill, being rewarded or punished—were by 1940 seen in groups, with family and peers, doing things and solving problems together.

Whatever the motivation for any specific textbook content, arguments about textbooks' social messages must ultimately face the murky question of what impact the texts actually had on children. Arguments about the influence of *McGuffey's Readers* illustrate the lack of consensus on this issue. Initially published in 1837, *McGuffey's* 1879 edition was in wide use during the early part of our period. Mark Sullivan, who devoted considerable space in *Our Times* to the *McGuffey's Readers*, maintained that "The moral precepts in McGuffey's First to Fourth Readers left their record in the ideals of conduct held, and to some extent lived up to, by several American generations."[34] In contrast, Henry Steele Commager questioned whether the *McGuffey's*-style moralisms "eventually did more harm than good," pointing out that the generation most heavily exposed to these readers "was probably the most materialistic generation in our history."[35]

Skepticism about whether children absorbed subtle messages from reading texts may be in order. On the other hand, one can think of the school classroom as a stage on which to dramatize the values and behaviors that educators think are important in the society. Thus, it seems that the readers' content likely added to the social lessons that many students heard about American society and the behaviors that adults considered proper. Beyond that, the history of reading hits a wall of evidentiary poverty.

Dick and Jane

By 1940 the texts encountered by third-grade readers were drastically different from the *Appleton's Readers* of 1880. Educators in the first four decades of the twentieth century developed a radical new approach to the reading process, the teaching of reading, and the introduction of children to the meanings and practices of modern life. The Curriculum Foundation Series, which came to be known as the "Dick and Jane" series, was used by more children than any other reading books of the time. Its authorial team was led by William S. Gray, the distinguished reading theorist and professor of education at the University of Chicago, who had studied with Thorndike.[36]

Streets and Roads, a third grade reader in the Dick and Jane series, presents a striking physical contrast to its 1880 progenitors. Although only slightly larger in height and width, it contained a multicolored illustration on almost every two-page spread. The stories averaged about 800 words, twice as long as *Appleton's* and no mention was made of pronunciation, intonation, or the power of letters. Although the authors condoned a few phonics decoding strategies in the early grades, they stressed training the eye rather than exercising the voice. The teacher's guide and other supplementary materials largely dismissed phonics in favor of the "look-say" method of teaching reading: the editors expected students to recognize words and phrases at a single glance. Forty reading selections included a balance of children's adventures, bits of American history, humor (including the "The Five Hundred Hats," by Dr. Seuss), animal stories, and a few folk tales. Generally, however, the series depicted life in tidy, prosperous towns or suburbs. Children were well dressed and scrubbed, mothers appeared mostly in aprons, and fathers were seen coming and going to work. Although published in 1942, the book is silent on war, the Depression, hunger, and ration-

FIGURE 21.3. [William S. Gray and May Hill Arbuthnot], "Uncle George and the Voices," in *More Streets and Roads*, Basic Readers: Curriculum Foundation Series (Chicago: Scott, Foresman, and Co. 1942), 6–7. From *Child Life Magazine*, copyright 1941 by Rand McNally; Department of Special Collections, Spencer Research Library, University of Kansas Libraries.

ing. There was ample gasoline for the car, a full stock of toys in Uncle Robert's department store, and a well-appointed passenger train to carry Bob, Molly Ann, and Patty from the Northfield station to the city (figure 21.3).

Reflections

During the period 1880 to 1940, the professionalization of authority in the education field and the national scale of the textbook industry combined to encourage the widespread diffusion of the pedagogy preferred by education professors reared in theories of the progressive education movement. Both the child-centered thrust and the social efficiency thrust of progressive education encouraged the shift to silent reading and an emphasis on comprehension not phonics. Reading for meaning, not pleasure, replaced reading for rhetorical expression. And the moral messages had become more implicit and softer. These reading books were about an ideal life in the suburbs, unruffled by bad behavior or dissolute people. They portrayed this ideal world because it was their ideal world; because the national, high-stakes textbook market and the statewide adoption policies of some states encouraged books that were bland in order to be uncontroversial, and because the consumerism of the day was rooted in the suburbs, so the basal readers—like the middle-class magazines of their day—portrayed that version of American life.

The revolution had been consolidated, and the message had become all warm and fuzzy, if also culturally biased. There was no national school system, but the increasingly standardized textbook industry insured that the revolution would diffuse across the country. It remained for later generations to question the narrow cultural base and to revive the old debate between phonics and whole-word teaching.

CHAPTER 22

The American Public Library
Construction of a Community Reading Institution

Wayne A. Wiegand

. . .

The Fiction Debate

On 4 October 1876, during the nation's centennial celebration in Philadelphia, 103 people gathered to discuss the status of libraries in the United States. Most of the attendees were librarians; most rightly sensed they were present at the start of something significant. Four things happened at the conference to mark the public library's role in American print culture history for the next half century. First, conference goers resolved to establish the American Library Association (ALA), which quickly became the national voice for librarianship. Second, they spent considerable time discussing Melvil Dewey's decimal classification system, a new scheme advocated for organizing all library collections. Third, they examined reports in the newly published *Public Libraries in the United States of America* that showed growing government interest in American library development.[1] Fourth, they engaged in a vigorous debate about what kinds of novels properly belonged in an American public library.

The last was unique among the four because it reflected a dilemma rather than an accomplishment. Although all conference participants agreed that dime novels like the Deadwood Dick series and tabloids like the *Police Gazette* had no place in a "public" library, they disagreed on novels of "marginal quality" like *Lady Audley's Secret* (1862) by Ouida (Mary Elizabeth Braddon) and *Trial for Her Life* (1869) by Mrs. E. D. E. N. Southworth. In a talk that occasioned the "most discussion of the conference," Chicago Public Library Director William Frederick Poole argued that it was more important for public libraries to foster reading than to limit access to marginal fiction. Once public library users formed the habit of reading, he reasoned, they would naturally solicit the librarian's advice to help them "elevate" their tastes. William Kite of the Friends' Library in Germantown, Pennsylvania, argued in contrast that novels did not belong in libraries. James W. Ward of the Grosvenor Library in Buffalo called for more discretion: "If the novel is a good book," it deserved a place in the public library. "If in any sense it is a bad or even useless book," however, "it should be rejected." In the course of discussion, New York City YMCA Library Director Reuben Pool cited an uncomfortable fact; in most public libraries at that time novels accounted for 75 percent of circulation, and—where libraries made them available—Ouida and Southworth were much more popular than Hawthorne and Emerson.[2]

Thus emerged the "fiction debate" that dogged American librarianship for the next half century and beyond. Librarians and library founders generally viewed the American public library as an educational institution with a responsibility to circulate freely the information required for informed and cultivated American citizenship. The public library's capacity to culturally uplift and politically inform, however, was compromised by its very nature. Because library use was voluntary, and because funding depended in large part on community use, librarians were constantly forced to yield to local public library users, whose preferences were evident in their reading selections.[3] Some librarians, like Kite, rejected these compromises; others, like Ward, saw them as unavoidable; still others, like Poole, viewed them as a means to build a relationship with users that would enable librarians eventually to do their best professional work.

Crafting the Library Profession

Although library leaders adjourned their 1876 conference without resolving the fiction question, published proceedings nonetheless suggest they shared a common vision for the public library. "Free Libraries," one of the essays in the Bureau of Education publication, depicts these goals, concluding that the public library "must be bequeathed to our successors as an instrument always working in the direction of moral and social development."[4]

That the American Library Association agreed with this vision was obvious. Three years later it adopted a motto Dewey drafted—"The best reading for the greatest number at the least cost."[5] The motto itself identifies a set of goals that public library leaders used to distinguish librarianship from other professional arenas emerging in the late nineteenth century. On the one hand, it was built on an ideology of reading shared with other middle-class professionals who believed that good reading led to good social behavior, bad reading to bad social behavior.[6] On the other hand, rather than duplicating jurisdictions, it allowed other professionals—especially those in the academic and literary establishment—the authority to identify "best reading."

In part, librarians chose not to compete for this authority in order to avoid confrontation. In part, their socioeconomic and cultural connections to these other professionals made it easier to abdicate responsibility for defining canonical literatures. Like most university professors and members of the East Coast literary establishment, library leaders tended to be middle-aged, white, Protestant male alumni of northeast colleges, born to northeastern families that had emigrated from northwestern Europe at least three generations earlier.[7] They deliberately crafted a profession independent of a publishing industry, which, they believed, was permanently tainted by the desire for profit. They structured it instead around responsibilities shared by their peers in other professions who wanted to improve society. Librarians sought a comfortable niche in the growing fraternity of these professions.

Given the voluntary nature of American public library use, however, the decision to allow other cultural authorities to define "best reading" did not eliminate the "fiction question." It continued for most of the next half century, with librarians in an ever-shifting literary middle ground between the printed works most cultural authorities agreed were good—that is, politically informing or culturally uplifting—and those they considered bad but which many library users wanted to read, such as dime novels. The debate reflected a complex set of gender, race, creed, and class biases present in the larger culture. Librarians encountered two specific problems: first, the cultural authorities to whom they looked for guidance in selecting new books frequently could not reach consensus; thus the library fiction debate often centered on works in the middle ground, like *Lady Audley's Secret* and Mark Twain's *Huckleberry Finn*. Second, local public library users frequently asserted their own cultural preferences at the circulation desk. Librarians were often uncomfortably caught in the middle.

Dewey and the Public Library Movement

Between 1876 and 1924, then, American public library history witnessed disconcerting disagreements on what was "the best reading." It also displayed efforts to reach "the greatest number at the least cost." This second function received much attention at professional conferences and in the professional literature. Leading these efforts were Melvil Dewey, whose energy and library reform interests largely defined librarianship's agenda, and Andrew Carnegie, whose philanthropy created a movement that encouraged local governments across the nation to support the public library as a community reading institution.

In the hope of centralizing and systematizing public library practices, Dewey envisioned in 1876 a national public library movement spreading outward from the Northeast. In June, less than two months after copyrighting his decimal classification scheme, he became managing editor of a new periodical, the *American Library Journal* (later *Library Journal*). In its pages he advocated efficient management, encouraging public librarians to adopt centralized systems like

FIGURE 22.1. New York State Library School, 1888 class portrait with Melvil Dewey (*top row, center*), New York State Library School Manuscript Collection, Rare Book and Manuscript Library, Columbia University.

a common classification scheme, and to develop "best reading" lists to guide acquisition decisions. Five years later, he organized the Library Bureau to market standardized library furniture, supplies, appliances, and forms. After becoming chief librarian at New York's Columbia College in 1883, he opened the School of Library Economy—the world's first—in January 1887 to train young professionals as book selectors, reference librarians, and library managers for institutions that, like so many others at the turn of the century, were becoming increasingly bureaucratized.[8]

Dewey's curriculum—and the faculty he chose to teach it—reflected the role he hoped librarians would play in American print culture in the twentieth century (see figure 22.1). The faculty came from three groups. Columbia College Library employees taught technique—how to manage the library, how to acquire books and periodicals, how to classify and catalog them, and how to circulate them to library patrons. A second group consisted of well-known but mostly local library professionals who gladly accepted Dewey's invitation to guest-lecture at his pioneering school. Most delivered practical information, but with the library faculty they were also expected to communicate to students what Dewey called "the library spirit"—an evangelical commitment to make the public library an "engine of civilization" by circulating "the best reading to the greatest number at the least cost." The third group, however, consisted of carefully selected Columbia faculty members. In late 1886 Dewey had asked them to discuss the best and most recent literature in their respective fields at the college's regular Saturday morning public lectures and then mandated that his students attend. For students, the curriculum conveyed the priorities of an efficient system evolving in a milieu of professional jurisdictions. The library faculty and practitioners provided inspiration and "how to" information, while the disciplinary authorities and literary luminaries outside of librarianship offered guidance on the "best reading."

In 1889 Dewey moved his library school to Albany when he accepted a joint position as director of the New York State Library and as secretary to the Board of Regents of the University of the State of New York. Between 1889 and 1926 (when the school returned to Columbia), it graduated hundreds of library students. By the turn of the century four other library schools were established, each headed by a Dewey library school graduate, at either Columbia or Albany. Each of these schools supported a curriculum largely cloned from its parent, and each hosted a student body of whom over 80 percent were women. Many of these graduates became "itinerant cataloguers," hired for a two to three-month period to organize a small collection of books that some new Carnegie building had inherited from a local social library. Most, however, took for granted the structure of the profession Dewey had outlined at Columbia in 1887. In library school they had learned how to manage a library—and the expertise necessary to run it efficiently—including collections acquisition, classification and cataloging, and circulation. Determination of the "best reading," however, continued to reside outside the profession's jurisdiction.[9]

The Model Library

Despite efforts to make printed materials other cultural authorities labeled "best" more available, heavy demand for popular fiction continued to plague public library leaders, impugning the argument that the public library was an educational institution whose users became better-informed and more cultivated citizens. In 1890 one anonymous librarian humorously captured this dilemma in a "Fiction Song."

> At a library desk stood some readers one day,
> Crying "Novels, oh, novels, oh, novels!"

And I said to them, "People, oh, why do you say
    Give us novels, oh, novels, oh, novels?"
Is it weakness of intellect, people, I cried,
Or simply a space where the brains should abide?
They answered me not, or they only replied,
    "Give us novels, oh, novels, oh, novels!"

Here are thousands of books that will do you more
      good
    Than the novels, oh, novels, oh, novels!
You will weaken your brain with such poor mental food
    As the novels, oh, novels, oh, novels!
Pray take history, music, or travels, or plays,
Biography, poetry, science, essays
Or anything else that more wisdom displays
    Than the novels, oh, novels, oh, novels!

A librarian may talk till he's black in the face
    About novels, oh, novels, oh, novels!
And may think that with patience he may raise the taste
    Above novels, oh, novels, oh, novels!
He may talk till with age his round shoulders are bent
    And the white hairs of time 'mid the black ones are sent,
When he hands his report in, still seventy per cent
    Will be novels, oh, novels, oh, novels![10]

The ALA conference at the 1893 World's Fair in Chicago highlighted two new strategies to bring "the best reading to the greatest number at the least cost." First, it structured conference sessions to address practical matters of library management and then engaged the Bureau of Education to publish the proceedings as a *Handbook of Library Economy*. Because the handbook was a government document, congressmen could be asked to send it free of charge to growing numbers of public libraries in their districts. ALA leaders hoped the new tome would bring librarians—especially those not educated in library schools—up to date on the best ways to run their libraries. Second, the ALA conference featured a Model Library, 5,000 of the "best books" recommended for every library. Most of the books had been solicited from publishers eager to exploit a growing public library market. The books were classified on cards, which were housed in a "public" catalog. Although visitors could not actually check books out of the exhibit, they could easily locate and browse titles from the "best reading" selections on the shelves.

Preceding the conference, for most of 1892, Mary Salome Cutler, vice director of the Albany Library School, had supervised a Model Library selection committee of disciplinary experts on the one hand, and several groups of librarians and library school students on the other. The latter especially looked to reviews in academic journals and literary establishment magazines to help them identify "the best reading." Only 15 percent of their selections were classified as "fiction," whereas fiction represented 75 percent of the circulation rates at most public libraries. The Model Library established itself both as a resource to foster an informed citizenry and as a cultural authority, connecting the ALA to the nation's literary establishment. At the conference the ALA announced that the Bureau of Education would publish a bibliography of the Model Library and make it available as a government document for public libraries across the country.[11]

Because the Model Library was exhibited at the World's Fair, it provided an opportunity for hundreds of people frequenting the Midway to observe modern-day library science. Many library board members and potential library founders who visited the exhibit used the exhibit's catalog as an authoritative guide by which to evaluate their own small collections. Many also converted to the decimal classification and adopted common forms, appliances, and furniture marketed by the Library Bureau in order to increase efficiency. Networks of public libraries arose in states and regions, and librarians formed associations for discussing common problems and sharing information. For example, shortly after several board members from the Osage, Iowa, public library returned from the World's Fair, their library began using Library Bureau accessions books; and in Wisconsin, the president of the new Wisconsin Library Association, Frank A. Hutchins, became a leading advocate for the modern library practice he had witnessed at the fair.[12]

New York led the way, however. To wean public libraries away from the popular fiction their patrons really wanted, the State Library offered matching grants up to $200 for titles selected only from its "Best Books" lists. Some local library officials, however, chafed at this heavy hand. On 5 August 1904, Louis Silberman, a lawyer representing the Albany (N.Y.) Free Library, reported to Andrew Carnegie that the library was "practically owned" by State Library officials. "They designate the character of the books we should buy and the amount we shall spend . . . and dictate our course of work."[13]

Carnegie and the Growing Library Network

By the early 1900s, the evolving public library community was supported not only by the American Library Association, *Library Journal*, five library schools, and the U.S. Bureau of Education, but also by twenty-five state library associations, eighteen state library commissions, and twelve local library clubs. In 1904 a growing number of public libraries—especially small public libraries—were arranged by the decimal classification. Many recorded their acquisitions in Library Bureau accessions books, cataloged the contents of their collections using ALA rules, adopted a card-and-pocket system sold by the Bureau, and checked out their books over a circulation desk purchased from the Library Bureau or one of its competitors. At the turn of the century, the library science Dewey had been advocating since 1876 had established a firm grip on professional practice. It easily fit the culture of incorporation that influenced so many other aspects of American daily life in the Progressive Era.

Dewey's library science could not have spread nearly so rapidly without Andrew Carnegie's library philanthropy, which contributed significantly to the growing infrastructure of American print culture institutions. Between 1890 and his death in 1919, Carnegie gave $41 million to construct 1,679 public library buildings in 1,412 communities in the United States. The scope of his generosity drew considerable attention to libraries, generated a competition between communities to establish them, and helped create a philanthropic environment that encouraged other donors to do the same. Between 1900 and 1906, for example, 3,099 individuals contributed more than $24 million to libraries, half of which went for buildings and sites.[14] Any member of a community could inquire about a Carnegie building grant, but to receive one a town had to provide a suitable site and pledge to support it by annually allocating from local taxes at least 10 percent of the construction costs.

Many communities also requested advice on how to design and construct a library (see figure 22.2). Therefore, in 1911 James Bertram, Carnegie's personal secretary, compiled a pamphlet containing such advice. Later editions identified six recommended floor plans. All arranged library services and collections around a circulation desk, the building interior's focal point. One wing of the building usually contained reference materials, periodical literature, and newspapers. Other wings contained children's reading materials and the regular stacks. The building's design was so efficient that one person—if she remained at the circulation desk—could usually monitor the entire floor (see figure 22.3).[15]

The situation in large urban public libraries was only marginally different. In places like Boston, Philadelphia, Baltimore, Chicago, and St. Louis, trustees frequently hired male professionals—more for their "natural" management skills or status as local cultural authorities—to preside over a large staff of (generally) female professionals and nonprofessionals. For the most part these library leaders, regardless of gender, agreed with and supported definitions of

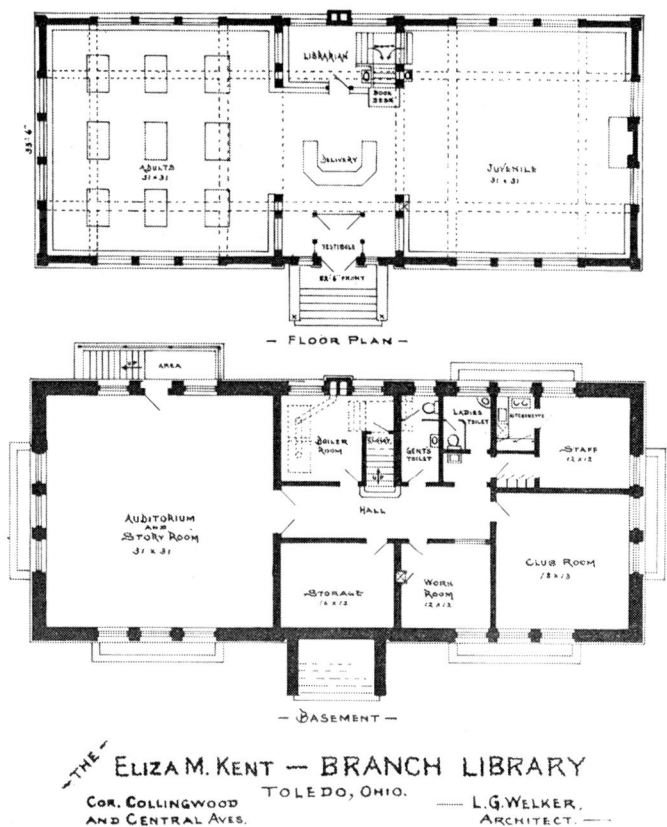

FIGURE 22.2. The Eliza Kent Branch (1917) of the Toledo Public Library was one of five branch library buildings for which ground was broken in 1916. The branches were funded by the Carnegie Corporation of New York; this branch was named for a longtime librarian who left a substantial bequest to establish a book fund. The branches were located following a series of public hearings for neighborhood organizations to make a case for library service. "Each building contains on the main floor a large open zone for delivery, adult and children's work, and a small office, and in the basement an auditorium seating 100 people, besides club rooms and rest rooms for the staff." *Five-Year Survey Toledo Public Library, 1914–1918* (Toledo: Commission of Publicity and Efficiency, 1919), 40–41. Courtesy Toledo-Lucas County Library.

FIGURE 22.3. Circulation desk, Chicago Public Library, ca. 1920. Courtesy Special Collections and University Archives, The University Library, The University of Illinois at Chicago.

"quality" that emanated from the canons of the middle-class culture in which they had been raised.[16] No matter the size of the library, most public library leaders still looked to other professional communities to guide their decisions about the "best reading" to put on the shelves. Meanwhile, most library patrons continued to express their own cultural preferences by checking out "novels, oh, novels, oh, novels."

The rapid proliferation of American public libraries in the first two decades of the twentieth century also prompted a variety of new services in this growing sector of the print culture infrastructure. In 1901, for example, the H. W. Wilson Company began issuing a *Reader's Guide to Periodical Literature* "for small libraries and reading clubs." In its initial issue the guide indexed twenty periodicals like *Atlantic Monthly*, *Current Literature*, *Dial*, and *North American Review*. As public libraries began to favor subscriptions to magazines covered by indexes, they granted "general interest" periodicals a distinct advantage over unindexed periodicals like the *Colored American Magazine* (1900-1904), the *Masses* (1911-17), and the *Woman's Journal* (1869-1917).

The Wilson Company's influence extended beyond magazine indexes. Its 1909 *Fiction Catalog* provided an annotated list of 350 titles of "the best novels" cited in guides like the ALA *Catalog* and the New York State Library "Best Books" series. That same year, Wilson published the first edition of *Children's Catalog*, an annotated list of 3,000 books intended as a "guide to the best reading for young people." Both catalogs featured the products of large publishers, mainly in New York, frequently overlooking local publishers and publishers outside the dominant culture—like radical publisher Charles H. Kerr and Company of Chicago and African American commercial book publisher J. A. Rogers Publications of New York City.[17]

Booklist *and Classification*

In 1905 ALA created *Booklist*, a monthly annotated guide to recently published books. *Booklist* emerged from the discontent among ALA members in the Midwest with the way directors of large eastern libraries were running the association. When New York Public Library director and ALA president John Shaw Billings convinced Andrew Carnegie in 1901 to endow an ALA publications fund with a gift of $100,000, the directors who controlled the fund began planning specialized bibliographies like *ALA Portrait Index*, a two-volume work costing $10 that mostly benefited patrons of large urban libraries.[18] The hundreds of small, struggling Carnegie libraries protested, voicing their concerns in the newly formed League of Library Commissions. In December 1905, the league's own publications committee noted that because smaller public libraries "do not have the books included in the A.L.A. *Portrait Index* . . . it is of no service to them." The league argued the money ought to be put to more practical uses.[19]

When he became secretary of the Wisconsin Free Library Commission in 1904, Henry Legler began pressing the ALA committee in charge of the Carnegie fund to issue serially a practical collections guide, promising that the League of Library Commissions would subsidize the guide by ordering subscriptions for hundreds of small public libraries. The committee responded by creating *Booklist*, but the directors of small public libraries complained that titles listed in its initial issues were still too expensive or too esoteric. Still unsatisfied, in 1906 Legler offered to pay half of an editor's salary from the Wisconsin committee's funds if the ALA committee allowed him to move all *Booklist* editorial work to Madison. When ALA agreed, Legler assigned Katharine McDonald, a commission employee, as editor. She quickly established working relationships with University of Wisconsin faculty to identify and review books that average citizens could read to become self-educated, cultivated, and informed.

Booklist's shift of focus was soon obvious. The title page of its January 1908 issue noted that it was not only "to aid public librarians in book buying" but also "to give assistance in cataloguing and classifying to librarians whose training or experience was limited." Each entry included a decimal classification number, cataloging information, and a lengthy annotation. Many citations were starred to identify books especially "recommended for small libraries, or for first purchase."[20]

Because the information in *Booklist* entries saved librarians considerable work, they tended to favor its recommendations. Thus, in a subtle, relatively unobtrusive way, professional library organizations, like the American Library Association and the League of Library Commissions, and the H. W. Wilson Company gradually created a filtering system for printed materials already privileged by cultural authorities outside librarianship. This system addressed the needs of small libraries created by Carnegie's philanthropy, was built on Dewey's library science, and was designed to counterbalance the worst features of a publishing industry all too willing to cater to some of the public's more debased reading interests.

Once publishers recognized this system, however, they worked to get their titles included. Larger houses with more renowned authors and better advertising and distribution capacity fared better than small, regional, or specialized publishers. Yet public library leaders were convinced that this "objective" system implemented by experts provided communities with guidance about "the best reading." They saw themselves as neutral professionals providing readers with self-education and enlightenment.

In most public libraries, however, fiction—and especially the popular fiction many cultural authorities pronounced worthless—continued to average 75 percent of circulation. Although most public librarians recognized that providing some popular fiction could "hook" patrons on reading, many also continued to hope that—if they only persisted—making the "best reading" available would eventually reverse these percentages. If not, many worried, it would be difficult to convince fellow professionals and library funders that library work truly deserved to be included in the growing fraternity of professions serving the public good.

Librarians continued to express this commitment to elevating the public reading tastes. At ALA's 1896 conference, Mary Salome Cutler organized members into groups to review lists recommended for an ALA *Catalog* supplement. In the fiction category, best-selling titles that most literary and academic authorities considered poorly written (including works by Horatio Alger and

Mrs. E. D. E. N. Southworth) or somehow "offensive" (including Stephen Crane's *Red Badge of Courage*) were not considered or were swiftly dismissed. Returning home from the conference, Hannah Packard James of the Osterhout Free Library in Wilkes-Barre, Pennsylvania, wrote that the session was "invaluable" because of "the tremendous weight of the influence of the Association in favor of purity in fiction." Over the decades, however, patrons stubbornly resisted moving from the popular fiction they favored to books that distant cultural authorities and library professionals prescribed for them as "best reading."[21]

Small-Town Libraries

Most library officials in small public libraries seemed less troubled about the "fiction question" than were ALA's leaders. At the Sage Public Library in Osage, Iowa, for example, librarians and trustees showed no visible concern that patrons were much more interested in E. P. Roe's *The Original*, the "Duchess's" *Airy, Fairy Lillian*, and Bertha M. Clay's *For Another's Sin* (titles not included in the ALA *Catalog*) than the works of Shakespeare, Milton, or Bancroft. All but three of the top sixteen circulating books at the Sage Public Library during this half decade were novels that most librarians generally categorized as "sensational" or "sentimental" fiction, and of the top ten titles checked out during this half decade, only four were cited in the *Catalog* — James Froude's *History of England*, Dinah Maria Mulock's *A Brave Lady*, Lew Wallace's *Ben Hur*, and George Eliot's *Daniel Deronda*.[22]

Hamlin Garland's autobiography, *A Son of the Middle Border* (1917), illuminates these attitudes. As a youth in the 1870s Garland lived in Osage. There he got his "first taste of Shakespeare" from a *McGuffey Reader* but also read action-filled popular fiction: stories of "hair-breadth escapes on the plain" from a stack of *New York Weekly* tabloids borrowed from "one of the older boys," Beadle's Dime Novels which he began "to purchase and trade" ("I took exquisite delight in *Old Sleuth* and *Jack Harkaway*"), and Edward Eggleston's *The Hoosier Schoolmaster*, which was serialized in *Hearth and Home*, to which his father subscribed. "My taste was catholic," he remembered, and although he acknowledged that "the pleasure" he took in sensationalist fiction "should fill me with shame," as an adult he had to admit "it doesn't — I rejoice in the memory of it."[23]

Garland's sense that he ought to have felt shame about part of his reading interests probably emanated from prescriptions about certain literatures articulated by high-culture authorities. His sense that he should not have to apologize for these youthful reading interests was validated by his later sense that they were delightful experiences. The Sage Library negotiated a middle ground between the local print culture described by Hamlin Garland and the cultural prescriptions delivered by elite easterners in bibliographies like the ALA *Catalog*. A close look at the leadership of another small-town public library may help explain the willingness of these institutions to buy and circulate popular fiction.

When the Bryant Library of Sauk Centre, Minnesota, moved into a new Carnegie building in November 1904, Miss Bessie Robbins served as librarian. Although from a prominent local family, she had no formal library training. Her job was not to select books (trustees exercised that responsibility), but to open and close the facilities and to monitor from the circulation desk patrons in the adult reading room to her left and the children's room to her right. She also managed the collection of 5,500 volumes (recently reclassified into the Dewey system by employees of the Minnesota State Library Commission). While the 1904 ALA *Catalog* recommended that collections include 16 percent fiction, 13.5 percent biography, and 13 percent history, the Bryant Library held 60 percent fiction, 6 percent biography, and 10 percent history.

Reasons for these differences are suggested by a profile of the Bryant Library Board, a cross section of the community elite, in 1904. As in other small communities, these leaders were connected to each other through a thick web of memberships in lodges, churches, and social clubs. The board was led by James A. Norris, a local agent for the Great Northern Railway, a Republican, Congregationalist, Mason, and chairman of the local Sunday school association. Among his colleagues was Edwin J. Lewis, a local physician, Mason, Episcopalian, Oddfellow, and father of nineteen-year-old Sinclair Lewis, at that time a Yale College student. Edwin's wife Grace was president of Sauk Centre's most prestigious women's club, to which Bessie Robbins also belonged. Grace Lewis had spearheaded club efforts in 1898 to open the library evenings to give local youths a healthful alternative to the local billiard hall.

Bryant Library board members acquired new books not only by consulting collection guides like the ALA *Catalog* but also by purchasing from booklists in Montgomery Ward and Sears catalogs, to which they also looked for various fashion suggestions. Local community leaders did not fear the effects of popular fiction. Board members and their families read the popular fiction their libraries collected. Their values helped set standards of community behavior. Popular fiction was serialized in local newspapers edited by men who in many cases were also public library board members. Charles F. Hendryx, editor of the *Sauk Centre Herald*, was a Bryant Library trustee from 1893 to 1903.[24]

In effect, small-town literary interests and library policies reflected two different canons — one determined by East Coast literary and academic elites and one incorporating cultural tastes of a local elite. This latter canon included popular fiction offered by major New York publishers, who, in turn, knew how to use existing national marketing devices that local folks had come to trust, like Montgomery Ward mail-order catalogs, which eschewed the avant-garde in both clothing and reading materials. Consequently, despite the best efforts of the American public library's professional community to discourage all but "the best reading," the small-town American public library evolved a different definition of "best," reflecting a more popularly based but locally determined literary canon. For every patron like Sinclair Lewis, who as a youth read voraciously through Bryant Library titles like Grote's *History of Greece* and Tolstoy's *War and Peace*,[25] there were at least five more who instead preferred Horatio Alger and E. D. E. N. Southworth for stimulation, enlightenment, and validation of locally endorsed moral codes.

Urban Libraries

Urban branch libraries provide other examples of the gap between elite intentions and patrons' print culture. Although the New York Public Library was founded in 1895 as a free public reference library and by 1911 was centrally located in a grand marble building at Fifth Avenue and Forty-Second Street, in the first decade of the twentieth century the Library's Circulation Department also expanded to monitor the thirty-nine branch buildings Andrew Carnegie had donated. Urban public libraries were usually run by men and usually by ALA officers, who often disparaged and sometimes disguised the high circulation rates of popular fiction. At the same time, however, they also served more culturally diverse clienteles, and some front-line library professionals reached out to embrace the cultural tastes of diverse groups they served. Ernestine Rose, whose experiences at the Chatham Square (1908–11) and Seward Park (1915–17) branches led her to write *Bridging the Gulf: Work with the Russian Jews and Other Newcomers* in 1917, moved to the 135th Street branch in 1920 to help make it a vital part of the Harlem Renaissance. Langston Hughes vividly remembered the "warm and wonderful librarian, white," who "made newcomers feel welcome." Rose's branch processed the Arthur A. Schomburg collection of Afro-Americana and sponsored a 160-voice chorus, literary and art workshops, a Little Negro Theatre, and a family relations institute for local teachers and social workers.[26]

Other librarians also distinguished themselves by developing services for specialized clienteles. At the turn of the century, for example, many public libraries organized and selected children's collections, both to extend services to "the greatest number" and to inculcate a desire for "the best reading" at an early age. At the Washington County Free Library in Hagerstown, Maryland, Director Mary Titcomb allocated most of her limited book budget to children's materials because she believed that over time the practice would create a greater community desire for reading good books.

The Cleveland Public Library organized a Children's Library League in 1897. Within a year membership jumped to 14,000, and by 1901—like public libraries in Buffalo, Toledo, and Milwaukee—Cleveland had established a separate children's room. Young members had to sign a pledge "to do all in our power to assist the librarian in keeping the books in good condition." It continued, "We promise to remember that good books contain the living thoughts of good and great men and women, and are therefore entitled to respect." The selection of printed materials for children differed significantly from the selection of materials aimed at adults. Because their gender supposedly equipped women uniquely for the task, male leaders, and the patriarchal culture dominating the turn-of-the-century world of library professionals, willingly gave women the responsibility for judging the quality of children's literature. Thus, by the early years of the century, children's librarians were exercising significant control over the canons of children's literature.[27]

Negotiating World War I

By the time that war broke out in Europe in 1914, the American public library community was led by a well-organized group of middle-class, Anglo-American, Protestant men and women. They had adopted common systems like the decimal classification, created organizations like the American Library Association, and subscribed to centralizing services provided by companies such as H. W. Wilson, all in order to increase public libraries' efficiency and effectiveness. At the same time, however, the public library community had to demonstrate community demand in order to justify its dependence on local funding. Yet most patrons wanted the very same materials the professional organizations were designed to combat.

While librarians were wrestling with this dilemma, the Great War erupted, providing an attractive service opportunity for public libraries across the nation to cement their role as an American institution of literacy. Although America's public libraries took no sides while the United States was a neutral power (August 1914–April 1917), they were inevitably affected in numerous ways. Partisan patrons often penned commentary into the margins of newspapers and periodicals to which libraries subscribed. Both Germany and Great Britain more subtly influenced library patrons by placing certain materials in U.S. library collections. Karl Alexander Feuhr of the German Information Service in New York bragged to his superiors that he had secretly distributed more than 400 titles like *Warlike England as Seen by Herself*, *The Truth about Germany*, and *Ger-*

many's Just Cause to American public libraries between 1915 and 1916 through organizations like the Friends of Peace (a New York-based German-Irish pacifist group) and the German-American Alliance. The British took a much more focused approach in getting 204 specific titles to 600 carefully selected public libraries. Sometimes these titles arrived in the mail marked "Donated by Author" from famous people like Sir Arthur Conan Doyle, Ford Madox Ford, and A. J. Toynbee, all of whom had been hired by the British government to write subtle propaganda favoring British viewpoints. Sometimes they came as donated documents, like the report of Lord Bryce's Committee on Alleged German Outrages, whose publication opportunely followed the sinking of the Lusitania on 7 May 1915. Sometimes the British would hide their connection to a publication altogether. For example, librarians receiving French professor Charles Marie Joseph Bedier's forty-eight-page pamphlet *How Germany Seeks to Justify Her Atrocities*, which was sent from Paris, never knew the British had funded its publication.[28]

Once America entered the war, however, any pretense of neutrality disappeared. Across the country, libraries provided meeting space for local chapters of the Red Cross, the Council on National Defense, and the Home Guards. They willingly circulated materials printed by George Creel's federal Committee on Public Information and welcomed Americanization programs whose literature and activities were designed to channel immigrants' loyalties. Libraries dispensed millions of food conservation pamphlets and participated in the ALA's Library War Service campaigns, functioning as local collection agencies for books and periodicals, which they then shipped to overseas troops through distribution centers. Book collecting campaigns attracted a lot of attention. In New York, for example, librarians framed a thirty-foot pyramid in front of the library on Fifth Avenue, urging New Yorkers to donate enough books to fill it to the top. Newspapers across the nation carried front-page pictures of the pyramid and regularly reported progress. Local public libraries used the publicity to press their own communities for more donations.

Public libraries were also active in discarding "disloyal" literature. In the January 1918 issue of the *Wisconsin Library Bulletin*, an editorial entitled "Seditious Publications in the Public Library" argued that "all questionable materials must be eliminated." Several public librarians in Iowa tossed all German-language materials into their library furnaces. State library commissions and agencies across the country also utilized the "Army Index," a list of pro-German or pacifist books that the military banned from libraries in its thirty-eight training camps. Several commissions reprinted these lists and sent them to local public libraries, where librarians dutifully removed cited titles from library shelves. The eagerness with which public librarians followed state and federal guidance suggests that they welcomed such clear signals from these reading authorities. These directives contrasted sharply with the perplexingly mixed messages sent by the academic and literary establishment before the war. Director Cornelia Marvin of the Oregon Free Library Commission even seized upon the censorship fever as an opportunity to stop buying fiction altogether for the duration of the war.[29]

However, the ALA campaign to supply soldiers and sailors with reading material could not be so selective. A book campaign volunteer in Hibbing, Minnesota, for example, claimed to know that soldiers really wanted titles that were "decent but not too highbrow," and shortly he delivered hundreds of *Red Books*, *Topnotches*, and *All-Story* books to his local library. Similar titles flooded distribution centers all over the country, and when the army made no objection, these materials found their way onto library shelves and into the hands of soldiers and sailors. Public library leaders, as a consequence, began to temper their criticism of light fiction. By war's end, training camp libraries averaged 65 percent fiction. In contrast, the latest prewar edition of the ALA *Catalog* had recommended 10.8 percent.[30]

The lesson here was unmistakable. If, within limits, an authority as powerful as the federal government thought it acceptable to circulate popular reading materials that most patrons wanted anyway, how could librarians object? After all, much of this type of literature was already circulating as serialized fiction either in national periodicals to which most libraries subscribed (e.g., *Saturday Evening Post* and *Ladies' Home Journal*) or in local newspapers edited by local elites from which public libraries drew their trustees. Wartime experiences ultimately confirmed the American public library as a local civic institution more in touch with popular reading tastes. Public library leaders finally came to accept the argument that the "light" reading they had reluctantly provided for a half century to attract new patrons was, at worst, harmless. No longer were they torn between prescribed canonical literatures advocated by cultural authorities and popular fiction demanded by their patrons and now sanctioned for wartime soldiers by the federal government.

Conclusion: Postwar Resolution

As a result, after the war librarians were less critical of popular fiction. In her preface to the 1923 edition of the *Fiction Catalog*, for example, compiler Corinne Bacon noted: "This is not a list of the best 2,350 novels, judged as literature, but a list of 2,350 of the best novels for public library use. This means it includes novels for highly educated and for comparatively uneducated readers, for those who like the older novels and for those who want to keep in touch with present day fiction."³¹ Once their niche among professional jurisdictions had solidified, public librarians focused more attention on running their libraries efficiently. They did not give up advocacy of the "best reading" entirely. Some initiated rental collections, which, they argued, satisfied patrons who wanted popular fiction but did not burden the library with permanent ownership of multiple copies of books with only temporary interest. Others restricted patrons to one work of fiction per library visit. Many did both. Despite their efforts, however, fiction remained popular. The Morris, Illinois, Public Library stuck to its rule about one work of fiction per patron per visit in 1918, but fiction still accounted for 78 percent of books drawn by adults that year. Five years later the board initiated a popular book rental service.³²

By 1924 public libraries across the country had settled into a routine with regard to book acquisitions. Many subscribed to *Booklist*, advertised as a "guide to the best new books," and used its recommendations to identify potential purchases.³³ Many also subscribed to *Reader's Guide to Periodical Literature*, which in 1924 indexed 112 periodicals, including professional journals like *American Historical Review*, *American Journal of Sociology*, and *Political Science Quarterly*, all of which had substantial review sections. In addition, many received Wilson's "Standard Catalog Series," which cited works selected either by experts in other fields or by librarians well trained in the canons of "the best reading." The exception was children's literature, where evaluative responsibility had been relinquished to the "natural" instincts of women who served on ALA selection committees that chose titles for new editions of H. W. Wilson's *Children's Catalog*. When new editions of any of these catalogs arrived, librarians checked their contents against library shelf lists. Titles not in their collections were often purchased; titles in the collection but not in the new catalog were often discarded.³⁴ Librarians cataloged and classified the new acquisitions by ALA rules; or they simply bought from the Library of Congress preprinted catalog cards that already contained Dewey numbers. They then filed the cards in a public catalog and placed the books on their shelves.

Although public librarians continued thus to collect and promote books belonging to high-culture canons in order to elevate the public taste and educate citizens, they quietly tolerated and, within socially acceptable limits, supplied the popular reading demanded by the vast majority of their patrons. Time—and now tradition—had combined to mute their objections. Unwittingly, perhaps, their willingness to accommodate popular reading allowed diverse patrons to determine their own canons and at the same time participate in a social infrastructure where they shared information.³⁵

America's public libraries worked hard to bring "the best reading to the greatest number at the least cost" in the mid-1920s, despite the fact that they competed locally with other sources of printed materials and with newer cultural forms. A local example can illustrate one such print culture context. In Morris, Illinois, the local schools sponsored a "pupils silent reading program" in 1924 that drew its material from newly acquired school library collections. Strawn's Drug Store regularly placed advertisements in the *Morris Daily Herald* announcing the popular fiction it sold. The *Herald* itself continued to publish serialized novels by authors like Edna Ferber, whose fiction also appeared regularly in magazines, subscriptions to which were available from door-to-door salesmen. The *Herald* also carried a column entitled "Radio Flashes" with a schedule of programs for that and the next day, and a second column entitled "The Screen" that summarized plots of silent movies playing at the Royal and Empire Theaters.

On a farm just outside Morris, young William Miller waited anxiously for the next issue of *Country Gentleman*, a periodical that regularly serialized Zane Grey fiction, and *Youth's Companion*, from which his mother often read stories to him and his siblings. And "every year," Miller later remembered, "relatives would give us a volume or two of the Horatio Alger books" and "two or three of the Rover Boys books."[36]

Amid this dynamic local print culture was the Morris Public Library. During the school year children's story hours took place every Saturday morning. Mary Gibson, Morris public librarian, ran a monthly column in the *Herald* entitled "Book Review" where she highlighted recently acquired titles and paraphrased annotations found in standard professional selection tools like *Booklist*, the ALA *Catalog*, and H. W. Wilson "Guides." Yet, when she issued her annual report in June 1925, she noted that 60 percent of Morris residents had used the library in 1924, and that each adult user averaged ten charges per year, but of that ten nearly 75 percent were fiction.[37]

By 1924 Melvil Dewey's library science had combined with Andrew Carnegie's library philanthropy to craft professional practice for a ubiquitous civic institution. On the one hand, the American public library prided itself on contributing to political democracy by making printed materials freely accessible in order to inform and cultivate local citizens who chose to use them. On the other, its users capitalized on the voluntary nature of the American public library ultimately to construct a community reading institution much more culturally democratic than library leaders and founders had originally intended. Because the public was not compelled to use the services of the American public library, users inevitably influenced the composition of the libraries' collections.

Thus, by 1924, the main lines of professional practice and user behavior in libraries were clear. In the succeeding two decades, libraries adjusted services to accommodate the impact of the automobile. Branch library systems followed urban commuters into the suburbs; new bookmobile services utilized a network of newly constructed highways. Reference librarians began answering telephone inquiries; some public library systems built film collections. Many booked time slots on local radio stations every Saturday morning for children's story hours. Despite these changes, the main purposes and institutional form of the public library remained relatively unchanged from the 1920s through the 1940s. Access in rural areas was sparse, and racial discrimination marred access, but otherwise the public library had attained its identity. Stable, low-profile, and ubiquitous, public libraries took their place in the cultural landscape of local communities.

CHAPTER 23

The Great Libraries

Phyllis Dain
. . .

Arguably, no great libraries existed in nineteenth-century United States. Rather, we can speak of a process, a movement toward greatness. Not until well into the next century could the largest American libraries compare with the immense European repositories that they emulated — the royal, ducal, ecclesiastical, and private collections and the university and national libraries derived from them. Such comprehensive libraries carry recognized cultural value as conservators of human history. They have acquired, preserved, and organized huge numbers of books, journals, and other forms of recorded knowledge, in a wide range of subjects and languages. In these institutions, quantity symbolized quality: usually containing only one copy of most titles and seldom discarding anything, the more items they had, the deeper and more varied the coverage.

In the United States, these "research" libraries have taken various institutional forms. They may be tax-supported public libraries, independent private nonprofit institutions, components of parent institutions such as universities, or national or state government establishments. As large, bureaucratized organizations bringing order to the world of recorded knowledge, their evolution corresponds to American corporate development and is related to the expansion of the book trade. Institutionally, however, they belong to the nonprofit sector, whether private or public or a combination of the two; their comprehensiveness distinguishes them from the large, specialized libraries established by historical societies, bar associations, academies of medicine, government agencies, and other entities.

In the modern, secular era, the great libraries of the Western world have had several key functions: to support scientific research, scholarship, and advanced study; to preserve society's intellectual heritage; and to document human thought and activity. They served as crucial repositories of both old and new knowledge, the latter growing exponentially by the late nineteenth century. Research libraries in the nineteenth century more consciously began to gather and retain information of utilitarian value to government, industry, and the newly emerging professions.

In the United States, these roles for large libraries developed to a limited degree before the end of the nineteenth century, when Americans finally emerged from intellectual colonialism and the scale and value of information in modern life demanded large repositories. Throughout much of the century, the major scholarly library collections, except at Harvard and Yale and a few others, had been outside of academe. By 1876 the largest was the Library of Congress, built into a de facto national library by ace collector Ainsworth Rand Spofford, Librarian of Congress from 1864 to 1897. Other considerable collections were in subscription libraries such as the Boston Athenaeum and in certain urban public libraries, most importantly the Astor Library in New York City and the Boston Public Library. These two pioneering institutions, free to the public, democratized access to recorded knowledge. The Astor Library had been the first privately endowed, free reference library in the country and the first large public library designed primarily for scholars and researchers. It was the model for other endowed free reference libraries, and it became a constituent part of the great New York Public Library, formed in 1895. The Boston Public Library, the first tax-supported free municipal library in the United States (but also having private funding), and with both popular and scholarly collections, was a prototype for other urban American public libraries founded after the Civil War, some as late as the 1890s. A number of such libraries—in Cleveland, Detroit, and Los Angeles, for example—became the major public collections in their regions.[1]

The Astor, Boston, and other large public libraries derived from the initiative of community leaders or wealthy people acting independently. Many of them believed that large public collections would educate the citizenry for informed participation in a republic and contribute to social stability. At a time when few persons went to secondary school, much less college, access to a broad range of books and journals could give serious learners the knowledge and skills needed in an industrial economy. Community leaders and philanthropists also wanted to have in the United States the intellectual and cultural resources commonly found in their sophisticated mother continent, including publications preserving the American experience and enabling study of its history. Such collections, and the monumental structures built to house them from the 1890s on, would be one more expression of the power of the secular, republican, capitalist New World. Knowledge is power: in the form of imposing book accumulations and buildings it also *signified* power.

Once established and regardless of founders' motivations, libraries take on a life of their own. People have their own reasons for reading or information seeking, and their own interpretations of what they see. This is as true of libraries as of other nodes in the communication of information and knowledge. Research libraries stand at the center of a feedback process in that communication. They collect society's records and accumulated knowledge, which people consult to help create new knowledge and new understandings, which, if issued in some form, find their way into libraries, where people consult them, and so on.

True, even the most comprehensive libraries would inevitably have been affected by paradigms of culture, knowledge, morality, gender, class, color, and nationhood that might influence collecting and, therefore, access to the human record. At the same time, the positivist intellectual outlook of late nineteenth-century Europe and the United States had a countervailing effect, one that could lead scholarly librarians to cast quite wide nets in the search for materials. They believed in the possibility of knowing and improving the world through systematic collection and investigation of published facts. A century later it became a truism that knowledge is variable and objectivity difficult if not impossible to achieve. Yet many librarians' positivistic pursuit of objectivity and comprehensiveness, however imperfect, yielded an inclusiveness that served current and future researchers well. Also at play was a human passion for collecting anything and everything and the desire to preserve and display the results. Much of the richness of great libraries derived from gifts or purchases of such private collections and from the collecting zeal of librarians.

Organization and Expansion

As Wayne Wiegand has documented in the previous chapter, the year 1876 marked a transition to modernity in the American library world. Librarians were developing rationalized, standardized modes of organization and a broad, common approach to managing the institutions and collections that were proliferating, along with increases in the industrializing world's publishing output and the growth of the reading public. By that point, American libraries and librarians had reached a critical mass, sufficient to constitute a separate field, a profession, which would bring high commitment, order, and thought to the tasks of accumulating and organizing materials for higher learning and research as well as popular education.

As tools for research, libraries needed not only books but ways for readers to find the books relevant to their interests. The larger and more scholarly the library, the more complex and vital the task of organization. It involved describing works bibliographically for identification and comparisons with other works, arranging such descriptions in accessible ways, and devising a practical, flexible system for the storage, retrieval, and use of the physical works. As libraries and collections multiplied and printed lists of holdings, or catalogs, began to come out, standardized rules to guide catalogers and facilitate use became crucial. European librarians had led the way; American librarians' contributions reflected the national propensity for practicality and for increasingly broad and unrestricted access to information resources.

Two significant American guides for bibliographic organization were published in 1876: *Rules for a Printed Dictionary Catalogue*, by the librarian of the Boston Athenaeum, Charles Cutter, issued as part 2 of the classic United States Bureau of Education Report, *Public Libraries in the United States*; and the young Melvil Dewey's new decimal classification system, which was summarized in part 1 of the special report.[2]

Cutter's *Rules* and his subsequent work on subject headings strongly influenced cataloging practice in American libraries. Books would be cataloged (bibliographically described) under standardized author, title, and specific subject headings, interfiled alphabetically, and with appropriate cross-references. Readers searching in such a catalog for books on particular subjects could go directly to the subject heading of interest. They did not have to be familiar with a hierarchical system for the classification of knowledge.

In contrast, Dewey's Decimal Classification, which would become ubiquitous in American libraries, was such a classification system, used not to arrange entries in the catalog but to arrange books on the shelves. It was a logical outline of the universe of knowledge, with a mnemonic decimal notation—that is, numerical symbols expressing the theoretically infinitely divisible subject categories, going from the general to the ever more particular and in sets of ten. Unlike earlier shelving arrangements, Dewey's scheme could accommodate growth of knowledge and collections. It also made possible a more democratic approach to library service by facilitating public browsing of bookshelves organized by topics and thus helped readers find books relevant to their interests.

The Decimal Classification, ingenious as it was, had its limitations, especially for scholarly use. Its hierarchical approach and the assumption that all branches of knowledge could be logically arranged in one system would become intellectually obsolete; the Baconian faculty psychology from which it was derived was on the way out by Dewey's time; and both life and knowledge exceed the sets of tens that the decimal system imposed. Finally, the scheme expressed the dominant American culture of its time—white, male, Christian, Western European. For example, all "other" religions, languages, and literatures were relegated in toto to the last of the ten subcategories under the main classes. Succeeding editions tried to remedy some of the shortcomings and provide for changes and growth in knowledge, but the built-in biases were not fully recognized until nearly a century after the first edition. Although most university libraries adopted Dewey's classification, many eventually switched to the Library of Congress classification, its first schedules published in 1901 and the rest in progress for years afterward. Expressing the new evolutionary thinking in its progression of subjects, the Library of Congress scheme was more scholarly, more pragmatic, more detailed, and more accommodating to new subjects than the Dewey Classification.

Concomitant with librarians' bibliographic innovations and also essential to their work were efforts of publishers and bibliographers to document the national publishing output, both current and retrospective. In the 1870s major new standard lists appeared. These included *Publishers' Weekly* (1872), which listed forthcoming titles; *Publishers Trade List Annual* (1873), comprising publishers' current catalogs; and the *American Catalogue of Books* (in print as of 1876).[3] As for periodicals, no published recurrent indexes existed in the nineteenth century. Although not yet as profuse and specialized as they would later be, periodicals were increasingly important for discussion of contemporary issues and special interests and as vehicles for popular literature. In 1876 the American Library Association agreed to sponsor a cooperative effort to update *Poole's Index*, the first general index to periodicals, originally published in 1848, with a second edition in 1853. The new update appeared in 1882, followed by several supplements, but consistent, current indexing would not come until the turn of the new century.

Academic Research Libraries

The year 1876 also signified the beginning of an academic sea change in the United States, one with serious implications for university library development. As described by Janice Radway and Marcel LaFollette earlier in this volume, that year saw the opening of the Johns Hopkins University, which emphasized, on the German model, graduate education, seminar study, and laboratory and documentary research. Although the Ph.D. was beginning to be offered in the United States at the time, and Harvard and other colleges had begun to add modern languages and science to the classical curriculum, it was Hopkins that set the standard for the elite colleges and premier state universities that would transform themselves into research universities.[4]

In doing so, these universities began their move to center stage in the cultivation and advancement of learning in the United States and as institutions vital to a modernizing society dependent on knowledge-based industrial processes and educated leaders and managers. Their growing faculties came to rely upon institutional research facilities, including libraries. As academic specialization increased, research methods developed, scholarly research broadened, and scholarly publishing multiplied, scholars' personal libraries would no longer suffice. And the Progressive Era belief in the necessity of knowledge to solve social and political problems entailed extensive library collections. Furthermore, undergraduates, no longer confined to rote learning and recitation, would, along with graduate students, need a wide array of books.

Creating academic empires, university presidents and trustees were persuaded to regard libraries as a measure of academic excellence. They devoted resources to library development and welcomed gifts of collections, monumental buildings, and money earmarked for libraries from persons seeking suitable objects of philanthropy upon which to expend the wealth that American capitalism was earning for them. Enterprising librarians sought to amass a broad range of publications, past and present. Whether such ingathering, which might include acquisition of entire collections, directly corresponded to the actual research activities of faculty and graduate students is a question. Some institutions with enlightened leadership and located in areas lacking substantial library resources (e.g., Illinois, Berkeley, and Michigan) developed policies designed to relate library holdings to research needs and to create balanced, comprehensive collections. In other universities, such efforts were uneven. The humanities might be better covered than "hard" sciences and the new social sciences, and collection growth would depend heavily on gifts or the differential power of academic departments and professors.

All this activity produced academic research library collections of some magnitude. From 1876 to 1891, holdings of major American university libraries, especially those that had started virtually from scratch, zoomed. Harvard and Yale, already decidedly ahead in 1876, kept their lead, as they always would. Other library collections—at Brown, Berkeley, Cornell, Columbia, Michigan, Pennsylvania, and Princeton—altogether more than doubled, some much more so. Still, no American library possessed a million volumes, and traditional humanistic interests of collectors, librarians, and many faculty members tended to dominate acquisitions. Scientific journals and other publications fundamental to scientific research remained underrepresented, as did primary and secondary materials for the study of ancient and medieval civilizations.[5]

Along with larger university collections came information services and liberalized provisions for use—longer opening hours, lending of books, and open stacks, resulting in problems of security, staffing, control, and the absence of books from shelves. Visiting scholars were usually welcomed, and in state universities the general public might have the right to use the libraries. Whether private or public, universities designated as United States Government Depositories (a system started in 1895) were obliged to make federal documents publicly available. Information or reference departments, which began seriously to develop in American university libraries in the early twentieth century, led by Columbia, extensively collected bibliographies and other reference works and helped individuals locate materials and extract relevant information. Books frequently circulated among institutions for scholars' use, a practice standardized in 1917 with the publication of the American Library Association's interlibrary loan code.

The commitment to assisting users rather than just administering a repository had originated in public libraries, which served a diverse clientele. This service orientation was uniquely American, and American research libraries came to share it. The great European libraries usually had closed-stack collections and tended to impose restrictions on users, who faced long delays in getting materials and little personal guidance in using them. American scholarly librarianship, along with higher education and scholarship generally, may have had a certain elite character, especially in the older eastern private institutions, but compared with their foreign counterparts, American libraries have been quite democratic, attentive to users, and progressively so.

The Bibliographic "System"

User services as well as acquisitions benefited from bibliographic developments in the early twentieth century that inaugurated a sort of national "system" or network of access to certain published materials. Librarians and publishers, working separately but often cooperatively, brought a measure of order to the burgeoning world of books and journals that knowledge seekers needed to enter. This was particularly important in the United States, given uneven library development and an expanding cohort of scholars, scientists, and intellectuals scattered about a vast and diverse country. Historian John Higham notes that such a diffuse environment, without the strong concentration of intellectual authority found in England or France, promoted the development of formal bibliographic devices—indexes, abstracts, catalogs, directories—to manage the outpouring of scholarly literature and increase its availability: "Instead of vesting leadership in an academy, Americans called on the neutral services of bibliographers and librarians."[6] Although total neutrality is impossible, librarians attempted to stand above the fray, and their professional ideology increasingly emphasized objectivity and comprehensiveness.

The bibliographic "system" in the United States developed as a pragmatic mix of private and public, profit and nonprofit, personal and organizational enterprise. Scientific and scholarly societies began to issue bibliographies, directories, and abstracting and indexing tools, as well as journals and proceedings for their constituencies. Libraries, some of which produced specialized bibliographies and printed lists of their holdings, also served as a key market for institutional publications. By the turn of the century two major companies, both in New York City, dominated American commercial bibliographic publishing: R. R. Bowker, which produced lists of published books, and the new H. W. Wilson Company. Entrepreneurial and innovative, Halsey W. Wilson perceived the emerging needs for bibliographic works and the potential of the library market, and he utilized the new Linotype technology to continuously and cumulatively update bibliographic entries. With the advice of librarians, his company launched important recurrent bibliographies: *Reader's Guide to Periodical Literature* (1900), the more scholarly *International Index to Periodicals* (1907) and then specialized subject indexes, *Cumulative Book Index* (1898), and *Book Review Digest* (1905). In 1895 the U.S. superintendent of documents started issuing the *Monthly Catalog of Government Publications* and from a year later until 1940 the *Document Catalog*, a complete list of federal publications. Soon thereafter librarian Charles Evans began to bring out his *American Bibliography* (1903–59), an indispensable work that eventually included virtually all publications produced in British colonial America (and then the United States) from 1639 to 1800. The proliferation of serial publications led to the publication of the *Union List of Serials in Libraries of the United States and Canada* (1927), a product of years of cooperative effort by the several hundred libraries whose holdings are listed.

American research libraries were, as a common formulation put it, being converted from storehouses to workshops, serving as active rather than passive participants in the intellectual endeavor. They also continued to be storehouses, charged with caring for their holdings through what was understood to be the proper construction of library buildings, suitable environmental conditions, and appropriate treatment of individual items. In the early twentieth century, librarians began to worry about decaying paper made from wood pulp, especially newsprint, and in the 1930s there was pioneering research in preservation of books and experimentation with microfilm as a preservation technique.

The Library of Congress

The Library of Congress was a vital actor in the new library and bibliographic order of the early twentieth century. Its status as a de facto national library was by then well established, symbolized by a great new building (see figure 23.1). A new chief, Herbert Putnam (former director of the Boston Public Library), who was appointed Librarian of Congress in 1899, proceeded to enlarge the library's national role. This path differed from that of the library's traditional European counterparts, which led the field through their prestige, unparalleled collections, and monumental printed catalogs (in progress for years). Putnam broadly conceived the Library of Congress's service to the nation: beyond manifesting cultural nationalism through its holdings, it

FIGURE 23.1. Library of Congress Building, 1897, exterior (*above*) and Great Hall (*opposite*). Library of Congress Prints and Photographs Division, Detroit Publishing Company Photograph Collection.

would systematically assist the nation's libraries and scholars. In addition to launching the new classification scheme and then, in 1908, the *List of Subject Headings*, the library began selling its printed catalog cards in 1901 and depositing sets in selected large libraries. These cards, with their authoritative descriptions, subject headings, and Library of Congress classification numbers, not only standardized and nationalized bibliographic description and subject cataloging in American libraries but spelled the end of printed book catalogs in favor of the more flexible and more easily updated (but not easily duplicated) card catalog, which retained its dominance until the advent of electronic catalogs at the end of the twentieth century. In the early 1900s, the Library of Congress developed an interlibrary loan service and the National Union Catalog, a critical location file of works in American research libraries. Under Putnam's forty-year administration, historian Jane Rosen-

berg concludes, "the scholarly world gained a map of American resources and keys to their organization."[7]

Putnam's successor, the poet Archibald MacLeish (1939–44), rationalized the library's sprawling organization and its collecting policy and presided over the launching of a new bibliographic era. From 1942 to 1946 the library published the 167-volume *Catalog of Books Represented by Library of Congress Printed Cards Issued to July 31, 1942*, an author catalog produced by the new photo-offset technology. This enterprise was followed by publication of later cumulations, including holdings of other research libraries, a subject catalog, and catalogs of other media. These publications, plus the later issuance in book form of catalogs of other research and specialized libraries, constituted key steps toward comprehensive access to cataloged American library holdings.

The national services of the Library of Congress can be seen as a form of indirect federal government subsidy of research libraries, along with tax-exempt status and special mailing rates. The library also played an important national role as a creature of Congress, particularly through its Legislative Reference Service (organized in 1914), which supplied information and analysis pertaining to legislation.

Of course, the basis for the Library of Congress's service to the scholarly world was its superb collections, overseen by specialist librarians and open to public use. Given the collections' comprehensiveness, the checklists and bibliographies produced by the different departments served as definitive guides and important contributions to their fields. The holdings ranged beyond copyright deposits of books, journals, music, maps, motion pictures, prints, and photographs to government documents, newspapers, publications of learned societies, rare books, manuscripts, and international acquisitions. Of the last, historian Neil Harris reminds us: "As a sense of world power emerged in the United States of the 1880s and 1890s, the conviction grew that its material possessions should represent the history and literature, not just of the United States, but of any culture which Americans might have business knowing about—and there was none exempt from this status."[8]

Putnam championed the library's duty to document the history of the nation and of the federal government: the Library of Congress should be "a library of record for the United States."[9] In 1903 he inaugurated the presidential papers collection, which, together with other Americana holdings, made the library a center for the study of American history and culture. Although congressional appropriations grew immensely, money for desired materials might be scarce. Gifts and exchanges provided much material, and endowment and gift funds helped with bibliographic projects and subsidized the salaries of curators and scholarly consultants. The premier library in the country, a grand cultural institution and a prime government entity, operated at that very American juncture of private and public sectors, philanthropy and tax support, in cultural and educational affairs.

When Putnam retired in 1939, the library's collections had grown from less than 1 million when he came in 1899 to more than 6 million books, plus millions of nonbook items. John Y. Cole, historian of the library and director of its Center for the Book, writes that the Library of Congress had become "one of the world's most complicated libraries: a legislative agency with executive functions; a government library open to the public; a national institution 'universal' in scope, collecting books and research materials from around the world; and a large bureaucracy serving diverse, often competing constituencies. These varied functions and roles have obscured the Library's substantial contributions to American scholarship, especially in American history, in cartography, in music, and in bibliographic work in several fields. . . ."[10]

The New York Public Library

The last decade of the nineteenth century also saw the creation of a new institution that would often be ranked second to the Library of Congress among American research libraries—The New York Public Library. The impetus for its founding derived from the successful challenge to the will of former Governor Samuel J. Tilden of New York, who died in 1886. He had designated a Tilden Trust to use his fortune to establish a public library in New York City, which, unlike other major cities, lacked a substantial popular library. The two major reference libraries in the city—the Astor and the Lenox (the latter an eclectic collection, founded in 1870 by James Lenox, of Bibles, rare books and manuscripts, Americana and New World exploration)—were free to users but considered aloof and elitist, and they badly needed an infusion of money and energy. Searching for partners to carry out Tilden's wishes after his will was broken and his funds diminished, the trustees finally settled on consolidation with the Astor and Lenox Libraries to form the New York Public Library in 1895.

The new institution, initially a reference library only, was a private nonprofit corporation with a self-perpetuating board of trustees made up of rich, prominent, white, mainly Anglo-Saxon, Protestant men, mostly attorneys and bankers. (A female trustee was not elected until 1950; no nonwhites and very few non-Protestants came on until the 1970s.) American libraries, universities, and other cultural and educational institutions rarely had diverse boards; few public library boards, however, were quite as exclusive or had so many nationally powerful members as at the New York Public Library, at its founding and for years afterward. The founders were nonetheless quite progressive, belonging to a new, more liberal generation of the city's high elite—philanthropic, interested in culture and education, and involved in civic affairs. They wanted the new library to be a New World British Museum or Bibliothèque Nationale de France, and they had the resources and connections to accomplish such a goal. They fulfilled their vision, and did so more generously than the European libraries: The New York Public Library would be freely open to anyone, with no questions asked, every day and every evening of the year. Books were delivered almost immediately, and the library responded to local interests as well as to the world of scholarship and research (see figure 23.2). The trustees' elite character notwithstanding, the library itself was profoundly democratic in its intellectual hospitality and open access. This reflected not only the trustees' sophistication

FIGURE 23.2. Main reading room, New York Public Library, opened in 1911. Picture Collection, The Branch Libraries, The New York Public Library, Astor, Lenox and Tilden Foundations.

but equally, if not more important, the broad-minded librarians' high professionalism and devotion to public service, with support from the municipality, generous donors, and a cosmopolitan clientele that helped shape the library's contents.

Like the Library of Congress, the New York Public Library was a complex institution. As of 1901, it became bifurcated into two separate units. The privately financed Reference Department contained the original Astor-Lenox collections, while a new Circulation Department oversaw a system of neighborhood lending libraries. Many of these branches were built with massive donations by Andrew Carnegie and supported thereafter by the municipality, which also constructed and maintained a landmark central building, mainly for the research collections, on a prime city-owned site on Fifth Avenue and 42nd Street.

The Reference Department (renamed The Research Libraries in 1966) grew quickly and was comprehensive in most fields. It gained vitality and particular strengths from its location in the most populous city in the country, the main port of entry into the United States, and a mecca not only of diverse cultures but of publishing, communications, art, literature, music, theater, design, advertising, and finance — all interests that the library served. Local demand accounted for outstanding performing arts collections, and, unusual for the time, notable specialized ethnic collections. The Jewish and Slavonic Divisions were established in the late 1890s, and in 1925 the Division of Negro Literature, History, and Prints (later the Schomburg Collection) was created in Harlem. Library use was phenomenal, more so than at the British Museum, and much more than the Library of Congress in Washington, a backwater city until the 1940s. The Reference Library's numerous clientele of independent and academic researchers and other information seekers was immensely augmented in the 1920s by hordes of students, whose college and university libraries, despite burgeoning enrollments, still had comparatively meager collections.

The professional leadership of the New York Public Library aimed to preserve the acknowledged world's cultural heritage and to create a historical record of human endeavors of all sorts. The pattern was set by the first director, Dr. John Shaw Billings, just retired from the United States Army Surgeon-General's Library, which he had built into one of the great world medical libraries. Under Billings and his successors Edwin Hatfield Anderson and Harry Miller Lydenberg, the New York Public Library Reference Department grew from fewer than 500,000 books and pamphlets in 1896 to nearly 3 million when Lydenberg retired in 1941.

The librarians knew they could not obtain everything, but they tried, and their devotion to comprehensiveness yielded collections that stood high among world libraries in both quantity and quality. They saw organized knowledge and information as necessary to modern society, and they believed in the importance of the life of the mind and the need for an informed people in a republic. Their outlook was not only modern but even, one might say, postmodern in its nonjudgmental attitude and unfearful appreciation of the multifaceted, limitless, and unpredictable nature of knowledge. Alert to incipient trends and concerned for posterity, librarians acquired materials traditionally neglected by conventional scholars: offbeat journals and pamphlets, avant-garde art and literature, popular music, ephemera, and the publications of the countless organizations and associations springing up at the turn of the century. Of course, other research libraries, Harvard and Yale, for example, also aspired to universality and collected such items, and the Library of Congress, which received all copyrighted items, also welcomed materials such as folk music and transcripts of slave narratives. The New York Public Library was known, though, for its systematic, consistent fulfillment of the documentalist role.[11]

Global Collecting

The Library of Congress, New York Public Library, and several university libraries were also exceptionally internationalist. Unlike most American academic institutions, where the study of world affairs was uncommon before the First World War and interest concentrated on western European society and culture, they welcomed non-European and non-Roman alphabet materials. Yale librarian Andrew Keogh alerted the library community to serious gaps in international holdings in 1919. He had seen this problem firsthand in his work with a research team collecting information, for example, on obscure Balkan areas, in preparation for the Versailles peace conference.[12] Yet, as late as the 1930s and 1940s, surveys showed that American university libraries lagged behind the Library of Congress and the New York Public Library in holdings of foreign imprints. The Second World War revealed the relative paucity of non-American, non western European information in this country, including geographic data vital to conducting the war. Notable exceptions were the Library of Congress, the New York Public Library, and Harvard, Michigan, Stanford, and Yale Universities, and even they had lacunae.

Ethnocentrism in American university libraries also extended, again with exceptions, to nonwhite and non–Anglo Saxon groups within the United States, as well as other nonmainstream subjects and groups. Not until the 1970s did contemporary interest in ethnicity, race relations, women, children, and gender issues point up the failure of many university libraries to collect material documenting these groups and subjects. Such interests had not previously been in the dominant intellectual ken on campuses; their neglect also no doubt stemmed from plain prejudice or narrow-mindedness.

Nonacademic institutions such as the Library of Congress and the New York Public Library were in a rather better position than most university libraries to acquire a very wide range of materials. The Library of Congress benefited from copyright deposit; as a national library, it also attracted numerous gifts and extensive international exchanges. And like the New York Public Library and other public libraries with research collections, it had a certain independence. Such libraries did have financial problems, they did compete with other agencies for private gifts and public monies, and their clienteles were less cohesive than in academe. But they did not have to contend with powerful intra-institutional budgetary rivals such as football stadiums, faculty salaries, laboratory equipment, or curriculum projects. True, university libraries were supported by an institutional structure and resident subject specialists. Librarians and curators in nonacademic institutions, however, many as expert in their subjects as university professors, did not suffer from the low status so often borne by librarians in academe. They could more easily exercise autonomous professional judgment and take a balanced approach that considered areas of knowledge beyond current mainstream intellectual and research interests or curricular demands.

Such independence characterized the privately endowed scholarly reference libraries that rose to prominence during the first half of the twentieth century, most of which focused on particular subjects or types of materials that reflected their founders' or trustees' own book collecting, cultural interests, ambitions, personalities, prejudices, or tastes. Special collections accumulated by private individuals did find their way into public and university libraries, and formed the basis there for distinguished rare book and manuscript collections. Other persons preferred to found independent libraries and study centers. These included the John Crerar Library (science) and Newberry Library (humanities) in Chicago; the Huntington Library in San Marino, California (rare books and manuscripts in American and English literature and history); the Folger in Washington, D.C. (Shakespeare and the Tudor and Stuart eras); and the Pierpont Morgan Library in New York City (rare books, manuscripts, and prints) — all founded in the 1890s or the early twentieth century. Such libraries, writes Louis R. Wilson in his classic study of American library resources, "brought to the use of American scholars a body and range of materials which tremendously reduced the difference between American and European libraries."[13] The collective contribution of these institutions to American scholarship remains to be studied and fully appreciated.

Academic Libraries on the Rise

In academe, the transformation of universities into research institutions, with their concomitant library needs, extended from the 1890s well into the twentieth century. The top research universities entered a golden age in the 1930s[14] and then, after World War II, reached new and higher levels of power and prestige. For the libraries of these research universities, a golden age came after the war, but even in the 1930s their efforts to catch up with Europe were quite successful, and research libraries came to constitute a distinctive entity within the North American library milieu. In 1932 the major academic libraries in the United States and Canada joined with several nonacademic institutions (including the Library of Congress, New York Public Library, and Boston Public Library) to form the selective Association of Research Libraries.

The geographic distribution of research library resources in the United States remained uneven. As Louis Wilson documented, in the mid-1930s they were heavily concentrated in traditional economic and cultural centers — the Northeast, the upper Midwest, and California. The Library of Congress, New

York Public Library, Harvard and Yale, Cleveland and Boston public libraries, and universities such as Columbia, Chicago, and Illinois each had considerably more than a million volumes (see figure 23.3). By 1939 Cornell, Michigan, Minnesota, and the combined campuses of the University of California also passed the million mark, but several other leading research universities had not yet done so.[15]

By then university librarians and interested faculty members had been trying for some years to systematically acquire current publishing outputs and documents from all levels of government and all sorts of organizations and corporations. Still, some major academic institutions continued to rely a good deal on gifts, shifting only gradually to substantial and regular budget appropriations. Of course, the many donations of money, buildings, and collections, and the often fortuitous acquisition of varieties of books and manuscripts, plus the tendency to take everything that was offered, gave university libraries much of their richness and diversity. Speaking of Harvard, Kenneth Carpenter remarks: "Librarians and others often acted with great wisdom to shape the Library; in other instances chance played a major role."[16] Special collections, fondly donated by scholars and book lovers, stimulated library development in diverse fields. Librarians endeavored to achieve balance and supply context. The Slavic scholar and chief librarian at Harvard from 1910 to 1928, Archibald Cary Coolidge, expressed this approach: "I have always believed in both quality and quantity, accepting cheerfully everything that comes our way but doing my best to guide carefully the expenditure of whatever funds I control or when I have any influence over the purchases of others."[17]

The large research libraries generally sought comprehensiveness individually. In bibliographic and other matters, collaboration had long been common, and by 1940 significant levels of technical standardization and professionalism had been achieved. This standardization, combined with a national outlook and cooperative spirit, the work of the Library of Congress, and the use of new technology, had set research libraries on the path toward an effective national bibliographic system. They thereby not only facilitated scholarly research but also mitigated the increasingly specialized, fractured character of the scholarly enterprise. By amassing materials of all kinds and issuing centralized information about their holdings, great research libraries can be seen as integrating, holistic intellectual forces at the same time as they accommodated particular local interests and needs.

The collections themselves did not, with some exceptions, reflect conscious national planning or regional collaborative efforts. Libraries did work together during the First World War to procure items from Europe, but subsequent proposals for sharing resources and improving national coverage faded. Again war

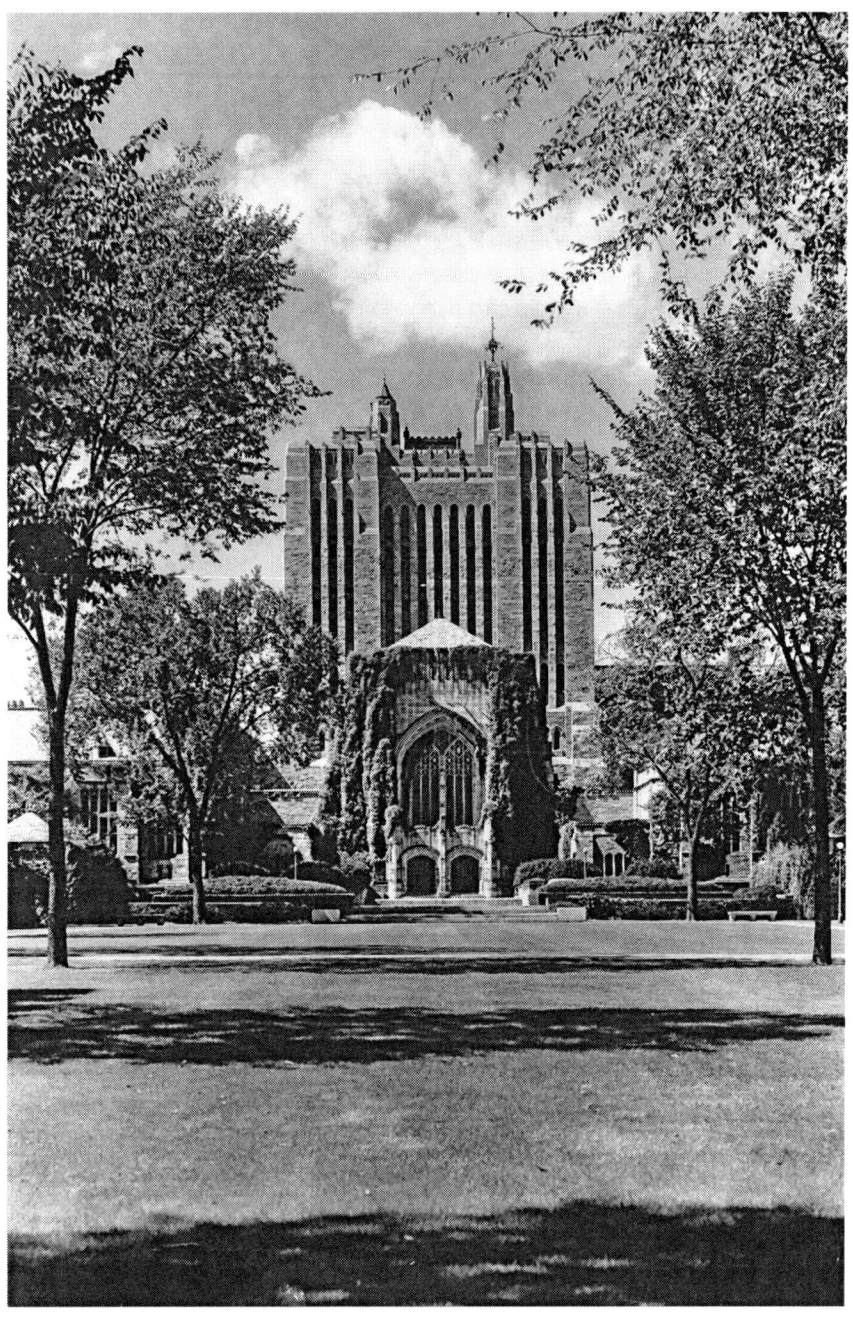

FIGURE 23.3. Sterling Memorial Library at Yale University, opened in 1930 (shown here in 1990). Yale University Manuscripts and Archives.

was the spur. During World War II, the problems of obtaining books and journals from Europe and the discovery of serious gaps in international collections sparked the first major American programs to jointly build collections to some degree. These included the Cooperative Acquisitions Project for Wartime Publications, led by the Library of Congress, which from 1945 to 1947 brought nearly 2 million pieces from Europe to American research libraries; and the Farmington Plan, conceived in 1942 and adopted by the Association of Research Libraries in 1947 to ensure that at least one copy of all international publications of research value would be in an American library and recorded in the National Union Catalog.

Conclusion: The "Information Explosion"

Research libraries, including newly developing ones in the South and West, would soon undergo dazzling growth. The country's wealth, cultural ambitions, and immensely increased scientific and scholarly activities, together with the worldwide "information explosion," the United States' emerging superpower status, and its hegemonic competition with the Soviet Union, all contributed to making American research libraries world leaders. The new expansionism generated strains, financial and otherwise, that would lead to unprecedented interlibrary cooperation. These trends were first played out in the context of traditional library technology, augmented by new microform and photocopying techniques. But by the time of the nation's bicentennial, research libraries stood on the cusp of another new era, the global electronic information age, which would parallel if not surpass the transformation begun in the industrial age a hundred years before.

Part B
Reading in Situ

Introduction

Carl F. Kaestle and Janice A. Radway

In some sense, statistics tell the story. Illiteracy among persons ten years and older declined from 7.7 percent in 1910, to 4.3 percent in 1930, to 2.9 percent in 1940.[1] In 1900 44 percent of the black population was illiterate. By 1930 that figure had been reduced to 16 percent.[2] High school attendance increased dramatically from less than 5 percent in 1880 to more than 50 percent in 1940.[3] The number of institutions of higher learning increased from 811 in 1880 to 1,706 in 1940, with enrollment increasing from 115,817 in 1880 to 1,494,203 in 1940.[4] The number of books imprinted expanded twice as fast as the population: from 2,076 titles in 1880 to 11,328 titles in 1940.[5] The number of English-language daily papers went from 850 in 1880 to 1,942 in 1930, while total daily circulation increased from 3.1 million in 1880 to 39.6 million in 1930.[6]

Taken together, statistics like these suggest that between 1880 and 1940, reading figured in the daily lives of substantially more Americans than ever before. By 1940, in fact, the United States had become a nation of readers. Both at work and at home, print was commonplace, nearly indispensable. Given the simultaneous expansion of print culture and of the American population, which rose from 11,328,000 in 1880 to 131,954,000 in 1940, even the most cursory effort at summarizing the history of reading in the United States during this period becomes a daunting, nearly impossible task.

A general history of reading between 1880 and 1940 is beyond the scope of this volume for other reasons as well. Reading, for example, is not in itself a uniform technology or practice that is identical from place to place, moment to moment, or person to person. As so many theorists and historians of the process have pointed out in recent years, although reading can be characterized simply as the decoding of text, the nature of that decoding varies enormously depending on the complexity of the text being read, on the literacy training and higher interpretive competencies of the reader, on the purpose of the task (e.g., for entertainment, excitement, gathering of information, or meditation), and on the social context within which it is carried out. Consequently, the meaning of the act of reading itself differs substantially from case to case. To understand, then, how reading changed during our period, one would need to investigate and compare the full range of reading practices employed in U.S. parlors, nurseries, churches, businesses, schools, universities and colleges, libraries, government agencies, commercial establishments, and other sites where reading played a central role.

Additionally, much basic research remains to be done on the changing nature of reading at the aforementioned sites. This lack of analysis reflects both the problems inherent in the documentary record itself and the long-standing disinterest in the reading activities of all but the most literate and elite of the population. Reading is a nearly ubiquitous practice in modern societies, essential to the nature of bureaucracies, corporations, and daily lives dominated by the manufacture, distribution, sale, and consumption of commodities. Given that reading is a cognitive and affective process that takes place internally, however, its effects are often invisible. Although most reading done on a daily basis leaves little in the way of a direct documentary record, some records do exist. Diaries, letters, and autobiographies often contain mention of the books their authors read; book margins and notebooks register student comments; more or less formal accounts of reading were produced by novelists, reviewers, and critics; and footnotes document the reading histories of scientists and academics. Readers of cookbooks, newspapers, magazines, government reports, business memos, and advertisements, however, left little account of how they understood the materials they read.

Reading occurs in an immediate context amid the particulars of a rich daily life and is intertwined with other activities. As such, reading informed cooking practices, voting behavior, particular purchases, agricultural practices, and accounting procedures. Because the role of reading in each of the latter actions cannot be known explicitly, it must be understood indirectly as mediated by a range of other factors and variables. Historians specialize in these complex and inferential investigations, but, until recently, few examined business memos, cookbook collections, ordinary diaries and letters, or postal or library circulation records for insight on reading practices. Previously, reading was conceived too uniformly, too much as a function of the texts themselves or as the consumption of ideas promulgated by authors to be analyzed so imaginatively. Only scholars and the literary and political elite took interest in this epiphenomenal practice.[7]

Rather than a highly abstract and generalized account of reading in the years between 1880 and 1940, we offer a small number of case studies, each of which approaches the topic of reading as a *social* practice that takes place in situ—at a particular place or site, in a given context, and at a given historical moment. These three essays strive to suggest that despite the apparently singular nature of the interaction between an individual reader and a text, reading always reflects and incorporates a reader's past experiences and training, ideological assumptions and expectations, shared desires, and, more often than not, fellow readers with whom one shared one's reading experiences. These essays treat reading as an intentional act in its own right, a form of agency rather than as passive consumption. Why, they ask, did specific people devote considerable time, energy, and expenditure to the reading of books? How did they manage this? Where, how, and with whom did they carry out this activity? What did they read and to what effect? Through these questions, readers become actors, people who turned to the culture of print to accomplish certain ends. Like the authors they read, these readers were *users* of print; they attempted to mobilize books, print, publishing, and the very act of reading itself for their own quite specific purposes.

Elizabeth Long, Elizabeth McHenry, and Joan Shelley Rubin consider a variety of readers and contexts, providing a textured view of specific reading practices and exploring the complex effects of reading on those who engaged in the practice. Literacy and its acquisition are invested with considerable meaning; thus, the impact of reading is of great interest to many in society. As Joan Rubin shows in her essay, this was especially the case between 1880 and 1940, because previously excluded individuals and groups were rapidly acquiring both basic and advanced literacy. Amid sweeping social, technological, and cultural change, social scientists, cultural critics, librarians, and government officials all wondered "what reading did to people." Although studies of the 1920s and 1930s focused largely on reading variations among different white social classes, modern interest in the effects of reading upon gendered, immigrant, and minority populations can be seen as a continuation and expansion of these earlier concerns.

In her essay on the explosion of the white women's literary club movement in the latter decades of the nineteenth century, Elizabeth Long explores the complicated relationship between women's cultural and literary activities and collective social action. She examines possible connections between the widespread club phenomenon and the white, educated, middle-class, progressive reform movement of the early decades of the twentieth century. Her analysis of the larger club phenomenon focuses on those that appeared in Texas in the last two decades of the century, resulting in an account that stresses the ironies and complexities of women's reading activities.

Texas women's book choices tended to reinforce the canonical and Anglophile thrust of the period's high-literary culture; but, as Long suggests, clubs also allowed their members to read, discuss, and even write about both historical and contemporary issues, thereby challenging prevailing definitions of femininity. In this case, as in many others during our period, reading at once consolidated aspects of the dominant culture and led to its alteration and diversification. Middle-class white women expanded their worlds and augmented their abilities despite facing structural constraints and traditional ideological frames that limited them to what Long calls "reformist initiatives that softened the harsh effects of an inequitable social order."

Elizabeth McHenry tackles similar questions in her account of "the literary activism" of black women. Although she examines reading and cultural activities as a stepping-stone into the public arena and social action, she is especially interested in black women's social solidarity and collective identity as developed by shared reading and literary activities. Like Long, McHenry analyzes reading as a technology of subject construction that enabled black women not only to contest stereotypes of highly promiscuous sexuality but to demonstrate their abilities at "critical argument, disciplined reason, and public expression." McHenry emphasizes the organizations and connections between clubwomen across the country, especially as demonstrated by the Women's Era Club of Boston. McHenry stresses that reading should never be conceived simply as a solitary activity nor used to neatly separate the literate and the illiterate. In the black community, those who could read often read to those who could not, allowing books and their messages to percolate slowly but definitively through the social order.

Whereas Long and McHenry focus on particular groups of readers, Joan Shelley Rubin looks at the genre of poetry "as a window through which to view the impact of site and practice." She explores the difference between literary history and a history of reading, finding that reading nearly always crosses aesthetic, chronological, and spatial boundaries and that texts can have multiple, even contradictory meanings for different readers. She argues that reading researchers of the 1920s and 1930s ignored these complexities, approaching reading with a kind of "desperate behaviorism." Rubin asserts that a researcher interested in the effects of print and reading cannot confine herself to statistical measures of simple effects but must consider the complex intersection between setting and the mode of reading through which particular texts are engaged and given meaning. She reminds her own readers that books actually circulate more widely than the emphasis on the actual physical object would suggest. Indeed, books circulate not only orally but also in anthologies, in sermons, and in quoted references of all sorts. Understanding the full impact of a given text, discourse, or genre, thus requires documenting the full history of its readers over time.

Rubin bases these generalizations on her research into the social life of poetry during the early twentieth century, when sales of individual volumes of poems were in decline. Americans, she demonstrates, continued to read and use poetry in a variety of settings. Although the form persisted over time, it did not always mean the same thing to those who adapted it to their own purposes. Thus, "[c]ultural needs, values, and principles, transmitted institutionally, intersected with the needs, values, and principles of individuals to shape a reading experience that cannot be recovered merely by chronicling titles, tabulating motives, or analyzing texts."

Rubin concludes that the researcher cannot simply correlate the interests and aims of readers with the literary materials published at the moment of their reading. People not only read best sellers and topical nonfiction but also peruse steady sellers and classic texts. To understand what these residual forms— Rubin borrows the term and the concept from Raymond Williams—meant at any given time, the researcher must make an effort, as she has, to recover how readers in one era encountered, used, and interpreted the work of another. Given the complexities of readers and the texts themselves, it is not always easy to pinpoint the effect of a particular act of reading.

Reading, as these three chapters suggest, is a richly layered practice in which readers engage deliberately and intentionally, but which is often unconsciously shaped by the context in which it occurs. Consequently, it has both multiple and unintended effects, only some of which are noticeable at the time of reading. Others, however, operate in subterranean, undetected fashion; their consequences can only be discerned over time. For example, the reading done by African American women and the families they introduced to "race literature" led eventually to a politicized social body that would demand its civil rights within a few short decades. Similarly, the continued reading of a canon of literature written largely by educated white men, in which poetry and verse figured centrally, might be taken to have perpetuated gender and race privilege at least into the 1960s and 1970s and even contributed to the conservation of an oppressive social order. To draw these conclusions too quickly and too neatly, however, would be to overlook the application of new reading strategies born of the political and intellectual struggle for equality. These new methods engaged the traditional canon in the 1980s and 1990s, using it not simply to recommend certain touchstones and moral and political beliefs but to critique them by witnessing their construction over time. The study of reading, it must be remembered, is always in some sense rereading—one must always know who reads, why, where, and to what end.

CHAPTER 24

Aflame with Culture
Reading and Social Mission in the Nineteenth-Century White Women's Literary Club Movement

Elizabeth Long

The late nineteenth century witnessed a remarkable consolidation of high culture, including the development of a canonical literary culture and the stratification of high culture from popular culture, blunting the populist thrust of such forms as opera and Shakespearean drama. As Lawrence W. Levine and Paul DiMaggio have argued, the American upper classes widely subscribed to a program of building museums, theaters, and concert halls, which became citadels of high culture and a regime of high seriousness.[1]

The newly "sacralized" culture, to use Levine's term, helped legitimate the cultural authority of the upper classes and underscored their commitment to the superiority of the English and German cultural heritage. The cultural themes of nationalism, individualism, and the Anglo-Saxon heritage contributed to a civil culture more broadly diffused through public schools and popular culture.[2]

This cultural and ideological development had some unintended consequences. The effort to establish the authority of high culture also diffused literacy, which could be used by diverse groups of people to explore their particular interests, expand their horizons, and craft their identity. However assiduously educators and members of the literary establishment tried to police what reading should be (what Roger Chartier called "the order of books"), the encounter between reader and text remained open-ended, maintaining the possibility, as Janice Radway terms it, of "going awry."[3] Moreover, as canonical literary works became quasi-sacred during this period, they perforce also became a cultural resource by which individuals and groups could achieve their own ends. Such processes of appropriation are complex. They are capable of reconfiguring identities, reworking cultural frames, even unsettling social hierarchies. The nineteenth-century white women's literary club movement exemplifies these ironies, demonstrating the transformative potential of reading, especially in association with other like-minded readers. Yet it also shows how powerfully social structures and ideological formations could constrain even social actors who were convinced that books and reading gave them the warrant to change the world.

Origins of the White Women's Literary Club Movement

After the Civil War, white women's book clubs spread from the urban centers of the Northeast across the American West almost as fast as the frontier.[4] (One group in Clarendon, Texas, began a scant seven years after initial white settlement.)[5] For the thousands of women who took up the torch, these were not merely local literary gatherings but a broad-based social movement, inspiring tremendous dedication, enthusiasm, and devotion. Although the idea and even the form of the literary association largely reflected late eighteenth-century white women's reading groups and the scattered legacy of free African American women's literary groups dating back to the 1830s, post–Civil War groups mainly recognized their more distant and glamorous predecessors: medieval women's religious associations, Anne Hutchinson's circle, or the French *salonières*. In the main, though, like most Americans of their day, book club members looked forward. The literary club movement meant progress and "a necessary step in the evolution of women."[6]

These literary women drew on organizational forms developed in charitable and reform associations that had involved thousands of women from the 1830s on, women's associations established to support both northern and southern efforts during the Civil War, and popular educational associations like the Chautauqua movement and local lyceums, which had generally been led by men but involved women as audiences.

When women immigrated to the frontier states, they brought with them both the idea and the format for book clubs. The New England Women's Club and Sorosis, a notable New York group, both established in 1868, were publicized by the press and by tireless lecturing of such stalwarts as reformer Julia Ward Howe, who presented her talk "How Can Women Best Associate?" to gatherings from New York to San Francisco. These eastern groups inspired dozens of literary clubs across the nation.

The Ladies Reading Club of Houston exemplifies the flavor and fervor of early Texas groups. Generally regarded as the first literary club in Texas, it was born in Adele Briscoe Looscan's drawing room in 1885.[7] As Mrs. Looscan later recalled, her friend Carrie Ennis Lombardi came to call and "opened a subject very near her heart. It so happened that her dominant thought had also been my thought for months, only awaiting an opportunity to broach it to her, and to a few others of our friends. The idea we wished to develop was the formation of a circle or club ... for the purpose of intellectual and social culture." Together, they set out by carriage across the brick and dirt streets of Houston (then a city of 23,000) to call upon "such intimate friends as we agreed ought to be interested," and they quickly enrolled nine members at the first meeting. By the end of the year, the group numbered twenty-four, with a slate of officers, a formal agenda, and careful minutes of each meeting.[8] Patterning itself after the Ladies Literary Club of Grand Rapids, Michigan (one of the founders had connections there), the Texas group began by studying the history, science, art, and literature of a specific country. For their first year's program they chose Egypt, "as at the time it was attracting the attention of the civilized world on account of the conflict in the Soudan [sic] and the tragic fate of the gallant Gordon."[9]

Book clubs became the "dominant idea" in the hearts of these two Texas ladies, as they did for thousands of other like-minded ladies across the country after the Civil War. Several factors stimulated this consciousness. First, a cluster of structural developments had given middle-class women more leisure time, narrowed their traditional sphere of domesticity, and widened the gap between the daily lives of men and women. Literary clubs offered such women a chance to partake of the broader world. As Megan Seaholm said, the literary club "added a dimension to 'true womanhood.'"[10]

Second, during the late nineteenth century, education was becoming crucially important for middle-class Americans, yet women maintained a tenuous relationship to the institutions of higher learning. In 1870 only about 750 B.A. degrees were granted to American women.[11] As one graduate put it, "a college woman was ... a curio."[12] For the large numbers of middle-class women who could not attend college, the literary club offered the possibility of lifelong learning. A member of the Dubuque (Iowa) Conversation Club said, "Our university must be in our homes. This country is too large to go to a place or a professor. The learned, inspiring minds must come to us."[13]

Third, just as women's higher education was beginning its tantalizingly slow expansion, some other sources of culture outside the home declined. The popular lyceum movement, for example, which had involved members of the Ladies Reading Club of Houston not only as audience members but also as librarians, began to wither as formal education grew. Finally, women turned to literature with moral and aesthetic fervor because high culture had itself been elevated to almost transcendent status in the late nineteenth century. As an unquestioned symbol of distinction, literary culture could presumably confer cultural authority upon the earnest women who made it their own.

The Literary Club Movement and Its Effects on Members' Ideology: Self-Culture for Enlightenment

The women who founded literary clubs were aflame with desire for education and "self-culture." Texas literary club mottoes capture some of this excitement. The Denton Woman's Shakespeare Club proclaimed: "Step by step, we gain the heights," and the Chautauqua Literary and Scientific Circle of Waxahachie urged its members: "Neglect not the gift that is in thee."[14]

Accounts of early literary clubs often include evidence that male authorities, from pastors to husbands, perceived such activities as a threat to domestic order. For instance, a 1938 description of the Dallas Shakespeare Club (founded in 1886 and distinguished as one of the first Shakespeare clubs in the United States) says of its early years: "Its members read Shakespeare for pure enjoyment and then hurried home to reach the fireside before the arrival of their husbands, most of whom had a very decided dislike for any kind of club. Later the club read Shakespeare more slowly and critically, the husbands still fumed, and some members, so the stories go, dropped out to keep peace in the family."[15] Husbands of the Rhode Island Woman's Club nicknamed it the Society for the Prevention of Home Industry; one New York journalist claimed that "Woman has laid down the broomstick to pick up the club."[16] Authors satirized women's literary clubs, and cartoonists caricatured them. Indeed, these clubs empowered their participants, changed their identity, and eventually inspired in them a strong sense of social mission.

Organization: Signaling Seriousness

Literary clubwomen signaled the seriousness of their endeavor through meticulous attention to organization and parliamentary procedure as well as by the substance and tone of their programs of study. Although each group was different, there were common elements. Most groups had a constitution and bylaws in place after only a few meetings.[17] These usually featured the club's purpose, membership requirements, officers, and election procedures. Leadership most commonly rotated intentionally among all members, allowing each to grow in confidence and skills. The bylaws established dues, meeting times, procedures, and penalties for absences or lateness. The Austin Pathfinders, for example, passed resolutions that rain and muddy streets were not an excuse for absence, that there would be no whispering during recitations, and that refreshments would be served only on special occasions.[18] Parliamentary procedure also demonstrated the solemnity of these literary endeavors and separated their work from more informal women's social groups. Some clubs appointed a parliamentarian, many held parliamentary "drills," and most conducted their meetings according to *Robert's Rules of Order* or Mrs. Shattuck's *Woman's Manual of the Parliamentary Law*.

The club year tended to run from fall to spring, following the school year, and a committee usually set out an entire year's program, which was often printed in a yearbook for members. Individual meetings followed an exacting format. The Order of Business in the 1917-18 yearbook of the Axson Club of Houston provides a typical example: Minutes of Last Meeting, Report of Corresponding Secretary, Treasurer's Report, Report of Committees, Unfinished Business, New Business, Critic's Report, Program, and Adjournment.[19]

These efforts gave gravity and definition to the enterprise, proclaiming its legitimacy in the public sphere.[20] This was a bold endeavor in the eyes of members, as well as for those who surveyed it from the sidelines. An account of the first annual meeting of the Texas Federation of Women's Literary Clubs in 1898 states that "gentlemen were in attendance, manifesting a quizzical interest, and . . . evident amusement, but the ready tact and wit of the president saved the day."[21] Women generally barred men from membership, fearing that their presence would intimidate or silence women. For much the same reason, although clubs did have guest speakers, reports were most often prepared by the members themselves, followed by questions and discussion. Women expended tremendous effort in reading and preparing written compositions for these meetings. About her second report, one clubwoman said: "Never before had I spent so much labor in the preparation of anything, nor, I presume, shall I ever do so again."[22]

Reading

Literary clubs' programs concentrated on branches of knowledge traditionally or potentially within women's sphere of interest and on topics that could be studied without specialized instruction or rare books. Book acquisition was a particular problem in Texas and other frontier states, which lacked sufficient libraries and easy means of transporting books. Books were usually shipped to Texas from publishing centers in the Northeast, arriving via New Orleans or, later in the period, from Galveston. In 1870 Texas could claim only 711 miles of railroad tracks, and even Austin, the state capital, was not connected to the railroad until 1877. By 1890, however, 8,000 miles of new track improved the situation dramatically.[23] This rail network was crucial for book circulation as well as for commerce in general.

Nonetheless, examining the Texas book trade in 1880, one wonders how literary clubs managed to find books for their discussions. Philip Metzger found that in Austin, between 1870 and 1900, "Fifteen or sixteen separate booksellers began business . . . most lasted only two or three years." Only one of those Austin booksellers offered a circulating library. It stocked 1,500 titles, and an annual subscription cost between $7.00 (if one checked out one volume at a time) and $22.00, for which the customer could check out up to four volumes at once. Most of those books were novels, usually English works published between the 1840s and the 1860s. Dickens and Sir Walter Scott were by far the most popular selections, with James Fenimore Cooper and Mrs. E. D. E. N. Southworth tying for seventh place on the list.[24]

Most bookstores in Austin and Houston also sold other goods. Of the six booksellers listed in the *Houston City Directory, 1895–1896*, none sold books alone. B. P. Bailey & Co. is listed as an agent for Remington typewriters; George T. Lathrop was a printer and rubber stamp manufacturer; and Miss Lizzie I. Moody sold not only books but also jewelry, hair goods, toys, bric-a-brac, and Butterick sewing patterns. Each sold stationery, newspapers, and periodicals as well.[25] The institution most resembling a city library during the period was the Houston Lyceum Library, whose holdings, thanks to the work of the Ladies Reading Club, became the initial stock of the Houston Public Library. By 1904, when the Houston Public Library opened, it held 10,000 volumes and more than 4,000 government documents.[26] By the end of the century, libraries were under construction, and the book trade was expanding in Texas as in other frontier states. New book distribution patterns helped connect local booksellers to the national trade, and *Publishers' Weekly* became, in Metzger's words, "a major form of communication in the book industry. Its columns offered, among other things, news of the latest books and complete ordering information for them."

One can assume that by the early 1900s it was somewhat easier for Texas women's literary clubs to acquire recently published or specialized books. Earlier in the period, and especially in smaller, more remote municipalities, it must have been very difficult. Women most likely utilized the personal libraries of family and friends as well as whatever semipublic collections existed in their hometowns. Books also circulated among club members, a pattern that Gere mentions as characteristic of less wealthy book clubs elsewhere in the country.[27] Acquisition problems likely limited early Texas book clubs to select reading material that was widely available, pushing them toward literary classics (Shakespeare, Wordsworth, Browning) or the kinds of worthy and popular fare, such as Dickens and Scott, that did well among patrons of the circulating libraries of the day. Material constraints, in other words, probably reinforced the canonical and Anglophilic thrust of the period's high-literary culture.

The majority of literary club programs centered on literature, history, or the fine arts. There was usually a leavening of issues of the day (including socialism, suffrage, and social reform) and some discussion of "home economics," the rubric under which Catharine Beecher had professionalized women's domestic concerns. In February 1888, for instance, the Ladies Reading Club discussed "Vinegar, Yeast, and Dust."[28] Of the "true" sciences, botany appeared with some regularity, but most women had only an elementary knowledge of mathematics and science, thereby limiting accessible fare. Some groups, however, heard lectures on evolution or astronomy, and psychology appears to have been of general interest.

Within these limits, programs were very ambitious. El Paso's Current Events Club, for example, set Roman history as a theme one year, but interspersed study of that subject with papers on "Women as Rulers," and "Can Criminals Be Reclaimed?"[29] Over time, most groups shed this miscellaneous approach to knowledge and settled into more systematic programs of study, as illustrated by the first yearbook of the Houston Ladies Reading Club, from the 1901–2 club year: American Literature was the topic, encompassing the Colonial Period, 1607–1764 (subdivided into early and late), the Revolutionary Period, 1765–87, and the Constitutional Period, 1787–1820. Meeting almost every week, the program began in October with Captain John Smith and William Bradford and ended in May with Daniel Webster and John C. Calhoun. The progression from a potpourri in 1888 that featured "Yeast" one month and Henry James the next to this kind of program in 1901 was quite typical for book clubs across the country, although some — such as Austin's History Club — were reputedly "brainy" from their inception.[30]

Book clubs quite consciously fostered women's ability to express themselves. Groups initiated the "roll call" that required some response from all present on a given topic, thereby ensuring that everyone would speak. Every member was assigned reports. As clubs began to organize across the nation, they disseminated program outlines, papers from other clubs, and even pamphlets on how to approach an author and his works to help new clubs and untrained members.[31]

Over time, standards for literary analysis began to improve. Clubs began to expect more original compositions. Some clubs introduced debates; others emphasized literary production, becoming forums for sharing members' essays, poems, or short stories as well as for book discussion.[32] And some clubwomen were so much in demand as writers and speakers that they made club lecturing and writing their lifework.

Analysts such as Karen Blair claim that these literary groups were engaged in a rather passive activity — as consumers of culture — and that few clubs produced scholars or career women. Such a perspective, however, neglects the important abilities and competences that literary clubs fostered. This "mild form of compulsory education" exposed women not only to the discipline of learning but also to intellectual analysis through defense of opinions and confident self-expression.[33] Reading thus helped women to expand their horizons, change their identities, and shape the values they imparted to their daughters (and sons), fostering significant generational change.

Studies of history or cultural geography provided many women their first opportunity to look beyond very limited personal horizons. Pursuing *general* knowledge (what Jane Croly called "knowledge of the history and development of races and peoples")[34] was itself a challenge to the ideology of pure domesticity. Nonetheless, most clubs functioned within quite constrained boundaries: they viewed Europe, especially England, as the dominant source of American traditions. Literary ventures to Asia or Latin America merely provided the pleasing sense of undertaking an exotic voyage or of journeying alongside colonizing figures like "the gallant Gordon."

Yet regarding women's issues, even relatively conservative reading clubs were apt to criticize the status quo. Blair cites groups giving papers on such topics as "Margaret Fuller," "New York State Laws Affecting Women," and "Women's Suffrage," and quotes a paper titled "Women in History," by Syracuse clubwoman Sarah Sumner Teall, which argued for reconceptualizing the meaning of history to include "woman's work, sufferings, [and] achievements."[35]

The reading clubs' literary studies, like their history studies, seem in retrospect both constraining and enabling. As might be expected, clubs' programs rarely included popular culture or avant-garde literature. The curriculum centered on the classics of English imaginative literature. Browning, the Brontes, Dickens, and George Eliot were among the most popular authors, but all were overshadowed by the immortal presence of the Bard. Seaholm calculates that Shakespeare was the topic of more than half of the programs of Texas reading groups in 1902–3.[36] Numbers alone cannot convey the awe his work inspired. Regarding their reading of Shakespeare in 1888, the Houston Ladies Reading Club chronicled: "We knelt humbly, hesitatingly, with most womanly reluctance, before the shrine of the inimitable, the incomparable, the greatest, the mightiest of all, William Shakespeare, poet by the grace of God. The depth of the mine opened was so great, the jewels so inexhaustible, so rare . . . that our ladies bring their tribute just a trifle timidly."[37]

If, however, this audience revered Shakespeare as an immortal and godlike figure, they were not merely succumbing to the orgasmic bliss of cultural consumption but were truly experiencing his genius for themselves. Reading and discussing Shakespeare changed them from passionate devotees into elite initiates. The quasi-religious significance of Shakespeare and lesser literary immortals conferred a generalized cultural authority on club members. Sacred texts could become, to varying degrees, the foundation on which to consider the crucial ethical dilemmas, to debate the nature of human nature, and to define identity.

Reading clubs frequently used Shakespeare to explore women's identities and social roles. According to Seaholm, almost every Texas club that studied Shakespeare discussed "Women in Shakespeare," or more specific topics such as "Shakespeare's Mothers," or "Women's Friendships in Shakespeare." *The Taming of the Shrew* inspired debates on "Was Katherine a Womanly Woman?" and "Katherine's Obedience." The Standard Club of Colorado City, Texas, claimed that "Shakespeare's women were for the most part, true, noble, and womanly." Nonetheless, Seaholm finds more discussions about Lady Macbeth than any other female character in Shakespeare. While such discussions usually condemned her, they demonstrated a fascination with the complexities of female power. It seems, then, that although Texas club women interpreted Shakespeare's female characters as "true women" and thus role models for their own lives, their processes of identification were quite complex.[38]

Like Lady Macbeth, Ibsen's heroines fascinated Texas clubwomen, who used them to discuss "wifehood," "Woman's Duty to Herself," and "the Woman Question." Although their reflections on Ibsen frequently reinforced relatively conservative views, readers were clearly interested in debating "the rights and responsibilities of woman and the meaning of modern womanhood." As Seaholm says, this was "education for identity." The clubwomen's desire to learn was driven partly by a hunger to elucidate woman's nature and potential place in the larger world.[39]

Literature not only gave women cultural authority and a projective screen on which to discern their identity but also inspired them to embrace a broad mission of social betterment that transcended their own self-development. If literature represented the highest accomplishments and the noblest ideals of the human spirit, then it demanded similarly noble efforts from the elect among its followers. For clubwomen, this was a direct and obvious connection. "The Club women who used to study Shakespeare have been looking around them upon life's Stage," said Mrs. A. O. Granger of Georgia.[40] Kate Cassatt MacKnight extended this line of thought:

> The literary and self-culture club is, as a rule, the beginning and support of all those important elements which . . . develop the interests of women in the forward movement of humanity. For after spending months studying the idealism of Tennyson, or the scathing arraignment of all that is sordid, found in Browning . . . one naturally begins to open one's eyes, to look about, and to inquire if we have any right to continue to live amid hideous surroundings; or to permit children of our "land of the free" to be

destroyed by drudgery, or vicious environment; or to stand idly by while the grandest . . . scenery in our country is destroyed by the blind greed of grasping commercialism.[41]

Sisterhood and the Transformation of Identity

Literary clubs enabled women to gain organizational skills; the ability to participate in serious, orderly, and rational discussion; the self-confidence of cultural authority; and the knowledge—both factual and ethical—to form opinions about the wider world and their own place and interests within it. It is equally clear that these groups gave their members a deeply felt sense of solidarity. The development of this solidarity and concomitant program of social reform cannot be explained solely by either affective sisterhood or rational analysis. The community of women in reading groups was bound together and empowered by both "love and ritual" and the force of textual analysis.[42] Simultaneously, they were able to revalue not only themselves as individual actors but also what womanhood might mean collectively. In turn, this allowed them to formulate a critical appraisal of the status quo. Their visionary program sought to reform it both in the interests of the literature, arts, and education they held so dear and in broader but still "womanly" arenas. For many of these readers, then, literary clubs were sites for developing not only literary skills but also strong and nurturing ties with other women that fostered a genuine feeling of sisterhood and an exhilarating sense of the powers and possibilities of womankind.

Meetings became a cherished event that brought women out of the narrow round of their domestic concerns. The extent of their devotion to these meetings is suggested by what happened when the Dallas Pierian Club's regularly scheduled meeting fell on Christmas Eve: "December 24, 1903, found the Pierians studying Japan and the Yoritamas feudal system."[43] Rituals and traditions were a central part of club life. Yearbooks feature club colors, flowers, and mottoes; literary programs and club minutes express the joy of beginning each club year in passionate perorations that celebrate their beloved clubs and their strong feelings for fellow members. Almost every club held at least one special meeting during the club year to celebrate not literature, but the fellowship of the reading club itself. Often these were anniversary celebrations, a yearly Gentlemen's Night, or—as for the Ladies Reading Club of Houston—an annual "pic-nic" held at the end of the club year.

Similarly, although many clubs forbade extensive refreshments, and some banned them altogether, clubwomen often mentioned that conversations "over the teacups" developed members' self-confidence. Stella Christian, historian of the Texas women's club movement, defended the generous hospitality that marked the first meetings of the state federation of literary clubs, "because, upon these occasions, clubwomen met face to face, with the leisure to go deeper into their problems, receiving practical aid and counsel from each other. Thus the teas, receptions, and luncheons became both sowing-time and reaping-time to these clubwomen."[44] Traditionally loath to speak in public, many women came to find and value their own voices in the welcoming environment of reading clubs.

Association also brought these women, often for the first time, out of the restricted circles of kin, neighbors, and those who shared political and religious sympathies and into egalitarian forms of contact with other women rather different from themselves. One clubwoman called her reading group "a democracy of brains," because status had so little meaning in their discussions, and many others claimed that participation in book clubs increased their sense of fellow feeling with and for other kinds of women.[45] For example, the Dubuque (Iowa) Ladies' Literary Association experienced "constantly growing fellowship [and] the disappearance of the class spirit."[46] Their aspirations for sisterhood were sincere; they achieved real "mixing" of local cliques, of society women and career women, of women from different denominations (even across the Protestant-Catholic or Jewish-Christian divide), and of single and married women.

From a historian's point of view, however, the groups are more notable for their homogeneity than their diversity. Almost all book clubs drew members from the "middling classes." Clubs were limited by racial as well as class boundaries. African American women of extraordinary achievement sometimes belonged to a white club, but African American clubs were often prohibited from joining state and national federations. African American women's book clubs thus led a separate existence and organized nationally in 1896 as part of the National Association of Colored Women.[47]

Reading club members were likely to be mature women; many joined only after their children were grown. Relative homogeneity of age, race, and class were common within individual clubs, unless they developed into the large "department clubs" that might boast upward of 200 members. Most reading clubs, however, stayed small enough to meet in each other's homes. Club members sometimes shared some common background: education, religion, neighborhood, or their husbands' occupations. Consequently, a social hierarchy of clubs prevailed in larger communities. Although this kind of homogeneity may have made it easier for women to speak in their book clubs, it also may have limited the ideology that emerged from them. Nonetheless, clubs did allow many women their first exposure to other women who differed from them to some degree.

The "semipublic" nature of book clubs provided an escape from what one clubwoman called a "tedious selfhood," a consciousness limited to purely "self-inclusive" thinking about subjects such as dress, family, neighbors, or the fads of the day.[48] Association and discussion could "dispel prejudices and broaden ... insight," thereby promoting tolerance, objectivity, and cooperation.[49] Accounts of club life consistently celebrate the new cooperation among women, and with it their newly heightened sense of the abilities and value of their sex that came from work in reading clubs. For example, state officers of literary clubs in Texas consciously used the power of their offices to nurture less established clubs or to spread the club idea into more remote communities. Also, as Christian reported, "Many ladies of strong clubs waived nominations that would doubtless have given them election, in order that the offices might be scattered geographically speaking, or given to weaker clubs that they felt needed the educative results of responsibility."[50]

"Harmony" is frequently mentioned in these accounts, encapsulating several qualities nurtured by club life: cooperation, loyalty, support for other women, and the pursuit of worthy goals without pettiness or self-seeking. "Harmony" also signified a union of head and heart, highlighting the emotional qualities of empathy, altruism, and the "sisterly pride and affection" of this new collective identity. According to one Texas clubwoman, "Long ago it was held up to women that they had little of the feeling of comradeship which is common among men . . . and that they could never accomplish anything of magnitude as a class, because they could not work together peaceably and effectively. Nearly all women will admit that this was true. The result was a lack of harmony until this club idea began to take root, and what a glorious boon it has been to women, as the use and beauty of organized work came to be known."[51]

A Tale with Two Endings

Reading Authorizes Reform: An Ambiguous Legacy

As literary clubs spread quickly across the country and formed broader federations, women realized their capacity for organized action. Further horizons of organization and collective ambitions became apparent. The "woman movement"—a loose conglomeration of groups (including suffragists and advocates of temperance) that, despite their differences, collectively agreed that women had something special to offer society—was gathering strength. Its representatives wrote prolifically in the national media and crisscrossed America on the lecture circuit.

Some local literary groups organized partly in response to these national currents; once organized, they were open to further such influence. For example, a local group might subscribe to a national reading service and then, like at least three Texas groups, send representatives to Boston for national meetings of the Anna Tichnor "Society to Encourage Studies at Home," bringing them into close communication with women from all over the country. Similarly, local groups became natural contacts for speakers on the national lecture circuit who sought audiences. In just such a fashion, Mrs. Adele Looscan and the Houston Ladies Reading Club hosted a meeting with two famous suffragists, Victoria Woodhull and Tennessee Claflin.

Such events brought local women into touch with ideas and personalities that encouraged their efforts to federate at the state and national level, and this broader organizational scope seemed to call for a larger collective purpose. As one chronicler put it: "Literary culture was the *raison d'être* of the . . . club, but it was felt that such an organization of women as the State Federation must stand for some united effort for social advancement in Texas."[52] The General Federation of Women's Clubs—which began both nationally and in Texas as an association of literary and culture clubs—became an important agent of Progressive Era reform, supporting and reflecting women's particular concerns.[53] They sought to supply the altruism and aesthetic women naturally possessed in order to shelter the entire social family, and especially its weaker members, from the effects of the competitive marketplace.

Clubs' early work centered on education and culture: they established almost 75 percent of the public libraries in the nation and more than 85 percent of those in Texas, began kindergartens, pushed for vocational education and other curricular reforms, supported higher education for women, and campaigned for universal compulsory education.[54] In Texas, clubwomen led efforts to establish a women's dormitory at the University of Texas at Austin, funded local and statewide scholarships for women, and were, in cooperation with the Women's Christian Temperance Union, instrumental in founding what is today Texas Women's University. Responding to the difficulty they themselves experienced obtaining books, they also sponsored fifty-three traveling libraries.[55] Expanding the definition of "education," many clubs addressed the provision of parks and playgrounds, the regulation of child labor, and the development of a juvenile justice system.[56]

Clubwomen felt that there was a direct connection between the hours they spent studying literary classics, the parliamentary seriousness of their meetings, and their ability to become effective (if nonvoting) citizens. Just as they did not question the elevated status of high culture, they rarely scrutinized either capitalism or their own privileged social position. Their reform initiatives softened the harsh effects of an inequitable social order without attempting to dismantle either the existing social hierarchy or its underlying causes. This is especially clear with regard to race and class. As noted earlier, African American women's clubs were prohibited from joining the General Federation of Women's Clubs. Clubs often supported legislation that had racist effects, such as the poll tax in Texas. Curricular reforms such as vocational education were intended to better the lives of the less privileged without granting them the same opportunities as middle-class youth.

Even regarding gender, clubwomen proved relatively conservative. Although many clubs had suffragist members and discussed women's issues, most clubs refused to let suffrage become an explicit part of their mission, and the General Federation did not endorse the vote for women until 1915.

Furthermore, club work legitimated the vocation of the "professional volunteer"—a way of life limited to the educated and affluent. The borders between social betterment and social control are often difficult to discern in Progressive initiatives, whether battles against municipal corruption, or the parks and playground movement. "Science" and "expertise," the supposedly disinterested watchwords of Progressivism, legitimated the status claims of a rising professional elite. Clubwomen were no less interested parties.

If womanhood gave these women strength and purpose, it also limited their endeavors. Their unique separateness grounded their social reform initiatives and enabled them to accomplish a great deal. It also ensured that they would not fundamentally challenge either the marketplace or the state; the dominant ideological frames that limited their ability to question either the cultural or the social hierarchy blunted their radical potential to refashion womanhood.

Women's Literary Associations: Twenty-First Century Reflections

By 1940 women's book clubs were very different from earlier clubs. Most were much more informally organized, and though a small fraction had links to formal or cultural politics, most book club members read and discussed books mainly for personal fulfillment. Participants focused more on interior exploration than social action.

There are several ways to understand this shift. First, the nineteenth-century reading groups—and the more politically oriented movement they generated—were a success, at least on their own terms. They facilitated women's entrance into higher education and agitated for a series of important reforms that established libraries, transformed schools, humanized the urban environment, and improved the legal and labor environment for children and women. All of these attainments changed what women needed from reading groups. The ideology of altruistic womanhood began to dissolve once women entered the public sphere. Furthermore, college education for middle-class women was commonplace by 1940.

In the second half of the twentieth century, the feminist movement and other challenges to the canonical tradition weakened the connection between literature and social reform that was so intrinsic to the nineteenth-century women's reading group experience. That connection was fostered by an earlier institutional and ideological constellation among writers and critics such as Matthew Arnold, Ralph Emerson, and Edward Bellamy, and it resonated among reading group members, who were looking for outlets for their own mobilized collective energy. Thus, by century's end, engagement with literature, which once signified in and of itself one path to an awakened social conscience, had, like education for women, lost some of its radicalizing power.

Reading cultures tend to be collectively harnessed to social activism only under certain conditions. Cultural meanings "frame" both literature and reading. Nonetheless, even today many reading clubs are communities that provide their members support, equality, and sharing and broaden their critical perspectives on themselves and their world. Thus, such groups are far more important both socially and for individuals than their contemporary status as "leisure time" activities might imply.

It is difficult to determine how reading clubs might impact constituencies currently outside the literary mainstream. Reading groups are voluntary associations, but understanding how and why reading group members read as they do may offer some insights for educators. The recent and rapid emergence of African American women's book clubs—clubs that often focus on books by African American writers—shows how a broader canon and a more ethnically diverse publishing effort can empower an important constituency.

CHAPTER 25

Reading and Race Pride
The Literary Activism of Black Clubwomen

Elizabeth McHenry

. . .

In a 1925 issue of *Publishers' Weekly*, Mary White Ovington reported the activities of a woman named Kathryn Johnson, who began her life as an "itinerant bookseller" after returning from a post abroad with the Young Men's Christian Association during World War I. Selling books out of the back seat of a little Ford coupe, Johnson had covered ten states and some 25,000 miles in two and a half years. She had sold more than 5,000 volumes of books, 100 volumes at a time, all she could fit in the back seat of the car. While door-to-door booksellers were not uncommon in the 1920s, Ovington's amazement is clear regarding this particular bookseller, whose sales pitch she described as "quite unlike any book agent's that I had ever heard." This story was newsworthy because Johnson was a black woman and she traveled the back roads of the north- and southeastern United States selling books by and about African Americans to an exclusively African American clientele. Although she sold books individually, she called her offerings a "Two Foot Book Shelf." "Two feet of books," her sales pitch proclaimed, "that you and all the colored people ought to read." Included in that collection were books by W. E. B. Du Bois, Carter Woodson, Benjamin Brawley, James Weldon Johnson, Paul Lawrence Dunbar, and Silas X. Floyd. "[M]y buyers don't want fiction," she told Ovington. "They look at such a book, say 'it's only a story,' and put it down. They want to spend their earnings for reality."

Ovington accompanied Johnson on one of her sales trips, during which a minister allowed Johnson ten minutes to address his congregation at the end of a Sunday service. She "prayed that [Johnson] might not be disappointed if she only sold a book or two." In fact, Johnson was "at once surrounded by people," taking orders for seventy books that day. "Was this [an] exceptional [day]?" Ovington asked, voicing her disbelief. "No," replied Johnson. "It was very good but not exceptional." When told by Ovington that she could "make her fortune as a regular book agent," Johnson underscored the distinction between her own efforts and the mere practice of peddling books. "I'm not first of all selling books," she said. "I am first of all creating a desire for reading." Recounting the story of a "clever book agent" who sold books to people who then kept them not to read but "for show," Johnson continued, "I want to sell books, I earn my living that way, but I want to sell to persons who will read them." By selling books that would be removed from the shelf, opened, and read, Johnson knew she was also selling something far greater in value: she was selling race pride. "I believed the way to change [the self-perception of Negroes in the United States] was to get the colored people reading. I knew the books that would help the Negro to understand his honorable place in America.... I knew the man or woman must handle the book, see what was in it, before he would put money down for it. So I bought my Ford and became an itinerant bookseller.... The Negro has got to get away from the past and he must do it as quickly as he can. A two foot book shelf is the best way I know of helping him."[1]

Johnson's "two foot book shelf" was similar in some ways to the "five-foot shelf of books" marketed by P. F. Collier & Son beginning in 1909, described by Ellen Garvey in chapter 10 and illustrated in figure 10.5. Also known as the Harvard Classics, that collection had been selected and promoted by Charles W. Eliot, president of Harvard University from 1870 to 1909, who had long supported the idea that every American should engage in self-guided reading for self-improvement. Although Johnson's project bore a striking resemblance to Collier's, she did not imply that owning her selections would lead to the acquisition of an educated self or to success and financial gain. Rather, the value of her books was in their ability to communicate race consciousness. In the development of such consciousness, she believed, lay the hope of group advancement.

Beyond the "Oral" Tradition

Historically, much has been written about the *absence* of literacy skills among African Americans. Although their verbal performance arts, from folktales and proverbs to testifying and rapping, have understandably received wide recognition, the identification of African American culture as "oral in nature" has overshadowed other language uses — especially those related to reading and writing. Recent celebrations of the black oral tradition and black vernacular have unwittingly undermined historical evidence that points to a long history of African Americans' literary interaction, not only as creators and readers of their own literature but as readers of the "canon" of European and European American authors as well. When told at all, stories of nineteenth-century black literacy are presented as rare cases, in which literacy often implies only the basic ability to read and write. As Ovington's article on Kathryn Johnson underscores, even in the heyday of the literary and artistic movement known as the Harlem Renaissance, the idea of a black bookseller with a black clientele was met with disbelief. Black readers have remained largely invisible even in our own time, as suggested by a 1992 *New York Times Magazine* headline proclaiming that "Publishers agreed that black people don't read."[2]

Students of African American literature, history, and culture have come to know, as Toni Morrison wrote, that "invisible things are not necessarily 'not there' . . . certain absences are so stressed, so ornate, so planned, they call attention to themselves."[3] Such is the case with the historical invisibility of black readers. The recent "recovery" and reprinting of various texts has made available the late nineteenth- and early twentieth-century literary creations of African American writers. Less is known, however, of the processes of intellectual exchange within African American communities, processes through which an African American readership was deliberately coordinated and maintained. While the reading of many European Americans is elaborately documented, sources that reflect the reading practices and literary habits of African Americans throughout the nineteenth and into the twentieth century are relatively few and scattered. Yet these readers existed, and their trails are important to establish.

The story of Kathryn Johnson and her two-foot bookshelf provides a useful vantage point from which to consider the meaning African Americans attached to books, reading, and literary practices in this period. Johnson's distinction between selling books and "creating a desire for reading" signals her understanding of the ideological significance of books for African Americans. She had no desire to sell books that would sit unused, valued primarily as cultural emblems for their ability to ornament the home and, by extension, augment the reputation of their owners. Rather, Johnson referred to her books as "seeds." They had practical value for individual advancement and group transformation. Books were not static objects but rather vehicles of self-fashioning and growth, a means of revisiting the past to introduce black people to new ways of thinking about themselves and their history. Johnson's two-foot bookshelf linked self-respect and advancement with reading works by African American authors about the race's progress from the degradation of slavery, countering the images perpetuated by racist stereotypes. Insofar as such reading might inspire race consciousness and instill pride, it carried with it the power to enlighten and elevate African Americans.

Black Women's Reading Clubs

Although we have little biographical information on Kathryn Johnson, this essay reaches back into the late nineteenth century to reveal a likely foundation for her equation of the intellectual advancement of black people as a group and the expansion of a black reading public. In the last decade of the nineteenth century, middle-class black women formed single-sex organizations in unprecedented numbers. Although few black women's clubs were exclusively literary, reading and association with printed texts took on great significance through what Evelyn Brooks Higginbotham has called the "politics of respectability."[4] Reading and publishing allowed black women to contest racist discourses and white America's representations of them as immoral and unworthy of respect. Through literary activities black women learned to assert agency by representing themselves as Americans as well as blacks and women. Their emphasis on the written word resulted in the increased production and circulation of printed texts in the form of newspapers, magazines, pamphlets, and bound books. Middle-class black women played a decisive role in linking these texts—especially those by and about African Americans—to the achievement of racial dignity and self-determination. A primary outgrowth of the black women's club movement was the belief that reading and discussing literary material would "[open] the door for the entry of a nobler and better way of thinking about ourselves."[5]

Black clubwomen communicated this understanding of reading to the larger black community with unique effectiveness, reaching even to some extent, the poor, working-class blacks, who made up the masses (figure 25.1). An emergent class of college-educated women provided leadership for the black women's club movement, and most members were middle-class. Through club work, they tried to disseminate their values and reading practices throughout black communities nationwide. Inherent in this effort was their condemnation of what they perceived to be inferior practices and attitudes among African Americans whose class and experience differed from their own. Nevertheless, despite their emphasis on reinforcing the manners and morals of the dominant society, black clubwomen were united by their determination to protest social injustice and to communicate a race consciousness that transcended distinctions of class to unite black men and women in their struggle for racial dignity.

Although African American women were denied the most visible forms of political agency well into the twentieth century, their impact on black communities nationwide was tremendous. As Cornel West has noted, the black women's club movement was one of the "most effective political forms of organizing and mobilizing black people" at the turn of the century.[6] Through their own literary activities and through the campaigns they initiated to disseminate their literacy and literature in black communities, clubwomen asserted their belief that reading was essential to the development of a racial dignity. Some clubwomen engaged with print culture as novelists, essayists, journalists, and public speakers; for many others, literary work was a gateway to teaching, a profession that, by the turn of the century, had assumed a feminine identity and proved to

FIGURE 25.1. Reading rooms of organizations such as the YMCA provided access to books, magazines, and other printed material for African Americans at the beginning of the twentieth century. YMCA Reading Room and Office, La Boca, Florida, circa 1900. Photographs and Prints Division, Schomburg Center for Research in Black Culture, The New York Public Library, Astor, Lenox, and Tilden Foundations.

be the most viable professional option for educated black women. Still others worked informally and for the most part, anonymously, to sustain the diverse community-based activities organized by their local clubs. As educators all, these women challenged the dearth of public schools and educational opportunities available to African Americans, especially African American adults.[7] Despite the class tensions inherent in the motto of the black women's club movement, "Lifting as We Climb," their leadership represents a significant historical force in the struggle for the rights of blacks and women. It also demonstrates the trust they placed in the power of print and their belief that reading could redefine identity, both their own and that of the larger black community as well.

The Woman's Era

Black women like Kathryn Johnson taught the importance of reading and printed texts through the first decades of the twentieth century. In the 1890s, during the height of the women's club movement, this lesson was one still to be learned. In this chapter, I look to recover the transmission of this lesson within the community of black clubwomen at the end of the nineteenth century. No organization better illustrates the urgency assigned to this project than the Woman's Era, a black women's club formed in Boston, Massachusetts, in 1893.[8] The club's commitment to reading and to the dissemination of print is apparent in the literary meetings that were an integral component of regular club activities. Within a year, the women decided to create a newspaper produced by and for African American women, underscoring the authority they conferred on the medium of print.[9] That paper, the *Woman's Era*, was not an economic venture; rather, it was a means by which to communicate their understanding of the link between reading and empowerment. This was illustrated in two ways. First, articles and literary columns explicitly outlined the importance of reading and implicitly offered directives on what and how to read; second, the newspaper functioned as "race literature," reflecting the accomplishments of its authors, inspiring pride in its readers and stimulating them to better themselves.

Here I wish to examine the content of the club's nationally distributed newspaper to explore the complex and often elusive reading habits and textual negotiations of black clubwomen as they came to equate individual and group advancement with the circulation of printed texts and the expansion of a black reading public. Through its published reports and its role as a vehicle for communication between clubs, the *Woman's Era* provides a remarkable example of the textual commitment of the black women's club movement. It reveals both the product and process of black women's developing understanding and use of reading and printed texts for collective self-representation at the turn of the century, and it is a point of departure from which to piece together other sources that reflect clubwomen's uses of print at that time.[10]

Prior to the organization of the Woman's Era, the "idea of a Woman's Club, not necessarily a colored woman's club, but a club started and led by colored women had been dormant in the minds of a few women of Boston." Florida Ridley, the daughter of the club's founder, Josephine St. Pierre Ruffin, noted that there seemed to be "no end" to the number of clubs in the last decade of the nineteenth century devoted to working for women's advancement. Yet, she felt, the particular concerns of African American women called for a unique "organization of colored women" able to speak to the many questions about racial matters that demanded "special treatment." Moreover, unlike other organizations, a black women's club would be able to attract those "numbers of women [who] would be over-looked unless some special appeal was made to them." That special appeal was made in February 1893, at the same time that Ida B. Wells was "[c]reating so much interest in her crusade against lynch-law."

FIGURE 25.2. Five women around a table with books, circa 1900. Photographs and Prints Division, Schomburg Center for Research in Black Culture, The New York Public Library, Astor, Lenox, and Tilden Foundations.

The initial membership of twenty soon grew to forty. The Woman's Era club was organized, as Ridley insisted, "not for race-work alone, but for work along the lines that make for women's progress."[11] Ridley was careful to position the Woman's Era both inside and outside the white women's club movement that was sweeping the country. The political, economic, and educational environment of the turn-of-the-century United States inspired middle- and upper-class women, both black and white, to form clubs based on their own activities and interests. While Ridley suggests that the founders of the Woman's Era had some desire to affiliate with their white sisters in recognition of the common goals of all women, she also implies that race-related needs and concerns distinguished black women from their white counterparts (see figure 25.2).

Visual artifacts serve as vivid reminders of the countless ways this was true. As Henry Louis Gates Jr. has noted, at the turn of the century "it would have been possible for a middle-class white American to see Sambo images from toaster and teapot covers on his breakfast table, to popular postcards in drug stores."[12] These stereotypical images reinforced white America's conception of African Americans as lazy, ugly, and, most fundamentally, intellectually inferior to whites. Public perception and media claims about black women were further complicated by their sexual victimization under slavery. The sexual persecution of black women by white men in the South remained rampant at the end of the nineteenth century, compelling thousands of black women to leave the South or urge their daughters to relocate in the North.[13] Myths of the black female's "innate" promiscuity, however, carried great weight in the North as well as in the South. The dominant white view of black women as morally vacuous left them, as Fannie Barrier Williams notes, "in the unfortunate position of being defenders of our name." Black women used their clubs to take on this task visibly and collectively. Ironically, as Williams noted, middle-class black women typically met more resentment than those who remained in "their place." She posed this rhetorical question to her mostly white audience: "Are we not justified in a feeling of desperation against that peculiar form of Americanism that shows respect for our women as servants and contempt for them when they become women of culture?"[14]

A retrospective report on the Woman's Era club written in 1899 states that the club "was not primarily started for Charity, nor yet for self-culture alone, and yet . . . our methods lead directly to these ends." Attempting to clarify the paradoxical unity of these dual goals, the report offered the following explanation: "The work for humanity in [the] way of interesting oneself in public affairs leads to self culture and an active interest in the laws of education, labor and morality [and] is the highest form of Charity." Meeting twice each month, the Woman's Era managed its general "business" at the first meeting; the second meeting could then be reserved as a "literary and public meeting."[15]

Publishing A New Voice

The Woman's Era sponsored a sewing circle and raised funds both for specific causes, like the establishment of a hospital for colored women, and for the more general and emergency needs of its membership. No activity was more important, however, than the production and publication of its club newspaper, the *Woman's Era*. Begun in 1894 as "the organ of the Woman's Era Club, and devoted to the interests of the Women's Clubs, Leagues, and Societies throughout the country,"[16] the newspaper was edited and published monthly by the mother-daughter team of Josephine St. Pierre Ruffin and Florida R. Ridley (who, readers are told in the December 1894 issue, "do their work gratuitously").[17] From its inception, the *Woman's Era* was run exclusively by African American women and filled with news of their organizations throughout the country. The editors targeted "women of the refined and educated classes," and boasted of a "large circulation in many of the large cities, notably Boston, New Bedford, Providence, New York, Chicago, Washington, and Kansas City."[18] This national circulation did more than keep the publication afloat financially by increasing the number of subscriptions; it allowed geographically dispersed readers to imagine themselves as part of a larger community.

The newspaper functioned as a forum that brought black women together, especially around the importance of literary activity as a means of self-improvement and affirmation. It is here that middle-class black women left the most complete record of their literary practices: reading was cast as one of the "opportunit[ies] for self-advancement" of which all black women should take advantage, and the *Woman's Era* fashioned itself as a primary source of both literary discussion and the printed texts that would allow readers to congregate and learn from each other. "We read daily of the progress women are making for the elevation of their sex and we are proud to note noble examples among us, who follow in their train, laboring earnestly, yet modestly for their sex and the upbuilding of the race," wrote S. Elizabeth Frazier in her introduction to one such text, a profile on the achievements of Victoria Earle Matthews that appeared in the *Woman's Era* in May 1894. She concluded by connecting the importance of reading to the particular need of African American women to display and lend authority to their past. This link between concrete presentation through print and the building of tradition would allow future generations to understand the central contribution of black women to the building of the nation: "Surely we cannot know too much of their genius and merits, for the inspiration of our girls."

For the clubwomen who produced the *Woman's Era*, reading and association with print were more than inspirational: they were transforming. Women were advised to take "[g]reat care . . . in cultivating the habit of reading, for without reading it is impossible to ever be [a] 'full man.'"[19] To the middle-class black women who aspired to Victorian standards of womanhood, this counsel signaled tremendous possibility. If, through reading, she could become a "full man," she would be authorized to reimagine herself in a variety of unfamiliar ways. Standards of Victorian womanhood located the power of ideal femininity in the domestic sphere and the nurturing, sensitivity, and empathy cultivated there. Reading and other literary work, however, allowed black women to hone skills conventionally associated with the masculine domain; these included critical argument, disciplined reason, and, ultimately, public expression. Clubwomen did not entirely cast aside the conventionally feminine for the conventionally masculine; on the contrary, allegiance to domestic rhetoric continued to cloak even their assertions of "full manhood." Rather, women were encouraged to develop and merge a powerful intellect with the conventional attributes of femininity, thus claiming the world of private and public, "feminine" and "masculine" politics as their domain. The resulting tension shattered the genteel silence that surrounded "proper" femininity and motivated and empowered black women to appropriate the necessary authority to carry out their own projects and purposes.

Challenges and Solutions

Despite the advantages of being supported by an organization, the anxieties associated with assuming a public voice and the posture of authority that accompanied it were not easily dismissed. Club reports occasionally revealed the difficulty of literary study for black women whose previous intellectual opportunities had been limited. In 1896 the Denver Branch of the National Colored Woman's League described itself as "crippled by the withdrawal of women of capabilities": one reason given for resigning from membership was "I am afraid that I may be called upon to write a paper and I do not want to be laughed at."[20] Another "mainly literary" club reporting in the same year revealed the initial insecurity of black women engaged in literary work: "some of our members are becoming quite brave and do not tremble any longer when it is their turn to face the audience."[21]

Although African American women were often encouraged to read "the masters" of English literature in order to "learn to appreciate the good and the beautiful," the connection between literary work and the development of critical thinking skills and the ability to articulate one's views was central to the development of black women's literary culture.[22] According to these women, "The chief benefit derived from the study [of literature] was . . . being able to form and hold one's own opinion."[23] "In order that the women may become educated in thought," reads one letter to the *Woman's Era*, "an original paper is presented and read by some member each week. A discussion follows."[24] Perhaps to discourage prospective members from mistaking their reading for a leisurely pastime, the *Woman's Era* increasingly referred to literary society meetings as "classes," even if informally organized and conducted by the members themselves.

The impulse to emphasize the academic nature of such meetings and to deny their possible social functions was especially characteristic of black women's literary societies during this time. While men's literary societies became more socially oriented between 1870 and 1910, women's clubs took measures to maintain and increase their focus on literature and, through it, the political and social justice issues of the time. Clubs maintained the intellectual coherence of their literary meetings in a variety of ways. "One distinct feature of these evenings," wrote Sara Iredell Fleetwood of her involvement in the Washington, D.C., Mignonette Club, "is the well-understood fact that no refreshments will be furnished, a decision that does much to ensure the permanency of these entertainments."²⁵ Missing a meeting was met with disapproval. The May 1895 issue of the journal reports that, at the Woman's Era's own literary meeting, two "thoughtful" papers were "prepared and eloquently presented"; both addressed the topic, "Our Opportunities." "Owing to small attendance," the announcement reprimanded, "it is proposed to have the papers read again, that a larger number may be heard in the discussion of this important subject."²⁶

A Network of Support

The benefit of literary study was rooted in the intellectual relationships and the atmosphere of sympathetic female peers found in collaborative literary groups. Members of the Woman's League of Denver, Colorado, wrote that "nothing so stimulates and creates enthusiasm as . . . contact and friction with other minds. To learn to work harmoniously is education of a higher order."²⁷ Black women relied on the combination of intellectual challenge and emotional sustenance for their developing talents. In the company of other black women, members found support for their thoughts and their ambitions; like-minded peers met their enthusiasm with enthusiasm. "The especial aim of this club," reads a notice in the *Woman's Era*, "is to promote and foster a spirit of unity and helpfulness in every needed direction among its members, to discover and uncover hidden capabilities." Through literary activities, the club aimed "to foster . . . ambition" and to bring "to the light talent among our women which had only to be discovered to reflect credit on any people."²⁸

A systematic analysis of the reports of other black women's clubs printed in the *Woman's Era* attests to the extent to which black women were reading together and otherwise engaged with print culture throughout the nation. One 1895 issue noted dozens of clubs in Denver alone, and highlighted the work of black women's literary societies in various other states, including Ohio's Dickens Club and Georgia's Phillis Wheatley Club.²⁹ Given the importance of literary exchange among these groups, the *Woman's Era* reserved space in each issue to share information about the literary endeavors of other societies. "The Greenwood Literary and Philosophical Club . . . has the History of German Literature under discussion for the year," offered one society by way of news; another reminded readers that the "Author's Interstate Literary Association of Missouri, Kansas and Iowa" would convene soon. Other announcements provided recommendations from avid readers. "Lovers of higher literary criticism should not fail to read Frederic Harrison's articles in the *Forum*," for discussions of "Carlyle, Macaulay, Thackeray and other writers," read one such announcement in the December 1894 issue.³⁰

This intellectual network connected middle-class black women throughout

FIGURE 25.3. Young woman reading, Athens, Georgia, 1880s. Photographs and Prints Division, Schomburg Center for Research in Black Culture, The New York Public Library, Astor, Lenox, and Tilden Foundations.

the country; the development of such a culture of readers was in fact the chief goal of the *Woman's Era* (see figure 25.3). In her inaugural editorial, Josephine Ruffin underscored the importance of eliminating the isolation of like-minded black women who, because of their race and their class affiliations as well as their aspirations, live in very "circumscribed sphere[s]" and confront "the impossibility of mingling freely with people of culture and learning."[31] Although denied access to many intellectual and cultural venues, clubwomen were able to "mingle" with one another, not only at meetings of their own local clubs or through the pages of the *Woman's Era* but also through their common reading.

To this end, the *Woman's Era* periodically reprinted in its pages the reading lists and study questions from the society's own meetings, making its local literary exchange available to subscribers nationwide.[32] Describing a class on the study of the novel, an announcement in the June 1896 issue read: "A few of the best novels were selected and studied carefully, the aim being not quantity but quality. Each member of the class was given a set of questions on the novel to be taken up, to which answers were to be formed according to one's opinion after careful reading. These questions and answers were afterwards discussed in the class." The column concluded with this promise: "The questions used in this class will be presented to the readers of the 'Era' from time to time as an incentive to pleasant and profitable study. No answers will be given, for many can simply be a matter of personal opinion." The first set of questions, on Scott's *Ivanhoe*, range from the general to the specific: "In an historical novel what should the novelist reject and what reproduce? What is the artistic effect of the introduction and notes? Compare Isaac of York and Shylock as delineations of Jewish character. How can we excuse ourselves for sympathizing with Locksley and his followers?"[33] The range of these questions suggests that readers of the *Woman's Era* were encouraged to consider texts not only in terms of setting, plot, and character; they were also prompted to compare characters from different texts and to analyze structural features and framing devices of a text as well as its place in broader literary traditions and the ethical issues it raised.

"To Succeed as a Race"

The *Woman's Era*'s literary ringleader was Medora W. Gould. Her regular column "Literature Notes" was a collection of literary trivia and shared discoveries, including everything from brief book reviews and reading suggestions to information on well-known and amateur authors and updates on the sales of their publications. Many of her comments were intended to facilitate her readers' choice of texts, encouraging them to focus their reading in particular directions. In December 1894 she listed *American Authors* by Mildred Rutherford as "a convenient reference book on American Literature" for readers of all ages, highlighting its "numerous half-tone portraits" and "the test questions at the end of each chapter."[34] While her columns are often filled with information on an array of literary gossip and information on new publications of interest to the black community, she also encouraged her readers to read and reread "our old favorite authors"; "however old," Gould advised, these texts "never cease to be new." Classical texts were especially important for shaping and nourishing readers' "noble characters." By exposing black clubwomen to "new beauties and . . . new lessons of life," these texts provided them with role models against whom to gauge their own lives and opportunities to critique and correct their moral standing.[35]

To Gould, reading could reinforce traditional notions of a woman's "proper" place and comportment that were essential to the black women's club movement. They emphasized conformity to the dominant society's understanding of "feminine sensibility" and its norms of manners and morals. A woman is most successful, Gould felt, when she transcends this conservative perspective and, through literary study, rises above the barrage of accusations of immorality and inferiority, and faces the complicated task of defining herself and her potential. Gould reveled in stories of women whose reading provided critical perspectives on their own lives and the lives of other women.

At the dawn of the twentieth century, educated black Americans believed, as Sutton Griggs wrote, that "to succeed as a race we must move up out of the age of the voice."[36] This statement implicitly condemns illiteracy and devalues oral communication in favor of the authority implied by printed texts that could be widely distributed. The power, scope, and influence of the printed word would be undermined if the text itself did not endure and circulate. The proliferation of ephemeral texts such as the *Woman's Era* stands as evidence of black clubwomen's belief that public distribution of their thoughts and awareness of their activities was crucial to their coming of age. "Let us not be content with being served up as others choose," wrote Ruffin in her inaugural editorial of the *Woman's Era*. "We are about old enough to speak for ourselves."[37]

The Woman's Era and the National Association of Colored Women

The extent to which black women's dedication to spreading literacy and literary expression was linked to their political concerns and organized activism is evident in the centrality of printed texts and literary discussion to the Conference of Colored Women of America, which took place in Boston, Massachusetts, in July 1895. This conference, which later evolved into the National Association of Colored Women, was prompted by an especially fierce attack on the morality of black women earlier that year. J. W. Jacks, president of the Missouri Press Association, published a letter in which he dismissed all African American women as "prostitutes" and accused them of "having no sense of virtue and being altogether without character."[38] The attack, coupled with the exclusionary policies of white women's clubs, prompted Woman's Era club president Josephine Ruffin to issue a call for a national meeting of African American clubwomen.[39] Although she refused to grant Jacks's letter undue authority by reprinting it in her call to meeting, she instructed African American women to "[r]ead this document carefully . . . and decide if it be not time for us to stand before the world and declare ourselves and our principles."[40]

Signaling their intent to use print as a primary means of representing themselves and asserting their critical perspective, the members of the new association made "THE WOMAN'S ERA . . . the official organ of the new federation."[41] Because the conference leaders understood reading and literary production as fundamental to the project of increasing black women's self-representation, the promotion of women's reading and a discussion of "Race Literature" was central to the assembly. The back cover of the program listed the most recent publications by black clubwomen; inside, delegates discovered that copies of the publications themselves could be "found on the literature table in the Reception Room."[42] In all, ten titles were listed, including Anna Julia Cooper's *A Voice from the South*, Mrs. N. F. Mossell's *The Work of Afro-American Woman*, Mrs. A. A. Casneau's *Guide to Artistic Dress Cutting and Making*, and Miss Rachel Washington's *A Guide to the Study of Harmony*. Delegates were encouraged to read these publications and share them with others, and to subscribe to the *Woman's Era*, where they would always have access to important reading material. The program promised that the "August number of 'The Woman's Era'" would be something of a collector's item, containing "synopses of all speeches made at the Conference, and cuts of many of the speakers."[43]

Victoria Earle Matthews's address to the conference, "The Value of Race Literature," proclaimed the literary campaign that was a central tenet of the black women's club movement. She began by defining "race literature" as the work of any black author, regardless of its subject matter, thus stressing the breadth and depth of black people's literary lives. For them, "literature" included "History, Biography, Scientific Treatises, Sermons, Addresses, Novels, Poems, Books of Travel, miscellaneous essays and . . . contributions to magazines and newspapers." These would provide "thoughtful, well-defined and intelligently placed . . . counter-irritants" to racist and demeaning presentations of African Americans by "supplying . . . influential and accurate information, on all subjects relating to the Negro, and his environments." Race literature, Matthews believed, could "undermine and utterly drive out . . . the subordinate, the servant as a type representing a race whose numbers are now far into the millions."[44]

This address lauded the *Woman's Era* for signifying women's responsibility for the advancement of both race and gender issues in their literary efforts. "[W]ithin the compass of one small journal," Matthews said, "we have struck out a new line of departure—a journal, a record of race interests gathered from all parts of the United States, carefully selected, moistened, winnowed, and garnered by the ablest intellects of educated colored women, shrinking at no lofty theme, shirking no serious duty, aiming at every possible excellence, and determined to do their part in the future uplifting of the race." The potential impact of this and other literary efforts by black women was immeasurable. "If twenty women, by their concentrated efforts in one literary movement, can meet with such success as has engendered, planned out, and so successfully consummated this convention, what much more glorious results, what wider spread success, what grander diffusion of mental light will not come forth at the bidding of the enlarged hosts of women writers, already called into being by the stimulus of your efforts?"[45]

Matthews's address is a manifesto of the women's club movement, espousing the belief that association with literature could ameliorate black women's condition and change what one writer for the *Woman's Era* identified as "the American scheme of life." Though literary work primarily allowed middle-class black women to establish their respectability, it could also transform the very structure of race relations. They used literature to wage war on lynching, the convict lease system, and job discrimination and to demand increased educational opportunities, civil rights, and the right to vote for all African Americans.

Clubs in the Spectrum of Literacy

The overall objective of most black women's clubs at the turn of the century was "the diffusion of accurate and extensive information relative to the civil and social status of the colored American citizen, that they may be directed to an intelligent assertion of their rights."[46] Countless organizations shared similar methods, which included both the "full and free discussion of existing evils [in American society], moral, physical and political" and "the circulation of printed matter relating to the colored American, whether written by them or not."[47] The efforts of black clubwomen fostered literacy among African Americans and facilitated their access to books and other printed materials by creating libraries and reading rooms, thus mitigating the dominant society's denial of these resources to black communities.

As Higginbotham has noted, black clubwomen used their interest in literature to promote their religious beliefs, which were intimately connected to their concepts of virtue and respectability; but dedication to the church was just one of the middle-class values that they intended to spread through the dissemination of literary texts.[48] In 1895 Katie V. Carmand, the corresponding secretary of the Woman's Loyal Union of New York and Brooklyn announced the availability of pamphlets on diverse subjects. "We have already printed for distribution, at a small price within the reach of all, leaflets addressed to 'Parents and Guardians,' and will soon have another, 'The Sanctity of Home,' to be followed by others—all of which are written by members of our association. In this way we hope to reach the masses, and do more effectual good than spoken words to the few."[49]

Many of the masses whom clubwomen hoped to reach, however, could not read. According to U.S. census data, 44 percent of the black population was illiterate in 1900. Although literacy increased dramatically among African Americans in the first decades of the twentieth century, more than 16 percent of the black population remained illiterate in 1930. Even among those who were nominally literate, reading skills varied greatly.⁵⁰ Yet black clubwomen did not consider illiteracy a barrier to the beneficial effects of literary study. They joined forces with others who shared their desire to "create an interest in racial expression through books."⁵¹ Such a partnership was formed in 1931, for instance, by Langston Hughes and a network of black female readers. Elizabeth Davey has described how Hughes, at the instigation of Mary Bethune, decided to expand the audience for his writing. He wrote a collection of poems for readers with varying literacy skills and developed new ways to circulate and distribute them. Throughout 1931 Hughes gave readings in black communities throughout the South. The text he read from, "The Negro Mother and Other Recitations," consisted largely of "recitation poems." Simple in diction and rhyme, inspirational in subject matter, these poems were not meant to be passively received but to engender further literary activity, such as memorization and performance. In this way, Hughes meant to "mobilize the audiences of [his] public readings into a reading public" that imagined itself through literary texts, through reading and listening to poetry.⁵²

Hughes knew he could reach only a small number of "the great masses of the colored people," even by traveling to far-flung communities to give public readings.⁵³ To reach a wider audience, he designed and printed two inexpensive texts to distribute at his readings: a pamphlet version of *The Negro Mother and Other Recitations*, which he sold for twenty-five cents, and illustrated broadside versions of single poems, available for ten cents each. Hughes also placed advertisements for these texts in black periodicals like the *Crisis*. Those who requested these materials were as determined as they were diverse. "[D]ear editor I me a reder of the Chris," begins one writer's 1932 request for several of the broadsides. Mrs. B. J. Anderson, president of the Periclean Club of Birmingham, Alabama, wrote to request a copy of Hughes's booklet, to be displayed as a part of a week-long exhibit "to acquaint the citizens of Birmingham with the achievement of Negroes in literature."⁵⁴ The large number of people who placed orders for the inexpensive pamphlets demonstrates the eagerness of black Americans at this time to take up the literary activity that Hughes offered. Still, as Davey notes, the most notable expansion of Hughes's efforts was accomplished by women from the communities he had visited, "who circulated the poems further, lending the booklet, lecturing on the poems and the poets, and reading the poems aloud."⁵⁵

Hughes's venture and the enthusiastic response to it illustrate the extent to which reading was not exclusively a solitary activity in the black community in the first decades of the twentieth century. Advocates of black literacy continued to endorse, to some extent, a notion of a combined oral and written tradition wherein those who could read would read to those who could not. This broad understanding of reading and literary practice had been a component of African American literacy and literary practice throughout the nineteenth century, allowing cohesive groups to develop despite widely divergent literacy skills. Because the silent, individual reading of texts was not privileged over oral performance, the benefits of literary study—inspiration, the development of critical thinking skills, the discussion of moral and political issues that arose from the reading—were available to those who listened to the text or recited it from memory as well as to those with the ability to read it for themselves.[56]

Well into the twentieth century, such an understanding of literacy and belief in the potential power of literature to form a black public was instrumental to the development of a black public sphere and to African Americans' expression of political desire. Black clubwomen were deeply aware of their need for self-representation and concerned about issues of citizenship and civil rights for African Americans, yet they were denied direct forms of resistance and were largely excluded from official structures of power and democratic participation. Black clubwomen at the end of the nineteenth century used reading and printed texts to unite around some political purposes. Their rhetoric at the founding conference of the National Association of Colored Women in 1895 underscored their understanding of the political and social implications of reading, literary production, and the distribution of printed texts. In the first decades of the twentieth century, clubwomen continued to focus on literacy initiatives and establishing libraries, further evidence of the deeply political nature of their literary work. Joined by others who shared their belief in literary activism, black clubwomen committed themselves to uniting and mobilizing black Americans toward the fulfillment of their political objectives. Principal among these objectives was a determination to make their activities more visible, both to a racist American society and to themselves (figure 25.4).

The literary activism of black women in the late nineteenth and early twentieth centuries nicely illustrates the crucial role of print as a vehicle by which subordinated social groups could imagine themselves as political bodies and unite themselves in coalition. The escalation of racial hostility in the 1890s left African Americans searching for solutions to the intractable problems of legalized violence, institutionalized racism, and widespread discrimination. Rayford Logan aptly described this period of intense political repression and brutal racial violence as the "nadir" of black experience in the United States. Largely because of the literary activism of black women, however, the same period is also described as "The Woman's Era." Unable to mount direct political or economic protests, black women turned their reading, literary study, and distribution of printed texts into forms of resistance against their own subordination and that of their

FIGURE 25.4. Older woman holding a book seated at a table with books, St. Augustine, Florida, 1880s. Photographs and Prints Division, Schomburg Center for Research in Black Culture, The New York Public Library, Astor, Lenox, and Tilden Foundations.

race. Reading and literary work offered black women throughout the nation a means of defending themselves and asserting their own agency. By empowering themselves, they were able to take the lead in establishing a black collective will, demanding broad structural changes in society, and pursuing more traditionally recognized forms of political activity, such as the right to vote. The achievement of these literary activists and the efficacy of their strategies to spread literacy and print throughout the black community are perhaps best measured by the escalating assault on race and gender discrimination begun in black women's clubs at the turn of the century.

CHAPTER 26

Making Meaning
Analysis and Affect in the Study and Practice of Reading

Joan Shelley Rubin

. . .

"It is at least cheerful to believe," the editor and Chautauqua publicist Edward N. Teall declared in 1921, "that newspaper readers can graduate to the magazines, and magazine readers to popular books and readers of popular books to Literature. The theory is not upset by the fact that the people you and I know read some newspapers, some magazines, some ephemeral books and some of the Great Books: even if only in a Library of Best Literature."[1] Teall's remark, which appeared in a volume of "friendly and informal counsel" he entitled *Books and Folks*, succinctly exemplifies the phenomenon scholars have denominated cultural hierarchy: the endowment of some forms of expression with greater value than others, and the accompanying belief that individual and social welfare depend on the upward movement of taste. Yet, notwithstanding his assertion to the contrary, the second part of Teall's statement undermines the first by eliminating what Roger Chartier called the "exclusive relationship" between a literary genre and a particular group. Hierarchy, Teall knew, coexisted with the eclecticism of the "omnivorous reader."[2]

Teall also distinguished between the works readers chose for their "social self" and those in their "Secret-Self collection." The first category included "the really great books," the ones that help people to "appear intelligent when talk of books is toward." Yet on an imagined desert island, or in the sanctum of the home, readers preferred the few texts they wanted "to have always handy, to fall back on when everything else fails": Henry Wadsworth Longfellow's most sentimental poems, a "battered old volume of Tennyson," Theodore Dreiser's *Hoosier Holiday*, "half a dozen Coopers," among others. Although likely to elicit laughter from a "highbrow," said Teall, these brought "true and lasting" pleasure.[3]

Teall's appreciation of both orderly progression and disorderly experience provides a useful framework for understanding book reading practices in late nineteenth- and early twentieth-century America. Much of historians' knowledge of American readers during those years comes from librarians, educators, and other social scientists who, in a number of local and regional studies, sought to quantify—and improve—the reading "habits" of their contemporaries. In the words of Carl F. Kaestle and Helen Damon-Moore, who integrated and evaluated the major early studies in 1991, such sources are "too tempting for the historian of reading to ignore."[4] Yet, impelled by their own anxieties, the authors of that body of work tended to focus on relatively manageable queries about frequency, motivation, and subject matter preferences. By contrast, this chapter (adopting Teall's dichotomous perspective) both resuscitates the social scientists' conclusions and raises new issues about the interplay between text and audience that are more difficult to discuss systematically; it addresses not only the matter of reading across aesthetic, chronological, and spatial boundaries but also the multiple meanings print can carry in various contexts.

Most of the investigators who scrutinized American readers between 1900 and 1930 were political progressives. They wanted to enlist reading in the service of both democracy and social stability, believing that widespread acquaintance with "desirable" material would have a salutary effect on American civic life. That agenda shaped the work of such figures as William S. Gray, Douglas Waples, Louis R. Wilson, and Robert L. Duffus and reflected their perception of the expanding flow of print into the American marketplace since the late nineteenth century and the resulting national variation in Americans' "reading proclivities." Although heartened that the United States was "rapidly becoming a nation of readers," the researchers overtly acknowledged the mixed character of the publications Americans encountered. When acknowledging the new variety of print available, however, they did so with equanimity; as Waples put it, "Most of us are both 'class' readers and 'mass' readers at the same time."[5] Yet, as that terminology implies, their tacit assent to a hierarchical view of print forms led Waples and his colleagues to criticize the general public's failure to prefer books to the ephemera of the periodical press.

Librarians and educators were also preoccupied with a second historical circumstance, the increase in leisure time enjoyed by relatively affluent Americans in the 1920s. In theory, greater leisure promoted edifying reading. Nevertheless, the attitudes accompanying New Era prosperity—the celebration of abundance, the gospel of relaxation—simultaneously threatened to undermine pastimes requiring effort and self-denial. Competition from mass culture—professional sporting events, movies, and eventually radio—compounded this risk. Adult education advocate Dorothy Canfield Fisher argued that Americans attracted to the "stifling multitude of mechanical comforts" and captivated by "ready-made amusement" risked "smother[ing] to death" beneath their "material possessions."[6]

Armed with faith in social science, the proponents of reading as democratic necessity thus set out to answer a series of related questions. In *The Reading Interests and Habits of Adults* (1929), Gray and Ruth Munroe summarized the evidence about which groups of Americans most often climbed to the top of the print hierarchy. Their answer, which has remained true in the intervening years, was that book readers were more often from the middle- or upper-classes than from the working class. That is, if class reflects education, occupation, and income, book readers have consistently possessed the best of these. As Wilson demonstrated in *The Geography of Reading* (1938), geographic location also affected print consumption; city-dwellers had easier access to materials and more leisure time, and thus read more books than rural inhabitants, especially those living in the South.

Whether or not one is surprised by the "simple truth" (to use Kaestle and Damon-Moore's language) of those observations, they add weight to the phrase publisher Henry Holt employed when, in 1911, he imagined the market for his firm's anthology *The Home Book of Verse*: its audience, he suggested to the volume's compiler, Burton E. Stevenson, was the "ordinary bourgeois family," one with perhaps a son or daughter in college.[7] Similarly, Henry Seidel Canby, longtime head of the Selecting Committee for the Book-of-the-Month Club and editor of the *Saturday Review of Literature*, defined the "average intelligent reader" as "your doctor, your lawyer, the president of your bank, and any educated business man who has not turned his brain into a machine."[8] Canby failed to notice, however, that, according to Gray and Munroe's data as well as later polls, between 1923 and 1949, book readers were predominantly female and, on average, younger than the typical bank president. Canby and Holt also neglected the importance of region, though their conceits do reflect a roughly realistic profile of American book readers.

Only one study from the interwar period explicitly challenged these assumptions, portraying working-class readers as more than foils for their white-collar counterparts. In the early 1930s, Charles H. Compton, a staff member at the St. Louis Public Library, collected data to produce a series of essays entitled *Who Reads What?* Compton's purpose was to dismantle the assumed connection between lower socioeconomic status and "lowbrow" taste. Discussing the circulation records of Thomas Hardy's works, for example, he contrasted "college graduates who have specialized in extra curricular activities, . . . who have time for golf, time for bridge . . . but no time to read" with ninety-one stenographers, six auto mechanics, four contractors, six electricians, and a number of other tradespeople—Hardy readers all. Compton's assumption that library users effectively represent the "masses" (his term) partially vitiates his conclusions, but the powerful stories of individual encounters with books in *Who*

Reads What? include ample testimony that many working-class Americans read more than just newspapers and magazines. A similar conclusion emerges from the second half of Gray and Munroe's account, which summarized interviews with two samples of readers: one from Chicago's Hyde Park area, the other from a northern suburb, Evanston, Illinois. Here, too (especially in less affluent Hyde Park), was evidence of working-class book reading.[9]

It is worth reiterating, however, that, regardless of education, income, occupation, or residence, most Americans did not read books. Seeking to reverse that trend, librarians and their colleagues posed additional queries: What was the content of the books Americans did select, or, alternatively, about what subjects would they read if they could? Why did they make those choices? Gray and Munroe offered preliminary answers to those questions in a 1924 study of silent reading among 900 individuals. Readers, they found, had many purposes: to gain information pertaining to work and social life; to stimulate and broaden the mind; to obtain pleasure and recreation; to satisfy curiosity. The authors observed that this list "emphasizes the more serious and valuable" objectives. Another study of 410 students and adults in largely professional occupations discovered 3,323 "uses" of recreational reading. Although many of the responses overlapped, the most common purposes included "for diversion"; "because one likes author"; "for recommendation of book"; "for interesting title"; "for physical rest"; "to relieve common every day experiences"; "to visualize"; "to get away from real life"; and "for pleasure."[10]

The most ambitious study of reader preference and motivation was *What People Want to Read About* (1931) by Douglas Waples and Ralph W. Tyler. Rather than actual reading practices, Waples and Tyler examined readers' interests, confining their purview to nonfiction and thus presuming the primacy of reading for information. They located preferences common across groups while also describing the differentiating effects of gender, schooling, and occupation on readers' choices. They discovered that both men and women, regardless of other variables, wished to read about "international attitudes and problems" and "personal hygiene," with nearly as many votes for "self-improvement" and "laws and legislation."[11]

Waples's interpretation of those results reflected his progressive orientation, as well as his own version of cultural hierarchy. Illiteracy, he concluded, was less a threat to civic participation than the lack of accommodation to the minimally literate. Given the "arrogance" of the "cultured," Waples claimed, "readable and authentic material" was scarcely available to "uncultured" groups. Likewise, "evidence concerning the topics in which they were least interested suggested cultural shortages on the part of the different groups which an effective educational program should seek to remove." Greater awareness would promote the state of "enlightened public opinion" on which the future of American democracy depended.[12]

One might suggest that Waples exhibited arrogance himself in seeing his respondents' dislikes as deficits and in deciding which especially required remediation. He announced, for example, that "for women of limited schooling to overcome their indifference to political and economic problems would do more to improve the condition of American society at large than for the men to take more interest in art."[13] Recreational reading, he believed, ought to be educational as well as pleasurable. Arguably, the researchers' premium on "readability" was also presumptuous in emphasizing simpler texts over improved reading skills.

In any event, Waples's subsequent work dissected readers' motivations for reading books in a time of economic crisis. His *People and Print* (1938) was chastened by both a newfound skepticism about the public's ability to transcend self-interest and by his discovery that "supply" (accessibility) rather than "demand" primarily influenced readers' choices. The resulting interpretation made no sweeping claims but posited a correlation between a book's popularity and its promise to alleviate the effects of the Depression. Waples speculated that, by helping readers to "escape," the book industry experienced only a slight change in the number of new fiction titles produced during the Depression. Readers, he hypothesized, also employed print to "follow the news" of the economy, "to find evidence" regarding current events, to "experience thrills" and thus offset suffering, to "improve vocational competence," and to "defend class interests" by learning what actions promised to restore financial security.[14]

A more subtle sense of readers' conscious and unconscious purposes characterized *What Reading Does to People* (1940). Greatly advancing reading research, the authors (Waples, Bernard Berelson, and Franklyn R. Bradshaw) insisted that terms like "information," "education," and "recreation" were vague, overlapping descriptors of print's "social effects." The authors carefully enumerated the factors influencing readers' "predispositions"—education, occupation, age, gender, and group membership, as well as the desire for prestige, "respite," experience, and security. Among contemporary studies, *What Reading Does to People* most precisely defined why people read: for instance, the "respite" motive was subdivided to encompass self-expression, aesthetic appreciation, and release of aggression. Those desires, the authors briefly recognized, might "determine" both the "meanings" readers "took from the content" and the "methods" they applied to interpret it.[15]

Yet, both *People and Print* and *What Reading Does to People* tended to impute a single meaning to a given text. That is, Waples and his colleagues largely implied that while historical conditions affected production, distribution, and consumption, texts remained static. A "definable literary stimulus" supplied a set of immutable "satisfactions" that readers either craved or spurned; thus, predisposition merely determined "why the same publication will incite one reader to revolutionary action, will be vigorously condemned by another, and will be ignored or read with apathy by a third." They failed to pursue the idea that, in different settings or ideological contexts, the "same publication" might deliver different messages—might yield itself to divergent or even contradictory appropriations. Concomitantly, the authors' view of American society included only higher and lower "groups" that competed but did not merge.[16]

It is tempting to speculate about the sources of that outlook and the attraction to social science from which it stemmed. From the moment they embarked on their projects, the progressive reading researchers incurred criticism for applying quantitative measures to the "art" of book selection and use. The librarians' and educators' affinity for scientific methodology may have been a matter merely of temperament and intellect. Yet their model, especially in the 1920s, seems itself a "social effect"—one arguably tinged with the fear of difference and disorder that many progressives shared. Amid the turbulence of immigration, anxieties about the spread of mass culture, and white, Anglo-Saxon Protestant displacement, the plan to foster democracy by promoting and measuring reading bespeaks an almost desperate behaviorism: give the American adult a good book and good citizenship will, indeed must, follow. Gray's, as well as Wilson's, use of the term "habits" (which, interestingly, proponents of book advertising also seized upon in the 1920s) likewise suggests an impulse to make reading the automatic activity of a compliant population. By labeling middle-class values as "ordinary" and "average," Holt and Canby displayed the same prejudices and needs. At the same time, however, the authors of *The Reading Interests and Habits of Adults* exhibited a strong animus against readers who gain too much empowerment from books. Verging on anti-intellectualism, the cases describe an interviewee who, "thwarted as a woman and a mother," turned to "books as a means of self-development"; a "somewhat docile" immigrant who collected poetry books and "evidently identifies himself . . . with the great men about whom he reads"; and another immigrant whose admiration for Byron reflected his delusions of "greatness."[17]

Early twentieth-century studies of American reading remain instructive for the composite picture they yield: undoubtedly, American book readers were, overall, a relatively small, relatively affluent population in search of knowledge and enjoyment. Yet the investigators' reductive search for order limits their contribution to the task Robert Darnton and others have set for the history of reading—to determine how readers make meaning from texts.[18] The following discussion attempts to gain fuller access to the experiences of the "average intelligent reader" by exploring the ideological and psychological factors that Waples et al. recognized but did not pursue. It illustrates not only why but also how and where Americans read books. Additionally, the ensuing examples suggest that some genres circulated by other means—the oral performance, the anthology, the quoted reference—that gave them an ongoing life in culture even when not read in their entirety from the printed page.

. . .

Some of the raw materials for such an analysis lie, interestingly, in the fifteen nonrepresentative case studies Gray and Munroe appended to *The Reading Interests and Habits of Adults*. Two of these are especially instructive. The first concerned a middle-aged business executive the authors called "Mr. M." Raised in a rural area by a mother who encouraged him to read, he completed one year of college after high school. Almost every evening after work, according to the case report, Mr. M. read books. He particularly relished mystery stories and also enjoyed biography, travel literature, and poetry. Reading was "a part of his quiet, happy home life." Once or twice a week, Mr. M. took down from his shelves certain "old favorites": Charles Dickens, Robert Burns, Henry Wadsworth Longfellow. Gray and Munroe observed the constancy "in his reading interests throughout his life," suggesting that Longfellow and Burns in particular were "perhaps a link with his early home and his mother." Those texts were "intimately connected with events of his whole life and have added the charm of old associations to their intrinsic appeal"; they possessed "a pervading richness from long use that no new books could have."

Mr. M.'s case is illuminating in several ways. First, Mr. M.'s reading repertoire displays great diversity, including mysteries and poems, domestic products and foreign imports, the "light" and the canonical, best sellers and "steady sellers," the old and the new. This case marks the difference between the history of reading—which must always account for such survivals and overlaps—and literary history, typically regarded as a series of discrete movements remaking high culture: romanticism, realism, modernism, and so on. Simultaneously, Mr. M.'s story captures how engagement with eclectic texts can nonetheless assume a reliable pattern: the reader night after night picking up a book to "relax," perhaps occupying the well-worn easy chair by the fireplace. Second, for Mr. M., the "quiet, happy" home not only shapes the pace and character of his involvement with the words on the page but also transforms books into tokens of the well-ordered household suffused with maternal love. Mr. M.'s reading routines likewise help to separate the home from the pressures of the workplace. Finally, the practice of rereading summons fond memories and provides continuity in life, functions that may (or may not) be extrinsic to a text's manifest content. In America, Gray and Munroe concluded, "There must be many Mr. M's."[19]

Similarly, the investigators singled out a twenty-eight-year-old man who spoke of liking poetry since the age of eight. Gray and Munroe noted: "He can recall—and does so with much animation—the literary gems" (i.e., memorized verse) he learned at school. In college, this man "met a friend who was interested in religion and poetry, and together they enjoyed Shelley, Keats, and Omar Khayyam because of their emotional quality. At night they roamed around together reciting their literary tidbits." Like Mr. M., this reader values the feelings aroused by books; however, his enjoyment is not merely silent and solitary but, rather, oral and communal.[20] Entangling youth, recollection, and ritual, both examples thus beautifully document how setting and mode of reading shape the construction of meaning. It is ironic, therefore, that poetry—the genre to which they each refer—was considered largely unpopular by progressive reading researchers. Mainstream publishing houses shared a similar view during the interwar period; editors at firms such as Scribner's repeatedly declared that poetry would not sell. That dictum was partly inaccurate and partly self-fulfilling: anthologies such as Stevenson's did sell, but production costs deterred publishers from promoting slim volumes by individual poets.

As the case studies demonstrate, however, poetry reading commanded a power and authority independent of the market. Like the cheap print that circulated in the colonial period, verse was everywhere and nowhere. Familiar poems remained alive in memory even for readers who lacked printed copies. The genre's considerable public dimension also supported its cultural pervasiveness. In the late nineteenth and early twentieth centuries, Americans were exposed to verse not only in the intimate surroundings of a lovers' tête-à-tête, but also, for example, in classroom recitations, family gatherings, speaking choir concerts, Boy Scout campfires, religious services, celebrity performances, and, eventually, radio broadcasts. Each of those venues supported ideologies and behaviors (such as rereading, reading aloud, and reading in groups) that eluded ledgers and statistics but that make poetry an especially good window through which to view the impact of site and practice.

The public school, for example, generally required all students—whether they belonged to the "classes" or the "masses"—to learn verse in every grade. Many poems acquired a fixity in the curriculum that transcended the vicissitudes of literary production. From 1890 to 1935, certain nineteenth-century British and American poems reappeared time and again in mandated state and local courses of study: William Cullen Bryant's "Thanatopsis," James Russell Lowell's "The Vision of Sir Launfal," Samuel Taylor Coleridge's "The Rime of the Ancient

Mariner," Alfred Lord Tennyson's "The Lady of the Lake," Matthew Arnold's "Sohrab and Rustum," John Greenleaf Whittier's "Snow-Bound," Rudyard Kipling's "If," William Ernest Henley's "Invictus," and William Wordsworth's "Daffodils (I Wandered Lonely as a Cloud)" were likewise ubiquitous. Curricula also included a limited infusion of innovative early modernist poetry, especially for high school students in "enrichment" programs. Nevertheless, a 1995 survey regarding poetry read in school demonstrated that the interwar period was as much the heyday of Longfellow as of T. S. Eliot.

Curricula based on such "steady sellers" (or at least enduring poetry assignments) promoted intergenerational bonds. "In 1939," a woman recalled, "I remember coming home from the fourth grade determined to memorize the poem about Columbus that begins, 'Behind him lay the gray Azores. . . .' As I was stumbling through the first few lines, my father began saying the poem, and said it to the end. . . . That glimpse of continuity and linkage . . . has stayed with me these fifty-six years."[21]

Yet one must not assume that the persistence of titles on a syllabus signaled an unvarying approach to reading, that the reasons educators prescribed them remained constant, or that teachers always transmitted them in the same fashion. In fact, the purposes and methods of poetry reading in school changed over time. Although late nineteenth- and early twentieth-century pedagogues always recognized multiple rationales for teaching the genre, their objectives decidedly fell outside Waples's 1931 paradigm of reading for information. Nor can they be entirely subsumed within Katherine Tinsley and Carl Kaestle's concept of "self-improvement."[22]

The title page of an 1883 volume of "memory gems," the anthologies of poetry and prose excerpts that became staples in American classrooms, makes clear a paramount goal of reading verse. Quoting the British essayist Sir Arthur Helps, it counsels: "We should lay up in our minds a store of goodly thoughts in well-wrought words, which should be a living treasure of knowledge, always with us, and from which, at various times, and amidst all the shifting circumstances, we might be sure of drawing some comfort, guidance, and sympathy." That injunction assumed that readers were both prudent bankers and connoisseurs of "goods"—an appealing image in a society where the upwardly mobile could suffer sudden reversals.[23]

Educators believed that the ability to stockpile such commodities required diligent training of particular mental qualities. Early poetry reading, for instance, cultivated the moral sense needed for "guidance" in future years. Thus, teachers stressed memorized recitation, which also taught elocution, often conducting exercises at the start of each school day, on Friday afternoons, or at holiday observances. Learning lines "by heart" ostensibly increased poetry's moral benefits by strengthening "the warp and woof of character," weaving ethical principles "into the very fibre" of the student's mind.[24] Other virtues—self-discipline and thoroughness—could be nurtured by carefully deciphering a poem's rhyme scheme, vocabulary, and message.

Similarly, "comfort" accrued to pupils who equipped themselves to retrieve not only the timeless moral rules poetry encapsulated but also the perspectives on human experience it transmitted. Beloved texts became "friends," mitigating students' sense of isolation.[25] In *The Choice of Books*, reprinted in the United States five times between 1891 and 1908, Frederic Harrison urged readers to make "friends" selectively by developing aesthetic standards. Learning to recognize the "best" literature—by which Harrison meant the superbly crafted as well as the morally sound—would place readers in the company of the "great spirits of the human race."[26] Finally, cultivating a sensibility for beauty of language promoted "sympathy" with humanity and attunement to nature.

The provision of emotional resources, moral direction, and "fellow feeling"— realized by means of self-discipline and conveyed through the catechism-like structure of the memorized recitation—affiliated schoolroom poetry reading with Christian worship. In this way, a prescribed mode (as well as an imputed function) of poetry reading made the secular and the sacred interchangeable. Harrison advised that "the immortal and universal poets of our race are to be read and re-read till their music and their spirit are a part of our nature; they are to be thought over and digested till we live in the world they created for us; they are to be read devoutly, as devout men read their Bible and fortify their hearts with psalms."[27] That ideal, consistent with the imagined virtues of repetition, made learning verse a source of rebirth, just as Christian conversion promised new life. In sum, the utility assigned to poetry dictated how it should be read. Those instructions, in turn, supported additional cultural values including a life of leisurely reflection and veneration of the Bible. Of course, the putative benefits of recitation and rereading conflicted with other outcomes of such practices. Parsing, explication, and drill might fragment the text, conceal its lessons, drive the shy or bored student away; the invitation to enter the poets' "world" could break as well as strengthen human connections; the "memory gem" compendium entailed a kind of cheating on disciplined training. It is also true that, as Richard Venezky details in this volume, silent reading eventually displaced vocalizing as a method of teaching children to associate letters and sounds. Yet, throughout this period, both the content and form of the poetry curriculum exhibited striking stability across locales ranging from Nebraska to New York.

By the early 1900s, however, disciples of progressive education, animated by their own moral priorities, began to promulgate an alternate approach to poetry reading in school. Rejecting the idea of education as storage, the curricular reformers most influential in the interwar years argued that children learned best when instruction derived from their natural inclinations and interests. Like their counterparts in librarianship, moreover, progressive teachers saw themselves as guardians of high culture and democratic citizenship against the growing threat from commercial amusements and the "large foreign element" in the nation's expanding high schools.²⁸

In some classrooms, those preoccupations led educators to discard *Evangeline* in favor of contemporary verse. More commonly, however, instructors introduced a new mode of reading for older and new texts alike—one in which students were expected to revel in the printed page rather than to analyze it. While sustaining other forms of recitation, progressives vehemently attacked the use of "memory gems" and rejected the obligation to "point a moral" after elucidating meaning. As one pedagogue, Sterling Andrus Leonard, insisted (in notable contrast to Harrison), "'[T]he literature of power' is rarely to be 'chewed and digested,'" but is instead "mainly to be 'apprehended'—taken hold of, that is, as genuine and living experience."²⁹ Moreover, the subordination of understanding to feeling meant that there was "nothing inherently hard" about poetry; the reader had only to submit to the "quickening and intensity of the emotions" that came from giving oneself over to the "mood" of a poet.³⁰ As one student at the progressive Lincoln School commented regarding Edna St. Vincent Millay's *The Harpweaver and Other Poems*, "It is cruel to review it. It is too lovely. Nothing can be said better than, 'Read it.'"³¹ (In her public performances, Millay herself made palpable the erotic overtones of the progressive model by sweeping onto the stage dressed in flowing scarves.) Paradoxically, such "surrender" ostensibly liberated and integrated the self, permitting the wholesome, free expression of "creativity"—a term that loomed large in the progressive educators' lexicon.

. . .

While reformist educators retained appreciation for poetry's lifelong benefits, they often substituted enhancement of consciousness for received wisdom. In 1935 the National Council of Teachers of English incorporated these assumptions into *An Experience Curriculum in English*, which perpetuated the assignment of such works as "Abou Ben Adhem" and Emerson's "Concord Hymn" but treated them as artifacts fostering the "enlargement of the individual." In this view, the English class was "a rather informal literary club in which the teacher is simply the most experienced member."³²

It must be emphasized, however, that progressive educators had a far greater influence on pedagogical theory than on the American public school during this entire period. Although individual teachers around the country implemented portions of the progressive program, only in wealthy districts such as Winnetka, Illinois, did public schools accomplish the sweeping curricular "transformations" pioneered by private schools such as Lincoln. Furthermore, even curricular innovators bound the idea of "experiencing" verse to aims that potentially retarded other kinds of change. Some of their phrases—"the spiritualization of public education," the promotion of "kinship with the lives of others"—were not so far removed from Helps's nineteenth-century vision of "comfort, guidance, and sympathy." One prominent progressive and Lincoln School teacher, Hughes Mearns, disavowed the erotic element in his method of reading by envisioning the appreciation of poetry as a weapon against the sexual promiscuity Samuel Hopkins Adams had portrayed in *Flaming Youth* (1923). Entitling his account of his English classes *Creative Youth* (1925), Mearns made "creativity" in the reading and writing of verse stand for opposition to everything the flapper symbolized.[33]

Reading poetry in school thus afforded—both successively and simultaneously—moral direction, communal linkage, religious inspiration, aesthetic sensitivity, self-discipline, personal growth, creative expression, social control, and democratic citizenship. For certain readers, Edna St. Vincent Millay's poem was "about" not only Columbus but also familial bonds; this meaning lay in both the depiction of particular behaviors and, more generally, the feeling venerated by the tone and delivery. Cultural needs, values, and principles, transmitted institutionally, intersected with the needs, values, and principles of individuals to shape a reading experience that cannot be recovered merely by chronicling titles, tabulating motives, or analyzing texts.

To understand how readers have historically made meaning, it is equally instructive to consider the appropriation of verse at sites where the religious impulse predominated—for example, in worship services. Of course, some religious poetry reading occurred in private surroundings, notably in daily devotions. In the late nineteenth and early twentieth centuries, both denominational presses like Abingdon and secular houses regularly issued volumes, frequently pocket-sized for portability, for that purpose. Beyond private employment, however, poetry also had a long-standing role in public services. Within American liberal Protestantism (to which this discussion is confined), it appeared in psalms and in the lyrics of hymns. As Henry Sloane Coffin remarked in 1946, "any definition of poetry that excludes altogether the simple congregational hymn is surely a narrow definition."[34] Scripture and song continued to fuse poetry and religion throughout the period between 1880 and 1940.

Furthermore, as theologians debated ways to enliven the churchgoer's experience, they also invoked the genre in the sermon, a ready showcase for the literary erudition of the clergy. Andrew W. Blackwood of Princeton Theological Seminary scornfully noted in 1939 that a minister may there "glibly refer to Milton and Dante, or Francis Thompson and Alfred Noyes, and perhaps repeat excerpts from Bartlett's *Familiar Quotations*, or Burton Stevenson's books." Instead of those perfunctory allusions, however, some liberal Protestant preachers in the post–World War I era offered from their pulpits sermons that dealt entirely with the message of a poem or a novel. Around 1918, for example, the Methodist minister William R. Stidger, who eventually published several works on the merits of reading, made a specialty of what he called the "dramatic book sermon."[35] Worshipers also encountered poetry at rites and observances marking the stages of life. At funerals, for example, the Christian romanticism of British Victorian poets evoked empathy and recollection.[36]

Finally (and perhaps most remarkably), some congregations communally recited verse as prayer. By the early twentieth century, the interpolation of poems into Protestant ritual offered great possibilities for augmenting a fixed liturgy. Religious educators targeted for experimentation the less formal services conducted at a time other than Sunday morning. For example, Margaret T. Applegarth integrated music, skits, and poems in her book of programs for women's church societies, *Bound in the Bundle of Life* (1941). Led by laity, the services interspersed lines from Wordsworth, Tennyson, Gibran's *The Prophet*, and Katherine Lee Bates, among others, with Bible passages and contemporary prose to address such themes as the family or the plight of farm laborers.[37]

Similarly, for proponents of "restoring worship," gatherings of church youth were appropriate settings for poetry as prayer, given that adolescents were "peculiarly ready for . . . and responsive to" the "religious nurture" that "vital" language and image supplied. Especially in church schools, a writer affiliated with an Indiana Evangelical and Reformed Church maintained, "bits of poetry, well chosen and well read, may fulfill the purpose of the call [to worship] more effectively than any other type of material." Thus, Alice Anderson Bays's *Worship Services for Youth* (1940) also excerpted *The Prophet*, together with Longfellow, Edwin Markham, and numerous selections from the popular British novelist and poet John Oxenham. The evangelical theologian Kirby Page's *Living Creatively* (1932) collected poems for use not only in daily devotions but also in "church services, schools of religions, education, young peoples' meetings, boys' clubs, summer camps, student conferences, and similar gatherings." Page's political activism extended his scope to include Oxenham and "God's World"; works by Countee Cullen, Langston Hughes, and James Weldon Johnson; and poems cognizant of working-class life—Margaret Widdemer's "Factories," Sandburg's "Prayers of Steel," Reginald Wright Kaufman's "The March of the Hungry Man"—that complemented Joyce Kilmer's "Trees."[38]

Perhaps the most suggestive of such works, however, was *Services for the*

Open (1923), arranged by Laura I. Mattoon, secretary of an association of girls' camps, and Helen D. Bragdon, general secretary of the Young Women's Christian Association at Mount Holyoke College. Designed primarily for young people at outdoor camps or schools, Mattoon and Bragdon's interdenominational Christian services targeted all who sought to commune with "the God of the open air." As Mattoon and Bragdon explained, "In such services, it has been felt that there is a rightful place—not only for passages from the greatest Book wrought out of human experience, but for the inspirations of seers and poets down to the present time." Giving equal weight to both biblical and poetic texts, Mattoon and Bragdon also sanctified Ralph Waldo Emerson, Henry David Thoreau, John Greenleaf Whittier, Wordsworth, and six naturalists as "apostles of the out-of-doors," around whose lives leaders could devise services of their own.[39]

The result was a series of thematic scripts in which the order of worship moved from the Doxology, for example, to a Bible quotation, The Lord's Prayer, and a hymn in praise of summer to stanzas by Edward Rowland Sill and Wordsworth. In a service for the planting of a tree, worshipers sang both "Fairest Lord Jesus" and a musical version of Kilmer's lines. Another, entitled "Growing Things," coupled the twenty-third psalm and a poem about meadows by Corinne Roosevelt Robinson (Theodore Roosevelt's sister). *Services for the Open* had a broad chronological and stylistic range, including William Shakespeare, Longfellow, Robert Lowell, the Presbyterian minister Henry Van Dyke, Edwin Markham, Edwin Arlington Robinson, the "little magazine" founder Alfred Kreymborg, and Robert Frost. These authors, however, were identified only in a list of references. Thus, while Mattoon and Bragdon sought to heighten the reader's experience of an unmediated spiritual encounter, they also diminished the possibility that readers would discriminate among the selections in literary terms.[40]

In fact, *Services for the Open*, like all such compilations, arranged texts to be read together around specific words or themes: God, Christ, the soul, prayer, nature. As in the schoolroom, eclecticism was limited: obscurity and pessimism were forbidden. Yet *Services for the Open* evades certain distinctions used by scholars to sort literary production: between the sacred and the secular, Victorian piety and early modernist revolt, the high and the popular. The stance of the poets who rejected the conventions of earlier generations disappeared in the process. Furthermore, poetry as worship forces a reconsideration of the argument that, by the nineteenth century, the authority of a text was inextricably bound to the construction of authorship. *Services for the Open* disseminated poetry without reference to the author; a text's authority derived from the weight of Protestant ritual—that is, from the site of the worship itself. One might alternatively propose that in this case the author was the ultimate authority, God.

That authority, moreover, inhered not merely in doctrine or in the impact of architecture but also in the modes of speech congregations habitually adopted. Worshipers were accustomed to delivering prayers at the slow pace and steady rhythm required for collective reading; reciting and pausing in unison created a homogenized voice that discouraged flamboyance and idiosyncratic theatricality. In tone and content, group services thus bestowed solemnity and stature on any text read aloud. Lines by Edgar Guest and Shakespeare acquired a common sound, which is to say that both sounded "good." Literal sacralization obviated any comparative judgments about a poet's use of form and language.[41]

These varied uses of verse in actual worship offered the same consolations as their quasi-religious public school counterparts. Poetry as prayer, however, more precisely defined "reading for inspiration" and reframed other motivations for classroom recitation in Christian terms. Here, "fostering community" meant achieving the unity of shared beliefs and oneness before God. It also referred to the equal standing of leader and congregation. As one commentator observed, nonliturgical denominations (i.e., Protestants apart from Episcopalians and Lutherans) minimized the "spiritual spectatorship and individualistic devotion" characteristic of Anglo-Catholicism.[42] Both the unison and responsive reading served community, but the latter device was especially suited to the antiphonal rendition of poetry. There was irony as well as fellowship in this practice. Like the verse-speaking choirs of the same era, congregations often used works by poets like Frost or Robinson to affirm social bonds, despite the authors' dominant messages regarding the solitariness of human existence.

Services for the Open also highlights a third arena in which American readers discovered (or rediscovered) verse: the summer camp. Although outdoor verse recitation requires greater consideration than allowed here, Girl Scout leaders, Young Men's Christian Association officials, and similar proponents of camping for young people affiliated poetry both with the free expression promoted in progressive schools and with Christian spirituality. In the summer camp setting, certain texts like *Hiawatha* or John Masefield's "Sea Fever" were used to assert the compatibility of simplicity, nature, and, for boys, manliness. In addition, however, reading verse made bookish campers (whether male or female) appear maladjusted to the group.[43] *Services for the Open* included in its plan of worship for the first day of camp a responsive reading from Wordsworth: "Up! Up! my friend, and quit your books; / Or surely you'll grow double; . . . Come forth into the light of things, Let Nature be your Teacher."[44] Thus, regardless of their content, poems recited around the campfire bespoke an enduring tension between contemplation and action in American culture.

The various modes and meanings attending the transmission of verse at school, church, and camp demonstrate how reading behaviors marginal to the quest for new information can sensitively register continuities, alterations, and contradictions in cultural norms and expectations. From a contemporary perspective in which some observers perceive electronic media as a threat to the practical print consumption Waples hoped to expand, the poetry reading of the interwar period may appear merely archaic. In Raymond Williams's terms, however, it is more useful to see the appropriation of verse as residual: that is, as a phenomenon that "has been effectively formed in the past, but is still active in the cultural process, not only and often not at all as an element of the past, but as an effective element of the present." Residual cultural forms may entail "alternatives" to the dominant culture, as when teachers and camp directors counterposed the wholesomeness of poetic sentiments to the materialism and individualism of the 1920s. Yet the residual also persists within the "dominant order," lending dynamism and complexity to historical development.[45] In the case at hand, poetry-reading practices argue against the customary depiction of the post–World War I America solely as an era in which Victorianism surrendered to modernism, or when "terrible honesty" obliterated sentimental and genteel values.[46]

Whether the incorporation of such practices into the "dominant order" eased the strains and dislocations of middle-class life under American industrial capitalism is another question. The metaphor of books as "friends" belongs to a long, uncharted tradition, yet when Frederic Harrison contrasted good book selection with the movement of a "lonely" man "aimlessly wandering about in a crowded city," he saw in the act of reading the capacity to repel the rootlessness and isolation endemic to the modern urban scene.[47] As progressive educators and ministers knew, the universal human quest for "comfort, guidance, and sympathy" was more urgent and specific when, for white Anglo-Saxon Protestants, economic growth brought with it the specter of class conflict and disturbing new mores. Betokening the familiar, reinvigorating religion, and offsetting anonymity through the construction of reading communities, the act of reciting verse both accommodated and resisted the rhythms of the assembly line and the dance hall. Even long-standing classroom procedures and yellowed syllabi might pick up new psychological and social functions as they came to be implemented under new conditions.

Still, poetry reading, though associated more with middle-class ideals of refinement than with vocational education, was never strictly a middle-class pursuit. The practices that overshadowed it with respect to the book market—reading for job advancement, speed reading, even escapist fiction reading—were more attuned to the requirements of a consumer economy. Furthermore, the challenge posed to older middle-class moralism by the poetry appropriations of liberal clergy and progressive educators cannot be ignored.

. . .

Raymond Williams's framework is perhaps most helpful in underscoring the competing outlooks cultures can encompass at a given time. As many of America's schoolchildren, campers, outdoor worshipers, and "Mr. M.'s" discovered, the "residual" *resides*;[48] it remains a vital and vibrant aspect of individual and social experience. A history of reading that incorporates sensitivity to "secret selves" and multiple ideologies, to psychic as well as economic profit and loss, offers the best hope of recovering that experience.

Epilogue

Carl F. Kaestle and Janice A. Radway
. . .

By 1940 the United States had become a nation of readers. Elementary and secondary education had expanded exponentially. Whereas, in 1880 only 2.5 percent of seventeen-year-olds had graduated from high school, by 1940 the figure was 51 percent.[1] Outright illiteracy, rated at 17 percent in 1880, had become so unusual by 1940 that the government began using the concept of "functional" literacy, defined by the U.S. Army during World War II as a fourth-grade reading level. The percentage of people in the United States who had less than five years of elementary schooling had decreased from 24 percent in 1910 to 6 percent in 1940.[2]

In chapter 2 of this volume, Carl Kaestle noted that the profile of literacy in the United States in 1880 approximated what Daniel and Lauren Resnick have called "industrial literacy," that is, a two-tiered system in which there is widespread rudimentary literacy across the population and a smaller elite corps of more extensively educated people with high literacy skills.[3] By 1940 the U.S. population was vastly more literate than this. All but a tiny fraction completed at least the fourth grade. High school graduation was by then the modal experience of youth. College attendance had expanded significantly. In this advanced stage of industrial literacy, there were more tiers of differently literate individuals. The middle class increasingly was high school educated. Many upper-middle-class workers had mastered higher levels of technical training and possessed both complex and specialized literacy skills that enabled them to labor intellectually rather than manually.[4] These people worked as professionals and managers in a now tightly integrated and heavily bureaucratized society and constituted, along with the upper class, the bulk of book readers. While 80 percent of the population reported reading newspapers regularly, only about one-fourth of the population reported reading books regularly.

Nonetheless, by 1940 a consumer culture organized around national brands and promoted at least initially by print advertising had been thoroughly established in the United States, contributing thereby to the creation of a national popular culture. That culture, which took shape during our period, was expressed not only by mass-market magazines and by the best sellers churned out by the publishing trades but also by widespread syndication in newspapers and by radio programs, professional sports, movies, and the entire Hollywood publicity apparatus. This popular culture was enabled by expanding school attendance and enhanced by faster transportation and improved communications networks, both of which in turn supported a loose but significant coupling of America's small towns during our period.

This did not mean, however, that everyone was part of a homogeneous national culture. Ethnicity, race, class, religion, region, and gender all mattered, often critically. The expanding technical and cultural elite trained in colleges and universities depended upon a constant stream of printed words. Print allowed them to conduct research, to communicate among themselves, and to disseminate the knowledge they generated. Governments, corporations, reformers, radicals, and religious denominations churned out print to organize their activities and promote their ideas, their intentions, and their accomplishments.

African Americans, Native Americans, political radicals, and labor activists built vibrant but sometimes divided movements and they risked considerable danger in their efforts to obtain justice, often enlisting print to advance their interests. Distinctive, diverse cultures thrived in neighborhoods, churches, and clubs as well. Although an increasingly corporate capitalism exerted standardizing tendencies, it also sought to profit by exploiting specialized niches. America's culture of print followed suit with a proliferation of periodicals aimed at Methodists, at ranchers, at African Americans, and at grocery store owners. Book merchants similarly sought to capitalize on difference and special tastes. Although the Book-of-the-Month Club and the Literary Guild sought to profit from the distribution of middlebrow cultural fare to a broad national audience, hundreds of smaller book clubs were spawned in their wake, seeking to reach groups with special interests, such as Catholics, freethinkers, book collectors, or readers with an interest in science.[5]

By 1940, at the close of our period, publishing in the United States had become a highly articulated system. Although dominated in the eyes of many by the traditional trade quartered in New York, the system was actually a good deal more varied than was popularly represented. Specialized sectors functioned more or less independently of the most commercial parts of the trade, publishing materials for targeted audiences. As our essays have documented, the religious and denominational presses, the publishing arm of the U.S. government, and the university presses all functioned largely independently of the traditional trade. Also, the commercial firms included many smaller publishing houses that focused their efforts on things like textbooks and reference works.

Within the trade itself, loose constellations of publishers, writers, distributors, audiences, and even genres were stratified and crystallized. They had become sufficiently distinguishable from each other that they were routinely discussed as the highbrow, the lowbrow, and the middlebrow. The pulp magazine industry, which targeted less educated, working-class readers, surged in the 1920s and 1930s, with much of the growth taking place first within the detective story genre and then later in science fiction (see figure E.1). The poetry and literary fiction circuit included little magazines, some of the most prestigious publishing houses in the country, and a relatively small group of highly educated readers. These categories were never as distinct in readership as contemporary commentators suggested, however. Many individuals read across brow levels, and many publishers sought ways to cross literary and class divides.

Publishers had intermittently introduced paperback books in previous eras to reach nontraditional readers, but in the late 1930s paperbacks emerged as a major feature of the culture of print, offering everything from Plato to Mickey Spillane (see figure E.2). Where previously the cheap paper format had been used to reach a large, popular audience, by the end of our period it was a means to expand the numbers of imprints in particular genres and persuade individual readers to buy more books and magazines.

Although the Depression negatively affected the entire publishing industry, most firms survived by reducing overhead and salaries and by keeping profit expectations relatively low, according to John Tebbel. Thus, the industry moved into the 1940s with relatively stable systems of acquisition, methods of marketing, and a strong, though impressionistic, sense of who its target audiences were.[6] Although overall title production declined in 1939, that was the first time it had since 1933. Title production increased again in 1940 when 11,328 titles were published in the United States, in Tebbel's words, "the largest number issued in any year in America."[7] In 1940, in fact, the publishing industry was so sure of its historically significant role that its industry organ, *Publishers' Weekly*, celebrated the 500th anniversary of the introduction of the printing press with the production of a special issue touting the contemporary trade as the culmination of the original invention.

Despite the self-congratulatory tone characteristic of the industry at the end of our period, old problems lingered and new ones loomed on the horizon. Worries that book buying was increasing insufficiently prompted the Joint Board of Book Publishers and Booksellers to pass a resolution in 1940 calling for a campaign to increase book reading in the United States and creating the American Book Council to foster such efforts.[8] The failure of earlier efforts to increase book sales prompted skepticism among some in the trade. Indeed, it had become common to bemoan the state of book distribution ever since the publication of O. H. Cheyney's *Economic Survey of the Book Industry* in 1929.

81. HOWARD V. BROWN *Einstein Express* 1935 (V.15 #2)

FIGURE E.1. The cover of *Astounding Stories* 15, no. 2 (April 1935) integrated an illustration by Howard V. Brown for J. George Frederick's story, "The Einstein Express," that appeared in the issue. Copyright circa 1935 by Street and Smith Publications, Inc. Reprinted by permission of Dell Magazines, a division of Crosstown Publications.

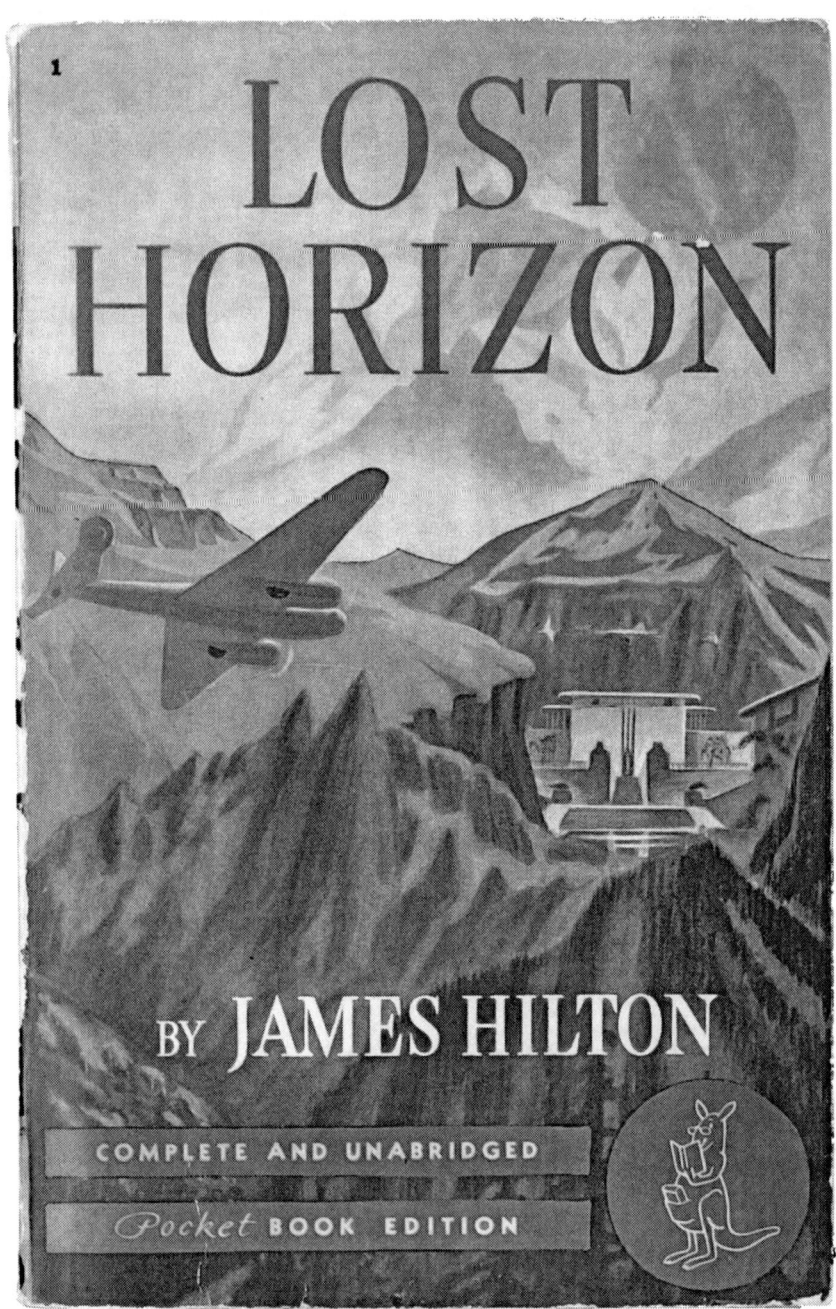

FIGURE E.2. Cover for paperback edition of James Hilton, *Lost Horizon* (New York: Pocket Books, 1939). Reprinted with the permission of Pocket Books, a division of Simon & Schuster, Inc.

Cheyney had concluded that the operations of the book industry were haphazard and wasteful, that book distribution was ineffective, that educational provisions were weak, and that more could be done to promote book buying and reading.[9] Supporting Cheyney's gloomy view, a 1935 study by Louis Wilson had found that despite an impressive expansion of public libraries, about 37 percent of the U.S. population still had no library service.[10] Nervously aware of the rise of fascism in Europe, many Americans worried that any limitations on people's access to reading might deprive them of the information necessary in a deliberative democracy.

Worries about the extent of reading in the United States were exacerbated not only by the political atmosphere but also by the appearance of new media. Radio and movies not only competed with books and print for the attention of Americans but also, some thought, seemed to provide more titillation than thoughtful analysis. As Joan Shelley Rubin has shown in this volume, various studies were undertaken in the 1930s and 1940s to consider who read what, for what purposes, and "what reading did to people." As the radio and movie industries captured more of Americans' leisure time and entertainment income, and as accounts of a new-fangled technology called "television" began to emerge, those involved in print culture and the publishing industry treated their competitors with a studied, albeit nervous, disdain.

Planning for the 1939 World's Fair in Flushing Meadow, New York, a collection of government officials, corporate executives, scientists, and educators sought to assess the nation's accomplishments. Many of the most prominent publishers declined to participate, however.[11] Last-minute arrangements eventually led to the inclusion of a "Book House" for children's literature and to several exhibits about print, including the Merriam dictionary company's "Pyramid of Knowledge" and an eighteen-foot tall, working, Underwood typewriter.[12] Perhaps not surprisingly, though, most of the emphasis at the 1939 Fair was on the newer, more eye-catching electronic media. Visitors could hear their own voices in stereophonic sound and listen to synthetic speech; they could see punch cards become printed reports, and tests graded by machine; they could watch a television set and hear about the history of the device.[13]

In the "Focal Exhibit" of the Communications Hall a twenty-foot tall, plastic talking head narrated the history of communications, beginning with sign language, moving through the postal service and printed books, then the telegraph, telephone, motion pictures and radio, ending with television. On the south wall of the hall, reflecting the unrelievedly optimistic projections of the fair's ideologues, a display summarized the achievements of that history: "Modern means of communication span continents, bridge oceans, annihilate time and space. . . . Servants of freedom of thought and action, they offer to all men the wisdom

FIGURE E.3. Televisions were exhibited in the RCA building—shaped like a giant radio tube—at the 1939 New York World's Fair. Television sets and TV transmission were introduced in the New York region at the time of the fair. The image was seen reflected in a mirror in the lid. Richard Wurts photograph, Wurts Brothers Photography Collection, Courtesy National Building Museum.

of the ages to free them from tyrannies and establish co-operation among the peoples of the earth."[14] Portrayed as the culmination of that history, television was the most popular communications display. Crowds thronged the main hall of the RCA pavilion, hoping to be caught by the cameras broadcasting images of the fair on receivers there (see figure E.3).[15]

Some commentators on the fair were unimpressed with the optimistic themes of technological advance in the cause of democracy and equality.[16] Yet, however naive or disingenuous the fair's ideologues, they did foretell the challenge that television would pose to print as a prime vehicle of communication. In the years to come, the dominant culture of print would give way to a mixture of competing media. Books would maintain their formal authority, and the profusion of print would continue to pour forth, but amid a cacophony produced by other media. People would increasingly get their knowledge of news from televisual and electronic sources, while newspaper reading would decline. The publication tie-ins of the prewar period would soon look modest compared to media deals that subordinated story books as "loss leaders" to toys, television programs, and video games.

In the subsequent war and postwar decades, communication would burst beyond national boundaries as the fair's prognosticators had predicted. Indeed the United States would emerge from World War II as one of the great ideological and commercial powers of the globe. These developments and their impact on the printed word, however, await the next volume of *A History of the Book in America*. For our part, we have attempted to grasp the developments of an earlier, pivotal era during which a culture of print was broadened and deepened. Recourse to print became both more ubiquitous and more essential, and struggles carried out *within* print were the central communication struggles of the era. Ever more in motion between 1880 and 1940, print circulated faster, more widely, and more effectively, yet much more contentiously. The culture of print became so important during this period that virtually anyone with an idea, point of view, aim, desire, or intention had to engage within its precincts.

NOTES

Prologue

1. John Tebbel, *A History of Book Publishing in the United States*, vols. 2 and 3 (New York: R. R. Bowker, 1975 and 1978).

2. See, for example, James L. W. West III, *American Authors and the Literary Marketplace since 1900* (Philadelphia: University of Pennsylvania Press, 1988).

3. Robert Darnton, "What Is the History of Books?" *Daedalus* 111 (1982): 65–83.

4. Roger Chartier, *The Order of Books: Readers, Authors, and Libraries in Europe between the Fourteenth and Eighteenth Centuries*, trans. Lydia G. Cochrane (Stanford: Stanford University Press, 1994).

CHAPTER 1
A Framework for the History of Publishing and Reading in the United States, 1880–1940

1. High school enrollment rates were calculated as a percentage of all persons age fifteen through nineteen. Private school enrollments for 1880 (not available) were estimated as equal to public enrollments. *Historical Statistics of the United States: Colonial Times to 1970*, pt. 1, no. 15 (Washington, D.C.: Bureau of the Census, 1975), 368–69.

2. Robert Wiebe, *The Search for Order, 1877–1920* (New York: Hill & Wang, 1967).

3. Alfred D. Chandler Jr., *The Visible Hand: The Managerial Revolution in American Business* (Cambridge, Mass.: Harvard University Press, 1977).

4. Nicholas Murray Butler, quoted in Alan Trachtenberg, *The Incorporation of America: Culture and Society in the Gilded Age* (New York: Hill & Wang, 1982), 84.

5. James R. Beniger, *The Control Revolution: Technological and Economic Origins of the Information Society* (Cambridge, Mass.: Harvard University Press, 1986); Emile Durkheim, *The Division of Labor in Society*, trans. George Simpson (1893; New York: Free Press, 1933).

6. Ellis W. Hawley, *The Great War and the Search for a Modern Order: A History of the American People and Their Institutions, 1917–1933* (New York: St. Martin's Press, 1979).

7. Sven Beckert, *The Moneyed Metropolis: New York City and the Consolidation of the American Bourgeoisie, 1850–1986* (Cambridge: Cambridge University Press, 2001); Claudia D. Goldin, *The Shaping of Higher Education: The Formative Years in the United States, 1890–1940* (Cambridge, Mass.: National Bureau of Economic Research, 1998); Michael Denning, *The Cultural Front: The Laboring of American Culture in the Twentieth Century* (New York: Verso, 1996).

8. George Rogers Taylor, *The Transportation Revolution, 1815–1860* (New York: Harper & Row, 1951), 79–80.

9. M. B. Schnapper, *American Labor: A Pictorial Social History* (Washington, D.C.: Public Affairs Press, 1975), 70.

10. Wiebe, *Search for Order*, 11.

11. James W. Cortada, "Progenitors of the Information Age," in *A Nation Transformed by Information: How Information Has Shaped the United States from Colonial Times to the Present*, ed. Alfred D. Chandler Jr. and James W. Cortada (New York: Oxford University Press, 2000), 188.

12. Richard R. John, "Recasting the Information Infrastructure for the Industrial Age," in Chandler and Cortada, *A Nation Transformed*, 76.

13. Beniger, *Control Revolution*, 19.

14. John, "Recasting the Information Infrastructure," 94.

15. Lisa Gitelman, *Scripts, Grooves, and Writing Machines: Representing Technology in the Edison Era* (Stanford: Stanford University Press, 1999), chap. 3.

16. Daniel J. Czitrom, *Media and the American Mind from Morse to McLuhan* (Chapel Hill: University of North Carolina Press, 1982), chap. 3. The Kaltenborn quotation, from 1926, is on p. 81.

17. Richard Ohmann, *Selling Culture: Magazines, Markets, and Class at the Turn of the Century* (London: Verso, 1996), 25-30.

18. Geoffrey Ashall Glaister, *Encyclopedia of the Book* (New Castle, Del.: Oak Knoll Press and the British Library, 1996), 295, 320.

19. Edwin Emery, *The Press and America: An Interpretative History of the Mass Media*, 3rd ed. (Englewood Cliffs, N.J.: Prentice-Hall, 1972), 337-430. Later editions of this venerable text include less detail on technological developments, so we are relying on the earlier edition.

20. Ibid., 343. See also Ted Curtis Smythe, *The Gilded Age Press, 1865-1900*, History of American Journalism Series, no. 4 (Westport, Conn.: Praeger, 2003), chap. 7.

21. See Sally F. Griffith, "Mass Media Come to the Small Town: The *Emporia Gazette* in the 1920's," in *Mass Media between the Wars: Perceptions of Cultural Tension, 1918-1941*, ed. Catherine Covert and John D. Stevens (Syracuse: Syracuse University Press, 1984), 141-58; Richard A. Schwarzlose, *The Rush to Institution: From 1865 to 1920*, vol. 2. of *The Nation's Newsbrokers* (Evanston: Northwestern University Press, 1990); Emery, *The Press and America*, chaps. 22 and 23.

22. Janice A. Radway, *A Feeling for Books: The Book-of-the-Month Club, Literary Taste, and Middle-Class Desire* (Chapel Hill: University of North Carolina Press, 1997); Joan Shelley Rubin, *The Making of Middlebrow Culture* (Chapel Hill: University of North Carolina Press, 1992).

23. E. L. Godkin, "Chromo Civilization," *Nation*, 24 September 1874. See Neil Harris, "Pictorial Perils: The Rise of American Illustration," in his *Cultural Excursions: Marketing Appetites and Cultural Tastes in Modern America* (Chicago: University of Chicago Press, 1990), 337-48.

24. Czitrom, *Media and the American Mind*, chap. 2.

25. Gerald Mast, ed., *The Movies in Our Midst: Documents in the Cultural History of Film in America* (Chicago: University of Chicago Press, 1982), 41.

26. Raymond Fielding, *The American Newsreel, 1911-1967* (Norman: University of Oklahoma Press, 1972), chaps. 1-9.

27. Arthur John, *The Best Years of the Century: Richard Watson Gilder, Scribner's Monthly, and Century Magazine, 1870–1909* (Urbana: University of Illinois Press, 1981), 182.

28. Emery, *The Press and America*, 340; Smythe, *Gilded Age Press*, 128.

29. John, *Best Years of the Century*, 237.

30. John, "Recasting the Information Infrastructure," 55; Schwarzlose, *Rush to Institution*, chaps. 1–3.

31. Frederick Jackson Turner, "The Significance of the Frontier in American History," in *American Historical Association Annual Report, 1893* (Washington, D.C.: Government Printing Office, 1894), 199–227.

32. David Wallace Adams, *Education for Extinction: American Indians and the Boarding School Experience, 1875–1928* (Lawrence: University Press of Kansas, 1995), 17.

CHAPTER 2
Seeing the Sites: Readers, Publishers, and Local Print Cultures in 1880

1. Dee Brown, *The Year of the Century: 1876* (New York: Charles Scribner's Sons, 1966), 116.

2. Ibid., 129–36.

3. Stanley Buder, *Pullman: An Experiment in Industrial Order and Community Planning, 1880–1930* (New York: Oxford University Press, 1967), 50–53.

4. On Ivory soap, see Vincent Vinikas, "Lustrum of the Cleanliness Institute, 1927–1932," *Journal of Social History* 22 (Summer 1989): 613–30; Ralph M. Hower, *The History of an Advertising Agency: N. W. Ayer & Son at Work, 1869–1949* (Cambridge, Mass.: Harvard University Press, 1939), 88–89.

5. Michel de Certeau, *The Practices of Everyday Life*, trans. Steven Rendall (Berkeley: University of California Press, 1984), xiv–xxii. See also Roger Chartier, *Forms and Meanings: Texts, Performances, and Audiences from Codex to Computer* (Philadelphia: University of Pennsylvania Press, 1995), 90–92.

6. Janice A. Radway, *Reading the Romance: Women, Patriarchy, and Popular Literature*, 2nd ed. (Chapel Hill: University of North Carolina Press, 1991); Christine Pawley, *Reading on the Middle Border: The Culture of Print in Late-Nineteenth-Century Osage, Iowa* (Amherst: University of Massachusetts Press, 2001); David Paul Nord, "Reading the Newspaper: Strategies and Politics of Reader Response, Chicago, 1912–1917," *Journal of Communication* 45 (Summer 1995): 66–93.

7. Saul Steinberg. "A View of the World from Ninth Avenue," *New Yorker*, 29 March 1976, cover illustration.

8. A. Gabriel Meléndez, *So All Is Not Lost: The Poetics of Print in Nuevomexicano Communities, 1834–1958* (Albuquerque: University of New Mexico Press, 1997), 28; Doris Meyer, *Speaking for Themselves: Neomexicano Cultural Identity and the Spanish-Language Press, 1880–1920* (Albuquerque: University of New Mexico Press, 1996), 8.

9. David Levering Lewis, *When Harlem Was in Vogue* (New York: Alfred A. Knopf, 1981), 99, 143; Isabel de Palencia, *I Must Have Liberty* (New York: Longmans, Green, 1940).

10. Lawrence W. Levine, *Black Culture and Black Consciousness: Afro-American Folk Thought from Slavery to Freedom* (New York: Oxford University Press, 1977), 231.

11. Houston A. Baker Jr., *Modernism and the Harlem Renaissance* (Chicago: University of Chicago Press, 1987), 37, 63, 71, 79, 93. On the transformative influence of bohemian culture on the mainstream, see Christine Stansell, *American Moderns: Bohemian New York and the Creation of a New Century* (New York: Metropolitan, 2000).

12. For a critique of the influential core-periphery model of Immanuel Wallerstein, see Steve J. Stern, "Feudalism, Capitalism, and the World-System in the Perspective of Latin America and the Caribbean," *American Historical Review* 93 (October 1988): 829-72.

13. The reference, of course, is to the oft-cited and seldom equaled "thick description" of Clifford Geertz. See his book of essays, *The Interpretation of Cultures* (New York: Basic Books, 1973), 3-33. See also Jonathan Boyarin, ed., *The Ethnography of Reading* (Berkeley: University of California Press, 1992). Conversations with Wayne A. Wiegand reinforced our emphasis on the "site" of literary activity.

14. George E. Pozzetta, "The Italian Immigrant Press of New York City: The Early Years, 1880-1915," *Journal of Ethnic Studies* 1 (1973): 32-46.

15. United States Census Bureau, *Historical Statistics of the United States: Colonial Times to 1970*, pt. 1, no. 15 (Washington, D.C.: Bureau of the Census, 1975), 370.

16. See Carl F. Kaestle and Maris A. Vinovskis, *Education and Social Change in Nineteenth-Century Massachusetts* (New York: Cambridge University Press, 1980), chap. 5.

17. United States Census Bureau, *Compendium of the Tenth Census* (Washington, D.C.: Bureau of the Census, 1880), 1638-53. For whites, the 1880 census marshals asked people both whether they could read and whether they could write; for colored citizens they asked only whether they could write. These therefore are the comparable figures across racial groups. They may be taken, at best, as a crude measure of people's willingness to describe themselves as having low literacy skills.

18. Daniel Resnick and Lauren Resnick, "The Nature of Literacy: An Historical Exploration," *Harvard Educational Review* 43 (1977): 370-85.

19. Richard A. Schwarzlose, *The Rush to Institution: From 1865 to 1920*, vol. 2 of *The Nation's Newsbrokers* (Evanston: Northwestern University Press, 1990), chap. 3. On "ready-print" pages, see Richard B. Kielbowicz and Linda Lawson, "Protecting the Small-Town Press: Community, Social Policy and Postal Privileges, 1845-1970," *Canadian Review of American Studies* 19 (Spring 1988): 27.

20. S. N. D. North, *The Newspaper and Periodical Press* (Washington, D.C.: Census Office, Department of the Interior, 1884), 73. See David J. Russo, "The Origins of Local News in the U.S. Country Press, 1940s-1870s," *JM: Journalism Monographs*, no. 65 (1980).

21. For an interesting study of how, later in our period, one newspaper editor tutored his readers about Republican reform ideas and the national political culture, see Sallie Foreman Griffith, *Home Town News: William Allen White and the Emporia Gazette* (New York: Oxford University Press, 1989).

22. Census Bureau, *Compendium of the Tenth Census*, 1628-31.

23. *Publishers' Weekly* 17 (31 January 1880): 85-86; *American Bookseller* 9, no. 1 (1 January 1880): 1, 6-8; *Publishers' Weekly* 18 (11 September 1880): 304.

24. *Publishers' Weekly* 453 (18 September 1880): 382; 454 (25 September 1880): 409.

25. See Donald Sheehan, *This Was Publishing: A Chronicle of the Book Trade in the Gilded Age* (Bloomington: Indiana University Press, 1952), chap. 7.

26. United States Bureau of Education, *Public Libraries in the United States of America: Their History, Condition, and Management* (Washington, D.C.: Department of the Interior, 1876), 796.

27. We have no data on library provision by race for 1880. We may assume that there were very few libraries open to nonwhites in the South, in light of the fact that much later, in 1935 there were only seventy-five libraries in the South providing service to African Americans. About 18 percent of the black population lived in the areas served. Louis R. Wilson, *The Geography of Reading: A Study of the Distribution and Status of Libraries in the United States* (Chicago: University of Chicago Press, 1938), 423. For whites as well, provision varied widely by section. Controlling for population, figures from 1870 show that provision of libraries was three times as great in the Northeast as in the South. Haynes McMullen, *American Libraries before 1876* (Westport, Conn.: Greenwood Press, 2000), 42.

28. Hope Summerell Chamberlain, *This Was Home* (Chapel Hill: University of North Carolina Press, 1938), 143, 169; see also 84–94, 175–76. For more details on Hope Summerell, see Katherine Tinsley and Carl F. Kaestle, "Autobiographies and the History of Reading: The Meaning of Literacy in Individual Lives," in Kaestle et al., *Literacy in the United States: Readers and Reading since 1880* (New Haven: Yale University Press, 1991), 229, 235, 236.

29. Chamberlain, *This Was Home*, 195–96.

30. Barbara Sicherman, "Sense and Sensibility: A Case Study of Women's Reading in Late-Victorian America," in *Reading in America: Literature and Social History*, ed. Cathy N. Davidson (Baltimore: Johns Hopkins University Press, 1989), 201–25.

31. Ibid., 207–14; see also *Alice Hamilton: A Life in Letters*, ed. Barbara Sicherman (Cambridge, Mass.: Harvard University Press, 1984).

32. Helen Lefkowitz Horowitz, *The Power and Passion of M. Carey Thomas* (Urbana: University of Illinois Press, 1999), chaps. 1–9.

33. Among the key texts were Théophile Gautier, *Mademoiselle de Maupin texte complet, 1835* (Paris: Garnier Frères, 1966), and Algernon Charles Swinburne, *Laus Veneris and Other Poems and Ballads* (New York: G. W. Carleton & Company, 1880). See Helen Lefkowitz Horowitz, "'Nous Autres': Reading, Passion and the Creation of M. Carey Thomas," *Journal of American History* 79 (June 1992): 68–95.

34. Horowitz, *Power and Passion of M. Carey Thomas*, 134.

35. Emma Goldman, *Living My Life* (1934; repr., New York: AMA Press, 1970), 1–25.

36. James D. Corrothers, *In Spite of the Handicap: An Autobiography* (Freeport, N.Y.: George H. Doran, 1916), 20.

37. Ibid., 137–38.

38. Ida B. Wells, *Crusade for Justice: The Autobiography of Ida B. Wells*, ed. Alfreda M. Duster (Chicago: University of Chicago Press, 1970), 9, 22.

39. Ibid., 8, 9.

40. Ibid.

41. For 1880 the percentage of the adult population who read, respectively, newspapers, magazines, and books is a matter of conjecture. But data on various population groups within the United States from the late 1880s to the 1950s demonstrate that newspaper reading was more prevalent than the reading of magazines and books, especially among working-class groups. See Lawrence C. Stedman, Katherine Tinsley, and

Carl F. Kaestle, "Literacy as a Consumer Activity," in Kaestle et al., *Literacy in the United States*, 164.

42. Recent authors have expressed contrary views on Whittaker's guilt or innocence. Stephen Ambrose, *Duty, Honor, Country: A History of West Point* (Baltimore: Johns Hopkins University Press, 1966), 234-35, took the verdict at face value and declared Whittaker guilty; while John F. Marszalek Jr., *Court-Martial: A Black Man in America* (New York: Charles Scribner's Sons, 1972), 276, concluded that Whittaker's guilt is "improbable." A popular film treatment of the incident, *Assault at West Point: The Court Martial of Johnson Whittaker* (Showtime, Made-for-Television Movie, 1994), is sympathetic to Whittaker; and in 1995 President Bill Clinton presented to Whittaker's heirs a posthumous commission as a second lieutenant in the U.S. Army.

43. *Atlanta Constitution*, 29 April 1880. Thanks and credit are due to Dina Stephens, formerly a graduate student at the University of Wisconsin, for much searching and many insights about the newspapers involved in this analysis.

44. *Atlanta Constitution*, 8, 10, 11 April 1880.

45. *Atlanta Constitution*, 10 April 1880.

46. *Atlanta Constitution*, 4 June 1880.

47. *San Francisco Evening Bulletin*, 2, 3 April 1880.

48. *San Francisco Evening Bulletin*, 17, 22, 23, 27, 29, 30 April 1880.

49. *Ogle County Press*, 10 April 1880.

50. *Quincy Daily Whig*, 8, 15 April 1880.

51. For examples, see *New York Times*, 1, 4, 8, 25 April; 15, 22 June 1880.

52. *New York Times*, 8, 10, 11, 12, 13, 14, 15, 16, 17, 18, 20, 21, 23, 24, 27, 28, 29, 30 April; 1, 2, 4, 5, 8, 13, 14, 16, 18, 19, 29 May 1880.

53. *New York Times*, 30 May 1880.

54. John Tebbel, *The American Magazine: A Compact History* (New York: Hawthorn Books, 1969), 119.

55. *American Agriculturalist* 39, no. 5 (May 1880): 179-80.

56. *American Newspaper Annual and Directory* (Philadelphia: N. W. Ayer & Son, 1880), 415-19.

57. *Illustrated Catholic American* 1 (17 January 1880): 1-2.

58. Ibid., 2, 15.

59. *New York Weekly*, 23 February 1880.

60. Quentin Reynolds, *The Fiction Factory; or, From Pulp Row to Quality Street* (New York: Random House, 1955), 44.

61. Ibid., 46.

62. Ralph D. Gardner, "Street & Smith," in *Publishers for Mass Entertainment in Nineteenth Century America*, ed. Madeleine B. Stern (Boston: G. K. Hall, 1980), 282.

63. Horatio Alger, *The Young Explorer; or, Among the Sierras* (Philadelphia: Henry T. Coates & Company, 1880), vii-viii.

64. Ibid., 275. For references to Mexican Americans as "greasers" in dime novels of the period, see Charles M. Harvey, "The Dime Novel in American Life," *Atlantic Monthly* 100 (July 1907): 43.

65. Reynolds, *Fiction Factory*, 38-40.

66. W. H. Bishop, "Story-Paper Literature," *Atlantic Monthly* 44 (September 1879): 392.

67. Nan Enstad, *Ladies of Labor, Girls of Adventure: Working Women, Popular Culture, and Labor Politics at the Turn of the Century* (New York: Columbia University Press, 1999), 37–42.

68. See, for example, *Illustrated Catholic American* 1 (17 January 1880): 2.

69. Bishop, "Story-Paper Literature," 384, 389.

70. Michael Denning, *Mechanic Accents: Dime Novels and Working-Class Culture in America* (London: Verso, 1987).

71. On the realism of James and Howells, see Nancy Glazener, *Reading for Realism: The History of a U.S. Literary Institution, 1850–1910* (Durham: Duke University Press, 1997), and Amy Kaplan, *The Social Construction of American Realism* (Chicago: University of Chicago Press, 1988).

72. On James's "bizarre performance" in his novel *Confidence*, see R. W. B. Lewis, *The Jameses: A Family Narrative* (New York: Farrar, Straus & Giroux, 1991), 308–9.

73. *New York Post*, quoted in an advertisement in *Publishers' Weekly* 80 (28 August 1880): 226.

74. On *A Tramp Abroad*, and Twain's struggles with *Huckleberry Finn*, see Justin Kaplan, *Mr. Clemens and Mark Twain: A Biography* (New York: Simon & Schuster, 1966), 217.

75. *Atlantic Monthly* 45 (May 1880): 693–99; *American Bookseller* 9 (1 January 1880): 8.

76. Henry Irving Block, "The Century, 1867–1886," in *The Century, 1847–1946*, ed. Geoffrey Parsons (New York: Century Association, 1947), 27.

77. Ibid., 38, quoting a memoir by James Herbert Morse, elected in 1877.

78. "The Holmes Breakfast," suppl., *Atlantic Monthly* 45 (February 1880): 3.

79. George Haven Putnam, *Memories of a Publisher, 1865–1915* (New York: G. P. Putnam's Sons, 1915), 73–75.

80. The American publication of Gaboriau's work occurred several years after their original publication in France; Gaboriau died in 1873. For Gaboriau's influence on Green, see Kathleen Woodward, "Anna Katharine Green," *Bookman* 70, no. 168 (October 1929): 168–70. The ad, from Estes and Lauriat of Boston, appeared in the *Dial*, no. 45 (June 1880), as well as in *Publishers' Weekly* 17 (1 May 1880), wherein the "prince" remark occurs.

81. *Nation* 31 (2 September 1880): 176.

82. *Publishers' Weekly* 17 (3 January 1880): 3. On the romanticization of white reconciliation and its disastrous effects on African Americans, see David Blight, *Race and Reunion: The Civil War in American Memory* (Cambridge, Mass.: Harvard University Press, 2001).

83. *Publishers' Weekly* 18 (7 August 1880): 164; 18 (21 August 1880): 212–13, 215.

84. *Publishers' Weekly* 17 (31 January 1880); 17 (20 March 1880): 277.

85. Canon Farrar, *The Life of Christ* (New York: E. P. Dutton, 1875), preface.

86. *Publishers' Weekly* 17 (20, 27 March, 17 April 1880); 18 (23 October 1880).

87. See, for example, *Publishers' Weekly* 17 (17 January 1880); 17 (24 January 1880): 42; 17 (29 May 1880): 64; 18 (3 July 1880); *American Bookseller* 9 (15 January, 2 February 1880).

88. *Nation* 46 (22 January 1880): 65.

89. *American Bookseller* 10 (2 August 1880): 90.

90. Samuel Green, "Sensational Fiction," *Library Journal* 4 (September–October 1879): 345–54.

91. American Library Association, Cooperation Committee, "Report on Exclusion," *Library Journal* 7 (1882): 28; I. L. Beardsley, "Fiction in Libraries," *Library Journal* 7 (July-August 1882): 176-76; Esther J. Carrier, *Fiction in Public Libraries, 1876–1900* (New York: Scarecrow Press, 1965).

92. William F. Poole, Discussion of Peter Cowell's paper, "On the Admission of Fiction in Free Public Libraries," *Library Journal* 2 (November-December, 1877): 7; Justin Winsor, "Reading in Popular Libraries," in United States Bureau of Education, *Public Libraries in the United States*, pt. 1, 431-33.

Section II. The Publishing Trades: Introduction

1. Janice A. Radway, *A Feeling for Books: The Book-of-the-Month Club, Literary Taste, and Middle-Class Desire* (Chapel Hill: University of North Carolina Press, 1997), 166-76.

2. Ibid.

CHAPTER 3
The Rise of a National Book Trade System in the United States

1. *Publishers' Weekly* 57 (6 January 1900): 8-9.

2. *Publishers' Weekly* 17 (3 January 1880): 6.

3. *Historical Statistics of the United States: Colonial Times to 1957* (Washington, D.C.: Bureau of the Census, 1960), 7-9, 419, 499; Hellmut Lehmann-Haupt, Lawrence C. Wroth, and Rollo G. Silver, *The Book in America: A History of the Making and Selling of Books in the United States*, 2nd ed. (New York: R. R. Bowker, 1951), 321.

4. In Lehmann-Haupt, Wroth, and Silver, *The Book in America*, see especially the essay by Lehmann-Haupt, "Book Production and Distribution from 1860 to the Present Day," 139-411. Donald Sheehan, *This Was Publishing: A Chronicle of the Book Trade in the Gilded Age* (Bloomington: Indiana University Press, 1952), and John Tebbel, *A History of Book Publishing in the United States*, vol. 2 (New York: R. R. Bowker, 1975) are the best general histories of the publishing trade during this period.

5. Eugene Exman, *The House of Harper: One Hundred and Fifty Years of Publishing* (New York: Harper & Row, 1967), 172-73, 180-89; Peter Lyon, *Success Story: The Life and Times of S. S. McClure* (New York: Charles Scribner's Sons, 1963), 159-74; Tebbel, *History of Book Publishing in the United States*, 2:195-201.

6. "Descriptive List of the Bibliographical Publications Issued by the Office of 'The Publishers' Weekly,'" in Adolf Growoll, *The Profession of Bookselling: A Handbook of Practical Hints for the Apprentice and Bookseller* (New York: Office of Publishers' Weekly, 1893-1913), [59]-65; Adolf Growoll, *Book Trade Bibliography in the United States in XIXth Century* (New York: Dibdin Club, 1898).

7. *A Portrait Catalogue of the Books Published by Houghton, Mifflin and Company* (Boston: Houghton, Mifflin, 1905-6), 176-214, and *Harper & Brothers' Descriptive List of Their Publications, with Trade-List Prices* (New York: Harper & Bros., 1888).

8. Sheehan, *This Was Publishing*, 41-45; see also chapter 6 by Ohmann in this volume.

9. Michael Winship, "Getting the Books Out: Trade Sales, Parcel Sales, and Book Fairs in the Nineteenth-Century United States," in *Getting the Books Out: Papers of the Chicago Conference on the Book in Nineteenth-Century America*, ed. Michael Hackenberg (Washington, D.C.: Center for the Book, Library of Congress, 1987), 4-25.

10. Sheehan, *This Was Publishing*, 158-68.

11. It is difficult to recreate the nature of the retail bookshop in this period; the description given in this paragraph is based chiefly on Growoll, *The Profession of Bookselling*.

12. Sheehan, *This Was Publishing*, 224-34; Tebbel, *History of Book Publishing in the United States*, 2:63-64, 67, 69-70, 78-79, 123-30.

13. Sheehan, *This Was Publishing*, 189.

14. Samuel Swett Green, *The Public Library Movement in the United States, 1853-1893* (Boston: Boston Book Co., 1913); William S. Learned, *The American Public Library and the Diffusion of Knowledge* (New York: Harcourt, Brace, 1924). See also Deanna B. Marcum, "The Rural Public Library in America at the Turn of the Century," and Joanne E. Passet, "Reaching the Rural Reader: Traveling Libraries in America, 1892-1920," in *Reading & Libraries*, Proceedings of Library History Seminar VIII, 9-11 May 1990, Bloomington, Indiana, ed. Donald G. Davis Jr. (Austin: University of Texas, 1991), 87-118.

15. For information on subscription publishing, see Robert Sterling Yard, *The Publisher* (Boston: Houghton Mifflin, 1913), 89-[138]; F. E. Compton, "Subscription Books," in Fourth of the *R. R. Bowker Memorial Lectures* (New York: New York Public Library, 1939), [56]-78; Tebbel, *History of Book Publishing in the United States*, 2:511-34; Sheehan, *This Was Publishing*, 189-95; Keith Arbour, *Canvassing Books, Sample Books, and Subscription Publishers' Ephemera, 1833-1951, in the Collection of Michael Zinman* (Ardsley, N.Y.: Haydn Foundation, 1996).

16. Walter A. Friedman, "Selling Ulysses S. Grant," in *Birth of a Salesman: The Transformation of Selling in America* (Cambridge, Mass.: Harvard University Press, 2001), 34-55. Tebbel, *History of Book Publishing in the United States*, 2:525. In 1887 Mark Twain, in an interesting comparison of sales figures between subscription publishing and trade publishing, claimed that the aggregate sales of the ten works that he had written and published by subscription were 618,000 (of which *Innocents Abroad* [1869] accounted for 160,000), while the aggregate sales of the two that he had published in the trade were only 16,000; see *Mark Twain's Letters to His Publishers, 1867-1894*, ed. Hamlin Hill (Berkeley: University of California Press, 1967), 232-35.

17. A small number of memoirs (often fictionalized) by subscription book agents were published and provided evidence of their methods; see Arbour, *Canvassing Books*, xii-xiii, n. 4.

18. "New Library Series American Authors" prospectus (Boston: Houghton Mifflin, n.d.), in possession of the author; Yard, *The Publisher*, 100-102.

19. Sheehan, *This Was Publishing*, 195-98. The distribution of books through the mails and private express companies became even more important in the next century with the rise of book clubs in the 1920s and 1930s and Amazon.com and other Internet distributors later in the century.

20. Tebbel, *History of Book Publishing in the United States*, 2:481-511; Raymond Howard

Shove, *Cheap Book Production in the United States, 1870 to 1891* (Urbana: University of Illinois Library, 1937).

21. Tebbel, *History of Book Publishing*, 2:539–59.

22. Ibid., 559–87; Sheehan, *This Was Publishing*, 45–49, 206–11.

23. Lehmann-Haupt, Wroth, and Silver, *The Book in America*, pp. 322–27; Tebbel, *History of Book Publishing in the United States*, 2:402–408, 417–18, 430–36.

24. Lehmann-Haupt, Wroth, and Silver, *Book in America*, 201–11; Tebbel, *History of Book Publishing in the United States*, 2:634–44; Sheehan, *This Was Publishing*, 56–74, 213–18. See also *The Question of Copyright*, comp. George Haven Putnam (New York: G. P. Putnam's Sons, 1891); Aubert J. Clark, *The Movement for International Copyright in Nineteenth Century America* (Washington, D.C.: Catholic University of America Press, 1960), 118–99.

25. Tebbel, *History of Book Publishing in the United States*, 2:130–49; Sheehan, *This Was Publishing*, 74–78; James Hepburn, *The Author's Empty Purse and the Rise of the Literary Agent* (London: Oxford University Press, 1968); James L. W. West III, *American Authors and the Literary Marketplace since 1900* (Philadelphia: University of Pennsylvania Press, 1988), [77]–102.

26. Michael Winship, "Anglo-American Literary Culture and the Transatlantic Book Trade in the Nineteenth Century," in *Reciprocal Influences: Literary Production, Distribution, and Consumption in America*, ed. Steven Fink and Susan S. Williams (Columbus: Ohio State University Press, 1999), 98–122, discusses the early years of this development.

27. For a discussion of the initial stages of the industrialization of American book production, see my "Manufacturing and Book Production" in *The Industrial Book, 1840–1880*, ed. Scott E. Casper, Jeffrey D. Groves, Stephen W. Nissenbaum, and Michael Winship, vol. 3 of *A History of the Book in America* (Chapel Hill: University of North Carolina Press, 2007), 40–69.

28. [W. W. Pasko], *American Dictionary of Printing and Bookmaking* (New York: H. Lockwood & Co., 1894), 376.

29. Lucien Alphonse LeGros and John Cameron Grant, *Typographical Printing-Surfaces* (London: Longmans, Green & Co., 1916), 429.

30. "Standardization," in E. J. Labarre, *Encyclopædia of Paper and Paper-Making*, 2nd ed., rev. and enl. (Amsterdam: Swets & Zeitlinger, 1952), 282–90.

CHAPTER 4
The Expansion of the National Book Trade System

1. See Bennett Cerf, *At Random: The Reminiscences of Bennett Cerf* (New York: Random House, 1977), 44–55.

2. Charles A. Madison, "Simon and Schuster," in Madison, *Book Publishing in America* (New York: McGraw-Hill, 1966), 346–47.

3. Charles A. Madison, "Jews in American Publishing," *Chicago Jewish Forum* 26 (Summer 1968): 282–87; Kenneth A. Lohf, "Publishers and Agents: The Columbia Connection," in *Dictionary of Literary Biography Yearbook, 1987* (Detroit: Gale Research, 1987), 36–46.

4. O. H. Cheney, *Economic Survey of the Book Industry, 1930–1931* (1931; repr., New York: R. R. Bowker, 1960).

5. Cerf, *At Random*, 77.

6. See Walker Gilmer, *Horace Liveright: Publisher of the Twenties* (New York: David Lewis, 1970); Tom Dardis, *Firebrand: The Life of Horace Liveright* (New York: Random House, 1995).

7. William Jovanovich, *Now Barabbas* (New York: Harper & Row, 1964), 123.

8. Madison, "The Paperback Explosion," in Madison, *Book Publishing in America*, 548; see also Daniel J. Miller, *Books Go to War: Armed Services Editions in World War II* (Charlottesville, Va.: Book Arts Press, 1996).

9. Joan Shelley Rubin, *The Making of Middlebrow Culture* (Chapel Hill: University of North Carolina Press, 1992); Janice A. Radway, *A Feeling for Books: The Book-of-the-Month Club, Literary Taste, and Middle-Class Desire* (Chapel Hill: University of North Carolina Press, 1997).

10. The restored text of *American Hunger* appeared first in 1991 from the Library of America and is published now in softcover by HarperCollins. See Arnold Rampersad, "Too Honest for His Own Time," *New York Times Book Review*, 29 December 1991, 3; James W. Tuttleton, "The Problematic Texts of Richard Wright," *Hudson Review* 45 (Summer 1992): 261–71.

11. Madison, "The Paperback Explosion," in Madison, *Book Publishing in America*, 547–56; Frank L. Schick, *The Paperbound Book in America* (New York: R. R. Bowker, 1958); Thomas L. Bonn, *Under Cover: An Illustrated History of American Mass-Market Paperbacks* (New York: Penguin, 1982).

12. Quoted in Robert Dahlin, "Men (and Women) Who Made a Revolution," *Publishers Weekly* 244 (July 1997): 52.

13. Ibid.

14. Internal memorandum, New American Library, 14 May 1951. Copy in Faulkner files, Random House collection, Butler Library, Columbia University, New York.

15. Frank Norris, "Fiction Writing as a Business," in *The Responsibilities of the Novelist* (New York: Doubleday, Page & Co., 1903), 164.

16. James L. W. West III, "The Agent," in *American Authors and the Literary Marketplace since 1900* (Philadelphia: University of Pennsylvania Press, 1988), 77–102. For a history of the literary agent in Great Britain, see James Hepburn, *The Author's Empty Purse and the Rise of the Literary Agent* (London: Oxford University Press, 1968).

17. See Frederick Lewis Allen, *Paul Revere Reynolds* (New York: privately published, 1944).

CHAPTER 5
Copyright in Transition

1. Eaton S. Drone, *A Treatise on the Law of Property in Intellectual Productions in Great Britain and the United States, Embracing Copyright in Works of Literature and Art, and Playwright in Dramatic and Musical Compositions* (Boston: Little, Brown & Co., 1879); Horace G. Ball, *The Law of Copyright and Literary Property* (Albany, N.Y.: Banks & Co. and Matthew Bender & Co., 1944).

2. The term "commodity-text" is borrowed from N. N. Feltes, *Modes of Production of Victo-*

rian Novels (Chicago: University of Chicago Press, 1986). See his definition of this important concept at 7–8.

3. Martha Woodmansee, "The Genius and the Copyright," *Eighteenth-Century Studies* 17, no. 4 (1984): 425–48; reprinted in *The Author, Art, and the Market: Rereading the History of Aesthetics* (New York: Columbia University Press, 1994), 34–55.

4. See Alvin Kernan, *Samuel Johnson and the Impact of Print* (Princeton: Princeton University Press, 1987); of the 1710 Statue of Anne, the first example of copyright legislation, Kernan writes that "it seems a likely inference that while it was the booksellers who were pushing the issue, they were using the author's rights as a blind for their own interests" (99). For the persistence of this pattern, see Martha Woodmansee, "The Cultural Work of Copyright: Legislating Authorship in Britain, 1837–1842," in *Law and the Domains of Culture*, ed. Austin Sarat and Thomas Kearns (Ann Arbor: University of Michigan Press, 1998), 65–96, and Peter Jaszi, "Toward a Theory of Copyright: The Metamorphoses of 'Authorship,'" *Duke Law Journal* 1991: 455–502.

5. On the Lockean position as a "natural law justification for recognizing property rights in works of authorship" enabling authors to reap the fruits of their creations, see Craig Joyce, Marshall Leaffer, Peter Jaszi, and Tyler Ochoa, *Copyright Law*, 7th ed. (New York: LEXIS Publishing, 2006), and Mark Rose, *Authors and Owners: The Invention of Copyright* (Cambridge, Mass.: Harvard University Press, 1993). Cathy Davidson relates Lockean individualism, the developing novel form, and the coming of copyright in eighteenth-century America. See *Revolution and the Word: The Rise of the Novel in America* (New York: Oxford University Press, 1986).

6. For an argument that in the earlier nineteenth century the Lockean position in the United States was subordinated to a "republican" ideology of print in which "private" ownership of a text is figured as a temporary alienation of public property, see Meredith McGill, "The Matter of the Text: Commerce, Print Culture, and the Authority of the State in American Copyright Law," *American Literary History* 9 (1997): 21–59. For an account that recasts this republican view as expressing a "utilitarian" concern with promoting the dissemination of knowledge, see Grantland S. Rice, *The Transformation of Authorship in America* (Chicago: University of Chicago Press, 1997). In addition, Rice acknowledges the influence of the Lockean form of "possessive individualism" (in C. B. MacPherson's terminology) on copyright developments.

7. For an account of such an enterprise, a "production factory for series books," see Deidre Johnson, *Edward Stratemeyer and the Stratemeyer Syndicate* (New York: Twayne, 1993).

8. Drone, *A Treatise on the Law of Property in Intellectual Productions*, 257.

9. Ibid., 259.

10. *Picture Music v. Bourne, Inc.*, 457 F.2d 1213 (2d Cir.), *cert. denied*, 409 U.S. 997 (1972), 1214. See the discussion of this case in Jaszi, "Metamorphoses," 458–59.

11. Ball, *Law of Copyright*, 479–80.

12. Richard C. DeWolf, *An Outline of Copyright Law* (Boston: John W. Luce & Co., 1925), 24–25.

13. The "work for hire" made another strategic appearance in the section of the 1909 act dealing with copyright renewal. The prior statute had granted the author (if alive), or the au-

thor's surviving spouse or children, the right to claim a fourteen-year renewal term of copyright at the conclusion of the initial twenty-eight-year term. In section 23 of the 1909 act, the renewal term was extended to twenty-eight years, and the right of renewal was allocated not to the author but to the proprietor (i.e., the owner, by operation of the statute, assignment, or otherwise) in the case of "a work copyrighted by . . . an employer for whom such work is made for hire." The effect was to assure that individual employed creators would be barred from asserting any claims to renewal of copyright in their literary and artistic productions.

14. See Bourge Varmer, "Works Made for Hire and on Commission," no. 13 in *Copyright Law Revision, Studies Prepared for the Senate Judiciary Subcomm. on Patents, Trademarks and Copyrights*, 86th Cong., 2nd sess., 123, 128 (Comm. Print, 1962). Even the authors' organizations that testified on other issues related to the legislation were silent on the "work-for-hire" provisions.

15. 189 F. 215 (C.C. M.D. Pa. 1911).

16. For another instance, see *Tobani v. Carl Fisher, Inc.*, 98 F.2d 57 (2d. Cir. 1938), at 58–59, dealing with rights in the work of a salaried musical arranger.

17. During this period, in contrast to their treatment of the works of salaried employees, courts continued to regard the right to claim copyright in specially commissioned works by "freelance" creators as a matter to be determined on a case-by-case basis, according to express or implied contractual understanding between the parties to the commission. By the 1960s and 70s, however, the Romantic conception of authorship had been mobilized to sweep increasing numbers of commissioned works into the ambit of the work-for-hire doctrine. See Jaszi, "Metamorphoses," 488–89.

18. For a good discussion of these techniques for getting around the law, and some of the pitfalls they entailed, see Simon Nowell-Smith, *International Copyright Law and the Publisher in the Reign of Queen Victoria* (Oxford: Oxford University Press, 1969), 70–72.

19. In the case of the most popular British authors, American houses also competed for the privilege of being designated as their "official" or "authorized" publishers, laying out sometimes considerable sums (like Harper's $27,000 payment to Charles Dickens in 1867) to enjoy this designation and to receive the British plates of their books. See John Tebbel, *Between Covers: The Rise and Transformation of American Book Publishing* (New York: Oxford University Press, 1987), 89. Significantly, however, these publishers had no legal right to complain (any more than did the authors by whom they were designated) about the activities of other firms that competed with them in the market for American reprints of British books.

20. Nowell-Smith, *International Copyright Law*, 69–70.

21. Ball, *Law of Copyright*, 216, 221. The first such proclamation of reciprocity was made, in favor of Belgium, France, Great Britain and her possessions, and Switzerland, on 1 July 1891. By 1905 additional proclamations had been made in favor of Germany, Italy, Denmark, Portugal, Spain, Mexico, Chile, Costa Rica, the Netherlands and possessions, Cuba, and Norway. See *Copyright Enactments of the United States: 1783–1906*, no. 3 (Washington, D.C.: Government Printing Office, 1906), 87–98.

22. Drone, *A Treatise on the Law of Property in Intellectual Productions*, 92–93. Drone discounts contemporary criticisms of international copyright as a likely "hindrance to the diffusion of knowledge. . . ." Ibid., 94.

23. Ibid., 95–96.

24. For the efforts of British authors (and publishers), including a fascinating account of organized efforts to bribe the American Congress to legislate in their favor, see James J. Barnes, *Authors, Publishers and Politicians: The Quest for an Anglo-American Copyright Agreement, 1815–1854* (Columbus: Ohio State University Press, 1974); for early lobbying efforts on behalf of American authors, see Aubert J. Clark, *The Movement for International Copyright in Nineteenth Century America* (Washington, D.C.: Catholic University of America Press, 1960), 70–77, which provides a description of the formation (in 1843) of the American Copyright Club, consisting of "about twenty-five men, chiefly well-known members of the New York *literati*, and about 125 'associate members' including every prominent author of the day, as well as a few well-known outsiders." Ibid., 70.

25. The United States had participated in some of the preliminary work leading up to the Berne Convention, but it did not sign or ratify the treaty, in large part due to the changes in the American law of copyright formalities it would have required; indeed, the United States would not join the Berne Union until 1989. For a discussion of the role that the Romantic conception of the author played in shaping the Berne Convention, see Peter Jaszi and Martha Woodmansee, "The Ethical Reaches of Authorship," *South Atlantic Quarterly* 95 (Fall 1996): 947–77.

26. George Haven Putnam's father, George Palmer Putnam, had addressed his first petition on the subject to Congress in 1843, with a respectable, but not overwhelming, list of cosignatories from the American publishing industry. See Clark, *The Movement for International Copyright in Nineteenth Century America*, 76. Some major firms, including Harper and Brothers, were conspicuous by their absence.

27. Representatives of the American Publishers' Copyright League to the Conference Committee formed in 1887 with the Authors' Copyright League included William H. and W. W. Appleton, George Haven Putnam, Charles Scribner, Joseph W. Harper, A. D. F. Randolph, Henry O. Houghton, Henry Holt, Craig Lippincott, and Dana Estes. In turn, some of the representatives of the Authors League, such as R. R. Bowker, seem to have been publishers in author's clothing. Ibid., 150. Publishers also took the initiative in organizing auxiliary branches of mixed membership in important cities, such as Chicago and Boston. Ibid., 152.

28. The activities of cheap reprint publishers undercut the "trade courtesy" that had developed among leading publishers "in lieu of international copyright," pursuant to which those publishers respected the arrangements between foreign authors and U.S. firms (described in note 19). See ibid., 95.

29. Stephen P. Ladas, *The International Protection of Literary and Artistic Property*, 2 vols. (New York: Macmillan, 1938), 1:26.

30. See Clark, *The Movement for International Copyright in Nineteenth Century America*, 100–101.

31. The advantages of the original clause for the typographical trades are obvious, because under it American publishers were effectively prevented from importing copies printed abroad and from printing U.S. editions from type set overseas. The advantages to the publishers themselves were less apparent, although some at the time believed that it represented a part of a design to bring the manufacture of books for the entire English-speaking world under the control of American firms. See Nowell-Smith, *International Copyright Law*, 69.

Still less clear is what effect the clause had on the cost of books in the American market. After 1904 Congress provided for temporary or *ad interim* protection of foreign works first published abroad, extendable to the full term of copyright upon compliance with the requirements of the Manufacturing Clause. The clause was extended in 1909 to require domestic printing and binding as well as typesetting. Thereafter, it was gradually relaxed, ultimately surviving in American law until July 1986.

32. See 17 U.S.C. Sec. 106(3).

33. 23 Fed. Cas. 201 (C.C.E.D.Pa. 1853) (No. 13514).

34. The translation in question, that of Adolf Strodtmann, was in competition with an inferior authorized translation by Hugo Rudolph Hutten. The German press in the United States and abroad was outraged by Stowe's attempt to force such an inadequate version on the German-reading public. See Robert E. Cazden, *A Social History of the German Book Trade in America to the Civil War* (Columbia, S.C.: Camden House, 1984), 350-51.

35. 23 Fed. Cas. 208.

36. Drone, *A Treatise on the Law of Property in Intellectual Productions*, 451-52. Drone also points out—correctly enough—that *Stowe v. Thomas* was something of an anachronism. British courts, at least, had abandoned this narrow view of the scope of copyright by the 1830s. For developments in the British case law, and their links to the Romantic conception of authorship, see Benjamin Kaplan, *An Unhurried View of Copyright* (New York: Columbia University Press, 1967), 19-25.

37. The same period saw the increasing use of "all-rights" contracts, which gave publishers control over various subsidiary rights. See Philip Wittenberg, *The Protection and Marketing of Literary Property* (New York: Julian Messner, 1937), 218.

38. Ball, *Law of Copyright*, 338-40.

39. 13 F. Cas. 910 (C.C.S.D.N.Y. 1850) (No. 7,437). The case involved alleged infringement of a musical composition entitled "The Serious Family Polka." In the pleadings, the defendants denied that they "have published or are engaged in selling any polka which is similar in plan or matter to, or is a substantial copy of that published by the plaintiff." Ball, *Law of Copyright*, 913.

40. See, for example, *Springer Lithographing Co. v. Falk*, 59 F. 707 (2d Cir. 1894), a case involving alleged infringement of a copyrighted photograph, in which the trial court is found to have correctly charged the jury that the only question before it was "whether these lithographs are copies or substantial copies, or whether the ideas, pose, and characteristics of the original photograph were substantially reproduced by the defendant. It is not necessary that the copies should be Chinese copies. You will observe that the statute says: 'If the infringer shall copy, either in whole or in part, or by varying the main design with intent to evade the law.' As I said, it is not necessary that the copies should be exact copies. It is necessary that the infringer should appropriate a substantial portion of the distinctive ideas and characteristic features of the original photograph to make up its lithographs." Ibid., 712.

41. 166 F. 589 (C.C.S.D.N.Y. 1908).

42. Ibid., 592.

43. See, for example, *Sid & Marty Krofft Televisions Prods., Inc. v. McDonald's Corp*, 562 F.2d 1157 (9th Cir. 1977). For the background of the case, see David Martindale, *Pufnstuf & Other Stuff* (Los Angeles: Renaissance Books, 1998), 74-75.

CHAPTER 6
Diverging Paths: Books and Magazines in the Transition to Corporate Capitalism

1. Richard Ohmann, *Selling Culture: Magazines, Markets, and Class at the Turn of the Century* (London: Verso, 1996). See the bibliographical essay for other sources.

2. Newspaper publishing went through a similar but more uneven change at about the same time; see Richard L. Kaplan, chapter 7 in this volume.

3. Gerald R. Wolfe, *The House of Appleton* (Metuchen, N.J.: Scarecrow Press, 1981), 27–30.

4. On the pre-1880 origins of these monthlies, see Eric Lupfer, "The Business of American Magazines," in *The Industrial Book, 1840–1880*, ed. Scott E. Casper, Jeffrey D. Groves, Stephen W. Nissenbaum, and Michael Winship, vol. 3 of *A History of the Book in America* (Chapel Hill: University of North Carolina Press, 2007), 248–58.

5. Wolfe, *The House of Appleton*, 175–76. On Scribner, see Donald Sheehan, *This Was Publishing: A Chronicle of the Book Trade in the Gilded Age* (Bloomington: Indiana University Press, 1952), 42–43. For Houghton Mifflin's experience, see Ellen B. Ballou, *The Building of the House: Houghton Mifflin's Formative Years* (Boston: Houghton Mifflin, 1970), 366. For Mifflin's letter to F. Hopkinson Smith in 1896, see p. 429. For the views of Scudder and Perry and for other information on Houghton Mifflin and the *Atlantic*, see pp. 444, 467, 295, 425, 433.

6. Quoted from the *Riverside Bulletin*, 1 September 1873, in Ballou, *Building of the House*, 350. On the *Atlantic* as prestigious money loser, see Ballou, 452–53. On *Scribner's* in the nineties, see Roger Burlingame, *Of Making Many Books: A Hundred Years of Reading, Writing and Publishing* (New York: Charles Scribner's Sons, 1946), 43.

7. Much of this information is from John Tebbel, *A History of Book Publishing in the United States*, vol. 2 (New York: R. R. Bowker, 1975).

8. See Peter Lyon, "The Syndicate-1884-1893," pt. 2 in *Success Story: The Life and Times of S. S. McClure* (Deland, Fla.: Everett-Edwards, 1967), 51–110.

9. See Sheehan, *This Was Publishing*, 190–95.

10. Janice A. Radway, *A Feeling for Books: The Book-of-the-Month Club, Literary Taste, and Middle-Class Desire* (Chapel Hill: University of North Carolina Press, 1997), 135; Carl F. Kaestle and Janice A. Radway, chapter 1 in this volume.

11. I abbreviate these ideas (and take the phrase "gentlemanly exchange") from Christopher P. Wilson, "The Rhetoric of Consumption: Mass-Market Magazines and the Demise of the Gentle Reader, 1880–1920," in *The Culture of Consumption: Critical Essays in American History, 1880–1980*, ed. Richard Wightman Fox and T. J. Jackson Lears (New York: Pantheon, 1983), 39–64.

12. Eugene Exman, *The House of Harper: One Hundred and Fifty Years of Publishing* (New York: Harper & Row, 1967), 180. For other information in this paragraph, see Tebbel, *History of Book Publishing in the United States*, 2:47, 149, and Ballou, *Building of the House*, 419, 445.

13. The standard work on this process is Alfred D. Chandler Jr., *The Visible Hand: The Managerial Revolution in American Business* (Cambridge, Mass.: Harvard University Press, 1977). See my *Selling Culture* for many details and references.

14. Sheehan, *This Was Publishing*, 21-22. See Michael Winship's ampler and somewhat different account of the book business, chapter 3 in this volume.

15. Sheehan, *This Was Publishing*, 224-37.

16. Ballou, *Building of the House*, 425-27. I rely for the picture drawn in this paragraph chiefly on Sheehan's chapter, "The Assault on the Consumer," and on Tebbel, *History of Book Publishing in the United States*, 2:150-70. The data are soft, at best.

17. Tebbel, *History of Book Publishing in the United States*, 2:153. For a further discussion of book advertising, see Ellen Gruber Garvey, chapter 10 in this volume.

18. Sheehan, *This Was Publishing*, 19-23.

CHAPTER 7
From Partisanship to Professionalism:
The Transformation of the Daily Press

1. Ted Smythe, "The Press and Industrial America," in *The Media in America*, ed. James Stovall, James Startt, and William Sloan (Scottsdale: Publishing Horizons, 1993).

2. See Thomas J. Leonard, *News for All: America's Coming-of-Age with the Press* (New York: Oxford University Press, 1995).

3. See Hazel Dickens Garcia, *Journalistic Standards in Nineteenth-Century America* (Madison: University of Wisconsin Press, 1989), 49; Michael McGerr, *The Decline of Popular Politics: The American North, 1865-928* (New York: Oxford University Press, 1986), 115-16.

4. See W. A. Swanberg, *Pulitzer* (New York: Scribners, 1967), 129-30.

5. McGerr, *Decline of Popular Politics*, 10-11, chap. 2; Michael Schudson, *The Good Citizen: A History of American Civic Life* (New York: Free Press, 1998), chaps. 3-4.

6. See the measure of partisan support in Detroit newspaper editorials in Richard Kaplan, "The American Press and Political Community: Reporting in Detroit, 1865-1920," *Media, Culture and Society* 19 (July 1997): 331-55.

7. Richard Kaplan, "Market Segmentation and Partisanship in the Detroit Press, 1865-1900: The Economics of Newspaper Politics," *American Journalism* 10 (1993): 84-101. On networks, see Richard L. Rubin, *Press, Party and Presidency* (New York: W. W. Norton, 1981), 23, 31, 34.

8. Lawrence Goodwyn, *The Populist Moment* (New York: Oxford University Press, 1978); Jean Folkerts, "The Functions of the Reform Press," *Journalism History* 12 (1985): 22-25; Alexander Saxton, *The Indispensable Enemy: Labor and the Anti-Chinese Movement in California* (Berkeley: University of California Press, 1971).

9. Harry Baehr Jr., *The New York Tribune since the Civil War* (New York: Octagon Books, 1972), 179-82; Richard Slotkin, *The Fatal Environment* (New York: Atheneum, 1985), 478-84; Richard Kaplan, "The Economics of Popular Journalism in the Gilded Age," *Journalism History* 22 (Summer 1995): 65-75; David Nord, "The Business Values of American Newspapers: The Nineteenth Century Watershed in Chicago," *Journalism Quarterly* 61 (Summer 1984): 363-66.

10. Edwin L. Godkin, *Unforeseen Tendencies of Democracy* (Westminster, U.K.: Archibald Constable & Co., 1898), 66-67, 76.

11. Michael Schudson, "The Politics of Narrative Form: The Emergence of News Conventions in Print and Television," *Daedalus* 111 (Fall 1982): 107-8; Michael Rogin, *McCarthy and the Intellectuals* (Cambridge, Mass.: MIT Press, 1967), 201-3; Lawrence Levine's *Highbrow/Lowbrow: The Emergence of Cultural Hierarchy in America* (Cambridge, Mass.: Harvard University Press, 1988) presents the most far-reaching account of this change.

12. E. G. Henry Watterson, "The Personal Equation in Journalism," and Francis Leupp, "The Waning Power of the Press," both in *The Profession of Journalism*, ed. Willard Bleyer (Boston: Atlantic Monthly, 1918), 97-111; 30-51.

13. Albert Britt, *Ellen Browning Scripps: Journalist and Idealist* (Oxford: Oxford University Press for Scripps College, 1960), 29, 61; Edward W. Scripps, *I Protest: Selected Disquisitions of E. W. Scripps*, ed. Oliver Knight (Madison: University of Wisconsin Press, 1966), 316-17.

14. Baehr, *The New York Tribune*, 234. Similar changes in England are known as "the Northcliffe Revolution." See Colin Seymour-Ure, *The Press, Politics and the Public* (London: Methuen, 1968), 22, 32, 98.

15. Richard Ohmann, "Where Did Mass Culture Come From? The Case of Magazines," *Berkshire Review* 16 (1981): 89-90; James D. Norris, *Advertising and the Transformation of American Society, 1865-1920* (New York: Greenwood Press, 1990), 31, 35-37.

16. On paper costs, see David C. Smith, "Wood Pulp and Newspapers, 1867-1900," *Business History Review* 4 (1964): 328-45.

17. Jon Udell, *Economics of the American Press* (New York: Hastings House, 1978), 118-25.

18. James E. Scripps, untitled essay beginning "In April 1871, . . ." [1875] in "James E. Scripps Letters, etc. 1906-7," Cranbrook Archives, Cranbrook, Michigan. Also, "Advertising then [1884] was only a modest source of income. Newspapers were expected to make a small profit over the cost of paper and printing . . . but a reduction in [newspaper] price hurt" (Swanberg, *Pulitzer*, 80).

19. Arthur Pound, *The Only Thing Worth Finding: The Life and Legacies of George Gough Booth* (Detroit: Wayne State University Press, 1964), 98.

20. Quoted in Scripps, *I Protest*, 53. See also R. Kaplan, "The Economics of Popular Journalism."

21. Alfred M. Lee, *The Daily Newspaper in America* (New York: Macmillan, 1937), 65-67, 82, 271, 278-79. And see Smith, "Wood Pulp and Newspapers," 341-43.

22. U.S. census figures as cited in Lee, *The Daily Newspaper*. The five cities are San Francisco, Chicago, Philadelphia, Cleveland, and Boston. On growth and circulation in New York City, see pp. 731-32, 778. For figures on Detroit, see R. Kaplan, "The Economics of Popular Journalism." For the United States in general, see Smith, "Wood Pulp and Newspapers," 341-42, 345.

23. Robert Lynd and Helen M. Lynd, *Middletown* (1929; repr., New York: Harcourt Brace Jovanovich, 1959), 514.

24. Michael Denning, *Mechanic Accents: Dime Novels and Working-Class Culture in America* (New York: Verso, 1987), 220-21, draws upon library reader surveys of the period.

25. William S. Gray and Ruth Monroe, *The Reading Interests and Habits of Adults* (New York: Macmillan, 1929), 35, 146, 176.

26. James Baughman, *The Republic of Mass Culture* (Baltimore: John Hopkins University Press, 1992), 11; Bernard Berelson, "What 'Missing the Paper' Means," in *Communications Research 1948–1949*, ed. Paul Lazarsfeld and Frank Stanton (New York: Harper & Brothers, 1949), 111–28.

27. By 1990 only 62 percent of the adult population said it had read the day's paper. Leonard, *News for All*, 178–79; Baughman, *Republic of Mass Culture*, 187–89.

28. William Leach, *Land of Desire: Merchants, Power and the Rise of New American Culture* (New York: Vintage Books, 1993), 17. See also Scripps's remarks on targeting market segments in R. Kaplan, "Market Segmentation and Partisanship."

29. Pound, *The Only Thing*, 112–13, 123–30, 136. Charles R. McCabe, *Damned Old Crank: A Self-Portrait of E. W. Scripps* (New York: Harper & Bros., 1951), chap. 18.

30. Edward W. Scripps to George Booth, 19 April 1889, George G. Booth Papers, Burton Historical Collection, Detroit.

31. Edward Scripps to James Scripps, 30 May 1889; see also his letter of 23 May 1889. Also relevant is Edward Scripps to George Booth, 22 May 1889. All in George G. Booth Papers.

32. R. Kaplan, "The Economics of Popular Journalism"; national figures come from the U.S. census as reported in Lee, *The Daily Newspaper*, 748–49. And see Ohmann, "Where Did Mass Culture Come From?" 96.

33. William Allen White, *The Autobiography of William Allen White* (New York: Macmillan, 1946), 377, 401; Sally Griffith, *Home Town News: William Allen White and the Emporia Gazette* (New York: Oxford University Press, 1989), 78–91. Sally Griffith, "Mass Media Come to the Small Town: The Emporia Gazette in the 1920s," in *Mass Media between the Wars*, ed. Catherine Covert and John Stevens (Syracuse: Syracuse University Press, 1984), 123–28, focuses on the 1920s.

34. See Leach, *Land of Desire*, chap. 1, 61–62, 123.

35. Ibid., 42–43, 45; and in general, see Frank Presbrey, *The History and Development of Advertising* (Garden City, N.Y.: Doubleday, Doran, 1929), chaps. 37 and 38; Michael Schudson, *Advertising, the Uneasy Persuasion* (New York: Basic Books, 1984), 161–68; Gerald Baldasty, *The Commercialization of the News in the Nineteenth Century* (Madison: University of Wisconsin Press, 1992), 52–80.

36. Ohmann, "Where Did Mass Culture Come From?" 93–94. See also Alfred D. Chandler Jr., *The Visible Hand: The Managerial Revolution in American Business* (Cambridge, Mass.: Harvard University Press, 1977), and Carl F. Kaestle and Janice A. Radway, chapter 1 in this volume.

37. See Marianne Salcetti, "The Emergence of the Reporter," in *Newsworkers*, ed. Hanno Hardt and Bonnie Brennen (Minneapolis: University of Minnesota Press, 1995), 51, 53. Donald Curl discusses the increased economic costs for the *Cincinnati Commercial* in the competition to obtain the news in the 1870s. Donald W. Curl, *Murat Halstead and the Cincinnati Commercial* (St. Augustine: University Presses of Florida, 1950), 91–92 and esp. 141.

38. Seymour-Ure, *The Press, Politics and the Public*; William Dean Howells, *A Modern Instance* (Boston: Houghton, Mifflin, 1957), 155–56, 209; Gerald Baldasty, "The Nineteenth-Century Origin of Modern American Journalism," *Proceedings of the American Antiquarian Society* 100 (1991): 408; Salcetti, "The Emergence of the Reporter," 51.

39. See the general discussion of barriers to market entrance in Richard Caves, *American Industry: Structure, Conduct, Performance* (Englewood Cliffs, N.J.: Prentice-Hall, 1977), 24-28. On comparable press dynamics in Great Britain, see Seymour-Ure, *The Press, Politics and the Public*, 105-8, 114-15.

40. Richard O'Connor, *Heywood Broun, a Biography* (New York: G. P. Putnam's Sons, 1975), 66.

41. Numbers from Lee, *The Daily Newspaper*, 732, 64-65, 718-19. Also see Smith, "Wood Pulp and Newspapers," 342-43. Also Oswald G. Villard, "Press Tendencies and Dangers," in Bleyer, *The Profession of Journalism*, 22-29.

42. Baughman, *Republic of Mass Culture*, 11.

43. See Phyllis Kaniss, *Making Local News* (Chicago: University of Chicago Press, 1991), 52-59; for example, George G. Booth to Edmund W. Booth, 19 January 1910, Cranbrook Archives.

44. Godkin, *Unforeseen Tendencies*, 195. And, Edward A. Ross, "The Suppression of Important News," in Bleyer, *The Profession of Journalism*, 79-96.

45. See Don C. Seitz, *Training for the Newspaper Trade* (Philadelphia: J. B. Lippincott Company, 1916), 93; John L. Given, *Making a Newspaper* (New York: Henry Holt and Co., 1912), 41.

46. Smith, "Wood Pulp and Newspapers," 342-43, 345; Lee, *The Daily Newspaper*, 322-26.

47. Griffith, *Home Town News*, 215-16. The Lynds in their survey of Middletown's newspapers measured shifts in the press content between their two dates of 1890 and 1920. See Baldasty, *Commercialization of the News*, 121-27.

48. Walter D. Scott, *The Psychology of Advertising* (Boston: Small Maynard & Co., 1913), 382; Given, *Making a Newspaper*, 307-8. For workers, evening papers were the journals of choice because, as the Lynds observed, "[W]orkers rising and getting to work an hour or two before [businessmen] seldom have time to read papers in the morning." Lynd and Lynd, *Middletown*, 471. The shorter, more sprightly written afternoon papers did not demand either the leisure time or concentration required by the morning blanket sheets. For more evidence of class differences in choosing newspapers, see Gray and Monroe, *Reading Interests and Habits of Adults*, 147-49, 177-79.

49. On the republican ideals of the press, see John Nerone, "A Local History of the Early U.S. Press: Cincinnati, 1793-1848," in *Ruthless Criticism*, ed. William Solomon and Robert McChesney (Minneapolis: University of Minnesota Press, 1993), 38-65.

50. Given, *Making a Newspaper*, 41.

51. On the gendered nature of nineteenth-century public space, see Mary Ryan, *Women in Public: Between Banners and Ballots, 1825-1880* (Baltimore: John Hopkins University Press, 1990). On the press, see Leonard, *News for All*, 19-28. On changing notions of the public with inclusion of women, see Michael Schudson, *Discovering the News: A Social History of American Newspapers* (New York: Basic Books, 1978), 128-31. On the orientation to women as readers, see Schudson, 99-101, and Baldasty, *Commercialization of the News*, 126-27, 153-55. On advertisers' desire to reach women, see Baldasty, *Commercialization of the News*, 117, 65. On department stores, see David Scobey, "Anatomy of the Promenade: The Politics of Bourgeois Sociability in Nineteenth-Century New York," *Social History* 17 (1992): 203-27.

52. Paul Weaver, *News and the Culture of Lying* (New York: Free Press, 1994), 46.

53. Baehr, *The New York Tribune*, 232. In reference to the dynamic expansion of magazine markets in the 1890s, Christopher P. Wilson describes how journals also rationalized their production of editorial material for the purpose of attracting readers. See his "The Rhetoric of Consumption: Mass-Market Magazines and the Demise of the Gentle Reader, 1880-1920," in *The Culture of Consumption: Critical Essays in American History, 1880-1890*, ed. Richard Wightman Fox and T. J. Jackson Lears (New York: Pantheon Books, 1983), 39-64.

54. As quoted in Catherine Covert, "A View of the Press in the Twenties," *Journalism History* 22 (Fall 1975): 66.

55. See, for example, Alan Trachtenberg, *The Incorporation of America: Culture and Society in the Gilded Age* (New York: Hill & Wang, 1982), chap. 4; Ben Singer, "Modernity, Hyperstimulus, and the Rise of Popular Sensationalism," in *Cinema and the Invention of Modern Life*, ed. Leo Charney and Vanessa Schwartz (Berkeley: University of California Press, 1995), 72-99.

56. See Amy Kaplan, *The Social Construction of American Realism* (Chicago: University of Chicago Press, 1988), 29 and chap. 1; Thomas Leonard, "Journalism and Its Discontents in the Gilded Age" (unpublished paper in author's possession, 26 October 1990). Schudson, *Discovering the News*, chap. 3, analyzes the 1890s press as divided into two status or class aesthetics. He also discusses the denunciation of the yellow press. And see Carl F. Kaestle et al., *Literacy in the United States: Readers and Reading since 1880* (New Haven: Yale University Press, 1991), 55-56.

57. As cited in Warren Susman, *Culture as History* (New York: Knopf, 1985), 258.

58. See Leonard, "Journalism and Its Discontents."

59. See Fredric Jameson, "Reification and Utopia in Mass Culture," *Social Text* 1 (Winter 1979): 130-48.

60. See Schudson, *Discovering the News*, 102-3, 130.

61. Roland Barthes, "Structure of the 'Faits Divers'" in *Critical Essays*, trans. Richard Howard (Evanston: Northwestern University Press, 1977), 185-99.

62. Tom Gunning, "An Aesthetics of Astonishment: Early Film and the (In)credulous Spectator," *Art and Text* 34 (Spring 1989): 31-45.

63. Thomas Elsaesser, "Tales of Sound and Fury: The Hollywood Family Melodrama," in *Film Theory and Criticism*, ed. G. Mast, M. Cohen, and L. Braudy (New York: Oxford University Press, 1992), 244-58.

64. Denning, *Mechanic Accents*. And see McGerr, *Decline of Popular Politics*, 126, 128-29, 136.

65. Richard Wald, "The News Market Place," *Media Studies Journal* 1 (Spring 1987): 7-20.

66. Lawrence Goodwyn, *The Populist Moment* (New York: Oxford University Press, 1978); Neil Schmitz, "Naturalism Undone," *American Literary History* 1 (Winter 1989): 897-907; Baehr, *The New York Tribune*, 255. And see Robert Wiebe, *The Search for Order, 1877-1920* (New York: Hill & Wang, 1967), chap. 4. William Livingstone, *The Republican Party* (New York: G. P. Putnam's Sons, 1904), 2:501. On the nation's papers leaving the Democratic Party, see Richard Jensen, *The Winning of the Midwest* (Chicago: University of Chicago Press, 1971), 272-75; David Sarasohn, *The Party of Reform: Democrats in the Progressive Era* (Jackson: University Press of Mississippi, 1989), 10-11.

67. Walter D. Burnham, *Critical Elections and the Mainsprings of American Politics* (New York: W. W. Norton, 1970).

68. Ibid., chap. 4.

69. See Gaye Tuchman, "Objectivity as Strategic Ritual: An Examination of Newsmen's Notions of Objectivity," *American Journal of Sociology* 77 (1972): 660-79.

70. American Society of Newspaper Editors, "Canons of Journalism," in *Mass Communications*, ed. Wilbur Schramm (Urbana: University of Illinois Press, 1960), 623-25.

71. Leach, *Land of Desire*, chap. 5.

72. George G. Booth to H. Chalmers, 7 November 1915, Cranbrook Archives.

73. On the intimate ties between the Progressive movement and newspapers in general, see Herbert Gans, *Deciding What's News* (New York: Vintage Books, 1979); Richard Hofstadter, *The Age of Reform* (New York: Vintage Books, 1955), 186-98; R. Kaplan "The American Press and Political Community"; David P. Nord, "Reading the Newspaper: Strategies and Politics of Reader Response, Chicago, 1912-1917," *Journal of Communication* 45 (Summer 1995): 66-94.

74. Jeffrey Alexander, "The Mass Media in Systemic, Historical, and Comparative Perspective," in *Mass Media and Social Change*, ed. Elihu Katz and Tamas Szesko (Beverly Hills: Sage, 1981), 17-51.

75. R. Kaplan, "The American Press and the Political Community."

76. Samuel Haber, *Efficiency and Uplift: Scientific Management in the Progressive Era, 1908-1920* (Chicago: University of Chicago Press, 1964).

77. Dan Hallin, *We Keep America on Top of the World* (New York: Routledge, 1994), chap. 6; Alexander, "The Mass Media," 35-37. The press throughout the century displayed a continuing tension between pluralizing the voices it publicized from civil society versus a relatively delimited range of formal political voices. The 1947 Hutchins Commission of Freedom of the Press recognized this defect to the objective press and called for greater social inclusion in its ethic of "press responsibility." See John Nerone, ed., *Last Rights: Revisiting Four Theories of the Press* (Urbana: University of Illinois Press, 1995).

78. Lynd and Lynd, *Middletown*, 476-77.

79. James Creelman, *On the Great Highway* (Boston: Lothrop Publishing, 1901), 61.

80. A. Kaplan, *Social Construction*, 116-17; O'Connor, *Heywood Broun*, 25-26, 31-32, 67.

81. Schudson, "Politics of Narrative Form," 105; *Discovering the News*, 212-13.

82. See William Solomon, "Newsroom Managers and Workers: The Specialization of Editing Work," *American Journalism* 10 (Winter-Spring 1993): 24-37. Given, *Making a Newspaper*, 203-4; Richard Kluger, *The Paper: The Life and Death of the New York Herald Tribune* (New York: Andrew A. Knopf, 1986), 218-19.

83. O'Connor, *Heywood Broun*, 22.

84. Richard Hofstadter, *The Paranoid Style in American Politics and Other Essays* (New York: Vintage Books, 1967), 196-98. On Stephen Crane's *The Red Badge of Courage*, see also A. Kaplan, *Social Construction*, 90.

85. Allen Churchill, *Park Row* (New York: Rinehart, 1958), 104-10.

86. Elmer Davis, *History of the New York Times, 1851-1921* (New York: New York Times, 1921), 228-29, and see 225-26, 245.

87. See Godkin, *Unforeseen Tendencies*, 204-9; Allan Nevins, *The Evening Post: A Century of Journalism* (1922; repr., New York: Russell & Russell, 1968), 510-11.

88. Baughman, *Republic of Mass Culture*, 32-33, 64, 112-13.

89. Walter Lippmann and Charles Merz, "A Test of the News," *New Republic* 23 (4 August 1920): 1-42.

CHAPTER 8
Persistence of Vision: Partisan Journalism in the Mainstream Press

1. Raymond Clapper, *Watching the World* (London: Whittlesey House, 1944), 15-16.

2. H. L. Mencken, *Thirty-five Years of Newspaper Work*, ed. Fred Hobson, Vincent Fitzpatrick, and Bradford Jacobs (Baltimore: Johns Hopkins University Press, 1994), 133. This memoir was written during World War II.

3. Edward McKernan, "Journalism Defined," *Quill* 13 (December 1925): 18-20.

4. Cited in Daniel W. Pfaff, *Joseph Pulitzer II and the Post-Dispatch* (University Park: Pennsylvania State University Press, 1991), 203.

5. See Michael Schudson, *Discovering the News: A Social History of American Newspapers* (New York: Basic Books, 1978), 61-87.

6. John S. Gilkeson Jr., *Middle-Class Providence, 1820-1940* (Princeton: Princeton University Press, 1986), 181.

7. Evans Johnson, *Oscar W. Underwood* (Baton Rouge: Louisiana State University Press, 1980), 171, 177, 178, 228.

8. Hugh Davis Graham, *Crisis in Print: Desegregation and the Press in Tennessee* (Nashville: Vanderbilt University Press, 1967), 36-37.

9. Johnson, *Oscar W. Underwood*, 385.

10. Susan E. Tifft and Alex S. Jones, *The Patriarch: The Rise and Fall of the Bingham Dynasty* (New York: Summit Books, 1991), 21.

11. James E. Cebula, *James M. Cox: Journalist and Politician* (New York: Garland Publishing, 1985), 21.

12. Kevin Cash, *Who the Hell Is William Loeb?* (Manchester, N.H.: Amoskeag Press, 1975), 21-36.

13. Elmer Davis, *History of the New York Times, 1851-1921* (New York: New York Times, 1921), 218.

14. Josephus Daniels, *Editor in Politics* (Chapel Hill: University of North Carolina Press, 1941), 88-89.

15. Ibid., 380.

16. Mark Lincoln Chadwin, *The Hawks of World War II* (Chapel Hill: University of North Carolina Press, 1968), 212.

17. Meyer Berger, *The Story of the New York Times, 1851-1951* (New York: Simon & Schuster, 1951), 424.

18. Martin Wattenberg, *The Decline of American Political Parties, 1952-1994* (Cambridge, Mass.: Harvard University Press, 1996), 151.

19. See Claude Bowers, *My Life: The Memoirs of Claude Bowers* (New York: Simon &

Schuster, 1962), 145-49, 192, 224-25, 232, 241-43. See also J. Joseph Huthmacher, *Senator Robert F. Wagner and the Rise of Urban Liberalism* (New York: Atheneum, 1968), 51.

20. Chadwin, *The Hawks*, 103.

21. Steven F. Lawson, *Black Ballots: Voting Rights in the South, 1944-1969* (New York: Columbia University Press, 1976), 62.

22. Ibid., 105.

23. "The Press and the Public," special section, *New Republic* 90 (17 March 1937): 185. See generally, Schudson, *Discovering the News*, 150-51, and Graham J. White, *FDR and the Press* (Chicago: University of Chicago Press, 1979), 27-32.

24. For some instances of newspapers rejecting columns, see White, *FDR and the Press*, 94-95.

25. Betty Houchin Winfield, *FDR and the News Media* (New York: Columbia University Press, 1994), 64, 82.

26. Robert W. Merry, *Taking on the World: Joseph and Stewart Alsop: Guardians of the American Century* (New York: Viking, 1996), 78.

27. Interestingly, the *New York Times* reviewer, Ralph Thompson, questioned the author's use of direct quotations in conversations that could not have been heard unless he was "hiding under the presidential bed." Ibid., 80. It is the same criticism later leveled by nearly everyone at Bob Woodward.

28. Ronald Steel, *Walter Lippmann and the American Century* (Boston: Atlantic Monthly Press, 1980), 388-89.

29. Chadwin, *The Hawks*, 90-91; Steel, *Walter Lippmann*, 384-85.

30. Steel, *Walter Lippmann*, 418-19. In his memoir, Reston offers a more circumspect account in which Lippmann's name does not appear. James Reston, *Deadline* (New York: Random House, 1991), 156-61.

31. Donald Bruce Johnson, *The Republican Party and Wendell Willkie* (Urbana: University of Illinois Press, 1960), 64-66.

32. Richard Kluger, *The Paper: The Life and Death of the New York Herald Tribune* (New York: Alfred A. Knopf, 1986), 328-29. See also James L. Baughman, *Henry R. Luce and the Rise of the American News Media* (Boston: Twayne, 1987), 120-23.

33. Marquis Childs, *Witness to Power* (New York: McGraw-Hill, 1975), 263.

34. Ibid., 54-55.

35. Mordechai Rozanski, "The Role of American Journalists in Chinese-American Relations, 1900-1925" (Ph.D. diss., University of Pennsylvania, 1974), 191-92.

36. Morrell Heald, *Transatlantic Vistas: American Journalists in Europe, 1900-1940* (Kent, Ohio: Kent State University Press, 1988), 95.

37. Quoted in Walter Johnson, *William Allen White's America* (New York: Henry Holt, 1947), 520.

38. Chadwin, *The Hawks*, 32-62.

39. Ibid., 114, 179.

40. Ibid., 81-84. Another organization, more moderate in its views, also emerged in 1940, the Committee to Defend America by Aiding the Allies, with William Allen White as its chairman. Where the Century Group was willing to advocate going to war, if necessary, to aid the allies, the Committee to Defend America justified support of the allies as the only way to stay

out of war. As the military situation in Europe turned worse and worse, committee leaders began to abandon their antiwar commitment; in December 1940, when White decided he could not alter his antiwar position, he resigned as committee chair. See Johnson, *William Allen White*, 546–50, and Walter Johnson, *The Battle against Isolation* (Chicago: University of Chicago Press, 1944; repr., New York: Da Capo, 1973), 181–87.

41. Cited in Hillier Krieghbaum, *Facts in Perspective* (Englewood Cliffs, N.J.: Prentice-Hall, 1956), 7.

42. Ibid., 9.

CHAPTER 9
Unruly Servants: Machines, Modernity, and the Printed Page

1. T. M. Cleland, "Harsh Words," in *Books and Printing: A Treasury for Typophiles*, ed. Paul A. Bennett (Cleveland: World Publishing, 1951).

2. Carl Rollins, *Fine Printing and the Small Shop* (Los Angeles: Plantin Press, 1935), 8.

3. Maggie Holtzberg Call, *The Lost World of the Craft Printer* (Urbana: University of Illinois Press, 1992), 98. See also Philip Gaskell, *A New Introduction to Bibliography* (New York: Oxford University Press, 1972), 274–88, and Maurice Annenberg, ed., *A Typographic Journey through the Inland Printer* (Baltimore: Maran Press, 1977).

4. For good overviews of the halftone process, see Gaskell, *A New Introduction to Bibliography*, 271–72, and James B. Carrington, "Some Modern Methods of Illustration," *Bookman* 21, no. 12 (August 1905): 645–50.

5. John Tebbel, *A History of Book Publishing in the United States*, 4 vols. (New York: R. R. Bowker, 1972–81), 2:482.

6. Gaskell reports that hand compositors averaged something less than 1,000 ens per hour (an en is a unit of measuring width in a typeset line, approximately half the width of a lowercase "m"). Linotype operators soon routinely achieved 6,000 ens per hour, and especially skilled workers might average 8,000 to 10,000 ens per hour. Gaskell, *A New Introduction to Bibliography*, 54–55, 278.

7. Carrington, "Modern Methods of Illustration," 648.

8. De Vinne's leadership in the American printing community was as broad as it was exemplary. He excelled as a typographic critic, historian, and type designer as well as printer. He was not only a practitioner of better typography but also its tireless advocate. See, for example, his pair of short essays written for a general audience and published serially in the *Independent*. Theodore Low De Vinne, "Typographical Effect," *Independent*, 19 November 1903, 2723–25; De Vinne, "Attractiveness in Books," *Independent*, 15 December 1904, 1374–77.

9. Beatrice Warde [Paul Beaujon], "The Machine in Book Composition," *Publishers' Weekly* 112 (2 February 1929): 573; James Wells, "Book Typography in the United States," in *Book Typography, 1815–1965: In Europe and the United States of America*, ed. Kenneth Day (Chicago: University of Chicago Press, 1966), 337.

10. See Michele H. Bogart, "Artistic Ideals and Commercial Practices: The Problem of Status for American Illustrators," *Prospects* 15 (1990): 225–81.

11. Rollins to Edmund G. Gress, 19 December 1923, Edmund G. Gress Papers, Manuscripts and Archives Division, New York Public Library.

12. See, for example, Jerome McGann, *The Textual Condition* (Princeton: Princeton University Press, 1990); McGann, *Black Riders: The Visible Language of Modernism* (Princeton: Princeton University Press, 1993); Roger Chartier, *Forms and Meanings: Texts, Performances, and Audiences from Codex to Computer* (Philadelphia: University of Pennsylvania Press, 1995).

13. Edward Marshall, "Machine-Made Freedom: An Authorized Interview with Thomas Edison," *Forum* 79 (October 1926): 492.

14. Jan Tschichold, *The New Typography*, trans. Ruari McLean (Berkeley: University of California Press, 1995), 7. See also Robin Kinross, *Modern Typography: An Essay in Critical History* (London: Hyphen Press, 1992).

15. Douglas McMurtrie, "Modernism in Design," *Publishers' Weekly* 115 (4 January 1930): 89.

16. Jim Clarke, "Modernism Has Come to Stay: Dump the Classics in the 'Hell-Box,'" *Direct Advertising*, Fall 1933, 17. (A hell-box is a container for worn or unusable type, which will later be melted down and recast into new type.) Although modernists were a minority among American typographers, they espoused their beliefs with rousing vigor. See, for example, Perry Walton's "Modern Type Best for Punch, Push and Howl," *Direct Advertising*, Winter 1934, 6-7, and the flurry of heated responses to it that were published in subsequent issues.

17. Ron Mendel, "Cooperative Unionism and the Development of Job Control in New York's Printing Trades, Labor History, 1886-1898," *Labor History* 32 (Summer 1991): 364.

18. Writing the judges' statement assessing the "Fifty Books" selected for the American Institute of Graphic Arts' annual competition for 1935, Rollins noted that "technical excellence is apparent, . . . but that elusive quality of artistic work — its spirit not its letter — is too often neglected in the effort to have the machine function smoothly." Preface to *Catalogue of the AIGA Fifty Books* (New York: AIGA, 1935).

19. See Susan Otis Thompson, *American Book Design and William Morris*, 2nd ed. (New Castle, Del.: Oak Knoll Press, 1996). For an excellent overview of the larger cultural context of wariness toward machinery and modernism, see T. J. Jackson Lears, *No Place of Grace: Antimodernism and the Transformation of American Culture, 1880-1920* (New York: Pantheon, 1981).

20. Will Ransom, "The Merrymount Press," *Publishers' Weekly* 111 (14 April 1928): 1619.

21. D. B. Updike, *Printing Types: Their History, Forms, and Use: A Study in Survivals* (1922; rev. ed., Cambridge, Mass.: Harvard University Press, 1937).

22. Warde [Beaujon], "Machine in Book Composition," 573.

23. Ibid., 576.

24. D. B. Updike, "Some Tendencies in Modern Typography" (1941), reprinted in Bennett, *Books and Printing*, 310.

25. Richard Ohmann, *Selling Culture: Magazines, Markets, and Class at the Turn of the Century* (London: Verso, 1996), 224.

26. Ellen Gruber Garvey, *The Adman in the Parlor: Magazines and the Gendering of Consumer Culture, 1880s to 1910s* (New York: Oxford University Press, 1996), 5.

27. Warde, "Printing Should Be Invisible" (1932), in Bennett, *Books and Printing*, 109-14.

28. Paul Johnston, "Modernism in Book Design," *Publishers' Weekly* 115 (1 March 1930): 1121.

29. On cultural sacralization in America, see Lawrence Levine, *Highbrow/Lowbrow: The Emergence of Cultural Hierarchy in America* (Cambridge, Mass.: Harvard University Press, 1988). On typographic sacralization more particularly, see Megan Benton, *Beauty and the Book: Fine Editions and Cultural Distinction in America* (New Haven: Yale University Press, 2000).

30. "Knowledge on Sight," *Nation*, 20 July 1893, quoted in Neil Harris, *Cultural Excursions: Marketing Appetites and Cultural Tastes in Modern America* (Chicago: University of Chicago Press), 342; J. L. Brown, "Picture Magazines and Morons," *American Mercury* 19 (1938): 405.

31. Frank Munsey Jr., "The Publisher's Desk," *Munsey's*, July 1897, 638, quoted in Garvey, *Adman in the Parlor*, 169.

32. "A Note on Typography," *Vanity Fair* 34 (March 1930): 31.

33. Ford Madox Ford, "The Fate of the Semiclassic," *Forum* 98 (September 1937): 128.

34. Cleland, "Harsh Words," 331.

35. The typographic tension between traditionalism and modernism was ideologically linked to larger debates about cultural hierarchies and the tastes and judgments of "the masses." Those debates crystallized in the 1950s as critics struggled to assess the value and authority of popular culture. See, for example, the collection of influential essays gathered in *Mass Culture: The Popular Arts in America*, ed. Bernard Rosenberg and David Manning White (Glencoe, Ill.: Free Press, 1957).

CHAPTER 10
Ambivalent Advertising: Books, Prestige, and the Circulation of Publicity

1. Christopher Wilson, *The Labor of Words: Literary Professionalism in the Progressive Era* (Athens: University of Georgia Press, 1985), 80.

2. Walter Hines Page, *A Publisher's Confession* (New York: Doubleday, Page, 1905), 109.

3. Horace Scudder on Henry Houghton, quoted in Wilson, *Labor of Words*, 69.

4. George Haven Putnam and John Bishop Putnam, *Authors and Publishers: A Manual of Suggestions for Beginners in Literature*, rev. 7th ed. (New York: G. P. Putnam's Sons, 1897), 175.

5. See Tom Dardis, *Firebrand: The Life of Horace Liveright* (New York: Random House, 1995), for more on sets.

6. Page, *A Publisher's Confession*, 8.

7. Robert Sterling Yard, *The Publisher* (Boston: Houghton Mifflin, 1913), 50.

8. Harper, Scribner, and Holt gave the cup to Putnam on his marriage. John Tebbel, *A History of Book Publishing in the United States*, 4 vols. (New York: R. R. Bowker, 1972–81), 2:11.

9. *The Book and News-Dealer* (San Francisco), January 1894, 16.

10. James M. Reid, *An Adventure in Textbooks, 1924–1960* (New York: R. R. Bowker, 1969), 12.

11. Eugene Exman, *The House of Harper: One Hundred and Fifty Years of Publishing* (New York: Harper & Row, 1967), 230.

12. Jack O'Bar, *The Origins and History of the Bobbs-Merrill Company*, Occasional Papers, 172 (Urbana: University of Illinois Press, 1985), 12.

13. "The Poster Rage of the 90's," *Publishers' Weekly* 137 (13 January 1940): 126.

14. "Book Advertising," *Billposter-Display Advertising*, March 1903, 18–19.

15. Page, *A Publisher's Confession*, 72.

16. Joan Shelley Rubin, *The Making of Middlebrow Culture* (Chapel Hill: University of North Carolina Press, 1992), 28–29.

17. Helen Woodward, *Through Many Windows* (New York: Harper, 1926), 273.

18. Ibid., 276–77.

19. Ibid., 284.

20. W. E. Woodward, *The Gift of Life* (New York: E. P. Dutton, 1947), 189.

21. Tebbel, *History of Book Publishing in the United States*, 2:231.

22. O. H. Cheney, *Economic Survey of the Book Industry, 1930–1931* (New York: National Association of Book Publishers, 1931), 127; Judith Applebaum, "Books that Sold a Million or More," *Book Research Quarterly*, Spring 1987, 41.

23. Cheney, *Economic Survey*, 125–26.

24. Edward L. Bernays, "Promotion Expert Urges New Sales Methods for Books," *Publishers' Weekly* 91 (20 March 1920): 933–36. See also Edward L. Bernays, *Biography of an Idea: Memoirs of a Public Relations Counsel* (New York: Simon & Schuster, 1965).

25. Bernays, "Promotion Expert."

26. Charles F. Bound, *A Banker Looks at Publishing* (New York: R. R. Bowker, 1950), 41.

27. Alfred Harcourt, talk at J. Walter Thompson Company, 3 March 1930; typescript, 12, Special Collections Library, Duke University, Durham, N.C.

28. Christopher Wilson, *White Collar Fictions: Class and Social Representation in American Literature, 1885–1925* (Athens: University of Georgia Press, 1992), 219.

29. *Publishers' Weekly*, 16 May 1925, 1910.

30. *Publishers' Weekly*, 9 March 1940, 1077.

31. Rubin, *Making of Middlebrow Culture*, 290.

32. Tebbel, *History of Book Publishing in the United States*, 3:331.

33. Ibid., 4:101.

34. John T. Winterich, *Three Lantern Slides: Books, the Book Trade, and Some Related Phenomena in America, 1876, 1901 and 1926* (Urbana: University of Illinois Press, 1949), 77; Rubin, *Making of Middlebrow Culture*, 277.

35. Rubin, *Making of Middlebrow Culture*, 292.

36. Ibid.

37. See Catherine Turner, *Marketing Modernism between the Two World Wars* (Amherst: University of Massachusetts Press, 2003).

Section III. *The Social Uses of Print:*
Introduction

1. We are indebted to David Nord for emphasizing (at our editorial seminars) the importance of subsidies in the history of print. For an elegant analysis of the process of pricing in a

subsidized publishing organization, see David Nord, "Free Grace, Free Books, Free Riders: The Economics of Religious Publishing in Early Nineteenth-Century America," *Proceedings of the American Antiquarian Society* 106 (1996): 241-72.

2. Robert E. Park, *The Immigrant Press and Its Control* (New York: Harper & Brothers, 1922).

CHAPTER 11
Learned and Literary Print Cultures in an Age of Professionalization and Diversification

1. Henry S. Canby, *Alma Mater: The Gothic Age of the American College* (1936; repr., New York: Arno Press, 1975), viii.

2. Ibid., xii.

3. Ibid., x.

4. On the changing definition and nature of scientific investigation during these years, see Derek J. de Solla Price's two books: *Science since Babylon* (New Haven: Yale University Press, 1961) and *Little Science, Big Science and Beyond* (New York: Columbia University Press, 1986). In the latter, Price traces the changing character of modern scientific publishing in journals in chapter 3, "Invisible Colleges and the Affluent Scientific Commuter," 56-81.

5. Canby, *Alma Mater*, 197-98.

6. On the relation between literary realism and the practices and ideologies of professionalization, see Amy Kaplan, *The Social Construction of American Realism* (Chicago: University of Chicago Press, 1988); Jonathan Freedman, *Professions of Taste: Henry James, British Aestheticism, and Commodity Culture* (Stanford: Stanford University Press, 1990); Phillip Barrish, *American Literary Realism, Critical Theory and Intellectual Prestige, 1880-1980* (Cambridge: Cambridge University Press, 2001).

7. On the subject of literary careers, see Richard Brodhead, *Cultures of Letters: Scenes of Reading and Writing in Nineteenth-Century America* (Chicago: University of Chicago Press, 1993). For a discussion of the rise of authorial celebrity in the United States, see Loren Glass, *Authors Inc.: Literary Celebrity in the Modern United States, 1880-1980* (New York: New York University Press, 2004).

8. For a discussion of the range of uses to which print was put in popular circles and the way such forms mimicked practices in learned culture in the last decades of the nineteenth century, see Neil Harris, "The Lamp of Learning: Popular Lights and Shadows," in *The Organization of Knowledge in Modern America, 1860-1920*, ed. Alexandra Oleson and John Voss (Baltimore: Johns Hopkins University Press, 1979), 430-39.

9. On the construction of this divide, see Lawrence Levine, *Highbrow/Lowbrow: The Emergence of Cultural Hierarchy in America* (Cambridge, Mass.: Harvard University Press, 1988).

10. On the rise and periodization of middlebrow culture, see Joan Shelley Rubin, *The Making of Middlebrow Culture* (Chapel Hill: University of North Carolina Press, 1992), and Janice A. Radway, *A Feeling for Books: The Book-of-the-Month Club, Literary Taste, and Middle Class Desire* (Chapel Hill: University of North Carolina Press, 1997).

11. Christine Stansell, *American Moderns: Bohemian New York and the Creation of a New*

Century (New York: Metropolitan Books, 2000), 74. The term "riot of words" comes from Burton J. Bledstein, *The Culture of Professionalism: The Middle Class and the Development of Higher Education in America* (New York: W. W. Norton, 1976), 78.

12. For a summary of this literature, see the bibliographical essay in this volume.

13. For a discussion of the more avocational culture of learning in the years prior to 1880, see David Hall, "Erudition and Learned Culture," in *The Industrial Book, 1840–1880*, ed. Scott E. Casper, Jeffrey D. Groves, Stephen W. Nissenbaum, and Michael Winship, vol. 3 of *A History of the Book in America* (Chapel Hill: University of North Carolina Press, 2007), 347–359.

14. Oleson and Voss, introduction to *Organization of Knowledge in Modern America*, vii–xxi.

15. See, for instance, Roger L. Geiger, *To Advance Knowledge: The Growth of American Research Universities, 1900–1940* (New York: Oxford University Press, 1976), 8.

16. On the history of land-grant colleges, see Roger L. Williams, *The Origins of Federal Support for Higher Education: George W. Atherton and the Land-Grant College Movement* (University Park: Pennsylvania State University Press, 1991); Coy F. Cross II, *Justin Smith Morrill: Father of the Land-Grant College* (East Lansing: Michigan State University, 1999); Roger L. Geiger, "The Rise and Fall of Useful Knowledge: Higher Education for Science, Agriculture, and the Mechanic Arts, 1850–1875," in *The American College in the Nineteenth Century*, ed. Geiger (Nashville: Vanderbilt University Press, 2000), 153–68.

17. Oleson and Voss, introduction to *Organization of Knowledge in Modern America*, xiii.

18. Geiger, *To Advance Knowledge*, 5.

19. Lincoln Steffens, "Sending a State to College," *American Magazine* 68 (1909), quoted in Laurence R. Veysey, *The Emergence of the American University* (Chicago: University of Chicago Press, 1965), 107–8.

20. On the transformation of the conception of learning, see Edward Shils, *The Order of Learning: Essays on the Contemporary University* (New Brunswick, N.J.: Transaction Publishers, 1997), esp. chaps. 1 and 2, 1–70. See also, Veysey, *The Emergence of the American University*, 124–49.

21. Hugh Hawkins, "University Identity: The Teaching and Research Functions," in Oleson and Voss, *Organization of Knowledge in Modern America*, 289.

22. For an account of the general reader and the role of the importance of nonfiction popularizations within middlebrow print culture, see Radway, *A Feeling for Books*. See also Radway, "Research Universities, Periodical Publication, and the Circulation of Professional Expertise: On the Significance of Middlebrow Authority," *Critical Inquiry* 10 (Autumn 2004): 203–28. See also Marcel Chotkowski LaFollette, chapter 12 in this volume.

23. Veysey, *The Emergence of the American Research University*, 135–36. I have drawn heavily on his discussion in "Research," chap. 3, 121–79.

24. The literature on professionalization is vast. The sources most relevant for the subjects under discussion in this chapter include Bledstein, *The Culture of Professionalism*; Magali Sarfatti Larson, *The Rise of Professionalism: A Sociological Analysis* (Berkeley: University of California Press, 1977); Samuel Haber, *The Quest for Authority and Honor in the American Professions, 1750–1900* (Chicago: University of Chicago Press, 1991).

25. Hugh Hawkins, *Pioneer: A History of the Johns Hopkins University, 1874–1889* (Ithaca, N.Y.: Cornell University Press, 1960), 6. My account here is heavily indebted to Hawkins's definitive history of Hopkins.

26. Ibid., 41 (emphasis added).

27. Daniel Kevles, "The Physics, Mathematics, and Chemistry Communities: A Comparative Analysis," in Oleson and Voss, *Organization of Knowledge in Modern America*, 140.

28. On the nature of modern scientific publication and its history, see Price, *Little Science, Big Science*, 57, where he argues and demonstrates that scientists moved to the regular publication of short research papers as a way of establishing and maintaining intellectual property. See Geiger's discussion of Ira Remsen's rejection by the *American Journal of Science*, founded initially in 1818, in Geiger, *To Advance Knowledge*, 26.

29. Hawkins, *Pioneer*, 74–75, 107–12.

30. Daniel Coit Gilman, quoted in John Tebbel, *A History of Book Publishing in the United States*, 4 vols. (New York: R. R. Bowker, 1972–80), 2:536.

31. Hawkins, *Pioneer*, 113–14.

32. For a table representing the distribution of the 1,000 leading American men of science in 1906, see Geiger, *To Advance Knowledge*, 39. It should be noted again that these new forms of scholarly production were largely confined to the major research universities and only later made inroads into smaller institutions and other geographical regions like the South.

33. Ibid., 22–24.

34. Ibid.

35. Ibid., 32–33.

36. On the relationship between speed, periodicity, and mass culture, see Richard Ohmann, *Selling Culture: Magazines, Markets, and Class at the Turn of the Century* (London: Verso, 1996), 48–61. For the way this new constellation affected cultural production more generally and middlebrow culture more specifically, see Radway, *A Feeling for Books*, 168–75.

37. Hawkins, *Pioneer*, 119.

38. Tebbel, *History of Book Publishing in the United States*, 2:537. On the history of the University of Chicago, see Richard Storr, *Harper's University* (Chicago: University of Chicago Press, 1966).

39. Tebbel, *History of Book Publishing in the United States*, 2:536.

40. Albert Muto, *The University of California Press: The Early Years, 1893–1953* (Berkeley: University of California Press, 1993), 43.

41. Robert Frederick Lane, "The Place of the American University Press in Publishing" (Ph.D. diss., University of Chicago, 1939; privately printed and distributed by the University of Chicago Libraries, 1942). Cited in Tebbel, *History of Book Publishing in the United States*, 2:535.

42. On the creation of a culture of the circulating book, see Radway, *A Feeling for Books*, 129–30, 136–37.

43. Wayne A. Wiegand, *Irrepressible Reformer: A Biography of Melvil Dewey* (Chicago: American Library Association, 1996), 29. See also Wayne A. Wiegand, chapter 22 in this volume.

44. John Higham has suggested that the card catalog was one of the great innovations of

American print culture during this period. See "The Matrix of Specialization," in Oleson and Voss, *Organization of Knowledge in Modern America*, 14.

45. Dorothy Ross, "The Development of the Social Sciences," in Oleson and Voss, *Organization of Knowledge in Modern America*, 113. See also her magisterial *The Origins of American Social Science* (Cambridge: Cambridge University Press, 1991). I have relied heavily on Ross's work for the brief account I give here of the development of the social sciences. See also Thomas L. Haskell, *The Emergence of Professional Social Science: The American Social Science Association and the Nineteenth-Century Crisis of Authority* (Urbana: University of Illinois Press, 1977).

46. Ross, "Development of the Social Sciences," 109.

47. Ibid., 112.

48. Ibid., 113.

49. Ibid., 121.

50. Ross, *Origins*, 157-59.

51. Christopher Wilson, *The Labor of Words: Literary Professionalism in the Progressive Era* (Athens: University of Georgia Press, 1985); Ohmann, *Selling Culture*.

52. Canby, *Alma Mater*, 196-97.

53. Laurence R. Veysey, "The Plural Organized Worlds of the Humanities," in Oleson and Voss, *The Organization of Knowledge in America*, 51-106.

54. See the bibliographical essay in this volume.

55. Sven Beckert, *The Monied Metropolis: New York City and the Consolidation of the American Bourgeoisie, 1850-1896* (Cambridge: Cambridge University Press, 2001). See also Stuart Blumin, *The Emergence of the Middle Class: Social Experience in the American City, 1760-1900* (New York: Cambridge University Press, 1989).

56. On the relation between the parlor and cultural aspirations, see Beckert, *Monied Metropolis*, 260. For a more general account of the new "guardians of culture" and their sponsorship of cultural institutions, see Alan Trachtenberg, *The Incorporation of America: Culture and Society in the Gilded Age* (New York: Hill and Wang, 1982), 144-53. See also Paul DiMaggio, "Cultural Entrepreneurship in Nineteenth-Century Boston: The Creation of an Organizational Base of High Culture in America," *Media, Culture and Society* 4 (1982): 33-50.

57. Thorstein Veblen, *The Theory of the Leisure Class: An Economic Study in the Evolution of Institutions* (New York: Macmillan, 1899).

58. On the emergence of the concept of "the humanities," see Veysey, "Plural Organized Worlds," 53-55. On the rise of the liberal culture defense more generally, see Veysey, *Emergence*, 18-251.

59. Gilman, quoted in Veysey, *Emergence*, 181.

60. On the social origins of the liberal culture advocates, see Veysey, "Plural Organized Worlds," 51-53.

61. Gerald Graff, *Professing Literature: An Institutional History* (Chicago: University of Chicago Press, 1987), 81.

62. On "chromo civilization," see Carl F. Kaestle, chapter 2 in this volume. Chromolithography could be used to make cheap, colored reproductions of art. E. L. Godkin famously ridiculed "chromocivilization" as a world of shallow art, accompanied by no deep understanding. See E. L. Godkin, "Chromo-Civilization," *Nation*, September 1874, 24; Neil Har-

ris, "Pictorial Perils: The Rise of American Illustration," in *Cultural Excursions: Marketing Appetites and Cultural Tastes in Modern America* (Chicago: University of Chicago Press, 1990), 337-48; Carl F. Kaestle and Janice A. Radway, chapter 1 in this volume.

63. Hiram Corson, *The Aims of Literary Study* (New York: Macmillan, 1896), 49.

64. On textbook publishing during this period, see Tebbel, *History of Book Publishing in the United States*, 2:559-87.

65. The term "genteel" was coined by George Santayana in 1911 in an essay "The Genteel Tradition in American Philosophy," *University of California Chronicle* 13, no. 4 (1911). On the "genteel" understanding of culture, see Trachtenberg, *Incorporation of America*, 143-49.

66. Trachtenberg, *Incorporation of America*, 155. Trachtenberg only incidentally connects Howells and colleagues with the academic defenders of liberal culture; the relation between the two groups is addressed at more length in Graff, *Professing Literature*, 81-93.

67. For a good summary description of the emergence of the new high-literary zone and the kind of career and social role it promoted, see Richard Brodhead, "Literature and Culture," in *Columbia Literary History of the United States*, ed. Emory Elliott et al. (New York: Columbia University Press, 1988), 467-81.

68. For a discussion of the appearance of the term "intellectual" in the United States, see Stansell, *American Moderns*, 43. See also Thomas Bender, *New York Intellect: A History of Intellectual Life in New York City, from 1750 to the Beginnings of Our Own Time* (Baltimore: Johns Hopkins University Press, 1987), 228. Both Bender and Stansell note that the term was generally used to describe the literary and cultural critics who began to work in New York in the first decades of the twentieth century, especially the group known as "the young intellectuals." My point in alluding to the term's later adoption here is to note that Howells and company actually pioneered the social role that subsequently had to be named explicitly as it was elaborated further.

69. Nancy Glazener, *Reading for Realism: The History of a U.S. Literary Institution, 1850-1910* (Durham: Duke University Press, 1997), esp. 23-47. Richard Brodhead also comments on the relationship between Boston elites and the creation of high-literary culture in Brodhead, "Literature and Culture," 470-73, and Brodhead, *Cultures of Letters*, 122-25. Both Glazener and Brodhead cite Paul DiMaggio's foundational work on the Boston elite's sponsorship of high cultural institutions in "Cultural Entrepreneurship in Nineteenth Century Boston."

70. Brodhead, *Cultures of Letters*, 124. On Gilder, see Arthur John, *The Best Years of the Century: Richard Watson Gilder, Scribner's Monthly and the Century Magazine, 1870-1909* (Urbana: University of Illinois Press, 1981).

71. Trachtenberg, *Incorporation of America*, 152-53, 172-73, 184-93.

72. On this point, see Brodhead, *Cultures of Letters*, 120-41; Kaplan, *Social Construction*, 8-14, especially her discussion of Howells, 15-64; and the discussion of the local colorists in Carl F. Kaestle, chapter 2 in this volume.

73. Glazener, *Reading for Realism*, 49.

74. On this point, see ibid., 43; Kaplan, *Social Construction*, 8-14. See also Ohmann, *Selling Culture*.

75. Phillip Barrish, *American Literary Realism, Critical Theory and Intellectual Prestige* (Cambridge: Cambridge University Press, 2001).

76. On the professionalism of the literary realists, see Jonathan Freedman, *Professions of Taste: Henry James, British Aestheticism, and Commodity Culture* (Stanford: Stanford University Press, 1990), esp. xix–xxviii, 177–82.

77. For a nuanced discussion of the professionalism of people working in the various precincts of the humanities at the end of the nineteenth century, see Veysey, "Plural Organized Worlds," esp. 57–66. On the complex relationship between the new social science disciplines, knowledge production in the universities, the desire to subdue the world's supposedly less civilized populations, and the imperialism of the West, see John Willinsky, *Learning to Divide the World: Education at Empire's End* (Minneapolis: University of Minnesota Press, 1998).

78. Brodhead, *Cultures of Letters*, 116.

79. See Carl F. Kaestle, chapter 2 in this volume, for the relevant statistics.

80. On the new magazines, see Wilson, *The Labor of Words*, and Ohmann, *Selling Culture*.

81. For a discussion of ethnic literature and its relationship to the ethnic press, see Werner Sollors, "Immigrants and Other Americans," in Elliott et al., *Columbia Literary History of the United States*, 568–88. See also Sally M. Miller, chapter 15 in this volume.

82. See James P. Danky, chapter 17 in this volume; Nicolás Kanellos, chapter 16 in this volume; Neil Harris, "The Lamp of Learning: Popular Lights and Shadows," in Oleson and Voss, *Organization of Knowledge in America*, 433.

83. On the development of localized cultures of bohemians, radicals, and intellectuals in a range of cities throughout the United States at this time, see Stansell, *American Moderns*, 11–69.

84. Elliott Shore, Ken Fones-Wolf, and James P. Danky, *The German-American Radical Press: The Shaping of a Left Political Culture, 1850–1910* (Urbana: University of Illinois Press, 1992), 3.

85. Frederic C. Jaher, "Nationalist," in *The American Radical Press, 1880–1960*, ed. Joseph R. Conlin, vol. 1 (Westport, Conn.: Greenwood Press, 1974), 33.

86. Conlin, introduction to *American Radical Press*, 7.

87. Paul M. Buhle, *Marxism in the United States*, rev. ed. (London: Verso, 1987), 87.

88. Ibid., 81; Conlin, *American Radical Press*, 54.

89. John Graham, *"Yours for the Revolution": The Appeal to Reason, 1895–1922* (Lincoln: University of Nebraska Press, 1990), x.

90. Ibid., 216.

91. Paul M. Buhle, "The Appeal to Reason, New Appeal," in Conlin, *American Radical Press*, 59.

92. *Bookseller and Stationer* 4 (July 1882): 45, quoted in Allen Ruff, *"We Called Each Other Comrade": Charles H. Kerr & Company, Radical Publishers* (Urbana: University of Illinois Press, 1997), 37.

93. Ruff, *"We Called Each Other Comrade,"* xiv–xv.

94. Stansell, *American Moderns*, 152. According to Stansell, more than 300 socialist periodicals flourished in the United States prior to the war and this figure does not include papers and journals of the women's movement, the anarchist journals, the progressive papers, or the nonsocialist labor papers.

95. On this subject, see Joanne Passet, *Sex Radicals and the Quest for Women's Equality* (Urbana: University of Illinois Press, 2003), and Stansell, *American Moderns*, 225-72.

96. Passet, *Sex Radicals*, 39.

97. Stansell, *American Moderns*, 74. For a discussion of the relationship between urban bohemias scattered throughout the United States and the increasingly important Greenwich Village scene in New York, see Stansell, *American Moderns*, 40-69. On the rise to prominence of New York as an intellectual and cultural center and the role commercial publishing played in that, see Bender, *New York Intellect*, 206-62. On literary Bohemia in Greenwich Village, see also Arthur Frank Wertheim, *The New York Little Renaissance: Iconoclasm, Modernism, and Nationalism in American Culture, 1908-1917* (New York: New York University Press, 1976).

98. Quoted in Bender, *New York Intellect*, 230-31.

99. Ibid., 223.

100. On the changing editorial positions of the *New Republic*, see Bender, *New York Intellect*, esp. 222-46.

101. Quoted in Sally Dennison, *Alternative Literary Publishing: Five Modern Histories* (Iowa City: University of Iowa Press, 1984), 2. On the little magazines, see Frederick Hoffman, *The Little Magazines: A History and a Bibliography* (Princeton: Princeton University Press, 1947).

102. Wertheim, *The New York Little Renaissance*. On World War I as a blow to the young intellectuals of New York, see Bender, *New York Intellect*, 241-49.

103. Stansell, *American Moderns*, 327.

104. The literature on modernism is vast. A good place to begin is Malcolm Bradbury and James MacFarlane, *Modernism, 1880-1930* (Harmondsworth: Penguin, 1978). See also Marshall Berman, *All That Is Solid Melts into Air: The Experience of Modernity* (New York: Simon & Schuster, 1982).

105. Alfred A. Knopf, quoted in Tebbel, *History of Book Publishing in the United States*, 3:114. On the rise of this new generation of publishers, see ibid., 2:388-93; James L. W. West III, chapter 4 in this volume; Stansell, *American Moderns*, 154-57.

106. Tebbel, *History of Book Publishing in the United States*, 3:114-16, 138.

107. On the marketing of modernism, see Jennifer Wicke, *Advertising Fictions* (New York: Columbia University Press, 1988); Lawrence Rainey, *Institutions of Modernism: Literary Elites and Public Culture* (New Haven: Yale University Press, 1998); Michael Levenson, *A Genealogy of Modernism: Constituents of a Literary Doctrine, 1908-1922* (New York: Cambridge University Press, 1984); Joyce Wexler, *Who Paid for Modernism?* (Fayetteville: University of Arkansas Press, 1997); Kevin J. H. Dettmar and Stephen Watt, *Marketing Modernisms: Self-Promotion, Canonization, and Rereading* (Ann Arbor: University of Michigan Press, 1996); Catherine Turner, *Marketing Modernism between the Two World Wars* (Amherst: University of Massachusetts Press, 2003).

108. On the development of this kind of journalistic criticism, see Rubin, *Making of Middlebrow Culture*, 34-92.

109. Quoted in Turner, *Marketing Modernism*, 15.

110. Quoted in James J. Martine, *Fred Lewis Pattee and American Literature* (University Park: Pennsylvania State University Press, 1973), 139.

111. On the nature of middlebrow aesthetics, see Rubin, *Making of Middlebrow Culture*, and Radway, *A Feeling for Books*, 221–304.

112. On the rise of the New Criticism, see Graff, *Professing Literature*, 145–161. See also John Fekete, *The Critical Twilight: Explorations in the Ideology of Anglo-American Literary Theory from Eliot to McLuhan* (London: Routledge & Kegan Paul, 1977), and Frank Lentricchia, *After the New Criticism* (Chicago: University of Chicago Press, 1980).

113. See James P. Danky, chapter 17 in this volume.

114. On the founding of the Seven Sisters, see Helen Lefkowitz Horowitz, *Alma Mater: Design and Experience in the Women's Colleges from Their Nineteenth-Century Beginnings to the 1930s* (Amherst: University of Massachusetts Press, 1984). See also Geiger, "The 'Superior Instruction of Women,'" in Geiger, *American College in the Nineteenth Century*, 189.

115. Horowitz, *Alma Mater*, 115.

116. Geiger, "The 'Superior Instruction of Women,'" 191. On the development of courses in American literature at the women's colleges, see also Elizabeth Renker, "American Literature in the Higher Curriculum: An Institutional History, 1870–1950" (unpublished manuscript, Ohio State University). I am grateful to Professor Renker for permission to read and cite from her study.

117. Barbara Sicherman, "Alice Hamilton," in *Notable American Women: The Modern Period*, ed. Sicherman and Carol Hurd Green (Cambridge: Harvard University Press, 1983).

118. Helen Lefkowitz Horowitz, "'Nous Autre': Reading, Passion and the Creation of M. Carey Thomas," *Journal of American History* 79 (June 1992): 68–95; Helen Lefkowitz Horowitz, *The Power and Passion of M. Carey Thomas* (Urbana: University of Illinois Press, 1999).

119. On women, libraries, literacy work, and the club movement, see Dee Garrison, *Apostles of Culture: The Public Librarian and American Society, 1876–1920* (New York: Free Press, 1979); Theodora Penny Martin, *The Sound of Our Own Voices, Women's Study Clubs, 1860–1910* (Boston: Beacon Press, 1987); Anne Ruggles Gere, *Intimate Practices: Literacy and Cultural Work in U.S. Women's Clubs, 1880–1920* (Urbana: University of Illinois Press, 1997); Elizabeth McHenry, *Forgotten Readers: Recovering the Lost History of African American Literary Societies* (Durham: Duke University Press, 2002); Elizabeth Long, chapter 24 in this volume; Elizabeth McHenry, chapter 25 in this volume.

120. On the changing nature of working-class femininity, see Kathy Peiss, *Cheap Amusements: Working Women and Leisure in Turn-of-the-Century New York* (Philadelphia: Temple University Press, 1985); Nan Enstad, *Ladies of Labor, Girls of Adventure: Working Women, Popular Culture, and Labor Politics at the Turn of the Twentieth Century* (New York: Columbia University Press, 1999).

121. Gere, *Intimate Practices*, 141.

122. Cecelia Tichi, "Women Writers and the New Woman," in Elliott et al., *Columbia Literary History of the United States*, 597.

123. Sharon O'Brien, *Willa Cather: The Emerging Voice* (New York: Oxford University Press, 1987). See also O'Brien's important discussion of Cather's changing reputation in "Becoming Noncanonical: The Case of Willa Cather," *American Quarterly* 40, no. 1 (1988): 110–26. There she documents the constant association between Cather's work, her gender, and her interest in small, domestic objects and spaces.

124. On Stein's self-conscious effort to construct herself as a literary "genius," see Barbara Will, *Gertrude Stein, Modernism, and the Problem of "Genius"* (Edinburgh: Edinburgh University Press, 2000).

125. On gender and modernism, see Margaret Dickie, ed., *Gendered Modernism: American Women Poets and Their Readers* (Philadelphia: University of Pennsylvania Press, 1996); Rita Felski, *The Gender of Modernity* (Cambridge, Mass.: Harvard University Press, 1995); Jayne E. Marek, *Women Editing Modernism: "Little" Magazines and Literary History* (Lexington: University Press of Kentucky, 1995); Bonnie Kime Scott, *Gender and Modernism: A Critical Anthology* (Bloomington: Indiana University Press, 1990).

126. James D. Anderson, *The Education of Blacks in the South, 1860–1935* (Chapel Hill: University of North Carolina Press, 1988), 239. See also Louis R. Harlan, *Separate and Unequal: Public School Campaigns and Racism in the Southern Seaboard States, 1901–1915* (New York: Atheneum, 1968).

127. August Meier, *Negro Thought in America, 1880–1915* (Ann Arbor: University of Michigan Press, 1969).

128. Donald Joyce, *Gatekeepers of Black Culture: Black Owned Book Publishing in the United States, 1817–1981* (Westport, Conn.: Greenwood Press, 1983), 20.

129. Ibid., 24.

130. On race literature and the founding of black libraries, see Janice A. Radway, "The Library as Place, Collection, or Service: Promoting Book Circulation in Durham, N.C., and at the Book-of-the-Month Club, 1925–45," in *Institutions of Reading: The Social Life of Libraries in the United States*, ed. Thomas Augst and Kenneth Carpenter (Amherst: University of Massachusetts Press, 2007), 231–63.

131. Victoria Earle Matthews, "The Value of Race Literature: An Address Delivered at the First Congress of Colored Women of the United States, July 30, 1895," *Massachusetts Review* 27 (1986): 170.

132. Joyce, *Gatekeepers of Black Culture*, 27.

133. Ibid., 42.

134. Ibid., 44.

135. Ibid., 53–66.

136. See especially Dickson D. Bruce Jr., *Black American Writing from the Nadir: The Evolution of a Literary Tradition, 1877–1917* (Baton Rouge: Louisiana State University Press, 1989), 11–55.

137. See also Jacqueline Jones Royster, *Traces of a Stream: Literacy and Social Change among African-American Women* (Pittsburgh: University of Pittsburgh Press, 2000), esp. 248.

138. *A Call for Afro-American Authors of America: To Meet with the American Association of Educators of Colored Youth in Wilmington, N.C., December 27–30, 1892*, pamphlet, quoted in Bruce, *Black American Writing*, 13.

139. Bruce, *Black American Writing*, 102.

140. Meier, *Negro Thought in America*, 256.

141. W. E. B. Du Bois, *The Souls of Black Folks* (1903; repr., New York: Dover Publications, 1994).

142. My discussion of Du Bois relies heavily on David Levering Lewis, *W. E. B. Du Bois: Biography of a Race, 1868–1919* (New York: Henry Holt, 1993).

143. For a discussion of the various terms used to encapsulate this literary movement of the 1920s, see Leon Coleman, *Carl Van Vechten and the Harlem Renaissance: A Critical Assessment* (New York: Garland Publishing, 1998), ix.

144. Harold Cruse, *The Crisis of the Negro Intellectual* (New York: Quill, 1984); Nathan Huggins, *Harlem Renaissance* (New York: Oxford University Press, 1971); David Levering Lewis, *When Harlem Was in Vogue* (New York: Albert A. Knopf, 1981); Houston A. Baker Jr., *Modernism and the Harlem Renaissance* (Chicago: University of Chicago Press, 1987); Anne Elizabeth Carroll, *Word, Image, and the New Negro: Representation and Identity in the Harlem Renaissance* (Bloomington: Indiana University Press, 2007); Cherene Sherrard-Johnson, *Portraits of the New Negro Woman: Visual and Literary Culture in the Harlem Renaissance* (New Brunswick: Rutgers University Press, 2007).

145. Lewis, *When Harlem Was in Vogue*, 91.

146. Ibid., 98.

147. Bender, *New York Intellect*, 254.

148. Michael Denning, *The Cultural Front: The Laboring of American Culture* (London: Verso, 1996), xv. See also Daniel Aaron, *Writers on the Left* (New York: Oxford University Press, 1977). The concluding section of this chapter is heavily indebted to Denning's extraordinary and well-documented account.

CHAPTER 12
Crafting a Communications Infrastructure:
Scientific and Technical Publishing in the United States

1. Boyd Childress, "Scholarly Periodicals in the Second World War," *Scholarly Publishing* 20 (January 1989): 93–106, notes that "There is very little secondary research on scholarly journals in the twentieth century" (96).

2. William H. Goetzmann, "Paradigm Lost," in *The Sciences in the American Context: New Perspectives*, ed. Nathan Reingold (Washington, D.C.: Smithsonian Institution Press, 1979), 24; John Tebbel, *A History of Book Publishing in the United States*, 4 vols. (New York: R. R. Bowker, 1972–80), 2:535; Nathan Reingold, "Reflections on 200 Years of Science in the United States," in Reingold, *The Sciences in the American Context*, 16, 18.

3. Genevieve Miller, "The Nineteenth Century Medical Press," in *Centenary of Index Medicus, 1879–1979*, ed. John B. Blake (Bethesda: U.S. Department of Health and Human Services, Public Health Service, 1980), 25.

4. Ibid., 27; Tebbel, *History of Book Publishing in the United States*, 1:372, 2:284.

5. Tebbel, *History of Book Publishing in the United States*, 1:319–20.

6. Edward Matthews Crane, *A Century of Book Publishing, 1846–1948* (New York: D. Van Nostrand, 1948), 16.

7. John Hammond Moore, *Wiley: One Hundred and Seventy-Five Years of Publishing* (New York: John Wiley & Sons, 1982), 82, 84; Tebbel, *History of Book Publishing in the United States*, 2:246.

8. Gerard R. Wolfe, *The House of Appleton* (Metuchen, N.J.: Scarecrow Press, 1981).

9. Ellen Gilbert, *The House of Holt, 1866–1946: An Editorial History* (Metuchen, N.J.: Scarecrow Press, 1993), 134; Tebbel, *History of Book Publishing in the United States*, 2:209, 312.

10. John Burnham, "How the Concept of Profession Evolved in the Work of Historians of Medicine," *Bulletin of the History of Medicine* 70 (1996): 5. Also see Roger L. Geiger, *To Advance Knowledge: The Growth of American Research Universities, 1900–1940* (New York: Oxford University Press, 1986), and Daniel J. Kevles, *The Physicists: The History of a Scientific Community in Modern America* (New York: Alfred A. Knopf, 1978).

11. Kevles, *The Physicists*, 76.

12. Geiger, *To Advance Knowledge*; Keith R. Benson, "Science and the Single Author: Historical Reflections on the Problem of Authorship," *Cancer Bulletin* 43 (July–August 1991): 326.

13. Kevles, *The Physicists*, 79.

14. See John C. Burnham, "The Evolution of Editorial Peer Review," *Journal of the American Medical Association* 263 (March 1990): 1323–29; Marcel C. LaFollette, *Stealing into Print: Fraud, Plagiarism, and Misconduct in Scientific Publishing* (Berkeley: University of California Press, 1992), chap. 3.

15. Elizabeth Knoll, "The American Medical Association and Its Journal," in *Medical Journals and Medical Knowledge: Historical Essays*, ed. William F. Bynum, Stephen Lock, and Roy Porter (London: Routledge, 1992), 159.

16. Frank Luther Mott, *A History of American Magazines*, 5 vols. (Cambridge, Mass.: Harvard University Press, 1930–68), 4:525; Knoll, "The American Medical Association," 159.

17. Knoll, "The American Medical Association," 159.

18. Michael M. Sokal, "*Science* and James McKeen Cattell, 1894–1945," *Science* 209 (4 July 1980): 43–52.

19. Ibid., 45.

20. Kevles, *The Physicists*, 283.

21. Reingold, "Reflections on 200 Years of Science," 12.

22. A. McGehee Harvey, *Science at the Bedside: Clinical Research in American Medicine, 1905–1945* (Baltimore: Johns Hopkins University Press, 1981), 115; Geiger, *To Advance Knowledge*, 80.

23. Benson, "Science and the Single Author," 327; Derek J. de Solla Price, *Science since Babylon* (New Haven: Yale University Press, 1961).

24. The first estimate is based on the author's analysis of *Publishers' Weekly* data given in "American Book Title Output, 1880–1918," appendix A, in Tebbel, *History of Book Publishing in the United States*, 2:673–708. The second estimate comes from Herbert A. Bloch, "An Analysis of National Publication Trends and Publishers' Best Sellers as an Index of Cultural Transition," *Journal of Educational Sociology* 22 (December 1948): 287–303. The third estimate draws from Robert Frederick Lane, "The Place of American University Presses in Publishing" (Ph.D. diss., University of Chicago, 1939; private edition, Chicago: University of Chicago Libraries, 1942), tables 11 and 12.

25. James Stacy Thompson, *The Technical Book Publisher in Wartimes* (New York: New York Public Library, 1942), 43.

26. Estimate based on the author's analysis of Pratt Institute Free Library, *Technical Books of 1908: A Selection* (Brooklyn, N.Y.: McGraw and Hill, 1909; subsequent editions by McGraw-Hill Book Company, through 1920). In 1909 the book departments of McGraw and Hill merged to form the McGraw-Hill Book Company.

27. Tebbel, *History of Book Publishing in the United States*, 2:240; Thompson, *The Technical Book Publisher*, 17.

28. Crane, *A Century of Book Publishing*, 27.

29. Wolfe, *The House of Appleton*, 79.

30. Crane, *A Century of Book Publishing*, 36; Tebbel, *History of Book Publishing in the United States*, 2:240.

31. Tebbel, *History of Book Publishing in the United States*, 2:240; Moore, *Wiley*, 146.

32. Moore, *Wiley*, 102.

33. Roger Burlingame, *Endless Frontiers: The Story of McGraw-Hill* (New York: McGraw-Hill, 1959), 178-79.

34. New York Public Library, *A Selected List of Books on Engineering, Industrial Arts and Trades* (New York: New York Public Library, 1913).

35. Ibid., 57-58; Tebbel, *History of Book Publishing in the United States*, 3:527.

36. Moore, *Wiley*, 98; Tebbel, *History of Book Publishing in the United States*, 2:240.

37. Moore, *Wiley*, 98.

38. Crane, *A Century of Book Publishing*, 40.

39. Ibid.

40. Tebbel, *History of Book Publishing in the United States*, 2:240.

41. Frederick S. Croft, "Textbooks Are Not Absolutely Dead Things," in New York Public Library, *Bowker Lectures on Book Publishing* (New York: R. R. Bowker, 1957), 44.

42. Thompson, *The Technical Book Publisher*, 43.

43. Colin Day, "The University Press: An Organic Part of the Institution," *Scholarly Publishing* 23 (October 1991): 31; Joseph A. Brandt, "The University of Every Man," in New York Public Library, *Bowker Lectures on Book Publishing*, 167.

44. Day, "The University Press," 30.

45. Albert N. Greco, *The Book Publishing Industry* (Boston: Allyn and Bacon, 1997), 72.

46. *The University of Chicago Press: Catalogue of Books and Journals, 1891-1965* (Chicago: University of Chicago Press, 1967), xv.

47. Day, "The University Press," 30.

48. Data from a study by Chester Kerr, cited in Paul Parsons, *Getting Published* (Knoxville: University of Tennessee Press, 1989), 28.

49. Tebbel, *History of Book Publishing in the United States*, 3:606; Moore, *Wiley*, 127.

50. *The University of Chicago Press*, xxiii; Chester Kerr, *A Report on American University Presses* (Washington, D.C.: Association of American University Presses, 1949), 18.

51. Donald Franklin Joyce, *Black Book Publishers in the United States: A Historical Dictionary of the Presses, 1817-1990* (New York: Greenwood Press, 1991), 108; Brandt, "The University of Every Man," 169.

52. Brandt, "The University of Every Man," 165, 171.

53. Lane, "The Place of American University Presses," 104-5, 107.

54. Kerr, *A Report on American University Presses*, 33; Brandt, "The University of Every Man," 173.

55. Garland Allen, "The Rise and Spread of the Classical School of Heredity, 1910-1930: Development and Influence of the Mendelian Chromosome Theory," in Reingold, *The Sciences in the American Context*, 210.

56. Burlingame, *Endless Frontiers*, 241, 243.

57. Ibid., 182.

58. Moore, *Wiley*, 82.

59. John L. Dusseau, *An Informal History of W. B. Saunders Company on the Occasion of Its Hundredth Anniversary* (Philadelphia: W. B. Saunders, 1988), 59.

60. Pnina G. Abir-Am, "The Assessment of Interdisciplinary Research in the 1930s: The Rockefeller Foundation and Physico-Chemical Morphology," *Minerva* 26 (Summer 1988): 169.

61. Crane, *A Century of Book Publishing*, 72-73.

62. Burlingame, *Endless Frontiers*, 234-35, 243.

63. Tebbel, *History of Book Publishing in the United States*, 3:252, 615; Moore, *Wiley*, 121; Crane, *A Century of Book Publishing*, 46-48.

64. Burlingame, *Endless Frontiers*, 249.

65. Tebbel, *History of Book Publishing in the United States*, 2:246.

66. Moore, *Wiley*, 75, 82.

67. *International Critical Tables of Numerical Data, Physics, Chemistry and Technology*, prepared under the auspices of the International Research Council and the National Academy of Sciences by the National Research Council (New York: McGraw-Hill Book Company, 1926).

68. Thompson, *The Technical Book Publisher*, 32-33; Burlingame, *Endless Frontiers*, 249.

69. Benson, "Science and the Single Author," 327, table 1.

70. James M. Reid, *An Adventure in Textbooks, 1924-1960* (New York: R. R. Bowker, 1969), 68-69.

71. Ella Thea Smith, *Exploring Biology* (New York: Harcourt Brace, 1938), iv.

72. Reid, *An Adventure in Textbooks*, 71.

73. Joseph J. Corn, "Educating the Enthusiast: Print and the Popularization of Technical Knowledge," in *Possible Dreams: Enthusiasm for Technology in America*, ed. John L. Wright (Dearborn: Henry Ford Museum and Greenfield Village, 1992), 21. Also see Ronald C. Tobey, *The American Ideology of National Science, 1919-1930* (Pittsburgh: University of Pittsburgh Press, 1971), 1-4.

74. Corn, "Educating the Enthusiast," 29.

75. Ibid., 62.

76. Mott, *A History of American Magazines*, 3:495-99.

77. Marcel C. LaFollette, *Making Science Our Own: Public Images of Science, 1910-1955* (Chicago: University of Chicago Press, 1990).

78. Annette M. Woodlief, "Science in American Culture," in *Handbook of American Popular Culture*, ed. M. Thomas Inge, 3 vols. (Westport, Conn.: Greenwood Press, 1978-81), 3:432.

79. John C. Burnham, *How Superstition Won and Science Lost: Popularizing Science and Health in the United States* (New Brunswick: Rutgers University Press, 1987), 170.

80. Marcel C. LaFollette, "Taking Science to the Marketplace: Examples of Science Service's Presentation of Chemistry during the 1930s," *HYLE: International Journal of Philosophy of Chemistry* 12 (2006): 69-74; David Rhees, "The Chemists' War: The Impact of World

War I on the American Chemical Profession," *Bulletin of the History of Chemistry* 13-14 (1992-93):41; Kevles, *The Physicists*, chaps. 12 and 13.

81. William E. Ritter to Charles B. Davenport, 10 December 1920, box 184, James McKeen Cattell Papers, Library of Congress, Washington, D.C.; E. W. Scripps in *Damned Old Crank: A Self-Portrait of E. W. Scripps Drawn from His Unpublished Writings*, ed. Charles R. McCabe (New York: Harper & Brothers, 1951), 231. Also see James C. Foust, "E. W. Scripps and the Science Service," *Journalism History* 21 (1995): 59.

82. William Emerson Ritter, "The Relation of E. W. Scripps to Science," *Science* 65 (25 March 1927): 292; Foust, "E. W. Scripps," 58-64.

83. John Tebbel, *Between Covers: The Rise and Transformation of Book Publishing in America* (New York: Oxford University Press, 1987), 320. See also Marcel Chotkowski LaFollette, *Reframing Scopes: Journalists, Scientists, and Lost Photographs from the Trial of the Century* (Lawrence: University Press of Kansas, 2008).

84. David Rhees, "The Chemical Foundation and Popular Chemistry between the Wars," *CHOC News* 3 (Spring 1985): 2; Rhees, "The Chemists' War," 46.

85. Crane, *A Century of Book Publishing*, 50.

86. Ibid., 45-46.

87. Ibid.

88. Ibid., 50.

89. LaFollette, *Making Science Our Own*.

90. Tobey, *The American Ideology*, 9-10. Also see Doug Russell, "Popularization and the Challenge to Science-Centrism in the 1930s," in *The Literature of Science: Perspectives on Popular Science Writing*, ed. Murdo William McRae (Athens: University of Georgia Press, 1993), and George Ehrhardt, "Descendants of Prometheus: Popular Science Writing in the United States, 1915-1948" (Ph.D. diss., Duke University, 1993).

91. Burnham, *How Superstition Won*, 189-90; Tebbel, *History of Book Publishing in the United States*, 3:303.

92. Frank Luther Mott, *Golden Multitudes: The Story of Best Sellers in the United States* (New York: Macmillan, 1947), 271.

93. Asa Don Dickinson, *The Best Books of the Decade, 1926-1935: A Later Clue to the Literary Labyrinth* (New York: H. W. Wilson, 1937), xi.

94. Alice Payne Hackett, *50 Years of Best Sellers, 1895-1945* (New York: R. R. Bowker, 1945); Mott, *Golden Multitudes*.

95. Charles E. Rosenberg, *No Other Gods: On Science and American Thought* (Baltimore: Johns Hopkins University Press, 1976), 124.

96. Burnham, *How Superstition Won*, 189-90.

97. Asa Don Dickinson, *The Best Books of the Decade, 1936-1945* (New York: H. W. Wilson Company, 1948), 10.

98. *Science, Popular Science, and Technical Books for Branch Libraries, January 1938-April 1940* (Baltimore: Enoch Pratt Free Library, Industry and Science Department, 1940) was compiled to address the wide-ranging interests of its patrons.

99. Dickinson, *Best Books of the Decade, 1926-1935*, 32, 39, 51.

100. Burnham, *How Superstition Won*.

101. Kevles, *The Physicists*, 218; Geiger, *To Advance Knowledge*, 233-34 and 241-42.

102. Louis de Broglie, *New York Times*, 11 May 1935, quoted in Kevles, *The Physicists*, 282.

103. Kevles, *The Physicists*, 218.

104. Harold C. Relyea, "Information, Secrecy, and Atomic Energy," *New York University Review of Law and Social Change* 10 (1980-81): 267.

105. Spencer Weart, "Scientists with a Secret," *Physics Today* 29 (February 1976): 23-30; Spencer R. Weart, *Scientists in Power* (Cambridge, Mass.: Harvard University Press, 1979).

106. Michael M. Sokal, "From the Archives," *Science, Technology & Human Values* 10 (Spring 1985): 24; Michael M. Sokal, "Restrictions on Scientific Publication," *Science* 215 (5 March 1982): 1182.

107. Thompson, *The Technical Book Publisher*, 13; Burlingame, *Endless Frontiers*, 330.

108. Robert E. Summers, ed., *Wartime Censorship of Press and Radio* (New York: H. W. Wilson Company, 1942), 115; Patrick S. Washburn, "The Office of Censorship's Attempt to Control Press Coverage of the Atomic Bomb during World War II," *Journalism Monographs* 120 (April 1990); and Michael S. Sweeney, *Secrets of Victory: The Office of Censorship and the American Press and Radio in World War II* (Chapel Hill: University of North Carolina Press, 2001), 195-206.

109. Childress, "Scholarly Periodicals."

110. Ibid.; "Science Hush-Hushed," *Time* 39 (11 May 1942): 90.

111. Tebbel, *History of Book Publishing in the United States*, 3:24, 218; Burlingame, *Endless Frontiers*, 21-14, 320.

112. Council on Books in Wartime, *A History of the Council on Books in Wartime, 1942-1946* (New York: The Council, 1946).

113. Burlingame, *Endless Frontiers*, 214-15.

114. Thompson, *The Technical Book Publisher*, 4. Also see Burlingame, *Endless Frontiers*.

115. Thompson, *The Technical Book Publisher*, 8.

116. Burlingame, *Endless Frontiers*, 326.

117. Thompson, *The Technical Book Publisher*, 5.

118. See, for example, Crane, *A Century of Book Publishing*, 67, and Thompson, *The Technical Book Publisher*, 14.

119. Burlingame, *Endless Frontiers*, 326; Thompson, *The Technical Book Publisher*, 9.

120. Moore, *Wiley*, 145.

121. Pamela Spence Richards, "Great Britain and Allied Scientific Information, 1939-1945," *Minerva* 26 (Summer 1988): 193.

122. Robert K. Stewart, "The Office of Technical Services: A New Deal Idea in the Cold War," *Knowledge: Creation, Diffusion, Utilization* 15 (September 1993): 46.

123. Ibid.

124. Burlingame, *Endless Frontiers*, 333.

125. Ibid., 334.

126. Hugh Stott Taylor, "In the Sciences," in *Putting Knowledge to Work, 1942-1952: A Tribute to Datus Clifford Smith, Jr., on the Occasion of His Tenth Anniversary as Director of the Princeton University Press* (Princeton: Princeton University Press, 1952), 58-59.

127. See Philip Dean Tegler, "The Amazing Half-Life of Atomic Science Writing," *American Book Collector* 4 (July-August 1983): 12-21.

128. Vannevar Bush, *Science — The Endless Frontier: A Report to the President on a Program for Postwar Scientific Research* (Washington, D.C.: Government Printing Office, 1945).

129. Stewart, "The Office of Technical Services," 45, 46.

130. Ibid., 57.

131. Science Division, Reference Department, *Science in the Library of Congress* (Washington, D.C.: Library of Congress, 1954), 1.

132. Ibid., 2.

133. Theodore Frederick Koop, *Weapon of Silence* (Chicago: University of Chicago Press, 1946), 285.

134. Ibid., 286.

135. Price, *Science since Babylon*, 103.

CHAPTER 13
The Government as Publisher

1. United States Government Printing Office, *Annual Report* (Washington, D.C.: Government Printing Office, 1896), 11.

2. United States Government Printing Office, *Annual Report* (Washington, D.C.: Government Printing Office, 1881), 13, 14. The range and number of government documents can be glimpsed in three publications: *Checklist of United States Public Documents, 1789–1909*, 3rd ed. (Washington, D.C.: Government Printing Office, 1911) and two serial catalogs: *Catalog of the Public Documents of the 53d to 76th Congress and of All Departments of the Government of the United States for the Period from March 4, 1893, to December 31, 1940* (Washington, D.C.: Government Printing Office, 1896–1945, 25 vols.) and *The Monthly Catalog* of government publications (title varies), which began in 1895 and continues today as an on-line resource with records from 1976 forward. ⟨http://catalog.gpo.gov/F⟩ query: Monthly Catalog (3 December 2007).

3. John Charles Frémont, *Report of the Exploring Expedition to Rocky Mountains in 1842, and to Oregon and North California in 1843–44* (Washington, D.C.: Gales and Seaton, 1845).

4. James Madison to W. T. Barry, 4 August 1822, in *The Writings of James Madison*, ed. Gaillard P. Hunt, 9 vols. (New York: G. P. Putnam's Sons, 1910), 9:103.

5. "What is the history of the GPO?" ⟨http://www.gpo.gov/factsheet/index.html⟩ (3 December 2007); Oz Frankel, *States of Inquiry: Social Investigations and Print Culture in Nineteenth-Century Britain and the United States* (Baltimore: Johns Hopkins University Press, 2006).

6. The USGPO began operations following authorization by Congressional Joint Resolution 25, passed on 23 June 1860 ⟨http://www.gpo.gov/aboutgpo/bld3.html⟩ (3 December 2007). On government printing from 1840 to 1880, see Scott E. Casper, "The Census, the Post Office, and Government Publishing," in *The Industrial Book, 1840–1880*, ed. Scott E. Casper, Jeffrey D. Groves, Stephen W. Nissenbaum, and Michael Winship, vol. 3 of *A History of the Book in America* (Chapel Hill: University of North Carolina Press, 2007), 178–93.

7. John Tebbel, *A History of Publishing in the United States*, 4 vols. (New York: R. R. Bowker, 1972–81), 2:177.

8. U.S. Government Printing Office, *Checklist of United States Public Documents, 1789–1909*.

9. Oz Frankel, "The State between Orality and Textuality: Nineteenth-Century Government Reports and Orature," in *Cultural Narratives: Textuality and Performance in the United States to 1900*, ed. Sandra M. Gustafson and Caroline F. Sloat (South Bend: University of Notre Dame Press, 2009).

10. See the introduction to Frankel, *States of Inquiry*, esp. 3-19.

11. Annual reports, quoted in Daniel R. MacGilvray, "Era of Reconstruction," *New Typeline*, 2:4 (May, 1986): 6-7, ⟨http://www.access.gpo.gov/su_docs/fdlp/history/macgilvray.html#quick⟩ (1 October 2007).

12. U.S. Bureau of Statistics, *Statistical Abstract of the United States*, Fifth Number, 1882, ⟨http://www2.census.gov/prod2/statcomp/documents/1882-01.pdf⟩ (29 April 2008).

13. Hoover's misplaced belief in the Department of Commerce statistics as a panacea for farmers' marketing problems is discussed by James H. Shideler, "Herbert Hoover and the Federal Farm Board Project, 1921-1925," *Mississippi Valley Historical Review* 42 (1956): 710-29.

14. U.S. Census Bureau, History, ⟨http://www.census.gov/prod/www/abs/decennial/1880.htm⟩ (3 September 2008).

15. Walter Francis Willcox, William Edward Burghardt Du Bois, and William Chamberlin Hunt, *Negroes in the United States*, Bulletin 8, United States Bureau of the Census (Washington, D.C.: Government Printing Office, 1904).

16. George B. Courtelyou, "Letter of Transmittal," Willcox, Du Bois, and Hunt, *Negroes in the United States*, 9.

17. Henry J. Dubester, *Catalog of United States Census Publications, 1790–1945* (Washington, D.C.: Government Printing Office, 1950).

18. U.S. Department of Labor, *Report on Condition of Women and Child Wage Earners in the United States*, 19 vols. (Washington, D.C.: Government Printing Office, 1910-13).

19. U.S. Women's Bureau, *The New Position of Women in American Industry*, Bulletin no. 12, *Report on Condition of Women and Child Wage-Earners in the United States*, 19 vols. (Washington, D.C.: Government Printing Office, 1920).

20. U.S. Women's Bureau, *Potential Earning Power of Southern Mountaineer Handicraft*, Bulletin no. 128 (Washington, D.C.: Government Printing Office, 1935).

21. Edward Drinker Cope, *The Vertebrata of the Tertiary Formations of the West*, vol. 3 of the *United States Geological Survey of the Territories Final Report* (Washington, D.C.: Government Printing Office, 1883).

22. John Wesley Powell, *Exploration of the Colorado River of the West and Its Tributaries, Explored in 1869, 1870, 1871, and 1872, under Direction of the Secretary of the Smithsonian Institution* (Washington, D.C.: Government Printing Office, 1875).

23. John Wesley Powell, *Canyons of the Colorado* (Meadville, Pa.: Flood and Vincent, 1895).

24. Clarence E. Dutton, *Tertiary History of the Grand Cañon District*, Monograph no. 2 of the *United States Geological Survey* (Washington, D.C.: Government Printing Office, 1882).

25. Franz Boas and John R. Swanton, "Siouan (Dakota)," *Handbook of American Indian*

Languages, Bureau of American Ethnology Bulletin, vol. 2, no. 40 (Washington, D.C.: Government Printing Office, 1911), 875-965.

26. Victor Mindeleff, "A Study of Pueblo Architecture: Tusayan and Cibola," in *Eighth Annual Report of the Bureau of Ethnology* (Washington, D.C.: Government Printing Office, 1891), 3-228.

27. Jesse Walter Fewkes, "Hopi Katcinas, Drawn by Native Artists," *Twenty-first Annual Report of the Bureau of American Ethnology* (Washington, D.C.: Government Printing Office, 1903), 3-126.

28. Robert Nicholson Scott, Henry Martyn Lazelle, and George Breckinridge Davis, *The War of the Rebellion: A Compilation of the Official Records of the Union and Confederate Armies* (Washington, D.C.: Government Printing Office, 1880-1902).

29. Clarence E. Carter, "The United States and Documentary Historical Publications," *Mississippi Valley Historical Review* 25 (1938): 16.

30. U.S. Bureau of the Census, *Compendium of the Eleventh Census: 1890*, pt. 1 (Washington, D.C.: Government Printing Office, 1892), xlviii.

31. Frederick Jackson Turner, "The Significance of the Frontier in American History," *American Historical Association Annual Report, 1893* (Washington, D.C.: Government Printing Office, 1894), 199-227.

32. Ibid., 199.

33. *Checklist of United States Public Documents, 1789-1909*, 203.

34. U.S. Department of Agriculture, *Yearbook of Agriculture, 1920* (Washington, D.C.: Government Printing Office, 1921), 127-46.

35. U.S. Dairy Industry Bureau, *Care of Milk Utensils on Farms* (Washington, D.C.: Government Printing Office, 1939).

36. U.S. Extension Service, *Home Economics Extension Objectives as They Relate to the Training of Extension Workers* (Washington, D.C.: Government Printing Office, 1939).

37. WorldCat search, au:Federal Writers' Project, 7 August 2007.

38. Federal Writers' Project, *Washington, City and Capital* (Washington, D.C.: Government Printing Office, 1937).

39. Federal Writers' Project, *New Mexico: A Guide to the Colorful State* (New York: Hastings House, 1940).

40. Dorothea Lange, *An American Exodus: A Record of Human Erosion* (New York: Reynal & Hitchcock, 1939).

CHAPTER 14
Gilded-Age Consensus, Repressive Campaigns, and Gradual Liberalization: The Shifting Rhythms of Book Censorship

1. The standard detailed history is the second volume of John Tebbel, *A History of Book Publishing in the United States*, 4 vols. (New York: R. R. Bowker, 1972-80). For a recent interpretation, see Michael Winship, chapter 3 in this volume.

2. Donald Sheehan, *This Was Publishing: A Chronicle of the Book Trade in the Gilded Age* (Bloomington: Indiana University Press, 1952), 104.

3. Lawrence C. Stedman and Carl F. Kaestle, "Literacy and Reading Performance in the

United States from 1880 to the Present," in *Literacy in the United States: Readers and Reading since 1880*, ed. Carl F. Kaestle et al. (New Haven: Yale University Press, 1991), 75–128, esp. 79, 127; Helen Damon-Moore and Carl F. Kaestle, "Surveying American Readers," in Kaestle et al., *Literacy in the United States: Readers and Reading since 1880*, 194–95 (on women readers); Carl F. Kaestle, *Pillars of the Republic: Common Schools and American Society, 1780–1860* (New York: Hill & Wang, 1983).

4. Quoted in Noel Perrin, *Dr. Bowdler's Legacy: A History of Expurgated Books in England and America* (Boston: David R. Godine, 1992), 237.

5. Richard H. Brodhead, "Literature and Culture," in *Columbia Literary History of the United States*, ed. Emory Elliott et al. (New York: Columbia University Press, 1988), 467–81.

6. Perrin, *Dr. Bowdler's Legacy*, 259; Paul S. Boyer, *Purity in Print: The Vice Society Movement and Book Censorship in America* (New York: Charles Scribner's Sons, 1968; new and expanded edition, Madison: University of Wisconsin Press, 2002), 16.

7. Kermit Vanderbilt, *The Achievement of William Dean Howells: A Reinterpretation* (Princeton: Princeton University Press, 1968), 106.

8. Though lacking footnotes, Perrin's *Dr. Bowdler's Legacy* is a readable, well-researched account of the nineteenth-century expurgation of many classical works. See also Tebbel, *History of Book Publishing in the United States*, 2:616–17.

9. Ibid., 2:162, 212; Boyer, *Purity in Print*, 15; Tebbel, *History of Book Publishing in the United States*, 2:162, 212, 268–69, 610.

10. Boyer, *Purity in Print*, 18; Perrin, *Dr. Bowdler's Legacy*, 188.

11. Quoted in Jack Salzman, "Literature for the Populace," in Elliott et al., *Columbia Literary History of the United States*, 559.

12. Thomas L. Tedford, *Freedom of Speech in the United States* (New York: Random House, 1985), 162.

13. Boyer, *Purity in Print*, 5–8.

14. Ibid., 22. Recent studies dealing with late nineteenth-century censorship and views of obscenity, written from differing interpretive perspectives, include Rochelle Gurstein, *The Repeal of Reticence: A History of America's Cultural and Legal Struggles over Free Speech, Obscenity, Sexual Liberation, and Modern Art* (New York: Hill & Wang, 1996); Alison M. Parker, *Purifying America: Women, Cultural Reform, and Pro-Censorship Activism, 1873–1933* (Urbana: University of Illinois Press, 1997); and Helen Lefkowitz Horowitz, *Rereading Sex: Battles over Sexual Knowledge and Suppression in Nineteenth-Century America* (New York: Alfred A. Knopf, 2002).

15. Horowitz, *Rereading Sex*, 20, 22; Tebbel, "American Book Title Output, 1880–1918," appendix A of *History of Book Publishing in the United States*, 2:619, 675–83.

16. Comstock, quoted in Salzman, "Literature for the Populace," 558.

17. Steven Marcus, *The Other Victorians: A Study of Sexuality and Pornography in Mid-Nineteenth Century England* (1966; repr., with a new introduction by the author, New York: Basic Books, 1975).

18. An exception was the suppression of Tolstoy's *Kreutzer Sonata* in 1890, which roused considerable protest in publishing and intellectual circles; see Tebbel, *History of Book Publishing in the United States*, 2:621.

19. Boyer, *Purity in Print*, 10–11.

20. Brodhead, "Literature and Culture," 476-77.

21. Daniel Aaron, "Literary Scenes and Movements [1910-1945]," in Elliott et al., *Columbia Literary History of the United States*, 733-57.

22. Boyer, *Purity in Print*, 19.

23. Ibid., 19; Tebbel, *History of Book Publishing in the United States*, 2:326.

24. Henry F. May, *The End of American Innocence: A Study of the First Years of Our Own Time, 1912-1917* (New York: Alfred A. Knopf, 1959), explores the cultural radicalism of these years.

25. Tebbel, *History of Book Publishing in the United States*, 2:337, 613. *The Old Wives' Tale* is the story of two English sisters, one of whom leads a turbulent life in Paris after being abandoned by her husband.

26. Boyer, *Purity in Print*, 30; Perrin, *Dr. Bowdler's Legacy*, 183.

27. Ellen Chesler, *Woman of Valor: Margaret Sanger and the Birth Control Movement in America* (New York: Simon & Schuster, 1992); Boyer, *Purity in Print*, 32-35, 37-39; Tebbel, *History of Book Publishing in the United States*, 2:383, 357.

28. Tebbel, *History of Book Publishing in the United States*, 2:383, 629-31.

29. Ibid., 24, 25.

30. Ibid., 55-56.

31. Ibid., 58-60.

32. Tedford, *Freedom of Speech in the United States*, 72-76.

33. Lynn Dumenil, *The Modern Temper: American Culture and Society in the 1920s* (New York: Hill & Wang, 1995).

34. Boyer, *Purity in Print*, 69-73. See James L. W. West III, chapter 4 in this volume.

35. Perrin, *Dr. Bowdler's Legacy*, 239.

36. Boyer, *Purity in Print*, 74-94.

37. Ibid., 99-134.

38. Ibid., 128-31; Jay A. Gertzman, *Bookleggers and Smuthounds: The Trade in Erotica, 1920-1940* (Philadelphia: University of Pennsylvania Press, 2002).

39. Boyer, *Purity in Print*, 107-17, 141 (quoted passage).

40. Ibid., 167-95.

41. Ibid., 196-206.

42. Ibid., 135 (emphasis in original).

43. Ibid., 210-42.

44. Ibid., 255-59; Tedford, *Freedom of Speech in the United States*, 163.

45. Felice Flanery Lewis, *Literature, Obscenity and Law* (Carbondale: Southern Illinois University Press, 1976), 120-24, 148-52, 162-66, 172-74.

46. Tedford, *Freedom of Speech in the United States*, 164-65.

47. Ibid., 165-71.

CHAPTER 15
Distinctive Media: The European Ethnic Press in the United States

1. Maldwyn Allen Jones, *American Immigration* (Chicago: University of Chicago Press, 1960), 179.

2. Joseph Velikonja, "The Periodical Press and Italian Communities," 1-3 (manuscript

in possession of author). I call these presses the "ethnic press," because "immigrant press" ignores their continuing functions beyond the first generation, and the term "foreign-language press" overlooks some English-language ethnic presses. See Lubomyr R. Wynar and Anna T. Wynar, *Encyclopedic Directory of Ethnic Newspapers and Periodicals in the United States*, 2nd ed. (Littleton, Colo.: Libraries Unlimited, 1976), 14-15.

3. Robert E. Park, *The Immigrant Press and Its Control* (New York: Harper & Brothers, 1922), 304-5, 330-32; Sally M. Miller, introduction to *The Ethnic Press in the United States: A Historical Analysis and Handbook*, ed. Sally M. Miller (Westport, Conn.: Greenwood Press, 1987), xiv-xv.

4. Miller, *The Ethnic Press*, xv-xvi.

5. Marion Tuttle Marzolf, *The Danish-Language Press in America* (New York: Arno Press, 1979), 29; Marion Tuttle Marzolf, "The Danish Press," in Miller, *The Ethnic Press*, 67.

6. Among recent strong studies are Ulf Jonas Bjork, "The Swedish-American Press: Three Newspapers and Their Communities" (Ph.D. diss., University of Washington, 1987); Jeffrey Alan Irvine, "Aspects of Identity: Evidence from the Irish-American Press, 1871-1925" (Ph.D. diss., University of Pittsburgh, 1994); Michael P. Mulcrone, "On Razor's Edge: The Irish-American Press, 1914-1918: A Case Study in Conflicting Loyalties" (Ph.D. diss., University of Oregon, 1988).

7. Bjork, "The Swedish-American Press," 17.

8. In "Bintel Brief," Cahan answered letters from readers, advising Jewish immigrants on life in America. For more, see Isaac Metzker, ed., *A Bintel Brief: Sixty Years of Letters from the Lower East Side to the Jewish Daily Forward* (Garden City, N.Y.: Doubleday, 1971).

9. Bjork, "Swedish-American Press," 194; Dorothy Burton Skaardal, *The Divided Heart: Scandinavian Immigrant Experiences through Literary Sources* (Lincoln: University of Nebraska Press, 1974), 157.

10. Mulcrone, "Irish-American Press," 9-11.

11. Miller, *The Ethnic Press*, xiii.

12. Ibid., xvii-xviii.

13. Joseph Velikonja, "Slovene Newspapers and Periodicals in America," paper presented at the Symposia Studijski Dnevi, New York, 1981.

14. James Bergquist, "The German-American Press," in Miller, *The Ethnic Press*, 140.

15. See chapters on the Norwegian, Irish, Danish, Swedish, and Dutch presses in Miller, *The Ethnic Press*. On Welsh, see "Welsh," in *Harvard Encyclopedia of American Ethnic Groups*, ed. Stephan Thernstrom (Cambridge, Mass.: Belknap Press, 1980), 1016.

16. Bergquist, "German-American Press," 134-43.

17. Frederick C. Luebke, "Legal Restrictions on Foreign Languages in the Great Plains States, 1917-1923," in *Languages in Conflict: Linguistic Acculturation on the Great Plains*, ed. Paul Schach (Lincoln: University of Nebraska Press, 1980), 2-3.

18. More than 120 such German-language labor newspapers were published between 1870 and 1900. See Dirk Hoerder, "The German-American Labor Press and Its Views of the Political Institutions in the United States," in *The German-American Radical Press: The Shaping of a Left Political Culture, 1850-1940*, ed. Elliott Shore, Ken Fones-Wolf, and James P. Danky (Urbana: University of Illinois Press, 1992), 184-85; Sally M. Miller, "Voices of Immigrant Labor," *Labor's Heritage* 2 (July 1990): 62-75. Also see Dirk Hoerder and Christiane Harzig,

eds., *The Immigrant Labor Press in North America, 1840s–1970s: An Annotated Bibliography*, 3 vols. (Westport, Conn.: Greenwood Press, 1987).

19. Bergquist, "German-American Press," 142–43.

20. Arlow W. Andersen, *The Immigrant Takes His Stand: The Norwegian-American Press and Public Affairs, 1847–1872* (Northfield, Minn.: Norwegian-American Historical Association, 1953); Lowell J. Soike, *Norwegian Americans and the Politics of Dissent, 1880–1924* (Northfield, Minn.: Norwegian-American Historical Association, 1991), 62–68.

21. Arlow W. Andersen, "The Norwegian-American Press," in Miller, *The Ethnic Press*, 265–70.

22. Jerzy Zubrzycki, "The Role of the Foreign-Language Press in Migrant Integration," *Population Studies* 12 (1958): 77.

23. A. J. Kuzniewski, "The Polish American Press," in Miller, *The Ethnic Press*, 276–90; Edmund G. Olszyk, *The Polish Press in America* (Milwaukee: Marquette University Press, 1940). The latter is a superficial study but see especially p. 25.

24. M. Mark Stolarik, "The Slovak-American Press," in Miller, *The Ethnic Press*, 354–68. Also see František Bieľcek, "Slovak Newspapers in the U.S. and Their Role in the Process of Acculturation of Slovak Emigrants," in *The Press of Labor Migrants in Europe and North America, 1880s to 1930s*, ed. Christiane Harzig and Dirk Hoerder (Bremen: University of Bremen, 1985), 505–17.

25. Andrew T. Kopan, "The Greek Press," in Miller, *The Ethnic Press*, 161–69.

26. Luebke, "Legal Restrictions on Foreign Languages in the Great Plains States, 1917–1923," 4–16. See also Joseph A. Ranney, "Aliens and 'Real Americans': Law & Ethnic Assimilation in Wisconsin, 1846–1920," *Wisconsin Law* (1997), ⟨www.wisbar.org⟩ (1 May 2007).

27. Bergquist, "German-American Press," 146–50; Zubrzycki, "Role of the Foreign-Language Press," 76.

28. Joseph S. Roucek, "Foreign-Language Press in World War II," *Sociology and Social Research* 27 (July–August 1943): 462.

CHAPTER 16

Exiles, Immigrants, and Natives:
Hispanic Print Culture in What Became the Mainland of the United States

1. Because other volumes in this series treating earlier periods in United States book history omit extensive treatment of Hispanic print culture, this essay looks back to its origins and early history. Developments in Hispanic print culture of the period 1880 to 1940 cannot adequately be understood without some knowledge of this earlier period.

2. Donald E. Chipman, *Spanish Texas, 1519–1821* (Austin: University of Texas Press, 1992), 243.

3. Bernard L. Fontana, *The Legacy of Spain and Mexico in the United States* (Albuquerque: University of New Mexico Press, 1994), 77.

4. Nicolás Kanellos, *Hispanic Firsts* (Detroit: Gale Research, 1997), 42.

5. Ibid., 292.

6. In fact, there were two editions of Las Casa's *Breve historia de la destrucción de las Indias* published in Philadelphia, in 1821 and 1822.

7. Ambrosio Fornet, *El libro en Cuba* (Havana: Editorial Letras Cubanas, 1994), 73-74.

8. Matias Montes-Huidobro, ed., *El laúd del desterrado* (Houston: Arte Público Press, 1995), 135.

9. Enrique Trujillo, *Apuntes históricos* (New York: Imprenta de "El Porvenir," 1890), 52.

10. Fornet, *El libro en Cuba*, 183.

11. For more on both revolutionaries, see Juan Gómez-Quiñones, *Roots of Chicano Politics, 1600-1940* (Albuquerque: University of New Mexico Press, 1994), 290-91.

12. At this point *Regeneración* was printing and distributing 30,000 copies. Yolanda Argudín, *Historia del periodismo en México desde el Virreinato hasta nuestros días* (Mexico City: Panorama Editorial, 1997), 111.

13. Ibid., 110.

14. See Clara Lomas, "The Articulation of Gender in the Mexican Borderlands, 1900-1915," in *Recovering the U.S. Hispanic Literary Heritage*, ed. Ramón Gutiérrez and Genaro Padilla (Houston: Arte Público Press, 1993), 293-308.

15. For further description for these newspapers, see Rafael Chabrán, "Spaniards," in *The Immigrant Labor Press in North America, 1840s-1970s*, ed. Dirk Hoerder and Christiane Harzig (Westport, Conn.: Greenwood Press, 1987), 151-90.

16. Robert E. Park, *The Immigrant Press and Its Control* (1922; repr., Westport, Conn.: Greenwood Press, 1970), 9-13.

17. Victoria Goff, "Spanish-Language Newspapers in California," in *Outsiders in 19th-Century Press History: Multicultural Perspectives*, ed. Frankie Hutton and Barbara Straus Reed (Bowling Green, Ohio: Bowling Green State University Popular Press, 1995), 64.

18. Ramón D. Chacón, "The Chicano Immigrant Press in Los Angeles: The Case of 'El Heraldo de México,' 1916-1920," *Journalism History* 4, no. 2 (Summer 1977): 48-50.

19. Ibid., 50.

20. Ibid., 62.

21. Onofre Di Stefano, "La Prensa of San Antonio and Its Literary Page, 1913-1915," *Dissertation Abstracts* 45, no. 1 (July 1984): 196A.

22. Rubén Munguía, "La Prensa: Memories of a Boy . . . Sixty Years Later," *Américas Review*, Fall-Winter 1989: 132.

23. Joseph P. Fitzpatrick, "The Puerto Rican Press," in *The Ethnic Press in the United States: A Historical Analysis and Handbook*, ed. Sally M. Miller (Westport, Conn.: Greenwood Press, 1987), 307.

24. Ibid., 308.

25. See Tomás Almaguer, *Racial Fault Lines: The Historical Origins of White Supremacy in California* (Berkeley: University of California Press, 1994), 183-203; Stuart Jamieson, *Labor Unionism in American Agriculture* (New York: Arno Press, 1976), 76-77; Carey McWilliams, *North from Mexico: The Spanish-Speaking People of the United States* (Philadelphia: Lippincott, 1949), 190; Sam Kushner, *Long Road to Delano: A Century of Farmworkers' Struggle* (New York: International Publishers, 1975), 20-21; F. Arturo Rosales, *Chicano! The History of the Mexican American Civil Rights Movement* (Houston: Arte Público Press, 1996).

26. Ann L. Henderson and Gary R. Mormino, *Spanish Pathways in Florida* (Sarasota, Fla.: Pineapple Press, 1991), 34.

27. Ibid., 40-45.
28. Fornet, *El libro en Cuba*, 185-86.
29. Chabrán, "Spaniards," 157.
30. Ibid.
31. Lubomyr R. Wynar and Anna T. Wynar, *Encyclopedic Directory of Ethnic Newspapers and Periodicals in the United States*, 2nd ed. (Littleton, Colo.: Libraries Unlimited, 1976), 18-19.
32. See Almaguer, *Racial Fault Lines*, 3, for the definition and use of the term "racialization," and the remainder of his book for details on how Mexicans became racialized.
33. John Melton Wallace, *Gaceta to Gazette: A Checklist of Texas Newspapers, 1812-1846* (Austin: University of Texas Department of Journalism Development Program, 1966), 74.
34. William B. Rice, *The Los Angeles Star, 1851-1864* (Berkeley: University of California Press, 1951), 17-24.
35. See Porter A. Stratton, *The Territorial Press of New Mexico, 1834-1912* (Albuquerque: University of New Mexico Press, 1969), 12.
36. Félix Gutiérrez, "Spanish-Language Media in America: Background," *Journalism History* 4 (Summer 1977): 39.
37. Ibid., 41.
38. Joseph Tardiff, *Dictionary of Hispanic Biography* (Detroit: Gale Research, 1995), 836.
39. See the introduction by Rosaura Sánchez and Beatrice Pita, in María Amparo Ruiz de Burton, *Who Would Have Thought It?* (1872; repr., Houston: Arte Público Press, 1996).
40. A. Gabriel Meléndez, *So All Is Not Lost: The Poetics of Print in Nuevomexicano Communities, 1834-1958* (Albuquerque: University of New Mexico Press, 1997), 24-25. Also see Juan Gómez-Quiñones, *Roots of Chicano Politics, 1600-1940* (Albuquerque: University of New Mexico Press, 1994), 323-28; E. B. Fincher, *Spanish Americans as a Political Factor in New Mexico, 1912-1950* (New York: Arno Press, 1974); Calvin Horn, *New Mexico's Troubled Years: The Story of the Early Territorial Governors* (Albuquerque: Horn and Wallace, 1963); Robert W. Larson, *New Mexico's Quest for Statehood* (Albuquerque: University of New Mexico Press, 1968).
41. Meléndez, *So All Is Not Lost: The Poetics of Print in Nuevomexicano Communities, 1834-1958*, 26.
42. Ibid., 28-29.
43. Ibid., 45.
44. Ibid., 58.
45. Ibid., 198.
46. Ibid., 201.
47. The standard text describing this process is Leonard Pitt, *The Decline of the Californios: A Social History of the Spanish-Speaking Californians, 1846-1890* (Berkeley: University of California Press, 1966).
48. Neri chooses the year 1868 as the turning point in Mexican American cultural identity in California. Michael C. Neri, "A Journalistic Portrait of the Spanish-Speaking People of California, 1868-1925," *Historical Society of Southern California Quarterly* 55 (Summer 1973): 193-208.

49. On Ramirez and *El Clamor Público*, see Nicolás Kanellos, "*El Clamor Público*: Resisting the American Empire," *California History* 84, no. 2 (Winter 2006-7): 10-18, 69-70.

50. Treviño examines the stance on English-Spanish language issues taken by the California Hispanic newspapers at length. Roberto R. Treviño, *Becoming Mexican American: The Spanish-Language Press and Biculturation of Californio Elites, 1852-1870* (Stanford: Stanford Center for Chicano Research, 1989), 8-13.

51. Ibid., 23-24.

52. F. Arturo Rosales, *Chicano! The History of the Mexican American Civil Rights Movement*, 99.

53. Gómez-Quiñones, *Roots of Chicano Politics, 1600-1940*, 291.

54. Matt S. Meier and Feliciano Ribera, *Dictionary of Mexican American History* (Westport, Conn.: Greenwood Publishing, 1981), 144.

55. See Henry A. J. Ramos, *The American G.I. Forum: In Pursuit of the Dream, 1948-1983* (Houston: Arte Público Press, 2002), 84-89, and Ignacio M. García, *Hector P. García: In Relentless Pursuit of Justice* (Houston: Arte Público Press, 1998), 222-24, for information on the impact of the forum's Viva Kennedy Clubs on the election. On the League of Latin American Citizens, see Rosales, *Chicano! The History of the Mexican American Civil Rights Movement*, 93-109.

56. See Virginia Sánchez Korrol, *From Colonia to Community: The History of Puerto Ricans in New York City, 1917-1948* (Westport, Conn.: Greenwood Press, 1983), which charts the development of a national minority consciousness among Puerto Ricans in New York.

57. See ibid., 153, for a complete list of the goals of the Liga.

CHAPTER 17
Reading, Writing, and Resisting:
African American Print Culture

1. *Colored Citizen*, 10 May 1878.

2. Recent works on African American history that focus on print culture extensively include Evelyn Brooks Higginbotham, *Righteous Discontent: The Women's Movement in the Black Baptist Church, 1880-1920* (Cambridge, Mass.: Harvard University Press, 1993); David Levering Lewis, *W. E. B. Du Bois: Biography of A Race, 1868-1919* (New York: Henry Holt, 1993); David Levering Lewis, *W. E. B Du Bois: The Fight for Equality and the American Century, 1919-1963* (New York: Henry Holt, 2000); Timothy B. Tyson, *Radio Free Dixie: Robert F. Williams and the Roots of Black Power* (Chapel Hill: University of North Carolina Press, 1999); Jacqueline Jones Royster, *Traces of a Stream: Literacy and Social Change among African American Women* (Pittsburgh: University of Pittsburgh Press, 2000); Elizabeth McHenry, *Forgotten Readers: Recovering the Lost History of African American Literary Societies* (Durham: Duke University Press, 2002).

3. Armistead S. Pride, "A Register and History of Negro Newspapers in the United States, 1827-1950" (Ph.D. diss., Northwestern University, 1950), 3; see also James P. Danky, "Newspapers and Selected Periodicals," in *The Harvard Guide to African-American History*, ed. Evelyn Brooks Higginbotham (Cambridge, Mass.: Harvard University Press, 2001), 77-93.

4. Robert T. Kerlin, *The Voice of the Negro: 1919* (1920; repr., New York: Arno Press, 1968),

ix, quoted in David Gordon Nielson, *Black Ethos: Northern Urban Negro Life and Thought, 1890–1930* (Westport, Conn.: Greenwood Press, 1977), 9.

5. The essential guide to Du Bois's voluminous writings is Herbert Aptheker, *Annotated Bibliography of the Published Writings of W. E. B. Du Bois* (Millwood, N.Y.: Kraus-Thomson Organization, 1973), which is vital to identifying appropriate materials within the complete edition of Du Bois works published by Kraus and the University of Massachusetts Press.

6. The quotation is from Lewis, *W. E. B. Du Bois, Biography of a Race*, 30.

7. The account of *Phylon* is taken from Lewis's study of Du Bois, ibid.

8. Janet Duitsman Cornelius, *"When I Can Read My Title Clear": Literacy, Slavery, and Religion in the Antebellum South* (Columbia: University of South Carolina Press, 1991), 142.

9. James D. Anderson, *The Education of Blacks in the South, 1860–1935* (Chapel Hill: University of North Carolina Press, 1988), 31; Woodson, quoted in Jacqueline Goggin, *Carter G. Woodson: A Life in Black History* (Baton Rouge: Louisiana State University Press, 1993), 11. On African American literacy in the United States from 1870 to 1920, see Sanford Winston, *Illiteracy in the U.S.* (Chapel Hill: University of North Carolina Press, 1930), 58, table 15. The illiteracy rate for all nonwhites was 16.4 percent in 1930 and 11.5 percent (compared to 2.0 percent for whites) in 1940. U.S. Department of Commerce, Census Bureau, *Current Population Reports*, 4 February 1960, Series P-20, no. 99, "Literacy and Educational Attainment: March 1959," 2, table A.

10. Dwight Oliver Holmes, *The Evolution of the Negro College* (New York: Teachers College, 1934); Anderson, *Education of Blacks in the South*, 59.

11. See John W. Blassingame and John R. McKivigan, eds., *Speeches, Debates, and Interviews*, vol. 4, 1864–1880, series 1 of *The Frederick Douglass Papers* (New Haven: Yale University Press, 1991), 232–33, and Jacqueline Jones, *American Work: Four Centuries of Black and White Labor* (New York: Norton, 1998), 328.

12. Linda O. McMurry, *Recorder of the Black Experience: A Biography of Monroe Nathan Work* (Baton Rouge: Louisiana State University Press, 1985), 39; Booker T. Washington, *The Negro in Business* (Boston: Hertel, Jenkins, 1907), 186–96. For publishing profiles of early African American publishers, see Donald Franklin Joyce, *Gatekeepers of Black Culture: Black-Owned Book Publishing in the United States, 1817–1981* (Westport, Conn.: Greenwood Press, 1983), appendix, esp. 200–201.

13. John Hope Franklin, *George Washington Williams: A Biography* (Chicago: University of Chicago Press, 1985); Adam Hochschild, *King Leopold's Ghost: A Story of Greed, Terror, and Heroism in Colonial Africa* (Boston: Houghton Mifflin, 1998).

14. Lawson Andrew Scruggs's collective biography *Women of Distinction: Remarkable in Works and Invincible in Character* (Raleigh, N.C.: L. A. Scruggs, Publisher, 1893) contains many sketches of prominent black women elocutionists. For biographical information on Frances Ellen Watkins Harper, see the introductions to the Schomburg Library reprint of *Iola Leroy*, ed. Francis Smith Foster (New York: Oxford University Press, 1988), and *Complete Poems of Frances E. W. Harper*, ed. Maryemma Graham (New York: Oxford Press, 1988). On Henrietta Vinton Davis, see Jo A. Tanner, *Dusky Maidens: The Odyssey of the Early Black Dramatic Actress* (Westport, Conn.: Greenwood Press, 1992), 30–33.

15. John Tebbel, *A History of Book Publishing in the United States*, 4 vols. (New York: R. R. Bowker, 1972–81), 2:452–53.

16. The 1879 Federal Census of Kansas, Bourbon County Population Schedules, 1870, lists James in Fort Scott along with his parents, Anna and Frank, plus Holson, a brother.

17. Rashey B. Moten, "The Negro Press of Kansas" (M.A. thesis, University of Kansas, 1936), 56–57.

18. Julius E. Thompson, "The Role of the Black Publisher as an Agent for Social Change," in *Africana History, Culture and Social Policy: A Collection of Critical Essays*, ed. James L. Conyers Jr. and Alva Barnett (Lanham, Md.: International Scholars Publications, 1999), 2.

19. Edwin Emery, *The Press and America: An Interpretative History of the Mass Media* (Englewood Cliffs, N.J.: Prentice-Hall, 1972), 337–39; Sally Foreman Griffith, *Home Town News: William Allen White and the Emporia Gazette* (New York: Oxford University Press, 1989), 76–77; Moten, "Negro Press," 33.

20. "Information to Emigrants—Where to Locate," *Colored Citizen*, 18 April 1878. Boosterism in the white press is well documented. For a contemporary example in a white Kansas paper, see Griffith, *Home Town News*, 36–41.

21. Penelope L. Bullock, *The Afro-American Periodical Press, 1838–1909* (Baton Rouge: Louisiana State University Press, 1981), 4; Moten, "Negro Press of Kansas," 60.

22. William M. Banks, *Black Intellectuals: Race and Responsibility in American Life* (New York: W. W. Norton, 1996), 56.

23. John Hope Franklin and August Meier, eds., *Black Leaders of the Twentieth Century* (Urbana: University of Illinois Press, 1981); Emma Lou Thornbrough, *T. Thomas Fortune: Militant Journalist* (Chicago: University of Chicago Press, 1972). On Wells-Barnett's childhood and youth, see Carl F. Kaestle, chapter 2 in this volume.

24. Ida B. Wells-Barnett, *Crusade for Justice*, ed. Alfreda M. Duster (Chicago: University of Chicago Press, 1970), 21–22.

25. Ibid.; Gail Bederman, *Manliness and Civilization: A Cultural History of Gender and Race in the United States, 1880–1917* (Chicago: University of Chicago Press, 1995), 38–39.

26. Henry Louis Gates Jr., "The Trope of the New Negro and the Reconstruction of the Image of the Black," *Representations* 24 (Autumn 1988): 129–55; Wilson J. Moses, "The Lost World of the Negro, 1895–1919: Black Literary and Intellectual Life before the 'Renaissance,'" *Black American Literature Forum* 21, nos. 1–2 (Spring–Summer 1987): 61–84.

27. Thornbrough, *T. Thomas Fortune: Militant Journalist*, 38–39, describes subsidy practices from the 1880s. The papers of Claude Barnett and the Associated Negro Press at the Chicago Historical Society contain a large box of Black Republican campaign papers from 1900 through the 1920s, demonstrating that the practice of subsidies continued into the twentieth century.

28. Alfred A. Moss Jr., *The American Negro Academy* (Baton Rouge: Louisiana State University Press, 1981), 1; Joyce, *Gatekeepers of Black Culture*, 27–30.

29. Goggin, *Carter G. Woodson*, 40–45; Sterling A. Brown, "The Negro Author and His Publisher," *Quarterly Review of Higher Education among Negroes* 9 (July 1941): 146.

30. *Durham Negro Observer*, 23 June 1906, quoted in Walter B. Weare, *Black Business in the New South: A Social History of the North Carolina Mutual Life Insurance Company* (Urbana: University of Illinois Press, 1973), 78.

31. African American insurance companies were among the most active of business publishers. Other serials produced by black insurance companies included the *Radiator* (Dur-

ham, N.C.: National Negro Insurance Association, 1922-?) and the *Guardian* (Chicago: Supreme Liberty Life Insurance, 1936-?).

32. For more detail on black women as activists and reformers, see Elizabeth McHenry, chapter 25 in this volume; Royster, *Traces of a Stream*, 176-238; Paula Giddings, *When and Where I Enter: The Impact of Black Women on Race and Sex in America* (New York: William Morrow, 1984), esp. 108.

33. Evelyn Brooks Higginbotham, *Righteous Discontent*, 12, 195.

34. Michael Fultz, "'The Morning Cometh': African-American Periodicals, Education, and the Black Middle Class, 1900-1930," in *Print Culture in a Diverse America*, ed. James P. Danky and Wayne A. Wiegand (Urbana: University of Illinois Press, 1998); Emery, *The Press and America*, 335-37; Guy Michael Fultz, "'Agitate Then, Brother': Education in the Black Monthly Periodical Press, 1900-1930" (Ed.D. diss., Harvard University, 1987), 186-91.

35. Linda O. McMurry, *Recorder of the Black Experience: A Biography of Monroe Nathan Work* (Baton Rouge: Louisiana State University Press, 1985), 75-76; Joyce, *Gatekeepers of Black Culture*, 40-47.

36. Donald Joyce, *Black Book Publishers in the United States: A Historical Dictionary of the Presses* (New York: Greenwood Press, 1991), 175-79; Wilson J. Moses, "Literary Garveyism: The Novels of Reverend Sutton E. Griggs," *Phylon* 40 (1979): 203-16; Hugh M. Gloster, "Sutton Griggs, Novelist of the New Negro," *Phylon* 4 (1943): 337.

37. Roi Ottley, *The Lonely Warrior: The Life and Times of Robert S. Abbott* (Chicago: Henry Regnery, 1955).

38. Emmett J. Scott, "Letters of Negro Migrants of 1916-1918," *Journal of Negro History* 4 (July 1919): 304.

39. James R. Grossman, "Blowing the Trumpet: The Chicago Defender and Black Migration during World War I," *Illinois Historical Journal* 78 (1985): 84.

40. Ottley, *Lonely Warrior*, 209.

41. Quoted from ibid., 142; Grossman, "Blowing the Trumpet," 84.

42. Quoted from Robert A. Hill, *The Crusader* (New York: Garland Publishing, 1987), xvi.

43. Kenyatta, quoted by Lawrence Levine, "Marcus Garvey and the Politics of Revitalization," in Franklin and Meier, *Black Leaders of the Twentieth Century*, 120; Edmund David Cronon, *Black Moses: The Story of Marcus Garvey and the Universal Negro Improvement Association* (Madison: University of Wisconsin Press, 1955), 45-49.

44. See Hill, *The Crusader*, v-xvi, and Frederick G. Detweiler, *The Negro Press in the United States* (1922; repr., College Park: McGrath, 1968), 165.

45. Lawrence Reddick, "Publishers Are Awful," *Negro Quarterly* 1 (Summer 1942): 1887-89.

46. Vishnu Oak and Eleanor Oak, "Children's Literature Dealing with Negro Life," *Journal of Negro Education* 8 (1939): 77-79; Dorothy B. Porter, "Recent Literature on the Negro," *Quarterly Review of Higher Education among Negroes* 8, no. 3 (1940): 118-22; Lawrence Reddick, "Methods of Combating Racially Derogatory Statements and Implications of American College Textbooks," *Quarterly Review of Higher Education among Negroes* 3 (1935): 207.

47. Olen Cole Jr., *The African-American Experience in the Civilian Conservation Corps* (Gainesville: University Press of Florida, 1999), 45.

48. African American camps are designated with a "C" (for colored) in *The Civilian Conservation Corps Camp Newspapers: A Guide* (Chicago: Center for Research Libraries, 1991).

49. "Marcus Garvey, 60, Negro Ex-Leader," *New York Times*, 12 June 1940; "Confirm Recent Report of Marcus Garvey Death," *Chicago Defender*, 22 June 1940; Cronon, *Black Moses*, 166-69.

CHAPTER 18
*An Outpouring of "Faithful" Words:
Protestant Publishing in the United States*

1. Martin E. Marty, John G. Deedy, David Wolf Silverman, and Robert Lekachman, eds., introduction to *The Religious Press in America* (New York: Holt, Rinehart, and Winston, 1963), vii; Martin E. Marty, "The Protestant Press: Limitations and Possibilities," in Marty et al., *Religious Press in America*, 8-11.

2. William R. Hutchison, "Protestantism as Establishment," in *Between the Times: The Travail of the Protestant Establishment in America, 1900-1960*, ed. Hutchison (Cambridge: Cambridge University Press, 1989), 3-20.

3. For a nice summary of these challenges, see Mark A. Noll, *A History of Christianity in the United States and Canada* (Grand Rapids, Mich.: Wm. B. Eerdmans, 1992), 311-12, 335-89.

4. Frank Luther Mott, *A History of American Magazines*, 5 vols. (Cambridge, Mass.: Harvard University Press, 1930-68), 4:288-89; Judith S. Duke, *Religious Publishing and Communications* (White Plains, N.Y.: Knowledge Industry, 1981), 162; Hendrik Edelman, "History of Religious Publishing and Bookselling in the United States and Canada, 1640-1985," in *Christian Book Publishing and Distribution in the United States and Canada*, ed. J. P. Dessauer, Paul D. Doebler, and Hendrik Edelman (Tempe, Ariz.: Christian Booksellers Association, 1987), 51; Paul A. Soukup, *Christian Communication: A Bibliographical Survey* (New York: Greenwood, 1989), 6.

5. Martin E. Marty, "Protestant Press," in *Encyclopedia of the American Religious Experience: Studies of Traditions and Movements*, ed. Charles H. Lippy and Peter W. Williams, 3 vols. (New York: Charles Scribner's Sons, 1988), 3:10-32; Martin E. Marty, "The Religious Press," in Lippy and Williams, *Encyclopedia of the American Religious Experience*, 2:1709.

6. For good summary statements in this regard, see Peter Williams, introduction to *America's Religions: From the Beginning to the Twenty-First Century* (Urbana: University of Illinois Press, 2001); David Moberg, "Denominationalism," in *Dictionary of Christianity in America*, ed. Daniel G. Reid, Robert Dean Linder, Bruce L. Shelley, and Harry S. Stout (Downers Grove, Ill.: InterVarsity Press, 1990), 350-52.

7. Edelman, "Religious Publishing and Bookselling," 51; Daniel G. Reid, Robert Dean Linder, Bruce L. Shelley, and Harry S. Stout, "Protestant Press," in Reid et al., *Dictionary of Christianity in America*, 935.

8. Marty, "Protestant Press," 62. The best directory of these periodicals is *Popular Religious Magazines of the United States*, ed. P. Mark Fackler and Charles H. Lippy (Westport, Conn.: Greenwood Press, 1995).

9. H. K. Carroll, ed., *The Federal Council Year Book: An Ecclesiastical and Statistical Di-

rectory of the Federal Council, Its Commissions and Its Constituent Bodies, and of all Other Religious Organizations in the United States, Covering the Year 1915 (New York: Missionary Education Movement, 1916), 44-154, 195-200.

10. Benson Y. Landis, ed., *Yearbook of American Churches* (Lebanon, Pa.: Sowers Printing Co., 1941), 1-85.

11. *N. W. Ayer and Son's American Newspaper Annual* (Philadelphia: N. W. Ayer and Son, 1890), 3-4; *N. W. Ayer and Son's American Newspaper Annual* (Philadelphia: N. W. Ayer and Son, 1909), 1074-82; *N. W. Ayer and Son's Directory of Newspapers and Periodicals* (Philadelphia: N. W. Ayer and Son, 1933), 1235-41; *N. W. Ayer and Son's Directory of Newspapers and Periodicals* (Philadelphia: N. W. Ayer and Son, 1943), 1223-30. Special thanks to Tim Dillon of the University of Dayton for his work in calculating circulation totals.

12. Dennis Voskuil, "Reaching Out: Mainline Protestantism and the Media," in *Between the Times: The Travail of the Protestant Establishment in America, 1900-1960*, ed. William R. Hutchison (Cambridge: Cambridge University Press, 1989), 74-75. Some of the more helpful sources regarding mainline periodicals include Alfred E. Degroot and Enos E. Dowling, *The Literature of the Disciples of Christ* (Advance, Ind.: Hustler Print, 1933); Anna Jane Moyer, "The Making of Many Books: 125 Years of Presbyterian Publishing, 1838-1963," *Journal of Presbyterian History* 41 (1963): 124-40; Elmer J. O'Brien, "Methodist Quarterly Review: Reflections on a Methodist Periodical," *Methodist History* 25 (1987): 76-90; Lawrence Slaght, *Multiplying the Witness: 150 Years of American Baptist Educational Ministries* (Valley Forge, Pa.: Judson Press, 1974); Walter Vernon, *The United Methodist Publishing House: A History*, vol. 2, *1870-1988* (Nashville: Abingdon, 1989).

13. Voskuil, "Reaching Out," 75; *Federal Council Year Book* (1915), 44-154, 195-200; *Yearbook of American Churches*, ed. Benson Y. Landis (Lebanon, Pa.: Sowers Printing Co., 1945), 5-86.

14. C. H. Phillips, *The History of the Colored Methodist Episcopal Church in America* (Jackson, Tenn.: Publishing House of the C.M.E. Church, 1898), 40, 127, 235-38.

15. Dennis C. Dickerson and Robert H. Reid Jr., *"Christian Recorder,"* in Fackler and Lippy, *Popular Religious Magazines of the United States*, 162-66; Reid et al., "Protestant Press," 935.

16. Richard T. Hughes, *Reviving the Ancient Faith: The Story of Churches of Christ in America* (Grand Rapids, Mich.: Wm. B. Eerdmans, 1996), 10, 242-43.

17. Gene A. Getz, *MBI: The Story of Moody Bible Institute* (Chicago: Moody Press, 1969), 149-52; William Vance Trollinger Jr., *God's Empire: William Bell Riley and Midwestern Fundamentalism* (Madison: University of Wisconsin Press, 1990), 120-22; Edith L. Blumhofer, *Aimée Semple McPherson: Everybody's Sister* (Grand Rapids, Mich.: Wm. B. Eerdmans, 1993), 119-25; Joel A. Carpenter, *Revive Us Again: The Reawakening of American Fundamentalism* (Oxford: Oxford University Press, 1997), 27-28; Reid et al., "Protestant Press," 935-36.

18. Paul B. Tinlin, *"Pentecostal Evangel,"* in Fackler and Lippy, *Popular Religious Magazines of the United States*, 380-85.

19. *Yearbook of American Churches* (1941), 6; Edelman, "Religious Publishing and Bookselling," 46; Monte B. McLaws, *Spokesman for the Kingdom: Early Mormon Journalism and the "Deseret News," 1830-1898* (Provo, Utah: Brigham Young University Press, 1977).

20. The tremendous diversity and doctrinal cacophony of Protestant journals impugns one of the predominant interpretive paradigms of American Protestantism, which holds that American Protestants can be classified as belonging to one of two irreconcilable camps: mainline versus evangelicals, or liberals versus conservatives. See Douglas Jacobsen and William Vance Trollinger Jr., introduction to *Re-Forming the Center: American Protestantism, 1900–Present* (Grand Rapids, Mich.: Wm. B. Eerdmans, 1998), 1-10.

21. Vernon, *United Methodist*, esp. 145-49, 199, 219-27, 266-71, 322 (quote), 338-41; Edelman, "Religious Publishing and Bookselling," 45.

22. John A. Hostetler, *God Uses Ink: The Heritage and Mission of the Mennonite Publishing House after 50 Years* (Scottdale, Pa.: Herald Press, 1958), 236-47.

23. Colleen McDannell, *Material Christianity: Religion and Popular Culture in America* (New Haven: Yale University Press, 1995), 230-46.

24. For a wonderful discussion of nineteenth-century religious communities and the "scripturalizing" process, see Stephen J. Stein, "America's Bibles: Canon, Commentary, and Community," *Church History* 64 (June 1995): 171-78. Also see Kent P. Jackson, "The Sacred Literature of the Latter-Day Saints," in *The Bible and Bibles in America*, vol. 1 of *Society of Biblical Literature: The Bible in American Culture*, ed. Ernest Frerichs (Atlanta: Scholars Press, 1988), 163-91; Ronald L. Numbers, *Prophetess of Health: A Study of Ellen G. White* (New York: Harper & Row, 1976); Robert Peel, "Science and Health with Key to the Scriptures: '. . . to gyve science and helthe to his people . . . ,'" in Frerichs, *The Bible and Bibles in America*, 193-213 (quote 193).

25. Linda-Marie Delloff, "C. C. Morrison: Shaping a Journal's Identity," *Christian Century* 101 (18 January 1984): 43-47.

26. Ibid., 43; Marty, "Religious Press," 2:1704; Voskuil, "Reaching Out," 76-77.

27. Marty, "Protestant Press," 58; Roxane Salyer Lulofs, "*Christian Herald*," in Fackler and Lippy, *Popular Religious Magazines of the United States*, 129-35; Reid et al., "Protestant Press," 936.

28. Margaret T. Hills, ed., *The English Bible in America: A Bibliography of Editions of the Bible and the New Testament Published in America, 1777–1957* (New York: American Bible Society and the New York Public Library, 1961), 292-401. The totals of new editions of the Bible break down as follows: 92 (1880s), 73 (1890s), 85 (1900s), 55 (1910s), 118 (1920s), 64 (1930s), 101 (1940s). Given that Hills missed some Bibles, the number of editions provided here is an understatement.

29. *New York Evening Post*, 21 May 1881, as quoted in Peter J. Thuesen, "Some Scripture Is Inspired by God: Late Nineteenth-Century Protestants and the Demise of a Common Bible," *Church History* 65 (December 1996): 609-23.

30. John Tebbel, *A History of Book Publishing in the United States*, 4 vols. (New York: R. R. Bowker, 1972-81), 2:542; Thuesen, "Some Scripture," 609.

31. Thuesen, "Some Scripture," 621-23.

32. For the wider impact of these ideas on American culture, see Paul Boyer, *When Time Shall Be No More: Prophecy Belief in Modern American Culture* (Cambridge, Mass.: Harvard University Press, 1991).

33. Ernest Sandeen, *The Roots of Fundamentalism: British and American Millenarianism, 1880–1930*; Boyer, *Time Shall Be No More*; Thuesen, "Some Scripture," 623.

34. Hills, *English Bible*, 300, 307, 315, 336, 372; Lawrence Slaght, *Multiplying the Witness: 150 Years of American Baptist Educational Ministries* (Valley Forge, Pa.: Judson Press, 1974), 54–55.

35. Hills, *English Bible*, 270, 317, 395; Philip L. Barlow, *Mormons and the Bible: The Place of the Latter-Day Saints in American Religion* (New York: Oxford University Press, 1991), 46–61 (quote 50); Stein, "America's Bibles," 182–83.

36. Hills, *English Bible*, 314, 319, 353–54, 364, 369, 383; Slaght, *Multiplying the Witness: 150 Years of American Baptist Educational Ministries*, 54–55; Harold P. Scanlin, "Bible Translation by American Individuals," in Frerichs, *The Bible and Bibles in America*, 49–50, 57–62.

37. Scanlin, "Bible Translation," 43–44.

38. R. Laurence Moore, *Selling God: American Religion in the Marketplace of Culture* (Oxford: Oxford University Press, 1994), 34–35.

39. Hills, *English Bible*, 293, 313, 354, 358, 374, 395; Wayne Elzey, "Popular Culture," in Lippy and Williams, *Encyclopedia of the American Religious Experience*, 3:1730, 1732.

40. Tebbel, *History of Book Publishing in the United States*, 2:542–43; 3:242, 485.

41. Hills, *English Bible*, 329 (quote); David Ewert, "Pocket Testament League," in Reid et al., *Dictionary of Christianity in America*, 914–15; Tebbel, *History of Book Publishing in the United States*, 2:544–45.

42. For an insightful discussion of the American Bible Society's publishing efforts, see David Paul Nord, "Free Grace, Free Books, Free Riders: The Economics of Religious Publishing in Early Nineteenth-Century America," *Proceedings of the American Antiquarian Society* 106 (October 1996): 241–72.

43. Hills, *English Bible*, 363; Tebbel, *History of Book Publishing in the United States*, 2:543.

44. Tebbel, *History of Book Publishing in the United States*, 2:544; Creighton Lacy, *The Word Carrying Giant: The Growth of the American Bible Society, 1818–1966* (South Pasadena: William Carey Library, 1977), 160–66.

45. Lacy, *Word Carrying Giant*, 159, 165.

46. Ibid., 162.

47. Not only was the data provided by publishers unreliable (particularly in the early years), but the definition of a "religious book" was neither precise nor consistently applied, and—perhaps most important—pamphlets were not counted. Counting the pamphlets would have radically increased the total of religious books. Tebbel, *History of Book Publishing in the United States*, 2:676–707; 3:238–39, 682–83; William Miller, *The Book Industry* (New York: Columbia University Press, 1949), 142–44.

48. Edelman, "Religious Publishing and Bookselling," 46–47, 53; Tebbel, *History of Book Publishing in the United States*, 2:555, 557–58; Paul C. Wilt, "Fleming Hewitt Revell," in Reid et al., *Dictionary of Christianity in America*, 1009.

49. Joan Shelley Rubin, "The Boundaries of American Religious Publishing in the Early Twentieth Century," *Book History* 2 (1999): 207–17; Edelman, "Religious Publishing and Bookselling," 52; Hendrik Edelman, "Religious Publishing," in Reid et al., *Dictionary of Christianity in America*, 962.

50. Rubin, "Boundaries of American Religious Publishing," 209–10.

51. Ruth Miller Elson, *Myths and Mores in American Best-Sellers, 1865-1965* (New York: Garland Publishing, 1985), 185-92; Allene Stuart Phy, "Retelling the Greatest Story Ever Told: Jesus in Popular Fiction," in *The Bible and Popular Culture in America*, ed. Allene Stuart Phy (Philadelphia: Fortress Press, 1985), 48-58; David S. Reynolds, *Faith in Fiction: The Emergence of Religious Literature in America* (Cambridge, Mass.: Harvard University Press, 1981), 203-8.

52. Edelman, "Religious Publishing and Bookselling," 52; Tebbel, *A History of Book Publishing in the United States*, 3:239-40; Alice Payne Hackett, *60 Years of Best Sellers, 1895-1955* (New York: R. R. Bowker, 1956), 84.

53. Rubin, "Boundaries of American Religious Publishing," 215-16.

CHAPTER 19
*Two Ambitious Goals:
American Jewish Publishing in the United States*

1. *American Hebrew* (8 June 1888): 70-71; *Announcement: The Jewish Publication Society of America* (Philadelphia, 1888), as cited in Jonathan D. Sarna, *JPS: The Americanization of Jewish Culture, 1888-1988* (Philadelphia: Jewish Publication Society, 1989), 20-22. The *Announcement* is reprinted in Sarna, *JPS*, 355-59.

2. Sarna, *JPS*, 357; Michael A. Meyer, *Ideas of Jewish History* (New York: Behrman House, 1974), 189-214; Michael A. Meyer, "German Jewish Identity in Nineteenth-Century America," in *Toward Modernity: The European Jewish Model*, ed. Jacob Katz (New York: Transaction Books, 1987); Naomi W. Cohen, "American Jewish Reactions to Anti-Semitism in Western Europe, 1875-1900," *Proceedings of the American Academy of Jewish Research* 45 (1978): 29-65.

3. Sarna, *JPS*, 355, 358.

4. Isaac M. Wise, *Reminiscences* (Cincinnati, 1901; repr., New York: Central Synagogue, 1945), 23-24; see also Isaac M. Wise, "The World of My Books," trans. Albert H. Friedlander, in *Critical Studies in American Jewish History*, ed. Jacob R. Marcus, 3 vols. (New York: Ktav, 1971), 1:154. First published in *American Jewish Archives* 6 (June 1954).

5. Cyrus Adler to the *American Hebrew*, 9 December 1894, in *Cyrus Adler: Selected Letters*, ed. Ira Robinson, 2 vols. (Philadelphia: Jewish Publication Society, 1985), 1:70.

6. Arthur Hertzberg, "'Treifene Medina': Learned Opposition to Emigration to the United States," *Proceedings of the 8th World Congress of Jewish Studies* (Jerusalem: World Congress of Jewish Studies, 1984), 1-30.

7. Jonathan D. Sarna, "The History of the Jewish Press in North America," in *The North American Jewish Press: The 1994 Alexander Brin Forum* (Waltham, Mass.: Cohen Center for Modern Jewish Studies, Brandeis University, 1995), 2-7; Arthur A. Goren, "The Jewish Press," in *The Ethnic Press in the United States: An Historical Analysis and Handbook*, ed. Sally M. Miller (New York: Greenwood Press, 1987), 203-28; Robert Singerman, "The American Jewish Press, 1823-1983: A Bibliographic Survey of Research and Studies," *American Jewish History* 73 (June 1984): 422-44.

8. Isaac Leeser, "Address of the Jewish Publication Committee to the Israelites of America," preface to *Caleb Asher*, no. 1 of *The Jewish Miscellany* (Philadelphia: Jewish Pub-

lication Society of America, 5605 [1845]), 1–4, reprinted in part in Paul Mendes-Flohr and Jehuda Reinharz, *The Jew in the Modern World: A Documentary History*, 2nd ed. (New York: Oxford University Press, 1995), 461–63. On the growth of religious journalism, see Nathan Hatch, "Elias Smith and the Rise of Religious Journalism in the Early Republic," in *Printing and Society in Early America*, ed. William L. Joyce, David D. Hall, Richard D. Brown, and John B. Hench (Worcester: American Antiquarian Society, 1983), 250–77.

9. Hatch, "Elias Smith," 250.

10. Rudolf Glanz, "Where the Jewish Press Was Distributed in Pre–Civil War America," *Western States Jewish Historical Quarterly* 5 (1972–73): 1–14, and "The Spread of Jewish Communities through America before the Civil War," *Yivo Annual of Jewish Social Science* 15 (1974): 7–45.

11. The index to Robert Singerman, *Judaica Americana: A Bibliography of Publications to 1900* (New York: Greenwood Press, 1990), includes a gazetteer of publishers and printers, making it easy to trace the output of individual firms.

12. Singerman, *Judaica Americana*, is the authoritative bibliography of publications to 1900.

13. Cecil Roth, "The People and the Book," in *Personalities and Events in Jewish History* (Philadelphia: Jewish Publication Society, 1953), 172–73.

14. Michael A. Meyer traces this development to the last third of the nineteenth century; see his "German-Jewish Identity in Nineteenth-Century America," in *Toward Modernity: The European Jewish Model*, ed. Jacob Katz (New Brunswick, N.J.: Transaction Books, 1987), 247–67.

15. Shuly Rubin Schwartz, *The Emergence of Jewish Scholarship in America: The Publication of the Jewish Encyclopedia* (Cincinnati: Hebrew Union College Press, 1991), esp. 16, 86–87.

16. Solomon Schechter to Mayer Sulzberger, 5 March 1900, in Meir Ben Horin, "Solomon Schechter to Judge Mayer Sulzberger: Part 1, Letters from the Pre-Seminary Period (1895–1901)," *Jewish Social Studies* 25 (October 1963): 276. More broadly, see Abraham J. Karp, "Solomon Schechter Comes to America," *American Jewish Historical Quarterly* 53 (September 1963): 44–62.

17. Israel Friedlaender, *Past and Present* (Cincinnati: Ark, 1919), 317.

18. Jonathan D. Sarna, "Two Traditions of Seminary Scholarship," in *Tradition Renewed: A History of the Jewish Theological Seminary*, ed. Jack Wertheimer, 2 vols. (New York: Jewish Theological Seminary, 1997), 2:55–63.

19. Additional volumes appeared in 1925, 1928, and 1938. Louis Ginzberg, of course, was an immigrant, and he wrote his original manuscript in German.

20. Sarna, *JPS*, 29–112; Joshua Bloch, *Of Making Many Books: An Annotated List of the Books Issued by the Jewish Publication Society of America, 1890–1952* (Philadelphia: Jewish Publication Society, 1953), 37–135.

21. *The Holy Scriptures*, ed. Max Margolis (1917; repr., Philadelphia: Jewish Publication Society, 1955), vi.

22. Menahem Blondheim, "Ha-Rabanut Ha-Ortodoksit Megaleh Et Amerikah" (The Orthodox Rabbinate Discovers America), in *Be-'ikvot Kolumbus: Amerikah 1492–1992*, ed. Miriam Eliav-Feldon (Jerusalem: Merkaz Shazar, 1996), 492–94.

23. Adolph S. Oko, "Jewish Book Collections in the United States," *American Jewish Year Book* 45 (1943-44): 67-96; Robert Singerman, "Books Weeping for Someone to Visit and Admire Them: Jewish Library Culture in the United States, 1850-1910," *Studies in Bibliography and Booklore* 20 (1998): 99-144.

24. Menahem Schmelzer, "Building a Great Judaica Library—at What Price?" in *Tradition Renewed: A History of the Jewish Theological Seminary of America*, ed. Jack Wertheimer, 2 vols. (New York: Jewish Theological Seminary of America, 1997), 1:679-97; Herman Dicker, *Of Learning and Libraries: The Seminary Library at One Hundred* (New York: Jewish Theological Seminary of America, 1988), 15-31; Alexander Marx, "The Library," in *The Jewish Theological Seminary of America Semi-Centennial Volume*, ed. Cyrus Adler (New York: Jewish Theological Seminary of America, 1939), 87-120.

25. Oko, "Jewish Book Collections in the United States," 73-87, esp. 76; Michael A. Meyer, "A Centennial History," in *Hebrew Union College: Jewish Institute of Religion at One Hundred Years*, ed. Samuel E. Karff (Cincinnati: Hebrew Union College Press, 1976), 72-74.

26. Grace Cohen Grossman with Richard Eighme Ahlborn, *Judaica at the Smithsonian: Cultural Politics as Cultural Model* (Washington, D.C.: Smithsonian Institution Press, 1997), 69-79, esp. 72; Simcha Berkowitz, "Ephraim Deinard: Bibliophile and Bookman," *Studies in Bibliography and Booklore* 9 (Spring 1971): 137-52; Abraham J. Karp, *From the Ends of the Earth: Judaica Treasures of the Library of Congress* (New York: Rizzoli, 1991), xv; Charles A. Madison, *Jewish Publishing in America* (New York: Sanhedrin Press, 1976), 60-62; Dan A. Oren, *Joining the Club: A History of Jews and Yale* (New Haven: Yale University Press, 1985), 329; Arthur A. Chiel, "The Kohut Collection at Yale," in *Jews in New Haven*, ed. Jonathan D. Sarna (New Haven, Conn.: Jewish Historical Society of New Haven, 1978), 80-94.

27. Cyrus Adler, *Jacob H. Schiff: His Life and Letters*, pt. 2 (Garden City, N.Y.: Doubleday, Doran, 1929), 64.

28. Sarna, *JPS*, 120-30, provides a full history of the Schiff Classics.

29. Norman Bentwich, *Solomon Schechter: A Biography* (Philadelphia: Jewish Publication Society, 1948), 259; Sarna, "Two Traditions of Seminary Scholarship," 59-61.

30. See, for example, Nathan M. Kaganoff, "American Rabbinic Books Published in Palestine," in *A Bicentennial Festschrift for Jacob Rader Marcus*, ed. Bertram W. Korn (New York: Ktav, 1976), 235-61.

31. Sarna, *JPS*, 127-28.

32. Madison, *Jewish Publishing in America*, 76.

33. Daniel Soyer, *Jewish Immigrant Associations and American Identity in New York, 1880-1939* (Cambridge, Mass.: Harvard University Press, 1997), 8.

34. Madison, *Jewish Publishing in America*, 77-84, 206-7.

35. Ibid., 84-100, 206-17; see also the annual bibliography of American Jewish books published in the *Jewish Book Annual*.

36. Sarna, "The History of the Jewish Press in North America," 6-7; *American Jewish Year Book* 43 (1941-42): 631-42.

37. *The Jewish Communal Register* (New York, 1918), iii-vi, 91-98; Arthur A. Goren, *New York Jews and the Quest for Community: The Kehillah Experiment, 1908-1922* (New York: Columbia University Press, 1970), 236-37.

38. Harry Schneiderman, "American Jewish Year Book, 1899-1948," *American Jewish Year Book* 50 (1948-49): 87-88.

39. *American Jewish Year Book* 43 (1941-42): 789.

40. Sarna, *JPS*, 183.

41. Ibid., 188.

42. Madison, *Jewish Publishing in America*, 64-67; Oscar I. Janowsky, *The JWB Survey* (New York: Dial Press, 1948), 348-49; Michael N. Dobkowski, *Jewish American Voluntary Organizations* (Westport, Conn.: Greenwood Press, 1986), 202-4; Philip Goodman, "A Chronicle of the Jewish Book Council of America," *Jewish Book Annual* 25 (1967-68): 366-89.

43. Salo Baron, "Report of the JWB Survey Commission," in Janowsky, *JWB Survey*, xiii; Sarna, *JPS*, 219-20.

44. Sarna, *JPS*, 224; Charles A. Madison, "The Rise of the Jewish Book in American Publishing," *Jewish Book Annual* 25 (1967-68): 81-86; Amnon Zipin, "Judaica from American University Presses," *Jewish Book Annual* 42 (1984-85): 172-82.

CHAPTER 20
*Running the Ancient Ark by Steam:
Catholic Publishing*

1. David J. O'Brien, *Isaac Hecker: An American Catholic* (New York: Paulist Press, 1992), 210-11.

2. Pastoral letter, Council of Bishops, in *The Memorial Volume: A History of the Third Plenary Council of Baltimore, 9 November-7 December 1884* (Baltimore: Baltimore Publishing Company, 1885), 7.

3. "Catholic" or "the church" should be understood in this essay as shorthand for "the Roman Catholic Church" rather than as a theological claim. By "Catholic publishing" I refer to any publishing efforts directed toward a Catholic audience, whether undertaken by Catholics or non-Catholics, as well as publications by Catholics directed at a general audience. For a discussion of Catholicism and print culture within the Hispanic United States, see Nicolás Kanellos, chapter 16 in this volume.

4. John G. Deedy Jr., "The Catholic Press: The Why and the Wherefore," in *The Religious Press in America*, ed. Martin E. Marty, John G. Deedy, David Wolf Silverman, and Robert Lekachman (New York: Holt, Rinehart and Winston, 1963), 65-121.

5. Charles H. Ridder, "The United States Catholic Press Exhibit at Vatican City, 1936," in *Historical Records and Studies* (New York: United States Catholic Historical Society, 1937), 35. Also see L. G. Happel, "The Freedom of the Catholic Press," *America* 6 (24 July 1920): 320-22.

6. Ridder, "The United States Catholic Press Exhibit," 48. See also Apollinaris W. Baumgartner, *Catholic Journalism: A Study of Its Development in the United States, 1789-1930* (New York: Columbia University Press, 1931), and William L. Lucey, S.J., *An Introduction to American Catholic Magazines* (Philadelphia: American Catholic Historical Society, 1952).

7. William L. Lucey, "Catholic Press, World Survey," *New Catholic Encyclopedia*, 16 vols. (New York: McGraw-Hill, 1967-79), 3:317.

8. Colleen McDannell, "Catholic Domesticity," in *The Christian Home in Victorian America, 1840–1900* (Bloomington: Indiana University Press, 1986), chap. 3.

9. O'Brien, *Isaac Hecker*, 212.

10. "Hierarchical authority" refers here to the authority of a given bishop in his diocese as well as the authority of canon law and of the pope. "Religious orders and congregations" refers to groups of religious men and women (i.e., priests, brothers and nuns, or sisters) committed to a consecrated life in service, usually, of a specific mission (e.g., education, mission work, care for the poor). They were subject to hierarchical authority, as were lay people.

11. As late as 1952, a bibliographer described a historian (John Paul Cadden) as saying, "The Catholic thought and feeling of any period is best expressed through the meetings of the hierarchy." Quoted in Mary Patricia Ruskin, "A Survey of Catholic Americana and Catholic Book Publishing in the United States, 1886–1890" (M.S.L.S. thesis, Catholic University of America, 1952), 8.

12. *The Memorial Volume*, 17–22 (third pagination).

13. John Tebbel, *A History of Book Publishing in the United States*, 4 vols. (New York: R. R. Bowker, 1971–82), 2:545–48; *Survey of Catholic Americana and Book Publishing, 1830–1895* (a microfilm edition of eleven master's theses in library science, issued by the Catholic University of America); Robert Healy, *A Catholic Book Chronicle: The Story of P. J. Kenedy & Sons, 1826–1951* (New York: P. J. Kenedy & Sons, 1951); Sr. Mary Stephana Cavanaugh, O.P., "Catholic Book Publishing in the United States," *Catholic Library World* 9, no. 5 (April 1938): 108–15; 10, no. 4 (January 1939): 125–28; 10, no. 5 (February 1939): 159–62; and 10, no. 7 (April 1939): 227–32.

14. *Survey of Catholic Americana* indicates both the concentration of publishing in New York City and the persistence of other significant publishing centers in Baltimore, Philadelphia, St. Louis, and Boston.

15. Josephine Ti Ti Chen, "A Survey of Catholic Americana and Catholic Book Publishing in the United States, 1891–1895" (M.S.L.S. thesis, Catholic University of America, 1956), 79. "S.J." designates a member of the Society of Jesus, commonly known as the Jesuits.

16. Fr. George Deshon, *Guide for Catholic Young Women, Especially for Those Who Earn Their Own Living*, 29th ed. (1897; repr., New York: Arno Press, 1978), 73–74.

17. Reprinting Alonzo Rodriguez's *Practice of Christian Perfection* established Patrick Kenedy as a Catholic publisher in 1834; a serialization of *Butler's Lives of the Saints* was D. & J. Sadlier's first success. Robert Orsi, *Thank You, Saint Jude: Women's Devotion to the Patron Saint of Hopeless Causes* (New Haven: Yale University Press, 1996), describes the later twentieth-century heyday of devotional culture (14–18).

18. Ann Taves, *The Household of Faith: Roman Catholic Devotions in Mid-Nineteenth-Century America* (Notre Dame, Ind.: University of Notre Dame Press, 1986).

19. See ibid., 93–94.

20. See Colleen McDannell, *Material Christianity: Religion and Popular Culture in America* (New Haven: Yale University Press, 1995).

21. Healy, *A Catholic Book Chronicle*, 28.

22. McDannell, *The Christian Home in Victorian America*, 106.

23. Deshon, *Guide for Catholic Young Women*, 78.

24. David O'Brien, *Public Catholicism*, 2nd ed. (Maryknoll, N.Y.: Orbis, 1996), 151–57.

25. Philip Gleason, "The Search for Unity and Its Sequel," in *Keeping the Faith: American Catholicism Past and Present* (Notre Dame, Ind.: University of Notre Dame Press, 1987), 136–51.

26. Two articles that have made useful attempts at describing this cultural work are James Emmett Ryan, "Sentimental Catechism: Archbishop James Gibbons, Mass-Print Culture, and American Literary History," *Religion and American Culture* 7 (Winter 1997): 81–119, and Penny Edgell Becker, "'Rational Amusement and Sound Instruction': Constructing the True Catholic Woman," *Religion and American Culture* 8 (Winter 1998): 55–90.

27. Ridder, "Catholic Press Exhibit," 48–49.

28. Sr. Mary Lonan Reilly, O.S.F., *A History of the Catholic Press Association, 1911–1968* (Metuchen, N.J.: Scarecrow Press, 1971); Ridder, "Catholic Press Exhibit," 49; Baumgartner, *Catholic Journalism*, 43–46, 60–62, 80–86.

29. Philip Gleason, *Contending with Modernity: Catholic Higher Education in the Twentieth Century* (New York: Oxford University Press, 1995), 96; Ridder, "Catholic Press Exhibit," 45–46; Baumgartner, *Catholic Journalism*, chap. 4.

30. Sr. Mary Charles Bryce, *The Influence of the Catechism of the Third Plenary Council of Baltimore on Widely Used Elementary Religion Text Books from Its Composition in 1885 to Its 1941 Revision* (Washington, D.C.: Catholic University of America, 1970).

31. "The Making of the Catholic Encyclopedia (1917)," *New Advent Catholic Encyclopedia*, ⟨http://www.newadvent.org/cathen/00001a.htm⟩ (25 September 2007). See also Paul H. Linehan, "The Catholic Encyclopedia," in *Catholic Builders of the Nation: A Symposium on the Catholic Contribution to the Civilization of the United States*, ed. C. E. McGuire (Boston: Continental Press, 1953), 4:204–18.

32. See John Murray Cuddihy, *No Offense: Civil Religion and Protestant Taste* (New York: Seabury, 1978).

33. The authors of *Catholic Gems; or, Treasures of the Church* wrote of the rosary in 1887 that "Nothing should deter Catholics from adhering to a devotion so holy, so consoling. Many, indeed, think it one for the ignorant only; but this is a grave error. Meditation on the life of our Lord is something to occupy the most exalted and most cultivated minds, and give them light and strength." Francis DeLigney, S.J., the Abbé Orsini, and John Gilmary Shea, *Catholic Gems; or, Treasures of the Church; A Repository of Catholic Instruction and Devotion* (New York: Office of Catholic Publications, 1887), 262.

34. *Ideal Catholic Reader* (New York: Macmillan, 1916; 14th printing, 1924); note that it includes an imprimatur though published by a secular publisher.

35. "Editorial Announcement," *America* 1 (17 April 1909): 5–6.

36. "An Introduction," *Commonweal* 1 (12 November 1924): 5.

37. "Editorial Announcement," 5.

38. Jessie L. Watson to Francis X. Talbot, 29 March 1928, *America* Magazine Archives, box 43, folder 41, Georgetown University, Washington, D.C.

39. Leon Hutton, "Catholicity and Civility: John Francis Noll and the Origins of Our Sunday Visitor," *U.S. Catholic Historian* 15 (Summer 1997): 11.

40. Ibid., 12; "Editorial Announcement," 5–6.

41. John Gilmary Shea, *History of the Catholic Church in the United States* (New York: J. G. Shea, 1886–1892). For a full bibliography of Shea's writings, see Peter Guilday, *John*

Gilmary Shea: Father of American Catholic History, 1824–1892 (New York: United States Catholic Historical Society, 1926), 155–71.

42. The period from 1784 to 1820 is covered in Joseph M. Finotti, *Bibliographia Catholica Americana, a List of Works Written by Catholic Authors, and Published in the United States* (New York: Catholic Publication House, 1872); Wilfrid Parsons, S.J., *Early Catholic Americana* (New York: Macmillan, 1939), covers the years 1729–1830; Walter Romig's *Guide to Catholic Literature* (Haverford, Pa.: Catholic Library Association, annual, 1888–1967) picked up the story in 1888; the *Survey of Catholic Americana* was explicitly undertaken to fill in the gap between the work of Parsons and Romig.

43. Dana Greene, *The Living of Maisie Ward* (Notre Dame, Ind.: University of Notre Dame Press, 1997), 85–91.

44. For Daniel A. Lord's specifically literary projects, see Arnold Sparr, *To Promote, Defend, and Redeem: The Catholic Literary Revival and the Cultural Transformation of American Catholicism, 1920–1960* (New York: Greenwood Press, 1990). Lord himself published an autobiography, *Played by Ear* (Chicago: Loyola University Press, 1956).

45. John M. Green, "Father Pamphlet," *Marianist* 46, no. 7 (September 1955): 6 (the quotation is attributed to Wilfrid Parsons, S.J., editor of *America* magazine); Sr. Mary Louis to Peggy Haney, 15 June 1955, Daniel Lord Papers, Midwest Jesuit Archives, St. Louis.

46. James Addison White, *The Founding of Cliff Haven: Early Years of the Catholic Summer School of America* (New York: United States Catholic Historical Society, 1950), 15–22; quote on 15.

47. Anne Klejment, "Catholic Digest and the Catholic Revival, 1936–1944," *U.S. Catholic Historian* 21 (Summer 2003): 89–110.

48. Letter from Francis X. Talbot, copy dated 18 April 1928, written to accompany a memo to members of the hierarchy soliciting their support for the Catholic Book Club, *America* Magazine Archives, box 43, folder 41.

Section IV. Readers and Reading;
Part A. Institutions:
Introduction

1. Magali Sarfatti Larson, *The Rise of Professionalism: A Sociological Analysis* (Berkeley: University of California Press, 1977).

2. See Lawrence Levine, *Highbrow/Lowbrow: The Emergence of Cultural Hierarchy in America* (Cambridge, Mass.: Harvard University Press, 1988), on the "sacralization" of high culture.

CHAPTER 21
From McGuffey to Dick and Jane:
Reading Textbooks

1. The *Appleton's School Readers* were originally published in 1877–78 as a five-volume series. Later the *Introductory Fourth Reader* was added. This series and its authors are discussed in John Nietz, *Old Textbooks* (Pittsburgh: University of Pittsburgh Press, 1961), 95–97, and Charles Carpenter, *History of American Schoolbooks* (Philadelphia: University of Pennsyl-

vania Press, 1963), 91–92. An older biography of William Torrey Harris is Kurt F. Leidecker, *Yankee Teacher: A Biography of William Torrey Harris* (New York: Philosophical Library, 1946). Lawrence A. Cremin has summarized the writings on Harris in *American Education: The Metropolitan Experience, 1876–1980* (New York: Harper & Row, 1988), 705–6.

2. William T. Harris, Andrew J. Rickoff, and Mark Bailey, *Appleton's School Readers: The Third Reader* (New York: D. Appleton and Co., 1881), ii, 209.

3. Ibid., 46–47.

4. Ibid., 18.

5. Ibid., 40–42.

6. On the values in *McGuffey's Readers*, see Richard Mosier, *Making the American Mind: Social and Moral Ideas in McGuffey Readers* (New York: Russell & Russell, 1965) and *The McGuffey Readers: Selections from the 1879 Edition*, ed. Elliott J. Gorn (Boston: Bedford/St. Martin's, 1998). For their devotion to instruction through phonics, see Douglas E. Mitchell and William L. Boyd, "Curriculum Politics in Global Perspective," *Education Policy* 15 (January 2001): 61; and A. W. Foshay, "Textbooks and the Curriculum during the Progressive Era," in *Textbooks and Schooling in the United States*, ed. L. Elliott and A. Woodward, Eighty-ninth Yearbook for the National Society for the Study of Education, pt. I (Chicago: University of Chicago Press, 1990), 23–41.

7. Statistics on school enrollment are taken from U.S. Department of Commerce, Bureau of the Census, *Historical Statistics of the United States: Colonial Times to 1970*, Part 1, no. 15 (Washington, D.C.: Bureau of the Census, 1975), 370.

8. Ibid., 379.

9. On the connections between the shift away from reading aloud and the shift away from phonics, see E. Jennifer Monaghan and E. Wendy Saul, "The Reader, the Scribe, the Thinker: A Critical Look at the History of American Reading and Writing Instruction," in *The Formation of the School Subjects*, ed. Thomas S. Popkewitz (Philadelphia: Falmer Press, 1987), 85–122.

10. See Nila Banton Smith, *American Reading Instruction*, rev. ed. (Newark, Del.: International Reading Association, 1965), 88–103; Mitford M. Mathews, *Teaching to Read Historically Considered* (Chicago: University of Chicago Press, 1976), 97–108.

11. On Francis Parker and the whole word method, see Monaghan and Saul, "The Reader," 143.

12. On the dominance of these "administrative progressives," see David B. Tyack, *The One Best System: A History of Urban Education* (Cambridge, Mass.: Harvard University Press, 1974), and Ellen Lagemann, *An Elusive Science: The Troubling History of Education Research* (Chicago: University of Chicago Press, 2000).

13. Monaghan and Saul, "The Reader," 97.

14. W. W. Thiesen, "Factors Affecting Results in Primary Reading," in *Twentieth Yearbook of the National Society for the Study of Education*, pt. 2 (Bloomington, Ill.: Public School Publishing, 1921), 3.

15. *The Heath Readers: Fifth Reader* (Boston: D. C. Heath & Co., 1903), 6.

16. E. Jennifer Monaghan, *A Common Heritage: Noah Webster's Blue-Back Speller* (Hamden, Conn.: Archon Books, 1983), 193.

17. William D. Lewis, Albert Lindsay Rowland, and Ethel H. Maltby, *The Silent Readers*

(Philadelphia: John C. Winston Co., 1924); Guy Thomas Buswell and William H. Wheeler, *The Silent Reading Hour, First Reader* (Chicago: Wheeler Publishing Co., 1923).

18. We owe this point to David Pearson of the University of California at Berkeley, who commented generously upon a draft of this chapter.

19. Bessie Blackstone Coleman, Willis L. Uhl, and James Fleming Hosic, *The Pathway to Reading: Eighth Reader* (New York: Silver, Burdett and Co., 1928), v.

20. Edmund Burke Huey, Ph.D., first published *The Psychology and Pedagogy of Reading* (New York: Macmillan, 1908). The work had as its extended title, "with a review of the history of reading and writing and of methods, texts, and hygiene in reading." It was reprinted eight times in the twenty years following its publication. See Magdelan D. Vernon, *The Experimental Study of Reading* (Cambridge: Cambridge University Press, 1931), xiv.

21. Surprisingly little has been written about the formation and growth of the American Book Company. Brief descriptions are found in John A. Tebbel, *A History of Book Publishing in the United States*, vol. 2 (New York: R. R. Bowker, 1975); Hellmut Lehmann-Haupt, Lawrence C. Wroth, and Rollo G. Silver, *The Book in America: A History of the Making and Selling of Books in the United States*, 2nd ed. (New York: R. R. Bowker, 1951), 360-61; Eugene Exman, *The House of Harper: One Hundred and Fifty Years of Publishing* (New York: Harper & Row, 1967), 172.

22. This statement from the *Chicago Daily Inter-Ocean* is reprinted in an undated pamphlet, *Facts Omitted in the Answer of the American Book Company to Its Defamers*, back cover.

23. Upton Sinclair, *The Goslings: A Study of the American Schools* (Pasadena: Author, 1924), 315. Sinclair documented a number of instances of corruption and bribery by the ABC and its agents but also claimed that, "The competitors of the American Book Company are forced to meet its methods and to buy their share of success" (315).

24. W. W. Livengood, *Our Heritage: An Address Delivered to the Entire Agency Force of American Book Company* (New York: American Book Company, 1947), 8-9.

25. Lehmann-Haupt, Wroth, and Silver, *The Book in America*, 360-61.

26. *Fifty Years of Publishing: A History of the Educational Department of Houghton Mifflin Company* (Boston: Houghton Mifflin Company, 1930), 6, 12, 14-16, 19.

27. The predecessor to the Curriculum Foundation Series at Scott Foresman was the Elson Basic Readers, written in the 1920s by William H. Elson, a transitional figure between the *McGuffey* generation and the Gray basal reader generation. Gray joined the authorial team in 1929, just as the first "Dick and Jane" book came out (in 1930). The series then became known as the Elson-Gray Basic Readers, and then, in the 1940s, the Curriculum Foundation Series, with Gray as lead author. See Allan Luke, "Making Dick and Jane: Historical Genesis of the Modern Basal Reader," *Teachers College Record* 89, no. 1 (Fall 1987): 91-116.

28. E. Jennifer Monaghan, "Gender and Textbooks: Women Writers of Elementary Readers, 1880-1950," *Publishing Research Quarterly* 10, no. 1 (1994): 28-46.

29. On the old-stock Protestant character of college faculties, see Steven J. Diner, *A Very Different Age: Americans of the Progressive Era* (New York: Hill & Wang, 1998), 185, 191.

30. See, for example, Michael W. Apple, *Teachers and Texts: A Political Economy of Class and Gender Relations in Education* (New York: Routledge & Kegan Paul, 1988), and Allan Luke, *Literacy, Textbooks, and Ideology* (London: Falmer Press, 1988).

31. Ruth Miller Elson, *Guardians of Tradition: American Schoolbooks of the Nineteenth Century* (Lincoln: University of Nebraska Press, 1964), 242.

32. Richard de Charms and Gerald Moeller, "Values Expressed in American Children's Readers: 1800-1950," *Journal of Abnormal and Social Psychology* 64 (1962): 136-42.

33. Bernard Wishy, *The Child and the Republic: The Dawn of Modern American Child Nurture* (Philadelphia: University of Pennsylvania Press, 1968). Writers who have treated children's literature historically include Gillian Avery, *Behold the Child: American Children and Their Books, 1621-1922* (Baltimore: Johns Hopkins University Press, 1994), and Mary F. Thwaite, *From Primer to Pleasure in Reading* (Boston: Horn Book, 1973).

34. Mark Sullivan, *America Finding Herself*, vol. 2 of *Our Times: The United States, 1900-1925* (New York: Charles Scribner's Sons, 1926-35), 45.

35. Henry Steele Commager, foreword to the Signet Classic reissue of *McGuffey's Fifth Eclectic Reader*, 1879 ed. (New York: New American Library, 1962), viii.

36. *The Curriculum Foundation Series* is described briefly in Nila Banton Smith, *American Reading Instruction* (Newark, Del.: International Reading Association, 1965), 224-25. A more extensive analysis of the series was done by Allan Luke, "Making Dick and Jane," and *Literacy, Textbooks, and Ideology*. A brief biography of William S. Gray is included in John T. Guthrie, ed., *Reading: William S. Gray; A Research Retrospective, 1881-1941* (Newark, Del.: International Reading Association, 1984). The body of this monograph is a reprint of Gray's 1941 article, "Reading," originally published in the *Encyclopedia of Educational Research*, ed. Walter S. Monroe (New York: Macmillan, 1941).

CHAPTER 22
The American Public Library:
Construction of a Community Reading Institution

1. The Bureau of Education reported that of the 3,600 libraries "accessible" to at least some members of the "public" in the United States in 1876, fewer than 300 could be categorized as free government-supported public institutions, and two-thirds of those were in the Northeast. See U.S. Bureau of Education, *Public Libraries in the United States of America: Their History, Condition, and Management; Special Report*, pt. 1 (Washington, D.C.: Government Printing Office, 1876), especially the statistics listed on 1010-1142. See also Haynes McMullen, "The Distribution of Libraries throughout the United States," *Library Trends* 25 (July 1976): 23-53.

2. Conference proceedings were published in *American Library Journal* 1 (November 1876): 98-99.

3. The "fiction problem" in American public libraries is covered in Dee Garrison, *Apostles of Culture: The Public Librarian and American Society, 1876-1920* (New York: Free Press, 1979), 67-101. Less analytical but exhaustive are two studies by Esther Jane Carrier: *Fiction in Public Libraries, 1876-1900* (New York: Scarecrow Press, 1965) and *Fiction in Public Libraries, 1900-1950* (Littleton, Colo.: Libraries Unlimited, 1985).

4. J. P. Quincy, "Free Libraries," in U.S. Bureau of Education, *Public Libraries*, 389-402. Quotations taken from 390, 393, 395, 396, and 399. A summary of the 1876 librarians' con-

ference can be found in Wayne A. Wiegand, *Politics of an Emerging Profession: The American Library Association, 1876–1917* (Westport, Conn.: Greenwood Press, 1986), 3–13.

5. See Melvil Dewey, "Origin of the A.L.A. Motto," *Public Libraries* 11 (February 1906): 55.

6. Authors whose works reveal the late nineteenth-century ideology of reading frequently cited by librarians include Francis Bacon, "Of Studies," in *The Essays or Counsels, Civil and Moral, of Francis Bacon*, ed. Samuel Harvey Reynolds (Oxford: Clarendon Press, 1890), 342; Ralph Waldo Emerson, "Books," in *Society and Solitude: Twelve Chapters* (Boston: Houghton Mifflin Co., 1912), 194; Frederick Harrison, *The Choice of Books and Other Literary Pieces* (London: Macmillan, 1896), 6; Newell Dwight Hilles, *A Man's Value to Society: Studies in Self-Culture and Character* (London: Oliphant, Anderson & Ferrier, 1897), 240.

7. See Wayne A. Wiegand, "American Library Association Executive Board Members, 1876–1917: A Collective Profile," *Libri* 31 (August 1981): 153–66; Wayne A. Wiegand and Geri Greenway, "A Comparative Analysis of the Socioeconomic and Professional Characteristics of American Library Association Executive Board and Council Members, 1876–1917," *Library Research* 2 (Winter 1980): 309–26; Wayne A. Wiegand and Dorothy Steffens, "Members of the Club: A Look at One Hundred ALA Presidents," *University of Illinois Graduate School of Library and Information Science Occasional Papers* 182 (April 1988): 1–29.

8. Much of the information on Dewey in this essay is taken from Wayne A. Wiegand, *Irrepressible Reformer: A Biography of Melvil Dewey* (Chicago: American Library Association, 1996).

9. It is no coincidence that the second number of *Library Notes*, a new serial that Dewey began publishing in 1886, carried large advertisements for *Political Science Quarterly*, *New England Magazine*, *Literary World*, and the *New Princeton Review*, all of which — readers were informed — routinely carried reviews of newly published books by academic and literary authorities. See *Library Notes* 1 (October 1886): 8, 11, 15, 17.

10. "The Fiction Song," *Library Journal* 15 (November 1890): 325. It is likely the lyrics were fashioned to fit "Titwillow" from Gilbert and Sullivan's *The Mikado* (1885).

11. See American Library Association, "Papers Prepared for the World's Library Congress," in U.S. Bureau of Education, Department of Interior, *Report of the Commissioner of Education for the Year, 1892–93*, pts. 1–2 (Washington, D.C.: Government Printing Office, 1895); U.S. Bureau of Education, Department of Interior, *Catalog of "A.L.A" Library: 5,000 Volumes for a Popular Library* (Washington, D.C.: Government Printing Office, 1893). The history of this publication is detailed in Wayne A. Wiegand, "*Catalog of 'A.L.A.' Library* (1893): Origins of a Genre," in *For the Good of the Order: Essays in Honor of Edward G. Holley*, ed. Delmus E. Williams et al. (Greenwich, Conn.: JAI Press, 1994), 237–54.

12. See Christine J. Pawley, *Reading on the Middle Border: The Culture of Print in Late-Nineteenth-Century Osage, Iowa* (Amherst: University of Massachusetts Press, 2001), 166; Bryant Library Board of Trustees, minutes for 12 December 1893, Bryant Library Archives, Sauk Centre, Minn.; Helen G. Lyman, "Hutchins, Frank Avery (1851–1914)," in *Dictionary of American Library Biography*, ed. George S. Bobinski (Littleton, Colo.: Libraries Unlimited, 1978), 257–59.

13. See Silberman to Carnegie, 5 August 1904 and 7 December 1904, Carnegie Library Correspondence, Rare Books and Manuscripts Reading Room, Columbia University, New

York. Under Dewey's direction the New York State Library had already established a precedent for "best book" bibliographies. See, for example, New York (State) Library Extension Division, *50 of the Best Books of 1899 for a Village Library* (Albany: New York State Library, 1900). Many of these lists were gathered in New York State Library, *Best Books of 1897-1925 Selected for a Small Public Library*, 2 vols. (Albany: University of the State of New York, 1898-1926).

14. For a descriptive study of Carnegie's library philanthropy, see George S. Bobinski, *Carnegie Libraries: Their History and Impact on American Library Development* (Chicago: American Library Association, 1969). Much more analytical is Abigail A. Van Slyck, *Free to All: Carnegie Libraries & American Culture, 1890-1920* (Chicago: University of Chicago Press, 1995). Scores of communities ultimately rejected Carnegie grants, for a variety of reasons. See Robert Sidney Martin, ed., *Carnegie Denied: Rejecting Carnegie Construction Grants, 1896-1928* (Westport, Conn.: Greenwood Press, 1993).

15. See Van Slyck, *Free to All*, 35-40. Dewey's library science and Carnegie's recommended building plans may have had much more to do with constructing the image of "Marion the 'Shushing' Librarian" than any gender or personality type.

16. This attitude appeared to show little regional variance. See, for example, Joanne E. Passet, *Cultural Crusaders: Women Librarians in the American West, 1900-1917* (Albuquerque: University of New Mexico Press, 1994), 116, and Deanna Marcum, *Good Books in a Country Home: The Public Library as Cultural Force in Hagerstown, Maryland, 1878-1920* (Westport, Conn.: Greenwood Press, 1994), 99.

17. *Fiction Catalog: A Selected List of about 350 Novels, Cataloged by Author and Title with Annotations* (Minneapolis: H. W. Wilson, 1909); Marion E. Potter, comp., *Children's Catalog: A Guide to the Best Reading for Young People Based on Twenty-Four Selected Library Lists* (Minneapolis: H. W. Wilson, 1909).

18. William Coolidge Lane, ed., *A.L.A. Portrait Index: Index to Portraits Contained in Printed Books and Periodicals* (Washington, D.C.: Library of Congress, 1906).

19. "Report of the League of Library Commissions Publication Committee, December, 1905," Matthew S. Dudgeon Papers, Manuscripts Division, Wisconsin Historical Society, Madison.

20. *Booklist* 4 (January 1908): 3.

21. James to Brett, 28 September 1896, William Howard Brett Papers, Cleveland (Ohio) Public Library Archives. See also *Proceedings of the American Library Association Conference, 1896*, 103, 125, and 155, and Marcum, *Good Books*, 107.

22. These data are reported in Pawley, *Reading on the Middle Border*, chap. 3.

23. Hamlin Garland, *A Son of the Middle Border*, edited with an introduction by Joseph B. McCullough (New York: Penguin Books, 1995), 92-93.

24. Biographical data are gleaned from the pages of the *Sauk Centre Herald*, 1865-1910. Many literary scholars have argued that the world Sinclair Lewis describes in *Main Street* is actually the turn-of-the-century Sauk Centre he experienced as a boy. See, for example, Mark Schorer, *Sinclair Lewis: An American Life* (New York: McGraw-Hill, 1961), and, more recently, Richard Lingeman, *Sinclair Lewis: Rebel from Main Street* (New York: Random House, 2002).

25. Schorer, *Sinclair Lewis*, 16.

26. The definitive work on the origins of the New York Public Library is Phyllis Dain, *The New York Public Library: A History of the Founding and Early Years* (New York: New York Public Library; Astor, Lenox, and Tilden Foundations, 1972). See also Bernice Selden, "Rose, Ernestine (1880-1961)," in Bobinski, *Dictionary of American Library Biography*, 447-48, and Dain, "Public Library Governance and a Changing New York City," *Libraries & Culture* 26 (Spring 1991): 219-58.

27. See Marcum, *Good Books*, 143; "Proud Prince under the Ban," *Cincinnati Post*, 6 February 1904, cited in Rosemary Ruhig Du Mont, *Reform and Reaction: The Big City Public Library in American Life* (Westport, Conn.: Greenwood Press, 1977), 88. Children's Library League pledge, quoted in Harriet G. Long, *Public Library Service to Children: Foundation and Development* (Metuchen, N.J.: Scarecrow Press, 1969), 129. See also Linda A. Eastman, "The Child, the School and the Library," *Library Journal* 21 (April 1896): 134-39; C. H. Cramer, *Open Shelves and Open Minds: A History of the Cleveland Public Library* (Cleveland: Press of Case Western Reserve University, 1972); Christine Jenkins, "'The Strength of the Inconspicuous': Youth Service Librarians, the American Library Association, and Intellectual Freedom for the Young, 1939-1955" (Ph.D. diss., University of Wisconsin at Madison, 1995), chap. 2.

28. "List Taken from Dr. Alexander Fuehr, Former Attache of the German Embassy in Japan," attached to Memo, Nicholas Biddle, Major, Office of Military Intelligence, New York, to R. H. Van Deman, Lt. Colonel, General Staff, Chief, Military Intelligence Section, box 2471, record group 165, Records of the War Department, General Staff, Military Intelligence Division, 1917-1941, file no. 9140-2755, National Archives, Washington, D.C. See also Wayne A. Wiegand, "British Propaganda in American Public Libraries, 1914-1917," *Journal of Library History* 18 (Summer 1983): 237-54.

29. A more complete story of the World War I American public library experience is in Wayne A. Wiegand, *"An Active Instrument for Propaganda": The American Public Library during World War I* (Westport, Conn.: Greenwood Press, 1989), 7-28. See also Passet, *Cultural Crusaders*, 116. A list of "Books and Pamphlets Banned by the War Department" can be found in Arthur P. Young, *Books for Sammies: The American Library Association and World War I* (Pittsburgh: Beta Phi Mu, 1981), 109-13.

30. Hibbing, Minnesota, incident reported in *Minneapolis Public Library Official Weekly* 6 (1917): 1. See also Young, *Books for Sammies*, 43.

31. Corinne Bacon, comp., *Standard Catalog: Fiction Section* (New York: H. W. Wilson Company, 1923), ii-iii.

32. Board Minutes, 5 May 1919, 31 May 1919, and 6 October 1924, Morris (Illinois) Public Library Archives.

33. *Booklist* 20 (April 1924): 245.

34. ALA published new editions of the *Catalogs* in 1922, 1927, 1932, 1936, 1942, and 1950. Over time, Wilson turned its "Series" into a set of quinquennially published editions (each with annual supplements). Eventually, *Public Library Catalog* and a resurrected *Fiction Catalog* grew out of *The Standard Catalog for Public Libraries*, first issued in 1934.

35. Recent scholarship on the history of reading suggests that over the centuries people have attached multiple values to and made multiple uses of their reading practices and behaviors. See, for example, Wolfgang Iser, *The Act of Reading: A Theory of Aesthetic Response*

(Baltimore: Johns Hopkins University Press, 1978); Stanley Fish, *Is There a Text in This Class? The Authority of Interpretive Communities* (Cambridge, Mass.: Harvard University Press, 1980); Stephen Greenblatt, *Renaissance Self-Fashioning: From More to Shakespeare* (Chicago: University of Chicago Press, 1980). Elizabeth Long, "Textual Interpretations as Collective Action," in *The Ethnography of Reading*, ed. Jonathan Boyarin (Berkeley: University of California Press, 1993), 180–211, makes the case for a "social infrastructure" among readers of certain types of fiction. Pierre Bourdieu, *Distinction: A Social Critique of the Judgment of Taste*, trans. Richard Nice (London: Routledge, 1986), is a fascinating discussion of the connections between social class and cultural taste. Michel de Certeau, *The Practice of Everyday Life*, trans. Steven Rendall (Berkeley: University of California Press, 1984), contains a close look at how in everyday life different people "appropriate" differently the cultural products and activities surrounding them. Finally, Jane Tompkins, *West of Everything: The Inner Life of Westerns* (New York: Oxford University Press, 1993), and Janice A. Radway, *Reading the Romance: Women, Patriarchy, and Popular Literature*, 2nd ed. (Chapel Hill: University of North Carolina Press, 1991), bring focus to multiple uses made by readers of two types of genre fiction that have accounted for heavy fractions of library patronage in the twentieth century.

36. William S. Miller, *Growing Up in Goose Lake* (Chicago: Open Lands Project, 1974), 55–56.

37. *Morris Daily Herald*, 4 October 1924; Board Minutes, 24 June 1925, Morris Public Library Archives.

CHAPTER 23
The Great Libraries

1. For further details on the Library of Congress, the Astor Library, and the Boston Public Library before 1880, see Kenneth E. Carpenter, "Libraries," in *The Industrial Book, 1840–1880*, ed. Scott E. Casper, Jeffrey D. Groves, Stephen W. Nissenbaum, and Michael Winship, vol. 3 of *A History of the Book in America* (Chapel Hill: University of North Carolina Press, 2007), 303–18.

2. United States, Bureau of Education, *Public Libraries in the United States of America: Their History, Condition, and Management; Special Report*, pt. 1 (Washington, D.C.: Government Printing Office, 1876), 623–48.

3. See Wayne A. Wiegand, chapter 22 in this volume.

4. On Johns Hopkins and the movement toward research, see Janice A. Radway, chapter 11 in this volume, and Marcel Chotkowski LaFollette, chapter 12 in this volume.

5. Samuel Rothstein, *The Development of Reference Services through Academic Traditions, Public Library Practices, and Special Librarianship*, ACRL Monographs, no. 14 (1955; repr., Boston: Gregg Press, 1972), 18; John Y. Cole, "Storehouses and Workshops: American Libraries and the Uses of Knowledge," in *The Organization of Knowledge in Modern America, 1860–1920*, ed. Alexandra Oleson and John Voss (Baltimore: Johns Hopkins University Press, 1979), 371; Louis R. Wilson, *The Geography of Reading: A Study of the Distribution and Status of Libraries in the United States* (Chicago: American Library Association, 1938), 118.

6. John Higham, "The Matrix of Specialization," in Oleson and Voss, *The Organization*

of Knowledge in Modern America, 1860–1920, 12–16 (quote on p. 13). On public librarians' attitudes toward objectivity and neutrality, see Wayne A. Wiegand, chapter 22 in this volume.

7. Jane A. Rosenberg, *The Nation's Great Library: Herbert Putnam and the Library of Congress, 1899–1939* (Urbana: University of Illinois Press, 1993), 165.

8. Neil Harris, "Public Funding for Rarity: Some American Debates," *Libraries & Culture* 31 (Winter 1996): 46.

9. Quoted in John Y. Cole, "The Library of Congress and American Scholarship, 1865–1939," in *Libraries and Scholarly Communication in the United States: The Historical Dimension*, ed. Phyllis Dain and John Y. Cole (New York: Greenwood Press, 1990), 52.

10. Ibid., 46.

11. Phyllis Dain, "Harry M. Lydenberg and American Library Resources: A Study in Modern Library Leadership," *Library Quarterly* 47 (October 1977): 451–60; Phyllis Dain, "'A Coral Island': A Century of Collection Development in The Research Libraries of The New York Public Library," *Biblion: The Bulletin of The New York Public Library* 3 (Spring 1995): 5–75.

12. Andrew Keogh, "Our Library Resources Shown by Some Government Needs in the War," *ALA Bulletin* 13 (July 1919): 270–73; Thomas F. O'Connor, "Library Service to the American Commission to Negotiate Peace and to the Preparatory Inquiry, 1917–1919" *Libraries & Culture* 24 (Spring 1989): 144–57.

13. Wilson, *Geography of Reading*, 120.

14. Roger L. Geiger, *To Advance Knowledge: The Growth of American Research Universities, 1900–1940* (New York: Oxford University Press, 1986), 229, 233.

15. Wilson, *Geography of Reading*, 118–25, 131–37; the 1939 figures are in Geiger, *To Advance Knowledge*, 276–77.

16. Kenneth E. Carpenter, *The First 350 Years of the Harvard University Library: Description of an Exhibition* (Cambridge, Mass.: Harvard University Library, 1986), ix, viii.

17. Quoted in William Bentick-Smith, *Building a Great Library: The Coolidge Years at Harvard* (Cambridge, Mass.: Harvard University Library, 1976), 140.

Section IV. Readers and Reading; Part B. Reading in Situ: Introduction

1. John A. Tebbel, *A History of Book Publishing in the United States*, 4 vols. (New York: R. R. Bowker, 1972–80), 3:4.

2. See Elizabeth McHenry, chapter 25 in this volume.

3. *Historical Statistics of the United States: Colonial Times to 1970*, 2 vols., pt. 1, no. 15 (Washington, D.C.: Bureau of the Census, 1975), 368–69.

4. *Digest of Educational Statistics, 2002* (Washington, D.C.: National Center for Education Statistics, 2003), 209.

5. Tebbel, *History of Book Publishing in the United States*, 2:676, 3:681.

6. Edwin Emery, *The Press and America: An Interpretative History of the Mass Media*, 3rd ed. (Englewood Cliffs, N.J.: Prentice-Hall, 1972).

7. See Elizabeth Long, *Book Clubs: Women and the Uses of Reading in Everyday Life* (Chicago: University of Chicago Press, 2003).

CHAPTER 24
Aflame with Culture:
Reading and Social Mission in the
Nineteenth-Century White Women's Literary Club Movement

1. Lawrence W. Levine, *Highbrow/Lowbrow: The Emergence of Cultural Hierarchy in America* (Cambridge, Mass.: Harvard University Press, 1988). Paul DiMaggio, "Cultural Entrepreneurship in Nineteenth-Century Boston, Part I: The Creation of an Organizational Base for High Culture in America," *Media, Culture and Society* 4 (1982): 33-50, and "Cultural Entrepreneurship in Nineteenth-Century Boston, Part II: The Classification and Framing of American Art," *Media, Culture and Society* 4 (1982): 303-22. On Lawrence Levine and "brow levels," see also Janice A. Radway, chapter 11 in this volume.

2. Robert Neelly Bellah et al., *Habits of the Heart: Individualism and Commitment in American Life* (New York: Harper & Row, 1985).

3. Janice A. Radway, "On the Sociability of Reading: Books, Self-Fashioning, and the Creation of Communities" (unpublished manuscript, Duke University); Roger Chartier, *The Order of Books: Readers, Authors, and Libraries in Europe between the Fourteenth and Eighteenth Centuries*, trans. Lydia G. Cochrane (Stanford: Stanford University Press, 1994).

4. This essay is centered on the white women's movement because most of its primary source materials are drawn from a larger research project on reading groups in Houston, Texas, and there are no extant records of nineteenth century African American women's reading groups for that city. For information on African American groups, see Elizabeth McHenry, *Forgotten Readers: Recovering the Lost History of African American Literary Societies* (Durham: Duke University Press, 2002), and McHenry, chapter 25 in this volume; Anne Ruggles Gere, *Intimate Practices: Literacy and Cultural Work in U.S. Women's Clubs, 1880-1920* (Urbana: University of Illinois Press, 1997); Anne Ruggles Gere and Sarah Robbins, "Gendered Literacy in Black and White: Turn-of-the-Century African American and European-American Club Women's Printed Texts," *Signs* 21 (1996): 643-78.

5. Megan Seaholm, "Earnest Women: The White Women's Movement in Progressive Era Texas, 1880-1920" (Ph.D. diss., Rice University, 1988), 212.

6. Mary A. Livermore (suffragist and New England Women's Club member), "The Club of the Future," *Arena* (August 1892): 386, cited in Seaholm, "Earnest Women," 92.

7. It was not the first. The Bronte Club of Victoria, Texas, had begun as a schoolgirls' literary club in 1855 and developed into an adult woman's club by 1885; historian John Boles (personal communication) also knows of a women's poetry club meeting somewhere in the Texas hill country, among German immigrants, by the 1830s. Certainly, though, the Ladies Reading Club was a flagship club for the late-century literary movement in Texas, and its programs, mailed out upon request, served as an inspiration for other clubs across the state.

8. Adele Briscoe Looscan, Speech, 29 November 1921, Ladies Reading Club Collection, box 2, folder 9, Houston Metropolitan Archives, Houston Public Library.

9. Adele Briscoe Looscan, "Club Life and Women's Review," Ladies Reading Club Collection, box 11, folder 39, Houston Metropolitan Archives.

10. Seaholm, "Earnest Women," 206.

11. Oberlin College had opened its doors to women in 1837, but by 1857 only 20 women

had entered the Collegiate Department, while 299 took the "ladies course" instead. Mary Sharp College in Tennessee (1851) may be the first true "college" for women. See Theodora Penny Martin, *The Sound of Our Own Voices: Women's Study Clubs, 1860–1910* (Boston: Beacon Press, 1987), 42–43.

12. The College Club, *Bi-annual Directory* (Boston: Samuel Usher, 1916), 4, cited in Martin, *The Sound of Our Own Voices*, 43.

13. Jane Cunningham Croly, *The History of the Women's Club Movement in America* (New York: H. G. Allen & Co., 1898), 452.

14. Seaholm, "Earnest Women," 2, 184; Martin, *The Sound of Our Own Voices*, 39.

15. Seaholm, "Earnest Women," 209.

16. Karen J. Blair, *The Clubwoman as Feminist: True Womanhood Redefined, 1868–1914* (New York: Holmes & Meier, 1980), 24.

17. Martin, *The Sound of Our Own Voices*, 65.

18. Seaholm, "Earnest Women," 222.

19. "Axson Club 1917–1918 Yearbook," 7, Houston Metropolitan Archives.

20. Seaholm, "Earnest Women," 221–23; Martin, *The Sound of Our Own Voices*, 65; Blair, *Clubwoman as Feminist*, 69.

21. Stella L. Christian, *The History of the Texas Federation of Women's Clubs* (Houston: Dealy-Adey-Elgin Co., Stationers and Printers, 1919), 23.

22. Martin, *The Sound of Our Own Voices*, 91.

23. Philip Allen Metzger, "Publishing and the Book Trade in Austin, Texas, 1870–1920" (Ph.D. diss., University of Texas at Austin, 1984), 59.

24. Ibid., 126, 81–83.

25. Ibid., 127; *Houston City Directory, 1895–1896* (n.p., n.d.), 371, 87, 88, 100, 180, 227, 256.

26. Orin Walker Hatch, "The Development of the Houston Lyceum and the Houston Public Library" (M.A. thesis, University of Houston, 1963), 60, 75.

27. Gere, *Intimate Practices*, 186.

28. Ladies Reading Club Meeting minutes for 7 February and 6 March 1888, Ladies Reading Club Collection, box 1, folder 1, Houston Metropolitan Archives.

29. Mary S. Cunningham, *The Woman's Club of El Paso* (El Paso: Texas Western Press, 1978), 19.

30. Seaholm, "Earnest Women," 213. Houston's Ladies Reading Club also established an early national reputation as a particularly serious club.

31. Gere, *Intimate Practices*.

32. Ibid. See also Gere and Robbins, "Gendered Literacy in Black and White."

33. Anne Firor Scott, *Natural Allies: Women's Associations in American History* (Urbana: University of Illinois Press, 1991), 118.

34. Croly, *Women's Club Movement in America*, 12.

35. Blair, *Clubwoman as Feminist*, 69–70.

36. Seaholm, "Earnest Women," 233.

37. Ladies Reading Club Meeting minutes, 6 March 1888.

38. Seaholm, "Earnest Women," 236–37. In *Clubwoman as Feminist*, Blair also notes that many of the discussions centered on people, speculating that women most easily made sense of the world through people.

39. Seaholm, "Earnest Women," 240.

40. Mrs. A. O. Granger, "The Effect of Club Work in the South," *Annals of the American Academy of Political and Social Science* 28, no. 2 (1906): 253.

41. Kate Cassatt MacKnight, "Report of the Civic Committee," *Annals of the American Academy of Political and Social Science* 28, no. 2 (1906): 293-94.

42. Carroll Smith-Rosenberg, "The Female World of Love and Ritual," in *Disorderly Conduct: Visions of Gender in Victorian America* (New York: Knopf, 1985), 53-76.

43. Seaholm, "Earnest Women," 225.

44. Christian, *Texas Federation of Women's Clubs*, 42.

45. Seaholm, "Earnest Women," 98.

46. Croly, *Women's Club Movement in America*, 459.

47. Blair, *Clubwoman as Feminist*, 108-12. For a discussion of the National Association of Colored Women, see Paula Giddings, *When and Where I Enter: The Impact of Black Women on Race and Sex in America* (New York: William Morrow, 1984), esp. 93-95.

48. Martha E. White, "The Work of the Woman's Club," *Atlantic Monthly* 99, no. 559 (1903): 620; Julia Ward Howe, "How Can Women Best Associate?" *Papers and Letters Presented at the First Woman's Congress of the Association for the Advancement of Woman, 1873* (New York: Association for the Advancement of Women, 1874), 6.

49. Martin, *The Sound of Our Own Voices*, 131.

50. Christian, *Texas Federation of Women's Clubs*, 41.

51. Seaholm, "Earnest Women," 92.

52. Ibid., 344.

53. After its inception, the Federation of Women's Clubs also drew on nonliterary constituencies, for example the popular Mothers' Clubs, which are referred to often as the progenitors of modern Parent-Teacher Organizations or Parent-Teacher Associations and which were especially interested in new ideas in early childhood education.

54. Seaholm, "Earnest Women," 272.

55. Ibid., 278.

56. Ibid., 296-98, 372-80.

CHAPTER 25
Reading and Race Pride:
The Literary Activism of Black Clubwomen

1. Mary White Ovington, "Selling Race Pride," *Publishers' Weekly* (10 January 1925): 111-14.

2. Daniel Max, *New York Times Magazine*, 9 August 1992, 20. For a more complete discussion of the literate underpinnings of African American "oral culture," see Elizabeth McHenry and Shirley Brice Heath, "The Literate and the Literary: African American Readers as Writers, 1830-1940," *Written Communication* 11, no. 4 (October 1994): 419-44.

3. Toni Morrison, "Unspeakable Things Unspoken: The Afro-American Presence in American Literature," *Michigan Quarterly Review* 23 (Winter 1989): 11.

4. Evelyn Brooks Higginbotham, *Righteous Discontent: The Women's Movement in the Black Baptist Church, 1880-1920* (Cambridge, Mass.: Harvard University Press, 1993), 186.

5. "The Bethel Literary," *People's Advocate*, 10 December 1881, 3.

6. Cornel West, "Black Strivings in a Twilight Civilization," in Cornel West and Henry Louis Gates Jr., *The Future of the Race* (New York: Random House, 1997), 67.

7. As Harvey Neufeldt and Leo McGee write in their introduction to the collection of essays *Education of the African American Adult* (Westport, Conn.: Greenwood Press, 1990), informal and alternative forms of adult education have historically complemented the more traditional educational settings of elementary and secondary schools and colleges in the black community.

8. There is some confusion over the exact date the Woman's Era Club was formed. My pinpointing of this club's organization in 1893 is based in part on a report of the second anniversary celebration of the Woman's Era Club on 25 January 1895 published in the February 1895 issue of the *Woman's Era*.

9. Given its national prominence and eventual status as the organ of the National Association of Colored Women, I would not call the *Woman's Era* a representative text. However, as Anne Ruggles Gere and Sarah R. Robbins argue about women's clubs in general in this period, the clubs' producing and circulating their own printed texts constituted one of the cultural practices that "fostered solidarity within groups and, in some cases, enhanced [women's] standing within the larger community." Many black women's clubs produced texts worthy of consideration in this context; some are a part of the Daniel Murray Collection at the Library of Congress. Gere and Robbins are interested in the textual negotiations undertaken by white and black clubwomen through their printed texts. See Gere and Robbins, "Gendered Literacy in Black and White: Turn-of-the-Century African American and European-American Club Women's Printed Texts," *Signs: Journal of Women in Culture and Society* 21 (1996): 644.

10. Roger Chartier asserts the importance of considering past reading practices by reconstructing them from what he calls the "sparse and multiple traces" that remain. Here I consider the *Woman's Era* and other sources for the fragments of information they offer toward the reconstruction of the elusive history of middle-class, African American readers at the turn of the century. That is not to say that *the Woman's Era* simply reflected the practices of its readers; setting themes for discussion and suggesting the foci of its readers' attention, the newspaper also contributed to the shaping of its readers' habits. See Chartier, "Texts, Printing, Readings," in *The New Cultural History*, ed. Lynn Hunt (Berkeley: University of California Press, 1989), 157.

11. *Woman's Era*, March 1894, 4. Better known by her pen name, "Iola," Ida B. Wells-Barnett waged an antilynching campaign in the last decades of the nineteenth century largely through fiery articles contributed to the press; her daring and influential writing inspired many black women to become activists. Florida Ridley's analysis of the founding of the Woman's Era was read before the members of the club before being printed in the inaugural issue of their newspaper.

12. Henry Lewis Gates Jr. puts together a remarkable visual essay of some of these images in his essay "The Trope of the New Negro and the Reconstruction of the Image of the Black," *Representations* 24 (Fall 1988): 150–55 (quotation from 150).

13. In 1904 Fannie Barrier Williams wrote: "It is a significant and shameful fact that I am constantly in receipt of letters from the still unprotected women in the South, begging me to

find employment for their daughters . . . to save them from going into the homes of the South as servants as there is nothing to save them from dishonor and degradation." See Williams, "A Northern Negro's Autobiography," *Independent* 57, no. 2902 (14 July 1904): 96, quoted in *Black Women in White America: A Documentary History*, ed. Gerda Lerner (New York: Pantheon Books, 1972), 165.

14. Fannie Barrier Williams, "The Intellectual Progress of Colored Women of the United States since the Emancipation Proclamation," in *The World's Congress of Representative Women*, ed. May Wright Sewall (Chicago: Rand, McNally, 1894), 702, 707. Sander Gilman's "Black Bodies, White Bodies: Toward an Iconography of Female Sexuality in Late Nineteenth-Century Art, Medicine, and Literature," in *"Race," Writing, and Difference*, ed. Henry Louis Gates Jr. (Chicago: University of Chicago Press, 1986), 223-40, offers a cogent analysis of how black women came to be seen, by the turn of the century, as "an icon for black sexuality in general."

15. "Report of the Woman's Era Club, 1899," Papers of the Woman's Era Club, Boston Public Library.

16. See, for instance, *Woman's Era*, December 1894, 1.

17. Ibid., 3. It is unlikely that any of the contributors to the *Woman's Era* were paid. Although she regularly contributed to the journal, Mary Church Terrell reported in her autobiography, *A Colored Woman in a White World* (1940; repr., New York: G. K. Hall, 1996), that "the *Colored American* [begun in 1900] was the first newspaper to pay me anything" (222). For unknown reasons, Terrell refers to the *Woman's Era* as the *New Era* in her autobiography.

18. "Advertise in *The Woman's Era*," *Woman's Era*, December 1894, 10.

19. Sarah E. Tanner, "Reading," *Woman's Era*, June 1895, 14.

20. Ida DePriest, "Report of the National Colored Woman's League, Denver Branch, 16 July 1896," reprinted in *A History of the Club Movement among the Colored Women of the United States of America* (1896; repr., Washington, D.C.: National Association of Colored Women's Clubs, Inc., 1902), 83.

21. Mrs. R. Aldridge and Mrs. Gertrude Brooks, "Report of the Frances E. W. Harper League of Pittsburgh and Allegheny, 15 July 1896," reprinted in *A History of the Club Movement among the Colored Women of the United States of America*, 105.

22. Tanner, "Reading," 14.

23. "The Woman's Era Literature Department," *Woman's Era*, June 1896, 2.

24. Elizabeth Piper Ensley, "Colorado," *Woman's Era*, May 1895, 9.

25. Sara Iredell Fleetwood, quoted in *We Are Your Sisters: Black Women in the Nineteenth Century*, ed. Dorothy Sterling (New York: W. W. Norton, 1984), 431-32.

26. "Notes and Comments," *Woman's Era*, May 1895, 1.

27. Ensley, "Colorado," 9.

28. "England's Attitude," *Woman's Era*, February 1895, 20. One of the "talents" introduced to the Woman's Era Club was Pauline Elizabeth Hopkins, who, on 15 November 1899, "presented [her new novel *Contending Forces*] before the Woman's Era Club of Boston"; the text was met with "instant success." A "Prospectus" for the novel, published in the September 1900 issue of the *Colored American Magazine*, indicated that Hopkins would be "glad to give readings before women's clubs in any section of the country." See "Prospectus . . .

of the New Romance of Colored Life," "Contending Forces," *Colored American Magazine*, September 1900, n.p.

29. Ensley, "Colorado," 8.

30. Untitled notice, *Woman's Era*, December 1894, 13.

31. Josephine St. Pierre Ruffin, editorial, *Woman's Era*, March 1894, 8.

32. See, for example, "The Woman's Era Literature Department," *Woman's Era*, June 1896, 2-3. If they were available, circulation figures for the *Woman's Era* would be deceptive. Like earlier productions of the black press, each issue of the *Woman's Era* might be shared by multiple readers. While some subscriptions represented an individual reader, clubs also subscribed to the *Woman's Era* and passed the newspaper from member to member.

33. Included here are questions 1, 2, 7, and 12. For a complete list, see "The Study of the Novel: Ivanhoe," *Woman's Era*, June 1896, 3. The method of review questions follows that of reference books of the time also mentioned in or recommended by the *Woman's Era*. See, for instance, Mildred Rutherford's *American Authors: A Handbook of American Literature from Early Colonial to Living Writers* (Atlanta: Franklin, 1894).

34. Medora Gould, "Literature Notes," *Woman's Era*, December 1894, 19.

35. Medora Gould, "Literature Department," *Woman's Era*, June 1895, 18.

36. Sutton Griggs, *Life's Demands; or, According to Law* (Memphis: National Public Welfare League, 1916), 51-52, 98.

37. Josephine St. Pierre Ruffin, *Woman's Era*, May 1894, 8.

38. J. W. Jacks, president of the Missouri Press Association, to Miss Florence Balgarnie, 19 March 1895. Jacks considered his letter a courtesy intended to inform Miss Balgarnie "what sort of people you are taking so much interest in." Of African Americans in general he writes: "The negroes [sic] in this country are wholly devoid of morality." The bulk of Jacks's letter comments on black women. His views are accurately summarized in the following sentence: "The women are prostitutes and all are natural liars and thieves." A copy of the letter is located in the *Woman's Era* Collection at the Boston Public Library.

39. For a discussion of the general exclusion of black women from white women's clubs and the exclusion of black women's clubs from the General Federation of Women's Clubs, see Karen J. Blair, *The Clubwoman as Feminist: True Womanhood Redefined, 1868-1914* (New York: Holmes & Meier, 1980), esp. 108-11.

40. Josephine Ruffin, "A Call," Mary Church Terrell Papers, Moorland-Spingarn Research Center, Howard University, Washington, D.C.

41. The immediate outgrowth of the 1895 Congress of Colored Women of the United States was the formation of the National Federation of Afro-American Women, which merged in 1896 with the National League of Colored Women to form the National Association of Colored Women. By 1897, when the new organization met in Nashville, its membership was 50,000. Fuller accounts of its origins are available elsewhere. See especially Elizabeth Lindsay Davis, *Lifting as They Climb: The National Association of Colored Women* (Washington, D.C.: National Association of Colored Women, 1933), and Paula Giddings, *When and Where I Enter: The Impact of Black Women on Race and Sex in America* (New York: Bantam Books, 1985), 85-117.

42. "Program of the First National Conference of the Colored Women of America, Boston, MA, July 29, 30, 31, 1895," the Woman's Era Papers, Boston Public Library.

43. Ibid.

44. Victoria Earle Matthews, "The Value of Race Literature: An Address Delivered at the First Congress of Colored Women of the United States, at Boston, July 30th, 1895," reprinted in *Massachusetts Review* 27, no. 2 (Summer 1986): 170, 173-74, 177.

45. Ibid., 183.

46. Katie V. Carmand, "Report of the Woman's Loyal Union of New York and Brooklyn," reprinted in *A History of the Club Movement among the Colored Women of the United States of America*, 13.

47. Ibid.

48. As Higginbotham notes in *Righteous Discontent*, her study of the women's movement in the Black Baptist Church, black Baptist women "linked literacy with the dissemination of middle-class values and religious proselytization" (45). Her observation serves to underscore the fact that, especially in the nineteenth and early twentieth centuries, the sacred and the secular were not discrete elements in the lives and experiences of black Americans.

49. Carmand, "Report of the Women's Loyal Union of New York and Brooklyn," 14.

50. U.S. Department of Commerce, *Negro Population, 1790-1915* (Washington, D.C.: Government Printing Office, 1918), 404; U.S. Department of Commerce, *Fifteenth Census of the United States, 1930*, vol. 2, *Population* (Washington, D.C.: Government Printing Office, 1933), 1223. The 1930 census was the last one to ask its respondents whether they could read and write; by 1940, literacy rates were so high that the question was no longer considered useful. Illiteracy rates for blacks and whites were higher in the South than in the North, and generally higher than the national average in the South. The precision of these data must be considered critically, as people were asked to record their own illiteracy. Of these data, Carl Kaestle has concluded: "At worst, census illiteracy statistics measure nothing more than people's willingness to admit illiteracy; at best they indicate a minimal estimate of illiteracy." See Carl F. Kaestle et al., *Literacy in the United States: Readers and Reading since 1880* (New Haven: Yale University Press, 1991), 24.

51. Langston Hughes to Walter White, executive secretary of the National Association for the Advancement of Colored People (NAACP), 3 August 1931, quoted in Elizabeth Davey, "Building a Black Audience in the 1930s: Langston Hughes, Poetry Readings and the Golden Stair Press," in *Print Culture in a Diverse America*, ed. James P. Danky and Wayne A. Wiegand (Urbana: University of Illinois Press, 1998), 223.

52. Davey, "Building a Black Audience in the 1930s," 238.

53. Langston Hughes, Promotional Letter, 13 October 1931, quoted in Davey, "Building a Black Audience in the 1930s," 224.

54. Florence Duke to the Golden Stair Press, 1932, quoted in Davey, "Building a Black Audience in the 1930s," 228; B. J. Anderson to the Golden Stair Press, 12 January 1932, quoted in Davey, "Building a Black Audience in the 1930s," 228-29.

55. Davey, "Building a Black Audience in the 1930s," 229.

56. For a more complete discussion of this phenomenon in the context of African American literary societies and reading practices in the antebellum United States, see Elizabeth McHenry, "'Dreaded Eloquence': The Origins and Rise of African American Literary Societies and Libraries," *Harvard Library Bulletin* 6, no. 2 (Spring 1995): 32-56.

CHAPTER 26
Making Meaning:
Analysis and Affect in the Study and Practice of Reading

1. Edward N. Teall, *Books and Folks* (New York: G. P. Putnam's Sons, 1921), 59–60.

2. Roger Chartier is quoted in David D. Hall, *Cultures of Print* (Amherst: University of Massachusetts Press, 1996), 178.

3. Teall, *Books and Folks*, 159–63.

4. Carl F. Kaestle et al., *Literacy in the United States: Readers and Reading since 1880* (New Haven: Yale University Press, 1991), 182.

5. William S. Gray and Ruth Munroe, *The Reading Interests and Habits of Adults: A Preliminary Report* (New York: Macmillan, 1929), 26, 260; Douglas Waples, *People and Print: Social Aspects of Reading in the Depression* (Chicago: University of Chicago Press, 1938), 7.

6. Dorothy Canfield Fisher, *Why Stop Learning?* (New York: Harcourt, Brace, 1927), 28.

7. Henry Holt to Burton E. Stevenson, 15 November 1911, Henry Holt Archives, Manuscripts Division, Department of Rare Books & Special Collections, Princeton University Library, Princeton, N.J. Reprinted by permission of Henry Holt & Co., LLC. Published with the permission of the Princeton University Library.

8. Henry Seidel Canby, *Definitions: Essays in Contemporary Criticism* (New York: Harcourt, Brace, 1922), 227.

9. Charles H. Compton, *Who Reads What?* (New York: H. W. Wilson, 1934), 25, 35–39.

10. Gray and Munroe, *Reading Interests*, 53, 62, 208.

11. Douglas Waples and Ralph W. Tyler, *What People Want to Read About* (Chicago: American Library Association and University of Chicago Press, 1931), 192.

12. Ibid., 7, 107.

13. Ibid., 82.

14. Ibid., 70, 158–59, 194–200.

15. Douglas Waples, Bernard Berelson, and Franklyn R. Bradshaw, *What Reading Does to People* (Chicago: University of Chicago Press, 1940), esp. 82–83.

16. Ibid., 9, 15, 19–20; Stephen Karetzky, *Reading Research and Librarianship* (Westport, Conn.: Greenwood Press, 1982), 113.

17. Gray and Munroe, *Reading Interests*, 215, 223–25, 230.

18. Robert Darnton, "First Steps toward a History of Reading," in *The Kiss of Lamourette: Reflections in Cultural History* (New York: Norton, 1990), 154–87.

19. Gray and Munroe, *Reading Interests*, 232–34.

20. Ibid., 250–54.

21. Mary Bingham, Los Alamos, New Mexico, to Joan Shelley Rubin, 14 May 1995.

22. Kaestle et al., *Literacy in the United States: Readers and Reading since 1880*, 233–34.

23. Sir Arthur Helps is quoted on the title page of W. H. Lambert, *Memory Gems: Graded Selections in Prose and Verse for the Use of Schools* (Boston: Ginn, Heath & Co., 1883).

24. W. H. Williams, *Memory Gems for School and Home* (New York: A. S. Barnes, 1907), v–vii.

25. John J. Goodwin, Bedford, N.Y., to Joan Shelley Rubin, 19 April 1995.

26. Frederic Harrison, *The Choice of Books* (Chicago: Albert, Scott, 1891), 21, 59. Macmillan published a London edition as late as 1925.

27. Ibid., 100.

28. James Fleming Hosic, comp., *Reorganization of English in Secondary Schools* (Washington, D.C.: Government Printing Office, 1917), 63-65, 97.

29. Sterling Andrus Leonard, *Essential Principles of Teaching Reading and Literature* (Philadelphia: J. B. Lippincott, 1922), 201-12 (quotation from 201-2).

30. *Course of Study in English for Rochester (N.Y.) Senior High Schools*, vol. 2, *Literature* (1929), 210, in Special Collections, Gottesman Libraries, Teachers College, Columbia University, New York.

31. Hughes Mearns, *Creative Youth* (Garden City, N.Y.: Doubleday, Doran, 1925), 94.

32. *An Experience Curriculum in English* (New York: D. Appleton-Century, 1935), 20, 22, 55-59.

33. Mearns, *Creative Youth*, 28, 128; Howard Francis Seely, *Enjoying Poetry in School* (Richmond, N.Y.: Johnson, 1931), 113, 137.

34. Henry Sloane Coffin, *The Public Worship of God* (Philadelphia: Westminster, 1946), 104.

35. Andrew W. Blackwood, *The Fine Art of Public Worship* (Nashville: Cokesbury Press, 1939), 232; William R. Stidger, *There Are Sermons in Books* (New York: Doran, 1922), xv; William R. Stidger, *The Place of Books in the Life We Live* (New York: George H. Doran, 1922), esp. 133; William R. Stidger, *Planning Your Preaching* (New York: Harper, 1932), 54.

36. Blackwood, *Fine Art of Public Worship*, 191.

37. Margaret T. Applegarth, *Bound in the Bundle of Life: Worship Services for Adult Church Groups* (New York: Harper, 1941).

38. Laura Armstrong Athearn, *Christian Worship For American Youth* (New York: Century, 1931), 29; Albert A. Susott, *A Practical Handbook of Worship* (New York: Fleming H. Revell, 1941), 134-35; Alice Anderson Bays, *Worship Services for Youth* (New York: Abingdon Cokesbury, 1940); Kirby Page, *Living Creatively* (New York: Farrar and Rinehart, 1932), esp. 99.

39. Laura I. Mattoon and Helen D. Bragdon, *Services for the Open* (New York: Century, 1923), esp. vii.

40. Ibid., 3, 28-29, 70-71.

41. Roger Chartier, *The Order of Books: Readers, Authors, and Libraries in Europe between the Fourteenth and Eighteenth Centuries*, trans. Lydia G. Cochrane (Stanford: Stanford University Press, 1994), 25-59; Mattoon and Bragdon, *Services for the Open*, 83.

42. Edwin H. Byington, *The Quest for Experience in Worship* (Garden City, N.Y.: Doubleday, Doran, 1929), 53.

43. Joshua Lieberman, *Creative Camping* (New York: Association Press, 1931).

44. Mattoon and Bragdon, *Services for the Open*, 3.

45. Raymond Williams, *Marxism and Literature* (Oxford: Oxford University Press, 1977), 122.

46. See Stanley Coben, *Rebellion against Victorianism* (New York: Oxford University Press, 1991); Ann Douglas, *Terrible Honesty: Mongrel Manhattan in the 1920s* (New York: Farrar, Straus, and Giroux, 1995); Henry F. May, *The End of American Innocence: A Study of the First Years of Our Own Time, 1912-1917* (New York: Alfred A. Knopf, 1950).

47. Harrison, *The Choice of Books*, 59.
48. The phrase is Daniel Borus's, a colleague of the author.

Epilogue

1. *Digest of Education Statistics, 1993* (Washington, D.C.: Department of Education, 1993), 108.
2. Sanford Winston, *Illiteracy in the United States from 1870 to 1920* (Chapel Hill: University of North Carolina Press, 1930), 9; Carl F. Kaestle "Literate America: High-Level Adult Literacy as a National Goal," in *Learning from the Past: What History Teaches Us about School Reform*, ed. Diane Ravitch and Maris A. Vinovskis (Baltimore: Johns Hopkins University Press, 1995), 337-38; *Digest of Education Statistics, 1993*, 17.
3. See Carl F. Kaestle, chapter 2 in this volume.
4. Ibid.
5. Janice A. Radway, *A Feeling for Books: The Book-of-the-Month Club, Literary Taste, and Middle-Class Desire* (Chapel Hill: University of North Carolina Press, 1997); John Tebbel, *A History of Book Publishing in the United States*, 4 vols. (New York: R. R. Bowker, 1972-81), 3:305-7.
6. For a good summary of the state of the larger book publishing industry as the forties began, see Tebbel, *History of Book Publishing in the United States*, esp. 3:427-57.
7. Ibid., 4:7.
8. Ibid., 5.
9. O. H. Cheney, *Economic Survey of the Book Industry, 1930-1931* (New York: R. R. Bowker, 1960), 9.
10. Louis R. Wilson, *The Geography of Reading: A Study of the Distribution and Status of Libraries in the United States* (Chicago: University of Chicago Press, 1938), 191.
11. Tebbel, *History of the Book Publishing in the United States*, 3:454.
12. *Official Guide Book of the New York World's Fair, 1939* (New York: Exposition Publications, 1939), 75-76; Larry Zim, Mel Lerner, and Herbert Rolfes, *The Worlds of Tomorrow: The 1939 New York World's Fair* (New York: Harper & Row, 1988), 61.
13. *Official Guide Book*, 77-82.
14. Ibid., 73-75.
15. Stanley Appelbaum, ed., *The New York World's Fair, 1939/1940 in 155 Photographs by Richard Wurts and Others* (New York: Dover Publications, 1977), 38-45.
16. Warren I. Susman, "The People's Fair: Cultural Contradictions of a Consumer Society," in Helen A. Harrison, *Dawn of a New Day: The New York World's Fair, 1939/40* (New York: New York University Press, 1980), 24.

BIBLIOGRAPHICAL ESSAY

Theoretical and General Works

The study of print history has developed into a thriving, interdisciplinary subfield over the past two decades. Creative collaborations among social historians, literary theorists, library studies experts, bibliographers, communications scholars, and others are common. Such teamwork has been essential to the conception and completion of this volume in the five-volume project, *A History of the Book in America*. The empirical knowledge, theories, and practices of these various contributing disciplines are quite disparate. This makes conversations interesting and the construction of a bibliography difficult. Also, the period treated in this volume was a time of profound turbulence and change in American life, which has inspired a massive amount of analysis work by historians and literary scholars intent on understanding how "modern" America evolved. For both of these reasons, a bibliographical essay can only sketch the parameters and cite the works that we have found most helpful.

Theoretical Works

Roger Chartier is one of the most influential theorists working on the history of books and reading. He has been cogent about efforts to create order through books and, conversely, the considerable potential for readers to make their own interpretations of what they read. See Chartier, *The Order of Books: Readers, Authors, and Libraries in Europe between the Fourteenth and Eighteenth Centuries*, trans. Lydia G. Cochrane (Stanford: Stanford University Press, 1994); Chartier, *Forms and Meanings: Texts, Performances, and Audiences from Codex to Computer* (Philadelphia: University of Pennsylvania Press, 1995); and Chartier, "Frenchness in the History of the Book: From the History of Publishing to the History of Reading," *Proceedings of the American Antiquarian Society* 97 (1987): 299–329. Robert Darnton, another historian of France, has also published influential monographs and theoretical articles on the history of the book. See *The Business of Enlightenment: A Publishing History of the Encyclopédie, 1775–1800* (Cambridge, Mass.: Harvard University Press, 1979); *The Great Cat Massacre and Other Episodes in French Cultural History* (New York: Basic Books, 1984); and the article in which his famous "circuit" metaphor is developed, "What Is the History of Books?" *Daedalus* 111 (1982): 65–83. Chartier's interest in the work of Michel de Certeau has helped popularize de Certeau's work among historians of print in the United States, particularly *The Practices of Everyday Life*, trans. Steven Rendall (Berkeley: University of California Press, 1984), which theorizes about the "strategies" of print producers and the "tactics" of readers. Sociologists who have tackled print culture include Herbert Gans, in *Popular Culture and High Culture: An Analysis and Evaluation of Taste* (New York: Basic Books, 1974), and, earlier, Robert Escarpit, *Sociology of Literature*, trans. Ernest Pick (Painesville, Ohio: Lake Erie College Studies, 1965). Another classic whose influence made its way across the

Atlantic is Raymond Williams, *The Long Revolution* (New York: Columbia University Press, 1961). There are many relevant works by theorists of popular culture. See, for example, those of Fredric Jameson, "Reification and Utopia in Mass Culture," *Social Text* 1 (Winter 1979): 130-48.

In the late 1970s and early 1980s, literary scholars produced "reader response" theories. The foundational works included Stanley Fish, *Is There a Text in This Class? The Authority of Interpretive Communities* (Cambridge, Mass.: Harvard University Press, 1980), and Wolfgang Iser, *The Act of Reading: A Theory of Aesthetic Response* (Baltimore: Johns Hopkins University Press, 1978). These studies appeared at approximately the time of the marriage of book history with the history of reading. Reader-response theory reinforced the notion that there could be no meaning to a text without a reader. For the most part, however, reader-response theorists were uninterested in evidence about actual readers in the past; furthermore, they tended to treat readers as generic, rather than as male or female, black or white, rich or poor. Subsequently these studies were superseded within the field of print culture history by works that examine social context and the social identity of actual readers, such as Janice A. Radway, *Reading the Romance: Women, Patriarchy, and Popular Literature*, 2nd ed. (Chapel Hill: University of North Carolina Press, 1991); Michael Denning, *Mechanic Accents: Dime Novels and Working-Class Culture in America* (London: Verso, 1987); and Elizabeth McHenry, *Forgotten Readers: Recovering the Lost History of African American Literary Societies* (Durham: Duke University Press, 2002).

Many broader theories prodded our imaginations and enhanced our understanding at various points. Jürgen Habermas, *The Structural Transformation of the Public Sphere: An Inquiry into a Category of Bourgeois Society*, trans. Thomas Berger (1962; reprint, Cambridge, Mass.: MIT Press, 1989), has proved provocative in print culture studies. See Michael Warner, *The Letters of the Republic: Publication and the Public Sphere in Eighteenth-Century America* (Cambridge, Mass.: Harvard University Press, 1990), and Houston A. Baker Jr., "Critical Memory and the Black Public Sphere," *Public Culture* 7, no. 3 (1994): 3-33. Pierre Bourdieu's work on cultural capital has obvious relevance; see Bourdieu, *Distinction: A Social Critique of the Judgment of Taste*, trans. Richard Nice (Cambridge, Mass.: Harvard University Press, 1984), and Pierre Bourdieu and Jean-Claude Passeron, *Reproduction in Education, Society and Culture*, trans. Richard Nice (Beverly Hills, Calif.: Sage Publications, 1977). Other theorists too numerous to discuss but relevant to print culture studies include Stuart Hall, Paulo Freire, Mikhail Bakhtin, Theodore Adorno, Werner Sollors, and others.

United States Cultural, Economic, and Social History, 1880-1940

Between the immediate post–Civil War years, often labeled "Reconstruction," and the accelerated and self-consciously modern transformations of "the Progressive Era," lies the "Gilded Age," what might be characterized as the Victorian plateau of an Anglo-dominated society with its full share of class and racial conflict but with an elite public life of relative complacency and pride. Secondary works illuminating the cultural and political conditions of that period include John Tomsich, *A Genteel Endeavor: American Culture and Politics in the Gilded Age* (Stanford: Stanford University Press, 1971); Stow Persons, *The Decline of American Gentility* (New York: Columbia University Press, 1973); Larzer Ziff, *The American*

1890s: Life and Times of a Lost Generation (New York: Viking Press, 1966); John Kasson, *Rudeness and Civility: Manners in Nineteenth-Century Urban America* (New York: Hill & Wang, 1990); and Lawrence Levine, *Highbrow/Lowbrow: The Emergence of Cultural Hierarchy in America* (Cambridge, Mass.: Harvard University Press, 1988).

For the transition from that world into the twentieth-century, see Alan Trachtenberg, *The Incorporation of America: Culture and Society in the Gilded Age* (New York: Hill & Wang, 1982); Robert Wiebe, *The Search for Order, 1877–1920* (New York: Hill & Wang, 1967); John Higham, "The Reorientation of American Culture in the 1890s," in *The Origins of Modern Consciousness*, ed. John Weiss (Detroit: Wayne State University Press, 1965), 25–48; Henry F. May, *The End of American Innocence: A Study of the First Years of Our Own Time, 1912–1917* (New York, Alfred A. Knopf, 1959); and David M. Kennedy, *Over Here: The First World War and American Society* (New York: Oxford University Press, 1980). For the economic and technological changes that drove this "incorporation of America," see Alfred D. Chandler Jr., *The Visible Hand: The Managerial Revolution in American Business* (Cambridge, Mass.: Harvard University Press, 1977); Chandler is nicely complemented by James R. Beniger, *The Control Revolution: Technological and Economic Origins of the Information Society* (Cambridge, Mass.: Harvard University Press, 1986). On communications, see Alfred D. Chandler Jr. and James W. Cortada, eds., *A Nation Transformed by Information: How Information Has Shaped the United States from Colonial Times to the Present* (New York: Oxford University Press, 2000), and on literacy and education, Carl F. Kaestle et al., *Literacy in the United States: Readers and Reading since 1880* (New Haven: Yale University Press, 1991).

Publishing and Print Production

Philip Gaskell, *A New Introduction to Bibliography* (New York: Oxford University Press, 1972), and entries in [W. W. Pasko], *American Dictionary of Printing and Print-Making* (New York: H. Lockwood & Co., 1894), are useful accounts of book production. The development and early use of hot-metal composition machines are documented in Theodore L. De Vinne, *Modern Methods of Book Composition* (New York: Century Co., 1904), and Alphonse LeGros and John Cameron Grant, *Typographical Printing-Surfaces* (London: Longmans, Green & Co., 1916). An indispensable guide to the identification and understanding of the numerous photomechanical techniques for the multiplication of images is Bamber Gascoigne, *How to Identify Prints* (New York: Thames & Hudson, 1986).

The Book Trades

The best general histories of the publishing trade during this period are Hellmut Lehmann-Haupt, "Book Production and Distribution from 1860 to the Present Day," in Lehmann-Haupt, Lawrence C. Wroth, and Rollo G. Silver, *The Book in America: A History of the Making and Selling of Books in the United States*, 2nd ed. (New York: R. R. Bowker, 1951); Donald Sheehan, *This Was Publishing: A Chronicle of the Book Trade in the Gilded Age* (Bloomington: Indiana University Press, 1952); and John Tebbel, *A History of Book Publishing in the United States*, vol. 2, *The Expansion of an Industry, 1865–1919* (New York: R. R. Bowker, 1975), and vol. 3, *The Golden Age between Two Wars, 1920–1940* (New York: R. R. Bowker, 1978).

Publishers' Weekly provides an indispensable, detailed record of the book trade and its activities. This journal includes weekly listings of new publications, which were cumulated and indexed both monthly and annually. From 1886 the annual accumulations were issued separately as bound volumes. Beginning in 1873, the Office of Publishers' Weekly also issued the *Publishers' Trade List Annual*, which gathered and bound together the trade lists of individual publishers. These resources should be supplemented by *The United States Catalog: Books in Print* (Minneapolis: H. W. Wilson, 1900, 1903, 1912, 1928) and the same firm's serial *Cumulative Book Index* (1900–).

Other important sources from the period include George Haven Putnam and John Bishop Putnam, *Authors and Publishers: A Manual of Suggestions for Beginners in Literature* (New York: G. P. Putnam's Sons, 1883; and rev. 7th ed., 1897); Adolf Growoll, *The Profession of Bookselling: A Handbook of Practical Hints for the Apprentice and Bookseller* (New York: Office of Publishers' Weekly, 1893-1913); Frederick H. Hitchcock, ed., *The Building of a Book: A Series of Practical Articles Written by Experts in the Various Departments of Book Making and Distributing* (New York: Grafton Press, 1906); and Robert Sterling Yard, *The Publisher* (Boston: Houghton Mifflin, 1913). Very much worth studying is O. H. Cheney, *Economic Survey of the Book Industry, 1930-1931* (New York: National Association of Book Publishers, 1931).

Worthwhile article-length studies are Bernard DeVoto, "Writing for Money," *Saturday Review of Literature*, 9 October 1937, 4; John Farrar, "Publishing: Industry and Profession," *American Scholar* 19 (Winter 1949-50): 31-39; Henry Holt, "The Commercialization of Literature," *Atlantic Monthly* 96 (1905): 577-600; Alfred R. McIntyre, "The Crisis in Book Publishing," *Atlantic Monthly* 180 (October 1947): 107-10; and Charles A. Madison, "Jews in American Publishing," *Chicago Jewish Forum* 26 (Summer 1968): 282-87.

Of the many publishing memoirs, biographies, and house histories that cover the period, among the most useful are J. Henry Harper, *The House of Harper: A Century of Publishing in Franklin Square* (New York: Harper & Bros., 1912); Eugene Exman, *The House of Harper: One Hundred and Fifty Years of Publishing* (New York: Harper & Row, 1967); Ellen B. Ballou, *The Building of the House: Houghton Mifflin's Formative Years* (Boston: Houghton Mifflin, 1970); Bennett Cerf, *At Random: The Reminiscences of Bennett Cerf* (New York: Random House, 1977); Cass Canfield, *Up and Down and Around: A Publisher Recollects the Time of His Life* (New York: Harper's Magazine Press, 1971); Hiram Haydn, *Words and Faces* (New York: Harcourt Brace Jovanovich, 1974); William Jovanovich, *Now Barabbas* (New York: Harper & Row, 1964); Victor Weybright, *The Making of a Publisher: A Life in the 20th Century Book Revolution* (New York: Reynal, 1967); and Roger Burlingame's history of Charles Scribner's Sons, *Of Making Many Books: A Hundred Years of Reading, Writing and Publishing* (New York: Charles Scribner's Sons, 1946). Also of interest may be various volumes in the *Dictionary of Literary Biography* series, especially *The House of Scribner*, vol. 13, *1846-1904*, and vol. 16, *1905-1930*, ed. John Delaney (Detroit: Gale Research, 1995, 1997), and *The House of Holt, 1866-1946: A Documentary Volume*, vol. 284, ed. Ellen D. Gilbert (Detroit: Thomson Gale, 2003).

Scholarly treatments include Richard Fine, *Hollywood and the Profession of Authorship, 1928-1940* (Ann Arbor: University of Michigan Research Press, 1985), and James L. W. West III, *American Authors and the Literary Marketplace since 1900* (Philadelphia: University of Pennsylvania Press, 1988). On Book-of-the-Month Club, see Joan Shelley Rubin, *The Making of Middlebrow Culture* (Chapel Hill: University of North Carolina Press, 1992), and Janice A. Radway, *A Feeling for Books: The Book-of-the-Month Club, Literary Taste, and Middle-Class Desire* (Chapel Hill: University of North Carolina Press, 1997). On the thirties and forties, see Ellen D. Gilbert, "*Publishers Weekly*, the Depression, and World War II," *Princeton University Library Chronicle* 59 (Autumn 1997): 59-82. Standard histories of softcover publishing are Frank L. Schick, *The Paperbound Book in America* (New York: R. R. Bowker, 1958), and Thomas L. Bonn, *Under Cover: An Illustrated History of American Mass-Market Paperbacks* (New York: Penguin, 1982). On the Armed Services Editions, see Daniel J. Miller, *Books Go to War: Armed Services Editions in World War II* (Charlottesville: Book Arts Press, 1996). Two useful histories of paperback houses are William H. Lyles, *Putting Dell on the Map* (Westport, Conn.: Greenwood, 1983), and Thomas L. Bonn, *Heavy Traffic and High Culture: New American Library as Literary Gatekeeper in the Paperback Revolution* (Carbondale: Southern Illinois University Press, 1989). A summary of paperback trends since the thirties is provided by Robert Dahlin, "Men (and Women) Who Made a Revolution," *Publishers Weekly*, special anniversary issue (July 1997): 51-60.

Magazines, Books, and Advertising

Publications addressed to the publishing industry offer backstage talk. *Publishers' Weekly* is the defining news organ for the publishing community, containing a conversation about advertising and promotion taking place over decades, between very differently situated players. In its earlier decades it largely ignored stationery and newsstand booksellers and the cheap original and reprint publishers that served them. For these, such journals as *American Newsman*, *American Bookseller* (which later became *Bookseller, Newsdealer and Stationer*), and the *Book and News-Dealer* of San Francisco are more useful.

Some memoirs of publishers and editors discuss their uses of and attitudes toward advertising and publicity, including those by Irving Bacheller, Henry Seidel Canby, Cass Canfield, Bennett Cerf, Frank Doubleday, Emmanuel Haldeman-Julius, Henry Holt, William Janovich, Walter Hines Page, Charles Scribner Jr., Peter Schwed, Helen Woodward, and W. E. Woodward.

The standard work on magazines in the United States is Frank Luther Mott, *A History of American Magazines*, 5 vols. (Cambridge, Mass.: Harvard University Press, 1930-68). Mott did not complete work on his final volume, and the standard history for that period is Theodore Peterson, *Magazines in the Twentieth Century* (1956; 2nd ed., Urbana: University of Illinois Press, 1964). Three recent works study the transformation of magazine publishing in some depth: Ellen Gruber Garvey, *The Adman in the Parlor: Magazines and the Gendering of Consumer Culture, 1880s to 1910s* (New York: Oxford University Press, 1996); Richard Ohmann, *Selling Culture: Magazines, Markets, and Class at the Turn of the Century* (London: Verso, 1996); and Matthew Schneirov, *The Dream of a New Social Order: Popular Magazines in America, 1893-1914* (New York: Columbia University Press, 1994). Studies of individual magazines are too numerous to mention.

Older histories of advertising tended to be anecdotal and celebratory. The fullest of these—and still indispensable for its detail—is Frank Presbrey, *The History and Development of Ad-*

vertising (Garden City, N.Y.: Doubleday, Doran, 1929). Recently, modern advertising has received attention from a number of scholars, including Jackson Lears, *Fables of Abundance: A Cultural History of Advertising in America* (New York: Basic Books, 1994); Daniel Pope, *The Making of Modern Advertising* (New York: Basic Books, 1983); Pamela Walker Laird, *Advertising Progress: American Business and the Rise of Consumer Marketing* (Baltimore: Johns Hopkins University Press, 1998); Juliann Sivulka, *Soap, Sex, and Cigarettes: A Cultural History of American Advertising* (Belmont, Calif.: Wadsworth, 1998); and Michael Schudson, *Advertising, the Uneasy Persuasion: Its Dubious Impact on American Society* (New York: Basic Books, 1984). Roland Marchand, *Advertising the American Dream: Making Way for Modernity, 1920-1940* (Berkeley: University of California Press, 1985), is particularly illuminating on the advertisers' own attitudes toward advertising.

Short essays on the development of book advertising decade by decade in Tebbel's *A History of Book Publishing in the United States*, volumes 2 and 3, are a useful starting point. Several scholars have explored the complex relationship of book advertising and promotion in more complex relation to middle-class self-construction. These include Radway, *A Feeling for Books*; Rubin, *Making of Middlebrow Culture*; and two of Christopher Wilson's books, *The Labor of Words: Literary Professionalism in the Progressive Era* (Athens: University of Georgia Press, 1985) and *White Collar Fictions: Class and Social Representation in American Literature, 1885-1925* (Athens: University of Georgia Press, 1992).

Printing and Typography

The best source for detailed explanations of the technologies of both hand-based and mechanical print production remains Philip Gaskell, *A New Introduction to Bibliography* (New York: Oxford University Press, 1972), while Robert Bringhurst's *Elements of Typographic Style*, 2nd ed. (Point Roberts, Wash.: Hartley and Marks, 1996) has quickly become the most highly regarded introduction to the fundamental components and principles of typography. For theoretical perspectives on the relation between typography, text, and cultural context, see Jerome McGann, *The Textual Condition* (Princeton: Princeton University Press, 1990) and his *Black Riders: The Visible Language of Modernism* (Princeton: Princeton University Press, 1993).

For a fascinating portrait of the triumph of mechanical type composition, see Maurice Annenberg, ed., *A Typographic Journey through the Inland Printer* (Baltimore: Maran Press, 1977). Good accounts of the impact on labor of the transition to mechanical typesetting include William S. Pretzer, "Tramp Printers: Craft Culture, Trade Unions, and Technology," *Printing History* 6, no. 2 (1984): 3-16, and Elizabeth Faulkner Baker, *Displacement of Men by Machines: Effects of Technological Change in Commercial Printing* (New York: Columbia University Press, 1933).

Several important essays written by leading practitioners and critics of the printing trades and typography between 1880 and 1940 are gathered by Paul A. Bennett, ed., in *Books and Printing: A Treasury for Typophiles* (Cleveland: World Publishing, 1951). Of particular interest are the essays by William A. Dwiggins (1919), Beatrice Warde (1932), Robert Josephy (1935), T. M. Cleland (1940), and Daniel Berkeley Updike (1941). Other key leaders in American printing and typography during this era include Theodore Low De Vinne and Carl Purington Rollins. See Michael Koenig, "De Vinne and the De Vinne Press," *Library Quarterly* 41 (January 1971): 1-24, and Rollins's influential biweekly column in the *Saturday Review of Literature* from 1927 to 1937.

On traditionalism in American book design and the influence of the arts-and-crafts movement in the late nineteenth and early twentieth centuries, see Susan Otis Thompson, *American Book Design and William Morris*, 2nd ed. (New Castle, Del.: Oak Knoll Press, 1996). On typographic modernism, see Jan Tschichold's influential 1928 *Die Neue Typographie*, available in English as *The New Typography*, trans. Ruari McLean (Berkeley: University of California Press, 1995). Modernism's most enthusiastic early endorsement in the United States was Douglas McMurtrie's *modern typography and layout* (Chicago: Eyncourt Press, 1929). For a knowledgeable and astute critical assessment of both modernist and traditionalist design, see also Robin Kinross, *Modern Typography: An Essay in Critical History* (London: Hyphen Press, 1992).

Newspapers and Journalism

Michael Schudson's now classic account of U.S. journalism history, *Discovering the News: A Social History of American Newspapers* (New York: Basic Books, 1978), traces shifts in the cultural and professional status of the news industry in the period covered by this volume. Contending views are ventured in Dan Schiller, *Objectivity and the News: The Public and the Rise of Commercial Journalism* (Philadelphia: University of Pennsylvania Press, 1981), and David T. Z. Mindich, *Just the Facts: How "Objectivity" Came to Define American Journalism* (New York: New York University Press, 1998). Schudson has significantly reworked his perspective: see Michael Schudson, *The Good Citizen: A History of American Civic Life* (New York: Martin Kessler Books, Free Press, 1998) and *The Power of the News* (Cambridge, Mass.: Harvard University Press, 1995).

Gerald J. Baldasty has innovatively probed the economic aspects of late nineteenth- and early twentieth-century newspapers in his clearly written and innovative *E. W. Scripps and the Business of Newspapers* (Urbana: University of Illinois Press, 1999) and *The Commercialization of News in the Nineteenth Century* (Madison: University of Wisconsin Press, 1992). Richard Kaplan's *Politics and the American Press: The Rise of Objectivity, 1865-1920* (New York: Cambridge University Press, 2002) focuses on the shifting politics and economics of the press. David Paul Nord gives an accounting of journalism's ties to progressivism in his *Newspapers and New Politics: Midwestern Municipal Reform, 1890-1900* (Ann Arbor: University of Michigan Research Press, 1981). Also important on politics is Richard L. Rubin, *Press, Party and Presidency* (New York: W. W. Norton, 1981). Michael McGerr, *The Decline of Popular Politics: The American North, 1865-1928* (New York: Oxford University Press, 1986), offers an incisive account of the partisanship of the nineteenth-century news media and the decline of such outright political alignment.

Thomas J. Leonard, *News for All: America's Coming-of-Age with the Press* (New York: Oxford University Press, 1995), provides a broad survey of newspapers and their readers; his *The Power of the Press: The Birth of American Political Reporting* (New York: Oxford University Press, 1986) analyzes changing narrative visions and politics of the press in this era. Kevin Barnhurst and John Nerone, *The Form of the News: A History* (New York: Guilford, 2001), views newspaper history through the optic of journalism's visual presentation or "form." Still informative is the textbook by Edwin Emery, *The Press and America: An Interpretive History of the Mass Media*, 3rd ed. (Englewood Cliffs, N.J.: Prentice-Hall, 1972).

The relationship of the press to politics in the first half of the twentieth century is not systematically or comprehensively examined anywhere. An attempt at a general overview would have to pursue works on individual politicians, individual journalists, and individual news institutions. For politicians, the literature is most extensive on presidents. George Juergens covers Theodore Roosevelt, William Howard Taft, and Woodrow Wilson in *News From the White House* (Chicago: University of Chicago Press, 1981). Stephen Ponder's *Managing the Press: Origins of the Media Presidency, 1897–1933* (New York: St. Martin's, 1999) is valuable. There are several good works on Franklin D. Roosevelt's relations with the press, including Graham J. White, *FDR and the Press* (Chicago: University of Chicago Press, 1979), and Betty Houchin Winfield, *FDR and the News Media* (New York: Columbia University Press, 1994). Also of interest is Maurine Beasley, *Eleanor Roosevelt and the Media: A Public Quest for Self-Fulfillment* (Urbana: University of Illinois Press, 1987). Political scientists have contributed significant historical works, notably Samuel Kernell, *Going Public: New Strategies of Presidential Leadership* (Washington, D.C.: Congressional Quarterly Press, 1993), and Jeffrey K. Tulis, *The Rhetorical Presidency* (Princeton: Princeton University Press, 1987). For changing forms of political reporting in this era, see Schudson, *The Power of News*.

Ronald Steel's biography of Walter Lippmann, *Walter Lippmann and the American Century* (Boston: Atlantic Monthly Press, 1980), is an astute study of the most influential political journalist in the country from the 1920s into the 1950s. Robert W. Merry's biography of the Alsop brothers also gives a very good sense of an era when patrician journalists wielded unusual influence in Washington and could think of themselves as policy makers as much as commentators. See *Taking on the World: Joseph and Stewart Alsop; Guardians of the American Century* (New York: Viking, 1996). David Nasaw's *The Chief* (Boston: Houghton Mifflin, 2000) is a scrupulous account of the influential but idiosyncratic publisher, William Randolph Hearst.

Works on individual newspapers include several histories of the *New York Times*, each with some merits of its own. The most recent and the most thorough in examining the owners' families is Susan E. Tifft and Alex S. Jones, *The Trust* (Boston: Little, Brown, 1999). Richard Kluger's study, *The Paper: The Life and Death of the New York Herald Tribune* (New York: Alfred A. Knopf, 1986), is likewise important and valuable.

Copyright

There exist no general histories of United States copyright law comparable to the treatments of British law by L. Ray Patterson, *Copyright in Historical Perspective* (Nashville: Vanderbilt University Press, 1968), and John Feather, *Publishing, Piracy and Politics: An Historical Study of Copyright in Britain* (New York: Mansell, 1994). For a baseline understanding of the origins of copyright law in the United States and some of the features of its early doctrine, the best choice remains Benjamin Kaplan, *An Unhurried View of Copyright* (New York: Columbia University Press, 1967).

Excellent sources of information on copyright doctrine and attitudes related to copyright during the period we treat remain the contemporary treatises: Eaton S. Drone, *A Treatise on* the Law of Property in Intellectual Productions in Great Britain and the United States, Embracing Copyright in Works of Literature and Art, and Playwright in Dramatic and Musical Compositions (Boston: Little, Brown & Co., 1879), and Horace G. Ball, *The Law of Copyright and Literary Property* (Albany, N.Y.: Banks & Co. and Matthew Bender & Co., 1944). See also Richard C. De Wolf, *An Outline of Copyright Law* (Boston: John W. Luce & Co., 1925). A fair amount has been written about the coming of international copyright, especially as it relates to the book trade between the United States and Great Britain. Useful sources include Simon Nowell-Smith *International Copyright Law and the Publisher in the Reign of Queen Victoria* (Oxford: Clarendon Press, 1968); James J. Barnes, *Authors, Publishers and Politicians: The Quest for an Anglo-American Copyright Agreement, 1815–1854* (Columbus: Ohio State University Press, 1974); and Aubert J. Clark, *The Movement for International Copyright in Nineteenth Century America* (Washington, D.C.: Catholic University of America Press, 1960).

There is also a useful and growing literature concerning developments in copyright as they relate to the evolution of the book trade in England during the period in question. See N. N. Feltes, *Literary Capital and the Late Victorian Novel* (Madison: University of Wisconsin Press, 1993), and Lee Erickson, *The Economy of Literary Form: English Literature and the Industrialization of Publishing, 1800–1850* (Baltimore: Johns Hopkins University Press, 1996). For the theoretical perspective that informs our treatment of the history of copyright during this period, see Martha Woodmansee, *The Author, Art, and the Market: Rereading the History of Aesthetics* (New York: Columbia University Press, 1994), and Martha Woodmansee and Peter Jaszi, eds., *The Construction of Authorship: Textual Appropriation in Law and Literature* (Durham: Duke University Press, 1994).

The Social Uses of Print

Two books are indispensable to any account of the rise of the research university in the United States. The first, notable for its magisterial sweep as well as for its attention both to dominant trends and countervailing forces, is Laurence R. Veysey, *The Emergence of the American University* (Chicago: University of Chicago Press, 1965). The second, a collection of essays by nearly all of the foremost commentators on the transformation of higher education during this period and still unsurpassed in the vigor of its analysis, is Alexandra Oleson and John Voss, *The Organization of Knowledge in America, 1860–1920* (Baltimore: Johns Hopkins University Press, 1979). Other useful sources on the early history of the American university include Julie A. Reuben, *The Making of the Modern University: Intellectual Transformation and the Marginalization of Morality* (Chicago: University of Chicago Press, 1996), and Roger L. Geiger, *To Advance Knowledge: The Growth of American Research Universities, 1900–1940* (New York: Oxford University Press, 1986). In addition, there are many institutionally based histories of American colleges and universities. Five are notable for their focus on especially significant institutions and figures: Hugh Hawkins, *Pioneer: A History of the Johns Hopkins University, 1874–1889* (Ithaca, N.Y.: Cornell University Press, 1960); Hugh Hawkins, *Between Harvard and America: The Educational Leadership of Charles W. Eliot* (New York: Oxford University Press, 1972); Merle Curti and Vernon Carstensen, *The University of Wisconsin: A History, 1848–1925* (Madison: University of Wisconsin Press, 1949);

Carl L. Becker, *Cornell University: Founders and the Founding* (Ithaca, N.Y.: Cornell University Press, 1944); and Richard Storr, *Harper's University* (Chicago: University of Chicago Press, 1966).

The literature on modern professionalism is essential to any understanding of the significance of the rise of the university in the United States. For a good introduction to the subject and to the vast literature that covers it, see the following: Magali Sarfatti Larson, *The Rise of Professionalism: A Sociological Analysis* (Berkeley: University of California Press, 1977); Thomas Haskell, *The Emergence of Professional Social Science: The American Social Science Association and the Nineteen-Century Crisis of Authority* (Urbana: University of Illinois Press, 1977); Samuel Haber, *The Quest for Authority and Honor in the American Professions, 1750–1900* (Chicago: University of Chicago Press, 1991); and Burton Bledstein, *The Culture of Professionalism: The Middle Class and the Development of Higher Education in America* (New York: W. W. Norton: 1976). In addition, see Dorothy Ross, *The Origins of American Social Science* (Cambridge: Cambridge University Press, 1991).

For related accounts of how American colleges were transformed during the period under discussion here, see Roger Geiger, ed., *The American College in the Nineteenth Century* (Nashville: Vanderbilt University Press, 2000), and Leslie Bruce, *Gentlemen and Scholars: Colleges and Community in the Age of the University, 1865–1917* (University Park: Pennsylvania State University Press, 1992). The now-standard volume on the early history of women's colleges is Helen Lefkowitz Horowitz, *Alma Mater: Design and Experience in the Women's Colleges from Their Nineteenth-Century Beginnings to the 1930s* (Amherst: University of Massachusetts Press, 1984). In addition, see the more focused but analytically useful volume by Patricia Palmieri, *In Adamless Eden: The Community of Women Faculty at Wellesley* (New Haven: Yale University Press, 1995).

The literature on higher education for African Americans and historically black colleges is substantial but often quite locally focused. For a more general account, the best place to begin is James D. Anderson, *The Education of Blacks in the South, 1860–1935* (Chapel Hill: University of North Carolina Press, 1988). See also Robert C. Morris, *Reading, 'Riting, and Reconstruction: The Education of Freedmen in the South, 1861–1870* (Chicago: University of Chicago Press, 1981); Eric Anderson and Alfred A. Moss Jr., *Dangerous Donations: Northern Philanthropy and Southern Black Education, 1902–1930* (Columbia: University of Missouri Press, 1999); and Henry N. Drewry and Humphrey Doermann, with Susan H. Anderson, *Stand and Prosper: Private Black Colleges and Their Students* (Princeton: Princeton University Press, 2001). In addition, see Louis R. Harlan, *Separate and Unequal: Public School Campaigns and Racism in the Southern Seaboard States, 1901–1915* (New York: Atheneum, 1968). On the educational debates between Booker T. Washington and W. E. B. Du Bois, see Jacqueline M. Moore, *Booker T. Washington, W. E. B. Du Bois, and the Struggle for Racial Uplift* (Wilmington, Del.: Scholarly Resources, 2003). On Washington, see Louis R. Harlan, *Booker T. Washington: The Making of a Black Leader, 1886–1901* (New York: Oxford University Press, 1972) and his *Booker T. Washington: The Wizard of Tuskegee, 1901–1915* (New York: Oxford University Press, 1983). The standard sources on the early years of W. E. B. Du Bois are the magisterial biography by David Levering Lewis, *W. E. B. Du Bois: Biography of a Race, 1868–1901* (New York: Henry Holt, 1993) and his *W. E. B. Du Bois: The Fight for Equality and the American Century, 1919–1963* (New York: Henry Holt, 2000). See also

Arnold Rampersad, *The Art and Imagination of W. E. B. DuBois* (Princeton: Princeton University Press, 1976).

On the subject of the literary field in the United States from 1880 to 1915, see the useful surveys in Emory Elliott et al., eds., *The Columbia Literary History of the United States* (New York: Columbia University Press, 1988), and in Elliot et al., eds., *The Columbia History of the American Novel* (New York: Columbia University Press, 1991). A more focused but highly important argument about how to conceptualize the literary field during these years can be found in Richard Brodhead, *Cultures of Letters: Scenes of Reading and Writing in Nineteenth-Century America* (Chicago: University of Chicago Press, 1993). On this subject, see also Levine, *Highbrow/Lowbrow: The Emergence of Cultural Hierarchy in America*. Although Ohmann, *Selling Culture: Magazines, Markets, and Class at the Turn of the Century* (New York: Verso, 1996), focuses on the rise of the mass-market magazine, Ohmann has significant things to say about how its emergence intersected with developments in the high-literary field. Similarly, although Alan Trachtenberg's still important book, *The Incorporation of America: Culture and Society in the Gilded Age* (New York: Hill & Wang, 1982), surveys political, economic, social, and cultural developments together, it has much to say on the development of high-literary culture during this period. For more on this subject, see the important accounts given in Nancy Glazener, *Reading for Realism: The History of a U.S. Literary Institution, 1850–1910* (Durham: Duke University Press, 1997), and June Howard, *Publishing the Family* (Durham: Duke University Press, 2001). On the subsequent rise of middlebrow culture, see Joan Shelley Rubin, *The Making of Middlebrow Culture* (Chapel Hill: University of North Carolina Press, 1992), and Radway, *A Feeling for Books*.

The literatures on American regionalism and local color writing as well as on American realism and naturalism are vast. For the former, two good places to begin are Elizabeth Ammons and Valerie Rohy, *American Local Color Writing, 1880–1920* (New York: Penguin Books, 1998), and Sherrie Inness and Diana Royer, *Breaking Boundaries: New Perspectives on Women's Regional Writing* (Iowa City: University of Iowa Press, 1997). On American literary realism and naturalism, there are several indispensable volumes in addition to Glazener. See Amy Kaplan, *The Social Construction of American Realism* (Chicago: University of Chicago Press, 1988); Warner Berthoff, *The Ferment of Realism: American Literature, 1884–1919* (Cambridge: Cambridge University Press, 1965); Michael Davitt Bell, *The Problem of American Realism* (Chicago: University of Chicago Press, 1993); Phillip Barrish, *American Literary Realism, Critical Theory and Intellectual Prestige, 1880–1890* (Cambridge: Cambridge University Press, 2001); June Howard, *Form and History in American Literary Naturalism* (Chapel Hill: University of North Carolina Press, 1985); Mark Seltzer, *Henry James and the Art of Power* (Ithaca, N.Y.: Cornell University Press, 1984) and *Bodies and Machines* (New York: Routledge, 1992); and Walter Benn Michaels, *The Gold Standard and the Logic of Naturalism* (Berkeley: University of California Press, 1987). For a general discussion of literary developments during the important but often neglected decade of the 1890s, see Larzer Ziff, *The American 1890s: The Life and Times of a Lost Generation* (New York: Viking Press, 1966). For a discussion of writing by African Americans during the period under discussion here, see Dickson D. Bruce Jr., *Black American Writing from the Nadir: The Evolution of a Literary Tradition, 1877–1915* (Baton Rouge: Louisiana State University Press, 1989). See also William L. Andrews, *The Literary Career of Charles Chesnutt* (Baton Rouge: Louisiana State University Press, 1980).

On the subject of literary bohemia and writing before World War I, see Christine Stansell, *American Moderns: Bohemian New York and the Creation of a New Century* (New York: Metropolitan Books, 2000), and Arthur Frank Wertheim, *The New York Little Renaissance: Iconoclasm, Modernism, and Nationalism in American Culture, 1908–1917* (New York: New York University Press, 1976).

Scientific and Technical Publishing

No comprehensive history of scientific book publishing in the United States exists for our period, though it was a time of considerable growth and change for that sector. Information about publishing strategies and organization may be found in the histories of firms that published some technical works, such as Edward Matthews Crane, *A Century of Book Publishing, 1846–1948* (New York: D. Van Nostrand, 1948); John L. Dusseau, *An Informal History of W. B. Saunders Company on the Occasion of Its Hundredth Anniversary* (Philadelphia: W. B. Saunders, 1988); and Ellen Gilbert, *The House of Holt, 1866–1946: An Editorial History* (Metuchen, N.J.: Scarecrow Press, 1993); and in the histories of two firms that specialized in technical works: Roger Burlingame, *Endless Frontiers: The Story of McGraw-Hill* (New York: McGraw-Hill, 1959), and John Hammond Moore, *Wiley: One Hundred and Seventy-Five Years of Publishing* (New York: John Wiley & Sons, 1982). James M. Reid's *An Adventure in Textbooks, 1924–1960* (New York: R. R. Bowker, 1969) provides insights to textbook publishing in the sciences and social sciences. University press involvement in science is discussed within such general histories as Roger L. Geiger, *To Advance Knowledge: The Growth of American Research Universities, 1900–1940* (New York: Oxford University Press, 1986), and Roger Shugg, *The Two Worlds of University Publishing* (Lawrence: University of Kansas Libraries, 1967).

Accounts of publishing in medicine include John B. Blake, ed., *Centenary of Index Medicus, 1879–1979* (Bethesda: U.S. Department of Health and Human Services, Public Health Service, 1980), and William F. Bynum, Stephen Lock, and Roy Porter, eds., *Medical Journals and Medical Knowledge: Historical Essays* (London: Routledge, 1992). Michael M. Sokal's historical essay "*Science* and James McKeen Cattell, 1894–1945," *Science* 209 (4 July 1980): 43–52, provides one of the few detailed profiles of an autocratic science journal editor of that period.

A more ripened literature exists for the popularization of science in the early twentieth century, beginning with John C. Burnham, *How Superstition Won and Science Lost: Popularizing Science and Health in the United States* (New Brunswick: Rutgers University Press, 1987). Discussion of popular magazine science may be found in Marcel C. LaFollette, *Making Science Our Own: Public Images of Science, 1910–1955* (Chicago: University of Chicago Press, 1990), and Murdo William McRae, ed., *The Literature of Science: Perspectives on Popular Science Writing* (Athens: University of Georgia Press, 1993).

During World War II, American publishers engaged in extraordinary efforts to publish thousands of technical books quickly and expediently. Useful histories of this endeavor include Boyd Childress, "Scholarly Periodicals in the Second World War," *Scholarly Publish-*

ing 20 (January 1989): 93-106; Michael S. Sweeney, *Secrets of Victory: The Office of Censorship and the American Press and Radio in World War II* (Chapel Hill: University of North Carolina Press, 2001); and James Stacey Thompson, *The Technical Book Publisher in Wartimes* (New York: New York Public Library, 1942).

Following the war, the U.S. government encouraged the dissemination of technical information that was potentially useful to industry and the general public. See Vannevar Bush, *Science—The Endless Frontier: A Report to the President on a Program for Postwar Scientific Research* (Washington, D.C.: Government Printing Office, 1945). Scientific and technical information continued to be subject to censorship and controls, however, as described in Robert E. Summers, ed., *Federal Information Controls in Peacetime* (New York: H. W. Wilson Company, 1949).

Government Publications

Because the literature on the government as publisher is sparse, the account given in this volume relies to a large extent upon primary sources. In addition to a recent important publication, Oz Frankel, *States of Inquiry: Social Investigations and Print Culture in Nineteenth-Century Britain and the United States* (Baltimore: Johns Hopkins University Press, 2006), readers may find useful the following general works: James L. Harrison, *100 GPO Years, 1861-1961* (Washington, D.C.: Government Printing Office, 1961); Robert E. Kling Jr., *The Government Printing Office* (New York: Praeger, 1970); Peter Hernon and Harold C. Relyea, "Government Publishing: Past to Present," *Government Information Quarterly* 12 (1995): 224-318; Stephen W. Stathis, "The Evolution of Government Printing and Publishing in America," *Government Publications Review* 7A (1980): 377-90; John V. Richardson, "The United States Government as Publisher since the Roosevelt Administration," *Library Research* 4 (1982): 224-27; and Sarah Jordan Miller, "Producing Documents for Congress and the Nation: Government Printing in the United States, Past and Present. Part I," *Printing History* 21, vol. 11, no. 1 (1989): 127-41, and "Part II," *Printing History* 21, vol. 11, no. 2 (1989): 40-46. Also, some more specialized studies exist; see, for example, William S. Cramer, "The Federal Writers' Project: Work Relief That Preserved a National Resource," *Publishing History* 18 (1985): 49-68, and Gay Walker, "Printing for the United States: Meriden Gravure and the U.S. Government," *Printing History* 21, vol. 10, no. 2 (1988): 19-33.

Censorship

General histories include Robert W. Haney, *Comstockery in America: Patterns of Censorship and Control* (Boston: Beacon Press, 1960); Paul S. Boyer, *Purity in Print: The Vice Society Movement and Book Censorship in America* (New York: Charles Scribner's Sons, 1968; new and expanded edition, Madison: University of Wisconsin Press, 2002); and Alan Hunt, *Governing Morals: A Social History of Moral Regulation* (Cambridge: Cambridge University Press, 1999).

Recent interpretive studies include Adam Parkes, *Modernism and the Theater of Censorship* (New York: Oxford University Press, 1996); Rochelle Gurstein, *The Repeal of Reticence: A History of America's Cultural and Legal Struggles over Free Speech, Obscenity, Sexual Libera-*

tion, and Modern Art (New York: Hill & Wang, 1996); Alison M. Parker, *Purifying America: Women, Cultural Reform, and Pro-Censorship Activism, 1873–1933* (Urbana: University of Illinois Press, 1997); Nicola Kay Beisel, *Imperiled Innocents: Anthony Comstock and Family Reproduction in Victorian America* (Princeton: Princeton University Press, 1997); Andrea Friedman, *Prurient Interests: Gender, Democracy, and Obscenity in New York City, 1909–1945* (New York: Columbia University Press, 2000); and Helen Lefkowitz Horowitz, *Rereading Sex: Battles over Sexual Knowledge and Suppression in Nineteenth-Century America* (New York: Alfred A. Knopf, 2002). See also Jay A. Gertzman, *Bookleggers and Smuthounds: The Trade in Erotica, 1920–1940* (Philadelphia: University of Pennsylvania Press, 2002), on the production and suppression of sexually explicit material between the wars.

The many works on movie censorship include Ira H. Carmen, *Movies, Censorship and the Law* (Ann Arbor: University of Michigan Press, 1966), and Francis G. Couvares, ed., *Movie Censorship and American Culture* (Washington, D.C.: Smithsonian Institution Press, 1996). Library censorship is considered in *Librarians, Censorship and Intellectual Freedom* (Chicago: American Library Association, 1968–69). On political censorship, see Zechariah Chafee Jr., *Free Speech in the United States* (Cambridge, Mass.: Harvard University Press, 1941), and William Preston Jr., *Aliens and Dissenters: Federal Suppression of Radicals, 1903–1933* (Cambridge, Mass.: Harvard University Press, 1966). On specific authors, see James L. W. West III, *A Sister Carrie Portfolio* (Charlottesville: University of Virginia Press, 1985); D. H. Lawrence, *Sex, Literature and Censorship*, ed. Harry T. Moore (New York: Viking Press, 1959); and Paul Vanderham, *James Joyce and Censorship: The Trials of Ulysses* (New York: New York University Press, 1997).

The European Ethnic Press

The basic monograph on this press is Robert E. Park's influential *The Immigrant Press and Its Control* (New York: Harper & Brothers, 1922). Little research was done thereafter until the current generation of scholars. The most common approach to the ethnic press has been to focus on the newspapers of one group and, thus, articles have often been written in a narrow context. The linguist Joshua Fishman did more comprehensive work in the 1960s. See his *Language Loyalty in the United States: The Maintenance and Perpetuation of Non-English Mother Tongues by American Ethnic and Religious Groups* (The Hague: Mouton, 1966). Useful resources include Lubomyr R. Wynar and Anna T. Wynar, *Encyclopedic Directory of Ethnic Newspapers and Periodicals in the United States*, 2nd ed. (Littleton, Colo.: Libraries Unlimited, 1976), and Hensley C. Woodbridge, "United States and Canadian National Bibliography: Foreign Languages," *Encyclopedia of Library and Information Science* 36, suppl. 1 (1983): 516–74. Sally M. Miller, ed., *The Ethnic Press in the United States: A Historical Analysis and Handbook* (Westport, Conn.: Greenwood Press, 1987), contains individual essays on twenty-eight different categories of ethnic presses.

There is no substitute for reviewing runs of the newspapers of the individual presses, but two serious problems complicate such an undertaking. First, it is difficult to locate such newspapers. They were typically excluded from newspaper directories and libraries seldom collected them. Second, scholars with the necessary language facility are scarce. A number of useful Ph.D. dissertations have been completed recently, though they tend to be based on samples rather than entire runs of newspapers.

The monographic literature includes Carl Wittke, *The German-Language Press in America* (Lexington: University Press of Kentucky, 1957); Marion Tuttle Marzolf, *The Danish-Language Press in America* (New York: Arno Press, 1979); Arlow W. Andersen, *The Immigrant Takes His Stand: The Norwegian-American Press and Public Affairs, 1847–1872* (Northfield, Minn.: Norwegian-American Historical Association, 1953); Robert A. Karlowich, *We Rise and Fall: Russian-Language Newspapers in New York City, 1889–1914* (Metuchen, N.J.: Scarecrow Press, 1991); and Jan Kowalik, *The Polish Press in America* (San Francisco: R & E Associates, 1978). The Works Progress Administration produced some relevant studies of the ethnic press in different locations, such as *History of Journalism in San Francisco*, vol. 1, *Foreign Journalism* (Washington, D.C.: Government Printing Office, 1939). Finally, Hanno Hardt, "The Foreign-Language Press in American Press History," *Journal of Communication* 39 (Spring 1989): 114–31, is a useful article.

Print and People of Color

African Americans

The starting point for research into all aspects of African-American history is a series of bibliographical guides produced in the last decade. *The Harvard Guide to African-American History*, ed. Evelyn Brooks Higginbotham (Cambridge, Mass.: Harvard University Press, 2001), is the most important survey of the field. *African-American Newspapers and Periodicals: A National Bibliography*, ed. James P. Danky (Cambridge, Mass.: Harvard University Press, 1998), is the definitive guide to serial publications. *Black Biography, 1790–1950: A Cumulative Index* (Alexandria, Va.: Chadwyck-Healey, 1991) provides access to thousands of African American lives. *Schomburg Library of Nineteenth-Century Black Women Writers*, ed. Henry Louis Gates Jr. (New York: Oxford University Press, 1988), makes available texts that were previously difficult to access. *The Norton Anthology of African American Literature*, ed. Henry Louis Gates Jr. and Nellie Y. McKay (New York: W. W. Norton, 1997), contains bibliographical guides to major and minor black American authors.

Afro American Press and Its Editors, ed. I. Garland Penn (Springfield, Mass.: Willey, 1891; repr., New York: Arno Press, 1969), still stands as a landmark, both as a history and a contemporary survey of the black press. Two subsequent studies highlight the post–World War I ascendance of the black press in white consciousness: Robert T. Kerlin, *Voice of the Negro: 1919* (New York: E. P. Dutton, 1920), and Frederick G. Detweiler, *The Negro Press in the United States* (Chicago: University of Chicago Press, 1922). More recent general histories of the black press include Maxwell R. Brooks, *The Negro Press Reexamined: The Political Contents of Ten Leading Negro Newspapers* (Boston: Christopher Publishing House, 1959); Martin E. Dann, ed., *The Black Press, 1827–1890: The Quest for National Identity* (New York: Putnam, 1971); Vishnu Oak, *The Negro Newspaper* (Westport, Conn.: Negro Universities Press, 1948); Armistead S. Pride and Clint C. Wilson II, *A History of the Black Press* (Washington, D.C.: Howard University Press, 1997); and Todd Vogel, ed., *The*

Black Press: New Literary and Historical Essays (New Brunswick: Rutgers University Press, 2001).

Biographies of editors and journalists are among the most numerous and rich sources of scholarship on the creation of African American print culture. These works include Jervis Anderson, *A. Philip Randolph: A Biographical Portrait* (New York: Harcourt Brace Jovanovich, 1973); Andrew Buni, *Robert L. Vann of the "Pittsburgh Courier": Politics and Black Journalism* (Pittsburgh: University of Pittsburgh Press, 1974); Lawrence Hogan, *A Black National News Service: The Associated Negro Press and Claude Barnett, 1919–1945* (Rutherford, Pa.: Fairleigh Dickinson University Press, 1984); Jane Rhodes, *Mary Ann Shadd Cary: The Black Press and Protest in the Nineteenth Century* (Bloomington: Indiana University Press, 1998); Rodger Streitmatter, *Raising Her Voice: African-American Women Journalists Who Changed History* (Lexington: University Press of Kentucky, 1994); and Emma Lou Thornbrough, *T. Thomas Fortune: Militant Journalist* (Chicago: University of Chicago Press, 1972). On Marcus Garvey, see Edmund David Cronon, *Black Moses: The Story of Marcus Garvey and the United Negro Improvement Association* (Madison: University of Wisconsin Press, 1955).

On children's books, see Violet J. Harris, "African American Children's Literature: The First One Hundred Years," *Journal of Negro Education* 59, no. 4 (Autumn, 1990): 540–55, and Louise S. Robbins, "Publishing Pride: The Jim Crow Series of Harlow Publishing Company," in *Defining Print Culture for Youth: The Cultural Work of Children's Literature*, ed. Anne Lundin and Wayne E. Wiegand (Westport, Conn.: Libraries Unlimited, 2003). On African American religious publishing, see Bobby Lovett, *A Black Man's Dream: The First 100 Years, Richard Henry Boyd and the National Baptist Publishing Board* (Jacksonville, Fla.: Mega Corporation, 1993), which chronicles one of the largest black publishing firms of its time.

For scholarship on African American magazines and periodical literature, see Penelope L. Bullock, *The Afro American Periodical Press, 1838–1909* (Baton Rouge: Louisiana State University Press, 1981); Walter Daniel, *Black Journals of the United States* (Westport, Conn.: Greenwood Press, 1982); and Michael Fultz, "'The Morning Cometh': African American Periodicals, Education, and the Black Middle Class, 1990–1930," *Journal of Negro History* 80, no. 3 (June 1995): 97–112.

Hispanic Americans

There is no comprehensive study of Hispanic book history in the United States. With the establishment of the Recovering the U.S. Hispanic Literary Heritage Project in 1992, a large corps of scholars has begun to consider the written culture of Hispanics in the present United States, beginning in the period of exploration and colonization in the sixteenth century. The first comprehensive anthology from this written tradition, *Herencia: The Anthology of Hispanic Literature of the United States*, ed. Nicolás Kanellos et al. (New York: Oxford University Press, 2002), includes literature written over the course of four centuries. The original Spanish-language texts can be read in a companion volume, *En otra voz: antología de la literature hispana de los Estados Unidos*, ed. Nicolás Kanellos et al. (Houston: Arte Público Press, 2003). See also the eight volumes of research papers published by the Project, under the title of *Recovering the U.S. Hispanic Literary Heritage*, vols. 1-8 (Houston: Arte Público Press, 1993-2008).

The study of Spanish-language literacy and the introduction of the printing press into particular regions of the Southwest have commanded considerable attention. See Lota M. Spell, *Pioneer Printer: Samuel Bangs in Mexico and Texas* (Austin: University of Texas Press, 1963); Bernardo P. Gallegos, *Literacy, Education, and Society in New Mexico, 1693-1821* (Albuquerque: University of New Mexico Press, 1992); and A. Gabriel Meléndez, *So All Is Not Lost: The Poetics of Print in Nuevomexicano Communities, 1883-1958* (Albuquerque: University of New Mexico Press, 1997).

Publishing newspapers and magazines was far more widespread and important in Hispanic communities than publishing books. On Hispanic periodicals, see Nicolás Kanellos and Helvetia Martell, *Hispanic Periodicals in the United States, Origins to 1960: A Brief History and Comprehensive Bibliography* (Houston: Arte Público Press, 2000), which documents the historical, social, and political roles played by historically Spanish-language periodicals in Hispanic communities. Of the studies mostly dedicated to periodicals in particular regions, see especially Joseph P. Fitzpatrick, "The Puerto Rican Press," in *The Ethnic Press in the United States: A Historical Analysis and Handbook*, ed. Sally M. Miller (Westport, Conn.: Greenwood Press, 1987), 303-14; Victoria Goff, "Spanish-Language Newspapers in California," in *Outsiders in 19th-Century Press History: Multicultural Perspectives*, ed. Frankie Hutton and Barbara Straus Reed (Bowling Green, Ohio: Bowling Green State University Popular Press, 1995), 55-70; Félix Gutiérrez, "Spanish-Language Media in America: Background, Resources, History," *Journalism History* 4, no. 2 (Summer, 1977): 34-41, 65-67; Raymund R. MacCurdy, *A History and Bibliography of Spanish Language Newspapers and Magazines in Louisiana, 1808-1949* (Albuquerque: University of New Mexico Press, 1997); and Doris Meyer, *Speaking for Themselves: Neomexicano Cultural Identity and the Spanish-Language Press, 1880-1920* (Albuquerque: University of New Mexico Press, 1996).

Four valuable studies of particular periodicals are Ramón D. Chacón, "The Chicano Immigrant Press in Los Angeles: The Case of 'El Heraldo de México,' 1916-1920," *Journalism History* 4, no. 2 (Summer 1977): 48-50, 62-64; Vernon A. Chamberlain and Ivan A. Shulman, *La Revista Ilustrada de Nueva York: History, Anthology and Index of Literary Selections* (Columbia: University of Missouri Press, 1976); Michael M. Smith, "The Mexican Immigrant Press beyond the Borderlands: The Case of El Cosmopolita," *Great Plains Quarterly* 10 (Spring 1990): 71-85; and Nicolás Kanellos, "*El Clamor Público*: Resisting the American Empire," *California History* 84, no. 2 (Winter 2006-7): 10-18, 69-70. For its volume 84, no. 2 (Winter 2006-7), *California History* dedicated the entire issue to studies of editor Francisco Ramírez and his *El Clamor Público*, and the *Américas Review* 17, nos. 3-4 (Winter 1989) was dedicated entirely to studies on San Antonio's *La Pensa*. Excellent studies of the exile press are Gerald Eugene Poyo, *With All and for the Good of All: The Emergence of Popular Nationalism in the Cuban Communities of the United States, 1848-1898* (Durham: Duke University Press, 1989), and Oscar U. Somoza and Armando Miguélez, *Literatura de la Revolución Mexicana en el exilio: Fuentes para su estudio* (Mexico City: Universidad Autónoma de México, 1997.

Religious Print Cultures

The Protestant Press

There is no comprehensive study of Protestant publishing in the United States. Hendrik Edelman comes closest in his compact but detailed "History of Religious Publishing and Bookselling in the United States and Canada, 1640-1985," in *Christian Book Publishing and Distribution in the United States and Canada*, ed. J. P. Dessauer, Paul Doehbler, and Hendrik Edelman (Tempe, Ariz.: Christian Booksellers Association, 1987).

Martin E. Marty provides an insightful introduction to Protestant periodicals in "The Protestant Press: Limitations and Possibilities," in *The Religious Press in America*, ed. Martin E. Marty, John G. Deedy, David Wolf Silverman, and Robert Lekachman (New York: Holt, Rinehart, and Winston, 1963), and his more general and more recent essay on "The Religious Press," in *Encyclopedia of the American Religious Experience: Studies of Traditions and Movements*, ed. Charles H. Lippy and Peter W. Williams (New York: Charles Scribner's Sons, 1988). See also Daniel G. Reid, Robert Dean Lindner, Bruce L. Shelley, and Henry S. Stout, "Protestant Press," in their *Dictionary of Christianity in America* (Downers Grove, Ill.: InterVarsity Press, 1990). For individual Protestant periodicals, the best place to start is the edited work by P. Mark Fackler and Charles H. Lippy, *Popular Religious Magazines of the United States* (Westport, Conn.: Greenwood Press, 1995), which contains informative vignettes of ninety-nine religious periodicals.

Two essays provide an excellent starting place for the study of the Bible and other sacred texts: Paul Gutjahr's bibliographic "The State of the Discipline: Sacred Texts in the United States" in *Book History* 4 (2001): 33-370, and Stephen J. Stein's captivating "America's Bibles: Canon, Commentary, and Community" in *Church History* 64 (June 1995): 169-84. The 1980s contribute significantly to the study of the Bible in American life. See, for example, *The Bible in America: Essays in Cultural History*, ed. Mark Noll and Nathan Hatch (New York: Oxford University Press, 1982), as well as the six-volume Bible in American Culture series produced by the Society of Biblical Literature. No scholar of the Bible in American life can ignore Margaret T. Hills's fascinating and remarkably thorough work, *The English Bible in America: A Bibliography of Editions of the Bible and the New Testament Published in America, 1777-1957* (New York: American Bible Society and the New York Public Library, 1961).

Joan Shelley Rubin helps us think more clearly about religious books in general in her provocative essay, "The Boundaries of American Religious Publishing in the Early Twentieth Century," *Book History* 2 (1999): 207-17. Also helpful for the years 1880-1940 are Allene Stuart Phy's essay on "Jesus in Popular Fiction," in *Bible and Popular Culture*, ed. Allene Stuart Phy (Philadelphia: Fortress Press, 1985), and David S. Reynolds, *Faith in Fiction: The Emergence of Religious Literature in America* (Cambridge, Mass.: Harvard University Press, 1981).

The Catholic Press

As in the case of the Protestant press, there is no comprehensive study of Catholic publishing in America. There was, however, a tremendous surge of scholarly activity in the early and middle decades of the twentieth century as Catholics newly conscious of the need to document their history began compiling studies of past and contemporary enterprises. The most significant undertakings in the realm of Catholic print culture bibliography for our period include Walter Romig's periodical *Guide to Catholic Literature* (Haverford, Pa.: Catholic Library Association, annual, 1888–1967), and a project at Catholic University entitled *Survey of Catholic Americana and Catholic Book Publishing in the United States*, for which Avelina Dawson covered the period 1881–85; Mary Ruskin, 1886–90; Josephine Chen, 1891–95; and Patricia Felten, 1896–1900.

Studies on more focused topics include Apollinaris W. Baumgartner, *Catholic Journalism: A Study of Its Development in the United States, 1789–1930* (New York: Columbia University Press, 1931); Sr. Mary Charles Bryce, *The Influence of the Catechism of the Third Plenary Council of Baltimore on Widely Used Elementary Religion Text Books from Its Composition in 1885 to Its 1941 Revision* (Washington, D.C.: Catholic University of America, 1970); William L. Lucey, S.J., *An Introduction to American Catholic Magazines* (Philadelphia: American Catholic Historical Society, 1952); and Sr. Mary Lonan Reilly, O.S.F., *A History of the Catholic Press Association, 1911–1968* (Metuchen, N.J.: Scarecrow Press, 1971). The *Catholic Encyclopedia*, in both its incarnations (1907–14 and 1967–79) is valuable both for its discussion of relevant topics and as an artifact of Roman Catholic print culture. The reemergence of the *Encyclopedia*'s 1907–14 edition as a Web site (http://www.newadvent.org/cathen/) is certainly one of the more remarkable instances of cyber-collaboration and a great resource for historians. Succinct descriptions of canon law governing publication and reading can be found in Francis Betten, *The Roman Index of Forbidden Books Briefly Explained for Catholic Booklovers and Students* (St. Louis: B. Herder, 1909), and Redmond Burke, *What Is the Index?* (Milwaukee: Bruce Publishing Company, 1952). *The Catholic Periodical and Literature Index* (Haverford, Pa.: Catholic Library Association, quarterly, 1968–) replaced *The Catholic Periodical Index* (Haverford, Pa.: Catholic Library Association, 1888–1967); both are invaluable resources for publications not indexed elsewhere.

The Jewish Press

Two excellent sources for material bearing on the history of Jewish books and publishing in America are the *Jewish Book Annual* (New York: Jewish Book Council of the National Jewish Welfare Board, 1942–), which also contains extensive bibliographies of Jewish books published each year, and *Studies in Bibliography and Booklore* (Cincinnati: Library of Hebrew Union College, 1953–), which publishes scholarly articles. The early monographic and serial literature has been brought under bibliographic control by Robert Singerman in his monumental *Judaica America: A Bibliography of Publications to 1900*, 2 vols. (New York: Greenwood, 1990). For early American Hebraica, see Yosef Goldman, *Hebrew Printing in America, 1735–1926: A History and Annotated Bibliography*, 2 vols. (Brooklyn: YG Books, 2006). See also Joshua Bloch, *Of Making Many Books: An Annotated List of the Books Issued by the Jewish Publication Society of America, 1890–1952* (Philadelphia: Jewish Publication Society, 1953). A list of American Jewish newspapers and periodicals appears annually in the *American Jewish Year Book* (Philadelphia: American Jewish Committee: 1900–).

Secondary sources bearing on the history of the Jewish book in America are few and far between. Charles A. Madison, *Jewish Publishing in America* (New York: Sanhedrin Press,

1976), represents an inadequate attempt to survey the entire field. Jonathan D. Sarna, *JPS: The Americanization of Jewish Culture, 1888–1988* (Philadelphia: Jewish Publication Society, 1989), supplies a cultural history of the Jewish Publication Society, long the foremost publisher of Jewish books in America. Shuly Rubin Schwartz, *The Emergence of Jewish Scholarship in America: The Publication of the Jewish Encyclopedia* (Cincinnati: Hebrew Union College Press, 1991), treats in detail one critical episode. Robert Singerman, "Books Weeping for Someone to Visit and Admire Them: Jewish Library Culture in the United States, 1850–1910," *Studies in Bibliography and Booklore* 20 (1998): 99–144, opens up the history of Jewish library collections. It may be complemented by Adolph Oko's dated but still important, "Jewish Book Collections in the United States," *American Jewish Year Book* 45 (1943–44): 67–96, and by Herman Dicker's history of the Jewish Theological Seminary's library, *Of Learning and Libraries: The Seminary Library at One Hundred* (New York: Jewish Theological Seminary of America, 1988).

No book-length history of American Jewish journalism exists, but see Robert Singerman, "The American Jewish Press, 1823–1983: A Bibliographic Survey of Research and Studies," *American Jewish History* 73 (June 1984): 422–44, which lists earlier sources. Secondary studies include Arthur A. Goren, "The Jewish Press," in *The Ethnic Press in the United States: An Historical Analysis and Handbook*, ed. Sally M. Miller (Westport, Conn.: Greenwood Press, 1987), 203–28, and Jonathan D. Sarna, "The History of the Jewish Press in North America," in *The North American Jewish Press: The 1994 Alexander Brin Forum* (Waltham, Mass.: Cohen Center for Modern Jewish Studies, Brandeis University, 1995), 2–7, reprinted in Luke Ford, *Yesterday's News Tomorrow: Inside American Jewish Journalism* (New York: IUniverse, 2004), 321–32; and Aviva Ben-Ur, "The Ladino (Judeo-Spanish) Press in the United States, 1910–1948," in *Multilingual America: Transnationalism, Ethnicity and the Languages of American Literature*, ed. Werner Sollors (New York: New York University Press, 1998).

For other subjects, the *Encyclopaedia Judaica* (1972; 2nd ed., 2007) is the best place to start. For recent monographic studies, see Nathan M. Kaganoff, *Judaica Americana: An Annotated Bibliography of Publications from 1960 to 1990*, 2 vols. (Brooklyn, N.Y.: Carlson Publishing, 1995).

Readers and Reading: Institutions

Reading Textbooks

The starting point for any study of reading textbooks is the textbooks themselves, which are scattered in minimally cataloged collections. The largest of these is at the Educational Research Library of the U.S. Department of Education. *Early American Textbooks 1775–1900: A Catalogue of the Titles Held By the Educational Research Library*, ed. Dolly Svobodny (Washington, D.C.: U.S. Department of Education, 1985), catalogs a sample of these texts to 1900. Other large collections are at the Center for Research Libraries in Chicago, Illinois, the University of Pittsburgh (Nietz Collection), Hofstra University (Nila Banton Smith Historical Collection), Columbia University (Plimpton Library), Trinity College (Bernard Collection), the University of Florida (Baldwin Library), and the University of Kansas (Monaghan Collection of Books on the History of Reading in the United States, Kenneth Spencer Research Library).

Archives from major textbook publishers are generally unavailable. One exception is the American Book Company Archives, located at Syracuse University. Substantial coverage on textbook publishing is found in Tebbel, *A History of Book Publishing in the United States*, vol. 2, *The Expansion of an Industry, 1865-1919*, and Lehmann-Haupt et al., *The Book in America*. Upton Sinclair, *The Goslings: A Study of the American Schools* (Pasadena, Calif.: Author, 1924), has a chapter on the textbook publishers of the early twentieth century, including the American Book Company.

Nila Banton Smith, *American Reading Instruction* (Newark, Del.: International Reading Association, 1965), gives extensive coverage to textbooks. Descriptions of readers throughout the history of schooling in the United States may also be found in John Nietz, *Old Textbooks* (Pittsburgh: University of Pittsburgh Press, 1961), and Charles Carpenter, *History of American Schoolbooks* (Philadelphia: University of Pennsylvania Press, 1963). Women authors of reading texts in the twentieth century have been studied by E. Jennifer Monaghan, "Gender and Textbooks: Women Writers of Elementary Readers, 1880-1950," *Publishing Research Quarterly* 10, no. 1 (1994): 28-46.

Ruth Miller Elson, *Guardians of Tradition: American Schoolbooks of the Nineteenth Century* (Lincoln: University of Nebraska Press, 1964), is the best of the content analysis studies of U.S. textbooks. More focused studies on reader content include Richard de Charms and Gerald Moeller, "Values Expressed in American Children's Readers: 1800-1950," *Journal of Abnormal and Social Psychology* 64 (1962): 136-42, and Allan Luke, *Literacy, Textbooks, and Ideology* (London: Falmer Press, 1988).

Libraries

There is no comprehensive history of the great research libraries in the United States. The essays in Alexandra Oleson and John Voss, eds., *The Organization of Knowledge in Modern America, 1860-1920* (Baltimore: Johns Hopkins University Press, 1979), in particular, John Y. Cole, "Storehouses and Workshops: American Libraries and the Uses of Knowledge," provide a context for modern research library development. Richard D. Johnson, ed., *Libraries for Teaching, Libraries for Research* (Chicago: American Library Association, 1977), is a useful group of articles on aspects of the history of academic and research libraries (including the independent endowed institutions). Phyllis Dain and John Y. Cole, eds., *Libraries and Scholarly Communication in the United States: The Historical Dimension* (New York: Greenwood Press, 1990), contains selected papers from a 1987 conference at the Library of Congress. The *International Dictionary of Library Histories*, ed. David H. Stam, 2 vols. (Chicago: Fitzroy Dearborn, 2001), which focuses on notable libraries, includes essays on numerous American research libraries. A good biographical source is *Dictionary of American Library Biography*, ed. Bohdan S. Wynar (Littleton, Colo.: Libraries Unlimited, 1978), and *Supplements* 1 and 2 (1990, 2003). General works on the New York Public Library are Phyllis Dain, *The New York Public Library: A History of Its Founding and Early Years* (New York: The New York Public Library, 1972), and a short history spanning 1895 to 2000, Phyllis Dain, *The New York Public Library: A Universe of Knowledge* (London: The New York Public Library in Association with Scala Publishers, 2000). On the Boston Public Library there is Walter Muir Whitehill, *Boston Public Library: A Centennial History* (Cambridge, Mass.: Harvard University Press, 1956).

A fairly recent account of university libraries is Arthur Hamlin, *The University Library in the United States: Its Origins and Development* (Philadelphia: University of Pennsylvania Press, 1981). Charles B. Osburn, *Academic Research and Library Resources: Changing Patterns in America* (Westport, Conn.: Greenwood Press, 1979), looks critically at university collection development; Orvin Lee Shiflett does the same for the status of librarians from 1876 to 1923 in *Origins of American Academic Librarianship* (Norwood, N.J.: Ablex, 1981); and the essays in Wayne A. Wiegand, ed., *Leaders in American Academic Librarianship: 1925-1975* (Pittsburgh: Beta Phi Mu, 1983), explore modern university library management. Two major historical views of Harvard's library are William Bentinck-Smith, *Building a Great Library: The Coolidge Years at Harvard* (Cambridge, Mass.: Harvard University Library, 1976), and Kenneth E. Carpenter, *The First 350 Years of the Harvard University Library: Description of an Exhibition* (Cambridge, Mass.: Harvard University Library, 1986). The best study of Yale's library is Thomas F. O'Connor, "The Yale University Library, 1865-1931" (D.L.S. diss., Columbia University, 1984), summarized in part in his "Collection Development in the Yale University Library, 1865-1931," *Journal of Library History* 22 (Spring 1987): 164-89. Berkeley's library is chronicled in Kenneth G. Peterson, *The University of California Library at Berkeley, 1900-1945* (Berkeley: University of California Press, 1970). For the Library of Congress, see John Y. Cole, *For Congress and the Nation: A Chronological History of the Library of Congress* (Washington, D.C.: Library of Congress, 1979), which documents the origins and growth of the library through 1975, with illustrations, and James Conaway, *America's Library: The Story of the Library of Congress, 1800-2000* (New Haven: Yale University Press, in Association with the Library of Congress, 2000).

No single book covers American public library history between 1880 and 1940 completely. Sydney Ditzion's *Arsenals of a Democratic Culture: A Social History of the American Public Library Movement in New England and the Middle Atlantic States from 1850 to 1900* (Chicago: American Library Association, 1947), set the tone for viewing the public library as an agency that promoted democratic culture and an informed citizenry. This perspective dominated the literature of public library history for the next quarter century. Mike Harris's 1973 essay, "The Purpose of the American Public Library: A Revisionist Interpretation of History," *Library Journal* 98 (September 1973): 2509-14, signaled a significant shift in public library historiography; he argued that American public libraries were agents of social control, through which the upper classes sought to influence the behavior of the masses. Rosemary Ruhig Du Mont, *Reform and Reaction: The Big City Public Library in American Life* (Westport, Conn.: Greenwood Publishing Group, 1977); Dee Garrison, *Apostles of Culture: The Public Librarian and American Society, 1876-1920* (New York: Free Press, 1979); and Evelyn Geller, *Forbidden Books in American Public Libraries, 1876-1939* (Westport, Conn.: Greenwood Press, 1984), also developed critical perspectives, paving the way for works like Wayne A. Wiegand, *Politics of an Emerging Profession: The American Library Association, 1876-1917* (New York: Greenwood Press, 1986); Joanne Passet, *Cultural Crusaders: Women Librarians in the American West, 1900-1917* (Albuquerque: University of New Mexico Press, 1994); and Deanna Marcum, *Good Books in a Country Home: The Public Library as a*

Cultural Force in Hagerstown, Maryland, 1878–1920 (Westport, Conn.: Greenwood Press, 1994). The best effort to incorporate the history of a public library into the history of print culture is Christine Pawley's pioneering *Reading on the Middle Border: The Culture of Print in Late-Nineteenth-Century Osage, Iowa* (Amherst: University of Massachusetts Press, 2001), which analyzes reading in a small town.

The literature surrounding the philanthropy of Andrew Carnegie also demonstrates the mid-1970s shift to critical perspectives. George Bobinski, *Carnegie Libraries: Their Histories and Impact on American Public Library Development* (Chicago: American Library Association, 1969), outlined the philanthropy but sidestepped issues of motive and intent. In contrast, *Carnegie Denied: Rejecting Carnegie Construction Grants, 1896–1928*, ed. Robert Sidney Martin (Westport, Conn.: Greenwood Press, 1993), presented essays that examine the reasons scores of communities rejected Carnegie grants. More recently, Abigail Van Slyck's *Free to All: Carnegie Libraries & American Culture, 1890–1920* (Chicago: University of Chicago Press, 1995), found gender and class distinctions built into the architecture of typical Carnegie library buildings.

The latest biography of Melvil Dewey is Wayne A. Wiegand's *Irrepressible Reformer: A Biography of Melvil Dewey* (Chicago: American Library Association, 1996), which examines Dewey in the context of his time, looking at both his accomplishments and his flaws, from his influential role in structuring the American library profession to his anti-Semitism and his sexual harassment of women. American public libraries during World War I are well covered in Arthur P. Young's *Books for Sammies: The American Library Association and World War I* (Pittsburgh: Beta Phi Mu, 1981) and Wayne A. Wiegand's *"An Active Instrument for Propaganda": The American Public Library during World War I* (Westport, Conn.: Greenwood Press, 1989).

Women's Literary Clubs

There are a surprising number of primary sources on women's book clubs and the General Federation of Women's Clubs, which not only grew from them but also incorporated other women's organizations. Many clubs kept minutes of their meetings, drafts of papers that members presented, and yearbooks that outlined annual programs, and these are often archived in local libraries or historical societies. Local newspapers often featured regular columns devoted to women's clubs. Clubs' organizational fervor, as well as their links to influential men — including newspaper editors — seem to have been important in ensuring them a life in print. A case in point is Houston's Ladies Reading Club. Its role in founding the Houston Public Library has earned its papers a favored place in the Houston Metropolitan Archive. Less socially elite book clubs generally did not leave such clear documentary trails.

Several fine books have discussed the nineteenth-century literary club movement. Anne Ruggles Gere, *Intimate Practices: Literacy and Cultural Work in U.S. Women's Clubs, 1880–1920* (Urbana: University of Illinois Press, 1997), is the most sophisticated, drawing fascinating connections between literary reception and literary production. Karen J. Blair, *The Clubwoman as Feminist: True Womanhood Redefined, 1868–1914* (New York: Holmes & Meier, 1980), and Theodora Penny Martin, *The Sound of Their Own Voices: Women's Study Clubs, 1860–1910* (Boston: Beacon Press, 1987), are also very interesting. Megan Seaholm discusses literary clubs in Texas and the transition to a Progressive women's movement in "Earnest Women: The White Women's Movement in Progressive Era Texas, 1880-1920" (Ph.D. diss., Rice University, 1988). In *Book Clubs: Women and the Uses of Reading in Everyday Life* (Chicago: University of Chicago Press, 2003), Elizabeth Long extends the work represented in her essay in this volume.

African American literary clubs also have a long history, but they have less representation in newspapers and municipal archives than most white women's groups. *Forgotten Readers: Recovering the Lost History of African American Literary Societies*, by Elizabeth McHenry (Durham: Duke University Press, 2002), analyzes such clubs, their differences from white women's clubs, and their importance for broadening our conceptualization of African American literacy. Research on African Americans and their relationship to print culture has traditionally been defined and limited by assumptions about pervasive African American illiteracy, which obscures the complexity of the history of African Americans' literacy and their literary legacy. Recent scholarship on African Americans has begun to reveal this complexity. Janet Duitsman Cornelius, *"When I Can Read My Title Clear": Literacy, Slavery, and Religion in the Antebellum South* (Columbia: University of South Carolina Press, 1991), offers evidence that restrictions against teaching slaves to read were far less effective than commonly thought. Her study looks at slave literacy as a vehicle of empowerment. In "The Word in Black and White: Ideologies of Literacy in Antebellum America," in *Reading in America: Literature and Social History*, ed. Cathy N. Davidson (Baltimore: Johns Hopkins University Press, 1989), 140-56, Dana Nelson Salvino argues that while literacy was often instrumental in leading slaves out of physical bondage, it could not free them from their cultural and economic subordination or social segregation.

Recent studies have shed new light on the significant black readership—free and slave—that existed in the nineteenth century. Frances Smith Foster's introduction to Frances E. W. Harper's *Minnie's Sacrifice, Sowing and Reaping, and Trial and Triumph: Three Rediscovered Novels* (Boston: Beacon, 1994) offers a cogent analysis of how nineteenth-century black print culture and a black readership came to be overlooked and how it might be recovered. Carla Peterson, *Doers of the Word: African-American Women Speakers and Writers in the North, 1830-1880* (New York: Oxford University Press, 1995) and her "Reconstructing the Nation: Frances Harper, Charlotte Forten, and the Racial Politics of Periodical Publication," in *Proceedings of the American Antiquarian Society* 107 (1997): 301-34, also speak to the importance of the periodical press in the history of African American print culture.

Many of the publications that influenced black readers are no longer extant or are located in collections of the personal papers of African Americans who were active in their creation. The most complete collection of the *Woman's Era* is in the Mary Church Terrell Papers at the Library of Congress; some of the issues missing in Terrell's collection can be found in the Woman's Era Club's Papers, located at the Boston Public Library. Other small, local literary efforts of black clubwomen, such as the *Literary Souvenir*, are a part of the Daniel Murray Pamphlet Collection at the Library of Congress. The scope and variety of the literary activism of African American women is extensively documented in the clubs' reports, reprinted in *A History of the Club Movement among the Colored Women of the United States of America* (Washington, D.C.: National Association of Colored Women's Clubs, 1902).

Evelyn Brooks Higginbotham, *Righteous Discontent: The Women's Movement in the Black*

Baptist Church, 1880–1920 (Cambridge, Mass.: Harvard University Press, 1993), argues the importance of literacy and the centrality of literary texts to the community work of the women she studies. In *Uplifting the Race: Black Leadership, Politics, and Culture in the Twentieth Century* (Chapel Hill: University of North Carolina Press, 1996), Kevin K. Gaines offers an analysis of the middle-class ideology of racial uplift and the intersections between race and gender in racial uplift ideology. Anne Meis Knupfer, *Toward a Tenderer Humanity and a Nobler Womanhood: African American Women's Clubs in Turn-of-the-Century Chicago* (New York: New York University Press, 1996), offers details about the operations of specific women's organizations.

During the Harlem Renaissance, African Americans' interaction with print became increasingly visible, and studies of the period abound. Especially important to scholars of African American print culture are two texts: David Levering Lewis's *When Harlem Was in Vogue* (New York: Alfred A. Knopf, 1981) and Nathan Huggins's *Harlem Renaissance* (New York: Oxford University Press, 1971). Abby Arthur Johnson and Ronald Maberry Johnson, *Propaganda and Aesthetics: The Literary Politics of African-American Magazines in the Twentieth Century* (Amherst: University of Massachusetts Press, 1991), is especially important for its detailed discussion of the "little magazines" produced by and for black readers during the 1920s and 1930s, such as *Black Opals, Fire!!*, and the *Saturday Evening Quill*.

Reading Practices

Studies of individual and collective reading experiences have begun to proliferate, frequently in the form of essays. In addition to Kaestle et al., *Literacy in the United States*, other efforts to chronicle real readers in the late nineteenth and early twentieth centuries include Barbara Sicherman, "Reading and Middle-Class Identity in Victorian America: Cultural Consumption, Conspicuous and Otherwise," in *Reading Acts: U.S. Readers' Interactions with Literature, 1800–1950*, ed. Barbara Ryan and Amy M. Thomas (Knoxville: University of Tennessee Press, 2002), 137–60, and several other essays in that volume; Christine Pawley's study of the uses of literacy and the library in Osage, Iowa, mentioned earlier; Ann Fabian, "Laboring Classes, New Readers, and Print Cultures," in *Perspectives on American Book History*, ed. Scott Casper, Joanne D. Chaison, and Jeffrey D. Groves (Amherst: University of Massachusetts Press, 2002), 285–310; David Paul Nord, "Working-Class Readers: Family, Community, and Reading in Late Nineteenth-Century America," *Communications Research* 13 (April 1986): 156–81; as well as the work of Elizabeth McHenry and Elizabeth Long on women's book clubs, mentioned previously.

Background on the 1920s context in which librarians and social scientists probed American reading practices appears in Robert and Helen M. Lynd's still useful *Middletown: A Study in American Culture* (New York: Harcourt, Brace & World, 1929) and in *Recent Social Trends in the United States*, 2 vols. (New York: McGraw-Hill, 1933). While the most important of the librarians' investigations are cited in the notes to Joan Shelley Rubin's essay in this volume, see Kaestle et al., *Literacy in the United States*, for a fuller list. Sociologists' concerns about the impact of new media on reading are epitomized by Paul Lazarsfeld, *Radio and the Printed Page* (New York: Duell, Sloan and Pearce, 1940).

A representative recent overview of American poetry between 1880 and 1945 is Jay Parini and Brett C. Millier, eds., *The Columbia History of American Poetry* (New York: Columbia University Press, 1993). Although most scholars continue to depict high modernism as an advance over sentimental and narrative verse, the following studies laudably attempt to recover the perspectives of contemporary readers: Dana Gioia, "Longfellow in the Aftermath of Modernism," in Parini and Millier, *Columbia History of American Poetry*, 64–96; David Perkins, *A History of Modern Poetry: From the 1890s to the High Modernist Mode* (Cambridge, Mass.: Harvard University Press, 1976); Cary Nelson, *Repression and Recovery: Modern American Poetry and the Politics of Cultural Memory* (Madison: University of Wisconsin Press, 1989); and Joseph Harrington, *Poetry and the Public: The Social Form of Modern U.S. Poetics* (Middletown: Wesleyan University Press, 2002).

A full account of poetry in the school curriculum and in religious settings appears in Joan Shelley Rubin, *Songs of Ourselves: The Uses of Poetry in America* (Cambridge, Mass.: Harvard University Press, 2007). See also Craig S. Abbott, "Modern American Poetry: Anthologies, Classrooms, and Canons," *College Literature* 17 (1990): 209–21.

Denominational periodicals such as the *Methodist Review* and the *Presbyterian Magazine* provide insight into the attitudes of nonfundamentalist Protestants toward the uses of verse as prayer. Floyd and Pauline Todd, *Camping for Christian Youth* (New York: Harper, 1963), offer a good summary of the history of camping. Ruth A. Brown, ed., *Magic Ring: A Collection of Verse* (Seattle: Newman-Burrows Co., 1926), documents poetry read at camp.

INDEX

Note: Page numbers in italics refer to figures or tables.

A.M.E. Sunday School Union and Publishing House, 343
Abbott, Robert S., 215, 351–54, 356
Abrams v. the United States, 288
Academic professionalization, 202–4, 208–9
Advertising: in African American press, 344–45; by book clubs, 12, 82; book trade and, 55, 103–5, 113–14, 165, 170–71, 173–75, 178; boom in, 178–82; in Catholic press, 398, 407; in *The Crisis* (periodical), 507; demand for space for, 123–25; display, 125–26; for Harper's New Books, *174*; in *Harper's Weekly*, *105*; human interest, 182–84; impact of, on newspapers, 128–30; in *Library Notes*, 607 (n. 9); mail-order publishers and, 173; in mass-market press, 16; for middlebrow books, 114–15; in monthly magazines, 10–11, 51, 102–4, 110, 114; national, 425; in newspapers, 450; by old-line publishers, 175–77; partisan journalism and, 130; Progressive Reformers and, 128; promotion of book "content" and, 185–86; promotion of multiple works, 172–73; on radio shows, 187–88; for *Refugee*, *180*; revenue from, 120, 126; in trade periodicals, 15–16, 175; traditional and modernist, *160–61*; typography in, *111*; word-of-mouth, 186–87
Advertising agencies, 22, 112
Advice columns, 300, 321
Aesthetic movements, 41–42, 198–99, 211–13, 220, 222–23. *See also* Modernism; Naturalism; Realism; Romanticism

African American press, 339–41, 344–45, 348–50, 354–57, 496; and religion, 362
African American print culture, 195, 228–31, 339–58, 506
African Americans: as authors, 33–34, 200, 229, 231, 340, 343–44, 351; as booksellers, 491–92; Civilian Conservation Corps and, 357; club women's newspapers, 496–98, 504–5, 508–10, 617 (n. 38), 618 (n. 48); corporate capitalism and, 14–15; cultural institutions of, 195, 229, 348, 350, 486, 504–8, 617 (n. 41); educated, beliefs of, 504; education for, 225, 228–29, 342, 448, 489; as elocutionists, 343; Great Migration and, 351, 354–58; Harlem Renaissance and, 230–31, 356, 445, 492–93; insurance companies and, 591–92 (n. 31); literacy of, 29, 342, 506–7; literature of, 229–32, 475; New Negro movement, 230–31; newspaper editors, 215; oral traditions of, 492–93; in printing trades, 347–48; professional associations of, 349; public perceptions of, 497; racial identity of, 345; reading and, 474, 491–95, *497*, 507–8; repression of, 227; sacred and secular in lives of, 618 (n. 48); soldiers, 341–46; talented tenth, 227–28; writing of, 27. *See also* Black women's reading club movement
African Methodist Episcopal Church, 343, 362
Agriculture Department, 266–68, 271–72, 274
ALA. *See* American Library Association (ALA)

Alberts v. California, 297
Alden, Henry Mills, 278–79
Alfred A. Knopf: authors published by, 221; book buyers and, 188–89; book design and, 164; censorship and, 293; cover art for *Shakespeare in Harlem*, 356; culture wars and, 289; emergence of, 70; Harlem Renaissance and, 26; modernist literature and, 222; text type and, 167
Alien and Sedition Acts (1798), 288
All-rights contracts, 551 (n. 37)
Alma Mater (Canby), 197, 209
Alperovich, Moses, 386–87
Alsop, Joseph, 146, 150
Alternative press. *See* Press: alternative
American Bible Society, 370–71, 374
American Book Company (ABC), 58, 69, 421–22, 605 (n. 23)
American Bookseller, 41–42, *176*
American Chemical Society, 238, 245
American Jews, 220–21, 376–85, 389–90. *See also Jewish entries*
American Library Association (ALA), 30, 64, 294, 431–32, 436, 441, 456
American Mercury, The (periodical), 221, 289, *290–91*, 295
American Negro Academy, The, 229, 348
Anderson, Margaret, 285–88
Andrews, Will, *246–47*
Antivice societies, 282–83, 287
Antiwar writing, 287
Apostolates, 395–96
Appleton, William H., 285, 420
Appleton (publisher), 57, 103, 115, 237
Appleton's School Readers, 415–17, 424–25, 603 (n. 1)
Armed Services Editions, 81, *82*
Arthur A. Schomburg collection of Afro-Americana, 445
Arts-and-crafts movement, 69, 74, 159
Asbury, Herbert, 293, *294–95*
Assimilation, 299–300, 321, 335, 402–3, 426
Association of Research Libraries, 467–68

Astor Library, 453, 463
Atlanta University, 342
Atlanta University Press, 229, 350
Atlantic group, 212–14
Atlantic Monthly, 103–4, 106, 115, 212, 278, 293
Author catalogs, 461
Authorial entitlement, Lockean views of, 91, 94
Authors: African American, 200, 229, 231, 340, 343–44, 351; avant-garde, 285–86; Book-of-the-Month Club and, 83; of Catholic revival, 406–7; as celebrities, 107, 178, 199; censorship and, 294–95; of Jewish Publication Society, *378–79*; lecture circuit and, 187; "literary," 198–99, 212–15, 232; literary agents and, 88; Mexican American, 337; movie rights and, 87; naturalist, 215, 284–85; of popular science books, 252–53; publishers' ties with, 241, 277; radio rights and, 87; of reading textbooks, 424–25; self-censorship by, 278; social criticism by, 196; for Spanish-language periodicals, 316; of textbooks and reference books, 234; women, 226; women's literary clubs and, 479
Authorship, 99–100, 142, 549 (n. 17)
Authors' League of America, 294, 550 (n. 27)
Awakening, The (Chopin), 226, 285
Ayer: Advertising Company, 22; circulation estimates, *38*; directory, 361. *See also* N. W. Ayer and Son

Backlists, 240
Bacon, Corrine, 448–49
Bailey, Mark, 416–17
Ball, Horace G., 90, 93, 95
Ballantine, Betty, 84–85
Ballantine, Ian, 84–85
"Banned in Boston," 293, 298
Bantam Books, 84–85, *86*
Barber, J. Max, 345, 350

Barnum, P. T., 66
Basal readers, 415
Bauhaus school of design, 156
Bellamy, Edward, 217, 490
Ben Hur (Wallace), 43, *373*
Berelson, Bernard, 515-16
Bernays, Edward, 185-86
Berne Convention, 96, 550 (n. 25)
Best sellers, 55, 253, 372, 388, 398, 442-43
Biases, institutional, 30, 425, 455
Bibles, 43-44, 366-71, 374-75, 384, 399-401, 595 (n. 28)
Bible study, 375
Bibliographical Essay: advertising, 627-28; censorship, 635-36; ethnic press, European, 636-37; government publications, 635; libraries, 643-45; magazines, 627; newspapers and journalism, 629-30, 636-38; print and people of color, 637-39; printing and typography, 628-29; publishing and print production, 625-27; readers and reading institutions, 642-43; reading practices, 647-48; religious print cultures, 640-42; scientific and technical publishing, 634-35; social uses of print, 631-34; theoretical and general works, 623-25; women's literary clubs, 645-47
Bibliographic systems and guides, 441-42, 455, 458-59, 468
Black women's reading club movement, 486, 488-90, 493-95, 500, 505-7
Bloch & Co. (Bloch Publishing Company), 381, 387
Bok, Edward W., 10, 102-3, 106, 112, 215, 284-85
Bolshevik Revolution, 139
Boni, Alfred, 221
Boni & Liveright, 70, 287-88
Book chat, 107
Book clubs, 81-84, 173, 252. *See also* Black women's reading club movement; White women's literary club movement
Book industry, 57, 78-79, 81, 481; pricing and, 62-64, 69, 78. *See also* Distribution systems
Booklist, 441-43, 449
Bookman (periodical), 107, *174*, 178, 184
Book-of-the-Month Club (BOMC), 12, 82-83, 222, 529
Book-of-the-Month Club, Catholic, 408
Book production, 91; design, 74, 164-67; illustration in, 76-77, 155, 167-68; industrialization in, 72, 418; Linotype machines in, 72-74, 154-55; overview, 11-12; typography, 167
Book publishing, 103-8, 169, 173-75, 177-78, 220-21, 276-78, 283
Book reviews: as library resource, 441-42; by literary men of *Atlantic* group, 213; in *Nation*, 43; in newspapers, 128, 184, 450; on radio programs, 187; scientific and technical, 248; shaping of, by old-line publishers, 172; of textbooks and reference books, 234
Books: auratic quality of, 54; best books lists and, 252-53, 436-37; "best reading," 432-33, 440, 448-50; best sellers, 184-85; "boomed" era of, 113; circulation of, 207, 432, 442, 450, 474-75, 480; commodity status of, 51-52, 171; commodity texts, 92-94; condensations of, 177; consumption of, 123, 165; devotional, 347-49; five-foot shelf of, 182, 184; as friends, 526; higher education and, 304-5; judgments of obscenity and, 296-98; multiple voices in, 142; as niche product, 115; problem of definition, 171; reissues of, 42-44; as sacramental artifacts, 393; for social self vs. secret self, 511; as source of salvation, 382; steady sellers, 43, 184; as subject matter and affective experience, 186; as weapons during war, 256
Booksellers: book clubs and, 83; censorship by, 294; door to door, 491-92; foreign-language, 69; independent, 80; retail, 63-64, 545 (n. 11); in Texas, 480-81

INDEX 651

Boston Public Library, 453, 468, 643
Bourgeois class, 178, 209-10, 213, 528
Bowen-Merrill (Bobbs-Merrill), 178
Bradon, Helen D., 524-25
Bradshaw, Franklyn R., 515-16
Bruce Publishing, 407
Bryan, William Jennings, 133, 296
Buffalo Bill stories, 39-40
Bureau of Education, 436-37
Bureau of Foreign and Domestic Commerce, 265
By-lines, 137, 142

Cahan, Abraham, 215, 284, 300
Caldwell, Otis W., *246-47*
California, 334-35
Canby, Henry Seidel, 197-98, 209, 513
Card catalogs, 460, 567 (n. 44)
Carnegie, Andrew, 433, 437-41, 450, 464
Carnegie Corporation, 64, *439*
Carnegie libraries, 438, *439*
Case studies in reading, 25, 31-34, 517-18
Catechisms, 403
Catholic Encyclopedia, 403-4, 407-8
Catholicism: American, 392, 402, 406-7; colleges and mission schools of, 313, 331; culture of, 393; history of, 401-2; piety of, 399-401; as religion and way of life, 393; revival in, 406-7; universities, 403; women, and reading circles, 408
Catholic press: American publishing and, 392-93; Catholic unity and, 406; devotional literature, 398, 404; journalists of, 395; lay-owned, 397; modern technology in, 403-4, 408; Newman, 407; in New Mexico, 331; newspapers, 393-95; news service, 402-3; Paulist, 371, 395; periodicals, 294, 395-96, 405-7; Spanish-language, 331, *332*
Catholic print culture, 393, 396-97, 399-401, 404-8
Catholic World (periodical), 395, *396*
Censorship: "Army Index," 447; battles of, 288-96; conviction rate in cases of, 283-84; Cultural Front and, 232-33; diverse forms of, 296-97; of foreign-language newspapers, 308-9; government, 354; legal, 279-84, 286-87; origins and use of word, 276; of print matter, 195; by public librarians, 442-43, 447-48; self-, 255, 278-79, 308-10; sources of impulse for, 296; as threat to publishers, 297-98; wartime, 255-57, 287-88; by white literary establishment, 231. *See also* Obscenity
Census Bureau, 29, 265-66, 271, 372, 506-7, 540 (n.17)
Centennial Exhibition (Philadelphia), 22, 23
Century Company, 103-4
Century Group (Fight for Freedom), 149-50, 560-61 (n. 40)
Century Magazine, 103-4, 212, 278
Cerf, Bennett, 78-80, 221-22, 297
Chace Act (International Copyright Act of 1891), 51, 71, 95, 97-98
Chap-Book (periodical), 70, 284
Charles H. Kerr & Company, 217, 441
Charles Scribner's Sons, 103-4, *249*, 253
Cheney, O. H., 79-80, 185, 530-33
Chesterton, G. K., 406-7
Chestnutt, Charles, 215, 229, 351
Chicago Defender (newspaper), 195, 345, 351, *352-53*, 356-57
Chicago Public Library, *440*
Chicago Sun, 144-45
Chicago World's Fair (1893), 436-37
Chicano movement, 324, 335, 337
Children's Catalog, 441, 449
Children's literature, 427, 445-46
Chopin, Kate, 215, 226, 284-85
Christadelphians, 361, 365
Christian Commercial Travellers Association (Gideons), 370, 374
Christian Recorder (newspaper), 345, 362
Christian Scientists, 365
Chromolithography, 12, 568 (n. 62)
Churches, 343, 361-63, 365. *See also* Catholicism; Protestantism

Cigar-manufacturing industry, 326
Circulating libraries. *See* Public libraries
Civil rights, 323; organizations, 345, 349–50
Civil War, government publications on, 269
Clamor Público, El (Public Clamor; newspaper), 329, 334–35
Clarke, Jim, 157, *160–61*
Class: of book readers, 513; bourgeois, 209–10, 213; in Catholic print culture, 404–6; consciousness, 7, 9; middle, 178, 478, 528; upper, cultural authority of, 476; upper-middle, literacy skills of, 528; in women's literary clubs, 486; working, 217, 232, 541 (n. 41)
"Clear and present danger" test, 288, 297
Cleland, Tom M., 151, 168
Clemens, Samuel (Mark Twain), 41, 65, 213–14, 278, 545 (n. 16)
Cleveland Public Library, 446, 453, 468
Cold-metal machines, 72
Cold War, 258, 310
Collected editions, 67
Colleges: African American, 342; Catholic, 313, 331; enrollments in, 29; Hebrew Union, 385; land-grant, 201, 225; liberal arts, 200; Morrill Land Grant Act and, 262
Collier's Harvard Classics, 182
Colonialism, and native press, 328
Colophons, 175, *379*
Colored Citizen (newspaper), 339–40, 344–45
Colored Episcopal Church (Christian Episcopal Church), 362
Columbia University library, 457, 468
Columbia University Press, 228, 243
Columnists, 137, 142, 146–47
Commercial travelers (salesmen), 62
Committee of Ten, 424
Commonweal (periodical), 405–7
Communications, in publishing, 9–10, 13–15, 202, 234, 481, 535
Competition in publishing, 109–10, 126–27

Compton, Charles H., 513–14
Comstock, Anthony, *282*, 282–83, 286–87
Congressional Joint Committee on Printing, 263–64
Consumer capitalism, 11, 110–12
Consumer culture, 14, 16, 528
Cooper, Anna J., 349, 505
Cooperative Acquisitions Project for Wartime Publications, 470
Copeland & Day, 69–70
Copy editors, 137
Copyright: American Publisher's Copyright League, 97, 550 (n. 27); coverage of, 50; on derivative works, 98–99; foreign authors and, 70–71; government publications and, 268; impounded, 256; international, 51, 70–71, 94–99, 171, 549 (n. 22); literary agencies and, 88; "motivating factors" and, 92–93; for photographs, 551 (n. 40); right of renewal, 548–49 (n. 13); romanticism and, 51, 90–91, 100; subscription sales and, 69
Copyright Act (1909), 93, 100, 548–49 (n. 13), 549 (n. 14)
Copyright deposit, 466
Corliss machine, 22
Cornell University, 205, 206, 237, 468
Corporate capitalism: great libraries and, 452–53; consumers and, 14–15; periodicals and, 112–13; in publishing, 26–27, 50–51, 57; sensationalism and, 130–31
Corporate revolution and magazines, 115–17
Corruption in textbook publishing trade, 421–22
Cosmopolitan (periodical), 102–3, 284–85
Council on Books in Wartime, 81, 256
Councils of Defense, 309–10
Courtesy of the trade, 71, 179, 550 (n. 28)
Covici-Friede, 289, 294
Crane, Stephen, 215, 219, 284–85
Creelman, James, 136, 138
Crime magazines, 279, 283

INDEX   653

Crisis (periodical), 195, 230, 340–41, 350, 507
Cristero War, 319
Criticism. *See* Book reviews
Criticism, New, 223
Croly, Herbert, 219–20
Cuban American labor press, 326
Cuban immigration, 326, 330, 337
Cuban independence movement, 316
Cultural authority, 333–34, 383, 391, 433, 442–43, 476, 484
Cultural Front, the, 232–33
Cultural hierarchy, 413, 511, 514–15
Cultural revolution, 285–86, 296–97
Cultura Proletaria (Proletarian Culture) newspaper, 321, 327
Culture: defined, 17; high, in late 19th century, 476, 478; learned, 200–11, 233; liberal, 210–11; literary, 211–14, 216–33, 314, 488; political, 135; popular, 15, 528–29; visual, 13–14, 233. *See also* Culture of Print; Print cultures; *specific ethnic and religious groups*
Culture industry, 21, 232–33
Culture of Print, 2, 8, 15–16, 18–19, 20, 24–25, 49, 53, 207–9
Culture wars, 288–92, 296–97
Curriculum Foundation Series (Dick and Jane series), 425, 428–29, 605 (n. 27)
Curriculum reform at women's colleges, 225
Curtis, Cyrus, 102–3, 215
Cutler, Mary Salome, 437, 442
Cylinder presses, 72

Dam v. Kirke La Shelle Co., 100
Darnton, Robert, 3, 515
Davis, William Morris, 268–69
Deinard, Ephraim, 384–85
De Kruif, Paul, 253, *254*
Derpression, impact on publishing, 80, 89, 272–74, 357–58
Deshon, George, 398, 401
Detroit Evening News, 121, 123

De Vinne, Theodore Low, 154, 561 (n. 7)
Dewey, John, 428
Dewey, Melvil, 431–35, 450, 455
Dewey's decimal classification system, 431, 433, 438, 455
Dick and Jane series, 425, 428–29, 605 (n. 27)
Dickinson, Asa Don, 252–53
Dime novels, 39–41, 279, 283, 431–32
Distribution systems: African American publishers, 350; Bibles, 369–71; book clubs, 545 (n. 19); book industry, 30, 50, 56, 62–64, 113, 173, 481; bookshops, 63, 64, 80, 173, 179, 481; department stores, 63; mail, 67, 81–84, 241; newspapers, 29, 116, 351; O. H. Cheney on, 79–80; periodicals, 108; subscription, 64–70. *See also* Booksellers
Douay New Testament, 371
Doubleday, Frank, 82, 372
Doubleday, McClure & Co., 58, 107
Doubleday, Page & Co., 285
Dreiser, Theodore, 215, 219, 284–86
Drone, Eaton S., 90, 92, 95–96, 99, 549 (n. 22)
Du Bois, W. E. B., 215, 228–30, 266, 340–41, 350, 491
Dunbar, Paul Lawrence, 33, 229, 357, 491
Dust jackets, 77, 107, 179, *181*, 184
Dutton, Clarence, 268, 274

Eastman, Max, 219, 285–86
Economic novels, 216
Economy, national, 80, 110–12, 123–24, 266, 271–74, 371, 418, 530
Edison, Thomas A., 10, 22, 156
Editorial writers, 145
Editors, 234
Education: in 1880, 28–29; from 1880 to 1940, 7; for African Americans, 225, 228–29, 342, 448, 489; broadening access to, 215; child-centered, 419; cultural, for working class, 217; curriculum reforms, 225; higher, 200–206, 342,

488–89; industrial, 227, 342; informal, of cigar workers, 326; middle-class Americans and, 478; mission schools and, 313, 331; profession of, 423–25, 429–30; progressive movement in, 418–21; vocational, 488–89; for women, 225–26, 342, 448, 489; women's literary club movement and, 488. *See also* Learning; Public schools; Research universities
"Einstein Express" (Frederick), 591
Elements of Electricity (Timbie), 240, 256
Eliot, Charles W., 182, 424, 492
Eliza Kent Branch, Toledo Public Library, *439*
Elocution, 419–20
Embargos, during World War II, 255
Emerson, Ralph Waldo, 85, 490, 524
Engineering and Science Management War Training program, 256
English-language periodicals, *12*, 335
Entrepreneurs in publishing, 107
Ernst, Morris, 289, 293, 296
Espionage Act (1917), 287–88
Ethnic minority consciousness, 334–35
Ethnic press: African American, 339–41, 344–45, 348–50, 354–57, 496; American electoral activities and, 311; coverage by, 300; Cuban American, 326; evolution of, 299–300; functions of, 302, 327–28; German, 302–4, 310; Greek, 308; Hebrew, 384, 386–88; Hispanic, 194, 315–17, 319, 321–25, 327–30, 334–35; immigrant groups and, 216, 299; impact of, 301–2; Irish, 300–301; Jewish, 301, 382–83, 387–89; Mexican, 317, 319; native, 328; Norwegian, 304–6; Polish, 306–7; Scandinavian, 308; self-censorship of, 308–10; Slovak, 307; use of term, 585 (n. 2); Yiddish, 219. *See also* Hispanic press; Spanish-language press
Ethnocentrism, 466
European libraries, 458
Experimental literary work, 219, 221
Extension services, 201, 272

Farmington Plan, 470
Farm Security Administration, 272, *273*, 274
Faulkner, William, 85, 297
Fauset, Jessie, 230, 350
Federal Writers' Project, 272
Feuhr, Karl Alexander, 446–47
Fiction: best-selling, 442–43; circulation of, by public libraries, 432, 437, 442, 450, 481; debate over, 431–33; demand for, 435–36, 443–44; factories, 108–9; modernist, 222–23; "new school" of, 411; offensive, 443; realist, 213–14; religious, 372; in training camp libraries, 448. *See also* Novels; Serializations
Fiction Catalog, 441, 443, 448–49
"Fiction Song," 435–36
First Amendment protection, 296
Fisk University, 342
Five-foot shelf of books, 182, 184, 492
Fleetwood, Sara Iredell, 500–501
Flores Magón, Ricardo, 215, 317–19, *318*
Folger Library, 467
Foreign affairs columnists, 147–48
Foreign correspondents, 143, 148
Foreign-language newspapers, *309*; Arabic, 302; censorship of, 308–9; German, 216, *303*, 585 (n. 18); Greek, 308; newsstand with, *124*; Norwegian, 304; number of, 301–4; Spanish, 314, 322, 328–29, 331, 334, 336
Foreign-language press, 308–11
Fortune, T. Thomas, 215, 345–46, 355
Forumeer (periodical), 336–37
Forverts (Jewish Daily Forward), 300–301
Freedom of the press, 395
Functional literacy, 528
Fundamentalism, 363
Funeral industry publications, 349

G. P. Putnam's Sons, 289, 343
Gaboriau, Émile, 42–43, 543 (n. 80)
Garvey, Marcus, 354–57
Gasparri, Donato M., 331, *332*
General Church of the New Jerusalem, 361

General Federation of Women's Clubs, 488-89
Genteel literary code, 277-79, 288-89
German Jewish immigrants, 220-21
German press, 216, 302-4, 310
Germany, 156, 446-48
Gideons, 370, 374
Gilded Age, 118-19, 122, 129, 276-77, 624
Gilder, Richard Watson, 13, 211, 278
Gilman, Daniel Coit, 203, 210
Ginsberg, Louis, 384, 598 (n. 19)
Godkin, E. L., 118, 128, 138-39, 568 (n. 62)
Golden Trumpet Company, 365
Goodman, Daniel Carson, 286-87
Gould, Medora W., 503-4
Government agencies, 258, 261-64, 266-69
Government censors, 354
Government publishing, 16, 201, 245, 260-72, 436, 459
Grapes of Wrath, The (Steinbeck), 181
Graphic design profession, 74
Graves, John Temple, 143, 149
Gray, William S., 425, 428, 512-14, 516-17, 605 (n. 27)
Great Britain, 446-48
Great Depression, 80, 266, 271-74, 371, 530
Great Gatsby, The (Fitzgerald), 86
Great Migration, 351, 354-58
Greek press, 308
Greenwich Village, 219, 285-86
Griggs, Sutton E., 350-51
Grosset and Dunlap, 85, 228

H. W. Wilson Company, 440-41, 449, 459
Hagar Revelly (Goodman), 286-87
Halftone: engravings, 153; photographic reproductions, 13, 76, 155
Hamilton sisters of Fort Wayne, Ind., 31-32, 225
Hampton Normal and Agricultural Institute, 227, 342
Hampton-Tuskegee model, 227-28
Hand compositors, 159, 561 (n. 6)
Harcourt, Alfred, 186, 221-22

Harcourt Brace, 177, 245-46
Harlem Renaissance, 230-31, 356, 445, 492-93
Harper Brothers, 57-58, 113, 115, 356, *373*
Harper magazines, 103-4, 110, 173, 278-79, 372
Harper's Monthly, 212
Harper's New Books, *174*
Harper's Weekly, *36*, *111*
Harris, William Torrey, 416, 424
Harrison, Frederic, 520, 526
Harvard Classics, 182, 184, 492
Harvard University, 385, 457, 465-66, 468
Harvey, George, 58-59
"Hatrack" (Asbury), 293, *294-95*
Hayes, Rutherford B., 35, 43
Haymarket bombing, 213
Hays, Arthur Garfield, 289, 293
Hearst, William Randolph, 11, 120, 130, 143
Hebrew press, 384, 386-88
Hebrew Union College library, 385
Hecker, Isaac, 392, 395
Henry Holt & Co., 237, 243, 252
Hicklin test, 282, 287, 296
Hierarchies: authority of, 601 (n. 10); of Catholic print culture, 396-97; cultural, 199-200, 413, 511, 514-15; of print forms, 512-13; social, of literary clubs, 486
Higham, John, 458-59, 567 (n. 44)
Higher education, 198, 342, 356-57, 488-89
High-literary sphere, 212-14
Hispanic Americans, 312-14, 319-21, 327-28, 330, 334, 337
Hispanicized Indians, 334
Hispanic journalism, native, 331
Hispanic labor unions, 326-27
Hispanic press, 194, 315-17, 319, 321-25, 327-30, 334-35. *See also* Spanish-language press
Hispanic print culture, 312-21, 330-38, 586 (n. 1)
Holiness movement, 363, 365
Holocaust, 390

Holt, Henry, 78, 109, 372, 513
Hopkins, Pauline Elizabeth, 350, 616 (n. 28)
Hot-metal composition machines, 72, 74
Houghton, Henry, 42, 67, 172
Houghton, Mifflin, 57, 59, 104-6, 113, 423
House magazines, 103-7, 177
Houston Public Library, 481
Howard University, 342
Howells, William Dean: ancillary literary rights and, 85; on Corliss engine, 22; genteel literary code and, 211, 278; high-literary sphere and, 212; Paul Dunbar and, 229; radical print cultures and, 217; realist fiction by, 41, 213-14; sensationalism and, 131; serialized novels and, 41; as social critic, 196; sympathy for labor movement, 213
Hughes, Langston, 230, 341, 356, 445, 507
Huntington Library, 467
Hurd & Houghton (Houghton, Mifflin), 103

Illustrations: in books, 76-77, 155, 167-68; cover art, *86*, 356; in Dick and Jane series, 428; dust jacket, *181*; image reproduction, 76; in monthly magazines, 112-13; in reading textbooks, 417
Il Progresso (newspaper), 28, 301
Immigrant press, 216, 337. *See also specific immigrant groups*
Immigrants: changing demographics and, 284; corporate capitalism and, 14-15; from Europe, 23, 220-21, 299, 305; exploitation of, 323; integration of, into economy, 7; intellectuals, 219; literacy of, 29, 301-2; religious diversity in U.S. and, 360; from Spanish-speaking countries, 321-22; World War II and, 310
Immigration, restrictions on, 301, 402
Impressionist painters, 284
Imprimatur (it may be printed), 398-99, *401*
Independence movements, 316-17

Industrial education, 227, 342
Industrial laboratories, and technical publishers, 244-45
Industrial literacy, 29, 528
Information commerce, 51
Intellectuals, 212, 219, 236, 316-17, 569 (n. 68)
Interlibrary loans, 458, 460
International Church of the Foursquare Gospel, 361
International Copyright Act of 1891 (Chace Act), 51, 71, 95, 97-98
International Typographical Union, 74
Irish Americans (Anglophobia), 300-301, 308
Irish press, 300-301

J. A. Rogers Publications, 441
J. P. Morgan & Co., 58
Jacks, J. W., 504, 617 (n. 38)
Jacobs, Maurice, 387, 390
James, Henry, 41, 67, 213-14, 279
Jehovah's Witnesses, 363
Jesuit College, Las Vegas, 331
Jewett, Sarah Orne, 42, 110
Jewish libraries, 384-86
Jewish press, 301, 382-83, 387-89
Jewish print culture, 194, 376-91
Jewish Publication Society, 194, 376-77, 378-79, 382-87, 390-91
Jewish Theological Seminary, 383, 385
John Crerar Library, 467
Johns Hopkins University, 201, 203-4, 206, 456
Johnson, Kathryn, 491-93, 495
John Wiley and Sons, 237, 239-40, 242, 244-45, 256
Jollie v. Jacques, 99
Jones Act (1917), 337
Journalism: assertion of objectivity, 135, 140-43, 144, 150; in Catholic universities, 403; elite vs. mass, 131-32; hierarchy of power in, 135-36; internationalism and, 148-49; partisan, 130, 138-39, 150;

political advocacy in, 143-50; popular, 132; professionalism in, 140-41; public-state relations and, 139
Journalists: of Catholic press, 395; as heroes, 137; Mexican American, 335; ostensible refusal of partisan politics by, 140; as political wordsmiths, 141-42; World War II and, 148-49
Journal Ring, 143
Journals. *See* Periodicals
Joyce, James, 289, *292-93*, 297
Judaica Americana, bibliography of, 381
Judson, Edward (Ned Buntline), 39-40

Kelmscott Press, 159
Kennerly, Mitchell, 221, 287
Kerr, Charles Hope, 217-18
Kinetograph camera, 12-13
Klopfer, Donald, 78-79
Knowledge production, 202-7, 246
Knox, Frank, 144, 149

Labor: movement, 213; periodicals, 303-4, 326-27; unions, 74, 97, 326-27, 342, 347
Ladies' Home Journal, 102-3, 106, 178, 284-85
Ladies Reading Club of Houston, 477-78, 481-84, 488, 612 (n. 7)
Laird & Lee, 344
Lamson, Wolffe & Co., 70
Land-grant colleges and universities, 201
Lange, Dorothea, *273*, 274
Lanston, Tolbert, 72, 152
Latent content, in textbooks, 426-27
Lawrence, D. H., 289, 293
League of Library Commission, 441
League of United Latin American Citizens (LULAC), 336
Learned culture, transformation of, 200-202; transmission of, 31-32
Learning, 195-98, 478; cultures of, 200-201; knowledge production and, 202-7, 456-57

Lectores, 326
Leisure time, 512
Lend-Lease bill, 147
Lenox Library, 463
Levine, Lawrence, 27, 625
Lewis, Sinclair, 184, 186, 217, 253, 293, 444-45
Lewis and Clark's expedition, 266
Liberal culture, 210-11
Liberal Reformist Association, 317-19
Librarians: book choices and, 432-33; *Booklist* and, 442; as censors, 296, 447; of New York Public Library, 465; public, and "best reading" advocacy, 448-50; scholarly, 454, 458; services for specialized clienteles, 445; status of, in nonacademic institutions, 466-67
Libraries: academic, 456-58, 467-70; consolidation of library practices and, 433-35; great, 452-53; leaders of, 432-33, 442; reference departments in, 457-58; technical, 239; transition to modernity, 454-56; traveling, 488; university, 466, 468. *See also* Public libraries; Research libraries
Library Bureau, 434, 437-38
Library Journal, 44, 59
Library of Congress, *461*; acquisition of wartime publications, 470; acquisitions of, 465; classification scheme, 455-56, 460; functions and roles of, 462-63; holdings of, 466-68; Judaica collection, 385; Science Division, 258; service to nation by, 459-60; Ainsworth Rand Spofford and, 453
Library science, professional practice of, 432, 438
Library series, 67, 69
Library staff, 438-40
Limited editions, 67
Lindley, Ernest K., 146-47
Linotype machines: in bibliographic publishing, 459; in book production, 72-74; debut of, 11; ethnic press and, 302;

features of, 152–53; invention and spread of, 35; Model, 9, *73*; in newspaper and magazine production, 154; operators of, *153*, 561 (n. 6)
Lippincott, 57, 243
Lippmann, Walter, 53, 139, 146–48
Literacy: in 1880, 28–29; from 1880 to 1940, 528; from 1910 to 1940, 471; in 1930 and 1940, 590 (n. 9); in 1940, 618 (n. 50); of African Americans, 342, 506–7; diverse uses of, 412; environment of, 31–35; functional, 528; of immigrants, 301–2; industrial, 29, 528; institutions of, 312; of middle class, 528; training in public schools, 412; of upper-middle class, 528; value of, to Baptist African American women, 618 (n. 48)
Literary activism, 508–10
Literary agencies and agents, 50, 71, 87–88, 108
Literary analysis, 482
Literary commodification, 109
Literary critics, and censorship, 294
Literary culture, 212, 312, 314, 488
Literary erotica, 278–79
Literary Guild, 82, 222, 529
Literary left, 232
Literary magazines, 277–78, 284
Literary men, 212–13, 220
Literary modernism, 200, 220–22
Literary movements. *See* Aesthetic movements
Literary News, 59
Literary policing, 199, 294
Literary property, 92, 99. *See also* Copyright
Literary studies, 500–501, 507–8; academic, 223
Literary women, 226–27
Literature: of African Americans, 228, 230–32; children's, 427, 445–46; devotional, 398, 404; for emerging audiences, 224–31; European, 277–78; for modern era, 219–24; in periodicals, 284; popular, 235–36; race, 228–29, 475, 505; serious, 212
Lithographers, 347
Little, Brown and Co., 187, 293
Little Blue Books, 173, 217
Little magazines, 219–20, 285–86
Little Review, The (periodical), 219, 220, 285–87, 289, *292–93*
Liveright, Horace, 78–80, 221
Loeb Classical Library, 385–86
Lombardi, Carrie Ennis, 477–78
London, Jack, 215, 284
Longfellow, Henry Wadsworth, 67, 85
Looscan, Adele Briscoe, 477–78, 488
Los Angeles Public Library, 453
Lovers Once but Strangers Now (Libbey), *176*
Lozano, Ignacio E., 323–25
Luce, Henry R., 149, 413
LULAC. *See* League of United Latin American Citizens (LULAC)
LULAC News (periodical), 336–37
Lyceum movement, 478
Lynchings, 346–47

M. R. Gately Company, 369
Machine-set type, 154, 156
MacKnight, Kate Cassatt, 484–85
Macmillan, 237, 239–40, 243, 256, 372
Magazines. *See* Periodicals
"Magazining," 108
Magnus, Lady Katie, 383–84
Mail-order: distribution, 81–84, 241; publishers, 170–71, 173, 182–84
Manhattan Project, 257–58
Manifest Destiny, 328, 334
Man in a Chemical World (Morrison), 248, *249*, *250–51*
Manufacturing Clause, 71, 97, 550–51 (n. 31)
Marín, Francisco Gonzalo (Pachín), 316–17
Marketing. *See* Advertising
Market surveys, 22
Masses (periodical), 219, 285–86

Matthews, Victoria Earle, 228, 499, 505–7
Mattoon, Laura I., 524–25
McClure, S. S., 10, 103, 106, 108, 112, 215
McClure's (periodical), 102–6, 110, 208–9
McDonald, Katharine, 441–42
McGraw-Hill, 239–40, 244–45, 256–57, 407
McGuffey, William Holmes, 415–17, 424–25
McGuffey's Readers, 415–17, 420, 427–28
McPherson, Aimée Semple, 363, *364*
Media, new, 13–14, 181
Mencken, H. L., 136, 140, 223, 289, *290–91*, 294–95
Mennonite Publishing House, 365
Men's literary societies, 500
Mergenthaler, Ottmar, 11, 72, 152
Mergenthaler Linotype Company, 262–63
Methodists, 360, 365
Mexican American civil rights movement, 324, 335
Mexican American journalists, 335
Mexican Americans, as ethnic minority, 40, 336
Mexican exile press, 317, 319
Mexican immigrants, 321–22, 328, 330
Mexican *mestizaje*, 335
Mexican Revolution, 319, 325, 335
Mexicans, as colonial subjects, 328
Microbe Hunters (De Kruif, Paul), 253, *254*
Middlebrow: authorities, 223; books, 42–43, 114–15; as category, 194–98; institutions, 222
Middle class, 178, 209–10, 213, 478, 528. *See also* Class
"Migrant Mother and Children" (Lange), 273
Migration toward American cities, 80, 351, 354–58
Milwaukee Leader, 287, 304
Mission schools, 313, 331
Mitchell Kennerley (publisher), 70
MIT Press (Technology Press), 242
Model Library, 435–37
Modernism: as aesthetic movement, 198, 222–23; artistic, 286; effect on print culture, 285; emergence of, 226–27; European, 157; literary, 12; typographic, 156–57, *158*, 164, 166, 168, 562 (n. 16)
Modern Library, 78
Modern typography and layout (McMurtrie), 157, *158*
Monotype machines, 72, 74–75, 152–53, 162, 386
Monroe, Harriet, 285–86
Monsieur LeCoq (Gaboriau), 42–43
Montgomery Ward catalogs, 444–45
Monthly Catalog of Government Publications, 272, 459
Moral censorship, 288
Moral teaching, 427
Mormons, 361, 363, 365
Morrill Land Grant Act (1861), 201, 262
Morris Public Library (Illinois), 449–50
Movie industry, 13, 181
Movie rights, 87
Munroe, Ruth, 513–14, 516–17
Munsey, Frank, 103, 106, 112, 127, 168
Munsey's (periodical), 102–3, 110, 178, 208–9
Mysteries, 42

N. W. Ayer and Son, *38*, 112, 361
Nana (Zola), 32, 41
Nation (periodical), 43, 133, 289
National Association for the Advancement of Colored People (NAACP), 195, 229, 350
National Association of Colored Women (NACW), 350, 486, 504–6, 508, 617 (n. 41)
National Baptist Publishing Board, 340, 343
National Baptist Union Review, 349–50
National Cloak & Suit Co. v. Kaufman, 94
Nationalism, 15, 301, 528–29
National Police Gazette, 279, *280*
National Union Catalog, 460, 470
National Urban League, 229, 350

Naturalism, as aesthetic movement, 41–42, 198, 215, 284–85
Nature of the World, The, 242–43
Negroes in the United States, 265–66
Negrotarians, 231
Negro World (newspaper), 355–56
Negro Year Book Publishing Company, 229
Net-pricing system, 50, 63–64
New American Library, 85
Newberry Library, 467
New Criticism, 223
New Decalogue of Science, The (Wiggam), 246–47, 253
New England Women's Club, 477
Newman, John Henry, *396*, 406
Newman Press, 407
New Mexico, 330–34
New Negro Renaissance, 230–31
New Republic (periodical), 146, 219–20
Newspaper columnists, 137, 142, 146–48, 300, 321
Newspaper industry: in 1910 to 1920, 52–53; hot-metal composition machines and, 74; mature stage in, 126–27; political and cultural authority of, 53; political revolution in, 116–17; production costs, 121, 127
Newspaper publishers, 141–44
Newspaper reading, 535, 541 (n. 41)
Newspapers: in 1880s and 1890s, 108; addition of sections to, 128; advertising and, 128–30; African American, 215, 345, 496; bilingual, 328–29; book publishers and, 277; circulation of, 121–22, 304, 498–99; consolidation of, 127; consumption of, 120, 123; as corporations, 116; cultural authority of, 150; economic forces and, 124–26, 130; editorial page, 145; in English, *12*; ethic of nonpartisanship, 133–36, 141; as guide in middle-class life, 178; interplay between national and local, 35; multiple voices in, 142; in 19th century, 29, 37; as outlets for black writers and editors, 344; political coverage by, 53; political parties and, 117–19; readership of, 555 (n. 27), 556 (n. 48); sensationalism in, 124; serialized books in, 450; syndicated material in, 11. *See also* Foreign-language newspapers
News syndicates, 17
New Testaments, 367, 369, 371
New York Age, 345–46
New York City, 218–19
New York Public Library, 385, 445, 453, 463–64, *464*, 464–68
New York State Library, *434*, 437
New York Times, 122, 139, 283, 289, 293
New York Times Book Review, 172, 184, 248
New York Tribune, 11, 139
New York *World*, 132, 138, *153*
New York World's Fair (1939), 255, 533–34, *534*
Nixon v. Condon, 145–46
Noll, John, 407–8
Norris, Frank, 85, 215, 284
North Carolina Mutual Provident Association, 348–49
Norwegian Press, 304–6
Novels: depicting Mexican Revolution, 319, 325; dime, 39–41, 279, 283, 431–32; economic, 216; in ethnic presses, 300; of Harlem Renaissance, 356; popular, 42; religious, 372; serialization of, 177; utopian, 216. *See also* Fiction
Nowell-Smith, Simon, 94–95
Nuevomexicanos, 330–33

Obrero, El (Worker), 319, 321
Obscenity, 282–83, 296–98. *See also* Censorship
Ochs, Adolph, 144–45
Old Wives' Tale, The (Bennett), 286, 584 (n. 25)
Oral reading, 416, 419–21
Oregon Free Library Commission, 448
Orion Publishing Company, 350–51
Ouida (Louise de la Ramée), 40, 42–43

Outlines of Jewish History (Magnus), 383–84
Overseas Editions, 81
Ovington, Mary White, 491–92
Oxford University Press, 367

P. F. Collier & Son, 252, 492
Page, Walter Hines, 171, 173, 179, 285
Palmer, A. Mitchell, 143–44
Panamanians, 328
Paperback books, 81, 84–85, 530
Paper production, 11, 77, 152
Paper stock, 120, 123–24, 154
Paris Peace Conference, 307
Park, Robert E., 130, 194, 299, 321
Parsons, Geoffrey, 145, 149
Partisan politics, 130, 140
Paulist Press, 371, 395
Pedagogical theory, 521–22
Peer review, 235, 237
Penguin Books, 84
Pentecostalism, 363, 365
Periodicals, 164; academic, 195–96, 203–6; active and adaptive uses for, 17–18; advertising and, 113; African American, 229–30, 348–50; agricultural, 38; as arena for intellectual debate, 236; book ads in, *104*; Catholic, 294, 395–96, *396*, 405–7; children's, 340; circulation of, 109; corporate capitalism and, 11; crime, 279, 283; distribution systems for, 108; English-language, 335; guides and indexes to, 449, 456, 459; illustrated monthly, 112–13; Jewish, 380, 388–89; labor, 303–4, 326–27; literary, 214–15, 277–78, 284; of literary houses, 49, 103–4; little, 219, 232, 285–87, 289–93, 530; machine technology and, 165; mass market, 102–3, 120, 178, 208–9, 279, 284–85; Mexican American civil rights, 335–38; monthly, 102–3, 106, 110; new media and, 181; partisan, 117–19; popular, 166, 212; popularized science, 246–47; publication of, 198; public libraries and, 440–41; religious, 39, 229, 360–66, 405–7; scholarly and association-sponsored, 204, 238, 255, 348, 356–57; scientific and technical, 235, 237–39, 243; selling books with, 107–8; serializations in, 41, 104, 177; as servant to readers, 168; socialist, 286, 570 (n. 94); Spanish-language, 316, 319, 321; trade, 15–16, 175, 179. *See also* Advertising; Newspapers
Perkins, Maxwell, 89, 222
Phonic method of reading, 416–17
Photographs, 13–14, 166, 272–74
Photo-offset lithography, 77, 461
Physical Review, 237, 239, 255–56
Pilot, The (periodical), 294, 363
Pocket Books, 84, 257
Poetry (periodical), 285–86
Poetry reading, 374, 518–25
Polish press, 306–7
Political press, 53, 116–17, 140–50, 262, 315–16
Ponce de León, Néstor, 215, 316
Poole's Index, 456
Popular literature, 235–36
Popular science books, 253
Population of U.S., 49–50, 57, 122
Populist Party, 133
Pornography, 278–79
Postal system, 67, 279–84, 356
Posters, 179, *181*
Prayer book for Jewish soldiers, 390
Prensa, La (The Press) newspapers, 324–25
Prentice-Hall, *180*, 407
Presidential papers collection, 462
Press: alternative, 119, 216–20, 223, 286, 317–21, 340, 348, 354–56, 570 (n. 4); foreign-language, 301–11, 312–38; freedom of, 395; political, 53, 116–17, 140–50, 262, 315–16; Protestant, 360–61, 363–66, 372–75, 595 (n. 20); religious, 39, 229, 342–43, 360–63, 371–72, 596 (n. 47); socialist, 570 (n. 94); tabloid, 279; technical, 235, 238–43, 257; yellow, 130, 132, 138. *See also* Catholic press;

Ethnic press; Trade press; University presses
Princeton University Press, 206, 207, 243, 257
Print: active and adaptive uses for, 18-19; aesthetic nature of, 155; as force for consolidation, 2-4, 9-10, 13, 17, 377, 392, 395, 528-29, 535; as force for diversification, 2-4, 14, 16-17, 49, 50, 199-200, 214-33, 382, 528-29, 535; genteel text for, 277; geographic location and consumption of, 513; growth of government and, 16, 261-64, 271; influences on producers of, 35; mechanized production of, 53-54; mobility of, 21; racist scholarship in, 228, 348; as vehicle of activism, 483-84, 485-89, 508-10
Print cultures: age of the expert and, 207-9; bound books in, 19-20; brow levels in, 40-43, 199, 387-88, 529-30; core/periphery model, 25-27; integration of, 20-21, 49, 50, 101, 111-13, 529; local, 2, 16-17, 20-21, 25, 109, 142; modernism in, 285; nationalism in, 21, 333; publishing trades and, 49; radical and alternative, 216-19; sites of, 27-28, 31-45, 472, 529; social change and, 7-15; as term, 15-17. *See also* Literary culture; *individual ethnic and religious groups, publisher entries*
Printing industry, 76, 97, 113-14, 151-64, 342, 347-48
Printing presses, 72-74, 127, *129*, 152-55, 312-13, 530
Printing Types (Updike), 162, *162-63*
Production, mechanized, 164, 169
Progressive Era: agenda for reading, 512; education movement, 418-21; initiatives of, 489; literary clubs and, 488; learned culture and, 208-9; political culture of, 133, 135, 287-88; popular interest in science, 248; public philosophy, 119; reading research methods of, 516; research libraries and, 456-57

Prohibition movement, 287
Protestantism, 359-61, 367
Protestant press, 360-61, 363-66, 372-75, 595 (n. 20)
Protestant print culture, 194
Public Education Law (1894), 334
Public libraries: access to, 542 (n. 27), 606 (n. 1); access to books, 414; "best reading" advocacy, 432-33, 440, 448-50; boards of, 463; book circulation and, 207, 481; bookmobile services, 451; branch systems, 450; cataloging and classification, 449; children's literature in, 445-46; class biases in, 30; collections of, 44; design and construction of, 438; differing visions for, 432; in distribution system, 64; establishment of, 261; fiction debate and, 431-33, 443-45; funding for, 466; municipal, 453; networks of, 437; policies of, vs. small-town literary interests, 443-44; power of readers in defining, 414; serialized books in, 448; social mission of, 413-14; support for, 437-38, 453; in Texas, 481, 488; urban, 445-46; women's literary club movement and, 488; World War I and, 446-48
Public library movement, 433-35
Public schools: class biases in, 30; cultural messages and, 412-13; elementary and secondary curricula, 411-12; English as language of instruction in, 303, 334; enrollment in, 418, 421; establishment of, 261; high school graduates, 418; literacy training programs, 412; poetry reading in, 518-19
Publishers: academic, 350; African American, 229-31; backgrounds of early 20th-century, 79; *Booklist* and, 442; in engineering and technology, 236-37; German Jewish immigrants as, 220-21; of Harlem Renaissance novels, 231, 356; Hispanic, 315; insurance companies as, 591-92 (n. 31); literary agents and, 88; literary modernist, 223; of medical,

surgical, and scientific books, 236; in mid-size cities, 127; in natural and physical sciences, 242; newspaper, 141–44; old-line, 170–72, 175; political activity of, 149; relationships with customers and authors, 241; relationships with experts, 244; reputations of, 177; self-censorship by, 255; text generation and, 108

Publishers' Trade List Annual, 59, 456

Publishers' Weekly: best-seller lists, 184; on book trade, 29–30, 56–57; Boston police department's clean-books campaign and, 293; celebration of printing press, 530; censorship and, 295; communication in book industry, 481; documentation of national publishing output, 456; general trade houses and, 61; mail orders and, 67; sense of community reflected in, 175; statistics on religious books, 371–72; on Tourgée novel, 43; trade books as percent of all new books, 239

Publishing: African Americans and, 347; control of, by mainstream elites, 195; cooperative, 244–46; entrepreneurs in, 107; growth of trade, 57–61, 78–79, 89, 90, 255; internationalization of, 71; nonprofit, 370–71; scholarly, 202–7; scientific and technical, 234–35; separation of printing from, 113–14; specialized sectors in, 193, 261, 274, 359, 370, 374, 529

Publishing industry, 16, 49–50; as club/community, 175, 188–89; corruption, 421–22; integration of trade, 49, 50, 55, 101, 111–13, 529; internationalization, 70–72; Puerto Rican immigrants, 325, 327–28, 330, 337; public relations and, 185–86

Puerto Rican independence movement, 316–17

Pulitzer, Joseph, 11, 120, 128–30, 132

Pulitzer, Joseph, II, 141, 147

Pulitzer Prizes, 145, 148

Pulp magazines, 530

Putnam, George Haven, 97, 172
Putnam, George Palmer, 289, 550 (n. 26)
Putnam, Herbert, 459–62

Queen v. Hicklin, 282

R. H. Macy, 63–64, 256
R. R. Bowker Company, 59, 459
Race literature, 228–29, 475, 505
Race riots, 346–47
Racialized romanticism, 231
Racism, 322, 328, 346–47, 508
Radio, 10, 123, 181–82, 187–88, 533
Radio Phone Receiving, 252
Radio rights, 87
Radway, Janice A., 109, 624
Railroads, 9, 26, 29, 480
Ramée, Louise de la (Ouida), 40, 42–43
Ramírez, Francisco P., 334–35
Random House, 78, 297
Reader-response theory, 624
Readers: advertising and, 130; characteristics of, 513–14; as consumers, 128; female, 277; Hispanic, 322; illustrated monthly magazine and, 112–13; influences on, 25, 473; interests of, 514–15; motivations of, 515; natural circle of, 172–73; of newspapers, 126; newspapers vs. books, 528; supply vs. demand in choices by, 515; of technical books and journals, 243; of textbooks and reference books, 234; of Thomas Hardy, 513; traditional typography and, 167; women authors and, 226

Reader's Guide to Periodical Literature, 440, 449, 459

Reading: in African American community, 474, 491, 493–95, 507–8; agenda for, 512; across brow levels, 530; case studies in, 473–75, 517–18; changing styles of, 109; characterizations of, 471–72; as democratic necessity, 513; as devotional and contemplative exercise, 375; experience of, with popular magazines, 166;

history of, 471-72; identity and, 31-34, 224-33, 484, 485-87, 508-10; instruction in, 413, 418-21, 424; middle-class, 178; poetry, 518-25; roles of, 472; setting and mode of, and construction of meaning, 517-18; silent, 420-21, 450, 514; as social practice, 473-74; statistics, 471; study of, 475; 20th-century studies of, 516-17. *See also* Black women's reading club movement; White women's literary club movement; Women's literary clubs
Reading circles, Catholic women and, 408
Reading material, nonreligious, 374
Reading programs, 450
Reading rooms, *461, 464, 495*
Reading textbooks: in 1880, 415-17; Anglo-American bias in, 425; authors of, 424-25; latent content in, 426-27; national marketing of, 423-24; progressive education and, 418-21; social change and, 417-18; social messages in, 413; textbook industry and, 424; vocabulary in, 417; women as authors of, 425
Readyprint pages, 29
Realism, as aesthetic movement, 198
Recitation poems, 507
Reference books, 234, 245-46
Reference departments in libraries, 464-65
Reference librarians, 451, 467
Regionalist fiction, 213-14, 226
Reid, Helen and Ogden, 147-48
Reissues of books, 42-44
Religious press, 39, 229, 342-45, 360-63, 371-72, 596 (n. 47). *See also* Catholic press; Jewish press; Protestant press
Reporters. *See* Journalists
Reprint publishers, 87, 94, 97, 170, 549 (n. 19), 550 (n. 28)
Research, 202, 207, 210, 234, 239, 516
Research libraries: acquisitions of, 457; evolution from storehouses to workshops, 459; forms of, 452; funding for, 466; geographic distribution, 467-68; Library of Congress services to, 462; New York Public Library, 464-65; of 19th century, 452-54; Progressive Era beliefs and, 456-57; service orientation of, 458; special collections of, 468; standardization and collaboration, 468
Research universities: cultures of learning in, 200-201; funding of, 468; government publishing and, 269; Johns Hopkins University as standard for, 201, 456; knowledge production and, 202-7; modern, 197; Morrill Land Grant Act (1861) and, 262; professionalization of expertise and, 237; scholarly publications of, *205-6*
Reston, James, 147, 150, 560 (n. 30)
Restoration movement, 362
Revista Católica, La (Catholic Review; magazine and publisher), 331, *332*
Reynolds, Paul Revere, 87-88
Ridley, Florida (Ruffin), 350, 496-98
Rollins, Carl Purington, 151-52, 155, 159, 562 (n. 18)
Romance of the reporter, 136-37
Romanticism, 90-91, 100, 136-39, 231, 549 (n. 17)
Roosevelt, Franklin D., 143-44
Rosaries, 401, 602 (n. 33)
Royes, R., 38-39
Ruffin, Florida. *See* Ridley, Florida (Ruffin)
Ruffin, Josephine St. Pierre, 350, 496, 498, 502, 504

S. S. McClure Company, 58
Sacred images, 398
Sacred texts, 365-66
St. Nicholas, 103-4
San Antonio, Tex., 324
Sanger, Margaret, 286, 288
Saturday Evening Post (periodical), 146, 182, 208-9, 253
Scandinavian Americans, 308
Schechter, Solomon, 383, 386
Schenck v. United States, 288
Schiff, Jacob, 385-86

Schiff Library of Jewish Classics, 385–87
Schneiderman, Harry, 389–90
Schomburg Collection, 465
School of Library Economy, 434–35
Schools. *See* Colleges; Mission schools; Public schools; Universities
Schudson, Michael, 52–53
Science, 199, 255–57, 266–67; popularized, 246–48, 252
Science and Health (Eddy), 365–66
Science Remaking The World (Caldwell and Slosson), 246–47
Scientific and technical publishing, 234–35, 239–41, 257–59, 268–69, 284, 457
Scientific lecture tours, 246
Scientific research, 207
Scientific societies, 203, 238
Scofield Reference Bible, 367, *368*
Scopes, John T., 248, 296
Scott, Sir Walter, 128, 481
Scribner, Charles, 26, 57, 67, 286
Scribner, Charles, II, 222
Scribner's Monthly Magazine, 103–4, 173, 253, 268
Scripps, Edward W., 119, 124–25, 248
Scripps, James, 120–21, 124–25
Scudder, Horace, 104, 106, 110
Sedition Amendment (1918), 287–88
Self-censorship, 255, 278–79, 308–10
Sendak, Maurice, 257–58
Sensationalism, 119, 124, 130–33, 351
Sephardic Jews, 313–14
Serializations: of African American authors, 351; of *The Jungle*, 217; in libraries, 448; of *Life on the Mississippi*, 278; in *The Little Review*, 220, 292–93; by magazine entrepreneurs, 107; in magazines, 41, 104, 177; in newspapers, 450; of novels of Mexican Revolution, 325; of popular science books, 253; in story papers, 39–40
Servant and master metaphor, 151–52, 155
Services for the Open (Mattoon and Bragdon), 524–25

Seventh-day Adventists, 363, 365
Sex radical movement, 218
Shakespeare, and women's literary clubs, 483–84
Sheed and Ward (publisher), 407
Sherman Antitrust Act, 64
Silent reading, 420–21, 450, 514
Simon and Schuster, 78, 184
Sinclair, Upton, 421, 605 (n. 23)
Singer, Isidore, 382–83
Sister Aimée, 363, *364*
Slosson, Edwin E., 246–47, 252
Slovak press, 307
Small, Maynard & Co., 70
Smith, Ella Thea, 245–46
Smoot-Hawley tariff, 296
Social criticism, 196
Social injustice, 30, 322, 328, 346–47, 425, 455, 494, 508
Socialist press, 217, 219, 286, 570 (n. 94)
Social sciences, 208, 269
Softcover houses, 84–85
Soldiers, 341–46, 369–71, 390
Southworth, E. D. E. N., 40, 42, 44, 431, 481
Spanish-American War, 137–39
Spanish immigration, 330
Spanish-language Catholic weekly, 331, *332*
Spanish-language press: educational publishing, 314; exile, 319–21; in New Mexico, 333–34; offerings of, 325; periodicals, 316; in San Antonio, 324. *See also* Hispanic press
Spanish working-class immigrants, 326–27
Speech writing, political, 145
Staats-Zeitung (Public News), 301, 304
Star Series, *246–47*
Statistical information in government publications, 264–66
Stereotype plates, 11
Stereotypes, 40, 139, 344. *See also* Readyprint pages
Sterling Memorial Library, Yale University, *469*

Story papers, 39-41, 107
Stowe, Harriet Beecher, 42, 551 (n. 34)
Stowe v. Thomas, 98-99, 551 (n. 36)
Subscription libraries, 453
Subscription publishers, 65, 108, 173
Subscription sales, of books, 344-45
Subsidiary rights market, 85-87
Substantial similarity doctrine, 98-100
Suffrage movement, 303, 305, 489
Sullivan, Mark, 146, 427-28
Summer camps, 525
Sumner, John S., 287, 289, 294
Syndicated political columns, 142, 146
Syndication of novels, 108

Tabloid press, 279, 431-32
Teaching, 349, 423, 494-95
Teall, Edward N., 511-12
Technical and cultural elite, 529
Technical libraries, 239
Technical press, 235, 238-44, 257
Technologies: developments in, 14, 69, 302; government publications and, 266-67; mass audiences and, 164-66; modernity and, 152-64; showcasing vs. subordination of, 166-67
Telegraphs, 10, 29
Telephone, 10
Television, 533-34
Temperance movement, 303, 305
Terrell, Mary Church, 349, 616 (n. 17)
Tertiary History of the Grand Cañon District (Dutton), 268, 274
Texas, 336-37, 480-81, 488
Texas literary clubs, 477-79, 481-84, 487-88, 612 (n. 7)
Textbook industry, 16, 413, 421-24, 429-30
Textbooks, 69, 81, 234, 240-41, 404, 423, 426-28
Third Plenary Council, 392-95, 397, 403
Thomas, M. Carey, 32-33, 225
Thomas Nelson and Sons, 370, 372
Thompson, James S., 241-42

Thorndike, Edward L., 419
Timbie, William Henry, 240, 256
Time Magazine, 413
Tobacco workers from Cuba, 326
Toledo Public Library, *439*
Trade courtesy, 71, 175, 550 (n. 28)
Trade fairs, 30
Trade press: book clubs and, 83; designed editions, 69-70; as general publishers, 59-60, 62; literary agents and, 88; periodicals, 15-16, 175, 179; popular literature and, 235-36; professional managers in, 57; *Publishers' Weekly* and, 61; religious publications and, 372-73; specialties of, 60; subscription departments of, 67; textbooks and, 69; works by foreign authors and, 71
Trade-sale system, 62
Trading with the Enemy Act (1917), 287, 308
Translations, 98, 551 (n. 34)
Turner, Frederick Jackson, 14, 271
Tuskegee Normal and Industrial Institute, 227, 342, 350
Twain, Mark, 22, 41, 65, 213-14, 278, 545 (n. 16)
Two-foot bookshelf, 491-93
Typesetting, 11, 152, 159, 263
Typography: in advertisements, *111*; in classic style, 162; ethic of invisibility and, 167; modern, 156-57, *158*, 159, 164, 166, 168-69, 562 (n. 16); modern vs. traditional, 54, 563 (n. 35); role of, in modern America, 151; traditional, 164; type styles, 154-55, 162

Ulysses (Joyce), 220, 289, *292-93*, 297
Unions. *See* Labor: unions
U.S. Geological Survey, 266-69
U.S. Government Depositories, 457
U.S. Government Printing Office (US-GPO), 260-62, 264, 270, 342, 580 (n. 6)
U.S. Office of Scientific Research and Development, 258

U.S. Postal Service officials. *See* Comstock, Anthony; Sumner, John S.
U.S. Postal System, 279–84, 356
USGPO. *See* U.S. Government Printing Office (USGPO)
United States v. One Book Called "Ulysses," 296
United States v. Roth, 297
Universal Negro Improvement Association (UNIA), 354–55
Universities, 197–98, 200–202, 224–25, 403. *See also* Research universities; University presses
University libraries, 466, 468
University presses, 206–7, 228–29, 235, 240–43, 257, 350, 367
Updike, Daniel Berkeley, 159–62, *162–63*

Van Nostrand, 236–37, 239–41, 244, 248, 252
Verse, appropriation of, 526–27
Victorian era, 32, 131, 277, 499–500
Viola Novelty Company, 324–25
Vocational education, 488–89
Voice of the Negro of Atlanta (weekly newspaper), 345, 350
Voting rights, 347
Voz de la Mujer, La (Woman's Voice), 319, *320*

Wallace, Lew, 43, *373*
Waples, Douglas, 512, 514–16
Ward, James W., 431–32
Washington, Booker T., 227–28, 345–46
Watch and Ward Society, 283–84, 286–87, 290, 294–95
Watchtower (periodical), 363
Wells-Barnett, Ida B. (Iola), 34, 346, 496, 615 (n. 11)
Wesley, Carter, 145–46
West, James L. W., 50–51
What People Want to Read About (Waples and Tyler), 514–15
What Reading Does to People (Waples, Berelson, and Bradshaw), 515–16

"When the Mob Comes and You Must Die, Take at Least One with You" (Abbott), 351–54
White, William Allen, 149, *254*, 560–61 (n. 40)
White supremacy theories, 347
White women's literary club movement, 476–77, 479–88, 504
Whitman, Walt, 278–79
Whittaker, Johnson, 35, 38, 542 (n. 42)
Wholesale trade system, 59, 62–63, 67
Who Reads What? (Compton), 513–14
Wiggam, Albert E., *246–47*, 253
Williams, Fannie Barrier, 346, 349, 498, 615–16 (n. 13)
Williams, Raymond, 526–27, 624
Willkie, Wendell, 146–47
Wilson, Edmund, 223, 297
Wilson, Louis R., 512–13, 533
Wilson, Woodrow, 354, 371
Wise, Isaac Mayer, 377–81
Womanhood, meaning of, 226, 484
Woman's Era (club), 495–98, 501, 615 (n. 8)
Woman's Era (newspaper), 350, 496, 498–506, 615 (n. 9–10), 616 (n. 17), 617 (n. 32)
Women, *497*, *502*, *509*; in 1880s, 23; advice for, in domestic service, 401; African American print cultures and, 349; as authors, 226, 425; barred from Century Association, 42; college-educated, 494; education and, 225, 342, 448, 478; importance of novels to, in Victorian world, 32; inclusion of, in newspaper reading audience, 129; literary, 226–27; public world and, 15; reading circles and, 408; selection of children's literature and, 445–46; standards of proper femininity and, 499–500; stereotypes of, according to genteel code, 284; volunteerism and, 489
Women's literary clubs: academic nature of meetings, 500–501; Catholic women and, 408; class and racial boundaries

in, 486; focus of, 481–82; harmony in, 487; lifelong learning and, 478; men's response to, 479–80; sisterhood and, 485–87; standards for literary analysis, 482; 21st-century reflections on, 489–90; woman movement and, 487–88; women's ability to express themselves and, 482–83. *See also* Black women's reading club movement; White women's literary club movement

Women's rights movement, 303, 305

Woodson, Carter G., 342, 348, 351, 491

Woollcott, Alexander, 187–88

Woolsey, John, 296–97

Work-for-hire doctrine, 51, 90, 92–94, 548–49 (n. 13), 549 (n. 14)

World War I: book collecting campaigns, 447; Catholic Americans in, 401–2; ethnic press on American intervention in, 304–7; foreign correspondence in, 148; Great Migration and, 351, 354–58; immigrant press and, 308–10; interlibrary collaboration during, 468–70; literary bohemians and, 220; public library collections and, 446–48; technical book publication following, 240–41; training camp libraries, 448

World War II: Bibles for soldiers of, 369; book industry during, 81; censorship and embargos, 255–57; destruction of European Jewry and, 390; gaps in international collections of libraries and, 466, 470; immigrants and, 310; journalists and, 148–49; obscenity laws following, 297

Writers. *See* Authors

Yale University, 385, 457, 465–66, 468, *469*

Yellow press, 130, 132, 138

Yiddish press, 219

Youmans, Edward L., 237

Ziff, Larzer, 624–25

Zola, Emile, 32, 41, *400*

CPSIA information can be obtained
at www.ICGtesting.com
Printed in the USA
FSOW01n0029260417
33566FS